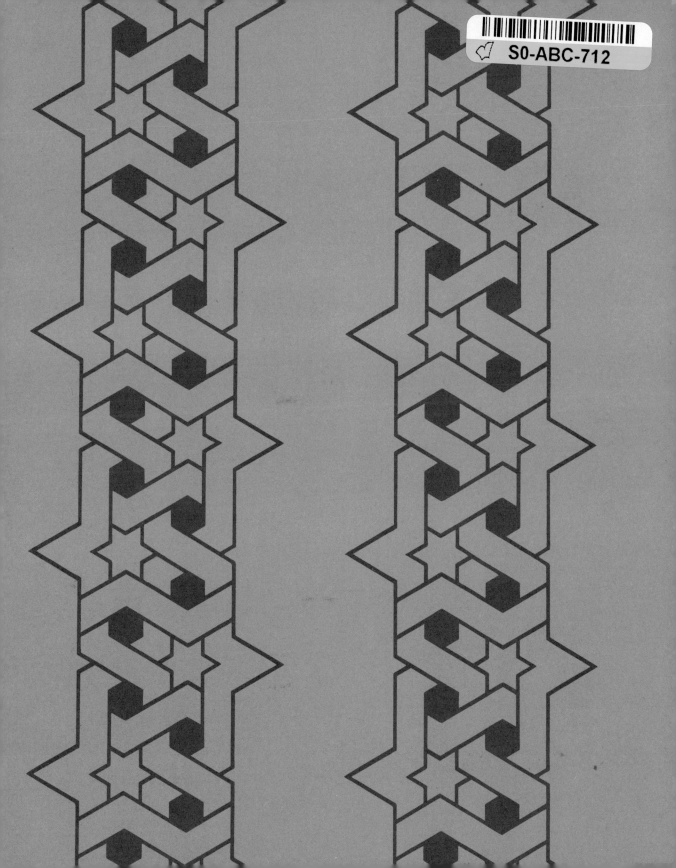

FOUNDATION COURSE IN
SPANISH

FOUNDATION
COURSE IN

FOURTH EDITION

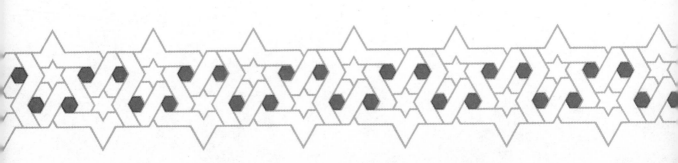

SPANISH

Laurel H. Turk

DePauw University

Aurelio M. Espinosa, Jr.

Stanford University

Carlos A. Solé, Jr.

University of Texas, Austin

D. C. HEATH AND COMPANY
Lexington, Massachusetts   Toronto

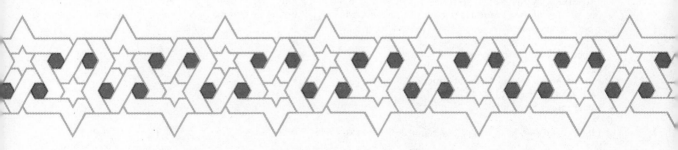

Color photographs in the "Viñetas Culturales" section between pages
160–161, by Peter Menzel.

Cover design by Rob Howard

Published simultaneously in Canada.

Printed in the United States of America.

International Standard Book Number: 0-669-00491-X

Library of Congress Catalog Card Number: 77-72889

Preface

Foundation Course in Spanish, Fourth Edition, is intended for beginning students who wish to understand and use Spanish. The materials presented will make possible a development of the language skills in their natural order—*listening, speaking, reading,* and *writing.* At the same time that the student learns to understand and say in Spanish many of the things he says every day in English, and learns to read and write simple Spanish, he will become informed of something of the civilization, culture, customs, and way of life of the peoples whose language he is studying.

Throughout the text, emphasis is placed on a practical vocabulary and oral use of the language. The dialogues deal with everyday situations, such as the classroom, the home, meals, shopping, travel, amusements, and other phases of daily life within the experience of the average student. Each lesson presents not only a number of new words and expressions, along with an explanation of the new grammatical points, but it also repeats systematically much of the material from earlier lessons. Individual words in the dialogues have been chosen for their frequency in everyday speech, rather than for their literary or aesthetic value. Most of the words and phrases introduced are those most commonly used. On the other hand, the *Lecturas* offer a vocabulary which will be of value in reading Spanish, whether it be novels, plays, short stories, essays, or newspaper articles.

This edition of *Foundation Course in Spanish* consists of two preliminary lessons on pronunciation, punctuation, and capitalization, followed by twenty-four lessons, five reviews, thirteen *Lecturas,* four *Conversaciones,* a short section on letter writing, three appendices, and the end vocabularies. The maps, illustrations, and the pictorial essay called *Viñetas culturales,* form an important part of the book, offering great variety in topics which supplement the story of the cultural background in the Spanish-speaking lands. The art section, *La pintura española,* is a special feature of the book. Through the use of carefully selected slides, films, filmstrips, and other visual materials, the teacher may give the student an even wider understanding of Hispanic culture.

The first ten lessons consist of six parts: (*a*) dialogues, preceded by a brief description of the setting; (*b*) *Conversación;* (*c*) *Notas gramaticales;* (*d*) *Ejercicios;* (*e*) *Ejercicios de pronunciación;* (*f*) *Vocabulario.* Beginning with Lesson 11 a *Composición* is included after the *Ejercicios.* The pronunciation section is not continued beyond Lesson 15, but it is assumed that the student will constantly apply the elementary principles acquired up to this point. The new words and expressions listed in each *Vocabulario* are placed at the end of each lesson as a means of encouraging the student to learn them in context.

Habits of speech are formed in the first few weeks of study, hence the dialogues are designed for concentration on the student's hearing and speaking the language. He should listen carefully to the pronunciation and intonation of the teacher, then imitate each phrase or sentence as closely as possible. As an aid to the teacher and student, tape recordings are available for the dialogues and oral exercises of the lessons. A Laboratory Manual, which contains additional drills on pronunciation and structures, is also provided. Students may memorize parts or all of the model passages, or they may retell similar situations using words already presented. Parts of these passages, or of the *Lecturas,* may be used for dictation.

The *Conversación* section of each lesson will facilitate oral work and comprehension, and it will serve to test the student's knowledge of words and phrases that he needs and wants to learn. In each *Conversación* there is a limited number of questions in Spanish which are based on the dialogue, and a second group which represent an application of this material.

The *Notas gramaticales* are grouped and presented in logical sequence as far as possible. Care has been taken to state the explanations simply, but adequately, and in terms easily understood by beginning students. Emphasis has been placed upon general principles which arise naturally from Spanish usage, and exceptions are held to a minimum. The examples, drawn largely from the dialogue, are given before the explanations so that the student may be encouraged to make deductions on his own initiative. Frequent cross references are made to similar or contrasting constructions. A short section called *Práctica* is included for further drill after the discussion of certain troublesome points of grammatical usage. The teacher may want to explain the grammatical items before the student works on the dialogue or other parts of the lesson. In any event, the student should study the *Notas gramaticales* carefully before working on the dialogues.

Recognizing the necessity of a thorough knowledge of verb forms and basic grammatical principles, regardless of the purpose for which Spanish is to be used, special attention has been placed first upon a gradual, logical, and clear presentation of the forms, and then upon adequate and varied drill exercises. Function and usage are gradually taught. The English sentences, for which the Spanish equivalent is to be given, appear as the last exercise in each regular lesson. This section may be used at the discretion of the teacher, depending on the emphasis placed on written work. In these sentences the student is asked to write only what he should have learned to understand, say, and read correctly. The *Composición,* of varied nature, serves to encourage more creative and original involvement of the student. This section may be assigned in addition to the English-Spanish sentences, or used as an alternate exercise. The *Repasos,* spaced at five-lesson intervals, provide further drill on the material of the preceding lessons.

The four *Conversaciones,* which follow Lessons 9, 13, 20, and 23, offer additional oral practice on topics which should be of interest to students. The new words in these selections are repeated in the lesson vocabularies if they are used again in the regular lessons.

The *Lecturas,* introduced after Lesson 6, are designed so that the student can read with understanding without conscious translation. They are closely correlated with the dialogues and grammatical notes, so that the student is not introduced to troublesome constructions before they have been used or explained in the regular lessons. The series of questions in Spanish will test the student's comprehension of the *Lecturas.* The short notes and exercises in the *Estudio de palabras* section, which follows the questions, should aid greatly in building a working vocabulary. Some five per cent of the individual words used in the *Lecturas* are identical cognates, and nearly sixty per cent are recognizable cognates, leaving only approximately thirty-five per cent which may not be recognized from the context. Many words in the latter group are listed in footnotes, to avoid vocabulary thumbing and to facilitate reading. Idioms and difficult phrases are also included in the footnotes. Words and phrases used first in the *Lecturas* are listed in the active vocabularies if used again in the dialogues. Thus, a teacher may omit the *Lecturas* entirely, he may assign them as outside reading, or he may take them up at any subsequent period of the year.

For those who may wish to carry on social or commercial correspondence in Spanish, some commonly used phrases and formulas are given in the special section on letter writing, called *Cartas españolas.*

Appendix A contains the Spanish alphabet, lists of expressions used in the classroom and the laboratory, grammatical terms, punctuation marks, and the abbreviations and signs used in the text; and Appendix B contains a complete list of verb forms used in the text, as well as a few additional verbs which may be encountered in later study of Spanish.

The Spanish-English vocabulary is intended to be complete with the exception of a few proper and geographical names which are either identical in Spanish and English or whose meaning is clear, a few past participles used as adjectives when the infinitive is given, titles of certain literary works mentioned in the *Lecturas,* the supplementary list of foods on pages 305–306, and Spanish examples translated in the *Cartas españolas* section. Idioms are listed under the most important word in the phrase, and, in most cases, cross listings are given. The English-Spanish vocabulary contains only the English words used in the English-Spanish exercises of the text.

In this fourth edition of *Foundation Course in Spanish* there are two preliminary lessons instead of one. The dialogues have been rewritten and updated in contents. In most cases they have been divided into two or three self-contained sequences to facilitate the introduction and preparation of the material, and also to provide more oral practice, as well as to afford flexibility of assignment. An effort has been made to clarify some of the more difficult matters taken up in the *Notas gramaticales.* Many of the drill exercises, both oral and written, have been revised. The two preliminary Lessons, along with the *Ejercicios de pronunciación,* constitute an elementary, but adequate, survey of the features of Spanish pronunciation and intonation which English-speaking students find most troublesome. The last regular lesson of the third edition has been dropped and most of the grammatical material contained in it has been spread through the last four lessons. The number of *Conversaciones* has been reduced from five to four. The *Lecturas* have been reorganized and rewritten. Two new ones have been added, several have been combined, and parts of others deleted. All the photographs included in the color section *Viñetas Culturales* and most of the reproductions in *La pintura española* are new.

The Workbook offers additional drills on pronunciation and intonation and on all the major grammatical structures, and contains exercises based on the reading material. Some of the exercises, including those dealing with pronunciation, have been revised.

To recapitulate, the teacher who wishes to stress hearing and speaking Spanish will emphasize the dialogues and will select from the exercises those which are entirely in the language. The *Conversaciones* will also be assigned. If the teacher does not agree with the conviction of the authors concerning the desirability of the presentation of cultural material in a beginning text, the *Lecturas* may be omitted partially or entirely.

For teachers and students who wish to use *Foundation Course in Spanish, Fourth Edition,* for individualized instruction, a complete individualized program has been prepared largely by Guadalupe Valdés-Fallis.

As the student begins the study of a foreign language, he should recall the years that he has spent gradually learning his own language. After completing this text, he will not be able to talk and read Spanish like a native; however, if he has learned what is included in these pages, he will be able to understand much of what a Spanish-speaking person says, he will be able to say in Spanish many of the ordinary things he wants or needs to say, and he will be able to read and write simple Spanish.

In the preparation of this edition the authors are grateful for reviews and constructive criticism offered by many colleagues who have used the earlier editions, especially to professors Armando F. Concheso and Blas A. Orozco, both from Bergen Community College, for their valuable comments on the audio components—Laboratory Manual and tapes—, of *Foundation Course in Spanish, Fourth Edition.* The authors are also grateful to the staff of the Modern Language Department of D.C. Heath and Company for bringing this project to a successful conclusion.

L.H.T.
A.M.E., JR.
C.A.S., JR.

Contents

ADDITIONAL MATERIALS

   Instructor's Manual
   Workbook/Laboratory Manual
   Individualized Instruction Program
   Tapes
      Number of reels: 17 7″ dual track
      Speed: 3¾ ips
      Running time: 19 hours (approximately)
   Cassettes
      (Same specifications)

FOUNDATION COURSE IN
SPANISH

Saludos y despedidas (*Greetings and farewells*)

SRTA.[1] VALDÉS —Buenos días, señor (señora) López.

"Good morning, Mr. (Mrs.) López."

SR. (SRA.) LÓPEZ —Buenos días, señorita Valdés.

"Good morning, Miss Valdés."

SRTA. VALDÉS —¿Cómo está usted?

"How are you?"

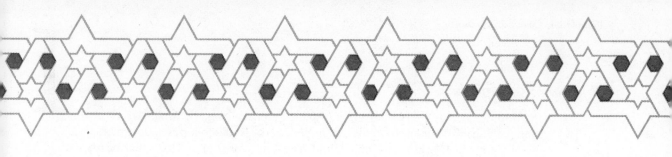

SR. (SRA.) LÓPEZ —Muy bien, gracias. ¿Y usted?	*"Very well, thanks (thank you). And you?"*
SRTA. VALDÉS —Bastante bien, gracias. Hasta luego.	*"Quite well, thanks. Until (See you) later."*
SR. (SRA.) LÓPEZ —Adiós. Hasta luego.	*"Goodbye. Until later."*

◆ ◆ ◆ ◆ ◆

FELIPE —Buenas tardes,[2] Carmen. ¿Cómo estás?	*"Good afternoon, Carmen. How are you?"*
CARMEN —¡Hola, Felipe! ¿Qué tal?	*"Hello, Philip! How goes it?"*
FELIPE —Bien, gracias. Y tú, Carmen, ¿cómo estás?[3]	*"Fine, thanks. And you, Carmen, how are you?"*
CARMEN —Así, así, gracias.	*"So-so, thanks."*
FELIPE —Hasta mañana, Carmen.	*"Until (See you) tomorrow, Carmen."*
CARMEN —Hasta mañana.	*"Until tomorrow."*

Repeat the Spanish dialogues after your teacher, listening carefully to the linking of words together and to the intonation patterns. Read the dialogues, either alone or with a classmate, and then memorize each expression.

---

[1] The abbreviation for **señorita** is **Srta. Señor (Sr.)** and **señora (Sra.)** also mean *sir* and *madam* (*ma'am*), respectively, when the family name is omitted.
[2] **Buenas tardes** may be used in some countries as a greeting in the very early evening, although **Buenas noches,** *Good evening,* is more common. This expression also means *Good night* when taking leave of persons.
[3] See Lesson 1 for a discussion of forms of address in Spanish: **tú** and **usted.** Also see Preliminary Lesson 2 for Spanish punctuation.

The Spanish alphabet[1]

In addition to the letters used in the English alphabet, **ch, ll, ñ,** and **rr** represent single sounds in Spanish and are considered single letters. In dictionaries and vocabularies words or syllables which begin with **ch, ll,** and **ñ** follow words or syllables that begin with **c, l,** and **n,** while **rr,** which never occurs at the beginning of words, is alphabetized as in English. **K** and **w** are used only in words of foreign origin. The names of the letters are feminine: **la be,** (*the*) *b;* **la jota** (*the*) *j.*

The Spanish alphabet is divided into vowels **(a, e, i, o, u)** and consonants. The letter **y** represents the vowel sound **i,** as in the conjunction **y,** *and,* or when final in a word: **hoy,** *today;* **muy,** *very;* **hay,** *there is, there are.*

The Spanish vowels are divided into two groups: strong vowels **(a, e, o)** and weak vowels **(i, u).**

Spanish sounds

Even though Spanish uses practically the same alphabet as English, few sounds are identical in the two languages. It will, however, be necessary to make comparisons between familiar English sounds and the unfamiliar Spanish sounds in order to show how Spanish is pronounced. Avoid the use of English sounds in Spanish words and imitate good Spanish pronunciation.

In general, Spanish pronunciation is much clearer and more uniform than the English. The vowel sounds are clipped short and are not followed by the diphthongal glide which is commonly heard in English, as in *no* (no^u), *came* (ca^ime), *why* (why^e). Even unstressed vowels are pronounced clearly and distinctly; the slurred sound of English *a* in *fireman,* for example, never occurs in Spanish.

Spanish consonants, likewise, are usually pronounced more precisely and distinctly than English consonants, although a few (especially **b, d,** and **g** between vowels) are pronounced very weakly. Several of them **(t, d, l,** and **n)** are pronounced farther forward in the mouth, with the tongue close to the upper teeth and gums. The consonants **p, t,** and **c** (before letters other than **e** and **i**) are never followed by the *h* sound that is often heard in English: *pen* (p^hen), *task* (t^hask), *can* (c^han).

Division of words into syllables

Spanish words are hyphenated at the end of a line and are divided into syllables according to the following principles:

a. A single consonant (including **ch, ll, rr**) is placed with the vowel which follows: **pa-pel, mu-cho, ca-lle, pi-za-rra.**

b. Two consonants are usually divided: **tar-de, es-pa-ñol, tam-bién.** Consonants followed by **l** or **r,** however, are generally pronounced together and go with the following vowel: **li-bro, pa-dre, a-pren-do.** By exception to the last principle, the groups **nl, rl, sl, tl, nr,** and **sr** are divided: **Car-los, En-ri-que.**

---

[1]See Appendix A, page 390, for the Spanish alphabet.

c. In combinations of three or more consonants only the last consonant or the two consonants of the inseparable groups just mentioned (consonant plus **l** or **r**, with the exceptions listed) begin a syllable: **ins-pi-ra-ción, in-glés, en-tra.**

d. Two adjacent strong vowels (**a, e, o**) are in separate syllables: **le-o, tra-e, cre-e.**

e. Combinations of a strong and weak vowel (**i, u**) or of two weak vowels normally form single syllables: **bue-nos, bien, es-tu-dio, gra-cias, ciu-dad, Luis.** Such combinations are called diphthongs. (See page 8 for further discussion of diphthongs.)

f. In combinations of a strong and weak vowel, a written accent mark on the weak vowel divides the two vowels into separate syllables: **dí-a, pa-ís, tí-o.** An accent on the strong vowel of such combinations does not result in two syllables: **lec-ción, tam-bién.**

Word stress

a. Most words which end in a vowel, and in **n** or **s** (plural endings of verbs and nouns, respectively), are stressed on the next to the last syllable. The stressed syllable or syllables are in italics: ***cla*-se, *to*-mo, *ca*-sas, *en*-tran, *Car*-men.**

b. Most words which end in a consonant, except **n** or **s**, are stressed on the last syllable: **pro-fe-*sor*, ha-*blar*, pa-*pel*, ciu-*dad*, es-pa-*ñol*.**

c. Words not pronounced according to these two rules have a written accent on the stressed syllable: **ca-*fé*, in-*glés*, lec-*ción*, tam-*bién*, *ár*-bol, *lá*-piz.**

d. The written accent is also used to distinguish between two words spelled alike but different in meaning (**si,** *if,* **sí,** *yes;* **el,** *the,* **él,** *he,* etc.), and on the stressed syllable of all interrogative words (**¿*cuán*-do?** *when?*) and of a few exclamatory words (**¡*Qué no*-che!** *What a night!*)

Vowels

a is pronounced between the *a* of English *ask* and the *a* of *father:* ***ca*-sa, *ha*-bla, *A*-na.**

e is pronounced like *e* in *café,* but without the glide sound that follows the *e* in English: ***me*-sa, *cla*-se, us-*ted*.**

i (y) is pronounced like *i* in *machine:* **Fe-*li*-pe, *sí*, *dí*-as, y.**

o is pronounced like *o* in *obey,* but without the glide sound that follows the *o* in English: **no, *so*-lo, cho-co-*la*-te.**

u is pronounced like *oo* in *cool:* **us-*ted*, *u*-no, a-*lum*-no.**

The vowels **e** and **o** also have sounds like *e* in *let* and *o* in *for.* These sounds, as in English, generally occur when the **e** and **o** are followed by a consonant in the same syllable: ***él, ser, con,* es-pa-*ñol*.** In pronouncing the **e** in **él** and **ser,** and the **o** in **con** and **español,** the mouth is opened wider; and the distance between the tongue and the palate is greater, than when pronouncing the **e** in **mesa** and **clase,** and the **o** in **no** and **solo.** These more open sounds of **e** and **o** occur also in contact with the strongly trilled **r (rr),** before the **j** sound (written **g** before **e** or **i,** and **j**), and in the diphthongs **ei (ey)** and **oi (oy).** Pay close attention to the teacher's pronunciation of these sounds.

Consonants

b and **v** are pronounced exactly alike. At the beginning of a breath-group (see page 8), or after **m** and **n,** the sound is that of a weakly pronounced English *b:* ***bien, bue*-nas, *ver*-de,**

vi-da. In other places, particularly between vowels, the sound is much weaker than the English *b*. The lips touch very lightly, leaving a narrow opening in the center, and the breath continues to pass between them. Avoid the English *v* sound. Examples: **li-bro, es-*cri*-bo,** *la*-vo, **Cu-ba.**

c before **e** and **i,** and **z** in all positions, are pronounced like the English hissed *s* in *sent* in Spanish America and in southern Spain. In northern and central Spain this sound is like *th* in *thin*. Examples: **cen-*ta*-vo,** *ci*-ne, **gra-cias, lá-piz.**

c before all other letters, **k,** and **qu** are like English *c* in *cat*, but without the *h* sound that often follows the *c* in English: *ca*-sa, *cla*-se, **ki-*ló*-me-tro, qué, par-que.** Note both sounds of **c** in *cin*-co, lec-*ción*.

ch is pronounced like English *ch* in *church*: **mu-cho, le-che, cho-co-*la*-te.**

d has two sounds. At the beginning of a breath-group or following **l** or **n,** it is pronounced like a weak English *d*, but with the tongue touching the back of the upper front teeth rather than the ridge above the teeth, as in English: *dos, dón*-de, **sal-*dré*.** In other places, particularly between vowels and at the end of a word, the sound is like a weakly articulated English *th* in *this*: *ca*-da, *to*-do, us-*ted*, **Ma-*drid*.**

f is pronounced like English *f*: **ca-*fé*, Fe-*li*-pe.**

g before **e** and **i,** and **j** in all positions, have no English equivalent. They are pronounced approximately like a strongly exaggerated *h* in *halt* (rather like the rasping German *ch* in *BUCH*): **gen-te, hi-jo, Jor-ge, re-*gión*.** (The letter **x** in the words **México** and **mexicano,** spelled **Méjico** and **mejicano** in Spain, is pronounced like Spanish **j.**)

g in other positions and **gu** before **e** or **i** are pronounced like a weak English *g* in *go* at the beginning of a breath-group or after **n.** In other cases, especially between vowels, the sound is much weaker, and the breath continues to pass between the back of the tongue and the palate. Examples: *gra*-cias, **gui-*ta*-rra, ten-go;** but **ha-go, lue-go, por-tu-*gués*.** (In the combinations **gua** and **guo** the **u** is pronounced like English *w* in *wet*: **len-gua, a-gua, an-*ti*-guo;** when the diaeresis is used over **u** in the combinations **güe** and **güi,** the **u** has the same sound: **ni-ca-ra-*güen*-se.**)

h is always silent: **ha-*blar*, has-ta, hoy.**

l is pronounced like *l* in *leap*, with the tip and front part of the tongue well forward in the mouth: *la*-do, **pa-*pel*.**

ll is pronounced like *y* in *yes* in most of Spanish America and in some sections of Spain; in other parts of Spain it is somewhat like *lli* in *million*: **e-lla, *ca*-lle, lla-*mar*.**

m is pronounced like English *m*: *to*-ma, **me-sa.**

n is pronounced like English *n*: **no, Car-men.** Before **b, v, m,** and **p,** however, it is pronounced like *m*: **un-po-co, con-*Bár*-ba-ra.** Before **c, qu, g,** and **j** it is pronounced like English *n* in *sing*: *blan*-co, **ten-go, *án*-gel.**

ñ is somewhat like the English *ny* in *canyon*: **se-*ñor*, ma-*ña*-na, es-pa-*ñol*.**

p is pronounced like English *p*, but without the *h* sound that often follows the *p* in English: *pe*-lo, **pa-*pel*.**

q (always written with **u**): see above and page 30, under **c, k,** and **qu.**

r and **rr** represent two different sounds. Single **r,** except at the beginning of a word, or after **l, n,** or **s,** is pronounced with a single tap produced by the tip of the tongue against the gums of the upper teeth. The sound is much like *dd* in *eddy* pronounced rapidly: *ca*-ra, *to*-ro, **ha-*blar*.** Initial **r, r** after **l, n,** or **s,** and **rr** are strongly trilled: *ri*-co, *ro*-jo, **Ro-*ber*-to, pi-*za*-rra, *co*-rre, En-*ri*-que.**

s is pronounced somewhat like the English hissed *s* in *sent:* **ca-sa, es-tos.** Before **b, d, g, l, ll, m, n, v,** and **y** the sound is like the English *s* in *rose:* **mis-mo, ras-go, es ver-***dad*, **los li-***bros.*

t is pronounced with the tip of the tongue touching the back of the upper front teeth (rather than the ridge above the teeth, as in English); it is never followed by the *h* sound that is often heard in English: **to-do, tar-des, tiem-po.**

v: see pages 3–4, under **b.**

x is pronounced as follows: (1) Before a consonant it is pronounced like English hissed *s* in *sent:* **ex-plo-***rar,* **ex-tran-***je***-ro;** (2) between vowels it is usually a double sound, consisting of a weak English *g* in *go* followed by a hissed *s:* **e-***xa***-men, é-***xi***-to.**

y is pronounced like a strong English *y* in *you:* **ya, yo, ma-yo.** The conjunction **y,** *and,* when combined with the initial vowel of a following word is similarly pronounced: **Car-los-***y* **A-na.**

EXERCISES

A. Vowel sounds. Pronounce after your teacher, following the explanations given on page 3:

a Ana, Amalia, hasta, casa, mañana, marchar, Marta, pasar.
e él, en, francés, inglés, José, leer, leche, qué.
o cómo, poco, señor, no, con, Carlos, español, profesor.
i dice, Felipe, libro, lista, así, señorita, y, día.
u alumno, escuchan, lectura, mucho, plumas, pregunta, uno, usted.

B. The sounds of Spanish **d.** Pronounce after your teacher, following the explanations given on page 4:

1. adiós, cada, estudiar, los dos, madre, padre, tarde, usted.
2. donde, día, el día, un día, leyendo, dos, con dos, saldré.

C. Rewrite the following words, dividing them into syllables by means of a hyphen (-), and underlining the syllable that is stressed; then pronounce:

1. Carmen, inglés, español, marchar, preparan, señorita.
2. día, lección, país, principio, pronuncian, siempre.

D. Pronounce the following given names after your teacher. If you cannot figure out the English meaning of each name, you will find it in the end vocabulary:

1. Marta, María, Carolina, Luisa, Inés, Julia, Isabel, Margarita, Elena, Beatriz, Juanita, Ana.
2. Felipe, Juan, Jorge, Tomás, Ricardo, Vicente, Ramón, Miguel, Jaime, Carlos, Eduardo, Roberto.

For further practice your teacher may ask you to divide the above names into syllables and underline the syllable that is stressed.

PRELIMINARY LESSON II

Frases para la clase[1] (*Classroom expressions*)

Escuche usted. Escuchen ustedes.	*Listen.*
Repita usted. Repitan ustedes.	*Repeat.*

◆ ◆ ◆ ◆

—Siéntense ustedes, por favor. Voy a pasar lista. ¿Carlos?

"Sit down, please. I am going to call the roll. Charles?"

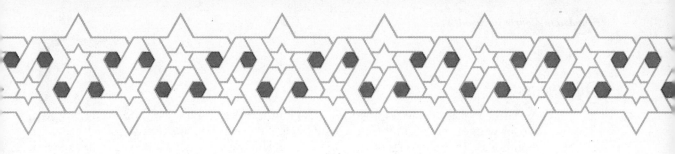

—Presente.   *"Present."*
—¿Qué lección tenemos hoy?   *"What lesson do we have today?"*
—Tenemos la Lección dos.   *"We have Lesson Two."*
—Abran ustedes sus libros. Carlos,   *"Open your books. Charles, read in*
     lea usted en español.   *Spanish."*

◆   ◆   ◆   ◆

—Está bien. ¿Quién quiere hacer   *"All right (That's fine). Who wants*
     una pregunta?   *to ask a question?"*
—¿Qué significa la palabra . . . ?   *"What does the word . . . mean?"*
—La palabra . . . significa . . . . La   *"The word . . . means . . . . The*
     clase ha terminado. Ustedes   *class has ended. You may leave*
     pueden marcharse.   *(You are excused)."*

Repeat the classroom expressions after your teacher, listening carefully to the linking of words together and to the intonation patterns. Memorize each expression.

---

[1] SPECIAL NOTE TO THE TEACHER. See Appendix A, pages 390–391, for a more complete list of classroom expressions which you may wish to introduce as they come up naturally. Others will be used in the regular lessons. Also in Appendix A you will find a list of expressions for use in the language laboratory.

Diphthongs

As stated on page 3, the weak vowels **i (y)** and **u** may combine with the strong vowels **a, e, o,** or with each other to form single syllables. Such combinations of two vowels are called diphthongs. In diphthongs the strong vowels retain their full syllabic value, while the weak vowels, or the first vowel in the case of two weak vowels, lose part of their syllabic value.

As the first element of a diphthong, unstressed **i** is pronounced like a weak English *y* in *yes,* and unstressed **u** is pronounced like *w* in *wet.* The Spanish diphthongs which begin with unstressed **i** and **u** are: **ia, ie, io, iu; ua, ue, uo, ui,** as in *gra*-cias, *bien,* a-*diós,* ciu-*dad*; *a*-gua, *bue*-no, an-*ti*-guo, *Luis.* (The sounds of the other diphthongs will be discussed later.)

Remember that two adjacent strong vowels within a word form separate syllables: *le*-e, *cre*-o. Likewise, when a weak vowel adjacent to a strong vowel has a written accent, it retains its syllabic value and forms a separate syllable: *dí*-a, pa-*ís.* An accent mark on a strong vowel merely indicates stress: **lec-*ción*, tam-*bién*.**

Triphthongs

A triphthong is a combination in a single syllable of a stressed strong vowel between two weak vowels. There are four combinations: **iai, iei, uai (uay), uei (uey),** as in **es-tu-*diáis,* pro-nun-*ciéis*, Pa-ra-*guay,* con-ti-*nuéis*.**

Linking

In speaking or reading Spanish, words are linked together, as in English, so that two or more may sound as one long word. These groups of words are called breath-groups. It is necessary to practice pronouncing phrases and even entire sentences without a pause between words. Frequently a short sentence will be pronounced as one breath-group, while a longer one may be divided into two or more groups. The meaning of what is being pronounced will help you to determine where the pauses ending the breath-groups should be made.

The following examples illustrate some of the general principles of linking. The syllabic division in parentheses shows the correct linking; the syllable or syllables italicized bear the main stress.

a. Within a breath-group the final consonant of a word is joined with the initial vowel of the following word and forms a syllable with it: **el alumno (e-la-*lum*-no).**

b. Within a breath-group when two identical vowels of different words come together, they are pronounced as one: **el profesor de español (el-pro-fe-*sor*-de es-pa-*ñol*).**

c. When unlike vowels between words come together within a breath-group, they are usually pronounced together in a single syllable. Two cases occur: (1) when a strong vowel is followed or preceded by a weak vowel, both are pronounced together in a single syllable and the result is phonetically a diphthong (see above): **su amigo (su a-*mi*-go), Juan y Elena (*Jua*-n y E-*le*-na), mi padre y mi madre (mi-*pa*-dre y-mi-*ma*-dre)**; (2) if both vowels are strong, each loses a little of its syllabic value and both are pronounced together in one syllable: **vamos a la escuela (*va*-mo-sa-la es-*cue*-la); ¿Cómo está usted? (¿*Có*-mo es-*tá* us-ted?).**

Intonation

The term intonation refers to the variations in pitch which occur in speech. Every language has its characteristic patterns of intonation. The intonation of Spanish is quite different from that of English.

The alternate rise and fall of the pitch depends upon the particular meaning of the sentence, the position of stressed syllables, and whether the sentence expresses command, affirmation, interrogation, exclamation, request, or other factors. In general, three meaningful levels of pitch can be distinguished in Spanish: one below the speaker's normal pitch (level 1), the speaker's normal tone (level 2), and a tone higher than the normal one (level 3). Study carefully these examples:

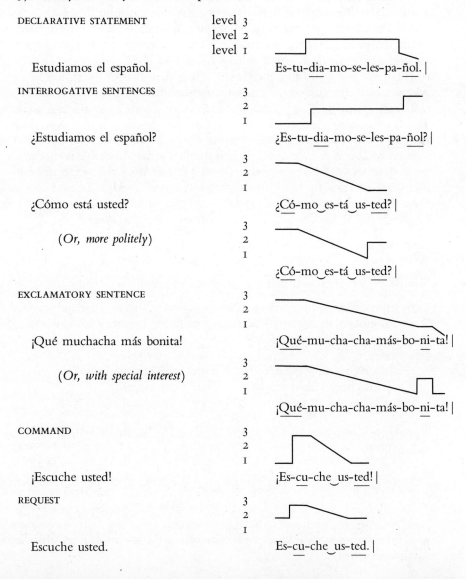

DECLARATIVE STATEMENT   level 3
                               level 2
                               level 1
Estudiamos el español.   Es–tu–dia–mo–se–les–pa–ñol. |

INTERROGATIVE SENTENCES   3
                               2
                               1
¿Estudiamos el español?   ¿Es–tu–dia–mo–se–les–pa–ñol? |

                               3
                               2
                               1
¿Cómo está usted?   ¿Có–mo es–tá us–ted? |

(*Or, more politely*)   3
                               2
                               1
                               ¿Có–mo es–tá us–ted? |

EXCLAMATORY SENTENCE   3
                               2
                               1
¡Qué muchacha más bonita!   ¡Qué–mu–cha–cha–más–bo–ni–ta! |

(*Or, with special interest*) 3
                               2
                               1
                               ¡Qué–mu–cha–cha–más–bo–ni–ta! |

COMMAND   3
                               2
                               1
¡Escuche usted!   ¡Es–cu–che us–ted! |

REQUEST   3
                               2
                               1
Escuche usted.   Es–cu–che us–ted. |

With respect to the use of these levels, the following basic principles should be observed:

a. At the beginning of a breath-group, the voice begins and continues in a relatively low pitch (level 1) as long as the first accented syllable is not reached.

b. When the first accented syllable of a breath-group is reached, the voice rises to the speaker's normal tone (level 2) and continues in the same pitch as long as the last accented syllable is not reached.

c. When the last accented syllable of the breath-group is reached, the voice falls or rises, depending on the following circumstances:

(1) At the end of a declarative statement, the voice falls to a pitch even lower than that of the initial unaccented syllable or syllables.

(2) At the end of an interrogative sentence, or of an incomplete sentence interrupted by a pause, the voice rises to a pitch above the normal tone (level 3).

d. In exclamations, and in questions which begin with an interrogative word, the voice begins in a pitch above the normal tone (level 3) and gradually falls in the following syllables as long as the final accented syllable is not reached; when the last accented syllable is reached, the voice falls to a pitch even lower than that of the initial unaccented syllable or syllables, as in the case of the end of a simple affirmative sentence, unless special interest or courtesy is intended, in which case the voice rises to the normal tone or even higher.

e. The pattern observed in an exclamatory sentence is also typical of commands and requests. In commands, the voice begins on a relatively low tone (level 1) as long as the first stressed syllable is not reached. When the first stressed syllable is reached, it is pronounced on a tone above the normal one (level 3), and then the voice descends notably in the following syllables; the last syllable (stressed or unstressed) is uttered on a tone below that of the initial unstressed syllable or syllables. Requests differ from commands in that the entire breath-group is usually uttered on a somewhat higher tone.

Punctuation

Spanish punctuation is much the same as in English. The most important differences are:

1. Inverted question marks and exclamation points precede questions and exclamations. They are placed at the actual beginning of the question or exclamation, not necessarily at the beginning of the sentence:

¿Hablan Carlos y Juan?   Are Charles and John talking?
¡Qué muchacha más bonita!   What a pretty girl!
Usted es español, ¿verdad?   You are a Spaniard, aren't you?

2. In Spanish a comma is not used between the last two words of a series, while in English it usually is:

Tenemos plumas, libros y lápices.   We have pens, books, and pencils.

3. A dash is generally used instead of the quotation marks of English and to denote a change of speaker in dialogue. It appears at the beginning of each speech, but is omitted at the end.

—**¿Es usted peruano?**   "Are you a Peruvian?"
—**Sí, señor. Soy de Lima.**   "Yes, sir. I am from Lima."

If quotation marks are used, they are placed on the line:

Juan dijo: «Buenos días».   John said, "Good morning."

Capitalization

Only proper names and the first word of a sentence begin with a capital letter in Spanish. The subject pronoun **yo** (*I* in English), names of months and days of the week, adjectives of nationality and nouns formed from them, and titles (unless abbreviated) are not capitalized. In titles of books or works of art, only the first word is capitalized.

Juan y yo hablamos.   John and I are talking.
Hoy es lunes.   Today is Monday.
Buenos días, señor (Sr.) Pidal.   Good morning, Mr. Pidal.
Son españoles.   They are Spanish (Spaniards).
El entierro del conde de Orgaz.   The Burial of the Count of Orgaz

EXERCISES

A. Review the sounds of Spanish **i** and **u**. Pronounce after your teacher:

  1. dice, Felipe, libro, lista, sí, siga, y, día.
  2. alumno, escuchan, lectura, mucho, plumas, uno, usted.

B. Spanish diphthongs. Pronounce after your teacher, following the explanations given on page 8:

  1. **i** + vowel   gracias, pronuncia; bien, siempre; lección, adiós, ciudad.
  2. **u** + vowel   cuaderno, cual, cuando; bueno, puede, puerta; muy, Luis.

C. Linking. Pronounce after your teacher, following the explanations given on page 8:

la alumna	clase de inglés	Ana habla bien.	¿Cómo estás?
los alumnos	clase de español	Hablo español.	Lea usted.
su hermano	Repitan ustedes.	Felipe estudia.	Siéntense ustedes.

D. Rewrite the following words, dividing them into syllables by means of a hyphen and underlining the syllable that is stressed; then pronounce:

  1. bastante, noches, amarillo, pizarra, escribir, universidad.
  2. gracias, cuaderno, biblioteca, avión, paseo, frío.

Present indicative of the first conjugation • **Use of subject pronouns** •
Gender and plural of nouns • **Use of the definite article** •
Negative and interrogative sentences

Conversaciones en la clase de español

La profesora de español habla con los alumnos.

SRTA.[1] VALDÉS —Buenos días (Buenas tardes), Carmen.
CARMEN —Buenos días (Buenas tardes), señorita Valdés.
SRTA. VALDÉS —Carmen, ¿habla usted español?
CARMEN —Sí, señorita, hablo español un poco.

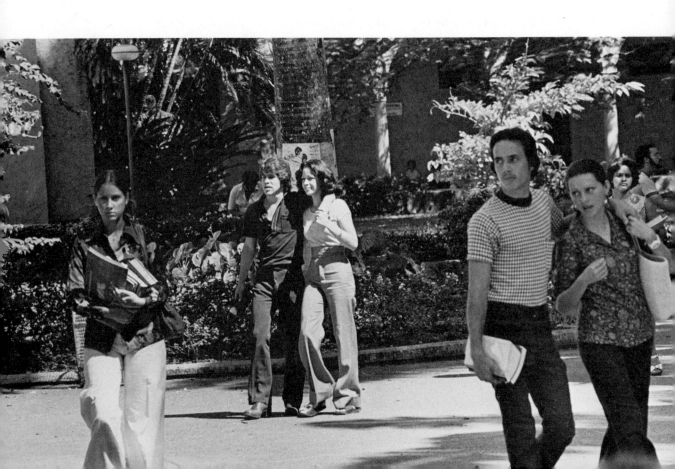

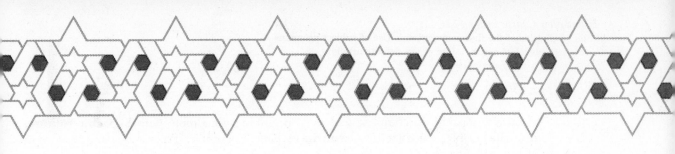

SRTA. VALDÉS —Felipe, ¿hablamos inglés en clase?

FELIPE —No, señorita, en clase no hablamos inglés. ¡Sólo hablamos español!

SRTA. VALDÉS —¿Qué lengua hablan ustedes con el profesor de inglés?

FELIPE —Hablamos inglés con el profesor de inglés.

◆ ◆ ◆ ◆

SRTA. VALDÉS —Ana, ¿estudia usted mucho?

ANA —Sí, señorita, estudio todos los días (todas las tardes, todas las noches).

SRTA. VALDÉS —¿Prepara usted la lección de español en clase?

ANA —No, señorita, siempre preparo la lección en casa.

SRTA. VALDÉS —Carlos, ¿qué lenguas estudian los alumnos en España?

CARLOS —En España los alumnos estudian (el) francés, (el) alemán . . . ¡Ah, y estudian (el) inglés!

SRTA. VALDÉS —¿Pronuncian bien las alumnas de la clase?

CARLOS —Sí, señorita, las alumnas pronuncian bastante bien.

SRTA. VALDÉS —Isabel, ¿pronuncian bien los alumnos?

ISABEL —Cuando estudian un poco, no pronuncian mal.

SRTA. VALDÉS —¿Prepara usted las lecciones con Carlos o con Carmen?

ISABEL —Preparo las lecciones con Carmen.

SRTA. VALDÉS —¡Muy bien! Ustedes hablan y pronuncian muy bien el español.

Conversación

Answer in Spanish in complete sentences, beginning your reply with **Sí, señor (señora, señorita)** or **No, señor (señora, señorita)** whenever possible. Follow the same practice in all subsequent lessons.

A. Preguntas sobre el diálogo (*Questions on the dialogue*)

1. ¿Habla Carmen español?   2. ¿Qué lengua hablan los alumnos en clase?   3. ¿Qué lengua hablan los alumnos con el profesor de inglés?   4. ¿Estudia Ana todos los días?   5. ¿Prepara Ana la lección en clase?   6. ¿Estudian (el) inglés los alumnos en España?   7. ¿Pronuncian bien las alumnas de la clase?   8. ¿Pronuncian bien los alumnos?

B. Aplicación del diálogo (*Dialogue adaptation*)

1. ¿Qué lengua habla usted?   2. ¿Estudia usted (el) francés?   3. ¿Qué lengua estudiamos en clase?   4. ¿Qué lengua hablan los alumnos en la clase de inglés?   5. ¿Estudia usted mucho?   6. ¿Hablamos mucho en clase?   7. ¿Estudia usted todas las noches (todas las tardes)?   8. ¿Preparan ustedes las lecciones en casa?   9. Y yo, ¿también preparo las lecciones?   10. ¿Qué lenguas hablo yo?

NOTAS GRAMATICALES (*Grammatical notes*)

A. Present indicative of the first conjugation

The infinitive of a Spanish verb consists of a stem **(habl)** and an ending **(-ar).** The three conjugations in Spanish end **-ar, -er, -ir,** and are usually referred to as the first, second, and third conjugations, respectively.

    To form the present tense of regular verbs of the first conjugation, add the endings **-o, -as, -a, -amos, -áis, -an** to the stem of the verb.

hablar, to speak	
singular	
(yo) **hablo**	I speak, do speak, am speaking
(tú) **hablas** (*fam.*)	you speak, do speak, are speaking
(él) **habla**	he speaks, does speak, is speaking
(ella) **habla**	she speaks, does speak, is speaking
usted **habla** (*formal*)	you speak, do speak, are speaking

plural	
(nosotros) **hablamos**	we speak, do speak, are speaking
(nosotras) **hablamos**	we (*fem.*) speak, do speak, are speaking
(vosotros) **habláis** (*fam.*)[1]	you speak, do speak, are speaking
(vosotras) **habláis** (*fam.*)	you (*fem.*) speak, do speak, are speaking
(ellos) **hablan**	they speak, do speak, are speaking
(ellas) **hablan**	they (*fem.*) speak, do speak, are speaking
ustedes **hablan** (*fam. and formal*)	you (*pl.*) speak, do speak, are speaking

Note that the present tense corresponds in English not only to the simple present, *I speak,* but also to the emphatic *I do speak* and to the progressive, *I am speaking.*

B. Use of subject pronouns

1. **Hablo español.**   I speak Spanish.
   Ella habla y él estudia.   She talks and he studies.
   Carlos y yo preparamos la lección.   Charles and I prepare the lesson.
   Usted estudia mucho.   You study hard (a great deal).

The subject pronouns (**yo,** *I;* **él,** *he,* etc.) are not always required in Spanish since the verb ending often indicates the subject. The subject pronouns, however, are used for emphasis (**hablamos,** *we speak,* but **nosotros hablamos,** *we speak*), for clearness (**él habla,** *he speaks;* **ella habla,** *she speaks*), or when a pronoun is combined with a noun or another pronoun to form a compound subject (**Carlos y yo hablamos,** *Charles and I speak*). For the sake of courtesy, the pronouns **usted** and **ustedes** (often abbreviated to **Ud.** and **Uds.** or to **Vd.** and **Vds.**) are usually expressed in Spanish. The subject *it* is rarely expressed.

2. Spanish has two forms for *you.* The familiar singular form **tú** is used when speaking to a relative, a child, or anyone with whom one is on a first-name basis. The formal **usted** (*pl.* **ustedes**) is normally used in addressing other persons. Since **usted** is a contraction of **vuestra merced,** *Your Grace,* it requires the third person of the verb, that is, the same form of the verb as **él, ella, Carlos.**

The plural of familiar **tú** is **vosotros, vosotras,** which take the second person plural forms of the verb. In Spanish America these forms are replaced by **ustedes,** which is used for the plural *you,* both familiar and formal.

C. Gender and plural of nouns

singular				*plural*			
Masculine		*Feminine*		*Masculine*		*Feminine*	
el alumno	the pupil	**la alumna**	the pupil	**los alumnos**	the pupils	**las alumnas**	the pupils
el profesor	the teacher	**la profesora**	the teacher	**los profesores**	the teachers	**las profesoras**	the teachers
el día	the day	**la lección**	the lesson	**los días**	the days	**las lecciones**	the lessons

---

[1] In Spanish America the second person plural forms in **-áis** are not used; the pronoun **ustedes** is used for the plural *you,* both familiar and formal. The second person plural forms may be omitted in the early stages of the study of Spanish; they will not be used in the exercises of this book until Lesson 24.

Nouns in Spanish are either masculine or feminine in gender. Most nouns which end in **-o** are masculine, and those which end in **-a** are generally feminine. An exception is **el día,** *the day.* Since many nouns have other endings, learn the definite article, *the* in English, with each noun. The masculine forms of the definite article are **el** (singular) and **los** (plural); the feminine forms are **la** and **las.** The definite article agrees in gender and number with the noun.

Certain masculine nouns ending in **-o** have a corresponding feminine form ending in **-a: el alumno, la alumna.** (See page 56 for other nouns of this type.) In the case of certain nouns ending in a consonant, **-a** is added for the corresponding feminine form: **el profesor, la profesora.**

Nouns which end in a vowel regularly add **-s** to form the plural; nouns ending in a consonant add **-es.**

Nouns which end in **-ción,** like **lección** and **conversación,** are feminine in Spanish. Remember that the accent mark is not required in writing the plural of such nouns: **lecciones, conversaciones.**

The masculine plural of nouns referring to persons may include both sexes: **los alumnos,** *the pupils* (boys and girls), **los profesores,** *the teachers* (men and women).

D. Use of the definite article

El profesor y el alumno hablan.　The teacher and (the) pupil talk.
Uds. preparan las lecciones en casa.　You prepare the lessons at home.

BUT: **En España hablan español.**　In Spain they speak Spanish.
¿Habla Ud. francés?　Do you speak French?
Hablo con la profesora de español.　I talk with the Spanish teacher.

The definite article is used more frequently in Spanish than in English. In general, the article is used whenever *the* is used in English, and it is repeated before each noun in a series.

The article is regularly used in Spanish with the name of a language, except after forms of the verb **hablar,** and the prepositions **de** and **en.** Many Spanish-speaking persons, however, also omit the article with a language after verbs meaning *to study, to learn, to read, to write,* and a few others to be introduced later:

Estudian inglés *or* **Estudian el inglés.**　They study (are studying) English.

The article must be used if the name of a language is separated from the verb by some form other than a subject pronoun:

Hablan muy bien el francés.　They speak French very well.
¿Estudian Uds. mucho el español?　Do you study Spanish hard?

Note the position of the adverbs **bien** and **mucho** in the last two examples.

E. Negative and interrogative sentences

 1. **Yo no estudio con Felipe.** I do not study (am not studying) with Philip.
    Ana no habla alemán. Ann does not speak (is not speaking) German.

To make a sentence negative in Spanish place **no** or some other negative word immediately before the verb. The English word *do* (*does*) is not expressed in a negative sentence in Spanish.

 2. **¿Habla Ud. español?** Do you speak Spanish?
    ¿Habla francés el profesor de español? Does the Spanish teacher speak French?
    ¿Estudian mucho los alumnos? Do the pupils study hard?
    ¿No prepara Ud. las lecciones en casa? Don't you prepare the lessons at home?

To formulate a question in Spanish a subject pronoun is usually placed immediately after the verb. If the subject is as long as, or longer than, the object, it is placed at the end of the question (second example). The word *do* (*does*) is not expressed in Spanish.

 3. **¿Qué lenguas estudian?** What languages do they study?
    Carmen, ¿habla Ud. español? Carmen, do you speak Spanish?
    ¿Qué prepara Ud.? What do you prepare *or* What are you preparing?

If an interrogative word introduces the question, it precedes the verb and always has a written accent. An inverted question mark is placed immediately before the question (second example).

EJERCICIOS (*Exercises*)

A. Substitution drill. Repeat the model sentence after your teacher. He/She will repeat your response, pause slightly, and then give a word or expression which you will substitute in your next response. (The teacher may ask part, or all, of the class to reply.)

MODEL: *Teacher.*[1] ¿Habla usted español?   *Student.* ¿Habla usted español?

    Teacher. ¿Habla usted español? ¿inglés? *Student.* ¿Habla usted inglés?

1. ¿Habla usted francés?   2. Estudiamos (el) español.
    alemán?   (el) francés.
    mucho?   (el) inglés.
    con Carlos?   todos los días.
    en clase?   en casa.

[1]Hereafter the model sentence given by the teacher will be listed at the left, and the student response(s) at the right in italics.

B. Substitution drill. Repeat the model sentence. When you hear a new subject, give a new sentence, making the verb agree with the subject:

MODEL: Yo hablo español.   *Yo hablo español.*
           Nosotros   *Nosotros hablamos español.*

1. Felipe habla español.
   Ellos
   Tú
   Usted
   Yo

2. Ella siempre prepara la lección.
   Yo
   Tú
   Nosotros
   Ustedes

3. Felipe no estudia mucho.
   Los alumnos
   Carlos y yo
   Tú
   Ella y él

4. Él pronuncia bien el español.
   Tú
   Ellos
   La alumna
   Felipe y yo

C. Repeat after your teacher; then change all possible forms to the plural:

MODEL: Yo estudio la lección.   *Yo estudio la lección.*
                                Nosotros estudiamos las lecciones.

1. Él prepara la lección.
2. Usted habla bastante bien.
3. Ella no pronuncia mal.

4. La profesora habla en español.
5. ¿Estudia mucho el alumno?
6. Yo hablo con el profesor de inglés.

D. Repeat after your teacher; then make each sentence negative:

MODEL: Carmen habla con Ana.   *Carmen habla con Ana.*
                              Carmen no habla con Ana.

1. Carlos habla con las alumnas.
2. Isabel prepara las lecciones.
3. El profesor de español habla bien.

4. Usted pronuncia bien el español.
5. Tú estudias (el) francés.
6. Yo estudio y él habla.

E. Answer affirmatively, beginning with **Sí, señor (señora, señorita):**

MODEL: ¿Estudia ella (el) español?   *Sí, señor (señora, señorita), ella estudia (el) español.*

1. ¿Hablan español Carlos y Ana?
2. ¿Estudian los alumnos en casa?
3. ¿Estudia usted en clase?

4. ¿Pronuncian ustedes muy bien?
5. ¿Hablo yo español en clase?
6. ¿Preparo yo las lecciones de español?

F. Put into questions, following the models:

MODELS: Carlos estudia (el) español. *¿Estudia Carlos (el) español?*
          La alumna pronuncia bien. *¿Pronuncia bien la alumna?*

1. Carmen prepara los ejercicios.   4. El profesor habla con las alumnas.
2. Los alumnos estudian mucho.   5. Usted prepara la lección de español.
3. Ustedes estudian en casa.   6. Los profesores pronuncian bien.

G. Say after your teacher; then repeat, substituting the name of another language:

MODEL: la clase de español   *la clase de español*
                               la clase de alemán (or *francés, etc.*)

1. la lección de inglés   4. la profesora de francés
2. las clases de alemán   5. las lecciones de alemán
3. el profesor de español   6. los profesores de inglés

H. Give the Spanish equivalent:

1. "Good morning, Charles. Do you speak Spanish?"[1] 2. "Yes, ma'am, I speak a little in class." 3. "Betty, are you studying English and Spanish?" 4. "Yes, ma'am, and I study the Spanish lessons well every night." 5. "Do you (*pl.*) speak Spanish in the English class?" 6. "No, ma'am, we do not speak Spanish with the English teacher." 7. "Ann, do you prepare the exercises in class?" 8. "No, I always study at home." 9. "What languages do the students study in Spain?" 10. "In Spain they study English, French, and German."

EJERCICIOS DE PRONUNCIACIÓN (*Pronunciation exercises*)

A. Spanish **b** and **v**

1. Spanish **b** and **v** are pronounced exactly alike. At the beginning of a breath-group, or after **m** and **n,** the sound is that of a weak English *b*. Pronounce after your teacher:

basta	bien	buenos días	Valdés
verde	vida	Vicente	también

2. In other places, particularly between vowels, the sound is much weaker. The lips touch very lightly, and the breath continues to pass through a narrow opening in the center. Avoid the English *v* sound. Pronounce after your teacher:

Roberto	hablamos	hablo	Isabel
libro	muy bien	beber	vivir

---
[1] Remember that in Spanish a dash is generally used instead of quotation marks and to denote a change in speaker in dialogue. It appears at the beginning of each speech, but is omitted at the end. (See the explanation and examples on pages 10 and 11.)

B. The sounds of Spanish **d**

Spanish **d** has two basic sounds: (1) at the beginning of a breath-group or when after **n** or **l**, it is pronounced like English *d*, but, as in Spanish **t**, the tip of the tongue touches the inner surface of the upper teeth, rather than the ridge above the teeth. Pronounce after your teacher:

donde	día	el día	un día
leyendo	dos	con dos	saldré

(2) In all other cases, the tongue drops even lower, and the **d** is pronounced like a weak English *th* in *this*. The sound is especially weak in the ending **-ado** and when final in a word before a pause. Pronounce after your teacher:

adiós	estudiar	los días	madre
tarde	todos	usted	verdad

C. Review linking, page 8, and pronounce as one breath-group:

en España	Buenas tardes, alumnos.	¿Hablan ustedes inglés?
con el profesor	Los alumnos estudian.	Hablamos inglés.
con las alumnas	No estudio alemán.	Ustedes hablan.

The oldest wooden schoolhouse in the United States, St. Augustine, Florida

VOCABULARIO[1] (*Vocabulary*)

¡ah!   ah! oh!
el **alemán**   German (*the language*)
la **alumna**   pupil, student (*girl*)
el **alumno**   pupil, student (*boy*)
Ana   Ann, Anna, Anne
bastante   *adv.* quite, quite a bit, rather
bien   *adv.* well, fine
bueno, -a[2]   good
Carlos   Charles
Carmen   Carmen
la **casa**   house, home
la **clase**   class, classroom
con   with
la **conversación** (*pl.* **conversaciones**)
   conversation
cuando   when
de   of, from, about
el **día** (*note gender*)   day
el **ejercicio**   exercise
en   in, on, at
España   Spain
el **español**   Spanish (*the language*)
estudiar   to study
Felipe   Philip

el **francés**   French (*the language*)
hablar   to speak, talk
el **inglés**   English (*the language*)
Isabel   Isabel, Betty, Elizabeth
la **lección** (*pl.* **lecciones**)   lesson
la **lengua**   language
mal   *adv.* badly
mucho   *adv.* much, hard, a great deal, a lot
muy   very
no   no, not
la **noche**   night, evening
o   or, either
preparar   to prepare
el **profesor**   teacher (*man*)
la **profesora**   teacher (*woman*)
pronunciar   to pronounce
¿qué?   what? which?
sí   yes
siempre   always
sólo   *adv.* only
también   also, too
la **tarde**   afternoon
todo, -a[2]   all, every
y   and

buenas tardes   good afternoon
buenos días   good morning (day)
clase de español (inglés)   Spanish (English) class
en casa   at home
en clase   in class
Lección primera   Lesson One
lección (lecciones) de español   Spanish lesson (lessons)
¡muy bien!   very well! (that's) fine!
profesor *or* **profesora de inglés (español)**   English (Spanish) teacher
todas las tardes (noches)   every afternoon (night, evening)
todos los días   every day (*lit.*, all the days)
un poco   a little

---

[1] See **Notas gramaticales,** sections **A** and **C** of this lesson, for the subject pronouns and definite articles.
[2] Agreement of adjectives will be explained in Lesson 2.

Present indicative of *ser* **and** *tener* • **The indefinite article** • **Use of
the definite article with titles** • **Forms and agreement of
adjectives** • **Use of** *hay* • **The adverbs** *aquí, ahí, allí* • **Uses of** *que*

LECCIÓN 2

¿Qué hay en la sala de clase?

El profesor Pidal habla de la sala de clase con los alumnos.

SR. PIDAL —Hoy vamos a hablar de la sala de clase. A ver, María, ¿qué hay en
la pared?

MARÍA —En la pared hay cuadros, dos mapas y una pizarra.

SR. PIDAL —¿De qué color es la pizarra? ¿Es negra?

MARÍA —No, señor, la pizarra no es negra, es verde.

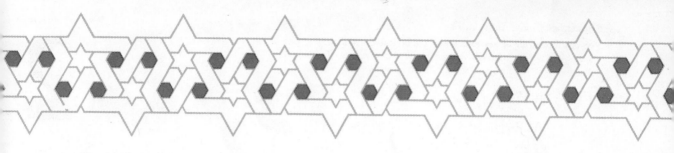

SR. PIDAL —¡Muy bien! ¿De qué países son los dos mapas?

MARÍA —Uno de los mapas es de España; el otro es de México.

◆　◆　◆　◆

SR. PIDAL —Carmen, ¿qué más hay en la sala de clase?

CARMEN —Hay mesas y sillas.

SR. PIDAL —¿Qué tiene Carlos allí sobre la mesa?

CARMEN —Carlos tiene papel, el libro de español y tres lápices.[1]

SR. PIDAL —Carmen, ¿son azules los lápices que Carlos tiene?

CARMEN —No, señor, dos son rojos y uno es amarillo. El lápiz que usted tiene es azul.

SR. PIDAL —Y usted, Carmen, ¿qué tiene ahí sobre la mesa?

CARMEN —Aquí tengo una pluma y un cuaderno. La pluma es roja y el cuaderno es blanco.

◆　◆　◆　◆

SR. PIDAL —Carlos, ¿son ingleses los alumnos de la clase de español?

CARLOS —No, señor, son de los Estados Unidos; son norteamericanos.

SR. PIDAL —¿De dónde soy yo? ¿De México?

CARLOS —Sí, señor, usted es mexicano.

SR. PIDAL —Y la profesora de francés, ¿es ella española?

CARLOS —No, señor, ella no es española; es francesa.

SR. PIDAL —¡Muy bien! Tenemos que hablar español todos los días.

---

[1]Final **z** changes to **c** before **-es.**

Conversación

A. Preguntas sobre el diálogo

1. ¿De qué habla el señor Pidal con los alumnos?   2. ¿De qué color es la pizarra?
3. ¿De qué países son los dos mapas que hay en la pared?   4. ¿Hay mesas y sillas en la sala de clase?   5. ¿Qué tiene Carlos sobre la mesa? ¿Y Carmen?   6. ¿Son ingleses los alumnos de la clase de español?   7. ¿Es de España el señor Pidal?   8. Y la profesora de francés, ¿es ella mexicana también?

B. Aplicación del diálogo

1. ¿Es usted alumno (alumna) o profesor (profesora)?   2. ¿Y qué soy yo?   3. ¿De dónde es usted, de México?   4. ¿Soy de los Estados Unidos?   5. ¿Qué hay en la sala de clase?   6. ¿Qué hay allí en la pared?   7. ¿Qué tiene usted ahí sobre la mesa?   8. ¿Qué tengo yo aquí sobre la mesa?   9. ¿Es amarillo el libro de español que tenemos?   10. ¿Tienen ustedes que estudiar mucho?

NOTAS GRAMATICALES

A. Irregular present indicative of **ser** and **tener**

ser, to be		**tener,** to have (*possess*)	
singular			
(yo) **soy**	I am	**tengo**	I have
(tú) **eres**	you (*fam.*) are	**tienes**	you (*fam.*) have
(él, ella) **es**	he, she, it is	**tiene**	he, she, it has
usted **es**	you (*formal*) are	**tiene**	you (*formal*) have
plural			
(nosotros, –as) **somos**	we are	tenemos	we have
(vosotros, –as) **sois**	you (*fam.*) are	tenéis	you (*fam.*) have
(ellos, –as) **son**	they are	**tienen**	they have
ustedes **son**	you are	**tienen**	you have

Forms of the irregular verbs must be memorized since there are few rules for conjugating them.

B. The indefinite article

1. **un libro y una pluma**   a book and (a) pen, one book and one pen
   Él tiene dos libros; yo tengo uno.   He has two books; I have one.

The word for *a* or *an* is **un** before a masculine singular noun and **una** before a feminine singular noun. These words also mean *one*. **Uno** (*m.*) and **una** (*f.*) are used when the word stands for a noun. The indefinite article is normally repeated before each noun in a series. (For the plural forms **unos, (-as,),** see footnote 3, page 129.)

2. **Carlos es español.**   Charles is a Spaniard (is Spanish).
   Ella es profesora.   She is a teacher.

After **ser** the indefinite article is not used with unmodified nouns which indicate nationality or profession.

C. Use of the definite article with titles

Buenos días, señorita Valdés.   Good morning, Miss Valdés.
El profesor Pidal habla de la sala de clase.   Professor Pidal talks about the classroom.

The definite article is used with titles, except when speaking directly to a person.

D. Forms and agreement of adjectives

1.

singular		*plural*	
masculine	*feminine*	*masculine*	*feminine*
blanco	blanca	blancos	blancas
mexicano	mexicana	mexicanos	mexicanas
verde	verde	verdes	verdes

Adjectives whose masculine singular ends in **-o** have four forms, and the endings are **-o, -a, -os, -as.** Most other adjectives have only two forms, a singular and a plural. The plurals of these adjectives are formed like those of nouns, by adding **-s, -es.**

2.

español	española	españoles	españolas
francés	francesa	franceses	francesas
inglés	inglesa	ingleses	inglesas

Adjectives of nationality which end in a consonant add **-a** to form the feminine; those which end in **-és** in the masculine singular drop the accent mark on the other three forms.

3. **La pared es blanca.**   The wall is white.
   Dos lápices son rojos.   Two pencils are red.
   Todas las casas son blancas.   All the houses are white.
   ¿Son azules las sillas?   Are the chairs blue?

Adjectives agree with the nouns they modify in *gender* and *number,* whether they modify the noun directly or are in the predicate. Numerals, except **uno,** do not change in form. In questions a predicate adjective (*e.g.*, after **ser**) is regularly placed immediately after the verb, and the subject follows the predicate; however, when the subject is shorter than the predicate, it follows the verb: **¿Es ella profesora?** *Is she a teacher?*

4. **El español habla inglés.**   The Spaniard speaks English.
   La mexicana es alumna.   The Mexican girl is a student.
   Ellas no son francesas.   They are not French (girls).
   ¿Es ella española?   Is she Spanish (a Spanish girl)?

Adjectives of nationality are often used as nouns. When used thus, they have the gender and number of the noun they are replacing.

E. Use of **hay**

   ¿Qué hay en la sala de clase?   What is there in the classroom?
   Hay dos cuadros en la pared.   There are two pictures on the wall.
   ¿Hay mapas en el libro?   Are there (any, some) maps in the book?

The form **hay** has no subject expressed in Spanish and means *there is, there are.* Do not confuse **hay** with **es,** (*it*) *is,* and with **son,** (*they*) *are.*
   Note in the third example that unemphatic *any* or *some* are not expressed in Spanish.

◆ *Práctica* (*Practice*).   Read in Spanish, keeping the meaning in mind:

   1. Hay mapas en el libro de español. 2. También hay cuadernos aquí. 3. ¿Hay cuadros en la sala de clase? 4. ¿Tienen Uds. papel? 5. ¿Tengo yo lápices o plumas sobre la mesa? 6. ¿Tienen Uds. libros de inglés?

F. The adverbs **aquí, ahí, allí**

   Aquí tengo un libro de español.   I have a Spanish book here.
   ¿Qué tiene Ud. ahí?   What do you have there?
   ¿Qué lengua hablan allí?   What language do they speak there?

The adverb **ahí,** *there,* usually refers to a place or to something near the person addressed (near *you*), and **allí,** *there, over there,* to a place or to something at a distance (away from the speaker and the person addressed). Rememer that **hay** is used when *there* is merely a part of the expression *there is, there are* (see section E): **Hay dos libros aquí,** *There are two books here.*

Adverbs normally are placed near the verb, but great variation is possible. Observe the position in Spanish sentences.

G. Uses of **que**

1. **El lápiz que Carlos tiene es azul.**   The pencil (that) Charles has is blue.
   El alumno que habla es español.   The pupil who is talking is Spanish.

The relative pronoun **que** refers to things or persons and may mean *that, which, who, whom.* Note that in English the relative pronoun is not always obligatory.

2. **Tengo que estudiar.**   I have to (I must) study.
   ¿Tiene Ud. que hablar mucho?   Do you have to talk much?

The idiomatic expression **tener que** plus an infinitive expresses necessity and means *to have to, must.*

EJERCICIOS

A. Repeat after your teacher; then say again, substituting **un (una)** for **el (la):**

1. Tengo el lápiz.   2. Tienes el libro.   3. Tenemos el mapa.   4. ¿Tiene Ud. la pluma?
5. ¿Tiene ella el cuaderno?   6. Es la mesa.   7. Es la sala de clase.   8. Es el mapa de México.

B. Repeat after your teacher; then make each sentence plural:

MODEL: La pizarra es verde.   *La pizarra es verde.*
                                Las pizarras son verdes.

1. El libro es verde.   2. El cuaderno es blanco.   3. La pared es blanca.   4. La mesa no es azul.   5. La pluma no es amarilla.   6. ¿Es verde el libro de español?   5. ¿Es rojo el lápiz?   8. ¿Es amarilla la casa?   9. El alumno no es mexicano.   10. La alumna es norteamericana.   11. La profesora es española.   12. Ella no es inglesa.

C. Substitution drill:

1. *Carlos* es de España.
   (*El señor Pidal, Ud., María y yo, Tú, Yo*)

2. *Yo* no soy mexicano.
   (*Tú, Ud., Uds., Carlos y Ana, Carmen y yo*)

3. *Yo* tengo dos lápices aquí.
(*Nosotros, Carmen, Tú, Uds., Ana y yo*)

4. *Los alumnos* tienen que estudiar.
(*Ana, Yo, Ud. y yo, Carlos y María, Tú*)

D. Answer affirmatively, following the models:

MODELS: ¿Es verde la pared?   *Sí, señor (señora, señorita),*[1] *la pared es verde.*
           ¿Es Ud. alumno?   *Sí, señor (señora, señorita), soy alumno.*

1. ¿Es Felipe mexicano?
2. ¿Es María norteamericana?
3. ¿Es blanca la casa?
4. ¿Es blanco el papel?
5. ¿Son ingleses los alumnos?
6. ¿Son alumnas María y Carmen?
7. ¿Son Uds. alumnos?
8. ¿Somos Ud. y yo norteamericanos?
9. ¿Soy yo profesor (profesora)?
10. ¿Tiene Ud. un libro de español?

E. Answer negatively; then, when you hear the cue, answer affirmatively, following the model:

MODEL: ¿Es Ana francesa?   *No, Ana no es francesa.*
         ¿Española?   *Sí, Ana es española.*

1. ¿Es María mexicana?
   ¿Norteamericana?
2. ¿Es Carmen inglesa?
   ¿Francesa?
3. ¿Es negra la casa?
   ¿Verde?
4. ¿Son blancas las sillas?
   ¿Azules?
5. ¿Son rojos los lápices?
   ¿Amarillos?
6. ¿Son ellos españoles?
   ¿Norteamericanos?

F. Read in Spanish, using the correct form of the verbs given:

(ser) 1. ¿De dónde _____ Ud.? 2. ¿De dónde _____ tú? 3. ¿De dónde _____ yo? 4. Los mexicanos _____ de México. 5. Ud y yo _____ norteamericanos. 6. Carlos y Ana no _____ mexicanos. 7. Carmen no _____ francesa. 8. ¿De qué color _____ la casa?

(tener) 9. Carlos _____ un cuaderno. 10. ¿ _____ Ud. papel? 11. ¿Qué _____ tú ahí? 12. ¿Qué _____ yo aquí? 13. ¿Qué _____ los alumnos? 14. Felipe _____ que preparar la lección. 15. Él y yo _____ que hablar mucho. 16. ¿ _____ Uds. que estudiar en casa?

G. Repeat after your teacher; then use the cue words to form new sentences, making the necessary changes in the verb and predicate:

---

[1] Hereafter only **Sí** or **No** will be given in the models, but for politeness be sure to include **señor, señora,** or **señorita,** in your reply.

1. La casa es blanca.   3. El profesor no es español.
   Las casas   La profesora
   El papel   Felipe y yo
   La silla   Carlos y María

2. Los cuadernos son rojos.   4. Ella es norteamericana.
   Las mesas   Los alumnos
   La pluma   Carmen y María
   El lápiz   Él

H. Form a sentence, making the necessary changes in the verb and supplying the definite article when required:

MODEL: azul / ser / lápices   *Los lápices son azules.*

1. todos los días / alumnos / lección / preparar
2. libro de español / Carlos / tener / allí
3. ser / de México y de España / mapas
4. tener / en la sala de clase / aquí / nosotros / mesas y sillas

I.   Give the Spanish equivalent:

1. Carmen is not [a][1] teacher; she is [a] pupil.   2. Philip is Spanish; [he] is from Spain.
3. Mary is [an] American; [she] is from the United States.   4. The Spanish book is green; [it] is not black.   5. "Is the house white?" "No, [it] is yellow."   6. The pencils are not blue; two are red and one is yellow.   7. "Is there a map of Mexico here in the classroom?"   8. "There are maps of Mexico and of Spain on the wall."   9. "Charles, what do I have here on the desk?"   10. "You[2] have there [some] books, paper, and two notebooks."   11. "Do you have to study hard?"   12. "Yes, I have to study every night."

EJERCICIOS DE PRONUNCIACIÓN

A. Sounds of Spanish **c** (and **z**), **qu,** and **k**

1. Spanish **c** before **e** and **i**, and **z** in all positions, are pronounced like English hissed *s* in *sent* in Spanish America and in southern Spain; in northern and central Spain the sound is like *th* in *thin*. Pronounce after your teacher:

ejercicio	francés	lápices	lección
pronunciar	azul	lápiz	pizarra
aplicación	hacer	gracias	conversación

---

[1] Words in brackets are not to be translated.
[2] Use the formal **usted** form of *you* in the exercises unless the context requires the familiar form.

2. Spanish **c** before all other letters, **qu** before **e** and **i,** and **k** (used only in words of foreign origin) are like English *c* in *cat,* but without the *h* sound that often follows the *c* in English (*c^hat*). The **u** in **que, qui** is never sounded as in English *quest, quick.* Pronounce after your teacher:

blanco	Carlos	casa	color
cuadro	lectura	aquí	que
kilo	kilómetro	parque	pequeño

B. Breath-groups, division of words into syllables, and word stress

Rewrite the first three exchanges of the dialogue of this lesson, dividing them into breath-groups and into syllables, and underlining the stressed syllables. Note that a conjunction **(y),** prepositions **(a, de, en),** and the forms of the definite article are not considered stressed words in Spanish.

VOCABULARIO

a   to, at
ahí   there (*near person addressed*)
allí   there (*distant*)
amarillo, -a   yellow
aquí   here
azul   blue
blanco, -a   white
el **color**   color
el **cuaderno**   notebook
el **cuadro**   picture
¿dónde?   where?
dos   two
español, -ola   *adj.* Spanish
francés, -esa   *adj.* French
hay   there is, there are
hoy   today
inglés, -esa   *adj.* English
el **lápiz** (*pl.* **lápices**)   pencil
el **libro**   book
el **mapa** (*note gender*)   map
María   Mary

más   more, most
la **mesa**   table, desk
mexicano, -a   Mexican
México   Mexico
negro, -a   black
norteamericano, -a   (North) American (*of the U.S.*)
el **país**   country (*nation*)
el **papel**   paper
la **pared**   wall
la **pizarra**   (black) board
la **pluma**   pen
que   that, which, who, whom
rojo, -a   red
ser   to be
la **silla**   chair
sobre   on, upon, about, concerning
tener   to have (*possess*)
tres   three
un, una, uno   a, an, one
verde   green

a ver   let's see
¿de qué color es?   what color is (it)?
el otro   the other (one) (*m.*)
libro de español   Spanish book
los Estados Unidos   the United States
¿qué más?   what else?
sala de clase   classroom
tener que + *inf.*   to have to (must) + *inf.*
vamos a (hablar)   we are going to (talk)

View of Fort San Marco, constructed by the Spaniards in the 17*th* century, St. Augustine, Florida.

Present indicative of the second conjugation • **Present indicative of** *ir* • **Preposition** *a* • **Possession** • **Cardinal numerals** • **Time of day** • **Use of** *¿(no es)* *verdad?*

LECCIÓN 3

Conversaciones entre estudiantes

En el cuarto de Jorge. Son casi las siete de la mañana.

LUIS —Buenos días, Jorge. ¿Adónde vas tan temprano?

JORGE —Voy al comedor a tomar el[1] desayuno. Luego voy con Felipe a la biblioteca.

LUIS —Pero, ¿qué hora es?

JORGE (*Mira el reloj que tiene sobre la mesa.*) —Pues, son las siete y media.

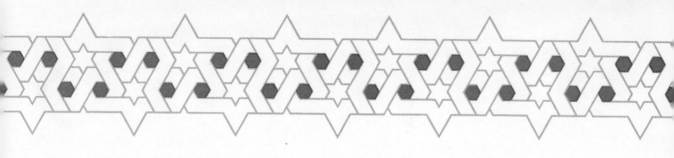

LUIS —¡No, hombre! El reloj que tienes ahí no anda bien. Son solamente las siete menos cinco.

JORGE —¿Verdad, Luis? Tengo el reloj de Felipe, que es viejo, pero casi siempre anda bien.

LUIS —Pero, ¡oye, Jorge! ¿Cuántas clases tienes por la mañana?

JORGE —Generalmente tengo dos, pero hoy tengo un examen a la una y . . .

LUIS —¡Ah . . . ! Pues, vas a estudiar en la biblioteca toda la mañana, ¿no es verdad?

JORGE —Sí, Luis. Felipe y yo vamos a estudiar allí desde las ocho hasta las doce. Luego vamos a tomar el almuerzo.[1]

◆ ◆ ◆ ◆

A las cinco y cuarto de la tarde.

LUIS —¡Hola, Jorge! ¿Qué tal el examen?

JORGE —Bastante bien, creo. Oye, Luis, ¿dónde vas a cenar hoy?

LUIS —Pues voy a la casa del señor Pidal, el profesor de español. Van todos los estudiantes de la clase.[2]

JORGE —¡Qué suerte! ¡Vas a comer muy bien hoy!

LUIS —Sí, sí . . . ¡pero ellos no comen hasta las nueve o las nueve y media de la noche!

JORGE —¡Hombre! ¡Cenan casi tan tarde como en España!

LUIS —Sí, es verdad; y tú, Jorge, ¿dónde vas a cenar?

JORGE —¡Pues, yo tengo que ir a la cafetería! Hasta luego, Luis.

LUIS —Hasta luego, Jorge.

---

[1] In contrast to English the definite article is used in certain set expressions, such as **tomar el desayuno (almuerzo)**, *to take, have,* or *eat breakfast* (*lunch*).

[2] The subject often follows the verb in Spanish, particularly when the verb does not have an object.

Conversación

A. Preguntas sobre el diálogo

1. ¿Adónde va Jorge tan temprano? 2. ¿Qué tiene Jorge sobre la mesa? 3. ¿Es de Jorge el reloj? 4. ¿Anda bien el reloj que tiene Jorge? 5. ¿Cuántas clases tiene Jorge por la mañana generalmente? 6. ¿Van a estudiar Jorge y Felipe toda la mañana? 7. ¿A qué hora van a tomar el almuerzo Jorge y Felipe? 8. ¿Y qué tiene Jorge a la una? 9. ¿A qué hora comen en la casa del profesor Pidal? 10. ¿Dónde va a cenar Jorge?

B. Aplicación del diálogo

1. ¿Tiene usted un reloj? 2. ¿Qué hora es? 3. ¿Dónde toman ustedes generalmente el desayuno? ¿Y a qué hora? 4. ¿Cuántas clases tiene usted por la mañana? ¿Y por la tarde? 5. ¿Cuántas clases tiene usted hoy? 6. ¿Tiene usted un examen hoy? 7. ¿Cena usted tarde o temprano? 8. ¿A qué hora comemos o cenamos generalmente en los Estados Unidos? 9. ¿A qué hora comen en España? 10. ¿Come usted en el comedor o en la cafetería?

NOTAS GRAMATICALES

A. Present indicative of the second conjugation

	comer, to eat. (Anytime)		
	singular		*plural*
como	I eat	**comemos**	we eat
comes	you (*fam.*) eat	**coméis**	you (*fam.*) eat
come	he, she, it eats	**comen**	they eat
Ud. **come**	you (*formal*) eat	Uds. **comen**	you eat

The present indicative endings of **-er** verbs (second conjugation) are: **-o, -es, -e, -emos, -éis, -en.** Compare with the endings of **-ar** verbs. Remember that the present tense corresponds in English not only to the simple present, *I eat,* but also to the emphatic *I do eat,* and to the progressive *I am eating.*

B. Irregular present indicative of **ir**

	ir, to go	
	singular	*plural*
	voy	**vamos**
	vas	**vais**
	va	**van**
Ud.	**va**	Uds. **van**

C. Preposition **a**

> **Voy al comedor.** I am going to the dining room.
> **¿Adónde vas tan temprano?** Where are you going so early?
> **Tengo que ir a la cafetería.** I have to (must) go to the cafeteria.
> **Vamos a estudiar la lección.** We are going to study the lesson.

Ir and other verbs of motion are followed by the preposition **a** before an infinitive or any other object.

When **a** is followed by the definite article **el,** the two words contract into **al.** The combinations **a la, a los, a las** do not contract: **Vamos a la biblioteca,** *We are going to the library.*

Note that when *where?* means *where to?* it is expressed by **¿adónde?** (literally, *to where?*) (second example; otherwise **¿dónde?** is used: **¿Dónde vas a cenar?** *Where* (i.e., in what place) *are you going to eat?*

D. Possession

> **Creo que el reloj es de Felipe.** I believe (that) the watch is Philip's.
> **¿Es viejo el reloj del estudiante?** Is the student's watch old?
> **Carlos tiene el libro del profesor.** Charles has the teacher's book.
>
> BUT: **a la casa del señor Pidal** to the house of Mr. Pidal (to Mr. Pidal's)
> **las plumas de los estudiantes** the students' pens

Spanish uses the preposition **de** to express possession. The apostrophe is not used in Spanish. When **de** is followed by the article **el,** the combination is contracted into **del;** however, **de la, de los, de las** are not contracted. **Del** and **al** are the only two contractions in Spanish.

E. Cardinal numerals

1	**uno**	9	**nueve**	17	**diecisiete**	25	**veinticinco**
2	**dos**	10	**diez**	18	**dieciocho**	26	**veintiséis**
3	**tres**	11	**once**	19	**diecinueve**	27	**veintisiete**
4	**cuatro**	12	**doce**	20	**veinte**	28	**veintiocho**
5	**cinco**	13	**trece**	21	**veintiuno**	29	**veintinueve**
6	**seis**	14	**catorce**	22	**veintidós**	30	**treinta**
7	**siete**	15	**quince**	23	**veintitrés**	31	**treinta y uno**
8	**ocho**	16	**dieciséis**	24	**veinticuatro**	32	**treinta y dos**

Cardinal numerals do not change their form, except that **uno** and numerals ending in **uno** drop **o** before a masculine noun: **un libro,** *a (one) book;* **veintiún cuartos,** *twenty-one rooms;* **treinta y un estudiantes,** *thirty-one students.* **Una** is used before a feminine noun: **una pluma,** *a (one) pen;* **veintiuna mesas,** *twenty-one tables;* **treinta y una casas,** *thirty-one houses.* Note the forms which require a written accent.

When a numeral ending in *one* follows a noun or is used alone, the numeral agrees in gender with the noun: **—¿Cuántos alumnos hay? —Veintiuno (Treinta y uno).** *"How many pupils are there?" "Twenty-one (Thirty-one)."* **—¿Cuántas mesas hay? —Veintiuna (Treinta y una).** *"How many tables are there?" "Twenty-one (Thirty-one)."*

The cardinal numerals precede the nouns they modify unless they are used in a descriptive sense: **tres lecciones,** *three lessons,* but **Lección tres (veintiuna),** *Lesson Three (Twenty-one).*

Numerals 16 through 19 and 21 through 29 are occasionally written as three words, but they are pronounced as one word: **diez y seis, diez y siete, veinte y uno, veinte y dos,** etc. Beginning with 31, numerals are written as separate words: **treinta y dos.**

F. Time of day

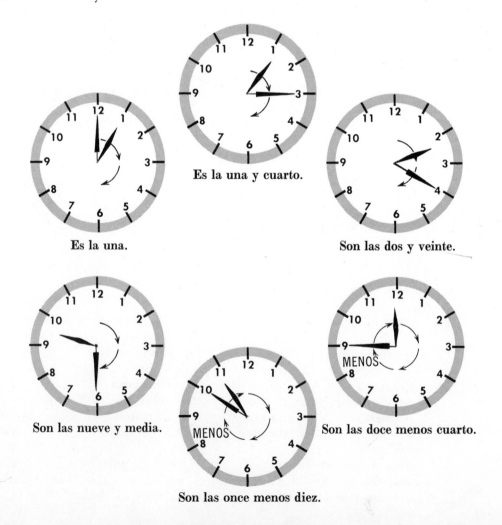

Es la una y cuarto.

Es la una.

Son las dos y veinte.

Son las nueve y media.

Son las once menos diez.

Son las doce menos cuarto.

¿Qué hora es?   What time is it?
¿A qué hora tomas el almuerzo?   At what time do you take (eat) lunch?
Es la una.   It is (It's) one o'clock.
Son las tres y veinte.   It is twenty minutes past three (It's 3:20).
Son las cuatro y media.   It is half past four (It's 4:30).
Son las diez menos cuarto.   It is a quarter to ten (It's 9:45).

The word **hora** means *time* in asking the time of day. In stating the time, the word **hora** is understood, and the feminine article **la** or **las** is used with the cardinal numeral corresponding to the hour. **Es** is used only when followed by **la una;** in all other cases **son** is used.

Up to and including the half hour, minutes are added to the hour by using the proper numeral after **y;** between the half hour and the next hour they are subtracted from the next hour by using **menos.** The noun **cuarto** is used for a quarter of an hour and the adjective **media** for a half hour. The word *minutes* is seldom expressed.

Son las siete y media de la mañana.   It is half past seven A.M. (in the morning).
Ella va a las tres de la tarde.   She is going at three P.M. (in the afternoon).
Estudio por la tarde (noche).   I study in the afternoon (evening).

When a specific hour is given, the word *in* is translated by **de;** when no definite hour is given, *in* is translated by **por.**

G. Use of **¿(no es) verdad?**

El reloj anda bien, ¿no es verdad?   The watch (clock) runs well, doesn't it?
Tú miras el mapa, ¿verdad?   You are looking at the map, aren't you?

The expression **¿no es verdad?** (literally, *is it not true?*) is the Spanish equivalent of English *isn't it? doesn't it? aren't you? doesn't he?* etc., depending upon the meaning of the verb in the preceding statement. The expression may be shortened to **¿verdad?** or even to **¿no?**

Es verdad means *It is true.* In a question or exclamation, **¿Verdad?** may mean *Is it true?*

EJERCICIOS

A. Substitution drill:

  1. *Luis* come a las seis.
     (*Luis y Jorge, Yo, Nosotros, Tú, Ud.*)
  2. *Jorge* toma el almuerzo a las doce.
     (*Yo, Nosotros, Jorge y yo, Tú, Tú y Jorge*)

3. *Jorge y Luis* van a la cafetería.
   (*Ella, Yo, Nosotros, El profesor Pidal, Tú*)
4. ¿Adónde vas *tú* tan temprano?
   (*Luis, Jorge y Luis, Ud., Uds., ella*)

B. Repeat after your teacher. When you hear a new subject, use it in a new sentence, making the verb agree with the subject:

1. Nosotros tomamos el desayuno temprano.   (Jorge)
2. Él toma el almuerzo a las doce. (Ellos)
3. Jorge come a las seis y cuarto. (Él y yo)
4. ¿A qué hora cenas tú? (ustedes)
5. Yo tengo sólo una clase por la tarde. (Carmen y Felipe)
6. Nosotros tenemos tres clases por la mañana. (La señora Pidal)
7. ¿Miras tú el reloj de Felipe? (ustedes)
8. Tú eres norteamericano, ¿verdad? (Usted)
9. María y yo vamos a la biblioteca hoy. (Yo)
10. ¿Tienes tú que cenar temprano? (usted y él)

C. Answer affirmatively, and then negatively, following the model:

MODEL: ¿Va usted al comedor?   *Sí, voy al comedor.*
                                 No, no voy al comedor.

1. ¿Va usted a la biblioteca?   4. ¿Van ustedes a la casa?
2. ¿Va Ana al cuarto de María?   5. ¿Miras tú el reloj del hombre?
3. ¿Vamos a la cafetería a tomar   6. ¿Tiene usted los libros de los
   el desayuno?   estudiantes?

D. Use **a, de, en,** or **por** to complete the following paragraph:

1. Tomamos el desayuno＿＿＿las siete＿＿＿la mañana. 2. ＿＿＿las ocho voy＿＿＿clase. 3. Tengo la clase＿＿＿español＿＿＿la tarde. 4. Tomo el almuerzo＿＿＿las doce; luego voy＿＿＿la biblioteca＿＿＿la una. 5. ＿＿＿la biblioteca preparo la lección＿＿＿español. 6. Generalmente estudio allí＿＿＿la tarde. 7. ＿＿＿ la seis y cuarto voy ＿＿＿ cenar con Luis. 8. Siempre comemos＿＿＿la cafetería. 9. ＿＿＿la noche preparamos la lecciones＿＿＿casa. 10. Casi siempre estudiamos desde las ocho hasta las diez y media ＿＿＿ la noche.

E. Read in Spanish:

1. 4 exámenes. 2. 5 casas. 3. 10 horas. 4. 15 días. 5. 14 cuadros. 6. 11 clases. 7. 13 lecciones. 8. 21 alumnos. 9. 21 alumnas. 10. 18 profesores. 11. 12 lápices. 12. 20 mesas.   13. 2 bibliotecas.   14. 3 mexicanos.   15. 25 norteamericanos. 16. 29 estudiantes.   17. 22 sillas.   18. 16 cuartos.

F. Listen to the hour given, and then to the question. Answer with a complete sentence:

MODELS: La una.   ¿Qué hora es?   *Es la una.*
          Las dos.   ¿Qué hora es?   *Son las dos.*

1. La una y cuarto.   5. Las ocho y diez.
2. Las cuatro y media.   6. Las nueve de la noche.
3. Las once menos cuarto.   7. Las tres de la mañana.
4. La una menos veinte.   8. Las dos de la tarde.

G. Form a sentence, making the necessary changes in the verb:

1. tomar el desayuno / en el comedor / Jorge / casi siempre
2. ser viejo / pero andar bien / el reloj de Felipe
3. veinte estudiantes / en la clase de español / hay
4. a las doce / nosotros tener que / tomar el almuerzo
5. a la biblioteca / yo ir / todos los días / por la tarde

H. Give the Spanish equivalent, using the familiar form for *you:*

1. "Listen, George, where are you going so early?" 2. "What time is it?" "It is a quarter
to seven." 3. "I have to go to the dining room to take breakfast." 4. "Do you have an
examination today?" 5. "Yes, I have one at eleven o'clock." 6. "Do you have to
study in the library until ten o'clock?" 7. "No, I am going to study there only until
nine." 8. "How many classes do you have in the morning?" 9. "Generally I have
two classes, but today I have only one." 10. "At what time do you take lunch?"
11. "I always take lunch late, at half past twelve." 12. "In Spain they eat (dinner) late,
at nine or ten P.M., don't they?"

EJERCICIOS DE PRONUNCIACIÓN

A. The diphthongs **ie** and **ei (ey)**

1. As the first element of a diphthong, unstressed **i** is pronounced like a weak English *y*
in *yes.* Pronounce after your teacher:

diez	siempre	siete	tiene
también	diecisiete	viejo	siéntese usted

2. **Ei (ey)** is pronounced like a prolonged English *a* in *fate.* Pronounce after your
teacher:

coméis	seis	tenéis	veinte
veintiséis	de inglés	doce y media	siete y cuarto

B. The sounds of Spanish **g** and **j**

1. Spanish **g** (written **gu** before **e** or **i**) is pronounced like a weak English *g* in *go* at the beginning of a breath-group or after **n.** Pronounce after your teacher:

gracias	inglés	lengua	gusto
guitarra	tengo	en guerra	un guisado

2. In all other cases, except when before **e** or **i** in the groups **ge, gi,** the sound is much weaker, and the breath continues to pass between the back of the tongue and the palate. Pronounce after your teacher:

agua	luego	negro	agosto
Miguel	la guerra	muchas gracias	una guitarra

3. When before **e** or **i** in the groups **ge, gi,** it is pronounced like Spanish **j,** that is, approximately like a strongly exaggerated *h* in *halt.* Pronounce after your teacher:

generalmente	gente	Jorge	ágil
ejercicio	rojo	viejo	gitano

C. Dictado (*Dictation*)

The teacher will select four exchanges of the dialogue of this lesson as an exercise in dictation.

Detail, Temple of Quetzalcóatl, Teotihuacán, Mexico.

VOCABULARIO

¿adónde? where? (*with verbs of motion*)
al = a + el to the
el **almuerzo** lunch
andar to run (*said of a watch*); to walk
la **biblioteca** library
la **cafetería** cafeteria
casi almost
cenar to eat supper (dinner-night)
el **comedor** dining room
comer to eat, dine, ~~have dinner~~ (Anytime)
como as, like; since
creer to believe, think
¿cuánto, -a? how much (many)?
el **cuarto** quarter; room
del = de + el of (from) the
el **desayuno** breakfast
desde from, since (*time*)
entre among, between
el (la) **estudiante** student
el **examen** (*pl.* **exámenes**) examination, exam, test
generalmente generally
hasta until, to, up to
¡hola! hello! hi!

el **hombre** man
la **hora** hour, time (*of day*)
ir (**a +** *inf.*) to go (to)
Jorge George
luego then, later, next
Luis Louis
la **mañana** morning
medio, -a half, a half
menos less
mirar to look at, watch
pero but
por during, through, along, by
pues well, well then, then
¡qué! how! what (a)!
el **reloj** watch, clock
solamente *adv.* only
la **suerte** luck
tan *adv.* so, as
tarde late
temprano early
tomar to take, eat, drink
la **verdad** truth
viejo, -a old

de *or* **por la mañana (tarde, noche)** in the morning (afternoon, evening)
desde . . . hasta from . . . to
(él) mira el reloj he looks at the (his) watch (clock)
es verdad it is true, that's true
hasta luego until later, I'll see you later
¡hombre! man (alive)!
¿(no es) verdad? isn't it? don't you? etc.
¡oye! listen! hey! (*fam. sing. form*)
¡qué suerte! what luck! how lucky (fortunate)!
¿qué tal . . . ? how about . . . ? how is *or* are (was *or* were) . . . ?
tan + *adj. or adv.* **+ como** as . . . as
toda la mañana all morning, the whole (entire) morning
tomar el desayuno (almuerzo) to take, have, *or* eat breakfast (lunch)

Present indicative of the third conjugation • Present indicative of
venir • Possessive adjectives • Position of adjectives • Phrases with
de plus a noun • Summary of uses of *ser*

LECCIÓN 4

Tomás habla de su familia

LUIS   —¡Hola, Tomás! ¿Qué lees? ¿Una carta de tu amiga María?

TOMÁS   —No, leo una carta que viene de México. Es de mi hermana
Carmen.

LUIS   —¿Dónde estudia ella ahora?

TOMÁS   —Estudia en la Universidad de México. Escribe muchas cartas muy
interesantes sobre la vida del país.

LUIS   —¿Vive tu hermana en una residencia de estudiantes?

TOMÁS   —No, ella vive con una familia mexicana.

LUIS   —Ah . . . ¡qué bien! Oye, ¿escribe tu hermana en español?

TOMÁS   —Todavía no; pero cada día aprende varias palabras nuevas.

❖   ❖   ❖   ❖   ❖

LUIS   —Tomás, ¿todavía viven ustedes en su casa de campo?

TOMÁS   —No, Luis. Ahora vivimos aquí en la ciudad, cerca del parque.

LUIS   —¡Qué lástima! La casa de campo es grande y hermosa . . .

TOMÁS   —Sí, es verdad. La casa de la ciudad es pequeña, pero es muy cómoda.

LUIS   —¿Quién vive ahora en la casa de campo?

TOMÁS   —Mi hermano Felipe vive allí con su familia.

◆   ◆   ◆   ◆

LUIS   —Tomás, ustedes hablan español en casa, ¿no es verdad?

TOMÁS   —Sí, un poco. Mi padre habla español con sus amigos mexicanos cuando vienen a nuestra casa.

LUIS   —¿Y no reciben tus padres periódicos en español?

TOMÁS   —Sí, y todas las tardes mi madre mira un programa de televisión, también en español.

LUIS   —¡Qué suerte, hombre! No es fácil aprender una lengua extranjera.

TOMÁS   —Es verdad. Es necesario trabajar mucho.

LUIS   —Bueno, tengo que ir a la biblioteca. Nuestra lección de español para mañana tiene una parte muy difícil.

TOMÁS   —Tenemos que escribir una carta a un estudiante mexicano, ¿no es verdad?

LUIS   —Sí. Yo voy a preparar la carta con mi amigo Carlos. Hasta mañana, Tomás.

TOMÁS   —Hasta mañana, Luis.

Conversación

A. Preguntas sobre el diálogo

1. ¿De dónde viene la carta que lee Tomás? ¿De quién es? 2. ¿Dónde estudia Carmen? 3. ¿Sobre qué escribe Carmen muchas cartas? 4. ¿Escribe Carmen sus cartas en español? 5. ¿Qué aprende Carmen cada día? 6. ¿Dónde viven los padres de Tomás ahora? ¿Es grande la casa de la ciudad? 7. ¿Quiénes viven en la casa de campo? ¿Es grande o pequeña? 8. ¿Habla español el padre de Tomás? ¿Qué mira la madre de Tomás todas las tardes? 9. ¿Adónde tiene que ir Luis? 10. ¿Qué tienen que escribir los estudiantes?

B. Aplicación del diálogo

1. ¿Escribe usted muchas cartas? 2. ¿Escribe usted sus cartas en español? 3. ¿Recibe usted muchas cartas? ¿De su familia? ¿De sus amigos? 4. ¿Dónde viven sus padres, en el campo? 5. ¿Vive usted con sus padres o en una residencia de estudiantes? 6. ¿Habla usted español o inglés con sus padres? 7. ¿Habla usted español con sus amigos? 8. ¿Qué periódicos lee usted? ¿Son periódicos en español? 9. ¿Cuántos programas de televisión mira usted cada día? 10. ¿Es fácil o es difícil aprender una lengua extranjera?

NOTAS GRAMATICALES

A. Present indicative of the third conjugation

vivir, to live			
singular		*plural*	
vivo	I live	vivimos	we live
vives	you (*fam.*) live	vivís	you (*fam.*) live
vive	he, she, it lives	viven	they live
Ud. vive	you (*formal*) live	Uds. viven	you live

The present indicative endings of **-ir** verbs (third conjugation) are: **-o, -es, -e, -imos, -ís, -en.** These endings are the same as those for **-er** verbs, except in the first and second persons plural. Remember that **Ud.** and **Uds.** require the third person of the verb; these forms will not be given separately hereafter. The present tense corresponds to the English *I live, I do live, I am living,* etc.

B. Irregular present indicative of **venir**

venir, to come	
singular	*plural*
vengo	venimos
vienes	venís
viene	vienen

C. Possessive adjectives

singular	*plural*	
mi	mis	my
tu	tus	your (*fam.*)
su	sus	his, her, its, your (*formal*)
nuestro, –a	nuestros, –as	our
vuestro, –a	vuestros, –as	your (*fam.*)
su	sus	their, your (*pl.*)

mi amiga, mis amigas   my (girl) friend, my friends
nuestra casa, nuestras casas   our house, our houses
su escuela   his, her, your, their school
sus padres   his, her, your, their parents
Él viene con sus amigos.   He is coming with his friends.

Possessive adjectives agree with the nouns they modify in *gender* and *number,* like other adjectives. Thus they agree with the thing possessed and not with the possessor. The possessive adjective never ends in **–s** unless the noun ends in **–s.** These forms precede the noun and are generally repeated before each noun modified. Forms will be given later to clarify **su** and **sus.**

D. Position of adjectives

una familia mexicana   a Mexican family
muchas cartas interesantes   many interesting letters
varios periódicos españoles   several Spanish newspapers
una casa grande y hermosa   a large, beautiful house

Adjectives which limit as to quantity (*the, a, an, much, several,* numerals, possessive adjectives, etc.) are placed before the nouns they modify.

Adjectives which describe a noun by telling its quality (color, size, shape, nationality, etc.) normally are placed after the noun.

When two adjectives of equal value modify a noun, they are usually placed after the noun and connected by **y** (last example).

E. Phrases with **de** plus a noun

> **el libro de español (inglés)**   the Spanish (English) book
> **la clase (lección) de español**   the Spanish class (lesson)
> **la casa de la ciudad**   the city house (home)
> **un programa de televisión**   a television (TV) program
> **una casa de campo**   a country house (home)
> **una residencia de estudiantes**   a student residence hall

Nouns are not normally used as adjectives in Spanish as they often are in English. An English noun used as an adjective corresponds in Spanish to **de** plus the noun.

Compare **un periódico español,** *a Spanish newspaper,* with **un profesor de español,** *a Spanish teacher* (teacher of Spanish). A native Spaniard who is a teacher would be **un profesor español,** and, depending on what he teaches, might be **un profesor de español, un profesor de francés,** etc. Also remember the expressions **la lección (la clase, el libro) de español.**

F. Summary of uses of **ser**

Ser has been used in this lesson and in the two preceding lessons without an explanation of its various uses. Note carefully the following summary, so that **ser** will not be confused with another verb meaning *to be* which will be given in Lesson 5.

Ser is used:

1. With a predicate noun or pronoun, or adjective used as a noun, to show that the subject and the noun or pronoun in the predicate refer to the same person or thing:

> **María es estudiante.**   Mary is a student.
> **No somos mexicanos.**   We are not Mexicans.

2. With the preposition **de** to denote *ownership, origin,* or *material;* and with the preposition **para** to indicate *for whom* or *for what* a thing is intended:

> **¿De quién es el libro?**   Whose book is it (*lit.,* Of whom is the book)?
> **Es de mi hermano.**   It is my brother's.
> **Son de España.**   They are from Spain.
> **El mapa es de papel.**   The map is of paper.
> **La carta es para Carmen.**   The letter is for Carmen.

3. In impersonal expressions (*it* + verb + adjective):

> **Es necesario estudiar mucho.**   It is necessary to study hard.

4. With an adjective to express an inherent, essential, or characteristic quality of the subject that is relatively permanent. This includes adjectives of color, size, shape, nationality, and the like:

La ciudad es grande.   The city is large.
La casa es amarilla.   The house is yellow.
Los programas son interesantes.   The programs are interesting.

5. To express time of day:

Son las nueve y cuarto.   It is a quarter after (past) nine.

EJERCICIOS

A. Substitution drill:

   1. *Yo* vivo en una casa pequeña.
     (*Tú, Tomás, Uds., Nosotros, Ana y Carmen*)
   2. *Ellos* escriben cartas interesantes.
     (*Luis, Yo, Ella y yo, Mi hermano, Tú*)
   3. *Jorge* viene a las ocho.
     (*Ana, Ana y yo, Yo, Tú, Mis amigos*)

B. Repeat after your teacher. When you hear a new subject, use it with the corresponding verb form to create a new sentence:

   1. Mis amigos y yo miramos un programa de televisión.   (La familia)
   2. Carlos no mira programas en español. (Mis hermanos)
   3. Felipe mira el mapa de España. (Los estudiantes)
   4. Ellos miran los cuadros del profesor. (Luis y yo)
   5. Cada día nosotros aprendemos palabras nuevas. (yo)
   6. Yo aprendo español en casa. (Tú)
   7. Tomás lee una carta de Carmen. (Mis padres)
   8. Mi madre no lee periódicos en inglés. (Mis hermanas)
   9. ¿Reciben ustedes cartas de países extranjeros?   (tú)
 10. Yo siempre recibo periódicos en español. (Mi hermano)
 11. Luis y yo tomamos el desayuno temprano. (Mis amigos)
 12. ¿A qué hora tomas tú el almuerzo? (tu familia)

C. Repeat after your teacher; then, when you hear the cue, say again, making the necessary changes:

MODEL: María va con *su amiga*.   *María va con su amiga.*
      (amigas)   *María va con sus amigas.*

1. Aquí tengo *mi cuaderno*. (pluma, libros, cuadernos)
2. Ahora escriben *sus lecciones*. (cartas, lección, carta)
3. Hablamos español en *nuestra clase*. (casas, clases, residencia de estudiantes)
4. Jorge y *su padre* leen mucho. (madre, hermanas, amigos)
5. ¿Vienen Tomás y *sus amigos*? (hermana, familia, hermano)
6. Hablamos siempre con *nuestros profesores* (profesora, amigo, familia)

D. Answer affirmatively, following the models:

MODELS: ¿Tiene Ud. su pluma? *Sí, tengo mi pluma.*
      ¿Tengo yo mi libro? *Sí, Ud. tiene su libro.*

1. ¿Habla Ud. con su madre?
2. ¿Hablas con tus amigos?
3. ¿Aprende Ud. su lección?
4. ¿Tienen Uds. sus lápices?
5. ¿Leen Uds. mi carta?
6. ¿Vienes con tus padres?
7. ¿Miro yo mi reloj?
8. ¿Tengo yo sus libros?

E. Answer negatively, following the model:

MODEL: ¿Tienen Uds. amigos nuevos? *No, no tenemos amigos nuevos.*

1. ¿Viven Uds. en casas viejas?
2. ¿Reciben Uds. cartas interesantes?
3. ¿Tienen Uds. casas de campo?
4. ¿Miran Uds. cuadros franceses?
5. ¿Miran Uds. programas de televisión?
6. ¿Aprenden Uds. palabras fáciles?
7. ¿Trabajan Uds. en ciudades grandes?
8. ¿Leen Uds. periódicos extranjeros?

F. Answer affirmatively, following the models:

MODELS: ¿Es rojo el lápiz? *Sí, es un lápiz rojo.*
      ¿Son fáciles las lecciones? *Sí, son lecciones fáciles.*

1. ¿Es hermoso el parque?
2. ¿Es grande la universidad?
3. ¿Es interesante la carta?
4. ¿Es mexicana la familia?
5. ¿Son difíciles las lecciones?
6. ¿Son cómodas las sillas?
7. ¿Son grandes las ciudades?
8. ¿Son nuevas las casas?

G. Read in Spanish, supplying the correct form of **ser**:

1. —¿No _____ tú amigo de Tomás? —Sí, _____ amigo de Tomás. 2. Él y yo _____ estudiantes en la clase de español. 3. La hermana de Tomás _____ estudiante en la Universidad de México. 4. —México _____ un país grande y her-

49   *Lección cuatro*

moso, ¿no _____ verdad? —Sí, y sus ciudades _____ viejas y nuevas.   5. No _____ fácil vivir en un país extranjero, pero _____ muy interesante.   6. —¿De quién _____ los cuadros que hay en la pared? — _____ de Felipe; _____ para su madre.   7. —Carlos, ¿qué hora _____ ahora? — _____ las ocho y media de la noche; todavía _____ temprano.   8. —¿De qué color _____ la casa del profesor Pidal? — _____ verde.

H. Give the Spanish for:

1. his television program
2. our student residence hall
3. their country home
4. my Mexican friends (*f.*)
5. your (*pl.*) Spanish newspaper
6. her interesting letters
7. my French class
8. our foreign students
9. her beautiful pictures
10. our new friends (*m.*)
11. my comfortable house
12. their beautiful cities

I. Give the Spanish equivalent:

1. Thomas is reading a letter from his sister.   2. He always receives letters from his family.   3. His sister lives in Mexico now and she is studying in the University of Mexico.   4. In her letters she writes about the interesting life of the country.   5. "Louis, there goes our friend Philip.   6. His parents speak Spanish, don't they?"   7. "Yes, a little, and his mother watches television programs in Spanish.   8. Also, they receive a Mexican newspaper, which they read every night."   9. "Do they still live in their country home?"   10. "No, they live near the park in a small and comfortable house."   11. "Well, we have a difficult lesson for tomorrow."   12. "Yes, it is necessary to work two or three hours."

EJERCICIOS DE PRONUNCIACIÓN

A. Spanish **x** and **j**

1. Before a consonant, the letter **x** is pronounced like English *s* in *sent*. Pronounce after your teacher:

extranjero   expresión   excursión   excelente

2. Between vowels, **x** is usually a double sound, consisting of a weak English *g* in *go* followed by a hissed *s*. Pronounce after your teacher:

examen   éxito   existencia   exhibir

3. In a few words, **x,** even when between vowels, is pronounced like English *s* in *sent* Pronounce after your teacher:

exacto   exactamente

4. The letter **x** in the words **México** and **mexicano,** spelled **Méjico** and **mejicano** in Spain, is pronounced like Spanish **j** (see Lesson 3, page 40). Spanish **j** is silent in **reloj,** but is pronounced in the plural **relojes.** Repeat after your teacher:

Jorge es mexicano.   Es de México.
Él tiene dos relojes.   El reloj que tengo es viejo.
Aprendo una lengua extranjera. Trabajo mucho.

B. Spanish intonation

Study the observations on Spanish intonation in Preliminary Lesson 2, pages 9–10; then rewrite the first two exchanges of the first dialogue of this lesson, dividing them into breath-groups and into syllables, underline the stressed syllables in each breath-group, and outline the intonation patterns.

VOCABULARIO

ahora   now
la **amiga**   friend (*f.*)
el **amigo**   friend (*m.*)
aprender   to learn
bueno *adv.*   well, well now, all right
cada (*invariable*)   each
el **campo**   country, field
la **carta**   letter
cerca de *prep.*   near
la **ciudad**   city
cómodo, -a   comfortable
difícil *adj.*   difficult, hard
escribir   to write
escuchar   to listen (to)
extranjero, -a   foreign
fácil   easy
la **familia**   family
grande   large, big
la **hermana**   sister
el **hermano**   brother
hermoso, -a   beautiful, pretty
interesante   interesting
la **lástima**   pity, shame
leer   to read
la **madre**   mother

mañana   tomorrow
mucho, -a   much, many; *pl.* many
necesario, -a   necessary
nuevo, -a   new
el **padre**   father; *pl.* parents
la **palabra**   word
para   for, in order to, to
el **parque**   park
la **parte**   part
pequeño, -a   small, little (*size*)
el **periódico**   newspaper
el **programa** (*note gender*)   program
¿quién? (*pl.* **¿quiénes?**)   who? whom?
recibir   to receive
la **residencia**   residence hall
la **televisión**   television, TV
todavía   still, yet
Tomás   Thomas, Tom
trabajar   to work
la **universidad**   university
varios, -as   several, various
venir (a + *inf.*)   to come (to)
la **vida**   life
vivir   to live

casa de campo   country house (home)
¿de quién es (el libro)?   whose (book) is it?
hasta mañana   until (see you) tomorrow
mirar un programa de televisión   to watch a television program
¡qué bien!   how fine (nice)!
¡qué lástima!   what a pity (shame)!
residencia de estudiantes   student residence hall
todas las tardes   every afternoon
todavía no   not yet

Present indicative of *estar, querer,* and *saber* • The present
participle • Uses of *estar* • Special uses of the definite
article • Feminine nouns • Use of *¿cuál?*

LECCIÓN **5**

Quieren trabajar en Suramérica[1]

Isabel, que vive en la Argentina, está visitando a sus padres en los Estados
Unidos. Está sentada en el patio de la casa de sus padres. Son las cinco y media
de la tarde. Llegan su primo Roberto y su esposa Diana, que quieren trabajar en
Suramérica.

ROBERTO —¿Qué tal, Isabel? ¡Qué gusto saber que estás aquí de visita!
ISABEL —Gracias, Roberto. ¡Hola, Diana! ¿No quieren pasar?
DIANA —Bueno, por un momento solamente. ¿Y tus padres?
ISABEL —Mamá está un poco enferma; está en su cuarto. Papá está en la oficina
todavía.
DIANA —Creo que tu madre trabaja demasiado . . . Necesita descansar más.
ROBERTO —¿Cuánto tiempo vas a pasar aquí, Isabel?
ISABEL —Dos semanas, creo. Estoy muy cansada . . . Pero también quiero ver
a toda la familia . . . a mi tía Ana, a mi prima Carmen y a su hija María.

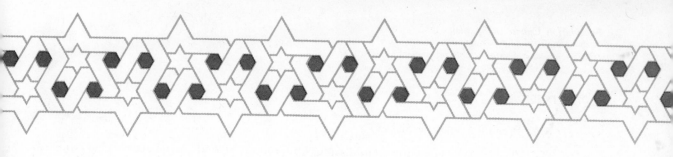

ROBERTO —¿No sabes que Diana y yo queremos trabajar en Suramérica?

ISABEL —¿De veras? ¿A qué país quieren ir?

ROBERTO —No sabemos todavía. Pero, oye, ¿es difícil hallar trabajo en la Argentina?

ISABEL —En las ciudades grandes, como Buenos Aires, no es fácil. Además, uno tiene que saber español perfectamente.

ROBERTO —¿Y cómo es[2] la ciudad de Buenos Aires?

ISABEL —¡Ah! Es una ciudad maravillosa. Y Montevideo, la capital del Uruguay, está muy cerca. Es una ciudad muy interesante.

DIANA —Tu madre cree que trabajas mucho. ¿Es verdad?

ISABEL —Bueno, sí . . . Y como tengo muchos amigos, estoy siempre muy ocupada. ¡La vida allí es tan agradable!

◆ ◆ ◆ ◆ ◆

ROBERTO —¡Qué bien! Necesitamos hablar más, ¿sabes?

ISABEL —¡Sí, claro! Pero, Diana, ¿no quieren tomar algo? ¿Algo frío?

DIANA —Gracias, pero ya es tarde y cenamos a las seis y media. Tú sabes, Roberto tiene que ir a la Universidad a las ocho.

ROBERTO —¿Por qué no pasas por nuestra casa mañana?

ISABEL —Sí, con mucho gusto, porque también quiero ver a tus hijos. Pero . . . ¿no están ustedes muy ocupados?

DIANA —No, no. Sabes cuál es nuestra casa, ¿verdad?

ISABEL —Creo que es la casa amarilla que está cerca del parque . . .

DIANA —Sí, todavía vivimos allí . . . Hasta mañana.

ISABEL —Hasta mañana. ¡Y gracias por la visita!

ROBERTO —No hay de qué, Isabel. Hasta mañana.

---

[1]Also used for *South America* are **la América del Sur** and **Sudamérica.**   [2]Compare **¿Cómo es la ciudad?** *How is the city* (*What is the city like?*) which inquires about what the subject is in essence, with **¿Cómo está usted?** *How are you?* which inquires about a state or condition of the subject.

Conversación

A. Preguntas sobre el diálogo

1. ¿Quién está de visita en los Estados Unidos? 2. ¿Dónde vive Isabel? 3. ¿Dónde está la madre de Isabel? ¿Cómo está ella? 4. ¿Dónde está el padre de Isabel? 5. ¿Cuánto tiempo va a pasar Isabel en los Estados Unidos? 6. ¿Quiénes quieren trabajar en Suramérica también? 7. ¿Saben a qué país quieren ir? 8. ¿Es difícil o fácil hallar trabajo en la Argentina? 9. ¿Cómo es la ciudad de Buenos Aires? ¿Cómo es la vida allí? 10. ¿Van a pasar Diana y Roberto por la casa de Isabel mañana? ¿Cuál es su casa?

B. Aplicación del diálogo

1. Usted trabaja y estudia, ¿verdad? 2. ¿Dónde está usted trabajando, en la biblioteca? ¿En la residencia de estudiantes? 3. Usted está muy ocupado (ocupada), ¿no? 4. ¿Es difícil trabajar y estudiar? 5. ¿Está usted muy cansado (cansada) ahora? 6. ¿Cuándo necesita usted descansar? 7. Usted tiene que estudiar todas las noches, ¿verdad? 8. ¿Quiere usted trabajar en un país extranjero? ¿En qué país? 9. ¿Y ya sabe usted español perfectamente bien? 10. ¿Lee usted muchos libros sobre Suramérica?

NOTAS GRAMATICALES

A. Irregular present indicative of **estar, querer,** and **saber**

estar, to be		
	singular	*plural*
	estoy	estamos
	estás	estáis
	está	están

querer, to wish, want		saber, to know, know how	
singular	*plural*	*singular*	*plural*
quiero	queremos	sé	sabemos
quieres	queréis	sabes	sabéis
quiere	quieren	sabe	saben

Note the accented forms of **estar. Querer** may be followed by an infinitive which is not preceded by a preposition: **Roberto quiere ir a la Argentina,** *Robert wants to go to Argentina.*

Followed by an infinitive, **saber** means *to know how to:* **Ella sabe hablar español,** *She knows how to speak Spanish.* **Necesitar** may also be followed by an infinitive: **Necesito descansar,** *I need to rest.*

B. The present participle

hablar:	**hablando**	*speaking*
comer:	**comiendo**	*eating*
vivir:	**viviendo**	*living*

The present participle, which in English ends in *-ing*, is regularly formed in Spanish by adding **-ando** to the stem of **-ar** verbs, and **-iendo** to the stem of **-er** and **-ir** verbs. The present participle always ends in **-o**. Forms of present participles which are irregular will be given later.

C. Uses of **estar**

Estar is used:

1. To express location or position, whether temporary or permanent:

Están en casa.   They are at home.
Montevideo está en el Uruguay.   Montevideo is in Uruguay.

2. With an adjective to indicate a state or condition of the subject, which may be noninherent, accidental, relatively temporary, or variable:

Mi tía está enferma.   My aunt is ill.
Todos están cansados.   All are tired.
No estoy muy ocupado.   I am not very busy.

3. With a present participle to express the progressive forms of the tenses:

¿Qué está Ud. escribiendo?   What are you writing?
Mi primo está trabajando allí.   My cousin is working there.

The progressive forms of the tenses in Spanish are less frequent and more emphatic than in English. They stress the fact that an action is or was in progress at a certain moment. The progressive forms of **ir** and **venir** are seldom used.

D. Special uses of the definite article

1. **La vida allí es agradable.**   Life there is pleasant.

The definite article is used in Spanish with abstract nouns, such as life, liberty, etc.

2. | **la Argentina** | **el Uruguay** | **el Perú** | **El Salvador** |
| **el Brasil** | **el Paraguay** | **el Ecuador** | **los Estados Unidos** |

The definite article regularly forms a part of a few place names, although today many Spanish-speaking people omit the article except with **El Salvador,** which means *The Savior,* and with **La Habana,** *Havana.*

Remember what has been stated in regard to the use of the definite article with the name of a language (page 16), and in certain set expressions (footnote 1, page 33).

E. Feminine nouns

el esposo husband		**la esposa** wife	
el hijo son		**la hija** daughter	
el hermano brother		**la hermana** sister	
el primo cousin (*m.*)		**la prima** cousin (*f.*)	
el tío uncle		**la tía** aunt	
el amigo friend (*m.*)		**la amiga** friend (*f.*)	
el alumno pupil (*m.*)		**la alumna** pupil (*f.*)	

Certain masculine nouns ending in **-o,** particularly those of relationship, have a corresponding feminine form ending in **-a.** Even though **el esposo** and **el tío** are not used in the dialogue of this lesson, remember their meanings, for the words will be used hereafter in the text.

Recall that the masculine plural of nouns referring to persons may include both sexes (see page 16): **los hijos,** *the sons, the son(s) and daughter(s)* or *the children;* **los padres,** *the fathers, the father and mother, the parents;* **los tíos,** *the uncles, the uncle(s) and aunt(s).*

The familiar forms **papá,** *papa, dad, father,* and **mamá,** *mama, mom, mother,* are commonly used without the article, as in English; however, one may say **mi papá, nuestra mamá,** etc.

F. Use of **¿cuál?** *which (one)? what?*

¿Cuál es la capital del Uruguay?   What is the capital of Uruguay?
¿Cuáles son países grandes?   Which (ones) are large countries?
Sabes cuál es nuestra casa, ¿verdad?   You know which (one) is our house, don't you?

BUT: **¿A qué país quieren ir?**   To what (which) country do they want to go?

¿Cuál? (*pl.* **¿Cuáles?**) is used as a pronoun, and it usually indicates a choice of one or more things from among several.

An accent mark must be written on interrogatives which introduce indirect questions, the same as in the case of direct questions (third example).

When English *which?* and *what?* modify nouns, the adjective **¿qué?** is used in Spanish (fourth example). Also compare **¿Qué libro tiene Ud.?** *Which (What) book do you have?* with **¿Cuál de los libros tiene Ud.?** *Which (one) of the books do you have?*

EJERCICIOS

A. Substitution drill:

1. ¿Cómo están *ustedes?*
(*tu familia, tú, Ud., su mamá, ellos*)
2. *Isabel* está trabajando mucho.
(*Yo, Mi papá y yo, Tú, El señor Pidal, Uds.*)
3. *Yo* quiero ir a la Argentina.
(*Mis amigos, Su hijo, Uds., Mi esposo y yo, La señora Pidal*)
4. *Nosotros* sabemos hablar bien.
(*Yo, Mi prima y yo, Mi amiga, Uds., Tú*)

B. Review the uses of **ser** in Lesson 4; then complete each sentence with the correct form of the verb:

1. —¿Cuál _____ la capital de la Argentina? 2. — _____ Buenos Aires; _____ una ciudad maravillosa. 3. La vida allí _____ muy agradable. 4. Roberto y su hermana _____ mexicanos. 5. Sus tíos _____ argentinos. 6. Yo _____ norteamericano. 7. ¿De dónde _____ usted, señor Pidal? 8. Y tú, Carlos, ¿de dónde _____? 9. Ahora yo _____ estudiante, pero quiero _____ profesor. 10. ¿Qué quieres _____ tú, Felipe? 11. ¿Qué _____ tu papá, Ana? 12. —¿Creen ustedes que el español _____ difícil? 13. —No, creemos que _____ bastante fácil. 14. Yo creo que _____ difícil aprender una lengua extranjera. 15. —Qué hora _____? —Ya _____ tarde; _____ las cinco y media. 16. —¿De quién _____ los periódicos? — _____ del profesor. 17. —Y la carta, ¿para quién _____? — _____ para la señora Pidal. 18. —¿De qué _____ el mapa? — _____ de papel.

C. Supply the correct form of **estar,** noting the uses of the verb:

1. Mi hermano _____ en la Argentina y mis padres _____ en el Uruguay. 2. Yo _____ aquí de visita. 3. Tomás, ¿dónde _____ tu familia? 4. —¿Dónde _____ ustedes ahora, Felipe? 5. —Nosotros _____ en el cuarto de Luis, pero él no _____ aquí. 6. ¿No sabes tú dónde _____ Luis? 7. —Creo que él y Tomás _____ en la biblioteca; _____ estudiando. 8. El señor Pidal _____ muy ocupado; _____ preparando un examen para los estudiantes. 9. —Carlos, ¿no _____ usted muy cansado hoy? 10. —Sí, _____ bastante cansado, pero ahora _____ descansando. 11. —¿Cómo _____ tus padres, Roberto? 12. —Mi mamá _____ bien, pero mi papá _____ un poco enfermo. 13. —¿Dónde _____ el mapa? Quiero saber dónde _____ Montevideo. 14. —¡Hombre! _____ en el Uruguay, que _____ cerca de la Argentina.

D. Answer affirmatively:

1. ¿Es profesora la señora Díaz?
2. ¿Es Diana tu prima?
3. ¿Es del Perú la carta?
4. ¿Son para María las plumas?
5. ¿Son interesantes los programas?
6. ¿Son ustedes estudiantes?
7. ¿Es Isabel tu hermana?
8. ¿Somos nosotros norteamericanos?

E. Answer affirmatively; then, when you hear the cue, answer again, making the necessary changes according to the model:

MODEL: ¿Está ocupado tu papá?   *Sí, mi papá está ocupado.*
        (¿Y tu mamá?)   *Mi mamá está ocupada también.*

1. ¿Está enferma tu prima? (¿Y tus primos?)
2. ¿Está cansado tu hermano? (¿Y tu hermana?)
3. ¿Están sentados tus amigos? (¿Y tus amigas?)
4. ¿Están de visita sus hijos? (¿Y su amiga?)
5. ¿Es difícil el trabajo? (¿Y las lecciones?)
6. ¿Es hermoso el campo? (¿Y la ciudad?)

F. Answer negatively, using the progressive form of the verb and **todavía:**

MODEL: ¿Trabajas tú ahora?   *No, no estoy trabajando todavía.*

1. ¿Descansan Uds. ahora?
2. ¿Cenan ellos ahora?
3. ¿Escribe Ud. la carta ahora?
4. ¿Miras la televisión ahora?
5. ¿Toman Uds. el desayuno ahora?
6. ¿Comen Carlos y Luis ahora?
7. ¿Prepara Felipe las lecciones ahora?
8. ¿Viven Uds. en Suramérica ahora?

G. Read in Spanish, supplying the correct form of the article (definite or indefinite), when required:

1. —Buenas tardes, ⎯⎯⎯ señor Díaz, ¿Sabe usted dónde está ⎯⎯⎯ señora Díaz?
2. —⎯⎯⎯ señora Díaz está hablando con ⎯⎯⎯ profesora Pidal. 3. ⎯⎯⎯ señora Pidal es ⎯⎯⎯ profesora muy buena. 4. Su esposo también es ⎯⎯⎯ profesor.
5. Mi amigo Felipe estudia ⎯⎯⎯ alemán; no es ⎯⎯⎯ lengua fácil. 6. Queremos hallar trabajo en ⎯⎯⎯ país extranjero. 7. ⎯⎯⎯ Uruguay es ⎯⎯⎯ país interesante, y ⎯⎯⎯ Argentina también. 8. ⎯⎯⎯ vida allí es muy agradable. 9. Carmen, que es ⎯⎯⎯ hermana de Tomás, viene de México mañana. 10. Ella estudia en ⎯⎯⎯ Universidad de México y es ⎯⎯⎯ estudiante muy buena.

H. Give the Spanish equivalent:

1. "How are you,[1] Mrs. Díaz? What a pleasure to know that you are visiting here! How is your daughter Betty? . . . And Mr. Díaz?" 2. "We are fine,[2] thank you, Diane. How are your parents?" 3. "My mother is a little sick, and my father is busy at (in) the office. I believe that he works too much now. 4. Mrs. Díaz, do you know that my cousin Robert and I want to go to South America?" 5. "Really? As you

⎯⎯⎯⎯⎯⎯⎯⎯

[1]Diane will use formal forms of address in speaking to Mrs. Díaz, and the latter will use familiar forms. [2]Use **bien.**

know, Betty is working in Buenos Aires, the capital of Argentina.   6. It is a beautiful city and I think (believe) that life is very pleasant there."   7. "Won't you take something, Mrs. Díaz?"   8. "No, thank you, Diane. It is late now and your mother needs to rest."   9. "Yes, of course! Won't you and your daughter come by our house tomorrow?   10. Robert and I want to talk with Betty."   11. "Yes, gladly. But it is nearly six o'clock already! Thank you, Diane."   12. "You're welcome, Mrs. Díaz. See you tomorrow."

EJERCICIOS DE PRONUNCIACIÓN

A. Spanish **h**

The letter **h** is silent in modern Spanish. Pronounce:

hasta	hay	hermoso	¡hola!
hijo	hoy	hermana	hora
dos horas	mi hermano	su hija	¿quién habla?

B. Spanish **t**

In the pronunciation of Spanish **t** the tip of the tongue touches the back of the upper front teeth, and not the ridge above the teeth, as in English; furthermore, the sound is never followed by a puff of air, as occurs in English *task* (*t*^h*ask*), for example. To avoid the puff of air, the breath must be held back during the articulation of the sound:

estar	parte	tengo	la Argentina
patio	tío	Tomás	perfectamente

C. Spanish **d**

1. Review the sounds of **d,** page 4, then pronounce:

Diana	difícil	¿dónde?	¿adónde?
desde	ciudad	estudiante	todavía

2. Pronounce each word individually after your teacher; then repeat, but as part of a breath-group introduced by the words indicated at the right, noting the change that occurs in the pronunciation of Spanish **d:**

a. doce dos diez	a las
b. descansar Diana	para
c. día desayuno	su
d. del profesor de mi padre difícil	es

VOCABULARIO

además *adv.* besides, furthermore
agradable pleasant, agreeable
algo something, anything
la **Argentina** Argentina
cansado, -a tired
la **capital** capital (*city*)
cerca *adv.* near, close by
¿cuál? (*pl.* **¿cuáles?**) which one (ones)? what?
demasiado *adv.* too, too much
descansar to rest
Diana Diana, Diane
enfermo, -a ill, sick
la **esposa** wife
estar to be
frío, -a cold
gracias thanks, thank you
el **gusto** pleasure, delight
hallar to find
la **hija** daughter
el **hijo** son; *pl.* children
llegar (a) to arrive (at), reach
la **mamá** mama, mom, mother
maravilloso, -a marvelous
el **momento** moment

necesitar to need
ocupado, -a busy, occupied
la **oficina** office
el **papá** papa, dad, father
pasar to pass *or* come (by), go, come in; to spend (*time*)
el **patio** patio, courtyard
perfectamente fine, perfectly
porque because, for
¿por qué? why? for what reason?
la **prima** cousin (*f.*)
el **primo** cousin (*m.*)
querer to wish, want
Roberto Robert
saber to know, know how
la **semana** week
sentado, -a seated
Suramérica South America
la **tía** aunt
el **tiempo** time (*in general sense*)
el **trabajo** work, employment, position, job
el **Uruguay** Uruguay
la **visita** visit, call
visitar to visit, call on
ya already, now

¡claro! of course! certainly!
con mucho gusto gladly, with great pleasure
¿cuánto tiempo? how much time? how long?
de veras really, truly
estar de visita to visit, be visiting, be on a visit
estar en (la oficina) to be at *or* in (the *or* his office)
gracias por (la visita) thanks for (the call *or* visit)
no hay de qué you're welcome, don't mention it
¿no quieren (Uds.) pasar? won't you come in?
por un momento for a moment, for just a moment
¡qué gusto! what a pleasure (delight)!
¿qué tal? how are you? how goes it?

REPASO[1] 1

A. Answer affirmatively:

1. ¿Sabes la lección?
2. ¿Tienes el mapa?
3. ¿Vas a la biblioteca?
4. ¿Quieres ir a la cafetería?
5. ¿Eres estudiante?
6. ¿Recibes muchas cartas?

7. ¿Son Uds. norteamericanos?
8. ¿Tienen Uds. papel?
9. ¿Van Uds. a tomar algo?
10. ¿Vienen Uds. a trabajar?
11. ¿Quieren Uds. mirar los cuadros?
12. ¿Viven Uds. en la ciudad?

B. Answer negatively:

1. ¿Viene Ud. temprano a la clase?
2. ¿Llega Ud. a las ocho?
3. ¿Recibe Ud. periódicos de México?
4. ¿Escribe Ud. muchas cartas?
5. ¿Quiere Ud. leer libros en español?
6. ¿Necesita Ud. descansar un rato?

7. ¿Están Uds. cansados?
8. ¿Aprenden Uds. lenguas extranjeras?
9. ¿Mira Ana cuadros hermosos?
10. ¿Mira Carlos la televisión?
11. ¿Tomamos Ud. y yo el desayuno?
12. ¿Leemos ella y yo los exámenes?

C. Repeat the model sentence; then substitute the cue words, making any necessary changes:

1. Voy con *mi amigo Roberto.* (amiga Ana, amigos, tío)
2. Diana come con *su papá.* (mamá, hermanos, amigas)
3. Cenamos con *nuestro primo.* (prima, padres, profesor)
4. El señor Díaz viene con *su hija.* (hijo, hijos, amigos)
5. ¿Siempre tienes *tu lápiz?* (lápices, cuaderno, plumas)
6. Ana habla con *su tía.* (amigos, primos, profesoras)

D. Repeat each sentence; then, when you hear another verb, make a new sentence using the corresponding form of that verb:

1. Tú escribes todas las palabras. (leer)
2. Los padres de Ana tienen una casa de campo. (querer)
3. Mi mamá trabaja en el patio. (descansar)
4. Nuestra familia cena muy tarde. (comer)
5. ¿Siempre llegan los estudiantes a la una? (venir)
6. ¿Estudia Ud. los ejercicios por la tarde? (preparar)
7. ¿Leen Uds. periódicos españoles? (tener)
8. Carlos y Ana pronuncian bien el español. (escribir)
9. Luis y yo queremos descansar un rato. (necesitar)
10. Nuestros primos no viven en el campo. (trabajar)

---

[1] **Repaso,** *Review.*

E. You will hear two sets of one or more words separated by a pause. Make a sentence using the correct form of **estar** or **ser** to join the two sets of words:

1. María . . . sentada en la silla.
2. Luis y yo . . . muy cansados.
3. Nosotros . . . de los Estados Unidos.
4. La capital del país . . . grande.
5. El profesor Díaz . . . de México.
6. Nuestra mamá . . . muy ocupada.
7. La señorita Valdés . . . en casa.
8. Creo que . . . las dos de lá tarde.

9. Las casas . . . hermosas.
10. El parque no . . . cerca de aquí.
11. Mi tía no . . . muy enferma.
12. María y yo no . . . mexicanos.
13. Tomás . . . trabajando demasiado.
14. Él y yo . . . mirando el mapa.
15. Ella no quiere . . . profesora.
16. Uds. necesitan . . . aquí temprano.

F. Listen to the question. After you hear an adjective or phrase, make an affirmative sentence repeating the subject:

MODEL: ¿Cómo está María? (muy bien) *María está muy bien.*

1. ¿Cómo está tu mamá? (bastante bien)
2. ¿Cómo están tus padres? (cansados)
3. ¿Dónde está la señora Gómez? (en casa)
4. ¿De dónde es el señor López? (de la Argentina)
5. ¿Qué es la señorita Valdés? (profesora de español)
6. ¿De quién es el reloj? (de mi hermano)
7. ¿Cómo está tu tío? (un poco enfermo)
8. ¿De qué color es la casa? (blanca)

G. Give the Spanish equivalent, using the formal forms for *you, your:*

1. "Good morning, Louis. How are you?" 2. "Very well, thanks, Mr. Valdés." 3. Miss Díaz is coming now. 4. There are twenty-one students (*m.*) in the Spanish class. 5. My sister is studying (*progressive*) in the University of Mexico. 6. Won't you (*pl.*) come in? 7. Charles and I watch the television program. 8. I arrive each morning at eight o'clock. 9. We have to study in the evening. 10. It is 3:15 P.M. 11. How many classes do you have in the morning? 12. What color is your new house? 13. We are going to the library to study. 14. We need to talk Spanish a little each day. 15. How long are you going to be here? 16. "Why does George arrive so late?" 17. "He works in his father's office every afternoon." 18. "Many thanks. See you tomorrow."

Patio, Museo Antropológico, México, D. F.

Present indicative of some irregular verbs • The personal *a* • Direct object pronouns • Position of object pronouns • Verbs which require a direct object without a preposition • The infinitive after a preposition • Meaning of *saber* and *conocer* • Demonstrative adjectives

LECCIÓN 6

Enrique busca a su amigo

Son las cuatro de la tarde. Enrique sale de la residencia de estudiantes, donde vive, y va a la casa de su amigo José. Llega y llama a la puerta. José la abre y, al ver a Enrique, lo invita a entrar. Los dos jóvenes entran en la sala.

JOSÉ —¿Qué hay de nuevo, Enrique?

ENRIQUE —Nada de particular. Estoy buscando a Tomás Ortega. ¿Sabes dónde está?

JOSÉ —No, no sé, pero pasa a menudo por aquí, especialmente si no me ve durante el día. ¿Por qué lo buscas?

ENRIQUE —Traigo una carta muy larga de Carlos Padilla. Sé que Tomás lo conoce bien.

◆ ◆ ◆ ◆ ◆

ENRIQUE —¿No vive Tomás en aquella casa nueva que podemos ver por esta ventana?

JOSÉ —Sí, Enrique. Pero estoy seguro de que[1] va a venir por aquí esta tarde. ¿Por qué no lo esperas un rato?

ENRIQUE —Con mucho gusto, si no estás ocupado.

JOSÉ —La verdad es que tengo que terminar la lección para mañana. Pero puedes leer el periódico. Aquí lo tienes.

ENRIQUE —Gracias. Siempre lo leo por la mañana, antes de salir de casa.

JOSÉ —¿No quieres mirar esa revista que está sobre la mesita? ¿La conoces?

ENRIQUE —Sí, la conozco. María Gómez trae revistas españolas a nuestra clase y todos los estudiantes las leen. Sabes quién es María ¿verdad?

JOSÉ —¡Sí, claro! La conozco bien. Visita a mi hermana muy a menudo.

ENRIQUE —¡Caramba, José! ¿Cuándo vas a terminar si te molesto tanto? Puedo pasar por aquí esta noche después de cenar.

JOSÉ —¡No, hombre! Aquí tengo mi cuaderno y ya estoy escribiendo las frases. Después de terminar la lección podemos charlar más.

---

[1]After **estar seguro, -a** the preposition **de** is regularly expressed in Spanish before an object, including a **que**-clause; however, in conversational Spanish it is often omitted in the latter case: **estar seguro, -a que**, instead of **estar seguro, -a de que**, *to be sure that*.

Conversación

A. Preguntas sobre el diálogo

1. ¿Quién llega a la casa de José? 2. ¿A quién está buscando Enrique? 3. ¿Qué trae Enrique? 4. ¿Dónde vive Tomás? 5. ¿Está ocupado José? 6. ¿Qué tiene que terminar José? 7. ¿Lee Enrique el periódico de José? 8. ¿Cuándo lee Enrique el periódico? 9. ¿Qué leen todos los estudiantes? 10. ¿A quién visita María?

B. Aplicación del diálogo

1. ¿Sale Ud. de casa a menudo? ¿Adónde va? 2. ¿Tiene Ud. muchos amigos en la universidad? 3. ¿Los visita Ud. a menudo? 4. ¿Cuándo visita Ud. a sus amigos? ¿Después de cenar? ¿Después de estudiar? 5. ¿Lee Ud. el periódico todos los días? ¿Cuándo lo lee? 6. ¿Qué traen generalmente los estudiantes a clase? 7. ¿Conoce Ud. a todas las estudiantes de su clase? 8. ¿Sabe Ud. dónde viven ellas?

NOTAS GRAMATICALES

A. Present indicative of some irregular verbs

conocer, to know, be acquainted with	poder, to be able, can	salir, to leave, go out	traer, to bring	ver, to see
singular				
conozco	puedo	salgo	traigo	veo
conoces	puedes	sales	traes	ves
conoce	puede	sale	trae	ve
plural				
conocemos	podemos	salimos	traemos	vemos
conocéis	podéis	salís	traéis	veis
conocen	pueden	salen	traen	ven

Poder, like **querer,** may be followed by an infinitive which is not preceded by a preposition: **Podemos ver la casa,** *We can see the house.*

B. The personal **a**

Enrique ve a su amigo. Henry sees his friend.
¿Buscas a José? Are you looking for Joseph?
¿A quién ve Ud.? Whom do you see?

BUT: **Tengo un amigo mexicano.** I have a Mexican friend.

An unusual feature of Spanish is the use of **a** before the direct object of a verb when the noun refers to a definite person. This word **a** is used with **¿quién?** to mean *whom?,* but it is not used after forms of **tener,** nor with direct object pronouns, which are given in section C.

◆ *Práctica.* Repeat after your teacher, noting the use of the personal **a:**

1. Conozco a Felipe. 2. ¿Conoce Ud. a mi hermana? 3. No veo a la señorita Ortega. 4. José está buscando al señor Padilla. 5. ¿A quién llama Ud.? 6. ¿Buscan a su madre? 7. ¿Espera Carmen a María? 8. No puedo escuchar a Tomás ahora.

C. Direct object pronouns

	singular		*plural*
me	me	**nos**	us
te	you (*fam.*)	**os**	you (*fam.*)
lo	him; you (*formal m.*); it (*m. and neuter*)	**los**	them (*m.*); you (*m.*)
la	her; it (*f.*); you (*formal f.*)	**las**	them (*f.*); you (*f.*)

Note carefully the third person direct object pronouns and do not confuse them with the definite articles. In addition to referring to masculine objects, **lo** may refer to an action, a statement, or an idea: **Lo creo,** *I believe it.*

In Peninsular Spanish **le** is regularly used instead of **lo** for *him, you* (formal). The **lo** form will be used in this text.

D. Position of object pronouns

José abre la puerta. Joseph opens the door.
José la **abre.** Joseph opens it.
Ella ve las revistas. She sees the magazines.
Ella las **ve.** She sees them.
Yo no busco a Tomás. I am not looking for Thomas.
Yo no lo **busco.** I am not looking for him.

Object pronouns are placed *immediately before the verb*. (Exceptions will be given later.) If the sentence is negative, object pronouns come between **no** and the verb.

◆ *Práctica.* Read in Spanish, noting particularly the object pronouns and their position with respect to the verb:

1. Yo tengo el cuaderno; yo lo tengo. 2. Ella tiene los lápices; ella los tiene. 3. Escribo la frase; la escribo. 4. José abre las ventanas; José las abre. 5. No veo a José; no lo veo. 6. Ellos buscan a los alumnos; ellos los buscan. 7. No miro a mi hermana; no la miro. 8. ¿No espera Ud. a María? ¿No la espera Ud.?

E. Verbs which require a direct object without a preposition

Diana busca el periódico.   Diane is looking for the newspaper.
Ella lo mira.   She is looking at it.
Escuchan el programa.   They listen to the program.
Esperamos a Roberto.   We are waiting for Robert.
Lo esperamos.   We are waiting for him.

Note that the prepositions *for, at, to* are included in the English meaning of the verbs **buscar, escuchar, esperar, mirar.** The personal **a** is used when the direct object is a person (fourth example).

However, just as **entrar** requires **en** before an object, **salir** requires **de.** If no object is expressed, **en** and **de** are omitted:

Salen de (Entran en) la casa.   They leave (enter) the house.
Los dos jóvenes salen (entran).   The two young men leave (enter).

F. The infinitive after a preposition

al ver   on (upon) seeing, when (he) sees
después de terminar las frases   after finishing the sentences
Estoy cansado de trabajar.   I am tired of working.

In Spanish the infinitive, not the present participle, is regularly used after a preposition. **Al** plus an infinitive is the equivalent of English *on* (*upon*) plus the present participle. This construction may also be translated as a clause beginning with *when*.

G. Meaning of **saber** and **conocer**

Sé que él viene esta tarde.   I know that he is coming this afternoon.
Lo conozco bien.   I know him well. (I am well acquainted with him.)
¿Conoces esa revista?   Do you know that magazine?

Foto de Sevilla, España, donde vemos la Torre del Oro y, al fondo, la Catedral con la torre de La Giralda.

Saber means *to know* facts or *to have knowledge* of something. Remember that with an infinitive **saber** means *to know how to:* **Sé leer español,** *I know how to (can) read Spanish.* **Conocer** means *to know* in the sense of *to be acquainted with* someone or something.

H. Demonstrative adjectives

	singular			plural	
masc.	*fem.*		*masc.*	*fem.*	
este	esta	this	estos	estas	these
ese	esa	that (*nearby*)	esos	esas	those (*nearby*)
aquel	aquella	that (*distant*)	aquellos	aquellas	those (*distant*)

A demonstrative adjective points out the noun to which it refers. (Do not confuse the demonstrative with the relative **que.**) It comes before its noun and, like all other adjectives in Spanish, it agrees with the noun in gender and number. It is repeated before each noun in a series. **Ese, esa, (-os, -as)** indicate persons or objects near to, or associated with, the person addressed; **aquel, aquella, (-os, -as)** indicate persons or objects distant from the speaker and the person addressed.

EJERCICIOS

A. Substitution drill:

1. *Mis amigos* conocen a José.
   (*Ud. y yo, Yo, Tú, Tomás y Carlos, Ana*)
2. ¿Puedes *tú* llamar a María?
   (*Uds., nosotros, Felipe, yo, Ud.*)
3. *Enrique* sale de casa a las ocho.
   (*Yo, Nosotros, Ud., Tú, Ellos*)
4. *Roberto* ve al señor Díaz.
   (*Tú, Tú y yo, Ella, Nuestros amigos, Yo*)

B. Say after your teacher. When you hear the question again, answer it affirmatively. Watch the possessives in sentences 7-12.

1. ¿Conoce Ud. a Felipe?
2. ¿Ve Ud. a la señorita Gómez?
3. ¿Sales de casa temprano?
4. ¿Puedes buscar a Tomás ahora?
5. ¿Tienen Uds. muchos amigos aquí?
6. ¿Quiere Ud. buscar trabajo?
7. ¿Busca Ud. sus lápices?
8. ¿Buscan Uds. a sus amigos?
9. ¿Quieren Uds. ir a ver a sus tíos?
10. ¿Puede José leer sus frases?
11. ¿Espera Carmen a mi hermana?
12. ¿Esperan Uds. a su papá?

C. Say after your teacher; then repeat, making the demonstrative adjective and the noun plural:

MODEL: Veo a ese hombre.   *Veo a ese hombre. Veo a esos hombres.*

1. Entran en este cuarto.
2. Quiero mirar esta revista.
3. Leen ese periódico.
4. Abren esa ventana.
5. No conozco a aquel hombre.
6. No vamos a aquella ciudad.
7. ¿Puedo traer este cuadro?
8. ¿Están saliendo de aquella casa?

D. Say after your teacher. When you hear a new noun, use it to form a new sentence, making the necessary change(s) in agreement:

1. ¿Quiere Ud. este lápiz?
   carta?
   periódicos?
   revistas?
   mapa?

2. Luis abre ese cuaderno.
   puerta.
   ventanas.
   libros.
   cartas.

3. No puedo ir a aquel parque.
   ciudad.
   países.
   programas.
   capital.

4. Esta casa es hermosa.
   casas
   patios
   ventanas
   mesita

E. Read in Spanish, supplying the personal **a** whenever necessary:

1. Veo _____ mis amigos a menudo.   2. ¿ _____ quién ves? ¿ _____ María?
3. Estamos buscando _____ un periódico en español.   4. José busca _____ su hermano. 5. ¿Estás mirando _____ mis revistas? 6. —¿ _____ quiénes mira José? —Mira _____ las estudiantes. 7. ¿Tiene Carlos _____ muchas amigas en la universidad? 8. ¿Estás esperando _____ Isabel? 9. Visito _____ mis amigos después de cenar. 10. ¿Conoces bien _____ la ciudad? 11. No conozco _____ la señorita Gómez. 12. ¿Miran Uds. _____ muchos programas de televisión?

F. Read each sentence in Spanish; then repeat, substituting the correct direct object pronoun for each noun object and modifiers:

MODEL: Yo abro la puerta.   *Yo abro la puerta. Yo la abro.*

1. José abre la ventana. 2. Felipe abre las ventanas. 3. José y yo vemos el cuadro.
4. Vemos los mapas también. 5. Enrique conoce al señor Ortega. 6. No conoce a los dos jóvenes. 7. No conozco a María Gómez. 8. Carlos llama a Tomás. 9. Los estudiantes escuchan el programa. 10. ¿Espera Ud. a sus padres? 11. Los hombres miran nuestras casas. 12. Isabel visita a María y a su hermana.

G. Repeat the question after your teacher; then answer affirmatively, substituting the correct direct object pronoun for each noun object and modifiers:

MODEL: ¿Abre Diana las ventanas?   *¿Abre Diana las ventanas?*
                                          Sí, las abre.

1. ¿Conoce Ud. a mi padre?   4. ¿Tienen Uds. sus cuadernos?
2. ¿Mira Ud. a las estudiantes?   5. ¿Abren Uds. sus libros?
3. ¿Visita Ud. a su amiga?   6. ¿Ven Uds. el cuadro?

Repeat after your teacher; then answer negatively, substituting the correct object pronoun for each noun object and modifiers:

7. ¿Ves a mi hermana?   10. ¿Miran Uds. el mapa?
8. ¿Buscan ellos a José?   11. ¿Visita Ana a María?
9. ¿Esperas a tus amigos?   12. ¿Leen Uds. las revistas?

H. Give the Spanish equivalent, using the familiar forms for *you* (except in 6), *your*:

1. Henry knocks at the door and Joseph opens it.   2. Upon seeing Joseph, Henry invites him to enter.   3. Joseph says: "I am looking for (*progressive*) Thomas. Do you see him often?"   4. "My friends Philip and Louis visit me nearly every afternoon. You know them, don't you?"   5. "Yes, they are students in (of) my Spanish class and I see them each morning."   6. "Do you know Spanish, Mr. Ortega?" "Yes, of course! I speak it perfectly well."   7. "Charles, do you bring a letter from your sister?"   8. "Yes, here I have it. Do you want it?"   9. After finishing my lesson, I want to visit Mary and Diane.   10. "Betty, do you visit your parents?" "Yes, I visit them on Sundays."   11. I don't know Carmen, but I know that she is your sister.   12. "Who are those men?" "I don't know them, but I am sure that they are coming to see my father."

EJERCICIOS DE PRONUNCIACIÓN

A. The sounds of **r** and **rr**

1. Single **r,** except when initial in a word and when after **l, n,** or **s,** is pronounced with a single tap of the tip of the tongue against the gums of the upper teeth; the sound is much like *dd* in *eddy* pronounced rapidly:

pared	eres	amarillo	hora
Carlos	largo	tres	charlar

2. When initial in a word, and when after **l, n,** or **s,** and doubled, the sound is strongly trilled, the tip of the tongue striking the gums in a series of very rapid vibrations:

un rato	recibir	el reloj	la revista
Roberto	rojo	pizarra	Enrique

B. Linking

Review linking, page 8, giving special attention to the linking of vowels between words, and pronounce as one breath-group:

1. Ella va a hablar. Busca a Tomás. ¿Mucho o poco?
   Tengo que estudiar. Es casi inglés. ¿Dónde vive el hijo?

2. la América española. Busco a Tomás. Vamos a estudiar.
   No hablo español. Escucho el programa. ¿Qué hay de particular?

C. Dictado

The teacher may select the first four exchanges of the dialogue of this lesson as an exercise in dictation.

Puerta del Cambrón, Toledo, España.

VOCABULARIO

abrir to open
antes de *prep.* before (*time*)
buscar to look for, seek, get, pick up, call for
conocer to know, be acquainted with, meet
charlar to chat
¿cuándo? when?
después de *prep.* after
donde where, in which
durante during
Enrique Henry
entrar (**en** + *obj.*) to enter, go *or* come in (into)
especialmente especially
esperar to wait, wait for; to hope
la **frase** sentence
invitar (**a** + *inf.*) to invite (to)
José Joseph, Joe
joven (*pl.* **jóvenes**) young

largo, -a long
llamar to call; to knock
la **mesita** small (little) table
molestar to bother, molest
nada nothing
particular particular, special
poder to be able, can
la **puerta** door
el **rato** while, short time
la **revista** magazine, journal
la **sala** living room
salir (**de** + *obj.*) to leave, go (come) out
seguro, -a sure, certain
si if, whether
tanto *adv.* as (so) much
terminar to end, finish
traer to bring
la **ventana** window
ver to see

a menudo often, frequently
al + *inf.* on, upon + *pres. part.*
aquí (lo) tienes here (it) is
¡caramba! gosh! dear me! good gracious! my goodness!
esta noche tonight
estar seguro, -a (de que) to be sure (that)
los dos jóvenes the two (both) young men (*adj. used as noun; see Lesson 7*)
nada de particular nothing special
¿qué hay de nuevo? what's new? what do you know?
salir de casa to leave home

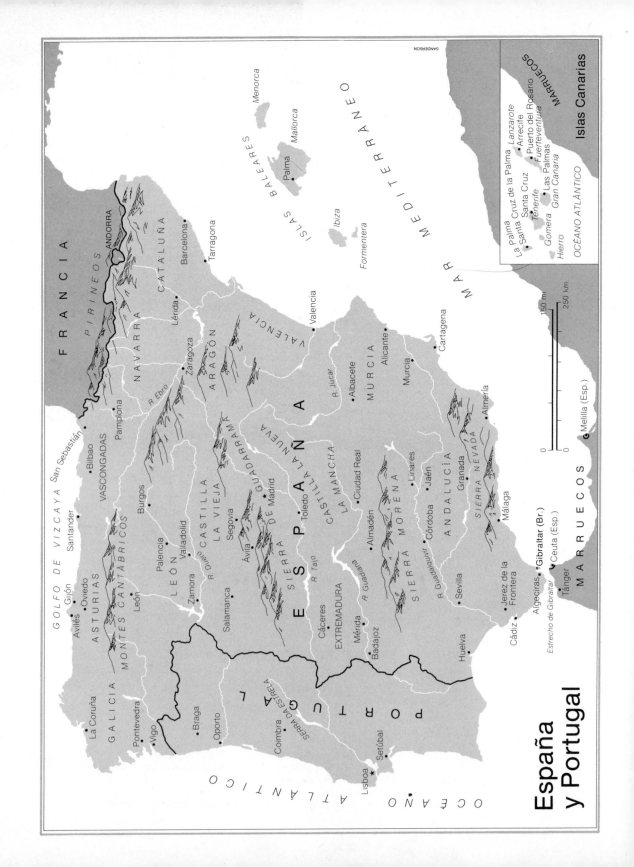

España
y Portugal

Islas Canarias

OCÉANO ATLÁNTICO

MARRUECOS

La Palma
La Cruz de la Palma
Santa Cruz
Tenerife
Gomera
Hierro
Gran Canaria
Las Palmas
Lanzarote
Arrecife
Puerto del Rosario
Fuerteventura

SANDERSON

FRANCIA

ANDORRA

PIRINEOS

NAVARRA

CATALUÑA

Barcelona
Tarragona
Lérida
Zaragoza
Pamplona

R. Ebro

ARAGÓN

VALENCIA

Valencia

MAR MEDITERRÁNEO

ISLAS BALEARES

Menorca
Mallorca
Palma
Ibiza
Formentera

GOLFO DE VIZCAYA
San Sebastián
Bilbao
VASCONGADAS
Santander
Gijón
Oviedo
Avilés
ASTURIAS
MONTES CANTÁBRICOS
GALICIA
La Coruña
Pontevedra
Vigo

Burgos
Palencia
Valladolid
León
Zamora
Salamanca
LEÓN
CASTILLA LA VIEJA
R. Duero
Ávila
Segovia
SIERRA DE GUADARRAMA
Madrid
Toledo
R. Tajo
CASTILLA LA NUEVA
Cáceres
Mérida
Badajoz
EXTREMADURA

R. Júcar
Albacete
MURCIA
Murcia
Alicante
Cartagena

ESPAÑA

LA MANCHA
Ciudad Real
Almadén
SIERRA MORENA
Linares
Jaén
Córdoba
R. Guadalquivir
Sevilla
Huelva
ANDALUCÍA
Granada
SIERRA NEVADA
Almería
Málaga
Jerez de la Frontera
Cádiz
Algeciras
Estrecho de Gibraltar
Gibraltar (Br.)
Ceuta (Esp)
Tánger
R. Guadiana

MARRUECOS

Melilla (Esp.)

0   150 mi
0   250 km.

PORTUGAL
SERRA DA ESTRELA
Braga
Oporto
Coimbra
Setúbal
Lisboa

OCÉANO ATLÁNTICO

Lectura 1

España en el siglo[1] veinte

Hoy vamos a estudiar un mapa que está en la
pared. Es un mapa de España y Portugal.
Los dos países forman la Península Ibérica,[2]
que está en el suroeste de Europa. Portugal
ocupa la parte occidental y España ocupa el
resto de la Península.

España tiene muchas montañas y cinco ríos
grandes. En el norte están los altos[3] Pirineos,
que forman la frontera con Francia. Hay
cordilleras paralelas en la parte central y en el
sur.

Estas montañas y los ríos dividen el país en
trece regiones naturales.[4] Estas divisiones
geográficas producen diferencias notables y
afectan el carácter[5] y la vida de la gente.

Las Provincias Vascongadas y Cataluña, en
el norte del país, son regiones muy ricas y
muy progresivas. Los habitantes de estas
regiones son muy industriosos y hasta[6] aspiran
a la autonomía política. Bilbao y Barcelona
son los centros industriales y comerciales más
importantes. Barcelona, que está en la costa
del Mar Mediterráneo, es el puerto principal
de España.

El interior de la Península es una meseta.[7]
Castilla la Vieja y Castilla la Nueva ocupan la
parte central de esta meseta. En general, las
tierras son áridas y la vida de los labradores[8]
en estas regiones es muy dura.[9]

Madrid, la capital de España, está en el
centro del país, en la región de Castilla la
Nueva. Es una ciudad moderna que tiene
más de[10] dos millones de habitantes.

Andalucía, ocupada durante siglos por los
musulmanes,[11] está en el sur de la Península.
Conserva en sus ciudades magníficos ejemplos
del arte árabe. La influencia árabe es evidente
también en la agricultura, las industrias, la
música y en otros aspectos de la vida andaluza. Sevilla, Cádiz, Granada y Málaga son
ciudades importantes de esta región.

---

[1]**siglo,** *century.*   [2]**Ibérica,** *Iberian.*   [3]See pages 285–286 for notes on the position of adjectives.
[4]The Spanish names of these regions are: Galicia, Asturias, León, Castilla la Vieja (*Old Castile*), las Provincias Vascongadas
(*Basque*), Navarra, Aragón, and Cataluña (*Catalonia*), in the northern part of the Peninsula, Extremadura, Castilla la Nueva, and
Valencia, in the central part, and Andalucía (*Andalusia*), and Murcia in the southern part.
[5]The plural of **carácter,** *character,* is **caracteres.**   [6]**hasta,** *even.*   [7]**meseta,** *tableland, plateau.*
[8]**labradores,** *farmers, peasants.*   [9]**dura,** *hard, rigorous.*   [10]**de,** *than.*   [11]**musulmanes,** *Moslems, Mussulmans.*

Como vemos, España es un país de contrastes. Tradicionalmente, el monarca español es «rey de las Españas» más bien que[12] «rey de España.» Cada región tiene costumbres[13] y tradiciones diferentes. Hasta en las comidas, por ejemplo,[14] podemos escoger entre el cocido madrileño,[15] el gazpacho andaluz,[16] la paella valenciana[17] . . .

Después de varios cambios[18] políticos en el siglo veinte, España es una monarquía otra vez.[19] El nuevo monarca, don Juan Carlos, promete iniciar[20] reformas importantes en el gobierno[21] del país. Los problemas políticos, económicos y sociales que España tiene que resolver son graves; pero parece que con el nuevo gobierno la nación puede esperar años de paz[22] y de progreso.

Preguntas

1. ¿Qué vamos a estudiar hoy?   2. ¿Qué forman España y Portugal?   3. ¿Dónde está la Península Ibérica?   4. ¿En qué parte de la Península están los Pirineos?   5. ¿Dónde hay cordilleras paralelas?

6. ¿Cuántas regiones naturales hay en España?   7. ¿Qué producen estas divisiones geográficas?   8. ¿Qué dos regiones son muy ricas y muy progresivas?   9. ¿A qué aspiran los habitantes de estas regiones?   10. ¿Qué ciudades son los centros industriales más importantes de estas regiones?   11. ¿Cuál es el puerto principal de España?

12. ¿Qué es el interior de la Península?   13. ¿Qué dos regiones ocupan la parte central de la meseta?   14. ¿Por qué es dura la vida de los labradores en estas regiones?   15. ¿Cuál es la capital de España?   16. ¿Dónde está Madrid?   17. ¿Cuántos habitantes tiene Madrid?

18. ¿En qué parte de la Península está Andalucía?   19. ¿Qué conservan sus ciudades?   20. ¿En qué aspectos de la vida andaluza es evidente la influencia árabe?

21. Más bien que "rey de España", ¿qué es el monarca español?   22. ¿Qué comidas españolas conoce Ud.?   23. Después de varios cambios políticos, ¿qué es España otra vez?   24. ¿Qué promete iniciar el nuevo monarca?

Estudio de palabras (*Word study*)

The ability to recognize cognates is of enormous value in learning to read a foreign language. In this section and in the "Estudio de palabras" section of subsequent Lecturas a number of principles for recognizing cognates will be introduced. Make every effort to figure out the meaning of new words by their use in the sentence, but if you are unable to do so, you will find them listed in the end vocabulary. A number of words not easily recognized are translated in footnotes. Many of the new words in the reading selections will

---

[12]**más bien que**, *rather than.*   [13]**costumbres**, *customs.*   [14]**por ejemplo**, *for example.*   [15]**cocido madrileño**, *Spanish stew, Madrid type.*   [16]**gazpacho andaluz**, *cold vegetable soup, Andalusian type.*   [17]**paella valenciana**, *Valencian paella* (a rice dish containing meat, vegetables, and shellfish).   [18]**cambios**, *changes.*   [19]**otra vez**, *again.*   [20]**promete iniciar**, *promises to initiate.*   [21]**gobierno**, *government.*   [22]**paz**, *peace.*

appear later in the active vocabularies. All examples listed below appear in the reading selection of Lectura I.

a. Exact cognates. Many Spanish and English words are identical in form and meaning, although the pronunciation is different. Pronounce these words in Spanish: capital, central, cordillera (*cordillera, mountain range*), general, grave, industrial, interior, natural, notable, occidental (*occidental, western*), Portugal, principal, social.

b. Approximate cognates. Three principles for recognizing near cognates are:

1. Many Spanish words have a written accent: división, península, región.
2. Many Spanish words lack a double consonant: comercial.
3. Many Spanish words have a final **-a, -e,** or **-o** (and sometimes a written accent) which is lacking in English: mapa, música, problema, reforma; arte, contraste, evidente, importante, parte; árido, aspecto, moderno, resto.

Pronounce the words listed in *b* and give the English cognates.

c. Less approximate cognates. Many words should be recognized easily, especially in context or when pronounced in Spanish. Pronounce the following words and then observe the English meaning: afectar, *to affect;* agricultura, *agriculture;* árabe, *Arabic;* aspirar, *to aspire;* autonomía, *autonomy;* carácter, *character;* centro, *center;* costa, *coast;* diferencia, *difference;* diferente, *different;* dividir, *to divide;* económico, *economic;* Europa, *Europe;* formar, *to form;* Francia, *France;* frontera, *frontier;* geográfico, *geographical;* habitante, *inhabitant;* industria, *industry;* industrioso, *industrious;* influencia, *influence;* Mediterráneo, *Mediterranean;* millón, *million;* monarca, *monarch;* monarquía, *monarchy;* montaña, *mountain;* nación, *nation;* norte, *north;* ocupar, *to occupy;* paralelo, *parallel;* Pirineos, *Pyrenees;* político, *political;* producir, *to produce;* progresivo, *progressive;* progreso, *progress;* provincia, *province;* puerto, *port;* resolver, *to resolve;* suroeste, *southwest;* tradición, *tradition.*

Castillo de San Servando, cerca del Puente de Alcántara, Toledo, España.

Arriba, a la izquierda, escena típica de las montañas de Asturias, una extensión de los Pirineos. La región de Asturias se encuentra al noroeste de la Península y sus costas dan al golfo de Vizcaya en el océano Atlántico.

A la derecha, la ciudad de Barcelona, el puerto más importante de España en el Mar Mediterráneo. En la foto vemos la Iglesia de la Sagrada Familia construida por el famoso arquitecto Gaudí.

A la izquierda tenemos los astilleros de Bilbao, también un puerto muy importante. Se encuentra en el país vasco, del lado del Atlántico.

A la derecha se ve el puente romano de Córdoba, que todavía se usa. Debajo podemos ver tres ejemplos de arquitectura que muestran muchas características de la vida y de la cultura española. Primero, el monasterio de El Escorial, cerca de Madrid, construido por el rey Felipe II en el siglo XVI, en el estilo renacimiento. El monasterio, que es también un palacio real, conmemora la victoria del ejército español contra los franceses en la batalla de San Quintín (1557).

Más abajo vemos la Torre de las Damas en la Alhambra de Granada y, a la derecha, La Giralda en Sevilla. Ambos monumentos son ejemplos del adelanto cultural y de la influencia de los moros en la Península Ibérica.

Present indicative of *dar* and *decir* • Indirect object
pronouns • Reflexive substitute for the passive • Use of
gustar • Adjectives used as nouns • Comparison of adjectives • Use
of the present tense for the future • Cardinal numerals

LECCIÓN 7

De compras en el centro

Carmen llama por teléfono a Julia y la invita a ir de compras.

CARMEN —¡Hola, Julia! Te habla Carmen. ¿Estás muy ocupada hoy?

JULIA —No, Carmen. Tengo que ir al mercado un momento, pero después
estoy libre.

CARMEN —Es que estoy cansada de estudiar y quiero ir al centro un rato. ¿Por
qué no me acompañas? Sé que te gusta ir de compras.

JULIA —Pues, ¡encantada! Con mucho gusto te acompaño. Pero oye, no
puedo salir antes de las diez. ¿A qué hora se abren las tiendas?

CARMEN —Creo que se abren generalmente a las nueve y media. Si salimos a
las diez y cuarto, tenemos bastante tiempo.

JULIA —Pues, yo te llamo después de venir del mercado. Podemos tomar el
autobús que pasa por tu calle.

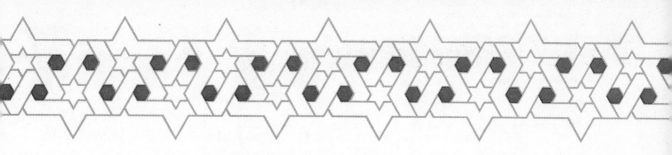

CARMEN —Bien. Te veo más tarde, Julia.

JULIA —Hasta la vista, Carmen.

◆　◆　◆　◆

Media hora más tarde las dos amigas toman el autobús y llegan al centro. Entran en una tienda muy cara y le dicen a la vendedora que quieren ver los vestidos que tienen a precio especial.

JULIA —¡Ay, Carmen! ¡Qué bonito es este vestido rojo! ¿No te gusta? (*Le enseña el vestido a su amiga.*)

CARMEN —Sí, me gusta mucho. Es más bonito que este azul que tengo aquí, ¿verdad?

JULIA —Creo que es el más bonito de todos. Señorita, ¿qué precio tiene este vestido rojo?

VENDEDORA —Esta semana lo damos a treinta y nueve dólares y noventa y cinco centavos.

CARMEN —¡Casi cuarenta dólares! ¡Qué barbaridad! ¿No te parece demasiado caro, Julia?

JULIA —No es barato, pero bueno . . . , este vestido es de algodón y ahora se usa mucho este estilo.

CARMEN —Sí, es verdad. Señorita, ¿de qué talla es? Me parece un poco grande.

VENDEDORA —Es talla diez. Aquel blanco que se ve en el escaparate es talla ocho, creo. ¿Lo quiere?

CARMEN —Sí, por favor. Me parece un vestido muy fino. Lo tomo. Aquí tiene el dinero.

VENDEDORA —Muchas gracias, señorita. ¿Les enseño algo más? Tenemos varias cosas a precio especial. ¿Un par de guantes, zapatos . . . ?

CARMEN —Hoy no, gracias. Tú, Julia, ¿no dices que necesitas comprar una cartera azul?

JULIA —Sí, y también quiero ver otras cosas. Pero, oye, ¿por qué no tomamos el almuerzo aquí?

CARMEN —Muy bien . . . ¡Veo que vamos a estar en el centro todo el día!

Conversación

A. Preguntas sobre el diálogo

1. ¿Quién llama por teléfono a Julia? 2. ¿Está Julia muy ocupada? ¿Adónde tiene que ir? 3. ¿A qué hora se abren las tiendas generalmente? 4. ¿Qué toman las dos amigas para ir al centro? 5. ¿Qué les enseña la vendedora a Carmen y a Julia? 6. ¿Les gusta el vestido rojo? 7. ¿Qué le parece este vestido a Julia? 8. ¿Cuál de los vestidos compra Carmen? 9. ¿Qué necesita comprar Julia? 10. ¿Dónde van a tomar el almuerzo las dos amigas?

B. Aplicación del diálogo

1. ¿Le gusta a Ud. ir de compras? 2. ¿Va Ud. al centro todas las semanas? 3. ¿Tiene Ud. que ir al centro hoy? 4. ¿Está el centro cerca de nuestra universidad? 5. ¿Toma Ud. un autobús para ir al centro? 6. ¿Le gustan a Ud. las tiendas del centro? 7. ¿A qué hora se abren las tiendas en esta ciudad? 8. ¿Qué le parecen a Ud. las tiendas de nuestra ciudad? ¿Le parecen buenas? ¿. . . caras? ¿. . . bonitas? ¿. . . grandes? 9. ¿Le gusta a Ud. comprar cosas caras o cosas baratas? 10. ¿Hay mercados cerca de aquí?

NOTAS GRAMATICALES

A. Irregular present indicative of **dar** and **decir**

dar, to give		**decir,** to say, tell	
singular	*plural*	*singular*	*plural*
doy	damos	**digo**	decimos
das	dais	**dices**	decís
da	dan	**dice**	**dicen**

B. Indirect object pronouns

singular		*plural*	
me (to) me		**nos** (to) us	
te (to) you (*fam.*)		**os** (to) you (*fam.*)	
le (to) him, her, it, you (*formal*)		**les** (to) them, you	

Carmen le escribe una carta. Carmen is writing him (her) a letter.
Ella les (nos) enseña varias cosas. She shows them (us) several things *or* She shows several things to them (us).

An indirect object tells *to* or *for* whom an action is done. In Spanish the indirect object pronoun includes the meaning *to* (sometimes *for:* e.g., **Carmen me abre la puerta,** *Carmen opens the door for me*). In English the word *to* is omitted if the indirect object precedes a direct object: *He gives me the money,* but *He gives the money to me.*

Be sure to observe that **le** is used for all third person singular indirect object pronouns and **les** for the plural, while **me, te, nos, os** are identical to the direct object pronouns. These forms are placed *immediately before the verb.* (Some exceptions will be given later.) The context of the sentence usually makes the meaning of **le** and **les** clear; however, when these pronouns mean (*to*) *you* (formal), singular and plural, **a usted(es)** is often expressed in Spanish also:

¿Le enseñan a Ud. muchos vestidos? Do they show you many dresses?
Les doy a Uds. los periódicos. I'm giving you the newspapers.

In Spanish the indirect object pronoun is regularly used in addition to the indirect object noun:

Carmen le da el dinero a la vendedora. Carmen gives the money to the clerk.
Yo le digo a Carlos la verdad. I'm telling Charles the truth.

◆ *Práctica.* Read in Spanish and indicate whether each pronoun in italics is a direct or an indirect object:

1. Carmen *la* llama por teléfono.
2. Julia *me* ve en la calle.
3. Yo *les* enseño mis compras.
4. *Le* gustan los vestidos y *los* compra.
5. Ella *nos* dice el precio.

6. Ella *me* escribe cartas y *las* recibo.
7. Él *le* abre la puerta y *lo* invita a entrar.
8. Ellas *nos* llaman a menudo.
9. Yo *te* espero en el centro.
10. *Te* dan el dinero. ¿*Lo* necesitas?

C. Reflexive substitute for the passive

Se abren las tiendas a las nueve. The stores are opened at nine o'clock.
Se ven varios vestidos en el escaparate. Several dresses are seen in the show window.
Se usa mucho este estilo. This style is worn a great deal.

In the active voice the subject acts upon an object: *The man opens the doors,* **El hombre abre las puertas.** In the passive voice the subject is acted upon by the verb: *The doors are opened,* **Se abren las puertas.**

In Spanish the passive is often expressed by using the reflexive object **se** before the third person of the verb, which is singular or plural, depending on the number of the subject. The subject often follows the verb in this construction. (See Lesson 8 for the explanation of reflexive verbs.)

D. Use of **gustar,** *to be pleasing, like*

	literal meaning	*usual English expression*
Me gusta la cartera.	The purse is pleasing to me.	I like the purse.
¿No te gusta?	Isn't it pleasing to you?	Don't you like it?
Nos gusta leer.	To read is pleasing to us.	We like to read.
Les gusta este vestido.	This dress is pleasing to them.	They like this dress.
Me gustan estos zapatos.	These shoes are pleasing to us.	We like these shoes.

Spanish has no verb meaning *to like* and uses, instead, the verb **gustar** meaning *to be pleasing.* An English sentence using the verb *to like* should be changed into one using *to be pleasing (to)* before it can be turned into Spanish. Instead of *I like the store,* say *The store is pleasing to me* **(Me gusta la tienda);** or instead of *I don't like those stores,* say *Those stores are not pleasing to me* **(No me gustan aquellas tiendas).**

Only two forms of the verb **gustar** are regularly used in the present tense: **gusta** if one thing or an action is pleasing, **gustan** if more than one. Only indirect object pronouns are used with this verb. English *it* and *them* are not expressed (second example), and the subject usually follows the form of **gustar.**

A Julia le gusta el vestido.   Julia likes the dress.
Le gustan a Julia los vestidos.   Julia likes the dresses.

When a noun is the indirect object of **gustar,** the indirect object pronoun (**le** in the last two examples) is also used. For greater emphasis, the noun indirect object may precede the verb.

Another Spanish verb which is used with an indirect object is **parecer,** *to seem, appear,* which indicates or asks about what a person thinks of something:

Me parece grande.   It seems large to me (I think it's large).
¿No te parece caro?   Doesn't it seem expensive to you (Don't you think it is expensive)?
Nos parecen bonitos.   They seem pretty to us (We think they are pretty).
¿Qué le parece a Ud. esta casa?   What do you think of this house? How do you like this house (How does this house seem to you)?

◆ *Práctica.*   Read several times in Spanish, noting the meaning:

1. Me gusta este vestido.   Me parece fino.
2. Me gustan estos vestidos.   Me parecen finos.
3. Nos gusta esta ciudad.   Nos parece hermosa.
4. Le gustan las tiendas.   Le parecen bonitas.
5. ¿Te gusta este estilo?   ¿Te parece bueno?
6. Les gusta esta cartera.   Les parece cara.

E. Adjectives used as nouns

> **Me gusta este rojo.**   I like this red one.
> **El blanco es muy bonito.**   The white one is very pretty.
> **No me gustan esos grandes.**   I don't like those large ones.
> **La joven (La señorita) compra un libro.**   The young woman buys a book.

Just as adjectives of nationality are used as nouns (page 26), so are many other adjectives, especially when used with the definite article or the demonstrative adjective. In such cases, the adjective agrees in gender and number with the noun understood. The word *one(s)* is often included in the English meaning.

F. Comparison of adjectives

> 1. **bonito**   pretty   **(el) más bonito**   (the) prettier, prettiest
>   **caro**   expensive   **(el) menos caro**   (the) less expensive, least
>   expensive

When we compare adjectives in English, we say *pretty, prettier, prettiest; expensive, more (less) expensive, most (least) expensive.* In Spanish we use **más** to mean *more, most,* and **menos** for *less, least.* The definite article is used when *the* is a part of the meaning, and the adjective must agree with the noun in gender and number: **el más bonito, la más bonita, los más bonitos, las más bonitas.** Sometimes the possessive adjective (**mi, tu,** etc.) replaces the definite article. Other examples are:

> **Este vestido es más bonito.**   This dress is prettier.
> **El blanco es el más bonito de todos.**   The white one is the prettiest of all.
> **Es el mercado más grande.**   It is the larger (largest) market.
> **Es mi cartera más nueva.**   It is my newer (newest) purse.
> **Este libro es el menos interesante.**   This book is the less (least) interesting.

You can tell from the context when an adjective has comparative or superlative force, that is, whether **más** means *more* or *most* and whether **menos** means *less* or *least.* Note the word order in the last two examples.

Adverbs are also compared by the use of **más** or **menos:** **Media hora más tarde Julia llama a Carmen.** *A half hour later Julia calls Carmen.*

> 2. **Este rojo es más bonito que el blanco.**   This red one is prettier than the white one.
>   **Ana tiene menos de diez dólares.**   Ann has less than ten dollars.

Than is translated by **que** before a noun or pronoun, but before a numeral it is translated by **de.**

> 3. **Es la ciudad más grande del país.**   It is the largest city in the country.

After a superlative, *in* is translated by **de.**

G. Use of the present tense for the future

Después estoy libre.   Later I'll be free.
Con mucho gusto te acompaño.   I'll gladly go with you.
Yo te llamo después de venir del mercado.   I'll call you after coming from the market.
Te veo más tarde.   I'll see you later.
¿Les enseño algo más?   Shall I show you anything else?

The present tense in Spanish is often used for the English future to give the action a more vivid or immediate character.

Ir a plus an infinitive also may refer to future actions or conditions: **Vamos a tener bastante tiempo,** *We are going to have enough time.*

H. Cardinal numerals

30 **treinta**	50 **cincuenta**	70 **setenta**	90 **noventa**
40 **cuarenta**	60 **sesenta**	80 **ochenta**	

Remember that beginning with 31 numerals are written as separate words, that numerals ending in **uno** drop **-o** before masculine nouns, and that **una** is used with feminine nouns: **treinta y un dólares,** *31 dollars;* **cincuenta y una carteras,** *51 purses.* (See pages 35–36.)

EJERCICIOS

A. Substitution drill:

1. *Carmen* le da el dinero.
   (*Yo, La vendedora, Nosotros, Uds., Tú*)
2. *El profesor* les abre la puerta.
   (*Ud., Yo, La señora, Nosotros, Julia y Ana*)
3. *Carlos* les dice la verdad.
   (*Tú, El señor Ortega, Uds., José y Luis, Ud.*)
4. *Diana* le enseña los zapatos.
   (*Mi tía, Uds., Yo, Mis hermanos, Tú*)

B. Read in Spanish, supplying the correct form of **gustar:**

1. Me _____ esta cartera pequeña; no me _____ aquellas dos carteras grandes.
2. —José, ¿te _____ las estudiantes de esta clase? —Solamente me _____ las bonitas.
3. —¿Les _____ a Uds. ir de compras a menudo? —No, no nos _____ ir de compras a menudo. 4. Me _____ estudiar después de cenar, pero a mi amigo Luis le _____ mirar la televisión. 5. A Julia y a María no les _____ esta cartera, pero a su mamá le _____ mucho.

C. Say each sentence as you hear it; then repeat, omitting the noun in your new sentence:

MODEL: Me gusta la casa grande.   *Me gusta la casa grande.*
                                    Me gusta la grande.

1. Le enseña el mercado pequeño. 2. No les da los guantes caros. 3. Le compra la cartera azul. 4. Me gustan estas sillas cómodas. 5. Este vestido blanco es fino. 6. El reloj nuevo es de Luis. 7. No les gustan los autobuses más viejos. 8. ¿Qué te parecen aquellos cuadros grandes? 9. Me parece bonita esta calle larga. 10. ¿Quién vive en la casa amarilla?

D. Say each sentence after your teacher; then make each one plural:

MODEL: Se abre la tienda tarde.   *Se abre la tienda tarde.*
                                    Se abren las tiendas tarde.

1. Allí se ve la casa nueva.   5. Aquí se compra el libro.
2. Se necesita esta cosa.   6. Se recibe la carta de México.
3. Se escribe la palabra difícil.   7. Se usa este estilo ahora.
4. Se aprende bien la lección.   8. Se termina la clase hoy.

E. Read each sentence in Spanish; then repeat, changing to the reflexive:

MODEL: Aquí hablan español.   *Aquí se habla español.*

1. Hablan inglés en este país. 2. Allí compran libros viejos. 3. Abren la biblioteca a las ocho. 4. Ven muchos autobuses en la calle. 5. Preparan programas interesantes. 6. Aprenden cosas nuevas. 7. Leen revistas y periódicos. 8. No necesitan mucho dinero. 9. Ven otro vestido en el escaparate. 10. Escriben las frases en español.

F. Repeat the question after your teacher; then answer the question affirmatively, following the model:

MODEL: ¿Le parece pequeña la casa?   *¿Le parece pequeña la casa?*
                                       Sí, me parece más pequeña que la otra.

1. ¿Le parece interesante el libro?   4. ¿Le parecen baratos los vestidos?
2. ¿Le parece fácil la lección?   5. ¿Le parecen finos los relojes?
3. ¿Le parece bonito el cuadro?   6. ¿Le parecen caros los zapatos?

G. Repeat the question after your teacher; then answer the question affirmatively, following the model:

MODEL: ¿Es nuevo ese mercado?   *¿Es nuevo ese mercado?*
                                  Sí, es el más nuevo de todos.

1. ¿Es hermosa aquella ciudad?   4. ¿Son cómodas estas sillas?
2. ¿Es bonita aquella tienda?   5. ¿Son nuevas estas mesas?
3. ¿Es grande aquel mercado?   6. ¿Son largas estas cartas?

H. Give the Spanish equivalent:

1. Carmen calls her friend Julia and tells her that she wants to go shopping. 2. Julia is not very busy and she accompanies her. 3. The stores open (are opened) early in the morning in this large city. 4. There is a bus which passes along Carmen's street; the two friends take it (in order) to go downtown. 5. A half hour later they arrive at a very expensive store. 6. Upon entering that store, Carmen tells a saleslady that she is looking for a dress. 7. The saleslady shows them several dresses which they have on sale that week. 8. Julia tells Carmen that she likes the red one and that it doesn't seem expensive to her. She likes the style. 9. Carmen believes that the red dress is prettier than the white one and she buys it. 10. After buying the dress, Julia and Carmen go to take lunch.

EJERCICIOS DE PRONUNCIACIÓN

A. The sounds of **ch, y, ll,** and **ñ**

1. **Ch** is pronounced like English *ch* in *church:*

| charlar | Chile | leche | mucho | noche |

2. **Y** is pronounced like a strong English *y* in *you;* the conjunction **y,** *and,* when initial in a breath-group before a vowel, or when between vowels within a breath-group, has the sound of Spanish **y:**

| ya | yo | desayuno | ¿y⌣usted? | blanco y⌣azul |

3. **Ll** is pronounced like *y* in *yes* in most of Spanish America and in some parts of Spain; in other parts of Spain and Spanish America it is pronounced somewhat like *lli* in *million:*

| allí | amarillo | llamar | llega | silla |

4. **Ñ** is an **n** pronounced with the same tongue position as **ch** and **y;** it sounds somewhat like the English *ny* in *canyon:*

| enseñar | España | mañana | pequeño | señor |

B. Spanish intonation

Review the observations on Spanish intonation, pages 9–10; then rewrite the first three exchanges of the dialogue of this lesson, dividing them into breath-groups and into syllables, and outline the intonation patterns. Read the exchanges, giving close attention to the intonation patterns.

VOCABULARIO

acompañar to accompany, go with
el **algodón** cotton
el **autobús** (*pl.* **autobuses**) bus
¡ay! oh! alas! ah!
barato, -a inexpensive, cheap
bastante *adj.* enough, sufficient
bonito, -a pretty, beautiful
la **calle** street
caro, -a expensive, dear
la **cartera** purse
el **centavo** cent (*U.S.*)
el **centro** center (of town), downtown
la **compra** purchase
comprar to buy, purchase
la **cosa** thing
dar to give *irregular verb*
decir to say, tell
después *adv.* afterwards, later
el **dinero** money
el **dólar** dollar (*U.S.*) *dolares*
encantado, -a delighted (to)
enseñar (a + *inf.*) to show, teach (how to)

el **escaparate** show window
especial special
el **estilo** style
el **favor** favor
fino, -a fine, nice, perfect
el **guante** glove
gustar to be pleasing, like
Julia Julia
libre free
el **mercado** market
otro, -a other, another; *pl.* other(s)
el **par** pair
parecer to seem, appear
el **precio** price
que than
la **talla** size (*of a dress*)
el **teléfono** telephone
la **tienda** shop, store
usar to use, wear
la **vendedora** saleslady, clerk (*f.*)
el **vestido** dress
la **vista** sight, view
el **zapato** shoe

a precio especial on sale, at a special price
algo más anything (something) else
en el centro downtown
es que the fact is (that)
hasta la vista until (I) see you, so long
hoy no not today
ir (llegar) al centro to go (arrive) downtown
(ir) de compras (to go) shopping
lo damos a we are offering (selling) it for
llamar por teléfono to telephone (call), call by telephone
más tarde later
media hora a half hour, half an hour
muchas gracias many thanks, thanks a lot
por favor please (*usually at end of statement or used alone*)
¡qué barbaridad! how terrible! what nonsense!
¿qué le (te) parece . . . ? what do you think of . . . ? how do you like . . . ?
¿qué precio tiene? what is the price of (it)?
te habla (Carmen) (Carmen) is talking to you, this is (Carmen) talking (speaking)
todo el día all day, the whole (entire) day

La Academia de la Lengua en Bogotá, Colombia, es una de las más importantes academias de la lengua en Latinoamérica. Hay academias de la lengua en cada uno de los países de habla española, incluyendo Puerto Rico y las Islas Filipinas.

Lectura 2

EL INGENIOSO
HIDALGO DON QVI-
XOTE DE LA MANCHA.

Compuesto por Miguel de Ceruantes
Saauedra.

DIRIGIDO AL DVQVE DE BEIAR,
Marques de Gibraleon, Conde de Barcelona, y Baña-
res, Vizconde de la Puebla de Alcozer, Señor de
las villas de Capilla, Curiel, y
Burgillos.

Año, 1605.

Con priuilegio de Castilla, Aragon, y Portugal.
EN MADRID, Por Iuan de la Cuesta.

Vendese en casa de Francisco de Robles, librero del Rey nro señor.

La lengua española

El español es una de las lenguas verdaderamente universales. Fuera de[1] España y sus
posesiones en África, se habla en extensas
zonas de los Estados Unidos, en México y la
América Central, en toda Suramérica menos[2]
en el Brasil y las antiguas[3] Guayanas, y en
Cuba, la República Dominicana y Puerto
Rico. Hay, además, una minoría hispanohablante[4] en las Islas Filipinas y en otras islas
del Océano Pacífico. Es la lengua oficial de
unos doscientos[5] millones de personas y más
de ciento cincuenta millones la tienen por
lengua materna.[6]

El español es una lengua romance. El portugués, el francés y el italiano también son
lenguas romances. Todas las lenguas romances
vienen del latín.

Como se habla español en tantas regiones,
la lengua no es exactamente uniforme en
todas partes.[7] Las lenguas son organismos
vivos y cambian según[8] el carácter y las
necesidades de las personas que las hablan.
Los cubanos no hablan como los chilenos y
los mexicanos no hablan como los argentinos.
Pero a pesar de[9] estas diferencias la unidad
básica de la lengua española es extraordinaria.

La base del español moderno es el dialecto
castellano. Pero es importante recordar[10] que
los otros dialectos españoles colaboran constantemente en su formación. La contribución
de los países americanos a la lengua común[11]
es especialmente importante. Por estas razones[12] es preferible dar a la lengua común el
nombre de «lengua española» en lugar del
de[13] «castellano», con que la designan en algunas partes.

Aunque el español es la lengua oficial de
España, no es la única lengua hablada[14] en el
país. Además del[15] castellano, otras lenguas
importantes son el gallego,[16] una forma del
portugués, que se habla en Galicia, y el
catalán, que se habla en Cataluña, Valencia y
las Islas Baleares.[17] El catalán tiene rasgos[18]
similares a la lengua provenzal del sur de

---

[1]**Fuera de,** *Outside of.* [2]**menos,** *except.* [3]**antiguas,** *former.* When it precedes the noun, the adjective **antiguo, -a,** often
means *former* rather than *ancient* (the sense it usually has, as on page 92, line 6). [4]**hispanohablante,** *Spanish-speaking.*
[5]**unos doscientos,** *some (about) two hundred.* [6]**la tienen por lengua materna,** *consider it as their mother tongue.* [7]**en** (*also*
por) **todas partes,** *everywhere.* [8]**según,** *according to.* [9]**a pesar de,** *in spite of.* [10]**recordar,** *to remember.* [11]**común,**
common. [12]**Por estas razones,** *For (Because of) these reasons.* [13]**en lugar del de,** *instead of that of.* [14]**la única lengua
hablada,** *the only language spoken.* [15]**Además de,** *Besides, In addition to.* [16]**gallego,** *Galician.* [17]**Islas Baleares,** *Balearic
Islands* (a group of islands in the Mediterranean Sea). [18]**rasgos,** *features, characteristics.*

Francia. Por último,[19] no debemos olvidar[20] que en las Provincias Vascongadas se habla todavía el vascuence,[21] una lengua no romance.[22] El origen del vascuence es desconocido.[23] Algunos creen que el vascuence representa la lengua de los antiguos iberos.

Aun sin incluir a Puerto Rico, la minoría hispanohablante de los Estados Unidos tiene mucha importancia. Millones de personas que hablan español viven en el suroeste, en Nueva York y sus alrededores[24] y en la Florida. El español del suroeste es una continuación del español de México. En el español de Nueva York la influencia de los puertorriqueños es evidente. En la Florida el español es predominantemente de tipo cubano.

Como vemos, aunque España es un país pequeño, su lengua es muy importante hoy día.[25] Hay que[26] saber comunicar con los hispanohablantes en nuestro país. Y, además, las relaciones comerciales, políticas y culturales entre los Estados Unidos y los países de habla española[27] tienen mucha importancia. La influencia de España y de los países hispanoamericanos en la vida diaria, la música, el arte, la arquitectura y en otros aspectos de la cultura en general es grande. Estudiamos el español para conocer y apreciar bien la cultura española e[28] hispanoamericana y su influencia en la vida moderna.

Preguntas

1. ¿En qué países de Suramérica hablan español? 2. ¿Qué lengua hablan en Cuba y en Puerto Rico? 3. ¿Cuántos millones de personas tienen el español por lengua materna? 4. ¿De qué lengua vienen las lenguas romances? 5. Fuera del español, ¿qué otras lenguas son lenguas romances?

6. ¿Es el español exactamente uniforme en todas partes? 7. ¿Hablan los cubanos como los chilenos? 8. A pesar de las diferencias, ¿qué puede decirse de la lengua española? 9. ¿Qué dialecto es la base del español moderno? 10. ¿Qué es importante recordar? 11. ¿Qué nombre es preferible darle a la lengua común?

12. ¿Es el español la única lengua hablada en España? 13. ¿Qué es el gallego y dónde se habla? 14. ¿Qué lengua tiene rasgos similares a la lengua provenzal del sur de Francia? 15. ¿Dónde se habla catalán? 16. ¿Dónde se habla vascuence? 17. ¿Es el vascuence una lengua romance? 18. ¿Qué creen algunos sobre el origen del vascuence?

19. ¿Tiene importancia la minoría hispanohablante en nuestro país? 20. ¿En qué regiones de los Estados Unidos hay millones de personas que hablan español? 21. ¿De qué es una continuación el español del suroeste? 22. ¿Qué influencia es evidente en el español de Nueva York? 23. ¿De qué tipo es el español de la Florida? 24. ¿Tienen mucha importancia las relaciones comerciales, políticas y culturales entre los Estados Unidos y los países de habla española? 25. ¿Para qué estudiamos el español?

---

[19]**Por último,** *Finally.* [20]**no debemos olvidar,** *we must not forget.* [2]**vascuence,** *Basque.* [22]**no romance,** *non-Romance.* [23]**desconocido,** *unknown.* [24]**sus alrededores,** *its environs.* [25]**hoy día,** *nowadays.* [26]**Hay que,** *One must.* [27]**de habla española,** *Spanish-speaking.* [28]Before words beginning with **i-, hi-,** Spanish uses **e,** *and,* for **y.**

Estudio de palabras

a. Exact cognates. Pronounce these words in Spanish: cultural, romance (*Romance,* designating a language or dialect developed from Latin), universal.

b. Approximate cognates. Additional principles for recognizing approximate cognates will aid you in understanding the reading selections. (Some of the examples listed below are taken from the reading selection of Lectura 1.)

1. Certain Spanish nouns ending in **-cia** end in *-ce* in English: diferencia, Francia, importancia, influencia, provincia.
2. Certain Spanish nouns ending in **-dad** end in *-ty* in English: necesidad, unidad.

c. In Spanish, adverbs of manner are often formed by adding **-mente** (the equivalent of English *-ly*) to the feminine singular of adjectives: exactamente, *exactly;* verdaderamente, *truly, really. What are the meanings of* constantemente, especialmente, predominantemente, tradicionalmente?

d. Many Spanish words can be recognized by comparing them with related words. *Compare:* Andalucía, *Andalusia, and* andaluz, *Andalusian;* cambiar, *to change, and* cambio, *change;* Castilla, *Castile, and* castellano, *Castilian;* cultura, *culture, and* cultural, *cultural;* día, *day, and* diario, *daily* (and also *diary*); forma, *form,* formación, *formation, and* formar, *to form;* habla, *speech, and* hablar, *to speak;* ibérico (*adj.*), *Iberian, and* ibero (*n.*), *Iberian;* importante, *important, and* importancia, *importance;* Madrid, *Madrid, and* madrileño, *Madrilenian, of Madrid;* tipo, *type, and* típico, *typical;* Valencia, *Valencia, and* valenciano, *Valencian;* vivir, *to live, and* vivo, *living.*

Present indicative of *hacer* and *poner* • Present indicative of stem-changing verbs, Class I • Reflexive pronouns • Present indicative of the reflexive verb *lavarse* • Position of pronouns used as objects of an infinitive • The definite article for the possessive • Omission of the personal *a*

LECCIÓN 8

Ricardo busca un compañero de viaje

Ricardo se prepara para bajar al comedor. Se lava las manos y la cara. Entra Pepe.

PEPE   —¿Qué te pasa, Ricardo? ¿Por qué estás tan serio?
RICARDO —Es que deseo ir a casa el mes que viene y no tengo bastante dinero. Hoy día cuesta tanto viajar en avión . . .
PEPE   —Oye, Ricardo, tengo una idea. ¿Por qué no pones un anuncio en el periódico de la universidad? Siempre hay estudiantes que viajan en coche durante las vacaciones.
RICARDO —¡Hombre! ¡Me parece una idea estupenda! ¿Podemos escribirlo ahora?
PEPE   —Con mucho gusto. Voy a buscar el periódico de hoy. Ahora vuelvo.

◆ ◆ ◆ ◆ ◆

Pepe vuelve con el periódico y se pone las gafas. Los dos jóvenes se sientan y piensan un poco antes de escribir.

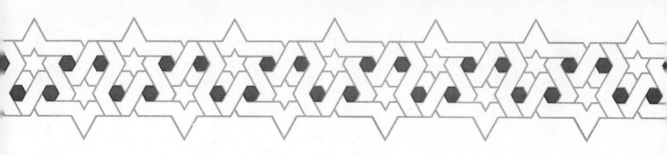

RICARDO   —Pepe, ¿qué dicen los anuncios generalmente?

PEPE   —A ver, Ricardo, ¿qué te parece si decimos: «Se necesita un compañero[1] para hacer un viaje en coche hasta Nueva York. Me llamo Ricardo López; mi teléfono es el 472-5136»?[2]

RICARDO   (*Lee el anuncio y se levanta.*)—Me gusta mucho y no lo encuentro[3] largo . . . Oye, Pepe, muchas gracias, ¿eh?[4]

PEPE   —No hay de qué, hombre. Ya sabes que me gusta hacerles favores a mis amigos.

◆ ◆ ◆ ◆ ◆

Al día siguiente el anuncio sale en el periódico. Ricardo está esperando en su cuarto . . . Suena el teléfono.

FELIPE   —Deseo hablar con Ricardo López. ¿Quiere Ud. decirme si está él allí?

RICARDO   —Sí, habla Ricardo.

FELIPE   —¡Ah! Me llamo Felipe Ortega. Veo que buscas[5] un compañero para hacer el viaje en coche hasta Nueva York.

RICARDO   —Es que no puedo hacer el viaje en avión. ¿Piensas ir en tu coche?

FELIPE   —Espero que sí, pero necesito encontrar un compañero. Como sabes, Ricardo, es un viaje muy largo. ¿Te gusta levantarte temprano?

RICARDO   —Siempre me acuesto y me levanto temprano.

FELIPE   —¡Qué bien! Pues, podemos salir temprano y viajar todo el día. Oye, quiero conocerte pronto.

RICARDO   —¡Sí, claro! Felipe, yo me desayuno a las siete más o menos . . .

PEPE   —¡Estupendo! Mañana te busco en tu cuarto. Nos desayunamos juntos y podemos charlar más.

---

[1] **Se necesita un compañero,** *Needed* (*Wanted*), *a companion.* In advertisements, signs, general announcements, etc., the reflexive substitute for the passive (see page 83) is used in Spanish, and the meaning is usually expressed in English by the past participle, with the verb *to be* understood.

[2] **el** = **el número,** *number.* Read: **cuatro siete dos—cinco uno tres seis** (*or* **cincuenta y uno, treinta y seis**).

[3] Today the verbs **hallar** and **encontrar** are used interchangeably when their meaning corresponds to English *to find.*

[4] In conversation **¿eh?** is often used similarly to **¿(no es) verdad?**

[5] Note the change to the familiar form of address when Ricardo realizes that a young man probably his own age answers the phone. This is customary, even though the young men may not have met.

Conversación

A. Preguntas sobre el diálogo

1. ¿Cómo se prepara Ricardo para bajar al comedor? 2. ¿Quién entra? 3. ¿Qué desea hacer Ricardo durante las vacaciones? 4. ¿Qué idea tiene Pepe? 5. ¿Qué hace[1] Pepe antes de escribir el anuncio? 6. ¿Qué dicen los anuncios generalmente? 7. ¿Cómo se llama el joven que llama a Ricardo? ¿Qué busca ese joven? 8. Al día siguiente ¿a qué hora se desayunan los dos jóvenes?

B. Aplicación del diálogo

1. ¿Cómo se llama Ud.? 2. ¿Le gusta a Ud. viajar? 3. ¿Hace Ud. viajes largos en coche? 4. ¿Hace Ud. viajes con su familia? 5. ¿Viaja Ud. mucho en avión? 6. ¿Cuesta mucho viajar en avión? 7. ¿Qué piensa Ud. hacer durante las vacaciones? 8. ¿Se pone Ud. gafas para leer? ¿Las usa Ud. siempre? 9. ¿A qué hora se acuesta Ud.? 10. ¿Se levanta Ud. tarde o temprano? 11. ¿A qué hora se desayuna Ud.? 12. ¿A qué hora toma Ud. el almuerzo? 13. ¿Cena usted antes de las seis? 14. Después de cenar, ¿se sienta Ud. a estudiar? ¿ . . . a leer? ¿ . . . a escribir cartas? ¿ . . . a pensar?

NOTAS GRAMATICALES

A. Irregular present indicative of **hacer** and **poner**

hacer, to do, make		**poner,** to put, place	
singular	*plural*	*singular*	*plural*
hago	hacemos	**pongo**	ponemos
haces	hacéis	pones	ponéis
hace	hacen	pone	ponen

B. Present indicative of stem-changing verbs, Class I

pensar, to think		**volver,** to return	
singular	*plural*	*singular*	*plural*
pienso	pensamos	**vuelvo**	volvemos
piensas	pensáis	**vuelves**	volvéis
piensa	**piensan**	**vuelve**	**vuelven**

---

[1] Note that **hacer** corresponds to the English *to do* as well as *to make:* **¿Qué hace Pepe?** *What does Joe do? What is Joe doing?*

Certain verbs have regular endings, but the stem vowel **e** becomes **ie** and **o** becomes **ue** when stressed, that is, in the three singular forms and in the third person plural. All stem-changing verbs of Class I end in **-ar** and **-er**. Verbs of this type are indicated thus: **pensar (ie), volver (ue)**.

C. Reflexive pronouns

singular		*plural*	
me	(to) myself	**nos**	(to) ourselves
te	(to) yourself (*fam.*)	**os**	(to) yourselves (*fam.*)
se	(to) himself, herself, yourself (*formal*), itself, oneself	**se**	(to) themselves, yourselves

The reflexive pronouns are used as direct and indirect objects. Notice that in the first and second persons singular and plural they are identical to the direct and indirect object pronouns.

D. Present indicative of the reflexive verb **lavarse**

lavarse, to wash (oneself)	
singular	
(yo) **me lavo**	I wash (myself)
(tú) **te lavas**	you (*fam.*) wash (yourself)
(él, ella) **se lava**	he, she washes (himself, herself)
Ud. **se lava**	you (*formal*) wash (yourself)
plural	
(nosotros, -as) **nos lavamos**	we wash (ourselves)
(vosotros, -as) **os laváis**	you (*fam.*) wash (yourselves)
(ellos, -as) **se lavan**	they wash (themselves)
Uds. **se lavan**	you wash (yourselves)

A verb is called reflexive when the subject does something to itself, either directly, **Ricardo se lava**, *Richard washes (himself)*, or indirectly, **Se compra un coche**, *He buys a car for himself, He buys himself a car*. Reflexive pronouns are in the same person as the subject of the verb.

Many intransitive verbs in English (that is, verbs that cannot have a direct object) are expressed in Spanish by using the reflexive pronoun **se** with a transitive verb. Note that all the reflexive verbs in this lesson, except **desayunarse,** are used transitively. The reflexive pronoun **se** attached to an infinitive indicates a reflexive verb: **lavarse**.

For position with respect to the verb, reflexive pronouns follow the same rules as other object pronouns.

The first person singular of reflexive verbs used in this lesson, except for **desayunarse,** is listed here with literal meaning; note, however, the usual meaning:

	literal meaning	*usual meaning*
me acuesto	I put myself to bed	I go to bed
me lavo	I wash myself	I wash
me levanto	I raise myself	I get up
me llamo	I call myself	I am called, my name is
me pongo	I put to (on) myself	I put on
me preparo	I prepare myself	I prepare
me siento	I seat myself	I sit down

Give the meanings of **¿Cómo te llamas? ¿Cómo se llama Ud.? ¿Cómo se llama el joven?** and **Se llama Felipe.**

E. Position of pronouns used as objects of an infinitive

Pepe, deseo hablarte.   Joe, I want (desire) to talk to you.
¿Podemos escribirlo ahora?   Can (May) we write it now?
¿Quiere Ud. decirme si él está allí?   Will you tell me whether he is there?
¿Te gusta levantarte temprano?   Do you like to get up early?
Quiero conocerte pronto.   I want to meet you soon.

Recall that object pronouns are regularly placed immediately before the verb. However, when they are used as *objects of an infinitive,* they are placed *after* the infinitive and *are attached* to it.

Note that **desear,** like **querer,** is followed by an infinitive (first example). Just as English *to desire* is used less than *to wish* or *to want,* so Spanish **desear** is used less than **querer.**

In the second example note that **poder** means *can* or *may:* **¿Podemos escribirlo?** *Can (May) we write it?*

In the third example **¿Quiere Ud.?** is used to express *Will you?* meaning *Are you willing to?* Similarly, one says **¿No quiere Ud.?** *Won't you?* In Lesson 5 the expression **¿No quieren (Uds.) pasar?** *Won't you come in?* was used.

F. The definite article for the possessive

Me lavo las manos.   I wash my hands.
Se lavan la cara.   They wash their faces.
Pepe se pone las gafas.   Joe puts on his glasses.

BUT: **Sus guantes están sobre la mesa.**   His gloves are on the table.

The definite article is often used instead of the possessive adjective with a noun which represents a part of the body or an article of clothing, and sometimes with other articles closely associated with the subject, when this noun is the object of a verb or preposition. Compare the first three examples with the fourth, in which case **sus guantes** is the subject of the verb. Note in the second example that Spanish uses the singular **la cara** to show that each person has one face.

G. Omission of the personal **a**

> **Busca un compañero de viaje.**   He is looking for a traveling companion.
> **Necesito encontrar un compañero.**   I need to find a companion.

The personal **a** is omitted in Spanish when the noun does not refer to a definite person. Compare the explanation on pages 66–67.

EJERCICIOS

A. Repeat after your teacher. When you hear the cue, make a new sentence:

MODEL: Enrique se desayuna.   *Enrique se desayuna.*
         (Yo)   *Yo me desayuno.*

1. Yo me acuesto temprano. (Tú)
2. Mis padres se acuestan tarde. (Ana)
3. Pepe se sienta a la mesa. (Yo)
4. Ud. no se llama Jorge. (Tú)
5. Tú te levantas tarde. (Ellos)
6. Los jóvenes se lavan la cara. (Nosotros)
7. Yo me pongo las gafas. (Ricardo)
8. Tú te pones los guantes. (Uds.)
9. Ud. no se lava las manos. (Luis)
10. Yo voy a sentarme. (Pepe y yo)
11. ¿Quiere Ud. lavarse? (Uds.)
12. Pepe y Ricardo se desayunan en el comedor. (Tú)

B. Answer affirmatively, watching the reflexive pronouns:

MODELS: ¿Se pone Ud. las gafas?   *Sí, me pongo las gafas.*
          ¿Van Uds. a ponerse las gafas?   *Sí, vamos a ponernos las gafas.*

1. ¿Se levanta Ud. temprano?
2. ¿Se lava Ud. las manos?
3. ¿Se sienta Ud. a la mesa?
4. ¿Se desayuna Ud. en el comedor?

5. ¿Va Ud. a levantarse?
6. ¿Va Ud. a lavarse?
7. ¿Va Ud. a sentarse?
8. ¿Va Ud. a desayunarse?

9. ¿Se levantan Uds. tarde?
10. ¿Se lavan Uds. la cara?
11. ¿Se sientan Uds. en la sala?
12. ¿Se acuestan Uds. a las diez?

13. ¿Quieren Uds. acostarse?
14. ¿Quieren Uds. lavarse?
15. ¿Pueden Uds. levantarse?
16. ¿Pueden Uds. sentarse?

C. Read in Spanish, placing the pronoun in its proper position:

1. (me) Yo siento. Voy a sentar. 2. (nos) Carlos y yo lavamos. Queremos lavar.
3. (se) Ana no pone los guantes. No puede poner los guantes. 4. (te) ¿Acuestas tú?
¿Piensas acostar? 5. (se) Ricardo levanta. Después de levantar, baja al comedor.
6. (se) Los hijos lavan las manos. Al lavar las manos, se sientan a la mesa. 7. (se)
Roberto acuesta tarde. Quiere acostar a las once. 8. (te) ¿Sientas tú allí? ¿No quieres
sentar aquí?

D. Repeat after your teacher. When you hear the cue, make a new sentence, following the
models:

MODELS: La abro.   *La abro.*   Nos levantamos.   *Nos levantamos.*
         Voy a   *Voy a abrirla.* Deseamos   *Deseamos levantarnos.*

1. Los veo. (Quiero)	5. Les traigo la revista. (¿No puedo?)
2. Se sientan. (Vienen a)	6. Te lavas las manos. (¿No quieres?)
3. Nos lavamos. (Necesitamos)	7. Nos dicen la verdad. (¿No van a?)
4. Me pongo el vestido. (Puedo)	8. ¿La llamas a menudo? (¿Deseas?)

E. Read in Spanish, using the correct form of the verb in italics:

1. Me *gustar* aquellos aviones.	Me *parecer* grandes.
2. Me *gustar* su idea.	Me *parecer* estupenda.
3. Nos *gustar* estas ciudades.	Nos *parecer* hermosas.
4. Les *gustar* tu coche.	Les *parecer* cómodo.
5. A los jóvenes les *gustar* viajar.	Les *parecer* interesante.
6. ¿Te *gustar* leer en español?	¿Te *parecer* fácil?
7. No nos *gustar* viajar en avión.	Nos *parecer* muy caro.
8. A María no le *gustar* el vestido.	No le *parecer* bonito.

F. Repeat after your teacher. When you hear a new verb, use the correct form in a new
sentence:

1. ¿Quieren Uds. ir al centro hoy? (Necesitar)
2. Los hombres no llegan a casa hasta las cinco. (volver)
3. Felipe piensa hacer el viaje en coche. (desear)
4. ¿Quiénes van a darle a Ricardo el dinero? (poder)
5. ¿A qué hora quieres levantarte? (pensar)
6. Carlos y yo necesitamos hablarle al profesor. (querer)
7. Yo deseo visitar a mi familia el mes que viene. (esperar)
8. Podemos viajar todo el día. (Tener que)

G. Give the Spanish equivalent:

1. Richard wants to visit his parents during (the) vacation. 2. Nowadays it is very
expensive to travel by plane. 3. Richard says that he doesn't have enough money to

make the trip next month.   4. Joe gives his friend an idea. He can put an ad in the university newspaper.   5. When Joe returns with a newspaper, he puts on his glasses and sits down near the table.   6. He does Richard a favor; he writes the ad.   7. Richard likes the ad; he says that it is not too long.   8. Philip also wants to find a traveling companion.   9. The two young men intend to make the trip to New York by car.   10. They go down to the dining room, where they take breakfast and chat more about the trip.

EJERCICIOS DE PRONUNCIACIÓN

A. The sounds of **m** and **n**

1. Spanish **m** is pronounced like English *m*:

mapa	comer	primo	mes

2. When initial in a syllable, when final before a pause, or when before any consonant other than those mentioned below, Spanish **n** is pronounced like English *n*:

grande	cansado	pronto	avión

3. When before **b, v, m,** and **p**, Spanish **n** is pronounced like **m**:

invitar	un par	un poco	un viaje
con papá	están bien	con mamá	un vestido

4. Before **c, qu, g,** and **j**, Spanish **n** is pronounced like English *n* in *sing*:

encontrar	¿con quién?	en casa	tengo
me pongo	lengua	inglés	con José

B. The sounds of **s**

1. Spanish **s** is pronounced somewhat like the English hissed *s* in *sent*:

demasiado	desear	desayuno	José
Luisa	televisión	visitar	mis padres

2. Before **b, d, g, l, ll, m, n, v,** and **y,** however, Spanish **s** is like English *s* in *rose*:

desde	buenas noches	es bueno	las manos
los llama	mis guantes	tres vestidos	varias lenguas

C. The variations of Spanish **s**

Pronounce each individual word after your teacher; then repeat, but as part of a breath-group introduced by the words indicated at the right:

1. grande	bueno	mexicano	viejo	es
2. gafas	mesas	lecciones	vacaciones	las
3. dólares	libros	meses	viajes	muchos

VOCABULARIO

acostarse (ue)   to go to bed, lie down
el **anuncio**   ad(vertisement)
el **avión** (*pl.* **aviones**)   (air)plane
bajar (**a** + *inf.*)   to go down(stairs)
la **cara**   face
el **coche**   car
el **compañero**   companion
costar (ue)   to cost
desayunarse   to take (eat) breakfast
desear   to desire, wish, want
¿eh?   eh? right?
encontrar (ue)   to meet, encounter; to find
estupendo, -a   stupendous, great, wonderful
las **gafas**   spectacles, (eye)glasses
hacer   to do, make
la **idea**   idea, thought
juntos, -as   together
lavar   to wash; *reflex.* to wash (oneself)
levantar   to raise, lift; *reflex.* to get up, rise

llamarse   to be called, be named
la **mano** (*note gender*)   hand
el **mes**   month
Nueva York   New York
pasar   to happen, be the matter (with)
pensar (ie)   to think; + *inf.* to intend
Pepe   Joe
poner   to put, place; *reflex.* to put on (oneself)
pronto   soon, quickly
Ricardo   Richard
sentarse (ie)   to sit down
serio, -a   serious
siguiente   following, next
sonar (ue)   to sound, ring
las **vacaciones**   vacation (*used in pl.*)
viajar   to travel
el **viaje**   trip
volver (ue)   to return, come back

ahora vuelvo   I'll be right back
al día siguiente   (on) the following *or* next day
compañero de viaje   traveling companion
(el mes) que viene   next (month)
en avión (coche)   by plane (car), in a plane (car)
espero que sí   I hope so
hacer un (el) viaje   to take *or* make a (the) trip
hacer un favor (hacer favores) a   to do a favor (favors) for
hoy día   nowadays
más o menos   more or less, approximately
periódico de hoy   today's (news)paper
periódico de la universidad   university (news)paper
¿podemos (escribirlo)?   may or can we (write it)?
¿qué te pasa?   what's the matter (what's wrong) with you?

Vista nocturna del castillo
de Chapultepec.

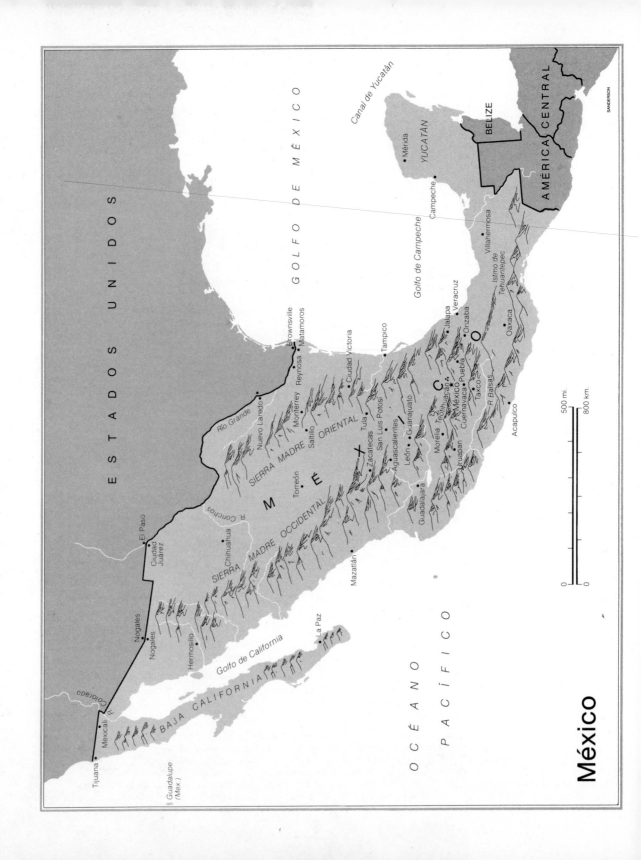

México

Lectura 3

México

Hoy vamos a estudiar otro mapa que tenemos en la pared. Es un mapa de México, nuestro buen vecino[1] al sur de los Estados Unidos. Cuatro estados de nuestro país, California, Arizona, Nuevo México y Texas, lindan con[2] México. El Río Grande, que pasa entre el estado de Texas y cuatro estados mexicanos, forma parte de la frontera con México.

La Carretera[3] Panamericana va desde Nuevo Laredo hasta Panamá. Pasa por Monterrey, un centro industrial de mucha importancia, y por la capital, la ciudad de México.

México es un país muy montañoso y hay que cruzar[4] muchas montañas para llegar a la capital, que está en la meseta central. Las dos cordilleras principales son la Sierra Madre Occidental, en el oeste, y la Sierra Madre Oriental, en el este. México tiene varios volcanes: el Popocatépetl y el Iztaccíhuatl se encuentran[5] cerca del valle central y están cubiertos de nieve[6] casi todo el año. El Orizaba, el pico más alto del país, está entre Puebla y Veracruz.

El norte de México es un gran[7] desierto. En el sur, en cambio,[8] en el istmo de Tehuantepec, la vegetación es abundante, porque el clima es tropical y llueve[9] mucho. La mayor parte de[10] los mexicanos viven en la meseta central, que tiene un clima muy agradable por la altura en que se encuentra.

La capital está situada en un valle de la meseta central y tiene más de once millones de habitantes. Es el centro comercial y cultural del país. Los magníficos edificios comerciales dan una buena idea del progreso y de la prosperidad de la ciudad. Por todas partes se ven árboles y flores[11] y numerosas fuentes,[12] especialmente en los parques que adornan la capital. Muchas de las colonias[13] tienen avenidas anchas[14] y casas nuevas de una arquitectura muy moderna, pero las colonias pobres tienen casas viejas y calles estrechas.[15]

---

[1]**buen vecino,** *good neighbor.* [2]**lindan con,** *border on.* [3]**Carretera,** *Highway.* [4]**cruzar,** *to cross.*
[5]**se encuentran,** *are found, are.* (**Encontrarse** often means approximately the same as **estar,** although it retains something of its original meaning, *to find itself, be found, be.*) [6]**cubiertos de nieve,** *covered with snow.* [7]**gran,** *great.* (When **grande** precedes a singular noun, it becomes **gran** and means *great.*) [8]**en cambio,** *on the other hand.* [9]**llueve,** *it rains.*
[10]**La mayor parte de,** *Most (of the).* [With this expression the verb may agree with the noun following **de** (**mexicanos,** in this case), rather than with **parte.**] [11]**árboles y flores,** *trees and flowers.* [12]**fuentes,** *fountains.* [13]**colonias,** *districts.*
[14]**avenidas anchas,** *wide avenues.* [15]**estrechas,** *narrow.*

Entre las ciudades principales se encuentran Monterrey, Guadalajara, Saltillo, San Luis Potosí, Puebla y Taxco. El puerto importante de Veracruz está en la costa del Golfo de México. El puerto de Tampico, famoso por la exportación de petróleo, también está en el este del país. Los puertos de Mazatlán y Acapulco, que se encuentran en la costa del Océano Pacífico, son famosos por sus playas bellas[16] y hoteles modernos.

El suelo de México es rico en minerales. En la producción de plata[17] México es la primera nación del mundo. Es importante la producción de cinc, mercurio, plomo[18] y petróleo. Abundan también el hierro[19] y el carbón.[20] Más de la mitad de la población[21] se dedica a la agricultura. Los productos principales son el algodón, el café, la caña de azúcar,[22] el maíz, y frutas y legumbres[23] de muchas clases.[24]

La civilización del país es una mezcla de la cultura indígena[25] y de la cultura de los españoles. Hay magníficos restos[26] de las civilizaciones precolombinas[27] en Tula, Teotihuacán, Oaxaca y la península de Yucatán. La influencia indígena es evidente en el arte, la arquitectura, las artes populares, la agricultura y en la lengua de los mexicanos.

El fenómeno característico que distingue a los mexicanos es la unificación racial. Una gran parte de los mexicanos son mestizos, es decir,[28] tienen sangre[29] india y española. Los indios que viven en las ciudades hablan español, pero en ciertas regiones aisladas[30] hay muchos que todavía hablan sus lenguas indígenas.

Preguntas

1. ¿Qué mapa vamos a estudiar hoy?   2. ¿Qué estados de nuestro país lindan con México? 3. ¿Qué río forma parte de la frontera entre los Estados Unidos y México?   4. ¿Hasta qué país llega la Carretera Panamericana?

5. ¿Qué es necesario cruzar para llegar a la capital de México?   6. ¿Cómo se llaman las dos cordilleras principales?   7. ¿Hay volcanes en México?   8. ¿Cuál es el pico más alto?

9. ¿Qué parte de México es un gran desierto?   10. ¿Cómo es el clima del istmo de Tehuantepec?   11. ¿Dónde viven la mayor parte de los mexicanos?   12. ¿Cómo es el clima de la meseta central?

13. ¿Dónde está situada la capital?   14. ¿Cuántos habitantes tiene la capital?   15. ¿Cómo son los edificios comerciales?   16. ¿Qué tienen muchas de las colonias?

17. ¿Cuáles son algunas de las ciudades importantes de México?   18. ¿Dónde está situada Veracruz?   19. ¿Por qué es importante Tampico?   20. ¿Por qué son famosos Acapulco y Mazatlán?   21. ¿Qué minerales hay en México?   22. ¿A qué se dedica más de la mitad de la población?   23. ¿Cuáles son los productos principales?

24. ¿Qué podemos decir de la civilización del país?   25. ¿Dónde hay magníficos restos de las civilizaciones precolombinas?   26. ¿En qué aspectos de la cultura es evidente la influencia indígena?   27. ¿Qué fenómeno característico distingue a los mexicanos? 28. ¿Hablan español todos los indios?

---

[16]**playas bellas,** *beautiful beaches.*   [17]**plata,** *silver.*   [18]**plomo,** *lead.*   [19]**hierro,** *iron.*   [20]**carbón,** *coal.* [21]**la mitad de la población,** *half of the population.*   [22]**caña de azúcar,** *sugar cane.*   [23]**legumbres,** *legumes,* also *vegetables.* [24]**clases,** *kinds.*   [25]**indígena,** *indigenous, native.*   [26]**restos,** *remains.*   [27]**precolombinas,** *pre-Columbian* (before the arrival of Columbus).   [28]**es decir,** *that is (to say).*   [29]**sangre,** *blood.*   [30]**aisladas,** *isolated.*

Estudio de palabras

a. Most Spanish nouns ending in **-ción** are feminine and end in *-tion* in English: civilización, continuación, contribución, exportación, formación, nación, producción, tradición, unificación, vegetación.

b. The Spanish ending **-oso** is often equivalent to English *-ous:* famoso, *famous. What are the meanings of* industrioso, montañoso *and* numeroso?

c. Many English words beginning with *s* followed by a consonant have Spanish cognates beginning with **es-** plus the consonant. Give the English for: España, español, estado, estudiante, estudio, estudiar.

d. Approximate and less approximate cognates. Pronounce the following words and then observe the English meaning: adornar, *to adorn;* arquitectura, *architecture;* clima, *climate;* desierto, *desert;* distinguir, *to distinguish;* edificio, *edifice, building;* fenómeno, *phenomenon;* isla, *island;* istmo, *isthmus;* maíz, *maize, corn;* parque, *park;* pasar, *to pass;* petróleo, *petroleum, oil;* pico, *peak;* volcán, *volcano.*

e. Compare the meanings of the following pairs of words: abundante, *abundant, and* abundar, *to abound, be abundant;* alto, *high, and* altura, *height, altitude;* carácter, *character, and* característico, *characteristic;* centro, *center, and* central, *central;* montãna, *mountain, and* montañoso, *mountainous;* producto, *product, and* producción, *production.*

Estudiantes de escuela primaria visitan el Museo Antropológico en la ciudad de México. En la foto se ve la maqueta que muestra la ciudad de México (Tenochtitlán de los aztecas) durante la época precolombina.

Tres ejemplos de arquitectura india precolombina en la ciudad maya de Chichén Itzá. Arriba, la pirámide de Cuculcán; a la izquierda y abajo, detalle y vista general del templo de Los Guerreros.

La plaza de Las Tres Culturas en la ciudad de México
ilustra muy bien la historia del país. Las ruinas aztecas
representan el aporte cultural de los indios, la iglesia de estilo
colonial representa la herencia española y los edificios
modernos, la integración de ambos en el México de hoy día.

Abajo, a la izquierda, un grupo de fotógrafos ambulantes
toman fotos enfrente del Santuario de Nuestra Señora de
Guadalupe. A la derecha vemos la famosa iglesia de Santa
Prisca en Taxco.

A la derecha, un artesano trabaja el vidrio en
una fábrica de la ciudad de México. México es
famoso por la calidad de los trabajos de artesanía,
no solamente en vidrio, sino también en cerámica,
cuero, madera, plata, cobre y piedra. Estos
trabajos se caracterizan por la armonía de su
colorido y la elegancia de su diseño, que se
inspiran por la mayor parte en la herencia india
precolombina.

Abajo, obreros trabajan el aluminio en una
fábrica de Guadalajara y, a la izquierda, se ve
una fábrica de motores. El gobierno mexicano
está haciendo grandes esfuerzos por desarrollar la
industria, sobre todo la metalúrgica y la del
petróleo, y así crear nuevas fuentes de trabajo
para combatir el desempleo.

La universidad de México, que se fundó en 1551, es una de las más antiguas de
América. Hasta la década de 1950–1960 los edificios de la Universidad se encontraban en
el centro de la ciudad de México, y muchos de ellos eran de estilo colonial. Hoy día, la
Universidad, que tiene más de 100.000 estudiantes, se encuentra en la ciudad Universitaria.

En la foto de arriba podemos ver algunos de los modernos edificios de la Universidad.
Muchos de ellos están cubiertos con murales por algunos de los grandes muralistas
mexicanos, como Diego Rivera, David Alfaro Ziqueiros, y muchos otros.

En la foto de abajo tenemos una vista del metro de la ciudad de México. El metro,
construido por ingenieros franceses, es uno de los más modernos del mundo.

El folklore mexicano es uno de los más ricos y variados de Latinoamérica. Cada región mexicana tiene sus bailes populares típicos que se inspiran en bailes indios precolombinos o en danzas populares españolas.

A la izquierda, una pareja baila en un festival en Oaxaca. Debajo, función de gala del Ballet Folklórico de México.

En México, como en España y algunos otros países sudamericanos, la corrida de toros es una fiesta popular.

Debajo, festival en Jocotepec cerca de Guadalajara, y a la derecha, los famosos jardines de Xochimilco cerca de la ciudad de México.

LECCIÓN

La última clase de la tarde

La señorita Valdés entra en la sala de clase y saluda a los estudiantes.

SRTA. VALDÉS —Buenas tardes. Siéntense Uds. Juan, hágame Ud. el favor de abrir la ventana.

MARTA —Pero Juan no está escuchando.

SRTA. VALDÉS —Marta, ¿quiere Ud. decirle a Juan que necesitamos aire fresco?

MARTA —Juan, abre la ventana, por favor. Necesitamos aire fresco. (*Juan abre la ventana.*)

SRTA. VALDÉS —Muchas gracias, Juan.

JUAN —No hay de qué, señorita.

◆ ◆ ◆ ◆ ◆

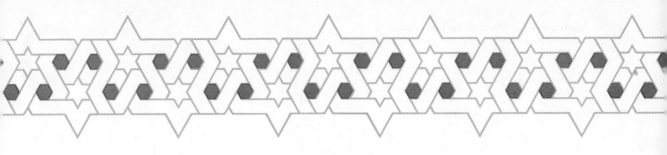

SRTA. VALDÉS —Ahora, cierren Uds. sus libros y pónganlos en las mesas. No los miren y escuchen con atención. Voy a hacerles algunas[1] preguntas.

MARTA —Debemos contestarlas en español, ¿verdad?

SRTA. VALDÉS —Sí, como siempre. Inés, ¿tiene Ud. frío?

INÉS —No, señorita. Siempre tengo mucho calor aquí.

SRTA. VALDÉS —Carlos, ¿tiene Ud. hambre o sed?

CARLOS —Tengo mucha hambre. Como me levanto tarde, generalmente no tomo más que café o un vaso de leche antes de venir a la universidad.

◆ ◆ ◆ ◆ ◆

SRTA. VALDÉS —Isabel, ¿llega Ud. a tiempo todos los días?

ISABEL —No, señorita. Cuando me despierto tarde, no llego a tiempo.

SRTA. VALDÉS —María, ¿tiene Ud. sueño en clase?

MARÍA —De vez en cuando tengo sueño. Pero si Ud. ve que no estoy escuchando, me hace alguna pregunta.

SRTA. VALDÉS —A veces lo hago, ¿verdad? Antonio, despierte Ud. a Carlos, por favor. El pobre tiene mucho sueño.

ANTONIO (*Despertando a su compañero.*) —¡Despiértate, Carlos! ¡Escucha a la profesora!

SRTA. VALDÉS —Muchas gracias. Carolina, ¿qué hace Ud. los domingos?

CAROLINA —Por la mañana voy a la iglesia. Por la tarde tengo mucho tiempo para estudiar. A veces doy un paseo con algunos amigos.

SRTA. VALDÉS —Muy bien; ya es la hora. Ahora levántense y tomen sus libros y sus cuadernos. No dejen[2] nada en las mesas. Salgan despacio, por favor. Hasta mañana.

ESTUDIANTES —Hasta mañana, señorita Valdés.

---

[1] Up to this point unemphatic *some* and *any* (*no* in a negative sentence, *e.g., I have no money,* **No tengo dinero**), so commonly used in English, have not been translated in Spanish. However, when emphasized, these words are expressed in Spanish.

[2] The transitive verb **dejar**, *to leave* (*behind*), requires a direct object. Do not confuse **dejar** with **salir**, *to leave, go out* (of a place).

Conversación

A. Preguntas sobre el diálogo

1. ¿Qué les dice la profesora a los estudiantes? 2. ¿Qué le dice Marta a Juan? 3. ¿Qué va a hacer la profesora? 4. ¿En qué lengua deben contestar los estudiantes? 5. ¿Tiene frío Inés? 6. ¿Por qué tiene hambre Carlos? 7. ¿Cuándo llega tarde Isabel? 8. ¿Qué hace la profesora cuando ve que María tiene sueño?

B. Aplicación del diálogo

1. ¿A qué hora se despierta Ud.? 2. ¿Tiene Ud. sueño en clase a veces? 3. ¿Les hago yo preguntas cuando veo que Uds. tienen sueño? 4. ¿Tiene Ud. hambre ahora? 5. ¿Qué hacemos cuando tenemos hambre? 6. ¿Qué hace Ud. los domingos? 7. ¿Qué les dice la profesora (el profesor) cuando es necesario abrir los libros? 8. ¿Qué les dice la profesora (el profesor) cuando es necesario escuchar? 9. ¿Qué le dice Ud. a su hermano cuando es necesario estudiar? 10. ¿Con quién da Ud. paseos a veces?

NOTAS GRAMATICALES

[handwritten: If there is an irregularity in first person singular — then it use it + employ the opposite vowel]

A. Commands

1. Formal commands

infinitive	*stem*	*singular*	*plural*	
hablar	habl-	hable Ud.	hablen Uds.	*speak*
comer	com-	coma Ud.	coman Uds.	*eat*
abrir	abr-	abra Ud.	abran Uds.	*open*
decir	**dig-**	**diga** Ud.	**digan** Uds.	*say, tell*
hacer	**hag-**	**haga** Ud.	**hagan** Uds.	*do, make*
poner	**pong-**	**ponga** Ud.	**pongan** Uds.	*put, place*
salir	**salg-**	**salga** Ud.	**salgan** Uds.	*leave, go out*
tener	**teng-**	**tenga** Ud.	**tengan** Uds.	*have*
traer	**traig-**	**traiga** Ud.	**traigan** Uds.	*bring*
venir	**veng-**	**venga** Ud.	**vengan** Uds.	*come*
ver	**ve-**	**vea** Ud.	**vean** Uds.	*see*
pensar	**piens-**	**piense** Ud.	**piensen** Uds.	*think*
volver	**vuelv-**	**vuelva** Ud.	**vuelvan** Uds.	*return*

To the stem of **-ar** verbs add the ending **-e** for the singular formal command and **-en** for the plural. For **-er** and **-ir** verbs the endings are **-a** and **-an**. In Spanish the stem for the formal command form of all but six verbs, four of which are given below, is that of the first person singular present indicative. Stem-changing verbs follow the same rule.

Poder cannot be used as a command, and the forms of **conocer, querer,** and **saber** are not used as commands in this text.

Ud. and **Uds.** are regularly expressed in commands and are placed after the verb; however, in a series of commands it is not necessary to repeat **Ud.** or **Uds.** with each one.

Four verbs whose first person singular present indicative ends in **-oy** do not follow the rule given above.

infinitive	*singular*	*plural*	
dar	**dé** Ud.	**den** Uds.	*give*
estar	**esté** Ud.	**estén** Uds.	*be*
ir	**vaya** Ud.	**vayan** Uds.	*go*
ser	**sea** Ud.	**sean** Uds.	*be*

◆ *Práctica.* Read in Spanish, noting the formal command forms:

1. Deje Ud. el libro aquí; dejen Uds. los cuadernos allí. 2. Lea Ud. la revista; lean Uds. el programa. 3. Escriba Ud. la carta; no escriban Uds. las frases. 4. Cierre Ud. la puerta; no cierren Uds. las ventanas. 5. Traiga Ud. el vaso; traigan Uds. el café. 6. No dé Ud. un paseo ahora; den Uds. un paseo mañana. 7. Salga Ud. del cuarto; no salgan Uds. de la casa. 8. No vaya Ud. a la biblioteca; vayan Uds. al centro.

2. Familiar singular commands

infinitive	*affirmative*		*negative*	
hablar	habla (tú)	*speak*	no hables (tú)	*don't speak*
comer	come (tú)	*eat*	no comas (tú)	*don't eat*
abrir	abre (tú)	*open*	no abras (tú)	*don't open*
pensar	**piensa** (tú)	*think*	no **pienses** (tú)	*don't think*
volver	**vuelve** (tú)	*return*	no **vuelvas** (tú)	*don't return*

The affirmative familiar singular command, often called the singular imperative, of regular and stem-changing verbs has the same form as the third person singular of the present indicative tense. The pronoun **tú** is omitted, except for emphasis.

To form the negative familiar singular command of these verbs, add **-s** to the formal singular command form: (formal) **No abra Ud. la puerta,** (familiar) **Carlos, no abras la puerta.** Certain verbs which have irregular affirmative singular command forms will be given later.

Remember that the **Uds.** form is used in this text for all plural commands, affirmative and negative.

In the case of reflexive verbs, the familiar **te** must be used:

levantarse:	levántate (tú)	*get up*	no te levantes	*don't get up*
sentarse:	**siénta**te (tú)	*sit down*	no te **sientes**	*don't sit down*

When object pronouns are attached to command forms in writing, an accent mark must be placed on the stressed syllable of a verb form of more than one syllable.

◆ *Práctica.*   Read in Spanish, noting the familiar command forms:

1. Compra tú el libro; no compres la pluma.   2. Llama tú a Marta; no llames a Diana. 3. Mira tú la iglesia; no mires los escaparates.   4. Aprende tú las palabras; no aprendas las frases.   5. Lee tú el periódico; no leas los precios.   6. Lávate tú las manos; no te laves la cara.   7. Acuéstate ahora; no te acuestes todavía.   8. Contesta en español; no contestes en inglés.

B. Position of object pronouns in commands

Ábrala Ud.; Ábrela (tú).   Open it.
No la abra Ud.; No la abras (tú).   Don't open it.
Siéntense Uds.; No se sienten Uds.   Sit down; Don't sit down.
Despiértate, Carlos.   Wake up, Charles.
Déjalo (tú) sobre la mesa.   Leave it on the table.
No lo dejes allí todavía.   Don't leave it there yet.

You have learned that object pronouns are placed immediately before the verb in Spanish except when used as the object of an infinitive, in which case they are attached to it (Lesson 8). Now remember that they are also *placed after* the verb and *are attached*

A View of Truxillo a City belonging to the Spaniards in the Bay of Honduras.

to it when used as the object of an *affirmative command*. In negative commands the object pronouns precede the verb.

◆ *Práctica.* Read in Spanish, noting the command forms:

1. Póngalo Ud. allí. 2. No lo ponga Ud. aquí. 3. Tráiganme Uds. sus cuadernos. 4. No me traigan Uds. sus libros. 5. Dénos Ud. café, por favor. 6. No nos dé Ud. café frío. 7. Hágame Ud. el favor de levantarse. 8. Levántese Ud., por favor. 9. Inés, acuéstate. 10. No te acuestes ahora. 11. Ciérrala tú, Carlos. 12. No la cierres todavía.

C. Expressions with **tener**

Juan tiene	**calor.** **frío.** **hambre.** **sed.** **sueño.** **suerte.**	John is	warm. cold. hungry. thirsty. sleepy. lucky.

Ellos tienen mucho frío.   They are very cold.
Marta y yo tenemos mucha hambre.   Martha and I are very hungry.
El pobre tiene mucho sueño.   The poor boy is very sleepy.

In describing certain physical and mental conditions of living beings, **tener** is used with *nouns* in Spanish to express the English equivalent of *to be* with adjectives.[1] **Juan tiene hambre** means literally *John has hunger.*

Since the words **calor, frío,** etc., are nouns in these expressions, they are modified by the adjective **mucho, -a,** not the adverb **muy.** The noun **la suerte** was introduced in Lesson 3: ¡**Qué suerte!** *What luck! How lucky!* **Hambre, sed,** and **suerte** are feminine nouns and require **mucha** for *very.*

In the sentence **El café está muy frío,** *The coffee is very cold,* note that the word **frío** is an adjective and it must be modified by **muy.**

The definite article **el** is used instead of **la** with a few feminine nouns which begin with stressed **a-** or **ha-;** thus, one says **el hambre,** *hunger.*

◆ *Práctica.* Read in Spanish, keeping the meaning in mind:

1. Yo tengo frío; tengo mucho frío. 2. Marta tiene sueño; tiene mucho sueño. 3. Juan y yo tenemos calor; tenemos mucho calor. 4. Inés y Carolina tienen hambre; tienen mucha hambre. 5. ¿Tienes sed? ¿Tienes mucha sed? 6. Tomás tiene suerte; tiene mucha suerte.

---

[1] Other expressions with **tener** + nouns will be introduced later in the text. Observe, for example, **tener . . . años,** *to be . . . years old,* as in ¿**Cuántos años tienes?** *How old are you?*

[handwritten margin note at top: Commana different in neg-goes before 2 forms ob Command (Tu, ud.)]

D. Spanish equivalents for the English word "time"

¿Qué hora es? What time is it?
Podemos charlar un rato. We can chat a short time (a while).
¿Siempre llega Ud. a tiempo? Do you always arrive on time?
Tengo mucho tiempo para estudiar. I have much time to study.
A veces doy un paseo. At times I take a walk.
Esta vez no puedo. This time I cannot.

You have already learned that **hora** is used to express *time of day* and that **un rato** is used for *a short time, a while.*

Tiempo refers to length of time or time in general (third and fourth examples). **Vez** (*pl.* **veces**) is used to express time in a series, such as *this time, the first time* (*occasion*), *at times,* etc. (last two examples).

◆ *Práctica.* Choose from **hora, rato, tiempo, vez,** or **veces** the correct word to complete each sentence:

[handwritten margin note: 6 sentences each Commana forms]

1. Marta no va al centro con su mamá esta vez ___ . 2. Mi papá no tiene mucho tiempo hoy. 3. ¿Sabe Ud. qué hora es? 4. Mi mamá va al mercado dos veces cada semana. 5. Las estudiantes charlan mucho todo el tiempo. 6. Los jóvenes pasan un rato aquí todos los días. 7. Yo veo a Juan de vez en cuando. 8. Hoy no tengo tiempo para dar un paseo. 9. ¿Van Uds. a la iglesia a esta hora de la mañana? 10. ¿Siempre llegan Uds. a tiempo?

EJERCICIOS

A. Say after your teacher; then change to a singular and a plural formal command, following the model:

MODEL: Carlos toma el papel. *Carlos toma el papel.*
Carlos, tome Ud. el papel. *Tomen Uds. el papel.*

1. Carolina compra ese vestido.
2. Carmen escribe las frases.
3. Inés contesta en español.
4. Ana lee el periódico.
5. Ricardo sale de casa.
6. Marta trae las cosas.
7. Juan pone los libros aquí.
8. María va a la biblioteca.

B. Say after your teacher; then change to a familiar singular command, following the model:

MODEL: Juan abre la ventana. *Juan abre la ventana.*
Juan, abre la ventana, por favor.

1. Carolina mira aquel cuadro.
2. Inés deja mi cuaderno allí.
3. Juan aprende estas palabras.
4. Marta abre la puerta.
5. Isabel cierra la ventana.
6. José vuelve a casa pronto.

When you hear the sentences again, make each one a negative familiar command:

MODEL: Juan abre la ventana.   *Juan, no abras la ventana.*

C. Say after your teacher; then repeat, making each sentence negative:

MODEL: Apréndalo Ud.   *Apréndalo Ud. No lo aprenda Ud.*

1. Tráigalos Ud. ahora.   5. Enséñenles Uds. los vestidos.
2. Póngalas Ud. aquí.   6. Siéntense Uds. allí.
3. Díganos Ud. la verdad.   7. Escríbanles Uds. mañana.
4. Levántese Ud. pronto.   8. Ciérrenlas Uds. esta noche.

D. Place the pronoun correctly with each verb:

1. (me) Ellos despiertan. Quieren despertar. Despierte Ud. No despierte Ud.
2. (la) Juan cierra. Va a cerrar. Cierre Ud. No cierre Ud.
3. (le) Inés escribe. Puede escribir. Escriba Ud. No escriba Ud.
4. (los) Yo hago. Tengo que hacer. Haga Ud. No haga Ud.

E. Listen to each question, then give formal affirmative and negative commands, using object pronouns for the noun objects:

MODELS: ¿Tomo el libro?   *Sí, tómelo Ud.* and *No, no lo tome Ud.*
          ¿Tomamos los libros? *Sí, tómenlos Uds.* and *No, no los tomen Uds.*

1. ¿Abro la puerta?   4. ¿Compramos los vestidos?
2. ¿Leo la carta?   5. ¿Ponemos las cosas allí?
3. ¿Cierro las ventanas?   6. ¿Traemos el dinero?

Answer, giving the familiar affirmative and negative singular commands:

MODELS: ¿Lo abro?   *Sí, ábrelo tú* and *No, no lo abras.*
          ¿Me lavo ahora? *Sí, lávate tú ahora* and *No, no te laves ahora.*

7. ¿La escribo?   9. ¿Me levanto ahora?
8. ¿Los dejo allí?   10. ¿Me siento allí?

F. Read in Spanish, using the correct form of **estar, ser,** or **tener:**

1. Hoy _____ un día muy fresco; Inés _____ en su cuarto; _____ mucho frío.
2. El señor López _____ profesor; _____ muchos estudiantes; ahora _____ en clase.   3. Nosotros _____ mucha hambre; ya _es_ muy tarde y el comedor no _____ cerca.   4. A veces Carolina _____ mucho sueño cuando _____ cansada, ¿no _____ verdad?   5. La hermana de Tomás _____ mucha suerte; _____ estudiando español y va a _ser_ estudiante en la Universidad de México.

G. Give the Spanish equivalent, using the formal forms in commands:

1. I bring the coffee. I bring it. Bring it. Do not bring it yet. 2. They sit down. They intend to sit down. Sit down (*pl.*). Don't sit down. 3. We wash our hands. We can wash our hands now. Wash (*pl.*) your hands. Do not wash your hands there.

H. Give the Spanish equivalent, using the formal forms of commands:

1. "Please (*pl.*) sit down and open your books. 2. After opening them, bring me your sentences for today. 3. Put them here on my table; do not leave them there. 4. John, close the door, please, and then open the windows." 5. When the teacher asks us questions, we always answer in Spanish. 6. "Martha, are you very cold here this morning?" "No, Miss Valdés, I am warm." 7. "Are you sleepy in class at times?" "Yes, if I go to bed late." 8. "Where do you go on Sundays?" "My friends and I go to church." 9. "What day is today?" "Today is the last day of the week." 10. "Very well. Take (*pl.*) your books in your hands; you must (should) not leave them here in the classroom."

EJERCICIOS DE PRONUNCIACIÓN

A. The pronunciation of **y,** *and*

The following principles govern the pronunciation of the conjunction **y:**

1. When initial in a breath-group before a consonant, or when between consonants, it is pronounced like the Spanish vowel **i: Y no la abras (Y-no-la-a-bras), dos y dos (do-s̯ y-dos).**

2. When initial in a breath-group before a vowel, or when between vowels, it is pronounced like Spanish **y: ¿y usted? (¿y͜ us-ted?), éste y aquél (és-te-y͜ a-quél).**

3. Between **d, s,** or **z** and a vowel within a breath-group, it is also pronounced like Spanish **y: usted y ella (us-ted-y͜ e-lla), alumnos y amigos (a-lum-nos-y͜ a-mi-gos).**

4. Between **l, n,** or **r** and a vowel within a breath-group, it is pronounced as the first element of a diphthong, with the preceding consonant, the **y,** and the following vowel in a single syllable: **hablan y escriben (ha-bla-n͜ y es-cri-ben), entrar y esperar (en-tra-r͜ y es-pe-rar).**

5. Between a vowel and a consonant, it forms a diphthong with the vowel that precedes it: **padre y madre (pa-dre͜ y-ma-dre).**

B. Apply the above principles as you read the following phrases and sentences in single breath-groups:

Hablan y pronuncian muy bien.	Vamos Carlos y yo.
España y América.	Y estudian español, también.
Tengo un lápiz y un libro.	Estudio inglés y francés.
Hablar y escribir.	Miren y escuchen.
Tengo hambre y sed.	Tengo sed y hambre.

VOCABULARIO

el **aire**   air
alguno, -a   *adj. and pron.* some, any, someone; *pl.* some, a few
Antonio   Anthony, Tony
la **atención**   attention
el **café**   coffee; café
el **calor**   heat, warmth
Carolina   Caroline
cerrar (ie)   to close
contestar   to answer, reply
deber   to owe, must, should, ought to
dejar   to leave (behind)
despacio   slowly
despertar (ie)   to wake up, awaken; *reflex.* to wake up (oneself)
el **domingo**   Sunday, on Sunday
fresco, -a   cool, fresh

el **frío**   cold
el **hambre** (*f.*)   hunger
la **iglesia**   church
Inés   Inez, Agnes
Juan   John
la **leche**   milk
Marta   Martha
el **paseo**   walk, stroll, ride; boulevard
pobre   poor
la **pregunta**   question
saludar   to greet, speak to, say hello to
la **sed**   thirst
el **sueño**   sleep
último, -a   last (*in a series*)
el **vaso**   glass
la **vez** (*pl.* **veces**)   time (*in a series*), occasion

el mandato – commands orders

a la iglesia   to church
a tiempo   on time
a veces   at times
con atención   attentively, carefully
dar un paseo   to take a walk (ride)
de vez en cuando   from time to time, occasionally
hacer una pregunta (a)   to ask a question (of)
haga (hágame) Ud. *or* **hagan (háganme) Uds. el favor de** + *inf.*
los domingos   (on) Sundays
no dejen nada   leave nothing, don't leave anything (*See Lesson 10 for explanation*)
no (tomar) más que   (to take) only, (to take) nothing but
tener tiempo para   to have time to (for)
ya es la hora   the hour is over, it is the end of the hour (period)

Conversación [1] 1

En un café español

Ana y Carmen son dos jóvenes norteamericanas que están estudiando en Madrid. Salen de su pensión a las cuatro de la tarde para ir a la universidad y pasan por un café al aire libre. Sentado a una mesa, con un compañero, está Carlos, un joven madrileño a quien conocen las muchachas.

CARLOS —¡Hola! ¡Qué sorpresa más agradable! ¿Adónde van Uds. a esta hora?

ANA —Pues pensamos dar un paseo antes de ir a la universidad. Tenemos una clase de arte a las seis.

CARLOS —Pues falta mucho tiempo para las seis. ¿Por qué no nos acompañan un rato? Quiero presentar a mi compañero, Felipe Morales.

ANA Y CARMEN —Mucho gusto.

FELIPE —El gusto es mío, señoritas. ¿No quieren Uds. sentarse?

ANA —Parece que en España todo el mundo va al café por la tarde.

CARLOS —Es verdad. Venimos al café para conversar con los amigos.

FELIPE —Aquí se habla de todo: de literatura, de música, de la situación política y económica . . . (*Se sientan las jóvenes y se presenta un camarero.*)

CAMARERO —Buenas tardes. ¿Desean Uds. tomar algo? ¿Café, té, chocolate, un refresco, un helado . . . ?

CARLOS —Ana, ¿qué va a tomar Ud.?

ANA —Café, por favor.

CAMARERO —¿Café solo o con leche?

ANA —Con leche, por favor.

CARLOS —En los Estados Unidos Uds. toman café con crema, ¿verdad? Mucho café y un poco de crema; en España tomamos mucha leche y poco café.

ANA —Sí, tomamos crema en el café y servimos el café en tazas. ¿Siempre toman Uds. el café en vasos?

FELIPE —No; en casa también usamos tazas, como en los Estados Unidos. Pero en los cafés generalmente sirven el café en vasos.

CARLOS —Y, ¿qué quiere tomar Ud., Carmen?

CARMEN —Voy a tomar té, como siempre.

---

[1]The teacher may assign the **Conversación** for close study, recognition, or comprehension, and students may compose similar dialogues. All new words listed at the end of each **Conversación** will be listed again when introduced in regular lessons.

CAMARERO —¿Con limón?

CARMEN —Sin limón, por favor, pero con un poco de azúcar.

CARLOS —Y tú, Felipe, ¿qué vas a tomar?

FELIPE —Por lo común tomo café con leche, pero hoy voy a tomar un helado.

CAMARERO —¿De vainilla o de chocolate?

FELIPE —De vainilla, por favor.

CAMARERO —¿Quiere Ud. café con el helado?

FELIPE —No, gracias. Un vaso de agua, solamente.

CARLOS —Pues, yo voy a tomar chocolate.

CAMARERO —¿Desean Uds. unos pasteles también?

CARLOS —Gracias, hoy no deseamos nada más.

CAMARERO —Muy bien. Vuelvo en seguida.

Preguntas

Sobre la conversación

1. ¿Son españolas Ana y Carmen?   2. ¿Quiénes están sentados a una mesa en un café al aire libre?   3. ¿Qué piensan hacer las muchachas?   4. ¿A qué hora tienen una clase de arte? 5. ¿Qué dice Ana del café español?   6. ¿De qué hablan los españoles en el café?

7. ¿Qué va a tomar Ana?   8. ¿Cómo toman el café en España?   9. ¿Qué toma Carmen? 10. ¿Cómo toma Carmen el té, con limón?   11. ¿Qué toma Felipe por lo común? 12. ¿Cuál es la última pregunta que les hace el camarero?

Aplicación de la conversación

1. ¿Hay un café al aire libre cerca de esta universidad?   2. ¿Van los estudiantes al café todos los días en los Estados Unidos?   3. ¿Vive Ud. en una pensión?   4. ¿Cuántas clases tiene Ud. por la tarde?   5. ¿Tiene Ud. clase a las seis de la tarde?   6. ¿Le gustan a Ud. las clases de literatura?

7. ¿Generalmente toma Ud. café o té?   8. ¿Tomamos el café con leche en los Estados Unidos?   9. ¿Toma Ud. mucha azúcar en el café?   10. ¿Le gusta a Ud. el té con limón? 11. ¿Tiene Ud. sed ahora?   12. ¿Qué toma Ud. por lo común por la tarde?

Práctica oral (Oral practice)

Groups of students will be selected to prepare a conversation of six to eight exchanges, using the vocabulary already given.

1. In one group two American students meet Spanish friends and speak briefly about their studies.

2. In other groups one student serves as waiter (waitress, **la camarera**) and takes the orders of other students.

VOCABULARIO

el **agua** (*f.*)[1] water
el (la) **azúcar** sugar
el **camarero** waiter
común (*pl.* **comunes**) common, ordinary, usual
conversar to converse, talk
la **crema** cream
el **chocolate** chocolate
faltar (*used like* **gustar**) to lack, be lacking
el **helado** ice cream
el **limón** (*pl.* **limones**) lemon
la **literatura** literature
el **pastel** pastry, pie

la **pensión** (*pl.* **pensiones**) boardinghouse
poco, -a little (*quantity*)
presentar to present, introduce
quien (*pl.* **quienes**) who, whom (*after prep.*)
el **refresco** cold *or* soft drink
servimos we serve
sin *prep.* without
sirven they serve
la **situación** (*pl.* **situaciones**) situation
la **taza** cup
el **té** tea
todo *pron.* everything
la **vainilla** vanilla

al aire libre outdoor, open-air
café solo black coffee
el gusto es mío the pleasure is mine
falta mucho tiempo para las seis it is a long time before six
mucho gusto (I am) pleased *or* glad to know you
no deseamos nada más we don't want anything else
por lo común commonly, generally
¡qué sorpresa más agradable! what a pleasant surprise!
se habla one talks, people talk
se presenta un camarero a waiter appears (presents himself)
todo el mundo everybody
vuelvo en seguida I'll be right back, I'll return at once

---

[1]See page 119 for explanation of the use of the definite article **el** with certain feminine nouns.

The preterit indicative of regular verbs • Preterit of *dar, ir,* and *ser* • Use of the preterit • Indefinite and negative expressions • Special uses of the definite article

LECCIÓN 10

En el comedor de estudiantes

José baja al comedor de la residencia de estudiantes y al entrar encuentra a Juan. José lo invita a sentarse a su mesa. Los dos jóvenes se desayunan juntos.

JOSÉ —¡Oye, Juan! ¿Qué pasó ayer? Traté de llamarte por teléfono a eso de las seis de la tarde, y nadie me contestó.

JUAN —Es que llevé[1] a mis padres al aeropuerto. Salieron para Los Ángeles en el avión de las cinco y media.

JOSÉ —No cenaste en la residencia, ¿verdad?[2]

JUAN —No, cené en el aeropuerto temprano y después fui a casa de María. Charlamos un rato y miramos unos[3] programas de televisión.

JOSÉ —¿Y te dio tu padre permiso para usar el coche?

JUAN —¡Sí, claro! Después dimos un paseo por el parque y tomamos un refresco en el café.

◆ ◆ ◆ ◆ ◆

JUAN —Y tú, José, ¿no saliste anoche?

JOSÉ —¡Hombre, nunca me quedo en casa los sábados por la noche! Llevé a Isabel al cine. Como salimos tarde, volvimos a casa sin visitar a nadie.

JUAN —¿Qué película vieron?

JOSÉ —Una estupenda[4] película mexicana. Hay algunos números de baile muy bonitos, especialmente el *jarabe tapatío,* el baile nacional de México.

JUAN —Mis padres la vieron la semana pasada. Dicen que hay una orquesta que toca canciones típicas. ¿Y les gustó esa película?

JOSÉ —Sí, nos gustó mucho. También hay dos jóvenes—un muchacho y una muchacha—que cantan y bailan bastante bien.

JUAN —¡Qué casualidad! María y yo vimos un magnífico programa de televisión sobre los bailes nacionales de España. Anunciaron que es el grupo que se presenta en Nueva York la semana que viene.

JOSÉ —¡Ah! Creo que es el grupo que se anuncia en un periódico que alguien me dio el otro día. Espero tener la oportunidad de verlo.

JUAN —Yo también, pues me gustan mucho los bailes típicos. Bueno, José, tengo que hacer muchas cosas hoy . . .

JOSÉ —Pues, sí . . . ¡Ya es hora de irnos! Pero escucha, Juan, a ver si te encuentro para cenar juntos . . .

---

[1] **Llevar** is used when *to take* means *to carry* or *take* (something or someone) to a place. **Tomar** means *to take* in the sense of *to take up* or *pick up* (*e.g.,* take something in one's hand) or *to take something to eat* or *drink.*

[2] After a negative, **¿verdad?** corresponds to *do* or *did (you)? will he (you, she,* etc.)? depending on the context of the sentence.

[3] In Lesson 9 you learned that **algunos, -as** means *some, a few.* **Unos, -as** also means *some, a few, several.*

[4] Note that the descriptive adjective **estupenda** precedes the noun; also note **magnífico** in line 11. There will be no drill on this point in the exercises. Note similar cases in later lessons and the explanation on pages 285–286.

Conversación

A. Preguntas sobre el diálogo

1. ¿Cuándo encuentra José a Juan? 2. ¿Quién contestó el teléfono en el cuarto de Juan cuando José llamó? 3. ¿Por qué fue Juan al aeropuerto? 4. ¿Cenó Juan en la residencia esa noche? 5. ¿Adónde fue Juan después de cenar? 6. ¿Adónde fueron Isabel y José el sábado por la noche? 7. ¿Les gustó la película que vieron? 8. ¿Qué se presenta en esa película? 9. ¿Qué vieron Juan y María en la televisión? 10. ¿Qué se anuncia en el periódico sobre ese grupo de bailes?

B. Aplicación del diálogo

1. ¿Qué hace Ud. los sábados por la noche? ¿Se queda Ud. en la residencia? ¿Visita a sus amigos? ¿Sale con alguna amiga? ¿Mira la televisión? ¿Prepara sus lecciones? 2. ¿No le gusta a Ud. ir al cine? ¿Qué hace Ud. después de salir del cine? 3. ¿Generalmente dónde se anuncian las películas? 4. ¿Lee Ud. los anuncios antes de ir al cine? ¿Por qué los lee Ud.? 5. ¿Qué películas le parecen más interesantes, las películas de bailes y canciones o las películas serias? 6. ¿Le gusta a Ud. bailar? ¿Qué bailes le gustan especialmente? 7. ¿Sale Ud. a bailar a menudo? ¿Qué orquesta le gusta a Ud.? 8. ¿Hay bailes aquí el sábado por la noche?

NOTAS GRAMATICALES

A. The preterit indicative of regular verbs

hablar		comer		vivir	
singular	*plural*	*singular*	*plural*	*singular*	*plural*
hablé	hablamos	comí	comimos	viví	vivimos
hablaste	hablasteis	comiste	comisteis	viviste	vivisteis
habló	hablaron	comió	comieron	vivió	vivieron

The preterit tense, sometimes called the past definite, is formed by adding the endings **-é, -aste, -ó, -amos, -asteis, -aron** to the infinitive stem of **-ar** verbs, or the endings **-í, -iste, -ió, -imos, -isteis, -ieron** to the stem of **-er** and **-ir** verbs. Remember that **-er** and **-ir** verbs have identical endings, except in the first and second persons plural of the present indicative tense. The stress is on the ending in the preterit, and the first and third persons singular of regular verbs have a written accent.

The preterit corresponds to the simple English past tense and the emphatic form with *did:* **hablé,** *I spoke, did speak;* **Ud. comió,** *you ate, did eat;* **vivieron,** *they lived, did live.* In questions and negative statements *did* is used in English, but not in Spanish:

¿Escribió Ud. la carta? Did you write the letter?
Juan no se quedó en casa. John didn't stay at home.

Stem-changing verbs that end in **-ar** and **-er** are regular in the preterit; for example, **pensar: pensé, pensaste, pensó,** etc.; **volver: volví, volviste, volvió,** etc.

B. Irregular preterit of **dar, ir,** and **ser**

	dar			ir, ser	
singular		*plural*	*singular*		*plural*
di		dimos	fui		fuimos
diste		disteis	fuiste		fuisteis
dio		dieron	fue		fueron

English equivalents for **di** are *I gave, did give* and for **fui** are *I went, did go,* or *I was.* **Ir** and **ser** have identical forms, but context makes the meaning clear.

Conocer and **salir** are regular in the preterit. Accents are omitted on **di, dio, fui, fue,** and **vi, vio** (preterit forms of **ver**).

C. Use of the preterit

Cené en el aeropuerto temprano. I ate supper early in (at) the airport.
Charlamos un rato. We chatted a while.
¿Qué pasó ayer? What happened yesterday?
Juan no se quedó aquí más que dos semanas. John stayed here only two weeks.

The preterit is the narrative past tense in Spanish. It indicates that an action began, that an action ended, or that a past action or state was completed within a definite period of time, regardless of the length of duration.

D. Indefinite and negative expressions

algo	something, anything	**nada**	nothing, (not) . . . anything
alguien	someone, somebody, anybody, anyone	**nadie**	no one, nobody, (not) . . . anybody (anyone)
siempre	always	**nunca**	never, (not) . . . ever

Los muchachos tienen algo. The boys have something.
No tengo nada *or* **Nada tengo.** I have nothing (I don't have anything).
Nadie me contestó *or* **No me contestó nadie.** No one answered me.
Yo nunca me quedo en casa. I never stay at home.
No hablé con nadie anoche. I did not talk with anyone last night.
Juan estudia más que nunca. John studies more than ever.

The negatives **nada, nadie,** and **nunca** may either precede or follow a verb. When they follow, **no** or some other negative must precede the verb. If these negatives come before the verb or are used without a verb, **no** is not required:—**¿Qué está Ud. haciendo? —Nada.** *"What are you doing?" "Nothing."* After **que,** *than,* a negative is used.

The pronouns **alguien** and **nadie** refer only to persons, unknown or not mentioned before, and the personal **a** is required when they are used as objects of the verb:

¿Ve Ud. a alguien? Do you see anyone?
No vimos a nadie. We did not see anyone (We saw nobody).
Volvimos sin visitar a nadie. We returned without visiting anyone.

Alguno, used as an adjective or pronoun (see footnote 1, page 115 and footnote 3, page 129), refers to persons or things already thought of or mentioned:

Hay algunos números de baile. There are some dance numbers.
Isabel cantó algunas canciones. Betty sang some (a few) songs.
Alguno de los hombres llamó. Someone of the men called.

E. Special uses of the definite article

1. **Espero ver la película el mes que viene.** I hope to see the film next month.
   Mis padres la vieron la semana pasada. My parents saw it last week.

When an expression of time, such as **semana, mes,** a day of the week, a month of the year, is modified by an adjective, the definite article must be used.
Contrast **pasado,** *last, past* (just passed), with **último,** *last* (in a series).

2. **Me gustan los bailes típicos.** I like typical dances.
   ¿Le gustan a Ud. las películas extranjeras? Do you like foreign films?

If a noun in Spanish denotes a general class, that is, if it applies to all dances, all foreign films, etc., the definite article is used with it.

EJERCICIOS

A. Substitution drill:

1. Ayer *yo* llamé a Juan.
   (*María, nosotros, Uds., tú, ellos*)
2. *José* no comió en la residencia.
   (*Yo, Ellos, Nosotros, Tú, Juan y tú*)
3. *Isabel* no volvió con nadie.
   (*Luis y yo, Tú, Carolina, Uds., Yo*)
4. *Alguien* fue a buscarlo.
   (*Nadie, Yo, Ellos, Juan y yo, Uds.*)
5. ¿Cerró *Ana* la puerta?
   (*Uds., tú, Carolina, nosotros, yo*)

B. Read each sentence in Spanish; then repeat, changing the verbs from the present tense to the preterit:

1. No me levanto hasta las siete y media. 2. Me lavo las manos y la cara. 3. Después, bajo al comedor y me siento a la mesa. 4. Mi hermano se despierta tarde y no se desayuna. 5. Salgo de casa y voy a mi clase de español. 6. Antes de sentarme, abro las ventanas. 7. El profesor entra y saluda a los estudiantes. 8. Nos habla en español y le contestamos. 9. Pero algunos estudiantes no contestan nada. 10. La clase termina a las nueve menos diez, y todos los estudiantes salen despacio. 11. Algunos toman sus libros en las manos y los llevan a casa. 12. Carlos y yo vamos a la biblioteca. 13. Nos quedamos allí hasta las doce menos cuarto. 14. No volvemos a la residencia hasta más tarde.

C. Answer affirmatively in Spanish:

1. ¿Se despertó Ud. temprano?
2. ¿Se levantó Ud. tarde?
3. ¿Te desayunaste en el comedor?
4. ¿Te sentaste a estudiar después?
5. ¿Te quedaste en casa hoy?
6. ¿Fueron Uds. a ver los bailes?
7. ¿Dieron Uds. un paseo ayer?
8. ¿Trataron Uds. de ver el programa?
9. ¿Cantaron Uds. algunas canciones?
10. ¿Bailaron Uds. anoche en el centro?

D. Repeat each negative sentence, and then make an affirmative one:

MODELS: Nadie canta ahora.   *Nadie canta ahora. Alguien canta ahora.*
         Nunca me dan nada.   *Nunca me dan nada. Siempre me dan algo*

1. Marta y yo no vimos a nadie.
2. Aquellos hombres no saben nada.
3. Inés no piensa ir con nadie.
4. Juan nunca da nada a nadie.
5. No hay nada en la mesa.
6. Nadie le lleva nada a Juan.

E. Repeat the question after your teacher. When you hear the question again, use the corresponding negative in your answer:

MODELS: ¿Ve Ud. algo?   *¿Ve Ud. algo?*
         ¿Ve Ud. algo?   *No, no veo nada.*

         ¿Viene alguien?   *¿Viene alguien?*
         ¿Viene alguien?   *No, nadie viene* or *No, no viene nadie.*

1. ¿Tiene Ud. algo?
2. ¿Está Ud. haciendo algo?
3. ¿Busca Ud. a alguien?
4. ¿Vas con alguien?
5. ¿Canta alguien ahora?
6. ¿Siempre llega Ud. a tiempo?
7. ¿Hay algo en la mesa?
8. ¿Tienes algo en la mano?
9. ¿Le llevó Ud. algo a Juan?
10. ¿Viste a alguien ayer?
11. ¿Fue alguien al cine?
12. ¿Le diste algo al profesor?

F. After reviewing the command forms in Lesson 9, read each sentence in Spanish. Then turn each sentence into a command, as indicated:

Fam. Sing.:
1. Marta baila un baile español.
2. Juan lleva a Inés al cine.
3. Isabel no escribe en inglés.
4. María no se queda en casa.

Formal Sing.:
5. Carlos me hace preguntas.
6. Inés se compra esa cartera.
7. Luis no da un paseo hoy.
8. José no toma mucho café.

Formal Pl.:
9. Se sientan en el comedor.
10. Los llevan al aeropuerto.
11. No traen nada.
12. No les dan permiso para ir.

G. When you hear the question, answer with a formal affirmative, and then with a formal negative command:

MODEL: ¿Me lavo aquí?   *Sí, lávese Ud. aquí, por favor.*
                            No, no se lave Ud. aquí, por favor.

1. ¿Me acuesto aquí?
2. ¿Me siento aquí?
3. ¿Me quedo aquí?
4. ¿Me pongo aquí?
5. ¿Me desayuno ahora?
6. ¿Me levanto ahora?
7. ¿Me voy ahora?
8. ¿Me presento ahora?

H. Give the Spanish equivalent, using the familiar forms for *you:*

1. "Charles, wait a moment. Where did you go yesterday?   2. No one answered when I tried to call you by telephone."   3. "Well, John, my parents left for New York, and I took them to the airport at four o'clock.   4. Afterwards I went to Mary's for dinner (in order to have dinner), and then I invited her to see a movie (film)."   5. "Didn't your parents give you permission to use their car?"   6. "Yes, I am very lucky. Before taking Mary home, we took a ride.   7. Did you stay at home or did you go to the movies too?"   8. "Man! You know that I never stay at home on Saturday nights.   9. Betty and I saw a film in which there are some Mexican dances.   10. There are a girl and a boy who sing and dance very well. The orchestra which plays is good also."   11. "Last week I saw a television program of typical dances from Spain.   12. I hope to have the opportunity to see a program of Spanish dances in New York next month."

EJERCICIOS DE PRONUNCIACIÓN

A. The diphthongs **ue** and **eu**

1. As the first element of a diphthong, unstressed **u** is pronounced like *w* in *wet:*

| luego | puedo | Nueva York | vuelvo |
| sueño | su hermano | su examen | tu hermana |

2. Spanish **eu** has no close equivalent in English. It consists of a Spanish **e**, followed closely by a glide sound which ends in English *oo*, to sound like *ehoo*:

Europa	¿quiere usted?	¿sabe usted?	busque usted
hable usted	pase usted	pronuncie usted	siéntese usted

B. Dictado

The teacher will select four exchanges of the dialogue of this or of the preceding lesson as an exercise in dictation.

VOCABULARIO

el **aeropuerto** airport
alguien someone, somebody, anybody, anyone
anoche last night
anunciar to announce, advertise
ayer yesterday
bailar to dance
el **baile** dance
la **canción** (*pl.* **canciones**) song
cantar to sing
el **cine** movie(s)
el **grupo** group
irse to go (away), leave
Los Ángeles Los Angeles
llevar to take, carry
magnífico, -a magnificent, fine
la **muchacha** girl
el **muchacho** boy
nacional national

nadie no one, nobody, (not) . . . anybody (anyone)
el **número** number
nunca never, (not) . . . ever
la **oportunidad** opportunity
la **orquesta** orchestra
pasado, -a past, last
la **película** film
el **permiso** permission
presentar to present, introduce; to give (*a performance*)
quedarse to stay, remain
el **refresco** refreshment, cold (soft) drink
el **sábado** Saturday, (on) Saturday
sin *prep.* without
típico, -a typical
tocar to play (*music*), touch
unos, -as some, a few, several

a eso de at about
avión de las cinco y media five-thirty (5:30) plane
comedor de estudiantes student dining room
dar permiso para (usar) to give permission to (use)
el sábado (los sábados) por la noche (on) Saturday night (nights)
en el aeropuerto at (in) the airport
es hora de it is time to
(ir) a casa de (María) (to go) to (Mary's)
número de baile dance number
¡qué casualidad! what a coincidence!
salir para to leave for
tener la oportunidad de + *inf.* to have the opportunity to + *verb*
tratar de + *inf.* to try to + *verb*

MAR CARIBE

OCÉANO ATLÁNTICO

Barranquilla
Cartagena •
Maracaibo
Caracas •
TRINIDAD
Puerto España

VENEZUELA

GUAYANA
Georgetown
SURINAM
Paramaribo
GUAYANA FRAN.
Cayenne

Medellín •
R. Orinoco

★ Bogotá
COLOMBIA

Cali •

Quito •
Ecuador

ECUADOR
Guayaquil •
Iquitos •
Manaus •
R. Amazonas
Belem •

CORDILLERA DE LOS ANDES

R. Madeira

B R A S I L

Recife •

PERÚ
Lima ★
Machu Picchu
Cuzco •

Arequipa •
L. Titicaca
La Paz •
BOLIVIA
Salvador •

Arica •
Iquique •
★ Sucre
Brasilia ★

Belo Horizonte •

PARAGUAY
Rio de Janeiro •

Antofagasta •
Asunción ★
São Paulo •
Santos •
Trópico de Capricornio

OCÉANO PACÍFICO

CHILE

Tucumán •
R. Paraná

Córdoba •
Pörto Alegre •

CORDILLERA DE LOS ANDES

Rosario •
URUGUAY

Valparaíso •
Mendoza •
Buenos
Aires ★
• Montevideo

Santiago •
La Plata •
Rio de la Plata

Concepción •
Bahía Blanca •

A R G E N T I N A

Puerto Montt •

Islas
Malvinas

Punta Arenas •
Estrecho de
Magallanes

Tierra del
Fuego
Cabo de
Hornos

| 0 | | 1000 mi. |
| 0 | | 1600 km. |

La América del Sur

SANDERSON

Lectura 4

La América del Sur

Otra parte muy importante del mundo hispánico es la América del Sur, o Suramérica. Como Uds. saben, Suramérica es un continente muy grande, con nueve repúblicas en que se habla español y una, el Brasil, en que se habla portugués.

El continente tiene montañas, llanuras,[1] desiertos y selvas,[2] y el clima varía según la altura. Hay tres ríos grandes en Suramérica: el Amazonas, que es el río más grande del mundo, el Orinoco, en el norte, y el sistema del Río de la Plata.

Venezuela y Colombia están en el norte del continente. Venezuela es un país muy rico en minerales. Abundan el hierro, el oro, la plata, el carbón y, sobre todo,[3] el petróleo. Caracas, la capital, es una ciudad moderna, con rascacielos y hoteles lujosos.[4]

Colombia tiene costas en el Mar Caribe[5] y también en el Océano Pacífico. La capital de Colombia es Bogotá. Además de Colombia, las repúblicas de la costa del Océano Pacífico son el Ecuador, el Perú y Chile. Las capitales de estos tres países son Quito, Lima y Santiago, respectivamente.

Como Uds. pueden ver, Chile es un país muy largo y estrecho. La exportación de cobre[6] es la base de su riqueza y de la economía del país.

Las bases de la economía del Perú son la industria minera y la industria del azúcar. Al este de Lima está la ciudad del Cuzco, la capital del antiguo imperio de los incas. Cerca del Cuzco están las ruinas de Machu Picchu, «la ciudad perdida de los incas».

La Argentina, en el sur, es un país muy rico. Por su extensión[7] es la segunda nación de Suramérica (después del Brasil). La agricultura y la ganadería[8] son las bases de la economía argentina. En las pampas, una región muy fértil, la producción de trigo,[9] maíz y lino[10] es muy grande, y se cría mucho ganado.[11] A pesar de la escasez[12] de hierro y carbón, la producción industrial también es importante. Buenos Aires, la capital, es una ciudad muy moderna, de más de nueve millones de habitantes.

El Uruguay es el país más pequeño de la América del Sur. La tierra es muy fértil. La tercera parte[13] de sus habitantes viven en la

---

[1]**llanuras**, *plains.* [2]**selvas**, *forests.* [3]**sobre todo**, *above all, especially.* [4]**lujosos**, *luxurious.* [5]**Caribe**, *Caribbean.* [6]**cobre**, *copper.* [7]**extensión**, *size.* [8]**ganadería**, *cattle (livestock) raising.* [9]**trigo**, *wheat.* [10]**lino**, *flax.* [11]**se cría mucho ganado**, *much cattle (livestock) is raised.* [12]**escasez**, *scarcity.* [13]**La tercera parte**, *One (A) third.*

capital, Montevideo. Cerca de la capital y en la costa del Río de la Plata hay hermosas playas que atraen a los turistas.

Bolivia y el Paraguay están en el interior del continente y no tienen costa. Aunque Sucre es la capital oficial de Bolivia, La Paz es la ciudad más importante de la nación y la sede[14] del gobierno. Asunción, una ciudad muy antigua, es la capital del Paraguay y es, además, el centro comercial del país.

Una gran parte de los habitantes de Colombia, el Ecuador, el Perú y Chile viven en las altas mesetas y en los valles de la Cordi-llera de los Andes. Es difícil ir de un país a otro, especialmente si uno tiene que cruzar las montañas y los ríos. Hoy día el servicio aéreo resuelve en gran parte[15] este problema.

La mayor parte de la población de la Argentina y del Uruguay es de origen europeo. En cambio, en el Ecuador, el Perú y Bolivia, hay muchos indios, especialmente en los pueblos y las ciudades de los Andes. En el Paraguay la población india es muy numerosa. En los otros países la mezcla de razas es la nota más característica de la población.

Preguntas

1. ¿Qué parte del mundo hispánico vamos a estudiar hoy? 2. ¿En cuántas repúblicas se habla español? 3. ¿Qué lengua se habla en el Brasil? 4. ¿Varía el clima del continente? 5. ¿Cuál es el río más grande del mundo? 6. ¿Dónde está el Orinoco?

7. ¿Qué países se encuentran en el norte del continente? 8. ¿Qué minerales abundan en Venezuela? 9. ¿Cuáles son las repúblicas de la costa del Océano Pacífico? 10. ¿Cuál es la capital de Colombia? 11. ¿Cuál es la capital de Chile? 12. ¿Cuál es la base de la economía de Chile?

13. ¿Cuáles son las bases de la economía del Perú? 14. ¿Cuál es la capital del Perú? 15. ¿Dónde está el Cuzco? 16. ¿Qué ruinas se encuentran cerca del Cuzco?

17. ¿Cuál es, por su extensión, la segunda nación de Suramérica? 18. ¿Cuáles son las bases de la economía argentina? 19. ¿Cuántos habitantes tiene Buenos Aires?

20. ¿Es grande o pequeño el Uruguay? 21. ¿Cuál es la capital del Uruguay? 22. ¿Qué hay cerca de la capital? 23. ¿Qué países se encuentran en el interior del continente? 24. ¿Cuáles son las capitales de Bolivia y del Paraguay?

25. ¿Dónde viven muchos de los habitantes de Colombia y de Bolivia? 26. ¿Es fácil ir de un país a otro? 27. ¿En qué países es de origen europeo la mayor parte de la población? 28. ¿En qué países hay muchos indios?

Estudio de palabras

a. Certain Spanish nouns ending in **-ia, -ía** end in *-y* in English: industria, autonomía, economía, monarquía.

b. Deceptive cognates. A number of Spanish and English words are similar in form, but quite different in meaning: largo, *long.*

---

[14]**sede,** *seat, headquarters*   [15]**en gran parte,** *largely.*

c. Many Spanish words can be recognized by comparing them with related words. *Compare:* económico, *economic, and* economía, *economy;* Europa, *Europe, and* europeo, *European;* pueblo, *town, village, and* población, *population;* rico, *rich, and* riqueza (*also* riquezas), *riches, wealth.*

d. An occasional Spanish noun, usually a compound noun which ends in **-s,** has the same form in the plural: el (los) rascacielos, *skyscraper(s).* In Lesson 18 see el (los) tocadiscos, *record player(s).*

*Caracas es una ciudad muy moderna, con altos edificios
y parques muy hermosos. Está rodeada de montañas.*

Maracaibo es otra ciudad muy importante de Venezuela. En la foto a la izquierda se ve un edificio en construcción en esta ciudad, donde la construcción de viviendas ha alcanzado un gran auge debido a la riqueza petrolera.

Debajo se ve el Capitolio Nacional en Caracas.

El Museo Nacional de Colombia está
en la ciudad de Bogotá. Tiene una de
las colecciones más importantes de arte
indio precolombino en Suramérica. En
la foto de arriba vemos algunas de las
famosas esculturas indias de San
Agustín. El museo es un bello
ejemplo de arquitectura colonial.

En la foto a la derecha, dos señores
conversan en un parque de Zipaquirá.
En la foto de abajo vemos la catedral
de Zipaquirá. Este pueblo es famoso
porque tiene también la catedral de sal,
construida dentro de una mina de sal.

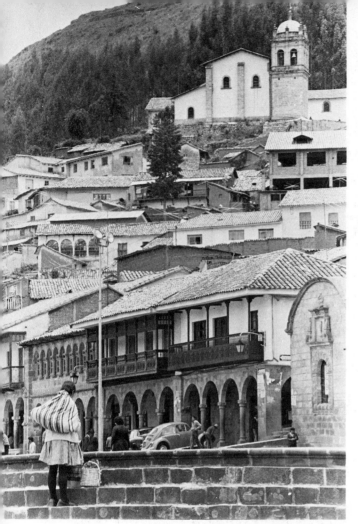

En esta página tenemos tres vistas del Perú. A la izquierda, El Cuzco, la famosa capital del imperio inca. Arriba, los Uros, que son unos indios que viven a orillas del lago Titicaca, muy conocidos por sus embarcaciones hechas de paja y por los tejidos tan bellos y coloridos que hacen. Abajo, por contraste, tenemos la moderna playa de Miraflores, que está cerca de Lima, la capital del país.

Arriba, la iglesia de la Compañía, construida por los jesuítas durante el período colonial, es una de las maravillas del barroco en Suramérica. Se encuentra en Quito, Ecuador.

Abajo se ve un mercado al aire libre de los indios Otavalo en el Ecuador.

La industria pesquera es una fuente de ingresos muy importante para Chile. En las dos fotos arriba, podemos ver un barco pesquero y a varios pescadores seleccionando el pescado.

A la izquierda se ven varias personas entrando en la catedral un domingo por la mañana, Santiago, Chile.

La zona del puerto de Buenos Aires se llama La
Boca. Buenos Aires, uno de los puertos más
activos de Suramérica, queda en el río de La
Plata. En la foto de arriba se ve un barco en el
puerto de Buenos Aires. A la derecha, una vista
de la Avenida 9 de Julio, una de las más
importantes de la ciudad.

A la izquierda vemos el monumento al patriota uruguayo José Artigas (1764–1850). Se encuentra en Montevideo, la capital del Uruguay.

En la foto de abajo tenemos una escena callejera en Asunción, la capital del Paraguay.

En esta página tenemos dos vistas de La Paz, la sede del gobierno de Bolivia. A la derecha, el monumento a Cristóbal Colón,—casi todas las capitales de la América Hispana tienen un monumento dedicado a Cristóbal Colón. También casi todas las capitales tienen un mercado al aire libre, semejante al que se encuentra en La Paz, como podemos ver en la foto de abajo.

REPASO 2

A. Say after your teacher; then repeat, changing the verb to the preterit:

1. Yo la veo. 2. Yo no le doy el dinero. 3. Tomás la lleva al baile. 4. Los muchachos van al cine. 5. Luis y Ana ven una película. 6. Después vuelven a casa. 7. Ud. se acuesta tarde, ¿verdad? 8. Ud. se levanta temprano. 9. Marta y yo salimos de casa. 10. Diana y yo damos un paseo. 11. Alguien llama a la puerta. 12. Nadie la abre. 13. ¿Buscas a alguien? 14. ¿Lo enseñas a bailar? 15. Las muchachas dejan los guantes sobre la silla. 16. ¿Baila Ud. mucho? 17. Se abren las puertas a las diez. 18. Se cierran a las cinco. 19. ¿Te despiertas tarde? 20. Yo llevo a Inés al mercado.

B. Choose from the verbs listed the correct form of the present tense to complete each sentence in the group:

1. **(dar, hacer, llevar, tomar)** *a.* Juan no _____ más que café. *b.* A menudo José _____ a Carolina a bailar. *c.* Mis padres no _____ un viaje a España. *d.* ¿ _____ Ud. un paseo con María todas las tardes? *e.* ¿Te _____ tu mamá dinero a veces?

2. **(estar, ser, tener)** *a.* Mi hermana _____ mucho frío. *b.* Esta leche no _____ fría. *c.* Ya _____ la hora. *d.* ¿ _____ mucha hambre las muchachas? *e.* Mi tía no _____ profesora. *f.* Los estudiantes _____ en el comedor. *g.* Ana y yo _____ sueño. *h.* La orquesta _____ buena. *i.* Ellas _____ cansadas. *j.* Hoy _____ el último día de la semana. *k.* Mi hermano _____ suerte. *l.* ¿Dónde _____ tu padre?

3. **(conocer, saber)** *a.* Creo que Juan _____ la lección. *b.* ¿ _____ ella la ciudad de México? *c.* Yo _____ bien al señor Valdés. *d.* ¿ _____ Uds. si Juan llega en el avión de las dos? *e.* ¿ _____ tú aquella película mexicana? *f.* Yo no _____ dónde están las muchachas.

4. **(dejar, salir)** *a.* Diana _____ sus gafas en casa. *b.* La vendedora _____ el vestido en el escaparate. *c.* ¿A qué hora _____ tú cada mañana? *d.* A veces el avión _____ tarde del aeropuerto. *e.* ¿Por qué _____ Uds. a Tomás en el parque?

C. Repeat after your teacher. When you hear a cue, substitute it and make the necessary changes in the sentence:

1. Me gusta *el vestido*. (los guantes)
2. Le gusta a Inés *la película*. (las dos orquestas)
3. No nos gustan *aquellos autobuses*. (aquel avión)
4. ¿Le gustan a Tomás *estas canciones*? (este baile)
5. Me parece bonito *este estilo*. (estos zapatos)
6. ¿Qué le parece a Ud. *aquella tienda*? (estas calles)
7. *Alguien* llamó a la puerta. (Nadie)
8. Escuchamos *unos* programas. (algunos)

D. Listen to each sentence; then change to a singular formal command:

1. Inés compra el vestido.
2. Ricardo vuelve a casa temprano.
3. Isabel se sienta en la sala.
4. Marta se pone el sombrero.
5. Carmen se levanta de la silla.
6. Enrique no da un paseo.

Change each sentence to an affirmative and negative singular familiar command:

7. Luis abre las ventanas.
8. Roberto deja su libro en la mesa.
9. María cierra la puerta.
10. Carmen se levanta de la mesa.
11. Felipe se lava las manos.
12. Diana se queda en casa.

E. Listen to each sentence; then change to an affirmative and a negative singular formal command, substituting object pronouns for the noun objects:

1. Jorge escribe la carta.
2. Marta lee las revistas.
3. Carlos mira los cuadros.
4. Tomás trae a su hermano.
5. Inés llama a su hermana.
6. Juan espera a sus amigos.
7. José cierra la ventana.
8. María escucha a su mamá.

F. Listen to each sentence; then repeat, substituting the correct object pronoun for the noun and modifiers:

1. Juan compró el coche. 2. María tomó los guantes. 3. ¿Vio Ud. a las muchachas? 4. ¿Esperó Ud. a Carolina? 5. ¿Llevó Ud. a Roberto al cine? 6. Deje Ud. los vasos aquí. 7. Cante Ud. las canciones ahora. 8. No despiertes al muchacho. 9. No traigas el dinero todavía. 10. Yo debo escuchar el programa. 11. Ella piensa comprar dos vestidos. 12. ¿Puedes dejar la revista aquí?

G. Answer each question affirmatively, following the models:

MODELS: ¿Es pequeña la casa? *Sí, es más pequeña que la otra.*
¿Son pequeñas las casas? *Sí, son más pequeñas que las otras.*

1. ¿Es hermoso el vestido?
2. ¿Es bonita la película?
3. ¿Está cansada la muchacha?
4. ¿Es interesante la idea?
5. ¿Son grandes los mercados?
6. ¿Son largas las calles?
7. ¿Son caros los relojes?
8. ¿Están fríos los refrescos?

H. Give in Spanish:

1. Are you (*pl.*) going to church tomorrow? 2. What's new? 3. What is his name? 4. Betty's sister is at (**en**) the university, isn't she? 5. Why are you (*pl.*) taking the trip by car? 6. John is leaving on the four-o'clock plane. 7. Joe went to Martha's. 8. I have only five dollars. 9. Sit down (*pl.*) here, please. 10. Please (*pl.*) arrive on time. 11. Don't try (*fam. sing.*) to call me tonight. 12. Write (*fam. sing.*) me from time to time. 13. Mr. Ortega wants to come next week. 14. I don't have time to go shopping. 15. My father gave me permission to use the car. 16. "What are you (*fam. sing.*) doing?" "Nothing special."

I. Answer in a complete Spanish sentence, using words which you have had:

1. ¿Qué lee Ud. todos los días? 2. ¿A qué hora sale Ud. de casa por la mañana? 3. ¿Le gusta a Ud. levantarse temprano? 4. ¿Se levanta Ud. a las seis? 5. ¿A qué hora se desayunó Ud. esta mañana? 6. ¿Toma Ud. un autobús todas las mañanas? 7. ¿Dónde compramos las cosas que necesitamos? 8. ¿A qué hora se cierran las tiendas aquí? 9. ¿Adónde vamos a menudo los domingos? 10. ¿Fue Ud. al cine la semana pasada? 11. ¿Dio Ud. un paseo el sábado pasado? 12. ¿Llamó Ud. a alguien por teléfono anoche?

Arcada central de la oficina de correos en Lima, Perú.

The imperfect indicative tense • **Uses of the imperfect
tense** • **Expressions with** *hacer* • **Use of the definite article with the
seasons**

LECCIÓN 11

Tema de composición

Pablo está sentado en su cuarto tratando de escribir una composición. Llega
Eduardo y le da una magnífica idea para el tema.

PABLO — ¡En buen momento llegas, Eduardo! Pasa, porque necesito tu ayuda.

EDUARDO — Pero, ¿qué hacías cuando entré?

PABLO — Trataba de comenzar una composición para mi clase de español, pero
no sé qué decir . . . ¿Quieres darme alguna idea?

EDUARDO — A ver . . . Piensa un poco en los años que pasaste en el campo.
Recuerda las cosas que hacías cuando eras pequeño.

PABLO — Sí, me parece un tema bonito. Teníamos una casa estupenda y
vivimos allí seis años . . .

◆ ◆ ◆ ◆ ◆

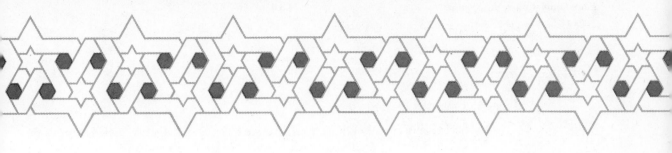

EDUARDO —¿Te gustaba vivir en el campo, Pablo?

PABLO —Me encantaba[1] la vida allí. Podíamos montar a caballo . . . Mi padre nos llevaba a veces a las montañas . . .

EDUARDO —Era especialmente agradable dar esos paseos en el verano, ¿verdad?

PABLO —Sí, cuando hacía sol, hacía mucho calor en casa.

EDUARDO —Pero en las montañas siempre hacía fresco, ¿verdad?

PABLO —Sí. Nos gustaba mucho pasearnos por los bosques bajo la sombra de árboles altos y hermosos.

EDUARDO —¿Y eran las otras estaciones tan agradables como el verano?

PABLO —En la primavera siempre hacía buen tiempo. Pero en el invierno hacía mucho frío, y entonces[2] las montañas estaban cubiertas de nieve.

◆　◆　◆　◆　◆

EDUARDO —Recuerdo que un día de otoño Uds. fueron a un sitio muy bonito en las montañas. Pero no fue un paseo muy agradable, creo . . .

PABLO —Es verdad. Salimos muy temprano y fuimos muy lejos. Cuando terminamos el almuerzo, vimos que había muchas nubes en el cielo y entonces comenzó a hacer mucho viento.

EDUARDO —¿Por qué no volvieron a casa en seguida?

PABLO —Porque mi hermano y yo insistimos en quedarnos un rato más. Pronto comenzó a llover. El agua corría por todas partes.

EDUARDO —El viaje a casa fue muy difícil, ¿verdad?

PABLO —Sí. ¡Sólo eran las cuatro y no podíamos ver el camino!

EDUARDO —Pues, mira, hombre, ya tienes muchas ideas para tu composición.

PABLO —Sí, es verdad. ¡Muchas gracias, Eduardo! ¡No sabes cuánto me gusta este tema!

EDUARDO —No hay de qué. ¡Ah! pero no va a ser fácil escribirla . . .

---

[1]**Me encantaba la vida allí,** *I loved life there* (literally, *Life there fascinated* or *charmed me*). The verb **encantar** is used like **gustar** (see page 84). [2]**Entonces** means *then* in the sense of *at that time* (*moment*). When *then* means *next, later,* **luego** is used.

Conversación

A. Preguntas sobre el diálogo

1. ¿Qué hacía Pablo cuando Eduardo entró en su cuarto? 2. ¿Dónde vivía la familia de Pablo? 3. ¿Le gustaba a Pablo vivir en el campo? 4. ¿Qué podían hacer Pablo y su hermano? 5. ¿Qué les gustaba hacer en el verano? 6. ¿En qué estación hacía siempre buen tiempo? 7. ¿Adónde fue la familia un día de otoño? 8. ¿Por qué no fue muy agradable el paseo ese día?

B. Aplicación del diálogo

1. ¿Hace buen tiempo hoy? ¿Hace frío o hace calor? 2. ¿Hace sol ahora o hay nubes en el cielo? 3. ¿Hace mal tiempo aquí en el invierno? 4. ¿Qué tiempo hace aquí en la primavera? ¿En el verano? ¿En el otoño? 5. ¿Qué estación del año le gusta a Ud. más? ¿Por qué? 6. ¿Le gustan a Ud. las montañas? ¿Por qué? 7. ¿Dónde cree Ud. que es más agradable la vida, en el campo o en la ciudad? ¿Por qué? 8. ¿Qué cosas se pueden hacer en el campo? ¿En la ciudad?

NOTAS GRAMATICALES

A. The imperfect indicative tense

1. Forms of the regular verbs:

hablar	comer	vivir
singular		
hablaba	comía	vivía
hablabas	comías	vivías
hablaba	comía	vivía
plural		
hablábamos	comíamos	vivíamos
hablabais	comíais	vivíais
hablaban	comían	vivían

The imperfect tense, **(yo) hablaba,** corresponds in English to *I was talking, used to (would) talk, talked* (habitually).

Note that **-er** and **-ir** verbs have the same endings in the imperfect tense. All forms of these two conjugations bear an accent mark, while only the first person plural of **-ar** verbs is accented. Since the first and third persons singular are identical in all verbs in the imperfect tense, the subject pronouns are used more than with other tenses.

2. Forms of the irregular verbs **ir, ser,** and **ver:**

> ir: **iba, ibas, iba, íbamos, ibais, iban**
> ser: **era, eras, era, éramos, erais, eran**
> ver: **veía, veías, veía, veíamos, veíais, veían**

Ir, ser, and **ver** are the only verbs in Spanish which have irregular forms in the imperfect tense. The meanings are: **iba,** *I was going, used to go, went;* **era,** *I used to be, was;* **veía,** *I used to see, was seeing, saw.*

B. Uses of the imperfect tense

The imperfect indicative tense, often called the past descriptive, is used to describe past actions, scenes, or conditions which were continuing for an indefinite period of time in the past. The speaker transfers himself mentally to the past and views the action or condition as taking place before him. There is no reference to the beginning or the end of the action or condition. The preterit, as we learned in Lesson 10, indicates that an action was completed or that an existing condition ended. The imperfect tense always translates English *used to* plus the infinitive, and usually *was (were)* plus the present participle. Note carefully the following examples in which the imperfect is used:

1. To express description in past time:

El agua corría por todas partes.   The water ran (was running) everywhere.
Hacía mucho calor en casa.   At home it was very warm.
Había muchas nubes en el cielo.   There were many clouds in the sky.
En los bosques siempre hacía fresco.   In the forests it was always cool.

2. To indicate repeated or habitual past action, equivalent to English *used to* or *would:*

¿Dónde vivías cuando eras pequeño?   Where did you (use to) live when you were small?
Vivíamos en el campo entonces.   We lived (used to live) in the country then.
A veces mi padre nos llevaba a sitios muy bonitos.   At times my father used to (would) take us to very pretty places.

3. To indicate that an action was in progress, or to describe what was going on when something happened (the preterit indicates what happened under the circumstances described):

¿Qué hacías cuando entré? What were you doing when I entered?
Yo estaba cansado cuando volví a casa. I was tired when I returned home.

4. To describe mental activity or a state in the past; thus, verbs meaning *to believe, know, wish, be able,* etc., are usually translated by the imperfect:

¿Sobre qué pensabas escribir la composición? On (About) what were you intending (did you intend) to write the composition?
Pablo sabía que yo quería quedarme en el parque. Paul knew that I wanted to stay in the park.

5. To express time of day in the past:

Eran las nueve cuando volvió Eduardo. It was nine o'clock when Edward returned.
¿Qué hora era? What time was it?

◆ *Práctica.* Read in Spanish, substituting the proper imperfect inflected form of each infinitive in italics. Observe carefully how the imperfect tense is used:

1. Cuando yo *ser* pequeño, mi familia *vivir* en el campo. 2. En el verano *hacer* mucho calor. 3. Generalmente *hacer* sol, y a veces *hacer* mucho viento. 4. Los domingos yo *levantarse* tarde. 5. Mis padres siempre me *llevar* a la iglesia. 6. Yo *saber* que *ser* necesario acompañarlos. 7. Después de comer, mi padre nos *llevar* en coche a las montañas, que no *estar* muy lejos. 8. Me *gustar* pasearme bajo los árboles altos. 9. Allí *hacer* fresco, y yo no *tener* mucho calor. 10. A menudo *ser* muy tarde cuando *volver* nosotros a casa.

C. Expressions with **hacer**

¿Qué tiempo hace? What kind of weather is it?
Hace buen (mal) tiempo. It is good (bad) weather.
Hace calor (frío, fresco, viento). It is warm (cold, cool, windy).
No hacía mucho calor (frío). It wasn't very warm (cold).
Hacía sol. It was sunny (The sun was shining).

Hacer is used impersonally with certain Spanish nouns to describe the temperature or weather. Since **frío, fresco, viento, calor, sol** are nouns when used with **hacer,** they are modified by the adjective **mucho,** not the adverb **muy.** (Compare the use of **tener** with certain nouns, page 119.) One also uses **Hay (Había) sol,** *The sun is (was) shining.*

Recall that **estar** is used with adjectives to express a temporary or changing condition of the subject: **El agua estaba fría,** *The water was cold.* However, one uses **ser** to express a characteristic quality: **La nieve es fría,** *The snow is cold (Snow is cold).*

Bueno and **malo** are shortened to **buen** and **mal** before masculine singular nouns; they retain their regular form otherwise: **un buen camino,** *a good road;* **dos buenos caminos,** *two good roads.*

D. Use of the definite article with the seasons

> **Me gusta la primavera (el invierno).**   I like spring (winter).
> **Es otoño (verano) ahora.**   It is fall (summer) now.

The definite article is regularly used with the seasons; however, it is usually omitted after **ser** or in a **de-**phrase: **un día de otoño,** *a fall day.* Also in daily speech it is often omitted after **en.**

EJERCICIOS

A. Substitution drill:

1. *Carmen* estudiaba en la Universidad de México.
   (*Mi primo, Nosotros, Yo, Tú, Ud.*)
2. *La familia de Pablo* tenía una casa en el campo.
   (*Mis padres, Yo, Nosotros, Tú, Uds.*)
3. *Isabel* vivía en la Argentina.
   (*Mis tíos, Tú, Carlos y Felipe, Mi hermana y yo, Yo*)
4. *Julia* iba de compras a menudo.
   (*Tú, Carmen y Julia, Yo, Nosotros, Uds.*)

B. Say after your teacher; then repeat, changing the verb to the corresponding preterit form, and finally change the verb to the imperfect:

1. Yo necesito tu ayuda.   2. Mis amigos viven en el campo.   3. Eduardo come a las seis.   4. Pablo va al centro.   5. ¿Escribes la composición?   6. ¿Espera Ud. a alguien? 7. Marta y yo no vemos a nadie.   8. Los muchachos cierran la puerta.   9. Carlos lleva a Carolina a bailar.   10. ¿Quién le da a Juan el dinero?   11. José insiste en quedarse. 12. Ana y yo montamos a caballo.

C. Read in Spanish, using the correct preterit or imperfect form of the verb in italics, as required:

1. Cuando yo *vivir* en California, *pasar* mucho tiempo en las montañas.   2. Todos los veranos mi familia *ir* a visitar varios parques nacionales.   3. Uno de los parques, que *ser*

muy hermoso, no *estar* lejos, y mi padre nos *llevar* en coche a sitios muy bonitos.   4.   En los bosques *haber* muchos árboles altos, y nosotros *poder* dar paseos muy agradables. 5.   Generalmente *hacer* fresco allí, y nos *gustar* pasearnos bajo la sombra de los árboles. 6.   El verano pasado yo *volver* a California.   7.   Un amigo y yo *querer* ver un sitio que *visitar* a menudo cuando *ser* jóvenes.   8.   *Ser* las ocho de la mañana cuando *salir* de casa. 9.   *Hacer* sol y mucho calor en la ciudad, pero en el parque *hacer* fresco.   10.   Después de comer allí, nosotros *dar* un paseo.   11.   A eso de las tres y media *sentarse* a descansar porque *estar* cansados.   12.   Pronto *ver* que *haber* muchas nubes en el cielo. 13.   Nosotros *volver* al coche, y en seguida *comenzar* a llover.   14.   No *llover* más que media hora, pero el agua *correr* por todas partes.   15.   Mi amigo y yo *salir* del parque a las cinco de la tarde y *llegar* a casa muy tarde.

D.   Complete each sentence with the correct present indicative form of **estar, hacer,** or **tener:**

1.   ¿Qué tiempo _____ hoy?   2.   _____ buen tiempo.   3.   _____ sol y yo no _____ mucho frío.   4.   Yo _____ calor y mucha sed.   5.   Yo _____ sentado aquí porque _____ muy cansado.   6.   _____ fresco bajo la sombra de este árbol.   7.   Esta agua _____ fresca.   8.   Carolina _____ sentada a la mesa porque _____ hambre. 9.   A veces _____ mucho viento en la primavera.   10.   También _____ mal tiempo, ¿verdad?   11.   A menudo yo _____ frío.   12.   Cuando _____ mucho sol, yo no _____ frío.

E.   Give the Spanish equivalent:

1.   When we were young, we used to live in the country.   2.   Our house was near the mountains, and our father often took us to some beautiful places.   3.   When it was warm at home in summer, it was always cool in the mountains.   4.   We liked to stroll through the forest because it was very pleasant there.   5.   Generally we ate under the shade of the beautiful trees in **(de)** the parks.   6.   We would not go to the mountains in the winter if the forest was covered with snow.   7.   I recall that one spring day my father took us to a park which was near our house.   8.   It was cool, but the sun was shining; really it was a beautiful day.   9.   Upon arriving at the park, we ate lunch and rested a while under a very tall tree.   10.   Then my brother and I went to take a walk with some friends.   Soon we saw that there were many clouds in the sky.   11.   We returned to the car, and at once it began to rain.   12.   It was six o'clock when we arrived home, and we were very tired.

F.   **Composición:**[1] Mis años en el campo

Write a short composition, using the questions as a guideline:

¿Vivía Ud. en el campo cuando era pequeño (pequeña)?
¿Estaba su casa cerca de las montañas? ¿Cerca de un parque nacional?

---

[1]The teacher who desires more personalized and original involvement of the student may assign the composition as an alternate of Exercise E, or assign it in addition to that exercise.

¿Lo (La) llevaba su padre a menudo a sitios bonitos?
¿Qué tiempo hacía en las montañas en el verano?
¿Qué le gustaba a Ud. hacer en los bosques? ¿Pasearse? ¿Comer bajo los árboles?
¿Adónde fue Ud. un día? ¿Cómo fue el paseo?

EJERCICIOS DE PRONUNCIACIÓN

A. The sounds of **c, qu,** and **k**

1. As we learned in Lesson 2, the sound of Spanish **c** before all letters except **e** and **i,** and of **qu** (also Spanish **k**), is similar to English *k*, but there is no aspiration. To avoid the aspiration, or puff of air, that follows the English sound (as in *c*[h]*at*), you must hold back your breath during the articulation of the Spanish sound. Remember, also, that the **u** in **que, qui** is never sounded as in English *quite:*

caballo	camino	cómodo	escuela	cuaderno
bosque	porque	quiero	orquesta	quedarse

2. Now watch the sound of Spanish **c** before **e** and **i** (and of **z**) as you pronounce these words:

entonces	estación	composición	precio	canción
cielo	parecer	ciudad	lápiz	almuerzo

B. The sound of **p**

Spanish **p** is similar to English *p*, but the explosion is weaker, and again there is no aspiration (as in *p*[h]*ast*):

Pablo	tiempo	primavera	película	pienso

Vista del volcán Cayambe–Urcu, uno de los puntos más altos de la Cordillera de los Andes. Se encuentra cerca de Quito, Ecuador.

VOCABULARIO

el **agua** (*f.*)[1] water
alto, -a tall, high
el **año** year
el **árbol** tree
la **ayuda** aid, help
bajo *prep.* under, beneath, below
el **bosque** woods, forest
el **caballo** horse
el **camino** road, way
el **cielo** sky
comenzar (ie) (a + *inf.*) to begin (to), commence (to)
la **composición** (*pl.* **composiciones**) composition, theme
correr to run
cubierto, -a (de) covered (with)
Eduardo Edward
encantar to enchant, delight, fascinate
entonces then, at that time (moment)
la **estación** (*pl.* **estaciones**) season
el **fresco** coolness
gustar más to like better (more, most), prefer

había there was, there were
insistir (**en** + *obj.*) to insist (on)
el **invierno** winter
lejos *adv.* far, distant
llover (ue) to rain
mal(o), -a bad
la **montaña** mountain
montar to mount, ride
la **nieve** snow
la **nube** cloud
el **otoño** fall, autumn
Pablo Paul
pasearse to walk, stroll
el **paseo** outing, excursion
la **primavera** spring
recordar (ue) to recall, remember
el **sitio** site, place
el **sol** sun
la **sombra** shade, shadow
el **tema** theme, topic, subject
el **tiempo** weather
el **verano** summer
el **viento** wind

día (de otoño) (fall) day
¡en buen momento llegas! you arrive just at the right time (moment)!
en seguida at once, immediately
montar a caballo to ride horseback
pasa, (Eduardo) come in, (Edward)
por todas partes everywhere
un rato más a while longer

---

[1]See page 119 for explanation of the use of the definite article **el** with certain feminine nouns.

Viñetas Culturales
UNA OJEADA AL MUNDO HISPÁNICO

España CIUDADES Y PAISAJES

En la página anterior: La iglesia inacabada de La Sagrada Familia, en Barcelona, la obra maestra del arquitecto catalán Antonio Gaudí (1852–1926). Los motivos de decoración naturalistas y las formas sinuosas son elementos típicos de su estilo.

A la izquierda: Otra obra de Gaudí es el Parque Güell, en la misma ciudad. Lleva el nombre de un rico industrial español, protector de las artes y de las letras.

Abajo: Vista de las Ramblas, en Barcelona. Se da este nombre a una serie de hermosas avenidas, con árboles, que atraviesan la ciudad. Barcelona es el puerto más importante de España, con industria y comercio muy activos.

Arriba: Vista, desde el Río Tormes, de la ciudad de Salamanca. Su famosa universidad, fundada en el siglo XIII, llegó en el siglo XVI a un período de gran esplendor, atrayendo miles de estudiantes de toda Europa.

Abajo: Vista parcial de las Murallas de Ávila, ciudad situada en la meseta castellana, al norte de Madrid. Su conservación es tan perfecta que se consideran como la más completa construcción militar de la Edad Media en Europa.

A la izquierda: El Palacio Real, Madrid. Construido durante el siglo XVIII, de estilo neoclásico, compite en extensión y magnificencia con los mejores de Europa. De interés especial, por la riqueza de sus muebles y adornos, son el Salón del Trono, el gran comedor de gala y la Capilla Real.

Abajo: Extensos olivares, como éste, son frecuentes en el paisaje andaluz. En la producción de aceite de oliva, España es la primera nación del mundo y este producto nunca puede faltar de la cocina española.

A la derecha: Interior de la Mezquita de Córdoba, el monumento más grandioso del arte del Califato de Córdoba. Su construcción comenzó en el siglo VIII y por el aumento de la población de la ciudad se amplió varias veces. Se hizo la última ampliación en el período de apogeo del Califato en el siglo X. El arco de herradura y la superposición de arcos que se ven en la Mezquita son elementos del arte árabe que los españoles llevaron a América.

Abajo: Exterior de la Mezquita. En primer término, el Patio de los Naranjos, y, en el centro, la catedral cristiana, construida durante los siglos XVI y XVII.

Hispanoamérica
PUEBLOS Y COSTUMBRES

A la izquierda: Pintura mural en uno de los edificios de la Universidad Nacional de México. Fundada en 1551, se trasladó a sus nuevos locales en la Ciudad Universitaria en 1954. Muchos de los edificios están decorados con mosaicos y pinturas murales que representan aspectos de la historia y cultura de México. La universidad es una de las más grandes del mundo, con más de cien mil estudiantes.

Abajo: Plaza y edificios modernos en una de las avenidas principales de la ciudad de México. La ciudad es el centro de las actividades económicas y culturales de la República. Tiene más de once millones de habitantes.

A la derecha: Plantación de una especie de maguey, a orillas del lago de Chapala. Del jugo del maguey se destila la tequila, una de las bebidas alcohólicas más populares entre los mexicanos. Situado al sudeste de Guadalajara, entre los estados de Jalisco y Michoacán, el lago de Chapala es el más grande de México. Es un hermoso centro turístico.

Abajo: Vista general de Taxco, pintoresca población del estado de Guerrero, al sur de la ciudad de México. Taxco es famosa por la belleza de los objetos de plata que se fabrican en sus numerosos talleres. Como ya hemos indicado, México es la primera nación del mundo en la producción de plata.

En la página anterior, arriba: Trabajadores cortando y acarreando caña de azúcar en Costa Rica. El país es básicamente agrícola y entre los cultivos sobresalen el café, el plátano y la caña de azúcar.

Abajo: Una iglesia en San José, capital de Costa Rica. La ciudad tiene unos 200,000 habitantes. La población de Costa Rica es casi totalmente de origen español.

En esta página, arriba: Mujeres indias caminan hacia Antigua Guatemala, capital de la región hasta su destrucción por los terremotos de 1773. Las ruinas de la ciudad dan testimonio de la importancia que había alcanzado. En el fondo, uno de los muchos volcanes que existen en la región.

A la derecha: Estelas que se encuentran entre las ruinas de la ciudad maya de Copán, en la parte occidental de Honduras. Antes de la llegada de los españoles, la ciudad era un importante centro de la cultura maya.

A la derecha: Mercado de artesanos en Cartagena, Colombia. Los artesanos son trabajadores que ejercitan su oficio por su cuenta, solo o con algún amigo o miembro de su familia. Cartagena es un puerto importante en la costa del Mar Caribe. Vista parcial de Bogotá, capital de Colombia, desde una de las carreteras modernas que conducen a la ciudad. Gracias a su riqueza agrícola y minera, Colombia es una de las naciones más prósperas de Suramérica. En el fondo, en lo alto de la montaña, se ve el Santuario de Monserrat, visitado los domingos por miles de bogotanos.

En la página siguiente, arriba: un grupo de jóvenes disfruta de un descanso en un parque de Zipaquirá, centro agrícola y minero a 35 millas de Bogotá. Debajo de esta población se halla una de las maravillas de Suramérica: la inmensa catedral de Zipaquirá, situada en una mina de sal, a media milla de la superficie.

Abajo: Iglesia y restaurante al aire libre en Caracas, capital de Venezuela. La ciudad es una de las más hermosas y prósperas de Suramérica, con avenidas anchas, rascacielos y hoteles lujosos.

Arriba: Paisaje en la Sierra peruana. El Perú se divide en tres regiones naturales, que se extienden de norte a sur en tres fajas paralelas: la Costa, al oeste; la Montaña o Selva, en la parte oriental, y, en medio de las dos, la Sierra, un altiplano dividido por valles profundos y dominado por los Andes. *A la izquierda:* Vista parcial de Machu Picchu, "la ciudad perdida de los incas," descubierta en 1912. Está situada en la cordillera de los Andes, a unos ciento diez kilómetros al noroeste del Cuzco. El imperio de los incas, establecido en el siglo XII, se extendía desde el sur de Colombia hasta el norte de Chile y la Argentina.

A la derecha: Frutas y cestas en un mercado de La Paz, capital de Bolivia. Situada en el Altiplano, entre dos ramales de los Andes, a 3600 metros de altitud, La Paz es la capital más alta del mundo.

Abajo: Mercado al aire libre delante de una iglesia en el Cuzco, en el sur del Perú. El Cuzco era la capital del imperio de los incas cuando se produjo la conquista española. Junto con restos de la cultura indígena, conserva edificios de la época colonial española.

Arriba: Vista aérea de Asunción, capital de la República del Paraguay. Situada a orillas del río del mismo nombre, es un puerto y centro comercial activo. Tiene medio millón de habitantes. La agricultura y la ganadería son las principales fuentes de riqueza del Paraguay. La industria está poco desarrollada. Una gran parte de los paraguayos son mestizos y la población india es muy numerosa. La lengua india de la región, el guaraní, es de uso frecuente en todo el país.

A la izquierda: Parque en Santiago, capital de la República de Chile. Fundada en 1541, la ciudad ha sido destruida varias veces por los terremotos. Santiago, que tiene más de dos millones de habitantes, es el centro de la vida comercial y cultural del país. Al lado de partes modernas, con avenidas anchas y parques hermosos, tiene barrios antiguos con edificios que datan de la época colonial.

A la derecha: Vista parcial de Montevideo, capital de la República del Uruguay. Situada a la entrada del río de la Plata, es el centro comercial e industrial del país. Tiene más de un millón de habitantes. Al lado de edificios antiguos, como el Cabildo, tiene construcciones modernas y hermosos parques. Por su excelente puerto es una de las ciudades más importantes de la América del Sur.

Debajo: Buenos Aires, a la luz de la luna. Además de ser un centro comercial de gran importancia, Buenos Aires es una de las ciudades más bellas del mundo, con grandes avenidas, hermosas plazas y numerosos rascacielos y construcciones modernas. Tiene más de nueve millones de habitantes.

Vista de las cataratas del Iguazú. Al desembocar en el río Paraná, el Iguazú, que constituye la frontera entre la Argentina y el Brasil, forma una de las cascadas más notables del mundo. El agua cae desde una altura de 70 metros. (La catarata del Niágara tiene 47 metros de altura.)

VIÑETAS CULTURALES
Aplicación

In addition to presenting a kaleidoscope of information about the Hispanic world, the preceding illustrated section is also intended to serve as a topical basis for oral and written composition. Assignments may be made at several points during the course of instruction. In each instance, students should include in their presentation the structures and the vocabulary learned so far. It might also be useful and productive to assign the same topic more than once to permit additional development and expansion of a previously completed composition. Some students may wish to use an English-Spanish dictionary in preparing the compositions.

Prácticas orales

Groups of students will be asked to prepare a conversation of 6 to 8 exchanges, using vocabulary already given, on one of the following topics:

1. Aspectos de la ciudad de Barcelona que atraen al turista.
2. Ávila y Salamanca como ciudades de interés histórico.
3. Restos de la dominación árabe en Andalucía.

Ejercicios escritos

Students will be asked to write a brief essay in Spanish (120-150 words) on one of the following topics:

1. Restos de civilizaciones precolombinas en la América Central y en el Perú.
2. La riqueza agrícola y minera de Hispanoamérica.
3. Algunas ciudades de la América del Sur que me gustaría visitar.

Hablan de algunas[1] fiestas y aniversarios

Terry, norteamericana, y Elena, colombiana, son compañeras de cuarto.[2] Terry se sienta a escribir una carta.

TERRY —Elena, ¿cuál es la fecha de hoy? Es el primero de octubre, ¿verdad?

ELENA —No, Terry, hoy es martes, tres de octubre . . . Y a propósito, la semana que viene se celebra en Hispanoamérica la fiesta del doce de octubre.

TERRY —También en los Estados Unidos nosotros celebramos el aniversario del día en que Cristóbal Colón descubrió el Nuevo[3] Mundo, en mil cuatrocientos noventa y dos . . .

ELENA —Creo que aquí se llama ese aniversario el Día de Colón, ¿verdad?

Columbus primus inuentor Indiæ Occidentalis.

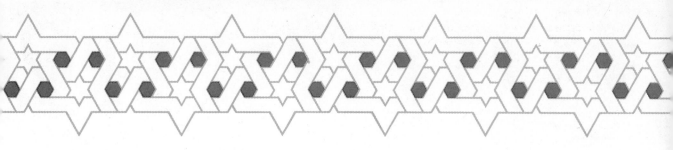

TERRY —Sí. Y como Colón era italiano, esa fecha se celebra aquí en las ciudades grandes, especialmente donde viven miles de habitantes de ese origen.

ELENA —¡Qué interesante! En nuestros países lo llamamos el Día de la Hispanidad[4] o el Día de la Raza.

TERRY —¡Claro! Así se celebra la contribución española al Nuevo Mundo. Como España trajo a las nuevas tierras su lengua, su religión, su cultura . . .

ELENA —Y hoy día algunas de las ciudades más importantes del mundo, como México[5] y Buenos Aires, se hallan en las tierras que Colón descubrió.

TERRY —¿Qué otras fiestas y aniversarios celebran los hispanoamericanos?

ELENA —Pues, las fiestas nacionales más importantes, como aquí. Por ejemplo, cada país celebra el día de su independencia.

TERRY —Ah, sí . . . Corresponde a nuestra fiesta nacional del cuatro de julio. En México es el dieciséis de septiembre, ¿verdad?

ELENA —Sí, Terry, y en el Perú es el veintiocho de julio y en la Argentina, el nueve de julio . . .

TERRY —En los Estados Unidos nosotros también celebramos el nacimiento de dos de nuestros presidentes famosos.

ELENA —Ya sé; el doce de febrero Uds. celebran el nacimiento de Lincoln, y el tercer lunes de ese mes, el nacimiento de Washington.

TERRY —¿Cuáles son algunas de las fiestas religiosas más importantes?

ELENA —Pues, en México la fiesta de Nuestra Señora de Guadalupe,[6] el día doce de diciembre, es una fiesta nacional.

TERRY —Nosotros tenemos algunas fiestas más o menos religiosas, como el Día de San Patricio,[7] el Día de San Valentín[8] . . .

ELENA —¡Ah . . . ! Y me parece tan interesante el origen de la fiesta que Uds. celebran el último jueves de noviembre, el Día de Acción de Gracias.[9]

---

[1]When two or more nouns refer to things and are in the plural, the adjective is plural and may agree with the nearest noun. [2]**compañeras de cuarto,** *roommates* (f.). The masculine for *roommate* is **compañero de cuarto.** [3]Before a noun **nuevo, -a,** means *new* in the sense of *another, different, other* (pl.), and after a noun *new, brand-new.* **Nuevo Mundo** is used for *New World* and **nuevas tierras** (see line 7, page 163), for *new lands.* [4]The **Día de la Hispanidad,** *Day of Spanish Solidarity* or *Union* (of Spain with the Americas), until recently was called the **Día de la Raza,** *Day of the Race.* [5]Even though **México** is used for the country as well as its capital, **la ciudad de México** is also used for *Mexico City.* [6]**Nuestra Señora de Guadalupe,** *Our Lady of Guadalupe,* patron saint of Mexico. [7]**Día de San Patricio,** *St. Patrick's Day.* [8]**Día de San Valentín,** *St. Valentine's Day.* [9]**Día de Acción de Gracias,** *Thanksgiving Day.*

Conversación

A. Preguntas sobre el diálogo

1. ¿Qué aniversario celebramos el doce de octubre?   2. ¿Cómo se llama ese aniversario en los Estados Unidos?   3. En los Estados Unidos, ¿dónde se celebra esa fecha especialmente? ¿Por qué?   4. ¿Por qué se llama esa fiesta en Hispanoamérica el Día de la Hispanidad o el Día de la Raza?   5. ¿Qué trajo España a las nuevas tierras?   6. ¿Qué otras fiestas celebran en Hispanoamérica?   7. ¿En qué fecha se celebra la fiesta nacional norteamericana?   8. ¿En qué fecha se celebra la fiesta nacional en la Argentina? ¿Y en México?   9. ¿Qué fiestas nacionales se celebran en los Estados Unidos durante el mes de febrero?   10. ¿Qué fiesta religiosa típica se celebra en México? ¿Y en los Estados Unidos?

B. Aplicación del diálogo

1. ¿Cuál es la fecha de hoy?   2. ¿Qué días de la semana viene Ud. a clases?   3. ¿Qué día de la semana fue ayer?   4. ¿Cuándo celebra Ud. el aniversario de su nacimiento?   5. ¿En qué fecha se celebra la fiesta de San Patricio?   6. ¿Qué fiesta o aniversario le gusta a Ud. más? ¿Por qué?   7. ¿Sabe Ud. cuántos habitantes tiene la ciudad de Nueva York? ¿La ciudad de Buenos Aires? ¿La ciudad de México?   8. ¿Cuántos estudiantes hay en esta universidad? ¿Y en esta clase?

NOTAS GRAMATICALES

A. Irregular preterit of **traer**

	singular	*plural*
	traje	trajimos
	trajiste	trajisteis
	trajo	trajeron

Note that in the first and third persons singular the stress falls on the stem, instead of on the ending; therefore, final **-e** and **-o** are not accented. Observe the spelling of **trajeron**. The English equivalent of **traje** is *I brought, did bring*.

B. Cardinal numerals

100	**cien(to)**		700	**setecientos, -as**
102	**ciento dos**		800	**ochocientos, -as**
200	**doscientos, -as**		900	**novecientos, -as**
300	**trescientos, -as**		1.000	**mil**
400	**cuatrocientos, -as**		2.000	**dos mil**
500	**quinientos, -as**		100.000	**cien mil**
600	**seiscientos, -as**		1.000.000	**un millón (de)**

cien (mil) casas   one hundred (one thousand) houses
cien mil estudiantes   a (one) hundred thousand students
ciento treinta y un días   one hundred thirty-one days
quinientas treinta y una muchachas   five hundred thirty-one girls
un millón de habitantes   a (one) million inhabitants
dos millones de hombres   two million men

Ciento becomes **cien** before nouns and the numerals **mil** and **millones,** but the full form is retained before numerals under a hundred.

Un is omitted before **cien(to)** and **mil,** but is used before **millón.** If a noun follows **millón** (*pl.* **millones**), **de** is used before the noun. Recall that **uno** and numerals ending in **uno** drop **-o** before masculine nouns, and that **una** is used before feminine nouns.

The plural **miles** means *thousands, many:* **miles de habitantes,** *thousands of (many) inhabitants.*

Numerals in the hundreds, such as **doscientos,** end in **-as** when used with feminine nouns.

In Spanish **y** is normally used only between the tens and units: **treinta y seis, cincuenta y ocho,** but **doscientos cinco.**

C. Ordinal numerals

1st	**primero, -a**	5th	**quinto, -a**	8th	**octavo, -a**
2nd	**segundo, -a**	6th	**sexto, -a**	9th	**noveno, -a**
3rd	**tercero, -a**	7th	**séptimo, -a**	10th	**décimo, -a**
4th	**cuarto, -a**				

la tercera frase   the third sentence
las primeras canciones   the first songs
el primer (tercer) viaje   the first (third) trip

The ordinal numerals agree in gender and number with the nouns they modify. **Primero** and **tercero** drop final **-o** before a masculine singular noun (third example); otherwise their regular forms are used.

Ordinal numerals are normally used only through *tenth;* beyond *tenth* the cardinal numerals replace the ordinals and they follow the noun: **Carlos Quinto,** *Charles V* (*Charles the Fifth*); **Alfonso Trece,** *Alfonso XIII* (*the Thirteenth*).

D. Days of the week

el domingo	(on) Sunday	**el jueves**	(on) Thursday
el lunes	(on) Monday	**el viernes**	(on) Friday
el martes	(on) Tuesday	**el sábado**	(on) Saturday
el miércoles	(on) Wednesday		

Hasta el lunes. Until Monday.
No tenemos clases los sábados. We have no classes on Saturdays.
Carolina, ¿qué hace Ud. los domingos? Caroline, what do you do on Sundays?
Hoy es viernes. Today is Friday.

The definite article is used with the days of the week, except after **ser.** The article also translates English *on.* The days of the week are not capitalized in Spanish and they have the same form for the singular and plural, except for **los sábados** and **los domingos.** (Spanish words of more than one syllable which end in unaccented **-es** and **-is** have the same form for the singular and plural.)

E. The months

enero	January	**mayo**	May	**septiembre**	September
febrero	February	**junio**	June	**octubre**	October
marzo	March	**julio**	July	**noviembre**	November
abril	April	**agosto**	August	**diciembre**	December

The months are not capitalized, except at the beginning of a sentence. They are masculine and do not require the definite article unless modified. (See section E, page 132.)

Memorize this jingle. You probably know the English version:

> **Treinta días tiene noviembre,**
> **con abril, junio y septiembre;**
> **veintiocho o veintinueve, uno;**
> **y los demás** (*the rest*) **treinta y uno.**

F. Dates

¿Cuál es la fecha (de hoy)?
¿Qué fecha es (hoy)? } What is the date (today)?

(Hoy) es el dos de diciembre.   (Today) is the second of December.
Ayer fue el primero de enero.   Yesterday was the first of January.
Yo salí el treinta y uno de mayo.   I left the thirty-first of May (May 31).

The cardinal numerals are used to express the day of the month, except for **el primero,** *the first.* The definite article **el** means *the, on the,* with the day of the month.

In counting and reading dates, use **mil** with numerals of one thousand or more: **el diez de abril de mil novecientos setenta y ocho,** *April 10, 1978.*

Also commonly used are:

¿A cuántos estamos (hoy)?   What is the date (today)?
Estamos a ocho de noviembre.   (Today) is the eighth of November.

G. The articles with nouns in apposition

Madrid, capital de España, . . .   Madrid, the capital of Spain, . . .
Hoy es martes, tres de octubre de 1978.   Today is Tuesday, October 3 (the third of October), 1978.

The definite article is usually omitted before a noun (or a numeral expressing the day of the month) in apposition if it is explanatory of a preceding noun. The use of the definite article, however, implies that the fact is well known: **Lima, la capital del Perú, . . .** *Lima, the capital of Peru, . . .*

The indefinite article with nouns in apposition usually follows the same rule as that for unmodified predicate nouns (see page 25):

Elena, colombiana, . . .   Helen, a Colombian, . . .

EJERCICIOS

A. Substitution drill:

1. *Mis padres* trajeron cosas importantes.
   (*Elena, Carlos y yo, Ud., Tú, Yo*)
2. *Los estudiantes* celebraron el cuatro de julio.
   (*Yo, Tú, Roberto, Elena y yo, Uds.*)
3. *Mi hermana* se sentó a escribir.
   (*Luis y yo, Yo, Tú, Ud., Los muchachos*)

B. Say after your teacher; then repeat, changing the verb to the imperfect tense:

1. Yo doy un paseo todos los días.
2. A menudo celebramos las fiestas religiosas.
3. Siempre les traigo algo a los muchachos.
4. Mi familia va a la iglesia todos los domingos.
5. Es un día muy hermoso.
6. Los estudiantes salen para sus casas.
7. Me acuesto tarde los viernes y los sábados.
8. Me gusta montar a caballo cuando tengo tiempo.
9. Generalmente la veo durante el verano.
10. Hace mucho fresco en las montañas.

C. Review the uses of the preterit and imperfect tenses in Lessons 10 and 11; then use the correct form of the infinitive in italics:

1. Ayer *ser* las tres de la tarde cuando yo *salir* de casa.   2. *Hacer* calor, pero *ser* un día hermoso.   3. Como yo *necesitar* comprar algunas cosas, *tomar* un autobús que me *llevar* al centro.   4. Cuando yo *entrar* en la tienda, todas las vendedoras *estar* ocupadas. 5. Después de un rato, una vendedora me *enseñar* varios vestidos.   6. Yo *comprar* uno que no *ser* muy caro.   7. Luego yo *ir* a otra tienda, pero *volver* a casa sin comprar nada más.   8. Al volver a mi cuarto, yo *tomar* algo frío y *sentarse* a descansar un poco.   9. Yo *estar* bastante cansado y *tener* mucha sed.   10. Entonces *llegar* mi compañero de cuarto y en seguida nosotros *ir* a cenar.

D. Read in Spanish:

1. 35 lápices.   2. 51 libros.   3. 41 bibliotecas.   4. 1.000 árboles.   5. 500 canciones. 6. 100 autobuses.   7. 100 películas.   8. 110 muchachas.   9. 2.000 estudiantes. 10. 750 caballos.   11. 365 días.   12. 1.000.000 dólares.   13. 10.000.000 de habitantes.   14. 500.000 teléfonos.   15. 41 cuadros.   16. 77 iglesias.   17. 444 palabras. 18. 201 años.   19. 121 semanas.   20. 666 jóvenes.   21. 711 muchachos.   22. 114 aviones.   23. 950 coches.   24. 21 países.   25. 888 hombres.

E. Give these dates in Spanish:

MODEL: January 2, 1979   *el dos de enero de mil novecientos setenta y nueve*

1. February 22, 1732
2. February 12, 1809
3. January 1, 1979
4. December 7, 1941
5. July 4, 1776
6. May 14, 1607
7. September 16, 1810
8. November 11, 1918
9. October 12, 1492
10. August 20, 1212
11. March 31, 1971
12. June 29, 1903

F. Answer each question in Spanish, using in your reply the next higher ordinal or cardinal numeral, as required:

MODELS: ¿Mira Ud. el primer cuadro?   *No, yo miro el segundo cuadro.*
          ¿Volvió Ud. el cinco de diciembre?   *No, yo volví el seis de diciembre.*

1. ¿Vive Juan en la cuarta casa?
2. ¿Prepara Ud. la primera lección?
3. ¿Hacen ellos el segundo viaje?
4. ¿Vas a leer la sexta frase?
5. ¿Tomó Ud. el primer autobús?
6. ¿Bailaron Uds. el tercer baile?

7. ¿Aprendieron Uds. la novena parte?
8. ¿Leía Ud. sobre Felipe Segundo?
9. ¿Estudiaba él la Lección once?
10. ¿Saliste el primero de noviembre?
11. ¿Salió Ana el diez de mayo?
12. ¿Tiene enero treinta días?

G. Give the Spanish equivalent:

1. Terry, an American, and Helen, a Colombian, who are roommates, talk about holidays and anniversaries. 2. It is Tuesday, October 3 (the third of October), and they know that the following week the holiday of October 12 is celebrated in Spanish America. 3. Christopher Columbus discovered the New World on that date in 1492. 4. Columbus Day is also celebrated in many parts of the United States. 5. Thousands of inhabitants of Italian origin live in many of our large cities. 6. Some of the most important cities in the world are found in the Spanish American countries. 7. In those countries holidays and anniversaries are celebrated, as in the United States. 8. For example, in each country the day of its independence from Spain is celebrated. 9. In Mexico the sixteenth of September corresponds to our national holiday of the Fourth of July. 10. In the United States we celebrate the birth of two famous presidents in February. 11. Besides, Thanksgiving Day is celebrated the last Thursday of November. 12. In the Spanish American countries there are religious festivals; for example, the festival of Our Lady of Guadalupe.

H. **Composición:** Un viaje a Nueva York

Assume that you spent Thanksgiving with your roommate's family in New York. By using the correct word order and the correct tense and form of each verb, you will end with a short composition:

1. el mes pasado / el Día de Acción de Gracias / nosotros celebrar / una fiesta norteamericana típica
2. mi compañero de cuarto / a visitar / a su familia / invitarme
3. el miércoles / después de clases / nosotros salir / en avión
4. en Nueva York / cinco días maravillosos / nosotros pasar
5. Nueva York ser / muy grande / una ciudad
6. tener más de / hoy día / doce millones de habitantes
7. ser / a esa ciudad / mi tercer viaje / y no conocerla bien / todavía
8. muchos sitios interesantes / tener / y / muchas cosas bonitas
9. hacer buen tiempo; / y no hacer mucho frío / todavía ser otoño
10. nosotros quedarse / el jueves / en casa / porque ser el Día de Acción de Gracias
11. los padres / ser muy agradables; / de mi compañero de cuarto / visitarlos / gustarme mucho
12. el domingo por la noche / a nuestra residencia / nosotros volver / y ahora / para los exámenes / tener que estudiar

EJERCICIOS DE PRONUNCIACIÓN

A. The diphthongs **ai (ay)** and **oi (oy)**

Ai (ay) is pronounced like a prolonged English *i* in *mine;* **oi (oy)** like a prolonged English *oy* in *boy:*

1. preparáis habláis hay
 estudiáis habla inglés ella y nosotros
2. hoy soy sois
 hablo inglés español o inglés blanco y negro

B. The diphthongs **ua** and **au**

As the first element of a diphthong, unstressed **u** is pronounced like *w* in *wet*. Spanish **au** is pronounced like a prolonged English *ou* in *out:*

1. cuaderno cuadro ¿cuánto? cuatro
 Juan su amiga su alumno su almuerzo
2. autobús la universidad la usamos abra usted
 ponga usted traiga usted venga usted vuelva usted

La basílica de Nuestra Señora de Guadalupe es uno de los santuarios más importantes de la América Hispana. Se construyó en el siglo XVI en el lugar donde, según la tradición, se apareció la Virgen a un indio llamado Juan Diego.

VOCABULARIO

el **aniversario** anniversary
así so, thus, that way
celebrar to celebrate
colombiano, -a Colombian
Colón Columbus
la **compañera** companion (*f.*)
la **contribución** (*pl.* **contribuciones**) contribution
corresponder to correspond
Cristóbal Christopher
la **cultura** culture
descubrir to discover
el **ejemplo** example
Elena Helen, Ellen
famoso, -a famous
la **fecha** date
la **fiesta** fiesta, festival, holiday, feast

el **habitante** inhabitant
la **Hispanidad** Spanish Solidarity (Union)
Hispanoamérica Spanish America
hispanoamericano, -a (*also noun*) Spanish American
importante important
la **independencia** independence
italiano, -a Italian
mil a (one) thousand
el **mundo** world
el **nacimiento** birth
el **origen** (*pl.* **orígenes**) origin
el **presidente** president
la **raza** race
la **religión** religion
religioso, -a religious
la **tierra** land

a propósito by the way
compañero (compañera) de cuarto roommate
Día de Acción de Gracias Thanksgiving Day
Día de Colón Columbus Day
Día de San Patricio St. Patrick's Day
Día de San Valentín St. Valentine's Day
Nuestra Señora de Guadalupe Our Lady of Guadalupe
Nuevo Mundo New World
por ejemplo for example, for instance

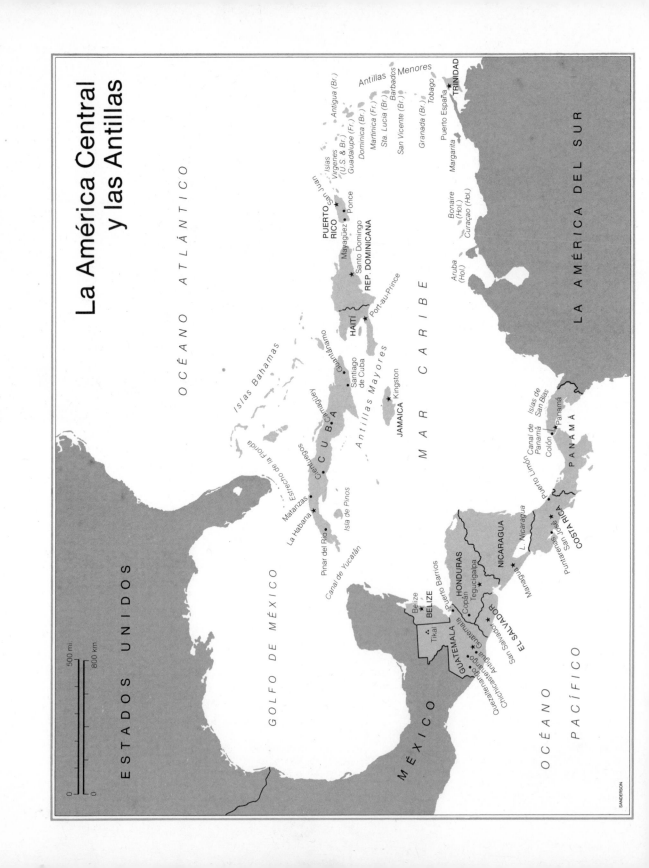

La América Central
y las Antillas

ESTADOS UNIDOS

OCÉANO ATLÁNTICO

Islas Bahamas

Estrecho de la Florida

GOLFO DE MÉXICO

500 mi.

800 km

Pinar del Río

La Habana

Matanzas

Cienfuegos

CUBA

Camagüey

Isla de Pinos

Canal de Yucatán

Santiago de Cuba

Guantánamo

Antillas Mayores

JAMAICA

Kingston

MAR CARIBE

HAITÍ

Port-au-Prince

REP. DOMINICANA

Santo Domingo

Mayagüez Ponce

San Juan

PUERTO RICO

Islas Vírgenes (U.S. & Br.)

Guadalupe (Fr.)

Dominica (Br.)

Martinica (Fr.)

Sta. Lucia (Br.)

San Vicente (Br.)

Granada (Br.)

Antigua (Br.)

Antillas Menores

Barbados

Tobago

TRINIDAD

Puerto España

Margarita

Bonaire (Hol.)

Curaçao (Hol.)

Aruba (Hol.)

LA AMÉRICA DEL SUR

Islas de San Blas

Canal de Panamá

Colón

Panamá

PANAMÁ

Puerto Limón

San José

COSTA RICA

Puntarenas

L. Nicaragua

Managua

NICARAGUA

L. Nicaragua

Tegucigalpa

HONDURAS

Copán

Puerto Barrios

Belize

BELIZE

Tikal

GUATEMALA

Guatemala

Quetzaltenango

Chichicastenango

Antigua

San Salvador

EL SALVADOR

MÉXICO

OCÉANO PACÍFICO

SANDERSON

Lectura 5

Puerto Rico

La isla de Puerto Rico es la más pequeña y la más oriental de las Antillas Mayores.[1] De forma casi rectangular, tiene unas cien millas de largo[2] por treinta y cinco de ancho.[3] Cruzada de este a oeste por la Cordillera Central, la isla está cubierta de montañas de poca altura.

Cristóbal Colón desembarcó en la isla en 1493 en su segundo viaje al Nuevo Mundo. Uno de sus compañeros, Juan Ponce de León (que después buscó la Fuente de la Juventud en la Florida), regresó[4] a la isla en 1508 y al año siguiente fue nombrado su primer gobernador.

A causa de su posición estratégica, los españoles convirtieron[5] la isla en una fortaleza para proteger las rutas marítimas del Caribe. «El Morro», a la entrada del puerto de San Juan, y «La Fortaleza», la residencia de los gobernadores de Puerto Rico, representan este aspecto de la historia de la isla. A pesar de los repetidos ataques de ingleses, franceses y holandeses,[6] los españoles lograron conservar[7] la isla en su poder[8] hasta 1898.

Desde los primeros tiempos los conquistadores españoles destinaron las tierras a la agricultura y a la ganadería. La caña de azúcar, el café y el tabaco eran los productos más importantes. Los últimos representantes de la raza india desaparecieron pronto y los españoles trajeron esclavos africanos para trabajar en el campo.

En 1898 España cedió el dominio[9] de Puerto Rico a los Estados Unidos. En 1950 Puerto Rico pidió el derecho[10] de establecer su propio[11] gobierno constitucional y dos años después se proclamó el Estado Libre Asociado[12] de Puerto Rico. Según el convenio[13] que originó el nuevo gobierno, se conserva la común ciudadanía,[14] el comercio libre y la autonomía fiscal.

La capital del Estado Libre Asociado de Puerto Rico es San Juan, en el norte de la isla. Los municipios de Santurce, Hato Rey y Río Piedras rodean la capital, con una población total, entre todos, de más de medio millón de habitantes.

---

[1]**Antillas Mayores,** *Greater Antilles.* (The West Indies Islands, except for the Bahamas, are composed of the Greater and the Lesser Antilles.)   [2]**tiene . . . de largo,** *it is about 100 miles long.*   [3]**de ancho,** *wide.*   [4]**regresó,** *returned.*   [5]**convirtieron** (*pret. of* **convertir**), *converted.*   [6]**holandeses,** *Dutch.*   [7]**lograron conservar,** *succeeded in holding (conserving).*   [8]**poder,** *power, hands.*   [9]**cedió el dominio,** *ceded the dominion (control).*   [10]**pidió el derecho de,** *asked the right to.*   [11]**su propio,** *its own.*   [12]**Estado Libre Asociado,** *Commonwealth (Associated Free State).*   [13]**convenio,** *covenant, pact.*   [14]**ciudadanía,** *citizenship.*

173

Fundada en 1521, la ciudad de San Juan tiene una parte vieja que data de la época colonial, con calles estrechas y edificios y fortificaciones antiguas. La parte nueva es el centro de la vida oficial y el centro comercial de la isla. Con su aeropuerto internacional y más de una docena de hoteles de lujo,[15] es también el centro de la industria turística.

Santurce y Río Piedras son importantes centros industriales. La Universidad de Puerto Rico tiene una moderna ciudad universitaria en Río Piedras.

Ponce, en la parte sur, y Mayagüez, en la costa occidental, son puertos importantes. Ponce, famosa por sus edificios blancos y bellos jardines, es el centro de la industria del azúcar.

En Mayagüez se halla la Escuela de Agricultura y de Ingeniería, que forma parte de la Universidad de Puerto Rico. Al sur de Mayagüez se encuentra la pequeña ciudad de San Germán, fundada en 1512. Tiene la iglesia cristiana más antigua del hemisferio occidental.

Hoy día Puerto Rico es uno de los países más densamente poblados de la tierra, con más de dos millones y medio de habitantes. Como la tierra cultivable no basta para mantener la población, el nuevo gobierno pone especial interés en la creación de nuevas industrias. Hoy la producción industrial es muy grande. Las fábricas de muebles,[16] de tejidos,[17] de calzado,[18] de artículos eléctricos y de productos químicos y farmacéuticos son las más importantes.

La educación y la vida cultural tienen mucha importancia en Puerto Rico. Más de la tercera parte del presupuesto[19] está destinada a la educación. Las universidades no son los únicos centros de la vida cultural. Los mejores concertistas del mundo y las mejores compañías de teatro visitan la isla en sus jiras[20] artísticas.

Preguntas

1. ¿Cuántas millas de largo y de ancho tiene la isla de Puerto Rico? 2. ¿Hay muchas montañas en la isla? 3. ¿Quién desembarcó en la isla en 1493? 4. ¿Quién fue nombrado su primer gobernador? 5. ¿En qué convirtieron la isla los españoles? 6. ¿A qué dedicaron las tierras los conquistadores españoles? 7. ¿Cuáles eran los productos más importantes?

8. ¿Cuándo cedió España el dominio de Puerto Rico a los Estados Unidos? 9. ¿Qué pidió Puerto Rico en 1950? 10. Según el convenio que originó el nuevo gobierno, ¿qué conservan los puertorriqueños?

11. ¿Cuál es la capital del Estado Libre Asociado de Puerto Rico? 12. ¿Cuántos habitantes tienen la capital y los municipios que la rodean? 13. ¿Cómo es la parte vieja de San Juan? 14. ¿Qué parte de la ciudad es el centro de la vida oficial?

15. ¿Dónde se encuentra la Universidad de Puerto Rico? 16. ¿Qué ciudades son puertos importantes? 17. ¿Qué ciudad es el centro de la industria del azúcar? 18. ¿En qué ciudad se encuentra la Escuela de Agricultura y de Ingeniería de la Universidad de Puerto Rico? 19. ¿Qué pequeña ciudad se halla al sur de Mayagüez? 20. ¿Qué edificio antiguo se encuentra en San Germán?

---

[15]**de lujo,** *de luxe.*   [16]**fábricas de muebles,** *furniture factories, factories of furniture.*   [17]**de tejidos,** *textile, of textiles.*
[18]**calzado,** *shoes, footwear.*   [19]**presupuesto,** *budget.*   [20]**jiras,** *tours, trips.*

21. ¿Cuántos habitantes tiene la isla de Puerto Rico? 22. ¿En qué pone especial interés el nuevo gobierno? 23. ¿Es grande la producción industrial hoy día? 24. ¿Qué clases de fábricas hay en Puerto Rico?

25. ¿Qué parte del presupuesto está destinada a la educación? 26. ¿Son las universidades los únicos centros de la vida cultural?

Estudio de palabras

a. Verb cognates

1. The ending of the Spanish infinitive is lacking in English: abundar, adornar, afectar, convertir, desembarcar (*to disembark*), formar, mantener (*to maintain*), pasar (*to pass*), proclamar (*to proclaim*), representar, visitar.

2. Spanish verbs in **-ar** often end in *-ate* in English: originar.

3. The English verb ends in *-e:* aspirar, ceder, conservar, datar, destinar, dividir, producir, resolver.

b. Compare the meanings of the following pairs of words: entrada, *entrance, and* entrar, *to enter;* gobierno, *government, and* gobernador, *governor;* joven, *young, and* juventud, *youth;* universidad, *university, and* universitario, *university* (adj.).

c. Pronounce the following words aloud, note the English cognates, and indicate the variations: comercio, *commerce, trade;* creación, *creation;* especial, *special;* farmacéutico, *pharmaceutical;* hemisferio, *hemisphere;* internacional, *international;* marítimo, *maritime;* químico, *chemical;* posición, *position.*

Vista aérea de la Fortaleza del Morro, San Juan, Puerto Rico. Esta fortaleza fue construida por los españoles durante el período colonial para proteger la ciudad de San Juan de los ataques de los piratas.

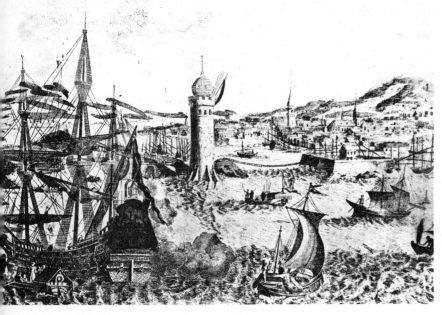

En la foto de arriba vemos un grabado antiguo que
muestra como era el puerto de La Habana alrededor del
año 1680. En la foto de la derecha se ve el monumento
al patriota Máximo Gómez, un dominicano que luchó
mucho por la independencia de Cuba. Abajo tenemos una
escena callejera que muestra la parte antigua de La
Habana, Cuba.

Arriba aparece la Fortaleza del Morro, esta vez en La Habana, Cuba. Los españoles construyeron varias fortalezas parecidas en distintas ciudades de la América Hispana, para protegerlas de los ataques de los piratas, como podemos ver en la foto de abajo tomada en el Morro de San Juan, Puerto Rico.

Puerto Rico es un isla que tiene hermosas playas y bellas ciudades que todavía conservan la influencia española. Arriba vemos una playa cerca de San Juan y abajo una calle de la misma ciudad donde se ven varios edificios de estilo colonial español. A la derecha, un grupo de estudiantes de la Universidad de Puerto Rico conversan en un parque cerca de la Universidad.

Estatua de Cristóbal Colón enfrente de la Basílica Metropolitana, la catedral de Santa María, donde se dice que está la tumba de Colón, Santo Domingo, República Dominicana.

Terraza del hotel Nicolás de Ovando, Santo Domingo, República Dominicana.

LECCIÓN 13

Preparando un viaje al Perú

Arturo piensa hacer un viaje por Suramérica con un grupo de estudiantes. Va a la oficina del Sr. Blanco, un amigo de su padre, para hacerle algunas preguntas.

SR. BLANCO —Pasa, Arturo. Siéntate un momento, por favor.

ARTURO —Gracias, Sr. Blanco. Me alegro mucho de poder hablar con usted.

SR. BLANCO —Pues, yo también me alegro de verte. Ayer por la tarde tu padre me dijo que estabas buscándome . . .

ARTURO —Es que pienso ir a Suramérica el mes que viene y lo que más me interesa[1] es visitar el Perú. Sé que usted conoce muy bien el país.

SR. BLANCO —Sí, el año pasado mi esposa y yo pasamos dos semanas viajando por el Perú. Lo conocimos[2] bastante bien.

ARTURO —¿Y qué parte del país les interesó más?

SR. BLANCO —Mira, nos interesó mucho Machu Picchu. Para mí, las ruinas de Machu Picchu son las más interesantes de América. Y claro, nos encantó el Cuzco, la antigua capital de los incas.

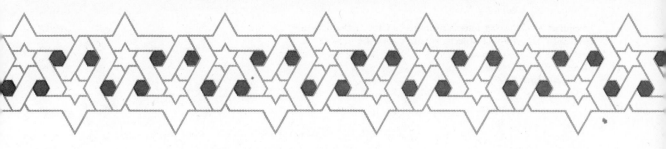

ARTURO —El Cuzco no está lejos de Lima, ¿verdad? ¿Cuánto tiempo toma el viaje?

SR. BLANCO —Volando directamente al Cuzco sólo se necesitan cincuenta minutos.

ARTURO —Creo que voy a tomar ese vuelo.

SR. BLANCO —Como vas a ver, el viaje del Cuzco a Machu Picchu es muy pintoresco.

◆ ◆ ◆ ◆ ◆

ARTURO —¿Es interesante la ciudad de Lima?

SR. BLANCO —¡Ya lo creo! La Universidad de San Marcos, por ejemplo, es la más antigua de Suramérica.

ARTURO —Lo sé. Anoche leí un libro que insistía precisamente en ese tema.

SR. BLANCO —Y si se quiere comprender el Perú en el siglo veinte, hay que[3] ver las fábricas, los edificios comerciales, los barrios modernos . . .

ARTURO —Pero todavía se ven muchas casas y edificios de estilo colonial, ¿verdad?

SR. BLANCO —Mira, Arturo, ¿por qué no vienes un día a casa y te enseñamos las fotografías que trajimos de nuestro viaje? Sacamos muchas fotografías y vas a disfrutar mirándolas.

ARTURO —¡Encantado, Sr. Blanco! Tengo muchos deseos de conocer mejor todos los aspectos de la cultura peruana.

---

[1]**Lo que más me interesa,** *What interests me most.* (The verb **interesar** is used like **gustar.**) In line 14 the meaning of **nos interesó mucho Machu Picchu** is *We were (became) much interested in Machu Picchu* (lit., . . . *interested us very much*). Machu Picchu, an old fortress-city of unknown origin, often called the "Lost City of the Incas," was discovered in 1911.

[2]**Lo conocimos,** *We came to know it.*   [3]**Hay que** plus an infinitive means *It is necessary to,* or the indefinite subject *One, We, You,* etc., *must* plus the infinitive.

Conversación

A. Preguntas sobre el diálogo

1. ¿Qué piensa hacer Arturo? 2. ¿Qué es lo que más le interesa? 3. ¿Por qué fue Arturo a hablar con el Sr. Blanco? 4. ¿Qué parte del Perú les interesó mucho al señor Blanco y a su esposa? 5. ¿Cuántos minutos se necesitan para volar de Lima al Cuzco? 6. ¿Cuál es la universidad más antigua de Suramérica? 7. ¿Qué hay que hacer si se quiere comprender el Perú en el siglo veinte? 8. ¿Qué puede enseñarle a Arturo el señor Blanco si Arturo viene a su casa?

B. Aplicación del diálogo

1. ¿Piensa Ud. hacer un viaje este verano? ¿Adónde piensa ir? 2. ¿Qué sitios le interesan más a Ud.? ¿Las ciudades grandes? ¿Las ruinas? ¿Las montañas y el campo? 3. ¿Cuál de las ciudades en los Estados Unidos conoce Ud. mejor? ¿Le parece bonita? ¿Interesante? ¿Agradable? ¿Demasiado grande? 4. ¿Conoce Ud. alguna ciudad extranjera? ¿Le gustó? ¿Por qué? 5. Qué países extranjeros desea Ud. visitar? 6. Cuando se viaja en avión, ¿se necesita mucho tiempo o se llega pronto? 7. ¿Cómo le gusta a Ud. viajar, en coche? ¿En avión? ¿Por qué? 8. ¿Le gusta a Ud. leer libros sobre viajes y sobre cultura? ¿Qué libros está Ud. leyendo ahora?

NOTAS GRAMATICALES

A. Irregular verbs having **i**-stem preterits

decir	hacer	querer	venir
singular			
dije	hice	quise	vine
dijiste	hiciste	quisiste	viniste
dijo	hizo	quiso	vino
plural			
dijimos	hicimos	quisimos	vinimos
dijisteis	hicisteis	quisisteis	vinisteis
dijeron	hicieron	quisieron	vinieron

The endings of these four verbs, which have **i**-stem preterits, are the same as for **traer** (Lesson 12). Note the spelling of **dijeron** and **hizo.**

The English equivalent of each first person singular preterit form is: **dije,** *I said, did say, I told, did tell;* **hice,** *I made, did make, I did;* **quise,** *I wanted, did want, I wished, did wish;* **vine,** *I came, did come.*

B. Uses of the present participle

1. In Lesson 5 the forms of the present participles of regular verbs were given and their use in the progressive forms of the tenses was explained: **Estoy (Estaba) leyendo un libro,** *I am (was) reading a book.*

Verbs already used which have irregular present participles are:

decir:	**diciendo**	*saying, telling*	creer:	**creyendo**	*believing*
ir:	**yendo**	*going*	leer:	**leyendo**	*reading*
poder:	**pudiendo**	*being able*	traer:	**trayendo**	*bringing*
venir:	**viniendo**	*coming*			

2. **Pasamos dos semanas viajando por el Perú.** We spent two months traveling through Peru.

   Vas a disfrutar mirándolas. You are going to enjoy looking at them.

   Volando directamente al Cuzco . . . (By) flying directly to Cuzco . . .

The present participle may be used alone in Spanish, as in English; it is also used to express *by* plus the present participle.

Remember that the infinitive, not the present participle, is used after a preposition: **Antes de verlos,** *Before seeing them.*

C. Position of object pronouns with the present participle

Ud. puede aprender mucho mirándolos. You can learn much by looking at them.

Juan está leyéndolos. }
Juan los está leyendo. } John is reading them.

Pronouns used as the object of the present participle are always attached to the participle, except in the progressive forms of the tenses, when the pronouns may be placed before **estar.** An accent mark must be written when a pronoun is attached to the present participle.

Remember that object pronouns are also attached to affirmative commands and to infinitives; otherwise they precede the verb.

◆ *Práctica.* Read in Spanish, noting the position of the object pronouns and the accented forms:

1. Arturo lo trae. Va a traerlo. Está trayéndolo. Tráigalo Ud. No lo traiga Ud.

2. Ellos las miran. Piensan mirarlas. Están mirándolas. Mírenlas Uds. No las miren Uds. 3. Yo les escribo. Quiero escribirles. Estoy escribiéndoles. Escríbales Ud. No les escriba Ud.

D. **Se** used as an indefinite subject

> They say
> **Se dice que es verdad.** People say ⎬ that it is true.
> It is said
>
> **Si se quiere comprender el Perú . . .** If one wishes to understand Peru . . .
> **Se puede decir** *or* **Puede decirse . . .** One can say . . . (It can be said . . .)
> **Se hace el vuelo . . .** One makes the flight . . . (The flight is made . . .)
> **¿Cuánto tiempo se necesita (necesita uno)?** How much time does one need (is needed)?

Sometimes an action is expressed without indicating definitely who is doing what the verb implies. In such cases in English we use subjects like *one, people, they, you,* which do not refer to a definite person, while in Spanish we use **se.** When used impersonally (that is, when no subject is expressed), the verb is in the third person singular, since **se** is considered the subject.

Compare this use of **se** with that explained on page 83, in which case the verb may be either third person singular or plural. When used with a singular verb form, **se** may be considered either as an indefinite subject or as a reflexive substitute for the passive (third and fourth examples).

Uno is also used as an indefinite subject (last example), particularly with reflexive verbs: **Uno se levanta tarde los domingos,** *One gets up late on Sundays.*

E. Pronouns used as objects of prepositions

I.	*singular*				*plural*		
para	mí	for	me	para	nosotros, –as	for	us
	ti		you (*fam.*)		vosotros, –as		you (*fam.*)
	él		him, it (*m.*)		ellos		them (*m.*)
	ella		her, it (*f.*)		ellas		them (*f.*)
	usted		you (*formal*)		ustedes		you

With the exception of the first and second persons singular, the forms which are used as objects of prepositions are the same as the subject pronouns. Note, however, the difference in meanings, and remember that direct and indirect object pronouns (**me, te, le,** etc.) are never used after prepositions.

Used with **con,** the first and second persons singular have the special forms **conmigo** and **contigo.**

Occasionally **mí, ti, nosotros, –as, vosotros, –as,** and **sí** (third person singular and plural) are used reflexively: **para mí,** *for myself;* **para nosotros, –as,** *for ourselves;* **para sí,** *for himself, herself, yourself* (formal), *itself, themselves, yourselves.* When used with **con, sí,** becomes **consigo,** *with himself,* etc. This form will be used later.

2. **Yo le doy a ella el dinero.** I give her the money.
   Él me enseñó a mí las fotografías. He showed *me* the photographs.
   ¿Le gustan a Ud.? Do you like them?
   Vi a su hermano y a la amiga de él. I saw your brother and his girl friend.

The prepositional forms are often used with the preposition **a** in addition to the direct and indirect object pronouns for emphasis and, in the third person, also for clearness. In the case of **usted(es)** it is more polite to use the prepositional form in addition to the object pronoun. See page 83.

The prepositional forms are also used with **de** (fourth example) to clarify the meaning of **su(s),** *his, her, your* (formal singular), *their, your* (plural).

EJERCICIOS

A. Substitution drill:

1. *El señor Blanco* le dijo varias cosas a Arturo.
   (*Mis padres, Yo, Tú, Juan y yo, Ud.*)
2. *Arturo* hizo un viaje al Perú.
   (*La profesora, Los estudiantes, Yo, Uds., Tú*)
3. *Marta* no quiso ver las ruinas.
   (*Los muchachos, Yo, Tú, Uds., Nosotros*)
4. *Elena* vino a sacar unas fotografías.
   (*Yo, Luis y yo, Nosotros, Tú, Los jóvenes*)

B. Read each sentence in Spanish; then repeat, changing the inflected verbs to the preterit:

1. Arturo viene a ver al Sr. Blanco y le hace algunas preguntas. 2. El señor Blanco y su esposa me dicen que traen muchas fotografías de su viaje. 3. Arturo no quiere hacer el viaje al Cuzco. 4. Yo no quiero ir al cine con ellos. 5. Se ve que Tomás dice la verdad. 6. Pablo se sienta a la mesa y escribe una composición. 7. Su amigo Eduardo viene al cuarto. 8. Tu mamá me dice que Uds. se levantan temprano.

C. Read in Spanish, placing the object pronouns in their proper position:

1. (nos) Ella escribe. Quiere escribir. Está escribiendo. 2. (lo) Arturo compra. Compre Ud. Trató de comprar. 3. (les) Enrique dice la verdad. Diga Ud. la verdad. Va a decir la verdad. 4. (le) Yo doy un caballo. No dé Ud. un caballo. No puedo comprar un caballo. 5. (te) Tú levantas. Piensas levantar. Estás levantando.

D. Answer each question, following the model:

MODEL: ¿Estás leyendo este libro? *No, no estoy leyéndolo todavía, pero voy a leerlo pronto.*

1. ¿Estás escribiendo una composición?
2. ¿Estás preparando las lecciones?
3. ¿Estás leyendo el periódico?
4. ¿Están Uds. mirando las fotografías?
5. ¿Están Uds. enseñando la película?
6. ¿Están Uds. presentando los bailes?

E. Read aloud, supplying the appropriate present participle selected from **pudiendo, sabiendo, viniendo, yendo:**

1. _____ hablar español se encuentra trabajo en Buenos Aires.
2. _____ temprano a clase se puede hablar con el profesor.
3. _____ en avión se llega pronto a México.
4. _____ estudiar todos los días se aprende mucho.
5. _____ a esta tienda a menudo se encuentran cosas baratas.
6. _____ ir al campo en el verano se descansa mucho.

F. Answer affirmatively, watching the prepositional pronouns in your answer:

MODEL: ¿Es para mí este periódico? *Sí, es para usted.*

1. ¿Es para ella esta revista?
2. ¿Son para nosotros estas cosas?
3. ¿Son para Uds. las cartas?
4. ¿Es para ti el cuadro?
5. ¿Es para Ud. el reloj?
6. ¿Son para mí las fotografías?

Answer negatively, substituting the correct pronoun for the noun which follows each preposition:

MODEL: ¿Baila Tomás con Elena? *No, no baila con ella.*

7. ¿Charla Ud. con los jóvenes?
8. ¿Vive Ud. cerca de mi tía?
9. ¿Es Ud. amigo de Arturo?
10. ¿Vino Ud. con sus amigas?
11. ¿Salió Pepe sin sus padres?
12. ¿Quisiste ir con tus primas?

G. Supply the correct form of the definite article where necessary:

1. Me gustan _____ películas extranjeras.   2. Hace buen tiempo en _____ verano.
3. _____ primavera es una estación agradable.   4. Ponemos _____ anuncios
en _____ periódico de vez en cuando.   5. _____ vida en España es agradable.
6. _____ agua es necesaria.   7. _____ exámenes son difíciles.   8. ¿Tiene
Ud. _____ hermanos?   9. Hoy día _____ teléfonos son de varios colores.
10. _____ norteamericanos trabajan mucho.   11. _____ peruanos disfrutan
de _____ vida.   12. Ayer volaron a _____ Suramérica.

H. Give the Spanish equivalent:

1. Arthur tells Mr. White that he intends to take a trip to Peru with a group of students during the summer.   2. Mr. White is glad to be able to talk with him a while.   3. Mr. White and his wife spent two weeks traveling through Peru last year.   4. He said that one of the most interesting places he visited was Cuzco, the old capital of the Incas.   5. Flying directly from Lima, only fifty minutes are needed (in order) to reach Cuzco.   6. The trip from Cuzco to the ruins of Machu Picchu is very picturesque and it fascinated them.   7. If one wants to understand Peru in the twentieth century, one must (it is necessary to) see the business buildings, the factories, the modern districts . . .   8. The University of San Marcos is the oldest in South America. It is an example of buildings of colonial style which are still seen in Lima.   9. Mr. White says that he can show Arthur many photographs which he took on his trip.   10. Arthur is very eager to see them; by looking at them, he can understand better all the aspects of Peruvian culture.

I. **Composición:** Una visita al Perú

Assume that you visited Peru last summer. By using the correct word order and the correct tense and form of each verb, you will end with a short composition:

1. el verano pasado / por Suramérica / yo hacer un viaje / muy interesante
2. con un grupo de estudiantes / yo visitar / de mi universidad / varios países
3. estudiar algunos aspectos / interesarle a este grupo / de la cultura hispanoamericana
4. especialmente / las culturas que ya encontrarse allí / a mí interesarme / en mil quinientos treinta y tres
5. vivir los incas / en el Perú / y hoy día / de su magnífica cultura / todavía / allí / poder verse aspectos
6. poder visitarse / por ejemplo / el Cuzco y las ruinas de Machu Picchu
7. en el Cuzco verse / de la vida colonial / también / aspectos muy interesantes
8. que estar en las montañas / cerca del Cuzco / encantarme / las ruinas de Machu Picchu
9. para comprender / el Perú estar haciendo / lo que / en el siglo veinte / las fábricas / los edificios comerciales / hay que ver / y los barrios modernos
10. en mi viaje / amigos hispanoamericanos / muchas cosas / yo aprender / sobre nuestros

EJERCICIOS DE PRONUNCIACIÓN

Review of the sounds of Spanish **g** and **j**

1. Remember that Spanish **g** (written **gu** before **e** and **i**) is pronounced like a weak English *g* in *go* at the beginning of a breath-group or after **n:**

gusto	grupo	guitarra	inglés	tengo

2. Also, remember that in all other cases, except when before **e** and **i (ge, gi),** the sound is much weaker (see Lesson 3):

siglo	siguiente	regalo	hago	traigan
digo	Miguel	luego	amiga	Santiago

3. When before **e** or **i** in the groups **ge, gi,** it is pronounced like Spanish **j,** that is, somewhat like a strongly exaggerated *h* in *halt* (see Lesson 4):

general	Jorge	viaje	lejos	dejan
mejor	dijimos	julio	viejo	agente

4. In the combinations **gua** and **guo** the **u** is pronounced like English *w* in *wet:*

lengua	agua	antiguo	guapo	guante

VOCABULARIO

alegrarse (de + *obj.*) to be glad (of)
América America
antiguo, -a old, ancient
Arturo Arthur
el **aspecto** aspect
el **barrio** district
claro *adv.* clearly, naturally, of course
colonial colonial
comercial commercial
comprender to comprehend, understand
el **Cuzco** Cuzco
el **deseo** desire
directamente directly
disfrutar (de + *obj.*) to enjoy
el **edificio** building
la **fábrica** factory
la **fotografía** photograph

el **inca** Inca
interesar to interest
lejos de *prep.* far from
lo que what, that which
mejor better, best
el **minuto** minute
moderno, -a modern
el **Perú** Peru
peruano, -a Peruvian
pintoresco, -a picturesque
precisamente precisely, exactly
las **ruinas** ruins
sacar to take, take out
San Marcos St. Mark
el **siglo** century
volar (ue) to fly
el **vuelo** flight

ayer por la tarde yesterday afternoon
lo sé I know
alegrarse (mucho) (de + *inf.*) to be (very) glad (to)
sacar fotografías to take photographs
tener muchos deseos de to be very eager (wish very much) to
venir a casa to come to (our) house
¡ya lo creo! of course! certainly!

*Restos de la fortaleza inca de Sacsahuamán,
cerca del Cuzco, Perú.*

Conversación 2

En un restaurante español

Carlos y Felipe, dos jóvenes madrileños, invitan a dos estudiantes norteamericanas, Ana y Carmen, a almorzar. Son las dos de la tarde, hora en que los españoles acostumbran tomar el almuerzo. Entran en un restaurante cerca de la Plaza Mayor. Se acerca un camarero.

CARLOS —¿Hay una mesa para cuatro?

CAMARERO —Hay una mesa libre cerca de la ventana. Pasen Uds. por aquí. (*Se sientan los jóvenes. El camarero trae la lista y, mientras los cuatro la examinan, trae vasos de agua, pan, mantequilla y entremeses.*)

CAMARERO —¿Qué desean tomar, señores?

CARLOS —¿Encuentran algo de su gusto, señoritas?

CARMEN —No es fácil escoger entre tantos platos. La selección es muy variada.

FELIPE —Es que cada región española tiene su plato típico.

CARMEN —Primero voy a tomar sopa. Y, después, paella valenciana.

CARLOS —¿No desea un plato de huevos después de la sopa? En España las tortillas son excelentes. Se hacen de patatas, de jamón, de verduras . . . No son como las mexicanas.

CARMEN —Gracias, hoy no.

ANA —Yo voy a tomar una tortilla española en vez de sopa. Luego no sé si tomar carne o pescado.

CAMARERO —Puede tomar las dos cosas, señorita. Tenemos muchas clases de pescado. La merluza con mayonesa es excelente.

FELIPE —El arroz con pollo es un plato español muy típico y muy sabroso.

ANA —Muy bien. Arroz con pollo, por favor.

FELIPE —Pues, yo voy a tomar sopa, pescado y, después, biftec con patatas fritas y una ensalada.

CAMARERO —Muy bien. Y, ¿usted, señor?

CARLOS —Como buen madrileño, voy a tomar el cocido. Primero la sopa y luego los otros elementos que contiene: garbanzos, patatas y albóndigas, con chorizo y tocino. Para terminar, un poco de lomo de cerdo y una ensalada.

CAMARERO —¿Desean vino, señores?

FELIPE —Naturalmente. Vino tinto. Una botella de vino de la Rioja, por favor. (*A las jóvenes.*) Como van a ver Uds., los vinos españoles son magníficos.

CAMARERO —¿Desean algún postre?

CARLOS —¿Qué postres hay?

CAMARERO —Además de los comunes—arroz con leche, flan, queso, membrillo, pasteles, helados y frutas—, en este restaurante tenemos varias especialidades, como los turrones, los bizcochos borrachos, almíbares de la Rioja. . .

CARMEN —Para mí, flan y una taza de café con leche y azúcar.

ANA —Pues, yo voy a tomar frutas y una taza de café solo.

FELIPE —Yo voy a tomar queso, frutas y café solo.

CARLOS —Y para mí, helado de fresa y una taza de café solo. (*Los jóvenes charlan mientras el camarero trae la comida. Terminan el almuerzo, lo pagan y le dan una buena propina al camarero.*)

CARMEN —Se come muy bien aquí, ¿verdad?

CARLOS —Tiene fama de ser uno de los mejores restaurantes de Madrid.

FELIPE —¿Por qué no cenamos aquí esta noche? Si cenamos a las nueve, podemos ir al teatro después.

CARMEN —¡Es una idea magnífica!

ANA —¡Encantada, porque deseo probar otros platos, como el gazpacho y el lechón y el cordero asados!

CARLOS —Pues, pasamos a recogerlas a las nueve. Vamos a tomar un taxi, porque a esa hora hay mucha gente en los autobuses.

FELIPE —Hasta las nueve, entonces.

ANA Y CARMEN —Muy bien, hasta las nueve. Y, ¡mil gracias por todo!

Preguntas

Sobre la conversación

1. ¿Quiénes son Ana y Carmen?   2. ¿Con quiénes van a almorzar?   3. ¿A qué hora acostumbran almorzar los españoles?   4. Mientras los jóvenes examinan la lista, ¿qué trae el camarero?   5. ¿Qué va a tomar Carmen?   6. ¿De qué se hacen las tortillas en España?   7. ¿Qué dice Felipe del arroz con pollo?   8. ¿Qué elementos contiene el cocido madrileño?   9. ¿Qué dice Felipe acerca de los vinos españoles?   10. ¿Qué postres son comunes a casi toda España?   11. ¿Qué postres recuerda Ud.?   12. ¿Dónde deciden cenar los jóvenes?

Aplicación de la conversación

1. ¿A qué hora acostumbramos almorzar en los Estados Unidos?   2. ¿Qué toma Ud. generalmente para el almuerzo?   3. ¿Cuáles son algunos platos típicos de los Estados Unidos?   4. ¿Conoce Ud. algunos platos típicos de otros países?   5. ¿Qué postres le gustan a Ud.?   6. ¿Cuál será el postre más común de los Estados Unidos?   7. ¿Qué ciudades norteamericanas tienen fama por sus restaurantes?   8. ¿Qué estados son famosos por sus vinos?   9. ¿Qué regiones tienen fama por sus frutas?   10. ¿Le gusta a Ud. la carne de cerdo?   11. ¿Le interesan a Ud. las comidas españolas?   12. ¿Sabe Ud. si se toma fría alguna sopa española?

Práctica Oral

Groups of students will be selected to prepare a conversation of eight to ten exchanges, using vocabulary already given.

1. Groups of students order a Spanish meal, with one acting as waiter (waitress) and others as customers.

2. In other groups two American students meet Spanish friends and discuss the variety of regional dishes in Spain and in the United States.

A la izquierda, camarero del hotel Viña del Mar, cerca de Santo Domingo, República Dominicana. Debajo vemos el famoso restaurante Los Caracoles, en Barcelona, España.

VOCABULARIO

acercarse (**a** + *obj.*) to approach
acostumbrar to be accustomed to
la **albóndiga** meat ball
algún (*used for* **alguno** *before m. sing. nouns*) some, any
el **almíbar** syrup
almorzar (**ue**) to have (eat) lunch
el **arroz** rice
el **arroz con leche** rice pudding
asado, -a roast(ed)
el **biftec** (**bistec, bisté**) steak
el **bizcocho borracho** tipsy (rum) cake
la **botella** bottle
la **carne** meat
el **cerdo** pork, pig
contener (*like* **tener**) to contain
el **cordero** lamb
el **chorizo** smoked pork sausage
el **elemento** element, ingredient
la **ensalada** salad
el **entremés** (*pl.* **entremeses**) side dish, hors d'oeuvre
la **especialidad** specialty
examinar to examine
excelente excellent
la **fama** fame, reputation
el **flan** custard
la **fresa** strawberry
frito, -a fried
el **garbanzo** chickpea
el **huevo** egg
el **jamón** (*pl.* **jamones**) ham
el **lechón** (*pl.* **lechones**) suckling pig
la **lista** (*or el* **menú**) menu
el **lomo** (**de cerdo**) (pork) loin
la **mantequilla** butter

la **mayonesa** mayonnaise
el **membrillo** quince (*fruit and paste*)
la **merluza** hake
mientras *conj.* while, as long as
pagar to pay (for)
el **pan** bread
la **patata** potato
el **pescado** fish
el **plato** plate, dish, course (*at meals*)
la **Plaza Mayor** Main Square (*in center of old Madrid*)
el **pollo** chicken
el **postre** dessert
primero *adv.* first
probar (**ue**) to try, sample, taste
la **propina** tip
el **queso** cheese
recoger to pick up
el **restaurante** restaurant
la **Rioja** *part of province of Logroño in northern Old Castile, famous for its wines*
sabroso, -a delicious, tasty
la **selección** (*pl.* **selecciones**) selection, choice
el **señor** gentleman; *pl.* gentlemen, ladies and gentlemen
la **sopa** soup
el **taxi** taxi
tinto, -a deep red; **tinto** (*m.n.*) red wine
el **tocino** bacon
la **tortilla** omelet (*Spain*)
el **turrón** (*pl.* **turrones**) nougat, almond candy
variado, -a varied
las **verduras** vegetables, greens
el **vino** wine

de su gusto to his (her, your, their) liking
en vez de instead of, in place of
hora en que the time (hour) when
mil gracias many (a thousand) thanks
para el almuerzo for lunch
pasar por aquí to pass (come) this way *or* by here
se come muy bien aquí the food is very good here (*lit.,* one eats very well here)
tener fama (de) to have the (a) reputation (of, as)
tener fama por to have a reputation for, be known for

Grupo de jóvenes almuerzan en un restaurante campestre en Urubamba, Perú.

Irregular verbs having *u*-stem preterits ● Verbs with changes in spelling in the preterit ● Combinations of two personal object pronouns ● Demonstrative pronouns ● Uses of *volver* and *devolver,* of *preguntar,* and of the idiom *acabar de* ● Use of the definite article in a general sense

LECCIÓN 14

Un encuentro inesperado

Al salir de una tienda, Marta se encuentra con su amiga Carolina.

MARTA —¡Carolina . . .! ¡Qué sorpresa encontrarte aquí en el centro! ¿Cuándo volviste de tu viaje?

CAROLINA —Llegué ayer al mediodía. Supe que estuviste en mi cuarto buscándome.

MARTA —Sí. Pregunté por ti ayer por la mañana, pero nadie sabía cuándo pensabas volver.

CAROLINA —Pues, decidí quedarme en casa un día más. Ah, y gracias por las flores.

MARTA —De nada. Como te esperábamos ayer, María y yo las pusimos en tu cuarto. ¿Y qué tal el viaje?

CAROLINA —Mucho mejor de lo que esperaba.[1] Además, encontré a toda la familia bien.

◆ ◆ ◆ ◆

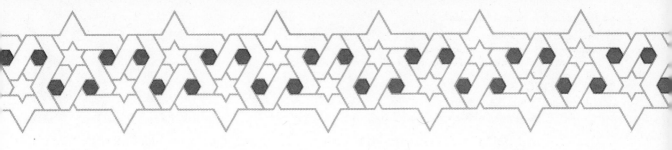

MARTA —Pero, ¿qué haces aquí en el centro?

CAROLINA —Es que la semana que viene es el cumpleaños de mi hermana Luisa . . .

MARTA —¿Cuántos años va a cumplir?

CAROLINA —Quince años. Mis padres van a regalarle un precioso reloj de oro.

MARTA —Lo entiendo muy bien. Es una fecha muy importante en la vida de las jóvenes. ¿Ya le compraste un regalo?

CAROLINA —Sí, empecé con una tarjeta muy bonita. Ahora acabo de comprarle una blusa que está muy de moda.

MARTA —Déjame verla . . . ¡Ay, qué bonita! ¿Cuánto pagaste?

CAROLINA —Pagué nueve dólares. Encontré también un prendedor de plata, pero no pude comprarlo porque no tenía bastante dinero.

◆ ◆ ◆ ◆ ◆

MARTA —Mira, aquí tengo un billete de veinte dólares que me mandó mi papá. Puedo prestártelo si quieres.

CAROLINA —¿De veras? ¡Qué amable eres, Marta! Te lo devuelvo esta noche. Ésta es la tienda. Entra conmigo.

MARTA —Si no tardas mucho, te acompaño. Pronto va a ser hora de almorzar. Tengo una cita con Tomás, que acaba de volver de la Florida.

◆ ◆ ◆ ◆ ◆

Entran en la tienda y se detienen frente al mostrador donde se venden los prendedores. Carolina le pregunta a la vendedora si son de plata.

CAROLINA —¿Te gusta éste, Marta? A mí me parece más fino que aquéllos.

MARTA —Sí, ése me gusta mucho. ¡Es precioso!

CAROLINA —Pues me lo llevo. (*Le da el dinero a la vendedora; ésta envuelve el prendedor y se lo entrega a Carolina.*)

MARTA —(*Mirando su reloj.*) Bueno, Carolina, ya es tarde; tengo que irme. Hasta luego.

CAROLINA —Gracias por todo, Marta. Te busco esta noche . . . Ah, y saluda a Tomás de mi parte.

---

[1]Before a verb, when an adjective, an adverb, or an idea is compared, **de lo que,** *than* (*what*), is used in Spanish. See page 85 for the explanation of the use of **que** and **de** for *than*.

Conversación

A. Preguntas sobre el diálogo

1. ¿Dónde se encuentra Marta con Carolina? 2. ¿Qué le pregunta Marta a Carolina? 3. ¿Quién puso las flores en el cuarto de Carolina? 4. ¿Qué está haciendo Carolina en el centro? 5. ¿Qué van a regalarle a Luisa sus padres? 6. ¿Por qué van a darle ese regalo? 7. ¿Cuántos años va a cumplir Luisa? ¿Cuántos años tiene Luisa[1] ahora? 8. ¿Qué compró Carolina con el dinero que le prestó Marta? 9. ¿Cuándo va a devolverle el dinero Carolina? 10. ¿Con quién va a almorzar Marta?

B. Aplicación del diálogo

1. ¿Cuándo celebra Ud. su cumpleaños? ¿Cuántos años va a cumplir Ud.? 2. ¿Qué regalos espera Ud. recibir? 3. Generalmente, ¿en qué fiestas se dan regalos? ¿A quiénes les da Ud. regalos? 4. Generalmente, ¿cuándo se mandan flores? ¿A quiénes les manda Ud. flores? 5. ¿Le mandan a Ud. mucho dinero de casa? 6. ¿Qué hace Ud. cuando recibe dinero de casa? ¿Va de compras al centro? ¿Va al cine? ¿Invita a una amiga? 7. Cuando Ud. no tiene bastante dinero, ¿quién se lo presta? ¿Un amigo? ¿Se lo devuelve Ud. pronto? 8. Cuando sus amigos necesitan dinero, ¿se lo presta Ud. a ellos? ¿Se lo devuelven ellos pronto?

NOTAS GRAMATICALES

A. Irregular verbs having **u-**stem preterits

estar	poder	poner	saber	tener
		singular		
estuve	pude	puse	supe	tuve
estuviste	pudiste	pusiste	supiste	tuviste
estuvo	pudo	puso	supo	tuvo
		plural		
estuvimos	pudimos	pusimos	supimos	tuvimos
estuvisteis	pudisteis	pusisteis	supisteis	tuvisteis
estuvieron	pudieron	pusieron	supieron	tuvieron

Note that these five verbs have **u-**stem preterits, and that the endings are the same as for the four verbs in Lesson 13 which have **i-**stems in the preterit. The English equivalents are: **estuve,** *I was;* **pude,** *I could, was able to;* **puse,** *I put, did put, I placed, did*

---

place; **tuve,** *I had, did have.* **Tuve** also may mean *I got, received.* The preterit of **saber** usually has a special meaning: **Cuando supe,** *When I learned, found out.*

B. Verbs with changes in spelling in the preterit

buscar: **busqué,** buscaste, buscó, etc.
llegar: **llegué,** llegaste, llegó, etc.
empezar: **empecé,** empezaste, empezó, etc.

Review the sounds of the consonants **c, g,** and **z;** then note that in order to keep the sound of the final consonant of the stem of a Spanish verb, a change in spelling is often necessary. Before the ending **-e** in the first person singular preterit, all verbs ending in **-car** change **c** to **qu;** those ending in **-gar** change **g** to **gu,** and those ending in **-zar** change **z** to **c.**

Note that **empezar** is also a stem-changing verb in the present tense: **empiezo, empiezas, empieza, empezamos, empezáis, empiezan. Comenzar** has the same changes.

C. Combinations of two personal object pronouns

| **Me lo llevo.** | I'll take it (with me). |
| **Ellos nos las escribieron.** | They wrote them to us. |

	⎧ a él.		to him. ⎫
	⎪ a ella.		to her. ⎪
Ella se lo vende	⎨ a Ud.	She sells it	to you (*formal sing.*). ⎬
	⎪ a ellos.		to them. ⎪
	⎪ a ellas.		to them (*f.*). ⎪
	⎩ a Uds.		to you (*pl.*). ⎭

| **Ella se lo entrega a Carolina.** | She hands it to Caroline. |
| **No se lo devolví (a ella).** | I didn't return it to her. |

The indirect object pronoun precedes the direct when two pronouns are used as objects of the same verb. When both pronoun objects are in the third person, **se** replaces the indirect **le** or **les.** Thus **se lo** replaces **le lo, les lo; se la** replaces **le la, les la,** etc. Never use two pronouns together which begin with **l.** Since **se** in this combination may mean *to him, her, you, it,* or *them,* the prepositional forms will often be required in addition to **se** for clearness.

María se los puso entonces.	Mary put them on then.
Vamos a llevárnoslas.	We are going to take them with us.
Tráigamelos Ud.	Bring them to me.
Poniéndoselos, ella salió.	Putting them on, she left.

A reflexive pronoun precedes any other object pronoun. When two pronouns are added to an infinitive, an accent mark must be written over the final syllable of the verb. Also note that an accent mark is written on the next to last syllable of an affirmative command form or of a present participle when either one or two pronouns are added.

◆ *Práctica.*   Say after your teacher:

1. Juan me lo da. Va a dármelo. Está dándomelo. (Me lo está dando.) Démelo Ud. No me lo dé Ud.
2. Yo se lo llevo a él. Quiero llevárselo. Estoy llevándoselo. (Se lo estoy llevando.) Lléveselo Ud. No se lo lleve Ud.
3. Luis no se los prestó a ellos. No pudo prestárselos. Prestándoselos. Présteselos Ud. No se los preste Ud.
4. ¿Se lavaron Uds. las manos? ¿Quieren lavárselas? ¿Están lavándoselas? (¿Se las están lavando?) Lávenselas Uds. No se las laven Uds.
5. ¿Se puso ella los guantes? ¿Se los puso? ¿Pudo ponérselos? ¿Estaba poniéndoselos? (¿Se los estaba poniendo?) Póngaselos Ud.

D. Demonstrative pronouns

éste, ésta, éstos, éstas	this (one), these
ése, ésa, ésos, ésas	that (one), those
aquél, aquélla, aquéllos, aquéllas	that (one), those
esto, eso, aquello	this, that (*neuter*)

estos regalos y ésos	these gloves and those (*near you*)
aquella blusa y ésta	that blouse (*yonder*) and this one
¿Qué es esto?	What is this?
Eso es interesante.	That is interesting.

The demonstrative pronouns are the same in form as the demonstrative adjectives, except for the written accent on the pronouns (see page 69). The use of the pronouns corresponds to that of the adjectives.

The three neuter pronouns are used when the antecedent is a statement, a general idea, or something which has not been identified. Since there are no neuter adjectives, an accent is not required on these three forms.

The demonstrative pronoun **éste (-a, -os, -as)** often translates *the latter* in Spanish:

Ella le da el dinero a la vendedora; ésta envuelve el prendedor.
She gives the money to the saleslady; the latter wraps up the pin.

E. Uses of **volver** and **devolver,** of **preguntar,** and of the idiom **acabar de**

1. **Marta volvió a casa.**   Martha returned home.
   Yo le devolví el dinero a ella.   I returned the money to her.

Volver means *to return, come back,* while **devolver** means *to return, give back,* e.g., something borrowed.

2. **Carolina le pregunta a la vendedora por el prendedor.**   Caroline asks the saleslady about the pin.
Pregunté por ti ayer.   I asked about you yesterday.

Preguntar means to ask (*a question*). The person of whom something is asked is the indirect object. To ask *about* a thing or person, **por** is used.

3. **Acabo de comprarle (a ella) una blusa.**   I have just bought a blouse for her.
Tomás acaba de volver de la Florida.   Tom has just returned from Florida.
Los muchachos acababan de salir.   The boys had just left.

The present and imperfect tenses of **acabar de** plus an infinitive are the equivalent of English *have* (*had*) *just* plus the English past participle.

F.   Use of the definite article in a general sense

Es una fecha muy importante en la vida de las jóvenes.   It is a very important date in the life of girls (young women).
Me gustan mucho las flores.   I like flowers very much.

Remember that if a noun in Spanish represents the entire class to which it belongs, that is, if it applies to all girls, all flowers, etc., the definite article is used with it (see Lección 10, page 132). Contrast this use with the omission of the article when unemphatic *some* or *any* are involved: **Le compré flores para Marta,** *I bought* (*some*) *flowers for Martha.*

EJERCICIOS

A. Say after your teacher; then repeat twice, changing the verb to the preterit tense and then to the imperfect tense:

1. Las jóvenes están en el centro.
2. Marta las pone sobre la mesa.
3. Yo les entrego las compras.
4. Yo comienzo a comer.
5. Nosotros llegamos a tiempo.
6. ¿Buscas a Carolina?
7. Juan le devuelve estas cosas.
8. Ella almuerza con Tomás.

B. Say after your teacher; then repeat, substituting the correct object pronoun for each noun (in italics) and placing it in the proper position:

1. Ella le escribió *una tarjeta.*
2. Sus padres le regalaron *un reloj de oro.*
3. La muchacha quería vendernos *las flores.*
4. Nosotros te dimos *las fotografías.*

5. Ud. nos trajo *las compras.*
6. Ellos le dieron a él *los billetes.*
7. Póngase Ud. *los zapatos.*
8. No se ponga Ud. *ese vestido.*
9. Carolina le devolvió a ella *el dinero.*
10. Los muchachos están lavándose *la cara.*

C. Answer affirmatively, substituting the correct object pronoun for the noun and making any other necessary changes:

MODELS:　¿Le llevó Ud. a ella el reloj?　*Sí, se lo llevé a ella.*
　　　　　¿Vas a darle a él el billete?　*Sí, voy a dárselo a él.*

1. ¿Le dio Ud. a él los billetes?
2. ¿Le compraste a ella esta blusa?
3. ¿Les mandaste a ellas las flores?
4. ¿Les trajo Ud. a ellos los regalos?
5. ¿Estás escribiéndole a él la tarjeta?
6. ¿Puedes darle a ella este dinero?

D. Say after your teacher; then repeat, using the demonstrative pronoun:

MODEL:　Mire Ud. aquella casa.　*Mire Ud. aquella casa. Mire Ud. aquélla.*

1. ¿Le gustan a Ud. estas blusas?
2. No quiero comprar esos guantes.
3. Enséñeme Ud. aquel prendedor.
4. Debes llevarles estas flores.
5. Yo le di aquel regalo.
6. Mi hermana me mandó esta tarjeta.
7. Juan me devolvió este billete.
8. ¿Se compró Ud. ese reloj?
9. No me regalaron estas flores.
10. Entraron en aquella tienda.

E. Answer each question, following the model:

MODEL:　¿Qué blusa le gusta a Ud.? ¿Ésta?　*No, no me gusta ésa.*

1. ¿Qué guantes acabas de comprar? ¿Éstos?
2. ¿Qué cartera vas a comprarle a Luisa? ¿Ésta?
3. ¿Cuáles de los prendedores de plata te gustan más? ¿Ésos?
4. ¿Cuál de las tarjetas vas a mandar? ¿Ésa?
5. ¿Qué fotografías puede Ud. prestarme? ¿Ésas?
6. ¿Cuál de los relojes de oro te parece más fino? ¿Ése?

F. Give the Spanish equivalent, using the formal forms in the commands:

1. The money. Give it to me; don't give it to her.　2. The photographs. Bring them to her; don't bring them to them (*f. pl.*).　3. The gifts. Do not take them to him; take them to her.　4. The car. He wants to sell it to us; he doesn't want to sell it to you (*pl.*).　5. The card. Martha is sending it to Louise; she has just sent it to her.

G. Give the Spanish equivalent, using the familiar forms for *you:*

1. Martha, who has just left a store, runs across Caroline. 2. Upon seeing her friend, Martha says: "What a surprise to see you downtown this morning! 3. I asked about you yesterday morning, but no one knew when you intended to return." 4. "I did not arrive until yesterday at noon, because I decided to stay at home one day longer than I expected." 5. Then Caroline tells her that she is looking for some gifts for her sister Louise's birthday. 6. "What did you buy?" Martha asks Caroline; the latter answers: "I began with a pretty card and a blouse which is very stylish. 7. Also I found a silver pin, but I couldn't buy it because I didn't have enough money." 8. Martha tells Caroline that she has a twenty-dollar bill that she can lend her. 9. They return to the store and stop in front of the counter where pins are sold. 10. Martha likes the pin; she says that [it] is darling. Then her friend says: "I'll take it (with me)." 11. She gives the money to the saleslady; the latter wraps up the pin, and hands it to Caroline. 12. Now it is time to eat lunch, and Martha has to leave. She has a date with Thomas who has just returned from Florida.

H. **Composición:** Un encuentro inesperado

Assuming that you are Martha and using the content of the dialogue as a guideline, complete the following sentences:

1. Esta mañana (yo) me _____ con Carolina. 2. Para mí _____ , porque yo no sabía que ella ya _____ en la ciudad. 3. Carolina no _____ antes (*before, sooner*) porque _____ en casa un día más. 4. Me _____ que el viaje _____ de _____ esperaba.
     5. Carolina _____ en el centro porque _____ algo para el cumpleaños de su hermana. 6. Empezó con_____. 7. También_____un prendedor de plata. 8. Como Carolina no _____ bastante dinero para _____ , yo le _____ veinte dólares. 9. Ella y yo _____ en la tienda y nos _____ frente al mostrador donde _____ los prendedores. 10. Cuando Carolina le _____ el dinero a la vendedora, ésta _____ el prendedor y _____ .

EJERCICIOS DE PRONUNCIACIÓN

1. Review the sounds of the diphthongs (see pages 3, 8, 39, 122, 134–135, and 170); then pronounce and divide into syllables:

miedo	principio	secretaria	vuelo	encuentra
iglesia	abierto	cuaderno	playa	autobús
baile	reina	veinte	traiga	sois
llevé uno	tengo una	ruinas	ciudad	muy

2. When a weak vowel adjacent to a strong vowel has a written accent, it retains its syllabic value and forms a separate syllable. Divide into syllables:

       traía   creí   había   ríos   país

3. An accent on a strong vowel merely indicates stress. Divide into syllables:

       diálogo   habéis   comió   avión   ayudáis

4. Two adjacent strong vowels form two separate syllables. Divide into syllables:

       paseo   idea   europeo   leemos   héroe

VOCABULARIO

acabar to end, finish
almorzar (ue) to have (eat) lunch
amable kind
antes *adv.* before, formerly, sooner
el **billete** bill, bank note
la **blusa** blouse
la **cita** date, appointment
el **cumpleaños** birthday
cumplir to fulfill, keep (one's word),
   reach (one's birthday), be (years old)
decidir to decide
dejar to let, allow, permit
detener (*like* **tener**) to detain, stop; *reflex.*
   to stop (oneself)
devolver (ue) to return, give back
empezar (ie) (a + *inf.*) to begin (to)
el **encuentro** encounter, meeting
entender (ie) to understand
entregar to hand (over), give
envolver (ue) to wrap (up)
esperar to expect
la **flor** flower
la **Florida** Florida

frente a *prep.* in front of
inesperado, -a unexpected
Luisa Louise
llevarse to take away, take with oneself
mandar to send, order
el **mediodía** noon
la **moda** style, fashion
el **mostrador** counter, showcase
el **oro** gold
pagar to pay, pay for
la **plata** silver
precioso, -a precious, darling, beautiful
preguntar to ask (*a question*), inquire
el **prendedor** pin, brooch
prestar to lend
regalar to give (*as a gift*)
el **regalo** gift
la **sorpresa** surprise
tardar to delay, be long
la **tarjeta** card (*postal, birthday, etc.*)
todo *pron.* everything
vender to sell

acabar de + *inf.* to have just + *p.p.*
al mediodía at noon
ayer por la mañana yesterday morning
billete de (veinte) dólares (twenty)-dollar bill
¿cuántos años tiene (ella)? how old is (she)?
¿cuántos años (va a cumplir ella)? how old (is she going to be)?
de lo que (yo esperaba) than (I expected)
de mi parte for me, on my part
de nada don't mention it, you are welcome, not at all
encontrarse (ue) con to meet, run across
estar (muy) de moda to be (very) stylish, be (very) fashionable
me lo llevo I'll take it (with me)
preguntar por to ask (inquire) about
(prendedor) de plata silver (pin)
¡qué sorpresa! what a surprise!
(reloj) de oro gold (watch)
tardar mucho to take long (a long time), be long
un día más one (a) day longer, one more day

Lectura 6

Fiestas y costumbres

Los países de habla española celebran muchas
fiestas. Algunas son nacionales; otras son
religiosas. Nosotros celebramos el aniversario
de nuestra independencia el cuatro de julio;
los mexicanos celebran el suyo[1] el dieciséis
de septiembre. En México esa fecha no conmemora el fin de la guerra de la independencia, sino el principio de una larga lucha[2]
contra los españoles. El día quince de septiembre de 1810, el padre Miguel Hidalgo,
un sacerdote[3] católico, pronunció las palabras
que al día siguiente iniciaron el movimiento
revolucionario. Todas las repúblicas
hispanoamericanas honran a sus héroes
nacionales y celebran el aniversario de su
independencia. Muchas veces[4] estas fiestas
duran dos o tres días.

El mundo católico dedica cada día del año
a uno o a varios santos. En muchos países
cuando se bautiza a un niño,[5] éste recibe el
nombre de un santo y cada año celebra el día
de su santo más bien que el aniversario de su
nacimiento. Es un día de mucha alegría[6] en
que hay regalos, tertulias y comidas.

En muchos países hispánicos se celebran las
procesiones religiosas de la Semana Santa, que
empieza el Domingo de Ramos[7] y termina el
Domingo de Resurrección.[8] En Sevilla,

España, se observa esta semana de[9] una
manera solemne y espléndida. Muchas
sociedades religiosas forman procesiones que
pasan por las calles llevando pasos[10] que
representan la Pasión de Cristo en forma
impresionante y hermosa. Las procesiones
terminan el Viernes Santo. Con el Sábado
de Gloria[11] vuelve la alegría y se tocan las
campanas de todas las iglesias. El Domingo
de Resurrección se llama la Pascua Florida
porque en todas las iglesias adornan de flores
los altares. Igual que[12] en nuestro país, la
gente se pone la ropa más elegante para ir
a la iglesia. Por la tarde generalmente hay
corridas de toros.[13]

En México las fiestas de Navidad[14] empiezan la noche del 16 de diciembre y no
terminan hasta la Nochebuena. Todas las
noches se celebran las «posadas», que representan los nueve días que pasaron José y

---

[1] **el suyo,** *theirs.*   [2] **lucha,** *struggle.*   [3] **sacerdote,** *priest.*   [4] **Muchas veces,** *Often, Many times.*
[5] **se bautiza a un niño,** *a child is baptized.* (When the reflexive construction used as substitute for
the passive has a personal subject, the reflexive verb is used impersonally, and the personal subject is
expressed as the indirect object.)   [6] **alegría,** *joy, happiness.*   [7] **Domingo de Ramos,** *Palm
Sunday.*   [8] **Domingo de Resurrección,** *Easter Sunday.*   [9] **de,** *in.*   [10] **pasos,** *floats.* (**Pasos** are
the heavy platforms on which life-sized figures representing Christ, the Virgin, and other persons
who figured in the Passion of Christ are carried through the streets of Seville during Holy Week by
members of the churches and religious societies.)   [11] **Sábado de Gloria,** *Holy Saturday.*
[12] **Igual que,** *The same as.*   [13] **corridas de toros,** *bullfights.*   [14] **Navidad,** *Christmas.*

María en su viaje a Belén.[15] En los pueblos y en ciertas colonias de las ciudades los amigos se reúnen[16] y forman una procesión. Van de puerta en puerta[17] llevando las figuritas[18] de José, María, el Niño Jesús, los pastores,[19] las mulas, las vacas y las ovejas. Una persona lleva la estrella[20] de Belén; las otras van detrás cantando. Llaman a cada puerta, pero una voz contesta que la posada[21] está llena. Cuando la procesión llega a la novena puerta, el dueño de la casa les da permiso para pasar la noche en el establo. Todos entran y colocan las figuritas en un altar que representa el nacimiento[22] del Niño Jesús.

En cada «posada», después de preparar el nacimiento, los niños rompen la piñata. Ésta es una olla de barro[23] adornada con papeles de muchos colores y llena de frutas, dulces, nueces[24] y juguetes.[25] Se cuelga[26] en el patio o en una sala de la casa. Con los ojos vendados,[27] uno de los niños trata tres veces de romper la piñata con un palo.[28] Si no la rompe, otro niño trata de hacerlo.

En España y en los países hispanoamericanos casi todas las familias ponen nacimientos durante las fiestas de Navidad, costumbre que también tienen muchas familias norte-americanas.

En general, en el mundo hispánico no hay árboles de Navidad y los niños no cuelgan sus medias[29] en las chimeneas. Los niños creen que, si han sido[30] buenos, los Reyes Magos[31] les traen regalos, pero no el día de Navidad, sino el seis de enero, día de la Epifanía.[32] La Epifanía conmemora la visita de los tres reyes de Oriente, Gaspar, Melchor y Baltasar, que siguieron[33] el camino que les indicó la estrella de Belén para ir a adorar al Niño Jesús y para llevarle ofrendas de oro, mirra e incienso. La verdad es que hoy día muchas familias han adoptado[34] la costumbre de poner árboles de Navidad.

El veintiocho de diciembre, Día de los Inocentes,[35] es para los españoles lo que el primero de abril es para nosotros. Todos tratan de dar bromas a[36] sus amigos y se divierten mucho.[37]

En España hay una costumbre muy extraña para celebrar la víspera[38] del Año Nuevo. Unos minutos antes de la medianoche todos toman doce uvas en la mano. A cada campanada del reloj[39] comen una uva para tener buena suerte durante el año nuevo. Al sonar la última campanada, todos aplauden mucho y gritan con entusiasmo: «¡Feliz Año Nuevo!» o «¡Próspero Año Nuevo!»

Preguntas

1. ¿En qué día celebramos el aniversario de nuestra independencia?   2. ¿Cuándo celebran el suyo los mexicanos?   3. ¿Quién fue Miguel Hidalgo?

4. Cuando se bautiza a un niño español, ¿qué nombre recibe generalmente?   5. ¿Qué celebran los españoles cada año?

---

[15]**Belén,** *Bethlehem.*   [16]**se reúnen,** *meet, gather.*   [17]**de puerta en puerta,** *from door to door.*   [18]**figuritas,** *small figures.*   [19]**pastores,** *shepherds.*   [20]**estrella,** *star.*   [21]**posada,** *inn.*   [22]**nacimiento,** *manger scene.*   [23]**Ésta . . . barro,** *This is a clay jar.*   [24]**nueces,** *nuts.*   [25]**juguetes,** *toys.*   [26]**Se cuelga,** *It is hung.*   [27]**Con . . . vendados,** *Blindfolded.*   [28]**palo,** *stick.*   [29]**medias,** *stockings.*   [30]**han sido,** *they have been.*   [31]**Reyes Magos,** *Wise Men (Kings), Magi.*   [32]**Epifanía,** *Epiphany.*   [33]**siguieron,** *followed.*   [34]**han adoptado,** *have adopted.*   [35]**Día de los Inocentes,** *Day of the Holy Innocents,* equivalent to April Fool's Day. (An **inocente** is a gullible person or one easily duped.)   [36]**dar bromas a,** *to play tricks on.*   [37]**se divierten mucho,** *they have a very good time (amuse themselves very much).*   [38]**víspera,** *eve.*   [39]**cada . . . reloj,** *each stroke of the clock.*

6. ¿Cuándo empieza la Semana Santa?   7. ¿Cuándo termina?   8. ¿Qué llevan en las procesiones de la Semana Santa en Sevilla?   9. ¿Qué hace todo el mundo el Domingo de Resurrección?

10. ¿Cuándo empiezan las fiestas de Navidad en México?   11. ¿Cuándo terminan? 12. ¿Qué representan las «posadas»?   13. ¿Qué forma la gente por la noche?   14. ¿Adónde va la procesión?   15. ¿Qué llevan las personas que van en la procesión?   16. ¿Qué contesta una voz cuando llaman a las puertas?   17. ¿Qué pasa cuando llegan a la novena puerta? 18. ¿Dónde colocan las figuritas?   19. ¿Qué representa el altar?

20. ¿Qué hacen los niños en cada posada?   21. ¿Qué es la piñata?   22. ¿De qué está llena la piñata?   23. ¿Dónde se cuelga la piñata?   24. ¿Qué trata de hacer uno de los niños?

25. ¿Dónde cuelgan sus medias los niños norteamericanos?   26. ¿Quiénes les traen regalos a los niños españoles?   27. ¿En qué día traen los regalos?   28. ¿Qué conmemora la Epifanía?   29. ¿Qué costumbre han adoptado algunas familias españolas e hispanoamericanas?

30. ¿Qué día es el veintiocho de diciembre?   31. ¿Qué tratan de hacer todos?   32. ¿Qué costumbre extraña hay en España para celebrar la víspera del Año Nuevo?   33. ¿Qué gritan todos al sonar la última campanada?

Estudio de palabras

a. Many Spanish nouns and adjectives ending in **-ario** end in *-ary* in English: aniversario, extraordinario, necesario, revolucionario.

b. Approximate cognates. Pronounce the following words aloud, give the English cognates, and indicate the principles involved in recognizing them: adorar, aplaudir, celebrar, dedicar, elegante, espléndido, héroe, independencia, indicar, observar, procesión, religioso, sociedad, solemne.

c. Less approximate cognates. Pronounce the following words aloud, note the English cognates, and indicate the variations: católico, *Catholic;* conmemorar, *to commemorate;* chimenea, *chimney, fireplace;* entusiasmo, *enthusiasm;* establo, *stable;* extraño, *strange;* movimiento, *movement.*

d. Compare the meanings of: campana, *bell, and* campanada, *stroke of bell* or *clock;* comer, *to eat, dine, and* comida, *meal, dinner, food;* noche, *night,* medianoche, *midnight, and* Nochebuena, *Christmas Eve;* puerta, *door, and* puerto, *port;* viaje, *trip, and* viajar, *to travel.*

La Feria de Abril en Sevilla es la feria más importante de Andalucía. En la foto de arriba vemos varias parejas de jóvenes paseando a caballo durante la feria. Abajo se ve una falla en la plaza del Dr. Collado en Valencia. Las fallas son grandes figuras de papel engomado, madera y otros materiales, que representan personajes alegóricos o caricaturas. Son típicas de Valencia, España.

Paso de la Virgen de los Dolores durante la Semana Santa de Sevilla, España. Una cofradía religiosa desfila durante la Semana Santa de Sevilla. Las cofradías son hermandades religiosas.

La vendimia cerca de Ciudad Real. Durante la vendimia se celebran grandes festivales en diversos lugares de la Península Ibérica, como en muchos otros países europeos, por ejemplo, en Francia, Alemania, Italia y Austria.

The past participles • **The present perfect and
pluperfect indicative tenses** • **The past participle used as an
adjective** • **Summary of other uses of** *haber* • *Hace* **meaning "ago,
since"**

LECCIÓN 15

Una tarde en la playa

Ricardo y Vicente, que están de vacaciones, se encuentran[1] en la calle.

VICENTE —¡Hola, Ricardo! ¿Dónde has estado toda la mañana? Te llamé hace
un par de horas y no había nadie en tu casa.

RICARDO —He estado trabajando en la oficina de mi padre. Su secretaria ha
tenido que volver a Nueva York y . . .

VICENTE —Hombre, hay que disfrutar un poco de las vacaciones de verano, ¿no
te parece?

RICARDO —¡Tienes razón! He estado trabajando demasiado. Pero mira, esta
tarde estoy libre. ¿Quieres ir a la playa conmigo?

VICENTE —¡Estupendo! No he ido a la playa esta semana y acabo de comprarme
un traje de baño nuevo.

◆　◆　◆　◆　◆

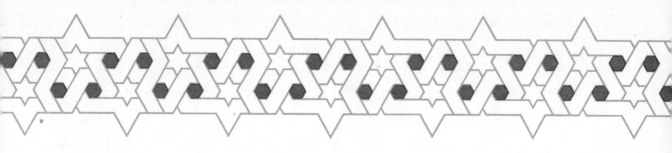

Al llegar a la playa los dos jóvenes se mudan de ropa. Caminan un rato por la arena; luego se sientan a tomar el sol.

VICENTE —Qué agradable es vivir en un sitio cerca del mar, ¿verdad? ¿Tú vienes a la playa a menudo?

RICARDO —Pues, vine hace dos semanas, pero entonces hacía mucho fresco. Y ahora que hace calor, he estado muy ocupado.

VICENTE —Cuando yo era pequeño y vivíamos en el campo, nadábamos en un lago que había cerca de casa.

RICARDO —Por aquí no hay ni lagos ni ríos. Hay piscinas, pero, en realidad, me gusta más nadar en el mar.

◆　◆　◆　◆　◆

VICENTE —El domingo pasado traje a mi hermanito a la playa.

RICARDO —¿Ya sabe nadar?

VICENTE —Estoy enseñándole y ya ha aprendido bastante. Al principio tenía miedo y no se atrevía a entrar en el agua solo.

RICARDO —¿Había mucha gente el domingo?

VICENTE —Nunca había visto tanta gente en la playa. Parecía que todo el mundo había venido a disfrutar del sol y del agua.

RICARDO (*Mirando a las chicas en traje de baño.*) —Y naturalmente, también es agradable poder mirar a tantas chicas bonitas, ¿verdad?

VICENTE —Pues ¡hombre! ¡Es lo que más me gusta hacer en la playa!

---

[1]**se encuentran,** *meet* (*each other*). The plural reflexive pronouns, **nos, os, se** may express a mutual or reciprocal action (one subject acting upon another).

Conversación

A. Preguntas sobre el diálogo

1. ¿Dónde estaba Ricardo cuando Vicente lo llamó? ¿Por qué estaba trabajando allí?
2. ¿Adónde fueron Ricardo y Vicente esa tarde? 3. ¿Qué hicieron cuando llegaron a la playa? 4. ¿Por qué no ha podido ir Ricardo a la playa a menudo? 5. ¿Dónde vivía Vicente cuando era pequeño? ¿Qué había cerca de su casa? 6. ¿Por qué no se atrevía el hermanito de Vicente a entrar solo en el agua? ¿Quién está enseñándole a nadar? 7. ¿Qué contestó Vicente cuando le preguntó Ricardo si había mucha gente en la playa ese domingo? 8. ¿Qué es lo que más le gusta a Vicente hacer en la playa?

B. Aplicación del diálogo

1. ¿Sabe Ud. nadar bien? 2. ¿En qué meses se puede nadar en esta parte del país? 3. ¿Dónde se puede nadar por aquí? 4. ¿Hay lagos o ríos cerca de aquí? 5. ¿Qué se pone uno para nadar? 6. ¿Piensa Ud. ir a la playa durante las vacaciones? ¿A qué playa piensa ir? 7. ¿Qué le gusta a Ud. hacer cuando va a la playa? ¿Tomar el sol? ¿Nadar? ¿Mirar a las chicas? 8. ¿Conoce Ud. algunas playas extranjeras?

NOTAS GRAMATICALES

A. The past participles

| hablar: **hablado** *spoken* | comer: **comido** *eaten* | vivir: **vivido** *lived* |

Past participles are regularly formed by adding **-ado** to the stem of **-ar** verbs and **-ido** to the stem of **-er** and **-ir** verbs.

If the stem ends in **-a, -e,** or **-o,** the regular ending **-ido** requires an accent:

| creer: **creído** *believed* | leer: **leído** *read* | traer: **traído** *brought* |

The following verbs which you have learned have irregular past participles:

abrir:	**abierto**	*opened*
decir:	**dicho**	*said*
descubrir:	**descubierto**	*discovered*
escribir:	**escrito**	*written*
hacer:	**hecho**	*done, made*
ir:	**ido**	*gone*
poner:	**puesto**	*put, placed*
ver:	**visto**	*seen*
volver:	**vuelto**	*returned*
devolver:	**devuelto**	*given back*
envolver:	**envuelto**	*wrapped (up)*

B. The present perfect and pluperfect indicative tenses

	Present Perfect		
he **has** **ha** Ud. **ha**	hablado	I have you (*fam.*) have he, she has you (*formal*) have	spoken
hemos habéis **han** Uds. **han**	hablado	we have you (*fam.*) have they have you have	spoken
	Pluperfect		
había habías había Ud. había	comido	I had you (*fam.*) had he, she had you (*formal*) had	eaten
habíamos habíais habían Uds. habían	comido	we had you (*fam.*) had they had you had	eaten

Nosotros lo hemos escrito. We have written it.
Ella no se lo ha puesto. She has not put it on.
¿No lo había hecho Ud.? Hadn't you (Had you not) done it?

The auxiliary verb **haber** is used with the past participle to form the compound or perfect tenses. The present tense of **haber** plus the past participle forms the present perfect tense, and the imperfect tense of **haber** plus the past participle forms the pluperfect tense, often called the past perfect tense in English.

Note the following points: (1) Following forms of **haber,** the past participle always ends in **-o;** (2) The form of **haber** and the past participle are seldom separated; (3) Negative words precede the form of **haber;** (4) Pronoun objects precede the form of **haber** or come between the negative and the form of **haber.**

◆ *Práctica.* Read in Spanish, keeping the meaning in mind:

1. he abierto; había abierto. 2. hemos puesto; habíamos puesto. 3. él ha escrito; había escrito. 4. ellos han hecho; habían hecho. 5. Ud. ha visto; había visto. 6. Uds. han dicho; habían dicho. 7. tú has vuelto; habías vuelto. 8. habéis ido; habíais ido. 9. yo no lo he creído; nosotros no lo hemos devuelto. 10. nosotros no la hemos leído; yo no me he sentado.

C. The past participle used as an adjective

> **Las ventanas estaban abiertas.**   The windows were open.
> **La puerta no está cerrada.**   The door isn't closed.
> **José se encontraba cansado.**   Joe was (found himself) tired.

Past participles may be used as adjectives, in which case they agree like other adjectives. Remember that certain reflexive verbs like **encontrarse, hallarse,** and **verse** are often substituted for **estar** with past participles, and that in such cases they normally retain something of their literal meanings. (See footnote 5, page 105.)

Do not confuse this use of **estar** with a past participle, used to describe a state or condition which is the result of a previous action, with the reflexive substitute for the passive, page 83, which is used when an action is involved:

> **Se cerró la puerta a las cinco,** *The door was closed at five o'clock.*

D. Summary of other uses of **haber**

1. Recall that the third person singular of **haber** is used impersonally, *i.e.,* without a definite personal subject: **hay** (used for **ha**), *there is, there are;* **había,** *there was, there were;* **ha habido,** *there has been, there have been.*

> **Por aquí no hay ni lagos ni ríos.**   Around here there are neither lakes nor rivers.
> **No había nadie en tu casa.**   There wasn't anyone (There was no one) at your house.

2. **Hay que llegar a tiempo.**   It is necessary to (One must) arrive on time.
> **Hay que disfrutar de las vacaciones.**   One (People) must enjoy vacations.

Hay que plus an infinitive means *It is necessary to* or the indefinite subject *One, You, We, People,* etc., *must.* The imperfect **había que** is less common:

> **Había que hablar despacio.**   It was necessary to talk slowly.

Remember that when *must = to have to,* expressing an obligation or necessity, **tener que** plus an infinitive is used:

> **Su secretaria ha tenido que volver a Nueva York.**   His secretary has had to return to New York.
> **Yo tengo que salir ahora.**   I must (have to) leave now.

For a moral obligation or duty, **deber** is used:

> **Debo practicar mucho.**   I must (should) practice a great deal.

E. **Hace,** meaning *ago, since*

> **Te llamé hace un par de horas** *or* **Hace un par de horas que te llamé.** I called
> you a couple of hours ago *or* It is a couple of hours since I called you.
> **Vine hace dos semanas** *or* **Hace dos semanas que vine.** I came two weeks ago *or*
> It is two weeks since I came.

When **hace** is used with an expression of time in a sentence which is in the past tense, it
regularly means *ago,* or *since.* If the **hace**-clause comes first in the sentence, **que** usually
(not always) introduces the main clause, but **que** is omitted if **hace** and the time
expression follow the verb.

EJERCICIOS

A. Say after your teacher; then repeat, using the present perfect tense, and then the
pluperfect tense:

1. Yo veo a Vicente.
2. Me escribe una carta.
3. Ellos abren la puerta.
4. Marta no dice eso.
5. Tomás me devuelve el dinero.
6. Él y yo vamos a la playa.
7. ¿Qué haces tú?
8. ¿Qué ponen Uds. allí?

B. Answer negatively in Spanish, following the model:

MODEL: ¿Ya le escribiste la carta?   *No, todavía no se la he escrito.*

1. ¿Ya le compraste los regalos?
2. ¿Ya le mandaste la tarjeta?
3. ¿Ya le pusiste los zapatos?
4. ¿Ya le diste el dinero?
5. ¿Ya les devolviste los libros?
6. ¿Ya les llevaste las cartas?
7. ¿Ya te pusiste el traje de baño?
8. ¿Ya te lavaste las manos?

C. Answer in Spanish, following the models in each group:

MODEL: ¿Ha cerrado Ud. la° puerta?   *Sí, está cerrada.*

1. ¿Ha escrito Ud. las frases?
2. ¿Ha abierto Ud. el cuaderno?
3. ¿Ha cerrado Ud. los libros?
4. ¿Ha terminado Ud. la composición?

MODEL: ¿Habían cerrado ellos las ventanas?   *No, ya estaban cerradas.*

5. ¿Había hecho María ese vestido?
6. ¿Había envuelto él los regalos?
7. ¿Habían abierto ellos la puerta?
8. ¿Habías puesto las cosas allí?

MODEL: ¿Cuándo llegó él?   ¿Hace dos días?   *Sí, llegó hace dos días* and *Sí,*
hace dos días que llegó.

9. ¿Cuándo volvieron?   ¿Hace una
hora?

10. ¿Cuándo salió Ana?   ¿Hace un
mes?

11. ¿Cuándo vino José?   ¿Hace media
hora?

12. ¿Cuándo la compró él?   ¿Hace un
año?

MODEL: ¿Qué hay que hacer?   ¿Sentarse?   *Sí, hay que sentarse.*

13. ¿Qué hay que hacer?   ¿Ir a casa
ahora?

14. ¿Qué hay que hacer?   ¿Esperar
aquí?

15. ¿Qué hay que hacer?   ¿Tomar el
autobús?

16. ¿Qué hay que hacer?   ¿Mudarse de
ropa?

MODEL: ¿Pudiste ir a la playa?   (trabajar)   *No, no pude; he tenido que trabajar.*

17. ¿Pudiste ir al cine?   (estudiar)
18. ¿Pudiste ir al lago?   (terminar la composición)
19. ¿Pudieron Uds. ir al centro?   (quedarse en casa)
20. ¿Pudieron Uds. llevar a Marta?   (esperar a Luisa)

D. Review the uses of the preterit versus the imperfect tense in Lessons 10 and 11; then
read aloud, supplying the appropriate form of each infinitive and making the necessary
changes in the reflexive pronouns:

1. El verano pasado yo (trabajar) _____ tres meses en un sitio que (estar) _____
cerca de una playa.   2. Todas las tardes cuando yo (terminar) _____ el trabajo,
(mudarse) _____ de ropa, (ponerse) _____ el traje de baño y (nadar) _____ un
rato.   3. También (gustarme) _____ tomar el sol y (sentarse) _____ en la arena para
descansar.   4. En el mes de agosto mis padres (hacer) _____ un viaje y
(venir) _____ a visitarme.   5. Yo les (enseñar) _____ todos los sitios bonitos que
(haber) _____ cerca de esa playa.   6. A ellos les (gustar) _____ mucho ver como yo
(pasar) _____ mis vacaciones de verano.   7. En realidad, yo (disfrutar) _____ mucho
de ellas.   8. ¡Y no (querer) _____ volver a clases!

E. Supply the definite article wherever required:

1. Nos gustan _____ flores.   2. No me gusta _____ invierno.   3. Elena va a cumplir
quince años _____ mes que viene.   4. Hoy es _____ jueves.   5. Mis padres quieren
salir _____ sábado por _____ mañana.   6. Mis tíos disfrutan de _____ vida
en _____ Perú.   7. Casi todos _____ estudiantes van a _____ iglesia _____
domingos.   8. Carolina se puso _____ zapatos.   9. Tenemos que mudarnos
de _____ ropa.   10. Las chicas se lavaron _____ manos.   11. Pasaron casi

todo _____ día en _____ agua. 12. _____ señor Ortega volvió de _____ Florida _____ semana pasada. 13. Buenas tardes, _____ señorita López. 14. _____ español es una lengua interesante.

F. Give the Spanish equivalent:

1. Where has Richard been all morning? 2. Vincent passed by his house an hour ago, and there was no one there. 3. Richard has been working at (in) his father's office. 4. The secretary has had to return to New York. 5. Richard believes that Vincent is right; he has not been enjoying his summer vacation. 6. That afternoon Richard and Vincent decided to go to the beach. 7. Vincent went to the beach two weeks ago. 8. Richard has not been able to swim because it has been cool. 9. When Vincent was small, he used to swim in a large lake. 10. Last Sunday there were many people on the beach. 11. It was hot then and it seemed that everybody was enjoying the sun and the water. 12. Vincent's little brother doesn't know how to swim yet. 13. At first he was afraid, but he has learned quite a bit. 14. Vincent likes to watch the pretty girls in their bathing suits.

G. **Composición:** Una semana en la playa

Assuming that the following experience has already taken place, rewrite the account in a past perspective, using the appropriate preterit or imperfect tenses:

1. Este verano mi familia y yo *vamos a hacer* un viaje a la playa. 2. *Vamos a ir* a un hotel (*hotel*) muy bonito que está cerca del mar. 3. *Vamos a salir* un jueves muy temprano por la mañana y *vamos a quedarnos* allí una semana.

4. Mi hermano y yo *vamos a levantarnos* muy temprano y en seguida *vamos a salir* de nuestro cuarto. 5. *Va a gustarnos* especialmente caminar por la arena y tomar el aire fresco de la mañana. 6. Luego *vamos a entrar* en el agua y *nadar* un rato. 7. Después, *vamos a volver* a nuestro hotel. 8. Allí *van a esperarnos* nuestros padres y *vamos a desayunarnos* con ellos.

9. Después, durante las otras horas de la mañana, *vamos a quedarnos* en el hotel. 10. *Vamos a leer* los periódicos, *escribir* algunas cartas, *nadar* en la piscina del hotel o *salir* a conocer algunos de los sitios interesantes que hay cerca de allí.

11. Por la tarde *vamos a acompañar* a nuestros padres a la playa. 12. A ellos les *gusta* ir a las cuatro o las cinco de la tarde, cuando no *hace* mucho calor. 13. Nosotros *vamos a sentarnos* en la arena, *charlar* y *disfrutar* del aire fresco y del sol. 14. Por la noche *vamos a salir* siempre a cenar. 15. Luego *vamos a ir* al cine a ver alguna película o *vamos a dar* un paseo en coche. 16. *Va a ser* una semana maravillosa para toda la familia.

EJERCICIOS DE PRONUNCIACIÓN

Review the observations on Spanish intonation (pages 9–10), then read the first three exchanges of the dialogue of this lesson, paying close attention to the intonation patterns.

VOCABULARIO

la **arena** sand
atreverse (a + *inf.***)** to dare (to)
caminar to walk, go
la **chica** girl
encontrarse (ue) to find oneself, be
found, be; *reciprocal* to meet (each other)
la **gente** people (*requires sing. verb*)
haber to have (*auxiliary*)
el **hermanito** little brother
el **hotel** hotel
el **lago** lake
el **mar** sea
el **miedo** fear
mudar to change
nadar to swim

naturalmente naturally
ni neither, nor, (not) . . . or
la **piscina** swimming pool
la **playa** beach
el **principio** beginning
la **razón** (*pl.* **razones**) reason
el **río** river
la **ropa** clothes, clothing
la **secretaria** secretary
solo, -a alone
tanto, -a (-os, -as) *adj. and pron.* as (so)
much; *pl.* as (so) many
el **traje** suit
el **traje de baño** bathing suit
Vicente Vincent

al principio at first, at the beginning
caminar por to walk in (through)
en realidad in reality, in fact
estar de vacaciones to be on vacation
mudarse de ropa to change clothes (clothing)
ni . . . ni neither . . . nor, (not) . . . . either . . . or
¿no (te) parece? don't (you) think *or* believe so?
por aquí around here
tener miedo (de + *obj.***)** to be afraid (of)
tener razón to be right
todo el mundo everybody (*requires sing. verb*)
tomar el sol to take a sun bath
un par de (horas) a couple of (hours)
vacaciones (de verano) (summer) vacation

Lectura 7

Los deportes[1]

En el mundo hispánico hay una gran variedad de deportes. No sólo los hombres, sino también las mujeres toman parte en los deportes, especialmente en el golf, el tenis y la natación.[2] Muchos deportes son de origen inglés o norteamericano, pero otros, como la pelota o el *jai alai* y la corrida de toros, son de origen español. El fútbol, de estilo *soccer,* es muy popular, y algunos de los estadios tienen una capacidad de 50,000 a 120,000 espectadores. También son populares el béisbol, el básquetbol, las carreras de caballos,[3] el polo, el boxeo, la caza,[4] la pesca,[5] y en realidad, todos los deportes que se conocen en los Estados Unidos y en el resto del mundo.

Muchas personas creen que hay corridas de toros en todos los países de habla española, pero la verdad es que se encuentran solamente en ciertos países, como en España, México, Colombia, Venezuela y el Perú. En España las corridas de toros constituyen[6] la fiesta nacional y son muy populares también en México y el Perú. En Venezuela y Colombia se celebran con menos entusiasmo y hay países, como el Uruguay y la Argentina, que no permiten este espectáculo.

Hasta fines del[7] siglo dieciocho las corridas eran una fiesta aristocrática, pero a fines de[8] ese siglo comenzó a perderse el gusto por los toros.[9] Hoy día pueden considerarse[10] como un espectáculo a la vez[11] popular y profesional.

En España el fútbol (o balompié) es un deporte muy popular, sobre todo en el norte. Tiene también miles de aficionados en casi todos los países hispanoamericanos, especialmente en México, la Argentina y el Uruguay. El desarrollo[12] de este deporte ha sido tan notable en el Uruguay que sus equipos[13] han ganado el campeonato mundial[14] en varias ocasiones. (Como se sabe, el Brasil también ha tenido equipos de fama mundial.)

La pelota es el famoso juego vasco,[15] del norte de España. Se juega[16] en un frontón[17] que tiene tres paredes: una alta, que está frente a los jugadores, otra a un lado y la tercera, detrás. Los espectadores se sientan en el lado abierto. Para lanzar la pelota, los

---

[1]**deportes,** *sports.*   [2]**natación,** *swimming.*   [3]**carreras de caballos,** *horse races.*   [4]**caza,** *hunting.*   [5]**pesca,** *fishing.*
[6]**constituyen,** *constitute.*   [7]**Hasta fines de,** *Up to the end of.*   [8]**a fines de,** *at the end of.*   [9]**comenzó . . . toros,** *the taste for bullfighting began to fade* (lit., *be lost*).   [10]**pueden considerarse,** *it* (= *bullfighting*) *can be considered.*   [11]**a la vez,** *at the same time.*   [12]**desarrollo,** *development.*   [13]**equipos,** *teams.*   [14]**el campeonato mundial,** *world championship.*   [15]**vasco,** *Basque.*   [16]**Se juega,** *It is played.*   [17]**frontón,** *court.*

"El Pato" es un deporte típico de la Argentina. Se parece un poco al polo, pero es mucho más peligroso.

jugadores usan una cesta[18] de forma curva. Una pareja de jugadores se opone a otra pareja. Es un juego muy rápido y para jugarlo bien es necesario ser muy ágil. Es popular no sólo en España, sino también en Cuba, en México y en otros países del Nuevo Mundo. También se juega en algunas ciudades de los Estados Unidos.

El béisbol, el deporte nacional de los Estados Unidos, es también el deporte nacional de Cuba. En Venezuela, en México, en la América Central y en la República Dominicana hay una gran afición por el béisbol. Varios equipos de estos países celebran concursos internacionales. Hoy día muchos jugadores de nuestros equipos profesionales son de la América española.

Las carreras de caballos parecen ser el deporte favorito en Chile y, sobre todo, en la Argentina. Son populares, también, en la República Dominicana y en Puerto Rico.

Hace muchos años los gauchos argentinos tenían un juego llamado «el pato».[19] Era un juego muy peligroso[20] y por eso[21] lo prohibieron las autoridades. Montados a caballo, los jugadores luchaban por la posesión de una pelota bastante grande y pesada[22] que tenía mangos.[23] Los jugadores se arrojaban[24] sobre sus adversarios, les pegaban con el látigo,[25] y con las boleadoras trataban de echar por tierra al caballo.[26] Para ganar la partida había que llevar la pelota unos seis o siete kilómetros. Ahora hay una forma moderna del juego, mucho menos peligrosa, que tiene elementos del polo y del básquetbol.

México parece ser el país hispanoamericano donde se practican más los deportes.[27] Es interesante recordar que en la época de los mayas y de los aztecas había un juego de pelota semejante al básquetbol. Sin usar los pies ni la cabeza, los jugadores tenían que pasar una pelota de hule[28] por un anillo[29] que estaba en una pared. La influencia de este juego en el origen del básquetbol moderno es dudosa.[30] Hoy día el básquetbol es muy popular en todos los países hispanoamericanos.

En Chile y en el Perú hay personas aficionadas al alpinismo,[31] puesto que estos dos países tienen magníficas sierras donde se puede practicar este difícil deporte.

---

[18]**cesta,** *wickerwork racket.* [19]**pato,** *duck.* [20]**peligroso,** *dangerous.* [21]**por eso,** *because of that.* [22]**pesada,** *heavy.* [23]**mangos,** *handles.* [24]**se arrojaban,** *threw themselves.* [25]**les pegaban con el látigo,** *they beat them with their whips.* [26]**trataban . . . caballo,** *they tried to throw the horse to the ground.* [27]**se practican más los deportes,** *sports are practiced (people go in for sports) most.* [28]**hule,** *rubber.* [29]**anillo,** *ring.* [30]**dudosa,** *doubtful.* [31]**alpinismo,** *mountain climbing.*

Preguntas

1. ¿Hay una gran variedad de deportes en el mundo hispánico?   2. ¿En qué deportes toman parte las mujeres?   3. ¿Cuáles son dos deportes de origen español?   4. ¿Qué otros deportes son populares?

5. ¿Hay corridas de toros en todos los países de habla española?   6. ¿Le gusta a todo el mundo la corrida de toros?

7. ¿Es popular el fútbol en España?   8. ¿Tiene muchos aficionados en los países hispanoamericanos?   9. ¿En qué países ha sido muy notable el desarrollo de este deporte?

10. ¿Dónde se juega a la pelota?   11. ¿Cuántas paredes tiene un frontón?   12. ¿Qué usan los jugadores para lanzar la pelota?   13. ¿Es rápido el juego?   14. ¿Dónde es popular?

15. ¿En qué países hay una gran afición por el béisbol?   16. ¿De dónde son muchos jugadores de nuestros equipos profesionales?   17. ¿Cuál parece ser el deporte favorito en Chile?

18. ¿Qué juego tenían los gauchos de la Argentina?   19. ¿Por qué lo prohibieron las autoridades?   20. ¿En qué país hispanoamericano se practican más los deportes?   21. ¿Qué juego había durante la época de los mayas y los aztecas?   22. ¿Qué tenían que hacer los jugadores?   23. ¿Es popular el básquetbol en los países hispanoamericanos?   24. ¿Dónde se practica el alpinismo?

Estudio de palabras

a. The Spanish ending **-dor** often indicates one who performs or participates in an action: espectador, *spectator;* conquistador, *conqueror;* gobernador, *governor;* jugador, *player.* It may express the means of an action: las boleadoras, *lariat with balls at one end, thrown so as to twist around an animal's legs.*

b. Observe the relation in meaning of the following words: afición, *fondness, and* aficionado, *fan, one who is fond of;* correr, *to run, and* corrida (de toros), *running (of bulls), bullfight;* espectáculo, *spectacle, and* espectador, *spectator;* jugar, *to play,* jugador, *player,* juego, *game, and* juguete, *plaything, toy;* varios, *various, several, and* variedad, *variety.*

c. Note the words with deceptive meaning: carrera, *race* (as well as *career*); concurso, *contest;* lanzar, *to throw.*

d. The adjectives of nationality **maya,** *Maya, Mayan,* and **azteca,** *Aztec,* have but one ending for both the masculine and the feminine. As we know, adjectives of nationality may be used as nouns: **el (la) maya,** *the Mayan;* **el (la) azteca,** *the Aztec.*

Las corridas de toros no son populares en todos los países suramericanos. En España, por supuesto, cuentan con muchos aficionados. En las dos fotos de arriba se ve una corrida en España: a la izquierda se ve el torero y a la derecha un rejoneador. Abajo, un grupo de aficionados juega un partido de soccer en el parque Alameda, Quito, Ecuador.

El fútbol de tipo soccer es uno de los deportes más populares de Suramérica. Se juega en casi todos los países, en la foto de arriba, un grupo de jóvenes juega un partido cerca de la fortaleza que guarda el puerto de El Callao, Perú. A la derecha, un padre juega al béisbol con su hijo en la ciudad de Oaxaca, México. El béisbol es popular en México, Venezuela y el área del Caribe. Debajo se ve un partido de tenis en la Universidad Central, Quito, Ecuador.

REPASO 3

A. Say after your teacher; when you hear a new subject, compose a new sentence using the same tense:

1. Ellos empiezan a leer. (Nosotros)
2. María se pone los guantes. (Yo)

3. José no encuentra nada. (Tú)
4. Ellos devuelven el dinero. (Ud.)

5. Mi papá llegó a las seis. (Yo)
6. Ellos buscaron a Marta. (Yo)
7. Tú no hiciste el viaje. (Ud.)

8. Él y yo le trajimos algo. (Ellos)
9. Los jóvenes no pudieron ir. (Él)
10. Yo no les dije nada. (Ellos)

11. Nosotros dábamos un paseo. (Tú)
12. Yo los veía a menudo. (Juan)

13. Ellos iban a la playa. (Ana y yo)
14. El traje era muy caro. (Los trajes)

15. ¿Has visto tú aquel lago? (Uds.)
16. ¿Les ha escrito Ricardo? (tú)
17. Ellos no han dicho eso. (Él y yo)

18. Ella no se lo había puesto. (Yo)
19. Pablo la había abierto. (Ellos)
20. Tú te habías mudado de ropa. (Ud.)

B. Read in Spanish, placing the pronoun objects correctly with each verb (as explained on page 183, in the progressive forms of the tenses there are two possibilities):

1. (me los) Trajeron. Han traído. Van a traer. Están trayendo. Traigan Uds.
2. (nos la) No dé Ud. Ha dado. Está dando. Quería dar. No dio. 3. (se los) Devuelven. Pueden devolver. Están devolviendo. Han devuelto. Devuelvan Uds.
4. (te lo) Enseñan. ¿No han enseñado? Tratan de enseñar. Estaban enseñando. No habían enseñado.

C. Read in Spanish, using the correct form of the verb selected from those in parentheses:

1. (*preterit tense of* dar, tomar, llevar) Ayer Marta _____ el libro en la mano. Yo me lo _____ . Entonces ellas _____ un paseo. 2. (*present of* haber, tener) Los muchachos no _____ visto la película. ¿La _____ visto Ud.? Yo _____ que irme. Ella _____ que cantar mañana. 3. (*preterit of* volver, devolver) Luis _____ anoche. No me _____ el dinero que le había prestado. 4. (*present of* conocer, saber) —¿ _____ Uds. a mi amigo Vicente? —No lo _____ , pero _____ dónde vive. ¿ _____ Uds. la ciudad de Nueva York? 5. (*preterit or imperfect of* estar, hacer, ser, tener) El reloj que _____ sobre el mostrador _____ precioso. _____ mucho calor en la tienda, y yo _____ mucha sed. La vendedora _____ razón; _____ sol y _____ un día muy agradable. _____ las cuatro cuando salí de la tienda. Había tanta gente en los autobuses que yo _____ que esperar mucho tiempo. Al llegar a casa, _____ muy cansada.

D. Complete with the necessary preposition:

1. El vestido de Luisa está muy _____ moda.   2. Algunos muchachos no se atreven _____ nadar solos.   3. Los estudiantes todavía están _____ vacaciones. 4. Arturo y yo nos alegramos _____ verlos.   5. José se mudó _____ ropa antes _____ salir.   6. Yo empecé _____ charlar con él.   7. Él y sus amigos no tienen miedo _____ entrar _____ el agua.   8. Luis se encontró _____ María en una tienda.   9. Los dos jóvenes acaban _____ volver _____ casa.   10. Ricardo tiene muchos deseos _____ ver el mar.   11. Él insiste _____ eso.   12. El señor López salió _____ aquí ayer _____ la mañana.   13. Mis amigos siempre disfrutan _____ la vida.   14. Casi es hora _____ almorzar.   15. Carlos nunca llega _____ tiempo.

E. Read in Spanish, supplying the preterit or imperfect tense of the verb in parentheses:

1. Esta mañana mi hermano (levantarse) a las ocho.   2. Generalmente (levantarse) más temprano.   3. Mis padres y yo (estar) sentados a la mesa y (desayunarse) cuando él (entrar) en el comedor.   4. (Tener) que comer rápidamente.   5. (Ser) las ocho y media cuando él (salir) de casa.   6. (Hacer) frío, pero él no (ponerse) los guantes.   7. Él (correr) a la calle Doce, donde (tomar) el autobús.   8. Más tarde yo (decidir) ir de compras, y (llegar) al centro a las diez.   9. (Haber) mucha gente en las tiendas, y todas las vendedoras (estar) muy ocupadas.   10. Yo (buscar) unos regalos y (poder) hallar varias cosas bonitas.   11. Al mediodía (almorzar) en el centro.   12. Yo (estar) muy cansado cuando (volver) a casa a las tres de la tarde.

F. Answer in Spanish:

1. ¿Le gusta a Ud. el invierno?   2. ¿Cuáles son las otras tres estaciones?   3. ¿Cuál de las estaciones le gusta a Ud. más?   4. ¿Dónde se puede nadar en el verano?   5. ¿Qué hay en las montañas durante el invierno?   6. ¿Hace buen tiempo hoy?   7. ¿Hizo sol ayer? 8. ¿Qué hora era hoy cuando salió Ud. de casa?   9. ¿Cuál es la fecha de hoy? 10. ¿Qué día de la semana es?   11. ¿Tiene Ud. clases los sábados?   12. ¿En qué días de la semana tiene Ud. clases?   13. ¿Cuántos estudiantes hay en esta clase?   14. ¿Cuántos estudiantes hay en esta universidad?   15. ¿En qué siglo vivimos?   16. ¿Qué hace Ud. cuando está de vacaciones?   17. ¿Ha hecho Ud. un viaje a México?   18. ¿Qué hizo Ud. el sábado pasado?

G. Give the Spanish for:

1. by the way.   2. at first.   3. a good road.   4. the first month.   5. the third week. 6. the ten-o'clock bus.   7. a five-dollar bill.   8. a bathing suit.   9. all afternoon. 10. at once.   11. at noon.   12. everybody.

   13. Mary took a sun bath then.   14. The blouse is very stylish.   15. They are right. 16. John came an hour ago.   17. These purses are prettier than those.   18. What kind of weather is it?   19. It is bad weather.   20. It is very windy this afternoon.   21. Yesterday they went to the beach to swim.   22. My father is on vacation.   23. I ran across Thomas downtown.   24. He has just returned from Spain.   25. You are welcome.

The future tense • **The conditional tense** • **Verbs irregular in the future and conditional** • **Uses of the future tense** • **Uses of the conditional tense** • **The future and conditional perfects** • **The future and conditional for probability or conjecture** • **Forms of *jugar*** • **Redundant use of the object pronoun *lo***

LECCIÓN 16

Aficionados a los deportes

Ha terminado el primer semestre. Para descansar un poco después de los exámenes, Carlos White, un estudiante norteamericano, ha hecho un viaje a México. Su amigo mexicano, Juan Molina, lo ha invitado a pasar unos días en la capital de su país. Los dos jóvenes acaban de comprar un periódico y se han sentado en el vestíbulo de un hotel de la ciudad de México para leerlo.

JUAN —¿Qué hay de nuevo en la sección de deportes?
CARLOS —Nada de particular. Estoy tratando de ver si se anuncia algún espectáculo de interés, pero no encuentro nada.

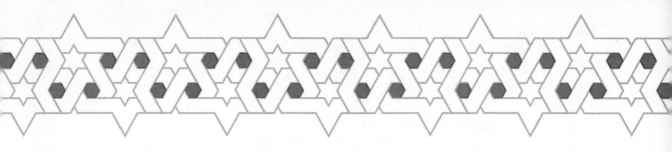

JUAN —¡Cómo! ¿No habrá un partido de fútbol[1] el domingo?

CARLOS —Yo diría que sí, pero mira tú, por favor. Así estaremos seguros. (*Se acerca a su amigo y le entrega el periódico.*)

JUAN (*Hojea rápidamente la sección de deportes.*) —Sí, hombre, jugará México contra el Uruguay. Comenzará a las once en punto.

CARLOS —Me alegro, pues tengo muchas ganas de ver un buen juego . . . y éste parece que será un partido magnífico.

JUAN —No te lo había dicho, pero hace varios días mi primo Pablo nos invitó a hacer una excursión a la sierra el domingo.

CARLOS —Y ya lo habrá preparado todo, ¿verdad? ¡Ah! Podríamos invitarlo y saldríamos después del partido. ¿Qué te parece?

JUAN —Lo llamaré en seguida y se lo diré.

◆ ◆ ◆ ◆ ◆

Juan llama a su primo y éste acepta la invitación.

JUAN —Pablo tendrá mucho gusto en acompañarnos . . . Pues, a ti te interesan mucho los deportes, ¿verdad, Carlos?

CARLOS —Sí, soy muy aficionado a casi todos. He jugado al béisbol, al básquet-bol, al golf, al tenis . . .

JUAN —Para mí el tenis resulta demasiado rápido. ¿Conoces el *jai alai,* o la pelota vasca? Se juega mucho aquí en México.

CARLOS —¡Ya lo creo! Es uno de los juegos más rápidos del mundo. Ya sé que aquí en México hay algunos jugadores vascos que son excelentes.

JUAN —¿No te gustaría ir conmigo a ver un partido? Podríamos comer en un restaurante vasco que está cerca del frontón.

CARLOS —Sería un gran placer. Me interesaría mucho . . .

JUAN —A propósito, me parece que debemos comprar en seguida los boletos[2] para el partido de fútbol. Le preguntaré al botones si hay un despacho de boletos cerca de aquí.

CARLOS —¡Tienes razón! Como el fútbol es tan popular, será difícil encontrar boletos.

---

[1] See page 221 for reference to the type of football played in Latin America and in other foreign countries. [2] In Mexico **el boleto** is normally used for *ticket.*

Conversación

A. Preguntas sobre el diálogo

1. ¿Por qué ha ido Carlos a la ciudad de México? 2. ¿Dónde están sentados Carlos y Juan? 3. ¿Qué sección del periódico le interesa más a Carlos? ¿Por qué? 4. ¿Habrá algún espectáculo el domingo? ¿A qué hora comenzará el partido? 5. ¿Qué podrían hacer Carlos y Juan el domingo? 6. ¿Qué deportes le interesan a Carlos? 7. ¿Qué es el *jai alai*? 8. ¿Qué deben comprar en seguida?

B. Aplicación del diálogo

1. ¿Es Ud. aficionado (aficionada) a los deportes? ¿Qué deportes le interesan? 2. ¿A qué deportes ha jugado Ud.? ¿A qué deportes juega Ud. ahora? 3. ¿Ha visto Ud. un partido de *jai alai*? 4. ¿Ha visto Ud. un partido de fútbol de estilo *soccer*? 5. ¿Se juega mucho al fútbol de estilo *soccer* en los Estados Unidos? 6. ¿Fue Ud. a los juegos de fútbol el otoño pasado? 7. ¿Cuándo se juega al básquetbol? ¿Y al béisbol? 8. ¿Le gusta a Ud. hacer excursiones? ¿Qué excursiones ha hecho? ¿A la sierra? ¿A las montañas? ¿A algún lago o a algún río?

NOTAS GRAMATICALES

A. The future tense

future endings		**hablar**	
-é	**-emos**	hablar**é**	hablar**emos**
-ás	**-éis**	hablar**ás**	hablar**éis**
-á	**-án**	hablar**á**	hablar**án**

The future indicative tense is regularly formed by adding the endings of the present indicative of **haber** to the full infinitive form. There is only one set of future endings for all verbs in Spanish.

Observe that three of the endings begin with **e** and three with **a,** and that all the endings except the first person plural have a written accent.

B. The conditional tense

conditional endings		**comer**	
-ía	**-íamos**	comer**ía**	comer**íamos**
-ías	**-íais**	comer**ías**	comer**íais**
-ía	**-ían**	comer**ía**	comer**ían**

The conditional indicative tense is formed by adding the imperfect endings of **haber** to the infinitive. As in the case of the future, there is only one set of conditional endings for all verbs in Spanish. All six forms are accented.

C. Verbs irregular in the future and conditional

infinitive	*future*	*conditional*
1. haber	**habré, -ás, -á,** etc.	**habría, -ías, -ía,** etc.
poder	**podré, -ás, -á,** etc.	**podría, -ías, -ía,** etc.
querer	**querré, -ás, -á,** etc.	**querría, -ías, -ía,** etc.
saber	**sabré, -ás, -á,** etc.	**sabría, -ías, -ía,** etc.
2. poner	**pondré,** etc.	**pondría,** etc.
salir	**saldré,** etc.	**saldría,** etc.
tener	**tendré,** etc.	**tendría,** etc.
venir	**vendré,** etc.	**vendría,** etc.
3. decir	**diré,** etc.	**diría,** etc.
hacer	**haré,** etc.	**haría,** etc.

The future and conditional tenses have the same stem, and the endings are the same as for regular verbs. The irregularity is in the infinitive stem used. In group (1) the final vowel of the infinitive has been dropped; in (2) the final vowel has been dropped and the glide **d** introduced to facilitate the pronunciation of the consonant groups **lr** and **nr**. Only two other verbs are irregular in these tenses.

◆ *Práctica.* Pronounce; then give the corresponding conditional form:

tomaré	saldrás	dirán	podremos
vivirán	tendréis	querrá	dirás
aprenderá	vendrán	habrá	saldrá
podrá	haremos	sabrán	haréis

D. Uses of the future tense

Juan dice que vendrá. John says that he will come.
Sabemos que él lo hará. We know that he will do it.
Habrá mucha gente allí. There will be many people there.

The meaning of the future tense is *shall* or *will* in English, and it is regularly used to express future actions or conditions. The impersonal form **habrá** means *there will be* (last example).

Up to this point substitutions have been used for the future, as is commonly done in English:

Voy a ver a Carlos esta noche.   I'm going to see Charles tonight.
Lo vemos a Ud. a las nueve.   We'll be seeing you at nine o'clock.
Yo sé que ella viene mañana.   I know that she is coming tomorrow.
¿Nos sentamos?   Shall we sit down?

When *will* means *be willing to,* it is translated by the present tense of **querer.** In the negative, it may mean *be unwilling to:*

¿Quiere Ud. ir conmigo?   Will you go with me?
No quieren jugar.   They won't (are unwilling to) play.

E. Uses of the conditional tense

Juan dijo que vendría.   John said that he would come.
Sabíamos que él lo haría.   We knew that he would do it.
Me gustaría ir con Uds.   I should like to go with you.
Yo creía que habría más tiempo.   I thought there would be more time.

The conditional tense is expressed by *should* or *would* in English. The impersonal form **habría** means *there would be* (last example).

As we learned in Lesson 15, when *should* means *ought to* (moral obligation), it is expressed by **deber:**

Debo escribirles.   I should (ought to, must) write to them.

Remember that *would* is sometimes used to represent a repeated past action in English, in which case it is translated by the imperfect indicative tense in Spanish (Lesson 11):

Me levantaba temprano.   I would (used to) get up early.

NOTE: The future and conditional tenses are used after **si** only when it means *whether,* never in a condition when it means *if:* **No sé (sabía) si vendrán (vendrían),** *I do not know (did not know) whether they will (would) come.*

F. The future and conditional perfects

	future perfect		*conditional perfect*	
	habré ⎫		**habría** ⎫	
	habrás ⎬ hablado		**habrías** ⎬ hablado	
	habrá ⎭		**habría** ⎭	
	habremos ⎫		**habríamos** ⎫	
	habréis ⎬ hablado		**habríais** ⎬ hablado	
	habrán ⎭		**habrían** ⎭	

These tenses are regularly used as in English, and are expressed by *shall* or *will have spoken,* and *should* or *would have spoken,* respectively.

G. The future and conditional for probability or conjecture

    Marta estará en casa.   Martha is probably (must be) at home.
    ¿Qué hora será?   I wonder what time it is. (What time can it be?)
    Serían las dos.   It was probably (must have been) two o'clock.
    Ya habrán llegado.   They have probably (must have) already arrived.

The future tense is used in Spanish to indicate probability, supposition, or conjecture concerning an action or state in the *present,* while the conditional indicates the same idea with respect to the *past.* The future perfect, and occasionally the conditional perfect, are also used to indicate probability in the past.

H. Forms of **jugar,** *to play* (a game)

present indicative tense	
singular	*plural*
juego	jugamos
juegas	jugáis
juega	**juegan**

Jugar is the only verb in Spanish in which **u** changes to **ue** when the stem is stressed. The first person singular preterit is **jugué.**

    In everyday conversation **jugar** is often used without **a** and the article: **jugar fútbol,** instead of **jugar al fútbol.**

I. Redundant use of the object pronoun **lo**

1. **Lo llamaré y se lo diré.** I shall call him and tell him (so *or* it).
   No te lo había dicho . . . I had not told you . . .

If no direct object is expressed with verbs such as **decir, preguntar, creer, saber,** and **pedir** (see Lesson 17), the neuter pronoun **lo** is normally added.

2. **Ya lo habrá preparado todo.** He probably has prepared everything already.

When **todo,** *everything,* is the direct object of a verb, the pronoun **lo** is also normally used.

EJERCICIOS

A. Substitution drill:

1. *Carlos* irá al juego el domingo.
   (*Nosotros, Uds., Carlos y Juan, Tú, Yo*)
2. *Los muchachos* saldrán al mediodía.
   (*Pablo, Ud., Uds., Ella y yo, Tú*)
3. *Tú* pondrás las flores en el cuarto de Luisa.
   (*Marta y María, Nosotros, Yo, Uds., Carolina*)
4. *Pablo* tendría mucho gusto en ir.
   (*Yo, Ellos, Tú, Carlos y yo, Ud.*)
5. *Nosotros* podríamos invitar a Ricardo.
   (*Ellos, Tú, Yo, Carlos y Juan, Carolina*)
6. *Yo* diría que sí.
   (*Carlos, Ellos, Tú, Nosotros, Marta*)
7. ¿Los habrá visto *Isabel?*
   (*tú, Ud., Uds., Vicente, ellos*)
8. *Carlos* juega al tenis ahora.
   (*Tomás y yo, Tú, Uds., Nosotros, Yo*)

B. Answer affirmatively:

1. ¿Comprará Ud. un periódico?
2. ¿Leerá Ud. la sección de deportes?
3. ¿Irás tú a ver el partido?
4. ¿Podrás encontrar boletos?
5. ¿Harás tú una excursión mañana?
6. ¿Tendrán Uds. mucho gusto en hacerlo?
7. ¿Saldrían Uds. al mediodía?
8. ¿Vendría Carlos también?
9. ¿Le gustaría a Ud. jugar al golf?
10. ¿Podría Ud. ir al juego?

C. Read in Spanish, changing the infinitive in parentheses to the tense indicated. Keep the meaning in mind:

(*Future*) 1. El sábado que viene nosotros (ir) al partido de pelota vasca. 2. Yo (comprar) los boletos mañana. 3. Yo lo (hacer) con mucho gusto. 4. Juan no (poder)

acompañarnos.   5. Dice que (tener) que trabajar esta noche.   6. Pablo y yo (salir) de casa temprano.   7. (Tomar) algo en el café antes de ir al frontón.   8. Algunos jugadores (estar) allí.   9. Nosotros (tener) mucho gusto en verlos.   10. (Ser) necesario salir en seguida porque a esa hora (haber) mucha gente en las calles.
(*Conditional*)   11. Carlos dijo que (venir) a mi casa a las tres.   12. Yo sabía que él (hacer) eso.   13. —¿Le (gustar) a Ud. ir con nosotros al partido de fútbol?   14. —Sí, gracias, (ser) un gran placer y yo (disfrutar) mucho.   15. ¿A qué hora (poder) nosotros ir?   16. Pues yo (decir) que Ud. (poder) venir a las cuatro.

D. Answer each question, following the models:

MODEL: ¿Qué hora es? ¿Las once?   *Sí, serán las once.*

1. ¿Quién es? ¿Tomás?
2. ¿Dónde está Carlos? ¿En casa?
3. ¿Cuándo salen ellos? ¿Mañana?

4. ¿Qué hora es? ¿Las diez?
5. ¿Cuándo vuelve Marta? ¿Hoy?
6. ¿Adónde van? ¿Al café?

MODEL: ¿Ha ido Juan al juego?   *Sí, Juan habrá ido al juego.*

7. ¿Ha llamado tu padre?
8. ¿Ha llegado la carta?

9. ¿Han salido ellos de casa?
10. ¿Lo han preparado todo?

MODEL: ¿Fue Carlos a jugar?   *Sí, creo que iría a jugar.*

11. ¿Salió Felipe a almorzar?
12. ¿Volvió ella a la residencia?

13. ¿Fueron Marta y María al centro?
14. ¿Compraron ellas muchas cosas?

E. Give in Spanish, using the familiar forms for *you:*

1. "What's new?"   2. "Nothing special."   3. "Do you like sports?"   4. "Of course!"   5. "I am fond of almost all [of them]."   6. "Can you (Do you know how to) play tennis?"   7. "Yes, but I like golf better (more)."   8. "Will you accompany me to a football game?"   9. "Gladly."   10. "I shall buy two tickets tomorrow."   11. "In Spain **(al)** *jai alai* is played a great deal."   12. "About what time is it?"   13. "It must be half past seven."   14. "I'll see you at nine o'clock, eh?"   15. "Yes, I'll be free."

F. Give the Spanish equivalent:

1. Charles is reading a newspaper in the lobby of a Mexico City hotel (hotel of Mexico City) when his friend John approaches.   2. The latter asks whether there will be a football game on Sunday.   3. As Charles is not sure, he looks at the sports section. 4. He sees that there will be a game which will begin at eleven o'clock sharp; Mexico will play against Uruguay.   5. Charles is very glad, since he is very eager to see a good game.   6. But John tells him that Paul, a cousin of John's, had already invited them to make an excursion to the mountains on Sunday.   7. Then Charles has an idea: "He has probably prepared everything already. Couldn't we invite him and leave after the

game?" 8. "Of course!" John answers. "He would be very glad to go with us. 9. He is fond of almost all sports. 10. He has played golf and baseball, but tennis was (turned out to be) too fast for him." 11. Then Charles tells his friend that he would also like to see a *jai alai* game, which is one of the fastest games in the world. 12. John says that they could see one that night after eating supper in a Basque restaurant which is near the court. 13. Since football is so popular, they must buy the tickets at once. 14. John says that he will ask a bellboy whether there is a ticket office near there.

G. **Composición:** Una visita a la ciudad de México

Assuming that you are Carlos, rewrite the following paragraph in Spanish. Be sure to use the appropriate first person forms for those which appear in italics:

1. Cuando terminó el primer semestre de clases, *Carlos White hizo*[1] un viaje a la ciudad de México. 2. *Lo*[1] había invitado un amigo mexicano que estudiaba *con él*[1] en la universidad. 3. *Carlos quería descansar* un poco después de *sus* exámenes y *se quedó* allí una semana. 4. Como *Juan y Carlos han sido* siempre muy aficionados a los deportes, *ellos decidieron* ir a ver varios partidos interesantes. 5. *Tuvieron* la oportunidad de ver un gran partido entre México y el Uruguay. 6. *Juan y Carlos habían estado* en el vestíbulo de un hotel de la ciudad leyendo la sección de deportes del periódico. 7. *Carlos* le *preguntó* a Juan si sería fácil encontrar boletos para ese partido. 8. *Carlos tenía* muchas ganas de verlo, pero Pablo, un primo de Juan, ya había preparado una excursión a la sierra. 9. *Carlos tuvo* una magnífica idea. 10. *Carlos llamó* a Pablo y lo *invitó* a ir *con ellos*. 11. Así, *los tres amigos irían* al juego y *saldrían* para la sierra después. 12. Como Pablo y Juan sabían que *a Carlos le* interesaban todos los deportes, también *lo* llevaron a ver un partido de *jai alai*. 13. *Carlos disfrutó* mucho en México y *está* seguro de que *volverá* pronto. 14. *Pasará* días muy agradables allí con *sus* amigos y *podrá* ver más partidos.

---

[1]Forms to be used in rewriting this paragraph are: *a.* **yo hice** *b.* **Me . . . conmigo**

VOCABULARIO

aceptar   to accept
acercarse (a + *obj.*)   to approach
el aficionado   fan
algún   (*used for* alguno *before m. sing. nouns*)
    some, any
el básquetbol   basketball
el béisbol   baseball
el boleto   ticket (*Mex.*)
el botones   bellboy
contra   against
el deporte   sport
el despacho   office
el espectáculo   spectacle, show
excelente   excellent
la excursión (*pl.* excursiones)   excursion,
    trip
el frontón (*pl.* frontones)   court (*jai alai*)
el fútbol   football
la gana   desire
el golf   golf
gran   (*used for* grande *before sing. noun*)
    great

hojear   to turn the pages of
la invitación (*pl.* invitaciones)   invitation
el interés (*pl.* intereses)   interest
el juego   game
el jugador   player
jugar (ue) (a + *obj.*)   to play (*a game*)
el partido   match, game
la pelota   ball
el placer   pleasure
popular   popular
el punto   point
rápidamente   rapidly
rápido, -a   rapid, fast
el restaurante   restaurant
resultar   to result, be, turn out (to be)
la sección (*pl.* secciones)   section
el semestre   semester
la sierra   mountains, mountain range
el tenis   tennis
vasco, -a   Basque
el vestíbulo   vestibule, lobby

aficionado, -a a los deportes   sports fan
¡cómo!   what (are you saying)! how!
decir que (sí)   to say (so, yes)
despacho de boletos   ticket office
en punto   sharp (*time*)
hacer una excursión   to take (make) an excursion
partido de fútbol   football game
¿qué te parece?   what do (you) think?
sección de deportes   sports section
ser aficionado, -a (a)   to be fond (of)
tener (muchas) ganas de   to be (very) eager *or* wish (very much) to
tener (mucho) gusto en   to be (very) glad to
¡ya lo creo!   of course! certainly!

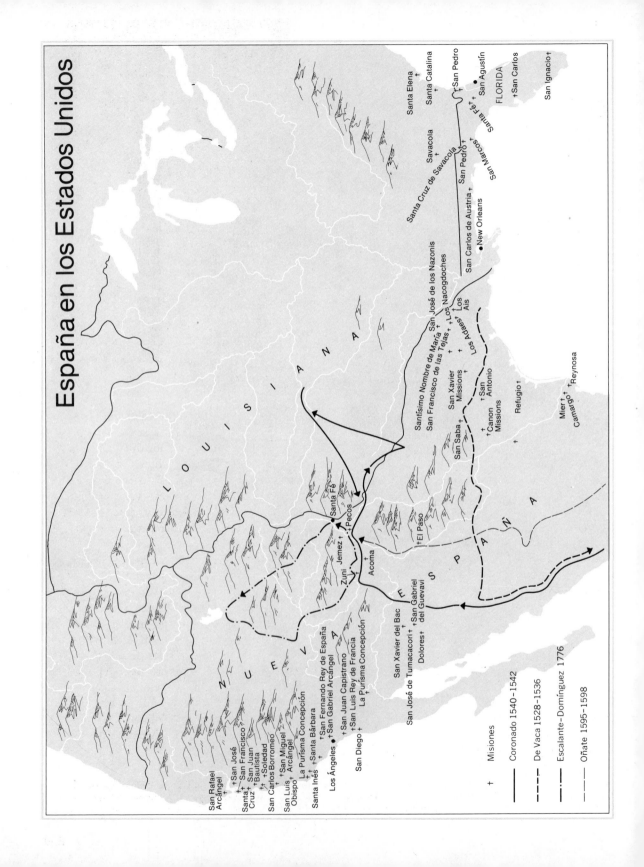

España en los Estados Unidos

Misiones †

Coronado 1540-1542

De Vaca 1528-1536

Escalante-Domínguez 1776

Oñate 1595-1598

Lectura 8

PEDRO MENÉNDEZ DE AVILÉS

Exploradores y misioneros

Durante la primera mitad del siglo XVI los españoles exploraron el territorio de los Estados Unidos que se extiende desde la Florida hasta California. El primer europeo que atravesó[1] el continente fue Cabeza de Vaca. Después de explorar el interior de la Florida con Pánfilo de Narváez en 1528, navegó por las costas del Golfo de México hasta llegar a la región que hoy se conoce como Texas. Una terrible tempestad destruyó su barco, quedando vivos sólo Cabeza de Vaca y tres compañeros. Los cuatro españoles vivieron varios años como esclavos de los indios, pero con el tiempo los indios llegaron a estimar mucho a Cabeza de Vaca como curandero.[2] Poco a poco,[3] caminando de pueblo en pueblo hacia el oeste, atravesó largas distancias y por fin[4] llegó a la costa del Pacífico, en el norte de México, en 1536.

Por desgracia,[5] los españoles creían que todo el Nuevo Mundo era tan rico como la Nueva España,[6] y los indios, sabiendo que nada les interesaba a los españoles tanto como el oro, hablaban de pueblos adornados de oro y de piedras preciosas. La más conocida de estas leyendas es la de las Siete Ciudades de Cíbola, situadas al norte de México, en donde las casas estaban cubiertas de oro puro. Al llegar a México Cabeza de Vaca, renació una vez más el interés en esta leyenda.[7] Fray

Marcos de Niza decidió ir en busca de estas ciudades para convertirlas a la fe católica. Después de caminar muchos días por lo que ahora son los estados de Nuevo México y Arizona, un día vio a lo lejos[8] lo que él creyó que eran las Siete Ciudades. Volvió a México a contar su descubrimiento y, naturalmente, cada vez que el relato se repetía, crecía más la riqueza imaginada.

Por fin se organizó una expedición que había de ser[9] una de las más notables de todas. En 1540 Francisco Vásquez de Coronado salió de México en busca de las Siete Ciudades de Cíbola. Llegó hasta donde ahora están los estados de Texas y Kansas, pero en vez de las fabulosas ciudades de oro y de piedras preciosas, sólo encontró tristes pueblos de adobe. Unos soldados de esta expedición fueron los primeros europeos que vieron el Gran Cañón del Río Colorado. A los dos años[10] Coronado volvió a México, triste y desilusionado.

---

[1]**atravesó,** *crossed.*   [2]**curandero,** *medicine man.*   [3]**Poco a poco,** *Little by little.*   [4]**por fin,** *finally.*   [5]**Por desgracia,** *Unfortunately.*   [6]**la Nueva España,** *New Spain* = **México.**   [7]**renació . . . leyenda,** *interest in this legend was revived once more.*   [8]**a lo lejos,** *in the distance.*   [9]**había de ser,** *was to be.*   [10]**A los dos años,** *After two years.*

239

La ciudad más antigua de los Estados Unidos fue fundada en la Florida el seis de septiembre de 1565 por Menéndez de Avilés. Éste construyó primero una fortaleza cerca del lugar donde ahora está San Agustín, el primer establecimiento permanente construido en nuestro país por los europeos.

El primer pueblo español en el valle del Río Grande fue fundado por Juan de Oñate en 1598, pero al poco tiempo[11] los españoles tuvieron que abandonarlo; once años más tarde establecieron la ciudad de Santa Fe. En seguida construyeron una iglesia, que es una de las más antiguas del país.

Entre otros muchos[12] exploradores bien conocidos hay que mencionar a Juan Rodríguez Cabrillo, un portugués que estaba al servicio del gobierno español, y que en 1542 descubrió la Alta California.[13]

Los españoles vinieron a América no sólo para buscar riquezas, sino también para convertir a los indios a la fe cristiana. Por eso los misioneros acompañaron a los exploradores por todas partes. Entre los misioneros se destaca[14] el padre Bartolomé de las Casas, el apóstol de los indios. Acompañó a Colón a América y se estableció primero en La Española.[15] Hombre de corazón noble y bondadoso, dedicó toda su vida a defender a los indígenas contra las injusticias de la esclavitud y contra su explotación por los españoles. En 1510 se ordenó de sacerdote y al poco tiempo ingresó en[16] la orden de los dominicos. Predicó[17] por todas partes de la Nueva España, defendiendo a los indios con la pluma y con la palabra.[18]

Los franciscanos también vinieron al Nuevo Mundo con los conquistadores y los exploradores, y durante más de dos siglos habían de acompañarlos por los dos continentes. La orden franciscana convirtió al cristianismo a miles de indios. Los franciscanos aprendieron las lenguas de los indios y les enseñaron artes y oficios[19] útiles y nuevos métodos para el cultivo de plantas y legumbres. Fundaron pueblos, iglesias, misiones, escuelas y universidades.

Las órdenes religiosas fundaron muchas misiones en Texas, Nuevo México, Arizona y California. El que ha visitado San Antonio ha visto sin duda el Álamo, que fue misión en los tiempos coloniales. O si uno ha estado en Tucson, Arizona, ha visto la famosa misión de San Xavier del Bac, fundada por el célebre padre jesuita, Eusebio Kino. El hermoso edificio que vemos allí hoy día se terminó a fines del siglo XVIII.

Cuando los jesuitas fueron expulsados de España y de sus colonias en 1769, muchas misiones que ellos habían construido pasaron a manos de los franciscanos. Fray Junípero Serra, que había venido a América desde la isla de Mallorca en la segunda mitad del siglo XVIII, fue nombrado presidente de las misiones de la Baja California y de todas las que habían de establecerse en la Alta California. Durante muchos años dio clases en las escuelas franciscanas de la Nueva España, pero por fin, en 1769, partió de México con don Gaspar de Portolá para establecer misiones en la Alta California. Empezando con la misión de San Diego, fundada en ese mismo[20] año, el padre Junípero Serra estableció una larga serie de misiones. En 1823 había veintiuna misiones entre San Diego y San Francisco. A lo largo del Camino Real[21] todavía se ven los restos de estos monumentos, que conmemoran la gloria de la obra de los misioneros españoles.

---

[11]**al poco tiempo,** *after (in) a short time.* [12]Adjectives of quantity and numerals preferably follow **otros, -as.**
[13]**la Alta California,** *Upper California* (the name used for the present state of California during the colonial period).
[14]**se destaca,** *stands out.* [15]**La Española,** *Hispaniola* (the name given to the island on which Haiti and the Dominican Republic are now situated). [16]**ingresó en,** *he entered, became a member of.* [17]**Predicó,** *He preached.*
[18]**con la pluma y con la palabra,** *writing and talking.* [19]**oficios,** *crafts, trades.* [20]**mismo,** *same.*
[21]**A lo largo del Camino Real,** *Along the King's Highway.*

Preguntas

1. ¿Qué territorio exploraron los españoles durante el siglo XVI?   2. ¿Quién fue el primer europeo que atravesó el continente?   3. ¿Por dónde navegó?   4. ¿Cuántos españoles quedaron vivos después de la tempestad?   5. ¿Cómo vivieron varios años?   6. ¿Adónde llegó por fin Cabeza de Vaca?

7. ¿Qué creían los españoles acerca del Nuevo Mundo?   8. ¿De qué hablaban los indios? 9. ¿Cuál es la más conocida de estas leyendas?   10. ¿De qué estaban cubiertas las casas? 11. ¿Quién decidió ir en busca de estas ciudades?   12. ¿Por dónde caminó?   13. ¿Halló las Siete Ciudades?   14. ¿Quién salió de México en busca de las Siete Ciudades en 1540? 15. ¿Qué encontró?   16. ¿Cuándo volvió a México?

17. ¿Cuál es la ciudad más antigua de los Estados Unidos?   18. ¿Qué fundó Juan de Oñate?   19. ¿Qué descubrió Cabrillo?

20. ¿Quiénes acompañaron a los españoles a América?   21. ¿Quién fue el apóstol de los indios?   22. ¿A qué dedicó toda su vida?   23. ¿En qué orden religiosa ingresó?   24. ¿Qué otra orden vino al Nuevo Mundo?   25. ¿Qué aprendieron los franciscanos?   26. ¿Qué les enseñaron a los indios?   27. ¿Qué fundaron los franciscanos?   28. ¿Qué fue el Álamo?   29. ¿Qué misión fundó el padre Eusebio Kino?

30. ¿Cuándo vino a América Fray Junípero Serra?   31. ¿De qué fue nombrado presidente?   32. ¿Qué expedición notable partió de México en 1769?   33. ¿Qué misión fundó Fray Junípero Serra en ese mismo año?   34. ¿Cuántas misiones había entre San Diego y San Francisco en 1823?

Estudio de palabras

a. Less approximate cognates. Pronounce the following words aloud, note the English cognates, and describe the variations: apóstol, *apostle;* dominico, *Dominican;* estimar, *to esteem;* fabuloso, *fabulous;* jesuita, *Jesuit;* mencionar, *to mention;* navegar, *to navigate, sail;* tempestad, *tempest, storm.*

b. Deceptive cognate. **Desgracia** means *misfortune,* as well as *disgrace.*

c. Compare the meanings of: camino, *road, way, and* caminar, *to walk, go, travel;* cristiano, *Christian, and* cristianismo, *Christianity;* esclavo, *slave, and* esclavitud, *slavery;* misión, *mission, and* misionero, *missionary;* relatar, *to relate, and* relato, *tale, story. Also compare:* la orden, *command, religious order (association),* ordenar, *to order, and* ordenarse (de sacerdote), *to be ordained, take orders (as a priest).* **El orden** means *order* in the sense of *arrangement.*

Arriba se ve la fortaleza de San Marco, cerca de San
Agustín en la Florida. Esta fortaleza fue construida por
los españoles en el siglo XVII. En la foto de abajo
aparece la parte antigua de San Agustín, y a la
derecha la estatua de Ponce de León, el descubridor y
explorador de la Florida.

Todavía se encuentran muchos edificios de la época colonial española en Santa Fe, New México. En la foto a la derecha se ve el Museo de Bellas Artes de esa ciudad. Abajo y a la derecha tenemos dos vistas de la misión de la Purísima Concepción en California.

En la foto de arriba se ve la misión de San Carlos Borromeo, en Carmel, California. Esta misión muestra el estilo colonial español, como muchos de los edificios construidos por los españoles en Hispanoamérica. Abajo, a la izquierda, la capilla de San Miguel, la iglesia más antigua de los Estados Unidos. A la derecha, la misión de San Juan Capistrano en California.

En esta página vemos arriba, la misión de Santa Bárbara y a la izquierda, la de San Gabriel, ambas en California. Como hemos podido ver en las fotos que acompañan esta Lectura, el estilo colonial español que se encuentra en el sur de los Estados Unidos es muy similar al de Hispanoamérica y al de España, donde se originó. La gran cantidad de pueblos y misiones fundadas por los españoles en territorios que hoy pertenecen a los Estados Unidos dan una idea de la extensión de la colonización española en América, y también del coraje y el valor de los exploradores y misioneros, que se aventuraron a llevar a efecto esa labor colonizadora.

Stem-changing verbs • Familiar singular commands of irregular
verbs • Irregular comparison of adjectives and adverbs • The
absolute superlative • Summary of comparison of
equality • Possessive adjectives that follow the noun

LECCIÓN 17

Juanita no se siente bien

Isabel ha notado que su amiga Juanita no ha ido a la oficina. Se imagina que debe[1] estar enferma. Aunque no quiere molestarla, decide pasar por su casa. Toca el timbre y Juanita abre la puerta.

JUANITA —¡Isabel! ¡Qué alegría me da verte! Estaba segura de que pasarías por aquí. Entra, por favor . . .

ISABEL —Le pregunté a tu jefe por qué no estabas[2] hoy. Sólo me dijo que habías pedido permiso para ausentarte.

JUANITA —Tengo un resfriado, y me duele la cabeza, aunque no tanto como ayer. Hoy ya me siento un poco mejor.

ISABEL (*Toca a Juanita en la frente.*) —Pero, mujer, todavía tienes fiebre. Dime, ¿por qué no te acuestas?

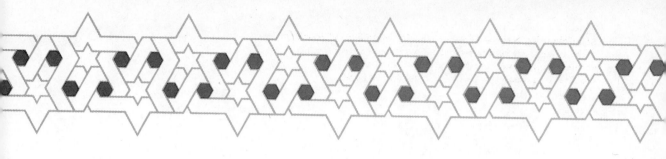

JUANITA —He pasado la mayor parte del día en la cama. Acabo de dormir una siesta de dos horas y si duermo más . . .

ISABEL —Lo sé . . . por la noche no podrás dormirte. ¿Qué te ha dicho el médico? ¿No le pediste nada?

JUANITA —Me ha recetado varias medicinas. Pero sobre todo me dice que debo descansar mucho.

ISABEL —Pues, mira, no quiero molestarte. Sólo me quedaré unos minutos. Vamos,[3] acuéstate.

◆ ◆ ◆ ◆ ◆

JUANITA —¿Has visto a Beatriz después que pasó el fin de semana en Nueva York?

ISABEL —Sí, ayer la acompañé a una joyería en el centro. Una tía suya le regaló una pulsera y tenía que buscarla.

JUANITA —¿Qué te ha contado de su viaje? ¿No se lo preguntaste?

ISABEL —Se divirtió tanto que quiere volver lo más pronto posible. Conoció[4] allí al hermano mayor del novio de Carmen.

JUANITA —Sí, Roberto Molina; lo conozco perfectamente. Es un muchacho guapísimo, muy simpático y, además, muy rico . . .

ISABEL —Me contó que el viernes fueron al teatro, y el sábado salieron a cenar y a bailar en un sitio muy elegante. Beatriz está contentísima.

JUANITA —¡Dios mío! ¿Se habrá enamorado tan pronto? ¡Cómo me gustaría verla!

ISABEL —Sí, creo que está muy enamorada. Bueno, Juanita, ya he pasado demasiado tiempo aquí.

JUANITA —No te imaginas,[5] Isabel, cuánto me ha ayudado tu visita. Te prometo que descansaré mucho y que pronto volveré a la oficina.

---

[1] In Lesson 16, section G, you learned that the future (or future perfect tense) may be used when *must* expresses probability; **deber** or **deber de** plus an infinitive is used similarly: **Se imagina que debe estar enferma,** *She imagines that she must be (is probably) ill.*   [2] When locality is clearly understood, **estar** may be used without **allí, aquí,** etc.   [3] **Vamos,** *Come now! Go on!* (as an interjection)   [4] The preterit tense of **conocer** means *met* (someone for the first time); the imperfect means *knew.*   [5] **No te imaginas,** *You can't imagine.*

Conversación

A. Preguntas sobre el diálogo

1. ¿Por dónde pasa Isabel al salir de la oficina? 2. ¿Por qué no ha ido Juanita a la oficina? ¿Cómo se siente ahora? 3. ¿Cómo ha pasado Juanita la mayor parte del día? 4. ¿Qué le ha dicho el médico a Juanita? 5. ¿A quién había visto Isabel? ¿Adónde la acompañó? 6. ¿Qué le contó Beatriz a Isabel de su viaje? 7. ¿Quién es Roberto Molina? ¿Cómo es él? 8. ¿Por qué le gustaría a Juanita ver a Beatriz? ¿Conoce Juanita a Roberto?

B. Aplicación del diálogo

1. ¿Ha estado Ud. enfermo (enferma) durante el fin de semana? 2. ¿Cómo se siente Ud. ahora? ¿Bien? ¿Mejor? ¿Todavía se siente mal? 3. ¿Qué tenía Ud.? ¿Un resfriado? ¿Fiebre? ¿Le dolía la cabeza? 4. Cuando Ud. no se siente bien, ¿viene Ud. a clases o se queda en casa y descansa? 5. ¿Conoce Ud. a un buen médico? ¿Llama Ud. a su médico cuando Ud. está enfermo (enferma)? 6. ¿Duerme Ud. la siesta todas las tardes? 7. ¿Qué hace Ud. para divertirse? ¿Va Ud. al teatro? ¿Sale Ud. a cenar? ¿Sale a bailar? 8. ¿Ha conocido Ud. a muchas muchachas (muchachos)? ¿Ya se ha enamorado?

NOTAS GRAMATICALES

A. Stem-changing verbs

	CLASS II		CLASS III
sentir, to feel	**dormir,** to sleep		**pedir,** to ask (for)

present indicative		
siento	**duermo**	**pido**
sientes	**duermes**	**pides**
siente	**duerme**	**pide**
sentimos	dormimos	pedimos
sentís	dormís	pedís
sienten	**duermen**	**piden**

preterit		
sentí	dormí	pedí
sentiste	dormiste	pediste
sintió	**durmió**	**pidió**
sentimos	dormimos	pedimos
sentisteis	dormisteis	pedisteis
sintieron	**durmieron**	**pidieron**

present participle		
sintiendo	**durmiendo**	**pidiendo**

When the stem of certain **–ir** verbs is accented, **e** becomes **ie** and **o** becomes **ue**, like Class I verbs, which end in **-ar** and **-er** (Lesson 8). In addition, the verbs of Class II change **e** to **i** and **o** to **u** in the third person singular and plural of the preterit and in the present participle. These verbs are designated in vocabularies: **sentir (ie, i), dormir (ue, u).**

Class III verbs, also of the third conjugation, change the stem vowel in the same forms as Class II verbs; the change, however, is always **e** to **i** (never to **ie**). Such verbs are designated: **pedir (i, i).**

The verb **preguntar** means *to ask* (a question); **pedir** means *to ask for, ask (request) someone to do something, ask a favor.*

B. Familiar singular commands of irregular verbs

inf.	*affirmative*		*negative*	
decir	**di** (tú)	*say, tell*	no **digas** (tú)	*don't say (tell)*
hacer	**haz** (tú)	*do, make*	no **hagas** (tú)	*don't do (make)*
ir	**ve** (tú)	*go*	no **vayas** (tú)	*don't go*
poner	**pon** (tú)	*put, place*	no **pongas** (tú)	*don't put (place)*
salir	**sal** (tú)	*go out, leave*	no **salgas** (tú)	*don't go out (leave)*
ser	**sé** (tú)	*be*	no **seas** (tú)	*don't be*
tener	**ten** (tú)	*have*	no **tengas** (tú)	*don't have*
venir	**ven** (tú)	*come*	no **vengas** (tú)	*don't come*

In Lesson 9 you learned that the familiar singular command is the same in form as the third person singular of the present indicative tense of all but a few verbs. Eight common verbs which have irregular forms are given above.

Review the formal command forms of these verbs in Lesson 9 and the formation of the negative familiar singular commands.

The familiar singular commands for the three model verbs in section A are:

inf.	*affirmative*		*negative*	
sentir	**siente** (tú)	*feel*	no **sientas** (tú)	*don't feel*
dormir	**duerme** (tú)	*sleep*	no **duermas** (tú)	*don't sleep*
pedir	**pide** (tú)	*ask (for)*	no **pidas** (tú)	*don't ask (for)*

C. Irregular comparison of adjectives and adverbs

1. In Lesson 7 we discussed the regular comparison of adjectives. The comparative of adverbs is also regularly formed by placing **más** or **menos** before the adverb. The definite article is not used in the superlative of adverbs, except that the neuter form **lo** is used when an expression of possibility follows:

> **Él habla más rápidamente que nunca.**   He talks more rapidly than ever.
> **Ella quiere volver lo más pronto posible.**   She wants to return as soon as possible
> (the soonest possible).

In the first example note that the negative **nunca** must be used after **que,** *than.*

2. Six adjectives and four adverbs, some of which have already been used, are compared irregularly:

adjectives

bueno good	(el) **mejor**	(the) better, best	
malo bad	(el) **peor**	(the) worse, worst	
grande large	(el) **más grande**	(the) larger, largest	
	(el) **mayor**	(the) greater, older, greatest, oldest	
pequeño small	(el) **más pequeño**	(the) smaller, smallest	
	(el) **menor**	(the) smaller, younger, smallest, youngest	

mucho(s) much (many)   **más**   more, most
poco(s)   little (few)   **menos** less, fewer

Grande and **pequeño, -a** have regular forms which refer to size; the irregular forms **mayor** and **menor** usually refer to persons and mean *older* and *younger,* respectively. **Mejor** and **peor** precede a noun, just as **bueno, -a** and **malo, -a** regularly precede it.

   Most (of), the greater part of, is translated **la mayor parte de: la mayor parte del día,** *most of the day.*

   Remember that **grande** becomes **gran** before a masculine or feminine singular noun and generally means *great.* The full form is used before plural nouns: **un gran hombre,** *a great man;* **una gran universidad,** *a great university;* **unos grandes jugadores,** *some great players.*

adverbs

bien	well	**mejor**	better, best	**mucho**	much	**más**	more, most
mal	badly	**peor**	worse, worst	**poco**	little	**menos**	less, least

D. The absolute superlative

   Beatriz está muy contenta (contentísima).   Beatrice is very happy.
   Ella se divirtió muchísimo.   She had a very good time.

A high degree of quality, without any element of comparison, is expressed by the use of **muy** before the adjective or adverb, or by adding the ending **-ísimo (-a, -os, -as)** to the adjective. When **-ísimo** is added, a final vowel is dropped. This form is emphatic; it is very common in Spanish. **Muchísimo** (never **muy mucho**) is used for the adjective or adverb *very much (many).*

   In order to keep the same sound of the final consonant of an adjective, a change in spelling is sometimes necessary: **rico, riquísimo; largo, larguísimo.** Compare certain verbs with changes in spelling in the preterit, page 199.

E. Summary of comparison of equality

   Ana tiene tantas cosas como yo.   Ann has as many things as I.
   Pablo es tan guapo como José.   Paul is as handsome as Joseph.
   Yo no hablo tan rápidamente como ella.   I don't talk so rapidly as she.

Tanto (-a, -os, -as) + a noun + **como** means *as (so) much (many) . . . as;* **tan** + an adjective or adverb + **como** means *as (so) . . . as.*

   Tanto is also used as a pronoun or adverb: **No tengo tantos,** *I don't have so many;* **No me duele la cabeza tanto como ayer,** *My head doesn't ache so much as yesterday.*

   Tan is used only as an adverb: **¿Se habrá enamorado ella tan pronto?** *Can she have fallen in love so quickly?*

F. Possessive adjectives that follow the noun

singular		*plural*
mío, mía	my, of mine	**míos, mías**
tuyo, tuya	your (*fam.*), of yours	**tuyos, tuyas**
suyo, suya	his, her, your (*formal*), its, of his, of hers, of yours, of its	**suyos, suyas**
nuestro, nuestra	our, of ours	**nuestros, nuestras**
vuestro, vuestra	your (*fam. pl.*), of yours	**vuestros, vuestras**
suyo, suya	their, your (*pl.*), of theirs, of yours	**suyos, suyas**

(1) **un amigo mío**   a friend of mine
aquella casa nuestra   that house of ours
Beatriz y una tía suya   Beatrice and an aunt of hers
dos hermanos suyos   two brothers of his (hers, yours, theirs)

(2) **¡Dios mío!**   heavens!

In Lesson 4 you learned the short forms of possessive adjectives, which always precede the noun. There is also a set of long forms which follow the noun, agreeing with it in gender and number. The long forms, which are emphatic, are most commonly used: (1) to translate *of mine, of his, of yours,* etc., and (2) in certain set phrases.

Since **suyo (-a, -os, -as)** has several meanings, the form **de él,** etc., may be substituted to make the meaning clear: **dos hermanos suyos = dos hermanos de él (de ella, de ellos, de ellas, de Ud., de Uds.),** *two brothers of his* (*hers, theirs, yours*). Do not use a prepositional form for any long possessive other than **suyo, -a, -os, -as.**

◆ *Práctica.*   Read in Spanish, noting the use of the possessives:

1. un compañero mío, dos compañeros míos, un compañero nuestro.   2. un traje de Carlos, este traje suyo, esos trajes suyos.   3. el vestido de Elena, ese vestido suyo, varios vestidos suyos.   4. una amiga nuestra, algunas amigas nuestras, algunas amigas mías.
5. Juanita y un primo suyo, Juanita y una prima suya, Juanita y unos primos suyos.
6. ese regalo tuyo, esos regalos tuyos, esa pulsera tuya.

EJERCICIOS

A. Substitution drill:

1. Hoy *yo* no me siento bien.
   (*el profesor, nosotros, tú, ellos, Uds.*)
2. *Ellos* se divierten durante el fin de semana.
   (*Juanita, Yo, Nosotros, Tú, él y ella*)
3. A veces *yo* duermo la siesta.
   (*ella, tú, nosotros, Uds., las muchachas*)

4. *Ella* pidió permiso para ausentarse.
   (*Juanita, Yo, Nosotros, Tú, Beatriz y Roberto*)
5. ¡*Beatriz* se ha enamorado!
   (*Roberto y Beatriz, Yo, Uds., Tú, Nosotros*)

B. Listen to each sentence; then change to a formal singular command and to a familiar singular command:

MODELS: Juan le pide algo.   *Juan, pídale Ud. algo.*   *Juan, pídele algo.*
          Juan no le pide nada.   *Juan, no le pida Ud. nada.*   *Juan, no le pidas nada.*

1. Isabel vuelve temprano.   4. Carlos viene conmigo.
2. Ana la llama por teléfono.   5. Juanita no toca el timbre.
3. José duerme la siesta.   6. Beatriz no le dice eso.

C. Listen to each sentence; then repeat, making it negative:

MODEL: Hazlo esta tarde.   *No lo hagas esta tarde.*

1. Dinos el precio de eso.   4. Duérmete en el coche.
2. Ponlas sobre la mesa.   5. Pregúntale si puedes ausentarte.
3. Ve al centro con ella.   6. Pídele permiso esta tarde.

D. Answer affirmatively, following the models:

MODELS: ¿Es grande la ciudad?   *Sí, la ciudad es más grande que ésta.*
          ¿Es bueno el camino?   *Sí, el camino es mejor que éste.*

1. ¿Es cómoda la silla?   4. ¿Es malo el periódico?
2. ¿Son finas las pulseras?   5. ¿Es buena la medicina?
3. ¿Son caros los regalos?   6. ¿Es simpático el muchacho?

MODEL: ¿Es hermosa María?   *Sí, es muy hermosa; es hermosísima.*

7. ¿Es guapo el novio de Ana?   9. ¿Están contentos tus padres?
8. ¿Es rica la familia?   10. ¿Está Marta enamorada?

MODEL: ¿Es alto el edificio?   *Sí, es el edificio más alto de la ciudad.*

11. ¿Es larga la calle?   13. ¿Son bonitas las tiendas?
12. ¿Es pequeño el parque?   14. ¿Son modernos los autobuses?

E. Substitution drill:

1. Isabel tiene tantas *flores* como Marta.
   (zapatos, tiempo, pulseras, ropa)
2. Juan no es tan *alto* como Roberto.
   (simpático, amable, inteligente, joven)

3. Beatriz baila *más* que nadie.
   (menos, mejor, peor, más rápidamente)
4. Carlos es *mayor* que yo.
   (menor, menos alto, más pequeño, más serio)

F. Say after your teacher; then repeat, replacing the **de-**phrase with **suyo, -a, -os, -as,** as required:

1. Felipe y una hermana *de él.*
2. Ricardo y un hermano *de él.*
3. Pablo y dos primos *de él.*
4. Beatriz y dos primos *de ella.*
5. Felipe y una tía *de él.*
6. Carmen y un tío *de ella.*
7. Las chicas y algunas amigas *de ellas.*
8. ¿Va Juanita con un amigo *de ella?*
9. Ana va a México con dos tías *de ella.*
10. Este reloj es *de Carlos.*
11. Esos trajes no son *de Ud.*
12. ¿Es *de Ud.* este coche?

G. Give the Spanish for the following phrases:

1. this watch of mine. 2. these bracelets of mine. 3. this car of ours. 4. those tickets of ours. 5. our father and two sisters of his. 6. Helen and two aunts of hers. 7. my brother and a friend (*m.*) of his. 8. my parents and some friends of theirs. 9. you (*fam. sing.*) and a (girl) friend of yours. 10. an uncle of hers (*two ways*).

H. Give the Spanish equivalent, using the familiar forms for *you:*

1. "Hello, Jane! How do you feel today? Do you still have a cold?" 2. "Yes, and my head aches, although not so much as yesterday." 3. When Betty touches Jane on the forehead, she knows that she has [a] fever. 4. Then she asks her: "Why don't you lie down? Have you taken a nap? 5. Have you seen the doctor? Has he said anything to you?" 6. "He has prescribed several medicines, and, above all, he has told me that I must rest a great deal. 7. Do you know whether Beatrice has returned from her trip to New York?" 8. "Yes; yesterday we went to a jewelry store downtown. Beatrice had to get (pick up) a bracelet that an aunt of hers had given her. 9. It seems that she fell in love with Carmen's younger brother. 10. Beatrice told me that he is very handsome and also very charming. She is so happy now that she talks about Robert most of the time. 11. They had a very good time dancing in one of the best hotels in the city Saturday night." 12. "Heavens! She must be in love!"

I. **Composición:** La visita de una buena amiga

Assuming that you are Juanita, rewrite the following paragraph. Be sure to use the appropriate first person forms for those which appear in italics:

1. *Juanita* no *se ha* sentido bien y hoy *pidió* permiso para no ir a trabajar. 2. *Ha* estado enferma y *se ha* quedado en casa. 3. Isabel, *su* mejor campañera de la oficina, decidió visitar*la* un rato. 4. Aunque Isabel no quería molestar*la*, ella quería saber cómo *se encontraba Juanita.* 5. *Juanita* le *contó* a Isabel que *tenía* un resfriado y que *le* dolía la cabeza. 6. Cuando Isabel tocó *a Juanita* en la frente, comprendió que *Juanita* todavía *tenía* fiebre. 7. Luego

Isabel *le* preguntó *a Juanita* por qué no *se acostaba.* 8. *Ésta contestó* que no *quería* dormir demasiado durante la tarde.

9. El médico *le* ha recetado *a Juanita* varias medicinas y *le* dijo que sobre todo era necesario descansar mucho, pero *Juanita quería* charlar con alguien.

10. Isabel *le* contó *a Juanita* que había visto a Beatriz, otra de *sus* amigas.

11. Aunque *Juanita* no *se sentía* muy bien, *le* gustaba escuchar las cosas que *le* contaba Isabel. 12. ¡La mejor medicina que *Juanita tuvo* fue la visita esa tarde de *su* buena amiga!

VOCABULARIO

la **alegría**   joy, happiness
aunque   although, even though
ausentarse   to be absent
ayudar (**a** + *inf.*)   to help, aid (to)
Beatriz   Beatrice
la **cabeza**   head
la **cama**   bed
contar (ue)   to tell, relate
contento, -a   happy, pleased, glad
demasiado, -a   *adj. and pron.* too much (many)
después que   *conj.* after
dime = di + me   tell me
Dios   God
divertir (ie, i)   to divert, amuse; *reflex.* to have a good time, amuse oneself
doler (ue)   to ache, pain
dormir (ue, u)   to sleep; *reflex.* to fall asleep, go to sleep
elegante   elegant
enamorado, -a   enamored, in love
enamorarse (**de** + *obj.*)   to fall in love (with)
la **fiebre**   fever
el **fin**   end

la **frente**   forehead
guapo, -a   handsome, good-looking
imaginarse   to imagine
el **jefe**   boss
la **joyería**   jewelry shop (store)
Juanita   Juanita, Jane
la **medicina**   medicine
el **médico**   doctor, physician
la **mujer**   woman, "dear"
notar   to note, observe
el **novio**   sweetheart, fiancé, boy friend
pedir (i, i)   to ask, ask for, request
posible   possible
prometer   to promise
la **pulsera**   bracelet
recetar   to prescribe
el **resfriado**   cold (*disease*)
rico, -a   rich
sentir (ie, i)   to feel, regret, be sorry
la **siesta**   nap
simpático, -a   charming, likeable, nice
el **teatro**   theater
el **timbre**   doorbell
tocar   to ring

¡Dios mío!   heavens!
divertirse (ie, i) tanto   to have such a good time
dormir (ue, u) la (una) siesta   to take a nap
estar (muy) enamorado, -a   to be (very much) in love
fin de semana   weekend
la mayor parte de   most (of), the greater part of
lo sé   I know
me duele la cabeza   I have a headache, my head aches (*lit.*, the head aches to me)
¡qué alegría me da verte!   how happy I am to see you!
sobre todo   above all, especially
sentirse (ie, i) (bien)   to feel (well)
vamos   come now! go on! (*as an interjection*)

The present subjunctive of regular verbs • The present subjunctive of irregular and stem-changing verbs • Theory of the subjunctive mood • The subjunctive in noun clauses

LECCIÓN 18

Celebran su aniversario de bodas

Ana y Roberto cumplen su primer aniversario de bodas. Deciden celebrar la ocasión con una fiesta en su casa. Diana, la hermana de Ana, acaba de conocer a Carlos Estrada, un estudiante venezolano que va a estudiar medicina en la misma universidad que Roberto. Ana y Roberto le piden a Diana que lo invite a la fiesta.

ROBERTO —Por fin llegas, Diana. Los estábamos esperando . . . (*A Carlos*) Usted debe ser . . .

DIANA —Sí, Roberto, quiero presentarte a mi amigo[1] Carlos Estrada. Va a estudiar contigo en la Escuela de Medicina.

ROBERTO —Encantado de conocerte, Carlos. ¡Bienvenido!

CARLOS —Gracias. Es un gran placer encontrarme en tu país. Sin duda estaremos en alguna clase juntos.

ROBERTO —Deseo mucho que sea así. Bueno, entren, por favor.

CARLOS —¡Tienen Uds. una casa muy bonita!

ROBERTO —Gracias. Como te habrá dicho Diana, mi esposa es colombiana. Hoy celebramos nuestro primer aniversario de bodas.

CARLOS —Deseo que celebren muchos más.

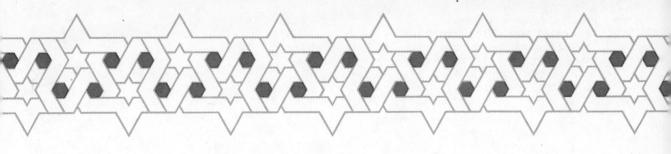

ROBERTO —Eres muy amable. Les ruego que pasen a la sala de recreo y que nos acompañen a celebrar nuestro aniversario.

◆ ◆ ◆ ◆ ◆

Ana se acerca y su marido le presenta a Roberto.

ANA —Mucho gusto en conocerte, Carlos. Ven, quiero que conozcas a los otros invitados.

ROBERTO —Un momento, por favor. Dime, Carlos, ¿qué te gustaría tomar?

CARLOS —Prefiero que no me traigas nada por ahora, gracias. Esperaré un rato.

◆ ◆ ◆ ◆ ◆

Entran en la sala de recreo y Ana hace las presentaciones. Charlan unos minutos y Diana se acerca al tocadiscos.

DIANA —¡Oye, Ana! ¿No quieres que pongamos unos discos de música popular?

ANA —Sí, pon un merengue. Como Carlos es venezolano, estoy segura de que . . .

LAS MUCHACHAS —Sí, sí . . . queremos que nos enseñe a bailar el merengue.

ANA —Carlos, aquí te piden que bailes. ¡Los otros muchachos no sabrán bailar el merengue tan bien como tú!

CARLOS —¡Caramba, qué gran honor! ¿No prefieren que bailemos una cumbia colombiana o un tango argentino?

◆ ◆ ◆ ◆ ◆

Todos se divierten mucho aprendiendo los diferentes pasos. A eso de las once Ana sirve algo de comer. Después de la medianoche se despiden los invitados.

LOS INVITADOS —Muchísimas gracias. Hemos pasado una noche muy agradable.

ANA Y ROBERTO —Pues, gracias a ustedes la fiesta ha sido muy divertida. Deseamos que todos vuelvan pronto. ¡Hasta la vista!

---

[1] To avoid confusion with the indirect object (**te,** *to you,* in this case), the personal **a** may be omitted before the direct object **(mi amigo),** unless the direct object is a proper noun, in which case the personal **a** must be used.

Conversación

A. Preguntas sobre el diálogo

1. ¿Cómo celebran Ana y Roberto su primer aniversario de bodas? 2. ¿A quién acaba de conocer Diana? 3. ¿Qué le piden Ana y Roberto? 4. ¿Por qué quiere Diana que Roberto conozca a Carlos Estrada? 5. ¿Por qué quiere Roberto que Carlos y Diana pasen a la sala de recreo? 6. ¿Qué disco le pide Ana a Diana que ponga? 7. ¿Qué le piden las muchachas a Carlos? 8. ¿Cómo ha sido la fiesta? ¿A qué hora se despiden los invitados?

B. Aplicación del diálogo

1. ¿Qué prefiere Ud., que lo (la) inviten a una fiesta o que lo (la) inviten al cine? 2. Cuando Ud. va a una fiesta, ¿prefiere que los invitados sepan bailar? ¿Por qué? 3. ¿Le gusta a Ud. la música? ¿Qué discos prefiere Ud. que pongan para bailar? 4. ¿Cuáles son los bailes más populares hoy día? 5. ¿Qué bailes hispanoamericanos conoce Ud.? ¿Sabe bailarlos? 6. ¿Cree Ud. que podrá aprenderlos? ¿Quiere Ud. que alguien le enseñe a bailarlos? 7. ¿Qué dice uno al presentar un amigo a otro? 8. ¿Qué dice uno al despedirse, después de una noche agradable?

NOTAS GRAMATICALES

A. The present subjunctive of regular verbs

	hablar		**comer**		**vivir**
sing.	*plural*	*sing.*	*plural*	*sing.*	*plural*
hable	hablemos	coma	comamos	viva	vivamos
hables	habléis	comas	comáis	vivas	viváis
hable	hablen	coma	coman	viva	vivan

In the present subjunctive tense the endings of **-ar** verbs begin with **-e,** while those of **-er** and **-ir** verbs begin with **-a.** In earlier lessons we have used the third person singular and plural forms of the present subjunctive in formal commands (Lesson 9), and the second person singular for negative familiar singular commands (Lessons 9 and 17). See section C for English equivalents of the present subjunctive tense.

B. The present subjunctive of irregular and stem-changing verbs

infinitive	1st sing. pres. ind.	present subjunctive
conocer	**conozco**	**conozca, conozcas, conozca,** etc.
decir	**digo**	**diga, digas, diga,** etc.
hacer	**hago**	**haga,** etc.
poner	**pongo**	**ponga,** etc.
salir	**salgo**	**salga,** etc.
tener	**tengo**	**tenga,** etc.
traer	**traigo**	**traiga,** etc.
venir	**vengo**	**venga,** etc.
ver	**veo**	**vea,** etc.

As we have learned in Lesson 9, in order to form the present subjunctive of all verbs in Spanish, except the following six verbs, drop the ending **-o** of the first person singular present indicative and add to this stem the subjunctive endings for the corresponding conjugation.

dar		estar		haber	
sing.	*plural*	*sing.*	*plural*	*sing.*	*plural*
dé	demos	**esté**	estemos	**haya**	**hayamos**
des	deis	**estés**	estéis	**hayas**	**hayáis**
dé	den	**esté**	**estén**	**haya**	**hayan**

ir		saber		ser	
vaya	**vayamos**	**sepa**	**sepamos**	**sea**	**seamos**
vayas	**vayáis**	**sepas**	**sepáis**	**seas**	**seáis**
vaya	**vayan**	**sepa**	**sepan**	**sea**	**sean**

Stem-changing verbs of Class I (ending in **-ar** and **-er**) have the same changes in the present subjunctive as in the present indicative, that is, throughout the singular and in the third person plural. This is also true of **poder** and **querer.**

pensar: **piense, pienses, piense,** pensemos, penséis, **piensen**
volver: **vuelva, vuelvas, vuelva,** volvamos, volváis, **vuelvan**

poder: **pueda, puedas, pueda,** podamos, podáis, **puedan**
querer: **quiera, quieras, quiera,** queramos, queráis, **quieran**

Stem-changing verbs of Class II and Class III (both of which end in **-ir**) have the same four changes in the present subjunctive which they have in the present indicative (throughout the singular and in the third person plural; see Lesson 17). In addition, Class II verbs change **e** to **i** and **o** to **u** in the first and second persons plural, and Class III verbs change **e** to **i** in these two forms also:

	CLASS II				CLASS III	
	sentir			**dormir**		**pedir**
sing.	*plural*	*sing.*	*plural*		*sing.*	*plural*
sienta	sintamos	duerma	durmamos		pida	pidamos
sientas	sintáis	duermas	durmáis		pidas	pidáis
sienta	sientan	duerma	duerman		pida	pidan

C. Theory of the subjunctive mood

Up to this point, the indicative mood, which indicates facts, has been used almost exclusively. The subjunctive mood has been used only in main clauses to express commands (see Lesson 9).

Spanish uses the subjunctive mood much more than English, particularly in dependent clauses. If the clause is used as a subject or direct object of a verb, it is called a noun clause. For example, in the sentence *I doubt that he knows it,* the words *that he knows it* make up a noun clause used as the direct object of the verb *I doubt.* The subjunctive mood is generally found in noun clauses that depend on verbs which express *uncertainty* or an *opinion,* an *attitude,* a *wish,* or a *feeling* of the speaker concerning the action of the dependent clause:

Yo no creo que él esté aquí. I do not believe that he is (will be) here.
Ella teme que Juan lo haga. She fears that John may (will) do it.
Ellos quieren que Ud. venga. They wish that you come, They want
                                        you to come.

Some of these uses are discussed further in section D; others will be taken up in Lesson 19. Note that the present subjunctive is expressed in several ways in English: (1) like the English present tense (*that he is, that you come*); (2) like the future (*that he will be here, that John will do it*); (3) with the word *may* (*that John may do it*), which carries the idea of something uncertain or not yet accomplished; and (4) by the infinitive (last example).

D. The subjunctive in noun clauses

Yo quiero ir. I want to go. (*Subjects the same*)
Ellos quieren que yo vaya. They want me to go (They wish that I go). (*Subjects different*)

José prefiere hacerlo.   Joseph prefers to do it.   (*Subjects the same*)
Él prefiere que ella lo haga.   He prefers that she do it.   (*Subjects different*)

In Spanish the subjunctive is regularly used in a noun clause when the main verb expresses ideas of the speaker such as those of *wish, request, command, order, necessity, permission, approval, advice, cause, suggestion, insistence,* and the like, as well as their negatives.

In English an infinitive is most commonly used after such verbs, but in Spanish a clause, usually introduced by **que,** is normally used if the subject of the dependent clause is different from that of the main verb. When there is no change in subject, or no subject is expressed for the English infinitive, the infinitive is also used in Spanish (first and third examples).

The present subjunctive is used for both present and future time in a dependent clause. And since the first and third person singular forms of the present subjunctive tense are the same, the subject pronouns should be used more often than in some other tenses.

With certain verbs, *e.g.,* **decir, pedir, rogar,** and others which require a personal object to be expressed as an indirect object, the subject of the infinitive in English is expressed as the indirect object of the main verb and understood as the subject of the subjunctive verb in the dependent clause. When you have a sentence like *Ask him to leave,* think of it literally as *Ask of (to) him that he leave:*

Pídale Ud. a Juan que salga.   Ask John to leave.   (*Subjects different*)
Les ruego a Uds. que pasen.   I beg you to come in.   (*Subjects different*)
Díganles Uds. que me lo den.   Tell them to give it to me.   (*Subjects different*)
Él nos dirá que volvamos.   He will tell us to return.   (*Subjects different*)

Decir is followed by the subjunctive when it is used to give an order (last two examples). Otherwise the indicative is used, since the verb indicates a fact (unless the verb is used negatively, in which case it becomes a verb which expresses uncertainty; see Lesson 19):

Juan dice que volverá.   John says (that) he will return.

EJERCICIOS

A. Answer each question with negative and affirmative formal commands, following the model:

MODEL: ¿Puedo hablar ahora?   *No, no hable Ud. ahora; hable más tarde.*

1. ¿Puedo leer ahora?   4. ¿Puedo comenzar ahora?
2. ¿Puedo cantar ahora?   5. ¿Puedo descansar ahora?
3. ¿Puedo salir ahora?   6. ¿Puedo volver ahora?

B. Say after your teacher; then repeat, changing to the negative:

1. Póngalos Ud. en la mesa.
2. Estúdienlas Uds. para mañana.
3. Levántense Uds. temprano.
4. Enséñeme Ud. los discos.

5. Dénoslo Ud.
6. Pónganselo Uds. pronto.
7. Siéntense Uds. allí.
8. Lávenselas Uds. aquí.

C. Repeat each familiar command; then change to the negative:

1. Beatriz, sirve el café.
2. Elena, sal en seguida.
3. Carolina, ve a la biblioteca.

4. Jorge, ponte los zapatos.
5. Tomás, tráeme la tarjeta.
6. Pablo, llévasela a ellos.

D. Answer each question according to the model, giving affirmative and negative formal commands and substituting the correct object pronouns for the noun objects:

MODEL: ¿Le doy a Juan el reloj? *Sí, déselo Ud. a él; no, no se lo dé a él.*

1. ¿Le traigo a Ana la blusa?
2. ¿Le mando a Luis el billete?
3. ¿Le doy a Marta la pulsera?

4. ¿Les llevo a las muchachas el dinero?
5. ¿Les vendo a sus amigos los discos?
6. ¿Les pido a Ana y a María el favor?

E. Substitution drill:

1. Juan quiere que *Uds.* hablen con el médico.
   (*tú, Marta y Luis, nosotros, ellos, Ud.*)
2. Prefieren que *tú* vengas temprano.
   (*Diana y Roberto, Ana y yo, ella, yo, Uds.*)

Listen carefully to the different patterns in the following:

3. *Pídale Ud.* que salga ahora.
   (*Pídales Ud., Ana me pide, José y Luis le ruegan, Yo le ruego*)
4. *Ellos me dicen* que lo haga.
   (*Dígale Ud., Marta nos dice, Yo les digo, Ella te dice*)

F. Listen carefully to the two questions; then compose an answer using the correct form of the verb, following the model:

MODEL: ¿Qué quiere Diana que Ana haga? *Sí, Diana quiere que*
       ¿Poner un disco?   *Ana ponga un disco.*

1. ¿Qué desea Ana que Diana haga? ¿Traer a Carlos a la fiesta?
2. ¿Qué quiere Roberto que Ana haga? ¿Servir algo de comer?
3. ¿Qué prefieren las muchachas que Carlos haga? ¿Bailar el merengue?
4. ¿Qué desean Ana y Roberto que los invitados hagan? ¿Volver pronto?

G. Answer each question negatively, and then affirmatively with a subjunctive clause, following the model:

MODEL: ¿Desea Ud. hacerlo?   *No, no deseo hacerlo; deseo que Ud. lo haga.*

1. ¿Desea Ud. traerlo?   4. ¿Quiere Ud. bailarlo?
2. ¿Desea Ud. servirlos?   5. ¿Prefiere Ud. ponerlo?
3. ¿Desea Ud. verla?   6. ¿Prefiere Ud. acompañarlas?

H. Give in Spanish, noting the change in subject in the second sentence in each group:

1. I desire to arrive early.   I desire that she arrive early.
2. Louis wants to return.   Louise wants John to return.
3. He and I want to meet her.   Helen wants us to meet her.
4. They prefer to stay here.   They prefer that I stay here.
5. Ask (*formal sing.*) him for   Ask him to give you permission
   permission to go.   to go.
6. Tell (*formal sing.*) her that we   Tell her to leave now.
   are going to leave now.

I. Give the Spanish equivalent, using the familiar forms for *you, your:*

1. Ann and Robert reach their first wedding anniversary and they decide to celebrate it with a party.   2. They ask Diane, Ann's sister, to bring Charles Estrada, a Venezuelan student.   3. He is going to study in the School of Medicine of the same university as Robert, and Diane wants them to meet him.   4. When Diane introduces Charles, Robert says: "Delighted to meet you! Welcome!"   5. Charles replies: "Many thanks. It is a great pleasure to be here in your country."   6. When Ann approaches, her husband introduces Charles to her.   7. After a moment Ann says to Charles: "Come with me; I want you to go (pass) to the recreation room to meet the other guests."   8. All chat a while. Finally Diane goes near the record player and asks her sister: "Don't you want us to put on some records?"   9. The girls ask Charles to teach them to dance the *merengue* and the *cumbia.*   10. After dancing a couple of hours, Ann serves them something to eat.   11. After midnight the guests take leave, saying: "We have spent a very pleasant evening."   12. Ann and Robert reply: "You (*pl.*) are very kind. We want all [of you] to return soon."

J. **Composición:** Nuevos amigos

Write a short composition, using the questions as a guideline:

1. ¿Fuiste anoche a casa de unos amigos, Diana y Roberto?
2. ¿Celebraban ellos su aniversario de bodas y tenían una fiesta?
3. ¿Conociste allí a un muchacho venezolano que se llama Carlos Estrada?
4. ¿Va a estudiar medicina en este país?
5. ¿Había muchos invitados en la fiesta?

6. ¿Recibieron Diana y Roberto muchos regalos?
7. ¿Estaban ellos muy contentos de celebrar esa ocasión con sus amigos?
8. ¿Sirvió Diana algo de comer a eso de las once?
9. ¿Qué hicieron Uds.? ¿Bailaron bastante? ¿Se divirtieron mucho?
10. ¿Le gusta a Carlos bailar?
11. ¿Sabe él bailar muy bien el merengue, la cumbia y otros bailes modernos?
12. Fue una fiesta agradable, ¿verdad?
13. Como tú también vas a estudiar medicina, ¿no deseas conocer mejor a Carlos?
14. ¿Deseas que él encuentre nuevos amigos en este país?

VOCABULARIO

argentino, -a Argentine
bienvenido, -a welcome
la **boda** wedding
la **cumbia** *popular Colombian dance*
despedirse (i, i) (**de** + *obj.*) to say goodbye (to), take leave (of)
diferente different
el **disco** record (*phonograph*)
divertido, -a entertaining, enjoyable
la **duda** doubt
la **escuela** school
el **honor** honor
el **invitado** guest
el **marido** husband
la **medianoche** midnight

el **merengue** *popular Caribbean dance*
mismo, -a same
la **música** music
la **ocasión** (*pl.* **ocasiones**) occasion
el **paso** step
poner to turn on, put on
preferir (ie, i) to prefer
la **presentación** (*pl.* **presentaciones**) introduction
rogar (ue) to ask, beg
la **sala de recreo** recreation room
servir (i, i) to serve
el **tango** tango
el **tocadiscos** record player
venezolano, -a Venezuelan

algo de comer something to eat
aniversario de bodas wedding anniversary
el (la) mismo (-a) . . . que the same . . . as
encantado, -a de conocerte delighted (pleased) to meet (know) you
Escuela de Medicina School of Medicine, Medical School
gracias a ustedes (ellos) thanks to you (them)
mucho gusto en conocerte (I am) very pleased (glad) to know (meet) you
pasar una noche muy agradable to spend a very pleasant evening
por ahora for now, for the present
por fin finally, at last
sin duda doubtless, without a doubt

La misión de Santa Bárbara en California es uno de los mejores ejemplos de arquitectura colonial en los Estados Unidos.

Patio de la casa donde nació Simón Bolívar, Caracas, Venezuela.

Lectura 9

España en América

La obra[1] de España en la exploración y la colonización de América fue de la mayor importancia. Hay que recordar que en realidad la palabra «América» no significa solamente los Estados Unidos, sino los dos continentes, la América del Norte y la América del Sur. A veces usamos la palabra «norteamericano» cuando hablamos de los habitantes de los Estados Unidos, pero este término tampoco es exacto,[2] porque México la América Central y el Canadá forman la América del Norte.

Para los norteamericanos las exploraciones que realizaron[3] los españoles en una gran parte de nuestro territorio tienen un interés especial. Exploradores como Ponce de León, Cabeza de Vaca, Hernando de Soto, Coronado y Cabrillo pertenecen también a la historia de los Estados Unidos. Desde San Francisco hasta el sur podemos ver hoy día las ruinas de las antiguas misiones españolas. Hay muchas misiones bien conocidas en California, como las[4] de Santa Bárbara y San Juan Capistrano.

En California, Arizona, Nuevo México, Texas, la Florida y otros lugares hay casas y edificios de estilo español. Sus balcones, corredores, portales, tejados,[5] y patios con flores y fuentes recuerdan la arquitectura española. La verdadera casa española tiene ventanas con rejas[6] de hierro y un patio, que está en el centro de la casa y que tiene una fuente, flores y pájaros.[7] En las ciudades y en los pueblos la plaza corresponde al patio de la casa. Muchas veces se encuentran cafés al aire libre en las plazas.

Varios estados de nuestro país tienen nombres de origen español: la Florida, la tierra de las flores; Nevada, la tierra de la nieve; Colorado, la tierra roja; y Montana, la montaña. California tiene el nombre de una isla que se menciona en una antigua novela española. Muchas ciudades tienen nombres españoles, como Fresno, El Paso, San Antonio, Santa Fe, Las Cruces, Las Vegas, San Diego, San José, San Francisco, Sacramento y Los Ángeles, cuyo nombre completo es El pueblo de Nuestra Señora, la Reina[8] de los Ángeles. También muchos ríos, valles y montañas tienen nom-

---

[1]**obra,** *work.* [2]**este término tampoco es exacto,** *this term is not exact either.* [3]**realizaron,** *carried out, realized.* [4]**las,** *those.* [5]**tejados,** *roofs (of tiles).* [6]**rejas,** *grills, gratings.* [7]**pájaros,** *birds.* [8]**Reina,** *Queen.*

bres españoles, como el Río Grande, el Sacramento, el Nueces, el Brazos y la Sierra Nevada.

Son innumerables las palabras españolas que se usan todos los días en inglés. Si no saben Uds. lo que significan las palabras siguientes, pueden buscarlas en un diccionario inglés: *adiós, amigo, arroyo, bolero, bronco, burro, cargo, cordillera, corral, fiesta, hacienda, hombre, mantilla, mesa, mosquito, parasol, paseo, patio, plaza, pronto, pueblo, rodeo, sierra, sombrero.*

Las palabras siguientes también son de origen español: *alligator* (el lagarto, *lizard*), *buckaroo* (vaquero, *cowboy*), *calaboose* (calabozo, *dungeon*), *canyon* (cañón), *desperado* (desesperado, *desperate, one in despair*), *hoosegow* (juzgado, *court of justice*), *lasso* (lazo), *lariat* (la reata), *mustang* (mesteño), *palaver* (palabra), *savvy* (¿sabe?), *vamoose* (vamos), *vanilla* (vainilla).

Entre las muchas palabras que los españoles tomaron de las lenguas indígenas de América, algunas han pasado al inglés, como *alpaca, canoe* (canoa), *coyote, chinchilla, chocolate, hurricane* (huracán), *maize* (maíz) y *tapioca.* Palabras como *banana* (de origen africano) y *adobe* y *tobacco* (tabaco), las dos de origen árabe, también llegaron al inglés por medio de[9] los españoles.

Debemos a los españoles muchas frutas y otros productos y varios animales que tenemos hoy día en las Américas. Las naranjas,[10] los limones, las aceitunas,[11] y las uvas, por ejemplo, son de España. De allí también son el trigo, el arroz, la caña de azúcar y otras plantas, y varios animales domésticos, como el caballo, la vaca, el toro, la oveja y el cerdo.

El resto del mundo también debe mucho a España por la introducción en Europa de frutas y legumbres como el maíz, el chocolate y la patata, que tuvieron su origen en América.

Se cree que la planta que hoy día conocemos con el nombre de maíz se originó en el sur de México o en algún lugar de la América Central. En los tiempos de los mayas, los indios que habitaban esa región antiguamente, había una planta silvestre[12] llamada *teocentli.* En la lengua de los mayas *teo* significaba divino y *centli,* maíz. Es evidente que la planta era para ellos una cosa divina, el maíz de los dioses. Poco a poco los mayas y otras tribus indígenas aprendieron a[13] cultivar el *teocentli,* que con el tiempo se convirtió en lo que hoy llamamos el maíz. El cultivo y el desarrollo de esta planta tuvieron una gran influencia en la vida de esas tribus, puesto que muchos hombres tuvieron que quedarse a vivir cerca de los campos de cultivo para cuidar y cosechar[14] el grano. Así se establecieron pueblos permanentes que, al necesitar leyes[15] y una organización social, dieron origen a[16] la civilización indígena. En realidad, puede decirse que el maíz fue la base de esa civilización. Todavía hoy, el maíz es uno de los productos más importantes del mundo.

Muchos años antes del descubrimiento de América los habitantes de México y de la América Central ya usaban el chocolate. Los aztecas usaban las semillas[17] del cacao para pagar el tributo a su emperador Moctezuma y como moneda en el comercio. Dice una leyenda que el chocolate era la única bebida que tomaba Moctezuma y que todos los días tomaba por lo menos[18] cincuenta jícaras.[19] El conquistador de México, Hernán Cortés, y sus soldados también tomaban chocolate. Fueron

---

[9]**por medio de,** *by means of, through.*   [10]**naranjas,** *oranges.*   [11]**aceitunas,** *olives.*   [12]**silvestre,** *wild.*   [13]Note that **aprender** requires **a** before an infinitive object.   [14]**cuidar y cosechar,** *to care for and harvest.*   [15]**leyes,** laws.   [16]**dieron origen a,** *originated.*   [17]**semillas,** *seeds.*   [18]**por lo menos,** *at least.*   [19]**jícaras,** *cups.*

los españoles del Nuevo Mundo quienes[20] llevaron el chocolate a Europa. El chocolate es hoy uno de los alimentos favoritos de todo el mundo.

Aquí no podemos mencionar todas las plantas que se originaron en las dos Américas. Algunas de ellas son la vainilla; el chicle, cuya leche se usa para hacer la goma de mascar;[21] la yuca, de que se saca la tapioca, y numerosas frutas tropicales que no tienen nombre en inglés. Y no debemos olvidar otros productos, como el chile, el tomate, el camote,[22] el tabaco, la calabaza[23] y la patata. La patata, que en muchas partes de la América española llaman papa, se originó en los Andes. Los españoles la llevaron a España a principios del[24] siglo dieciséis, y ha llegado a ser[25] uno de los alimentos más importantes del mundo.

Preguntas

1. ¿Qué significa la palabra «América»? 2. ¿Qué palabra usamos cuando hablamos de los habitantes de los Estados Unidos? 3. ¿Por qué no es exacto este término? 4. ¿Qué nombres de exploradores españoles recuerda Ud.? 5. ¿Dónde se ven hoy día ruinas de antiguas misiones españolas? 6. ¿Conoce Ud. los nombres de algunas misiones de California?

7. ¿Cómo son las casas y los edificios de estilo español? 8. ¿Cómo es la verdadera casa española? 9. En las ciudades, ¿qué corresponde al patio de la casa? 10. ¿Qué se encuentra muchas veces en las plazas?

11. ¿Cuáles de nuestros estados tienen nombres españoles? 12. ¿Qué significa la palabra «Colorado»? 13. ¿La Florida? 14. ¿Nevada? 15. ¿Qué ciudades tienen nombres españoles? 16. ¿Qué palabras españolas que se usan en inglés recuerda Ud.? 17. ¿Recuerda Ud. algunas palabras españolas de origen indígena?

18. ¿Qué productos debemos a los españoles? 19. ¿Qué animales domésticos debemos a España? 20. Mencione Ud. algunos productos que el resto del mundo debe a España.

21. ¿Dónde se originó el maíz? 22. ¿Cómo se llamaba la planta silvestre? 23. ¿Qué indios vivían en esa región? 24. ¿Qué era la planta para ellos? 25. ¿Por qué se quedaron los indios cerca de los campos? 26. En realidad, ¿cuál fue la base de la civilización indígena?

27. ¿Qué bebida hacían de las semillas del cacao los habitantes de México y de la América Central? 28. ¿Para qué usaban las semillas los aztecas? 29. Según una leyenda, ¿quién tomaba mucho chocolate? 30. ¿Lo tomaban también los españoles?

31. Mencione Ud. algunas plantas más que se originaron en América. 32. ¿Para qué se usa la leche del chicle? 33. ¿Cuáles son otros productos de las Américas? 34. ¿Dónde se originó la patata? 35. ¿Cuándo la llevaron a Europa los españoles?

---

[20]**Fueron . . . quienes = Los españoles del Nuevo Mundo fueron quienes** (*the ones who*). [21]**goma de mascar,** *chewing gum.* [22]**camote,** *sweet potato.* [23]**calabaza,** *pumpkin, squash.* [24]**a principios de,** *at the beginning of.* [25]**ha llegado a ser,** *it has become.*

Estudio de palabras

a. Approximate cognates. Pronounce the following words aloud, give the English cognates, and indicate the variations: civilización, completo, corredor, corresponder, diccionario, especial, introducción, misión, territorio.

b. Deceptive cognates. In Spanish **realizar** means *to realize, carry out,* and not *to realize, understand vividly.* **Recordar (ue)** has two meanings: with a personal subject it means *to remember;* with a thing as subject it means *to recall (to one), remind (one) of.*

c. Compare the meanings of the following pairs of words: cultivar, *to cultivate, and* cultivo, *cultivation;* exploración, *exploration, and* explorador, *explorer;* habitar, *to inhabit, and* habitante, *inhabitant;* interés, *interest, and* interesante, *interesting;* origen, *origin, and* originar(se), *to originate;* puerta, *door, and* portal, *doorway;* realidad, *reality, and* realizar, *to realize, carry out;* verdad, *truth, and* verdadero, *true, real.*

d. It will help you in increasing your vocabulary to take note of words of opposite meanings. How many of the following words do you recognize?

ancho—estrecho	ir—venir	pequeño—grande
bueno—malo	más—menos	recordar—olvidar
este—oeste	mucho—poco	también—tampoco
fácil—difícil	norte—sur	viejo—nuevo

e. **Santo** (not **Santa**) is shortened to **San** before all names of masculine saints, except those beginning with **Do-** or **To-:**

San Francisco St. Francis	**San José** St. Joseph	
BUT: **Santo Domingo** St. Dominic	**Santa Inés** St. Agnes	
Santo Tomás St. Thomas	**Santa María** St. Mary.	

Santa also means *Holy:* **Santa Fe,** *Holy Faith;* **Santa Cruz,** *Holy Cross.*

Try to give the meaning of: San Antonio, San Carlos, San Felipe, San Jorge, San Luis, San Pablo, Santa Ana, Santa Clara, Santa Rosa.

(Página de enfrente) *Reproducción de un grabado antiguo que muestra un central azucarero en la época colonial en Cuba. La industria del azúcar ha tenido gran importancia en la isla de Cuba desde el período colonial. Los españoles trajeron la caña de azúcar a la América desde la India. Pronto la producción de azúcar se convirtió, conjuntamente con el tabaco y el café, en una de las más importantes fuentes de ingreso de varias de las colonias españolas en América. Se construyeron muchos centrales azucareros, llamados también ingenios o trapiches, y el azúcar alcanzó un precio muy alto en el mercado internacional. En esta página se ven, primero, la recolección de la caña en un campo de caña en Costa Rica. La producción de azúcar continúa siendo una de las industrias principales en muchos países. A la derecha se ven unos campesinos recogiendo los granos de café que habían puesto a secar al sol. El café es otra de las fuentes de ingreso de varios países de Hispanoamérica. El Brasil es el mayor exportador de café del mundo.*

The present subjunctive of verbs with changes in spelling • The
subjunctive in noun clauses (continued) • The present perfect
subjunctive tense • More commands

LECCIÓN 19

José va de compras

Son las diez de la mañana. José sale a la calle y toma el autobús para ir al centro.
Al bajar del autobús tiene una sorpresa agradable. Se encuentra con su amigo
Jaime, que se ha detenido frente a los escaparates de un gran almacén.

JOSÉ —¡Cuánto me alegro de que hayas venido al centro esta mañana! ¿Puedes
ayudarme a hacer algunas compras?

JAIME —Puedo acompañarte un rato, pero es urgente que vuelva a la residencia
antes del mediodía. ¿Qué piensas comprar?

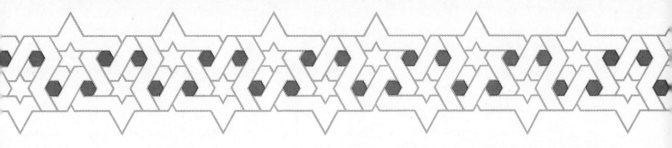

JOSÉ —Papá quiere que yo busque algunas cosas para mi cumpleaños: un par de zapatos, una camisa, una corbata, un sombrero, calcetines . . .

JAIME —¡Qué suerte tienes, José! Yo quiero un traje nuevo para el verano, pero mi padre me dice que no es preciso que lo compre ahora.

❖ ❖ ❖ ❖ ❖

JOSÉ —Entremos primero en esta zapatería aquí a la derecha. Voy a pedir que me enseñen unos zapatos como aquéllos. (*Señala un par que se exhibe en el escaparate. Entran en la zapatería.*)

JAIME —¡Qué extraño que haya tanta gente aquí tan temprano!

JOSÉ —Temo que tengamos que esperar un rato. Sentémonos aquí a la izquierda. (*Pasan cinco o seis minutos. Por fin se acerca un dependiente.*)

DEPENDIENTE —¿En qué puedo servirles, señores?

JOSÉ —Necesito comprar un par de zapatos. Me gusta el estilo que exhiben en el escaparate. ¿Podría enseñármelos, si me hace el favor?

DEPENDIENTE —A ver, ¿qué número usa Ud.? (*José se quita el zapato.*) Creo que le sentará bien el número nueve. (*Al poco tiempo.*) Pruébese éste, por favor.

JOSÉ —Es demasiado estrecho; no me sienta bien.

DEPENDIENTE —¿Quiere Ud. probarse éstos? Son medio número más grande, aunque el estilo es un poco diferente.

JOSÉ —Es cierto que éstos me sientan mucho mejor. ¿Qué precio tienen?

DEPENDIENTE —Veinticinco dólares. Dudo que encuentre Ud. otros mejores a este precio.

JOSÉ —Es posible que sea así, aunque es lástima[1] que no tenga los otros en mi número. Pero bueno, me quedo con ellos. Aquí tiene Ud. un billete de veinte dólares y otro de diez. (*El dependiente le da cinco dólares de vuelta, envuelve los zapatos y le entrega el paquete.*)

JAIME (*Mirando su reloj.*) —Ya es tarde. No puedo acompañarte más.

JOSÉ —Sí, es mejor que te vayas ahora. Siento que hayan tardado tanto.

JAIME —Hasta luego, José. ¡Que te diviertas!

---

[1] The indefinite article is sometimes used in this expression: **es una lástima,** *it is a pity, it's too bad.*

Conversación

A. Preguntas sobre el diálogo

1. ¿Con quién se encuentra José?   2. ¿Qué le pide José a Jaime?   3. ¿Qué le contesta Jaime?   4. ¿Qué quiere el papá de José?   5. Al entrar en la zapatería, ¿qué le parece extraño a Jaime?   6. ¿Qué teme José?   7. ¿Por qué compra José el segundo par de zapatos que se prueba?   8. ¿Qué le dice José a Jaime cuando éste mira el reloj?

B. Aplicación del diálogo

1. ¿Se alegra Ud. de que llegue el verano pronto? ¿Piensa Ud. hacer un viaje?   2. ¿Qué cosas es preciso que Ud. compre para su viaje?   3. ¿Le gusta a Ud. ir de compras solo (sola) o prefiere que alguien lo (la) acompañe?   4. ¿Le pide Ud. dinero a menudo a su padre para ir de compras? ¿Qué le dice él?   5. ¿Cuándo celebrará Ud. su cumpleaños? ¿Cuántos años cumplirá Ud.?   6. ¿Qué regalos espera Ud. que le den para su cumpleaños?   7. ¿Qué le decimos a un amigo cuando queremos que se divierta mucho?   8. ¿Qué le decimos cuando queremos que tenga mucha suerte?

NOTAS GRAMATICALES

A. The present subjunctive of verbs with changes in spelling

> buscar: **busque, busques, busque, busquemos, busquéis, busquen**
> llegar: **llegue, llegues, llegue, lleguemos, lleguéis, lleguen**
> empezar: **empiece, empieces, empiece, empecemos, empecéis, empiecen**

Just as in the case of the first person singular of the preterit tense, in all six forms of the present subjunctive all verbs which end in **-car** change **c** to **qu,** those in **-gar** change **g** to **gu,** and those in **-zar** change **z** to **c.** This change is made before the vowel **e** to keep the sound of the final consonant of the stem the same as in the infinitive. Note that **empezar** also has the stem change of **e** to **ie.**

Other **-car** verbs already used are: **acercarse, sacar, tocar;** other **-gar** verbs are: **entregar, jugar (ue), pagar, rogar (ue);** other **-zar** verbs are: **almorzar (ue), comenzar (ie).**

B. The subjunctive in noun clauses (continued)

1. **Me alegro de estar aquí.** I am glad to be here. (*Same subjects*)
   Me alegro (alegraré) de que no te vayas. I am (shall be) glad that you are not going (away).
   Es lástima que Ud. no los tenga. It is too bad (that) you don't have them.
   Temo que sean muy caros. I fear (that) they are very expensive.
   Esperamos que no lleguen tarde. We hope they will not arrive late.

¡Qué extraño que haya tanta gente aquí!   How strange that there are so many people here!

The subjunctive is used in noun clauses after verbs or expressions of emotion or feeling, such as *joy, sorrow, fear, hope, pity, surprise, strangeness,* and the like, as well as their negatives, provided that <u>the subject differs</u> from that of the main verb. Compare the first example, in which there is no change in subject, with those which follow. Remember that **que** regularly introduces a noun clause in Spanish, even though *that* is sometimes omitted in English.

Some common expressions of emotion are:

alegrarse	to be glad (that)	**sentir (ie, i)**	to regret, be sorry
(de que)		**temer**	to fear
es lástima	it is a pity, too bad	**tener miedo**	to be afraid (that)
esperar	to hope	**(de que)**	

2. **Creo que le sentará bien.**   I believe that it will fit you. (*Certainly implied*)
   No creo que tengamos que esperar.   I don't believe we will have to wait.
   Dudo que Ud. encuentre otros mejores.   I doubt that you will find other better ones.
   No estoy seguro de que vuelvan.   I am not sure that they will return.

The subjunctive is regularly used after expressions of *doubt, uncertainty,* or *belief in the negative.* Note that **creer** implies certainty and requires the indicative, while **no creer** implies uncertainty and requires the subjunctive. Likewise, **estar seguro de que** is followed by the indicative (or **estar seguro de** plus an infinitive is used if there is no change in subject), while **no estar seguro de que** requires the subjunctive. **Decir** used negatively also expresses uncertainty: **Yo no digo que Luis sepa eso,** *I do not say that Louis knows (may know) that.*

When **creer** is used in questions, the speaker may imply doubt on the action in the dependent clause, in which case the subjunctive is used. If no implication of doubt is made, the indicative is used. **No creer que** in a question implies certainty:

¿Cree Ud. que salgan hoy?   Do you believe (think) they will leave today? (*Doubt in the mind of the speaker*)
¿Cree Ud. que lo comprarán?   Do you believe they will buy it? (*The speaker has no opinion*)
¿No creen Uds. que lloverá?   Don't you believe it will rain? (*The speaker implies certainty.*)

The verb **negar (ie),** *to deny,* also requires the subjunctive, but this verb is not used in the dialogues: **Él niega que sea verdad,** *He denies that it is true.*

3. **Es fácil aprender eso.**   It is easy to learn that.
   Es urgente que yo vuelva a casa.   It is urgent that I return home (for me to return home).

Es mejor que te vayas ahora. It is better for you to leave (that you leave) now.
Es lástima que sean tan caros. It's too bad that they are so expensive.
No es preciso que él lo compre. It isn't necessary for him to buy it.
Es cierto (verdad) que él lo sabe. It is certain (true) that he knows it.
No es cierto que empiecen. It is not certain that they will begin.

The subjunctive is used after impersonal expressions (which usually begin with *it is*) of *possibility, necessity, probability, uncertainty, strangeness, pity,* and the like, provided that the verb of the dependent clause has a subject expressed. Impersonal expressions of certainty, such as **es cierto** and **es verdad,** require the indicative in the dependent clause; when these expressions are negative, they imply uncertainty and require the subjunctive (last example).

The infinitive *may* be used after most of these expressions if the subject of the dependent verb (expressed in English as the indirect object of the main verb) is a *personal pronoun,* not a noun:

Me (Les) es necesario salir. It is necessary for me (them) to leave.
BUT: **Es preciso que Juan salga.** It is necessary for John to go leave.

These impersonal expressions really fall under groups 1 and 2 of this section, and section D in Lesson 18, but they are listed separately for convenience and clarity.

Some common impersonal expressions which you have had are:

es difícil	it is difficult	**es mejor**	it is better
es extraño	it is strange	**es necesario**	it is necessary
es fácil	it is easy	**es posible**	it is possible
es importante	it is important	**es preciso**	it is necessary
es lástima	it is a pity, too bad	**es urgente**	it is urgent

C. The present perfect subjunctive tense

present perfect subjunctive	
haya **hayas** } hablado, comido, vivido **haya**	**hayamos** **hayáis** } hablado, comido, vivido **hayan**

¡Cuánto me alegro de que hayas venido! How glad I am that you have come!
Siento mucho que hayan tardado tanto. I am very sorry that it has taken them so long (that they have delayed so much).

The present perfect subjunctive tense is formed by the present subjunctive of **haber** with the past participle. After verbs in the main clause which require the subjunctive in the dependent clause, Spanish uses the present perfect subjunctive to express *have* or *has* with the past participle. The word *may* is sometimes a part of the English meaning: **(que) yo haya hablado,** (*that*) *I may have spoken.*

D. More commands

1. **Entremos en esta tienda.**   Let's (Let us) enter this store.
    Abrámosla.
    Vamos a abrirla.}Let's open it.
    No lo dejemos aquí.   Let's not leave it here.

The first person plural of the present subjunctive is used to express commands equal to *let's* or *let us* plus a verb. **Vamos a** plus an infinitive, in addition to meaning *we are going to,* may be used for *let's* or *let us* plus a verb if the intention is to perform the action at once.
   Vamos is used for the affirmative *let's* (*let us*) *go:* **Vamos a casa ahora,** *Let's go home now.* The subjunctive **vayamos** must be used in the negative for *let's not go:* **No vayamos a casa todavía,** *Let's not go home yet.* **No vamos a casa todavía** can only mean *We are not going home yet.*
   For *let's see,* **a ver** is often used without **vamos** (see Lesson 2).

    Vámonos.   Let's be going, Let's go.
    Sentémonos aquí.   (Vamos a sentarnos aquí.)   Let's sit down here.
    No nos levantemos.   Let's not get up.

When the reflexive pronoun **nos** is added to this command form, final **-s** is dropped from the verb. Remember that the reflexive pronoun must agree with the subject.

2. **Que lo traiga Juan.**   Have John (May John) bring it.
    Que te diviertas.   May you (I want you to, I hope you) have a good time.

Que, equivalent to English *have, let, may, I wish* or *I hope,* introduces indirect commands in the second and third persons. In such cases object pronouns precede the verb, and if a subject is expressed, it usually follows the verb. This construction is really a clause dependent upon a verb of *wishing, hoping, permitting,* and the like, with the main verb understood.
   Let, meaning *to allow* or *permit,* will be discussed later (see Lesson 22).

EJERCICIOS

A. Say after your teacher; then repeat, making the sentence negative:

1. Démelo Ud.   2. Tráiganoslos Ud. hoy.   3. Búsquenlo Uds.   4. Envuélvalo Ud.
5. Entrégueselo Ud. a Juanita.   6. Jueguen Uds. con ellos.   7. Tóquelo Ud. ahora.
8. Sentémonos.   9. Siéntese Ud.   10. Quitémonos los zapatos.   11. Cerrémosla.
12. Diviértanse Uds.   13. Póngaselo Ud.   14. Pongámoslo aquí.   15. Vámonos.

B. Say after your teacher; when you hear the cue, compose a new sentence using the subjunctive in the dependent clause:

MODEL: Jaime va a casa.   *Jaime va a casa.*
        Dudo que   *Dudo que Jaime vaya a casa.*

1. Yo busco un traje nuevo.
   (Quieren que, Se alegran de que, Es urgente que)
2. El jefe llega temprano a la oficina.
   (Desean que, Es importante que, No creen que)
3. Los estudiantes se sientan a la derecha.
   (Es mejor que, Es necesario que, Dudo que)
4. La vendedora no puede envolverlo ahora.
   (Temo que, Siento que, Es posible que)
5. Juan ha visto a Jaime hoy.
   (Esperamos que, No creo que, Es lástima que)

C. Repeat the sentence; when you hear the cue, include it in a new sentence:

MODEL: Yo temo no llegar a tiempo.   *Yo temo no llegar a tiempo.*
        que Jaime   *Yo temo que Jaime no llegue a tiempo.*

1. Yo siento no poder comprar los zapatos.   (que José)
2. Es mejor probarse otro par.   (que Ud.)
3. Juan espera encontrar trabajo.   (que tú)
4. Marta prefiere buscar otro vestido.   (que su hermana)
5. Los muchachos quieren tocar otros discos.   (que nosotros)
6. Nos alegramos de estar aquí.   (de que Uds.)
7. Es urgente empezar temprano.   (que Carolina)
8. No es preciso envolver el paquete.   (que yo)

D. Say after your teacher; when you hear the cues, expand the sentences, using the appropriate subjunctive tense:

MODEL: José viene esta tarde. Espero que   *Espero que José venga esta tarde.*
        José vino esta mañana. Espero que   *Espero que José haya venido esta*
                                              mañana.

1. Ella se pone su vestido nuevo. Me alegro de que . . .
   Ella se puso su vestido nuevo. Me alegro de que . . .
2. Tú no estás aquí ahora. Es lástima que . . .
   Tú no estuviste aquí hoy. Es lástima que . . .
3. Ellos no vuelven a tiempo. Temo que . . .
   Ellos no volvieron a tiempo. Temo que . . .
4. José no quiere comprar ese sombrero. Siento que . . .
   José no quiso comprar ese sombrero. Siento que . . .

5. Ellos empiezan las clases mañana. Es posible que . . .
Ellos empezaron las clases ayer. Es posible que . . .
6. Ella siempre se levanta temprano. No estoy seguro de que . . .
Ella se levantó temprano hoy. No estoy seguro de que . . .

E. Answer each question twice, using affirmative and negative replies, and (except in questions 5–8) substituting pronouns for the noun objects:

MODEL: ¿Escribimos la carta? *Sí, escribámosla. No, no la escribamos.*

1. ¿Llevamos a Felipe? 2. ¿Tomamos el autobús? 3. ¿Buscamos la zapatería? 4. ¿Compramos esos zapatos? 5. ¿Lo pagamos con este billete? 6. ¿Nos bajamos aquí? 7. ¿Nos sentamos a la izquierda? 8. ¿Nos vamos?

F. Listen to each direct command; then give an indirect command with **él,** preceded by the phrase **Yo no puedo:**

MODEL: Ciérrela Ud. *Yo no puedo, que la cierre él.*

1. Llévelo Ud. 2. Tráigalos Ud. 3. Siéntese Ud. 4. Búsquelos Ud. 5. Tóquelo Ud. 6. Pídaselo Ud. 7. Páguelo Ud. 8. Acérquese Ud.

G. Express in Spanish:

1. Let's open them (*two ways*). 2. Let's get up (*two ways*). 3. Let's not look for shirts today. 4. Let's not give it (*m.*) to him. 5. Let's go to the movie. 6. Let's see. 7. May he return the necktie. 8. Have him ring the doorbell. 9. Have Jane bring me the magazine. 10. Have her bring it (*f.*) to me.

H. Give in Spanish, noting the contrast in the use of the infinitive and the subjunctive forms:

1. I am glad to be able to go.	I am glad that she is able to go.
2. He hopes to return early.	He hopes that we return early.
3. I am afraid to arrive late.	I am afraid that they will arrive late.
4. It is better to wait here.	It is better for you (*pl.*) to wait here.
5. It is important to decide now.	It is important that we decide now.
6. It is a pity not to buy that house.	It is a pity you (*pl.*) do not buy that house.

I. Give the Spanish equivalent, using the formal forms for *you:*

1. John has just stopped in front of a department store when James passes along the street. 2. The latter asks his friend to go shopping with him. 3. He says that his father wants him to buy a pair of shoes, a hat, a shirt, a necktie, and some socks for his birthday. 4. First they enter a shoe store which is nearby, on the right. 5. There are so many people there that James fears that they will have to wait a while. 6. "Let's sit down here to the left," says James. 7. Finally a clerk approaches and asks: "What can

I do for you (*pl*)?" 8. James says: "Please show me a pair of black shoes. I like the style which you (*pl.*) are displaying in the show window." 9. Then the clerk asks him: "What size do you wear? Will you take off your shoe, please?" 10. The clerk believes that (the) size nine will fit him, but it is too tight. 11. James tries on other shoes which are a little larger. 12. Even though the style is different, he says: "I'll take them. Here is the money." 13. After wrapping up the shoes, the clerk hands the package to him. 14. Then John says that it is necessary for him to return to the residence hall at once. 15. James is sorry that his friend cannot accompany him longer (more).

J. **Composición:** De compras

Keeping in mind the dialogue of this lesson, complete the following paragraphs by supplying the correct form of the infinitive in parentheses in the present tense (indicative or subjunctive):

1. A Juan no le (gustar) _____ ir de compras. 2. Pero (ser) _____ necesario que él (comprar) _____ algunas cosas antes de volver a la universidad. 3. Por fin, un lunes por la mañana, Juan (ir) _____ al centro. 4. Él (acabar) _____ de detenerse frente a los escaparates de un gran almacén cuando (encontrarse) _____ con Jaime, un amigo suyo.

5. —¡Cuánto (alegrarse) _____ de que tú (haber) _____ venido al centro! —le (decir) _____ Juan a Jaime.[1] 6. Éste le (contestar) _____: —Como tú (saber) _____, yo (trabajar) _____ en la oficina de mi papá y casi nunca (estar) _____ por aquí a estas horas. 7. ¿Qué (estar) _____ haciendo en el centro, Juan? 8. ¿(Poder) _____ ayudarte en algo?

9. —(Ser) _____ que mi padre (querer) _____ que yo (hacer) _____ algunas compras. 10. Yo siempre (preferir) _____ que alguien (acompañarme) _____. 11. (Esperar) _____ que tú (poder) _____ ayudarme a buscar unos zapatos.

12. Jaime (decidir) _____ acompañar a su amigo a una zapatería que (estar) _____ cerca. 13. Juan (encontrar) _____ unos zapatos que le (sentar) _____ bien, aunque (ser) _____ muy caros. 14. Juan (necesitar) _____ comprar otras cosas, pero ese día (haber) _____ mucha gente en las tiendas. 15. Como no (ser) _____ urgente que Juan lo (comprar) _____ todo en seguida, Juan (decidir) _____ esperar y volver al centro con Jaime otro día.

---

[1]As we have learned, in Spanish dashes are used to introduce all direct quotations. If a direct quotation precedes its principal clause, another dash is used to enclose the quotation and set off the concluding portion of the sentence.

VOCABULARIO

el **almacén** (*pl.* **almacenes**)   department
   store
bajar (**de** + *obj.*)   to get off *or* out of
el **calcetín** (*pl.* **calcetines**)   sock
la **camisa**   shirt
cierto, -a   (a) certain, true
la **corbata**   necktie
el **dependiente**   clerk
derecho, -a   right
dudar   to doubt
estrecho, -a   narrow, tight
exhibir   to exhibit, show
extraño, -a   strange
izquierdo, -a   left
Jaime   James, Jim

el **número**   size (*of shoes*)
el **paquete**   package
preciso, -a   necessary, precise
primero   *adv.* first
probarse (**ue**)   to try on
quitar   to remove, take off; *reflex.* to take
   off (oneself)
señalar   to point at (out), indicate
el **señor**   gentleman
el **sombrero**   hat
temer   to fear
urgente   urgent
la **vuelta**   change (*money*)
la **zapatería**   shoe store

a la derecha (izquierda)   to (on, at) the right (left)
al poco tiempo   after (in) a short time
¡cuánto me alegro de (de que)!   how glad I am to (that)!
¿en qué puedo servirle(s)?   what can I do for you?
me quedo con (ellos)   I'll take (them)
¡qué suerte tienes!   what luck you have! how lucky (fortunate) you are!
salir a la calle   to go out into the street
sentar (ie) bien (a uno)   to fit (one) well
si me hace el favor   (if you will) please
tardar tanto   to take so long, delay so much (long)

Lectura 10

La España antigua

La historia de España presenta muchos contrastes. España ha tenido épocas de gloria y períodos de decadencia. En los párrafos siguientes vamos a repasar la historia de España desde sus orígenes hasta el descubrimiento de América, el hecho[1] más notable, sin duda, de su larga historia.

Los primeros pobladores de la península fueron los iberos, pero no se sabe ni su origen ni la época exacta en que entraron en la península. Cerca de Santander, en el norte de España, se conservan, en las cuevas[2] de Altamira, dibujos de animales pintados hace unos veinte o treinta mil años. Los fenicios,[3] considerados como los primeros comerciantes del mundo, llegaron a la península hacia el siglo XI antes de Jesucristo[4] y fundaron la ciudad de Cádiz. Hubo[5] otros invasores: los celtas,[6] en el norte, principalmente en Galicia; los griegos,[7] que se establecieron en la costa del Mar Mediterráneo; y los cartagineses,[8] que dominaron la península desde el siglo VI hasta el III antes de Jesucristo. Los romanos estuvieron en España unos seis siglos. Durante esa época la península llegó a ser una de las provincias más importantes del imperio romano. En España los romanos dejaron su lengua, sus costumbres, su religión, sus leyes y sus ideas sobre el gobierno; se construyeron teatros, acueductos, caminos, puentes[9] y otras obras públicas.

Buen ejemplo de la obra de los romanos es el acueducto de Segovia, que está en uso todavía. Está construido de piedras grandes, sin argamasa[10] de ninguna clase. Otra obra romana es el teatro de Sagunto, que está al norte de la ciudad de Valencia.

A la caída[11] del imperio romano, ocuparon la península los visigodos[12] y otras tribus germánicas. Los últimos invasores fueron los moros,[13] que entraron en España en 711 y no fueron expulsados hasta 1492. Córdoba fue el centro de la civilización de los moros, considerada en el siglo X como la más avanzada de Europa. No lejos de Córdoba está Granada, que fue la última capital de los moros. Allí se encuentra la famosa Alhambra,

---

[1]**hecho,** *event, deed.* [2]**cuevas,** *caves.* [3]**fenicios,** *Phoenicians.* [4]**antes de Jesucristo,** *B.C.* [5]**Hubo** (*pret. of* **haber**), *There were.* [6]**celtas,** *Celts.* [7]**griegos,** *Greeks.* [8]**cartagineses,** *Carthaginians.* [9]**puentes,** *bridges.* [10]**argamasa,** *mortar.* [11]**caída,** *fall.* [12]**visigodos,** *Visigoths.* [13]**moros,** *Moors.*

con sus magníficos patios, sus bellos jardines y sus alegres fuentes. Al abandonar a[14] España, los moros dejaron en ella influencias decisivas en la lengua, la literatura, la arquitectura, el arte, la música, el comercio y la agricultura.

Durante la guerra de la reconquista, que duró casi ocho siglos, surgieron los reinos[15] de León, Navarra, Aragón, Galicia y Castilla. Castilla, que se llamó así por la gran cantidad de castillos que se construyeron para la defensa contra los moros, llegó a ser, con el tiempo, el reino principal del país. En el siglo XI el castellano empezó a predominar sobre los demás dialectos romances hablados en la península. Se comenzó a cantar en la nueva lengua la vida guerrera[16] de la época. En ese siglo vivió el Cid, el gran héroe nacional de España, cuya tumba está en la catedral de Burgos, una de las más bellas de Europa.

Para ver la más grande de todas las catedrales góticas de Europa hay que ir a Sevilla. La torre de la catedral, la Giralda, construida por los moros, tiene fama de ser una de las más hermosas del mundo. Hay un refrán[17] español que dice: «Quien[18] no ha visto a Sevilla, no ha visto maravilla». Hay otro que dice: «Quien no ha visto a Granada, no ha visto nada».

Con el matrimonio de Fernando de Aragón con Isabel de Castilla, en 1469, consiguió[19] España la unidad política; poco después[20] los Reyes Católicos terminaron la conquista de Granada para realizar la unidad espiritual. El año de 1492 representa para los españoles el fin de la guerra contra los moros y el principio de una época de gloria y poderío.[21] En el siglo XVI España llegó a ser la nación más poderosa del mundo.

Conseguida[22] la unidad religiosa y política, los Reyes Católicos comenzaron a interesarse en la expansión del país y por fin decidieron ayudar a un pobre explorador italiano, Cristóbal Colón. Colón salió de España con tres carabelas, la Pinta, la Santa María y la Niña; y el doce de octubre de 1492, después de unos setenta días de viaje, llegó a una pequeña isla del Mar Caribe. Tomó posesión de ella en nombre de los Reyes Católicos, y la llamó San Salvador.[23]

Antes de volver a España, Colón exploró otras islas y estableció el primer pueblo español del Nuevo Mundo el 25 de diciembre, por lo cual[24] dio al pueblo el nombre de Navidad. Como Colón creía que había llegado a la India, dio el nombre de «indios» a los habitantes de las islas.

En el segundo viaje de Colón los españoles trajeron semillas, árboles frutales y varios animales domésticos. Los frailes,[25] los obreros[26] y los agricultores que acompañaron a Colón iniciaron la gran obra de la exploración y la colonización del Nuevo Mundo.

La América española ha dado el nombre del gran descubridor a una nación, Colombia, y a dos ciudades de Panamá, Cristóbal y Colón. En los Estados Unidos también hay ciudades que llevan el nombre de *Columbia* o *Columbus*. El mundo debe mucho a Cristóbal Colón. Este hombre enérgico y valiente sentó[27] un buen ejemplo para los hombres que vinieron a América durante las épocas siguientes.

---

[14]The personal **a** is often used before unmodified place names.   [15]**surgieron los reinos,** *(there) appeared the kingdoms.* [16]**guerrera,** *warlike.*   [17]**refrán,** *proverb.*   [18]**Quien,** *He (The one) who.*   [19]**consiguió,** *attained.*   [20]**poco después,** *shortly afterward.*   [21]**poderío,** *power, dominion.*   [22]**Conseguida,** *After having attained.*   [23]**San Salvador,** *Saint (Holy) Savior.* [24]**por lo cual,** *for which reason.*   [25]**frailes,** *friars.*   [26]**obreros,** *workmen.*   [27]**sentó,** *set.*

Preguntas

1. ¿Quiénes fueron los primeros pobladores de la península?   2. ¿Qué se conserva cerca de Santander?   3. ¿Quiénes fueron los fenicios?   4. ¿Cuándo llegaron a la península?   5. ¿Qué ciudad fundaron ellos?   6. ¿Quiénes fueron otros invasores?   7. ¿Cuántos siglos estuvieron en España los romanos?   8. ¿Qué dejaron allí?   9. ¿Qué construyeron?   10. ¿Cuáles son dos ejemplos de la obra de los romanos?

11. ¿Quiénes ocuparon la península después de los romanos?   12. ¿Quiénes fueron los últimos invasores?   13. ¿En qué año entraron en España?   14. ¿Hasta cuándo vivieron allí?   15. ¿Por qué fue importante Córdoba?   16. ¿Cuál fue la última capital de los moros? 17. ¿Qué se encuentra allí?

18. ¿Cuántos siglos duró la reconquista?   19. ¿Cuál es el origen del nombre de Castilla? 20. ¿Quién fue el Cid?   21. ¿Dónde está su tumba?   22. ¿Cuál es la catedral gótica más grande de Europa?   23. ¿Qué es la Giralda?   24. ¿Qué refrán hay sobre Sevilla? 25. ¿Sobre Granada?

26. ¿Cómo consiguió España la unidad política?   27. ¿Qué llegó a ser España en el siglo XVI?   28. ¿A quién decidieron ayudar Fernando e Isabel?   29. ¿Cómo se llamaban las tres carabelas de Colón?   30. ¿En qué día llegó Colón a una pequeña isla?   31. ¿Qué nombre dieron a la isla?

32. ¿Cuándo fundó Colón el primer pueblo del Nuevo Mundo?   33. ¿Qué nombre dio a los habitantes de las islas?   34. ¿Quiénes acompañaron a Colón en su segundo viaje? 35. ¿Qué trajeron estos españoles a América?   36. ¿Qué nación lleva el nombre de Colón?

Estudio de palabras

a. Less approximate cognates. Pronounce the following words aloud, note the English cognates, and indicate the variations: acueducto, *aqueduct;* avanzado, *advanced;* cantidad, *quantity;* castillo, *castle;* enérgico, *energetic;* espiritual, *spiritual;* establecer, *to establish;* gobierno, *government;* imperio, *empire;* invasor, *invader;* maravilla, *marvel;* matrimonio, *matrimony, marriage;* ocupar, *to occupy;* reconquista, *reconquest;* teatro, *theater;* unidad, *unity.*

b. Compare the meanings of: agricultor, *agriculturist, farmer, and* agricultura, *agriculture;* comercio, *commerce, and* comerciante, *merchant;* descubrir, *to discover,* descubridor, *discoverer, and* descubrimiento, *discovery;* explorar, *to explore,* exploración, *exploration, and* explorador, *explorer;* guerra, *war, and* guerrero, -a, *warlike;* nombrar, *to name, appoint, and* nombre, *name;* obra, *work, and* obrero, *workman;* poder, *to be able,* poderío, *power, and* poderoso, -a, *powerful;* pueblo, *town, and* poblador, *settler.*

Notas sobre el uso de los adjetivos

In the grammar lessons we have followed the general principle that limiting adjectives (numerals, demonstratives, possessives, a few indefinites, and the like) precede the noun, and that descriptive adjectives which single out or distinguish a noun from another of the same class (adjectives of color, size, shape, nationality, and the like) follow the noun.

Descriptive adjectives may also precede the noun when they express a quality that is generally known or not essential to the recognition of the noun. In such cases there is no desire to single out or to differentiate:

<table>
<tr><td>**los altos Pirineos**</td><td>**algunos de los famosos exploradores**</td></tr>
<tr><td>**las hermosas flores**</td><td>**la nueva lengua**</td></tr>
</table>

Whenever an adjective is changed from its normal position, the speaker or writer gives a subjective or personal interpretation of the noun. Therefore, position of adjectives may vary according to subject matter, style, and individual feeling or emotion. You have observed that **bueno** and **malo** usually precede the noun, although they may follow to distinguish characteristics of the noun. Other common adjectives like **hermoso, bonito, pequeño,** and the like, may precede or follow the noun. The following sentence from this Lectura offers a good example of adjectives which express qualities which are generally thought of in connection with the nouns in this particular situation:

la famosa Alhambra, con sus magníficos patios, sus bellos jardines y sus alegres fuentes . . .

In footnote 4, page 129, we called attention to the fact that a descriptive adjective often precedes the noun: **una estupenda película mexicana; un magnífico programa de televisión.**

Other examples are: **una terrible tempestad; las fabulosas ciudades de oro.** In the Lecturas which follow observe similar cases of adjective position.

Mercaderes catalanes, probablemente traficantes en seda, viajando de regreso a Cataluña en el siglo XIV.

Teatro romano de Mérida en
la provincia de Badajoz.

Vista del famoso acueducto
romano de Segovia.

El Patio de los Leones en la
Alhambra de Granada y la Torre de
la Giralda en Sevilla, son dos de los
monumentos más famosos de la
Península y también dos de los
ejemplos más puros del arte árabe en
España.

La Puerta del Sol en Toledo es uno de los
mejores ejemplos de arte mudéjar de la ciudad.
Se le da el nombre de mudéjar porque
contiene elementos arquitectónicos de
inspiración árabe y cristiana.

A la izquierda aparece la estatua del Cid,
Don Rodrigo Díaz de Vivar, en la ciudad de
Burgos, en cuya catedral está enterrado. El
Cid fue un personaje real, que luchó mucho
por el triunfo de los cristianos contra los
invasores moros. Muchos de los hechos que
narra el famoso Poema del Cid y varios de
los romances ocurrieron en la realidad.

A la izquierda se ve la página titular de la famosa crónica del rey Don Rodrigo. Debajo aparece el Alcázar de Segovia, durante largo tiempo residencia de los reyes de Castilla.

A la izquierda de ve la tumba de los Reyes Católicos, Isabel y Fernando, en la capilla de su nombre en Granada. La reja forjada, obra de Bartolomé de Jaén, es de estilo plateresco (1520).

A la derecha aparece la catedral de Burgos, uno de los más importantes monumentos del período gótico en España.

Adjective clauses and relative pronouns • The subjunctive in
adjective clauses • *Hacer* in time clauses • Verbs ending in
-ducir • Forms of *valer*

LECCIÓN 20

Un puesto en México

El señor Carter acaba de recibir una carta por correo aéreo del gerente de una
empresa comercial de México. Necesitan un joven que entienda algo de
agricultura y de maquinaria agrícola y que pueda trabajar como agente de la
empresa. También prefieren un joven que sepa algo de las costumbres del país
y que haya tenido algunos años de experiencia. El señor Carter se imagina que
su secretaria conoce a alguien; inmediatamente la llama a su despacho.

SR. CARTER —Ana, ¿conoce Ud. a alguien que podamos recomendar para el
  puesto en México?
ANA —Me imagino que necesitan a alguien que hable español, ¿verdad?

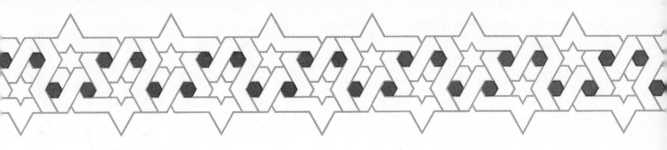

SR. CARTER —Sin duda para un puesto como éste, será absolutamente necesario que la persona lo sepa muy bien.

ANA —Puedo recomendarle a Ricardo Smith. Hace años que trabaja con Blanco y Compañía. No hay nadie que sea tan trabajador y tan responsable como él.

SR. CARTER —Sí, claro. ¿Cuánto tiempo hace que el Sr. Smith habla español?

ANA —Creo que lo habla desde hace unos diez años, por lo menos. Estudió parte de la escuela superior en México; ha vivido allí varios años y creo que su novia es mexicana.

SR. CARTER —¿No sabe Ud. cuáles son sus responsabilidades en el trabajo que ahora tiene?

ANA —No podría decírselo exactamente. Sé que Ricardo traduce al inglés toda la correspondencia que viene en español, cuida de muchos asuntos importantes y lleva algunas cuentas.

◆ ◆ ◆ ◆ ◆

SR. CARTER —¿Quién podría darme más informes acerca de él?

ANA —Creo que Ud. conoce a los señores Jones, con quienes Ricardo vive desde hace un año. Supongo que ellos . . .

SR. CARTER —¡Por supuesto! Mire, Ana, en vista de que Ud. conoce bien a este joven, ¿quiere Ud. preguntarle si le interesa el puesto?

ANA —Muy bien. Ahora estoy ocupada con otro asunto urgente, pero voy a telefonearlo más tarde.

SR. CARTER (*La secretaria está para volver a su despacho.*) —¡Ah, escuche, Ana! Me he dado cuenta de que el gerente quiere que el nuevo empleado comience a trabajar el próximo mes, lo cual me sorprende un poco.

ANA —No sé si Ricardo podría irse tan pronto. Será mejor que lo llame en seguida, y le pida que venga mañana a verlo a Ud.

SR. CARTER —No, valdrá más que venga esta tarde, si es posible. Si le interesa el puesto, le pondré un telegrama al gerente, dándole los informes.

ANA —Tiene Ud. razón. Lo llamaré inmediatamente. Espero que obtenga el puesto. Parece una magnífica oportunidad.

Conversación

A. Preguntas sobre el diálogo

1. ¿Qué acaba de recibir el Sr. Carter? 2. ¿Qué le dicen en la carta? 3. ¿Por qué llama el Sr. Carter a su secretaria a su despacho? 4. ¿Por qué recomienda Ana a Ricardo Smith para el puesto? 5. ¿Cuántos años hace que Ricardo habla español? ¿Cómo es que lo habla tan bien? 6. ¿Cuáles son las responsabilidades de Ricardo en el trabajo que tiene ahora? 7. ¿Qué le pide el Sr. Carter a su secretaria? ¿Por qué es urgente que Ana llame a Ricardo en seguida? 8. ¿Qué hará el Sr. Carter si le interesa a Ricardo el puesto?

B. Aplicación del diálogo

1. ¿Conoce Ud. a alguien que haya trabajado en Suramérica? 2. ¿Le interesaría a Ud. obtener un puesto allí? 3. ¿Qué trabajo le gustaría a Ud. hacer allí? ¿Ser agente de una empresa comercial? ¿Ayudar a las personas pobres? ¿Enseñar inglés? 4. ¿Qué cosa es absolutamente necesaria para poder trabajar en Suramérica? 5. ¿Cuánto tiempo hace que Ud. estudia español? 6. ¿Ha trabajado Ud. en alguna oficina? ¿Qué trabajos ha tenido Ud.? 7. ¿Cuáles han sido sus responsabilidades? 8. ¿Qué cosas son necesarias para obtener un buen puesto?

NOTAS GRAMATICALES

A. Adjective clauses and relative pronouns

An adjective clause modifies a noun or pronoun and is introduced by a relative pronoun, usually **que.** In the sentence *I know a man who can do it,* the clause *who can do it* modifies the noun *man.* *Who* is a relative pronoun, and *man* is the antecedent of the clause.

1. **Que,** *that, which, who, whom:*

    (*a*) **el agente que me escribió**   the agent who wrote to me
    (*b*) **el puesto que obtuvo**   the job (that) he got
         la joven que conocí   the young woman (whom) I met
    (*c*) **la empresa de que hablaban**   the firm of which they were talking

Que, which is invariable, is the commonest of all the relative pronouns. Introducing a clause, **que** may be: (*a*) the subject; (*b*) the object of the verb in a clause, and refer to persons or things; or (*c*) used as the object of a preposition, referring to things only. The relative **que** may be omitted in English, but not in Spanish.

2. **Quien** (*pl.* **quienes**), *who, whom:*

    (*a*) **Los hombres, con quienes habla Juan, . . .**
        The men, with whom John is talking, . . .

(*b*) **El gerente, quien (que) me ha escrito, desea . . .**
    The manager, who has written to me, desires . . .

(*c*) **Son los señores que (a quienes) vi en la oficina.**
    They are the gentlemen (whom) I saw in the office.

Quien (*pl.* **quienes**), which refers only to persons, is used: (*a*) mainly after prepositions; and (*b*) sometimes instead of **que** when *who* is separated from the main clause by a comma. The personal **a** is required (*c*) when **quien(es)** is the direct object of the verb. **Que** may replace **a quienes** in the last example, and in conversation is more commonly used.

3. **El cual** and **el que,** *that, which, who, whom:*

(*a*) **La hermana de Ricardo, la cual (la que) trabaja allí, . . .**
    Richard's sister, who works there, . . .

    . . . los señores Jones, con quienes Ricardo vive, . . .
    . . . Mr. and Mrs. Jones, with whom Richard lives, . . .

(*b*) **Los edificios cerca de los cuales (los que) dejamos el coche . . .**
    The buildings near which we left the car . . .

The longer forms of the relative pronouns, **el cual (la cual, los cuales, las cuales)** and **el que (la que, los que, las que),** are used: (*a*) to make clear which one of two possible antecedents the clause modifies; and (*b*) after prepositions other than **a, con, de, en.** (Often, however, and particularly in literary style, these long relatives are also used after these short prepositions. In elegant style the forms of **el cual** are preferred to those of **el que,** as you will see in the Lecturas and other readings). Be sure that the long relative agrees with its antecedent.

> **Quieren que comience a trabajar el próximo mes, lo cual (lo que) me sorprende.**
> They want him to begin to work next month, which (fact) surprises me.

The neuter form **lo cual** or **lo que,** *which (fact),* is used to sum up a preceding idea, statement, or situation.

B. The subjunctive in adjective clauses

Necesitan un joven que entienda algo de agricultura.
    They need a young man who understands something of agriculture. (*Any young man*)

¿Buscan una persona que hable español?
    Are they looking for a person who speaks Spanish? (*Any person*)

¿Conoce Ud. a alguien que podamos recomendar?
    Do you know anyone (whom) we can recommend? (*Indefinite antecedent*)

No hay nadie que sea tan trabajador como él.
    There is no one who is so industrious as he. (*Negative antecedent*)

When the antecedent of an adjective clause is *indefinite* or *negative* and refers to no particular person or thing, the verb in the dependent clause is in the subjunctive. If the antecedent refers to a certain person or thing, the indicative mood is used: **Busco al muchacho que llamó a la puerta,** *I am looking for the boy who knocked at the door.*

The personal **a** is omitted in the second example, since the noun does not refer to a specific person. However, the pronouns **alguien, nadie,** also **alguno** and **ninguno** when referring to a person, and **quien,** require the personal **a** when used as direct objects.

C. **Hacer** in time clauses

> **Hace tres años que él trabaja aquí** *or* **Él trabaja aquí desde hace tres años.**
> He has been working here three years (*lit.,* It makes three years that he works here).

> **¿Cuánto tiempo hace que habla español?**
> How long has he been speaking (*lit.,* How long does it make that he speaks) Spanish?

> **Lo habla desde hace unos diez años** *or* **Hace unos diez años que lo habla.**
> He has been speaking it (for) about ten years.

In Spanish, **hace** followed by a word indicating a period of time (**hora, día, mes, año,** etc.) plus **que** and a *present tense* verb, or a *present tense* verb plus **desde hace** plus a period of time, is used to indicate an action begun in the past and *still in progress.* The present perfect tense is used in English in this construction.

> **Hacía muchos años que él lo hablaba** *or* **Él lo hablaba desde hacía muchos años.**
> He had been speaking it (for) many years (*lit.,* It made many years that he spoke it).

Hacía followed by a period of time plus **que** and a verb in the *imperfect tense,* or the *imperfect tense* plus **desde hacía** plus a period of time, is used to indicate an action which *had been going on* for a certain length of time and *was still continuing* when something else happened. The pluperfect tense is used in English.

Recall that **hace** plus a verb in a past tense means *ago* or *since* (see Lesson 15): **Hace dos horas que llegué** *or* **Llegué hace dos horas,** *I arrived two hours ago* or *It is two hours since I arrived.*

D. Verbs ending in **-ducir: traducir,** *to translate*

Pres. Ind.	**traduzco,** traduces, traduce, traducimos, traducís, traducen
Pres. Subj.	**traduzca, traduzcas, traduzca, traduzcamos, traduzcáis, traduzcan**
Preterit	**traduje, tradujiste, tradujo, tradujimos, tradujisteis, tradujeron**

The imperfect, future, and conditional indicative tenses are regular.

E. Forms of **valer,** *to be worth*

    Pres. Ind.   **valgo,** vales, vale, valemos, valéis, valen
    Pres. Subj.   **valga, valgas, valga, valgamos, valgáis, valgan**
    Future   **valdré, valdrás,** etc. Conditional **valdría, valdrías,** etc.

The other forms are regular. The impersonal **vale** (**valdrá,** etc.) **más,** *it is* (*will be,* etc.)
better, is followed by the subjunctive when the dependent clause has a subject: **Valdrá
más que (él) venga hoy,** *It will be better for him to come* (*that he come*) *today.*

EJERCICIOS

A. Substitution drill:

   1. *Ricardo* traduce la correspondencia.
      (*Yo, Uds., Ana y yo, Tú, Mi secretaria*)
   2. ¿Tradujo *Ud.* la carta al inglés?
      (*Uds., María, tú, tu hermana, las muchachas*)
   3. Esperamos que *Ricardo* obtenga el puesto.
      (*Ud., Uds., los estudiantes, mi mamá, tú*)
   4. *Ud.* se dio cuenta de eso.
      (*Yo, Tú, Nosotros, Los señores Blanco, Ana*)

B. Say after your teacher; when you hear the cue, compose a new sentence, following the
    model:

MODEL: Buscan al joven que habla español.   *Buscan al joven que habla español.*
          Buscan un joven   *Buscan un joven que hable español.*

   1. Tengo una secretaria que escribe bien.   (Necesito una secretaria)
   2. Ricardo tiene un puesto que le gusta.   (Ricardo quiere un puesto)
   3. Tiene un despacho que es más grande que éste.   (Desea un despacho)

4. Quiero conocer al muchacho que trabaja en México. (Quiero conocer a alguien)
5. ¿Buscas al joven que lleva las cuentas? (¿Buscas un joven . . . ?)
6. Conozco a alguien que es tan trabajador como él. (No conozco a nadie)
7. Hay alguien que puede recomendar a Juan. (¿Hay alguien . . . ?)
8. Hay alguien que está libre ahora. (No hay nadie)
9. Busco al profesor que ha vivido en España. (Busco un profesor)
10. Prefieren a la persona que sabe traducir cartas. (Prefieren una persona)

C. After you hear a phrase and the cue, combine them in a sentence which requires the subjunctive in the adjective clause:

MODELS: Busco una casa *a.* Debe *ser* grande. *Busco una casa que sea grande.*
  b. Debe *estar* cerca. *Busco una casa que esté cerca.*

1. Necesitan una secretaria *a.* Debe *escribir* rápidamente. *b.* Debe *hablar* español. *c.* Debe *saber* traducir. *d.* Debe *ser* responsable.
2. Para ese puesto buscan a alguien *a.* Debe *haber* sido gerente. *b.* Debe *haber* tenido mucha experiencia. *c.* Debe *haber* vivido en México. *d.* Debe *haber* trabajado varios años.
3. Quiere una persona joven *a.* Debe *ser* muy trabajadora. *b.* Debe *poder* llevar las cuentas. *c.* Debe *entender* algo de agricultura. *d.* Debe *conocer* las costumbres.

D. After your hear two separate sentences, combine them into one sentence using the relative pronoun **que,** following the model:

MODEL: El libro tiene un mapa de España. *El libro que tiene un mapa de España*
  Es nuevo. *es nuevo.*

1. El señor viene ahora. Es mi tío. 2. El telegrama llegó esta mañana. Es de Roberto. 3. La casa tiene un patio. Es de estilo español. 4. El joven está visitándonos. Vive en México.

Combine, using **quien (quienes)** and **a quien (quienes),** following the model:

MODEL: Vimos a la joven. Es española. *Vimos a la joven, quien es española* and
  La joven a quien vimos es española.

5. Yo saludé al joven. Es mexicano. 6. Vimos a la profesora. Enseña francés. 7. Ella llamó a la estudiante. Está enferma hoy. 8. Hablamos con aquellos señores. Son profesores de otra universidad.

Combine, using **el (la) cual, los (las) cuales** or **el (la) que, los (las) que:**

MODELS: El padre de Ana es médico. *El padre de Ana, el cual (el que) es médico,*
  Estudió en México. *estudió en México.*
  Viven cerca de un parque. *El parque cerca del cual (del que)*
  Es muy hermoso. *viven es muy hermoso.*

9. La prima de Carlos salió ayer. Espera volver pronto.   10. El tío de María tiene una empresa comercial. Vive en México.   11. Ricardo me escribió acerca de esas costumbres. Son muy interesantes.   12. Dejamos el coche cerca de aquellos edificios. Son muy altos.

E. After you hear the question and the cue, answer affirmatively:

MODEL: ¿Lee Ud. el libro?   (Hace una hora)   *Sí, hace una hora que leo el libro.*

1. ¿Mira ella la televisión?   (Hace media hora)
2. ¿Escucha Marta unos discos?   (Hace quince minutos)
3. ¿Estudian Uds. español?   (Hace siete meses)
4. ¿Juega Ud. al golf?   (Hace varios años)
5. ¿Está enferma su tía?   (Hace dos días)
6. ¿Conocen Uds. al señor López?   (Hace mucho tiempo)
7. ¿Viajan tus padres por México?   (Hace dos semanas)
8. ¿Duerme tu mamá la siesta?   (Hace veinte minutos)

Give two answers to each question:

MODEL: ¿Cuánto tiempo hace que Ud. lee?   (una hora)   *Hace una hora que leo* and *Leo desde hace una hora.*

9. ¿Cuánto tiempo hace que Uds. juegan?   (media hora)
10. ¿Cuánto tiempo hace que conoces a Marta?   (tres años)
11. ¿Cuánto tiempo hacía que Ud. estudiaba español?   (varios meses)
12. ¿Cuánto tiempo hacía que ellos estaban en la cafetería?   (veinte minutos)

F. Read in Spanish, supplying the correct form of the infinitive in parentheses:

1. Una empresa mexicana está buscando personas que (entender) _____ algo de maquinaria agrícola.   2. El señor Carter no conoce a nadie que (estar) _____ preparado para ese puesto.   3. Su secretaria conoce bien a alguien que (ser) _____ responsable y que (haber) _____ tenido mucha experiencia.   4. Es necesario (saber) _____ bien el español.   5. También es muy importante que las personas (saber) _____ algo de las costumbres del país.   6. El señor Carter quiere (recomendar) _____ a alguien para el puesto.   7. Su secretaria espera que él (recomendar) _____ a su amigo Ricardo Smith.   8. Ana cree que (poder) _____ interesarle el puesto a Ricardo, pero ella no cree que él (poder) _____ ir a México tan pronto.   9. El señor Carter le pide a Ana que (hablar) _____ con Ricardo.   10. Ella le dice a su jefe que lo (telefonear) _____ y le pedirá que (venir) _____ en seguida.   11. Ricardo se alegra de (tener) _____ esa oportunidad.   12. Ana, por supuesto, se alegra de que su amigo (haber) _____ obtenido el puesto.

G. Give the Spanish equivalent:

1. "Richard, do you (*fam.*) know an agent who sells farm machinery?" 2. "No, John, but I hope to sell it some day." 3. "I do not know anyone who has worked with **(en)** a foreign firm." 4. "My mother's cousin (*m.*), who lives in the country, recommends that I study agriculture. 5. My father has just received a letter in which a friend of his writes of the good opportunities of work that there are in Mexico. 6. Also he has asked my father to look for a secretary who knows Spanish well. 7. He wants a person who has had two or three years of experience. 8. Dad will telephone (to) Mr. White, who has an office in New York, (in order) to ask him for information about his daughter. 9. The latter is trying to find a position in South America, but it is possible that she may want to go to Mexico. 10. It is a pity that Joe's sister, who wants to work there, is still studying in the university."

H. **Composición:** Una magnífica oportunidad

Assume that you are interested in finding a position in Spanish America. By using the correct word order and the correct form of each verb, you will end with a short composition:

1. que (yo) estudiar / tres años / español / hacer
2. perfectamente / algún día / (yo) esperar hablarlo
3. porque / esta lengua / un puesto en Suramérica / (yo) querer obtener / interesarme mucho
4. desde hacer varios meses / a algunas empresas comerciales / (yo) escribir cartas / acerca de este asunto
5. para extranjeros / (yo) darse cuenta de que / haber pocas / en algunos países de Suramérica / oportunidades de trabajo
6. haber muchas / pero como / (yo) poder obtener trabajo / con alguna de ellas / es posible que / empresas norteamericanas / en los países hispanoamericanos
7. del gerente de una / hacer algunos días / mi tío recibir una carta / en México / empresa norteamericana
8. un joven / el gerente buscar / que entender / y que saber inglés y español / algo de agricultura
9. con esa empresa / trabajo / no poder obtener / porque (yo) conocer / muy poco / (yo) temer / de agricultura
10. que (yo) le escribir / pero mi tío insistir en / al gerente / y le pedir más informes
11. bien el español / mi tío me dice / que como (yo) hablar / es posible que / por lo menos durante / (ellos) me dar / las vacaciones de verano / otro puesto
12. que mi tío tener razón / (yo) esperar / pues para mí / una magnífica oportunidad / ser

VOCABULARIO

absolutamente absolutely
acerca de *prep.* about, concerning
aéreo, -a air
el **agente** agent
agrícola (*m. and f.*) agricultural, farm (*adj.*)
la **agricultura** agriculture
el **asunto** matter, affair
la **compañía** company
el **correo** mail
la **correspondencia** correspondence
la **costumbre** custom
la **cuenta** account, bill
cuidar (**de** + *obj.*) to look after, care for, take care of
el **empleado** employee
la **empresa** company, firm, house
la **escuela superior** high school
exactamente exactly
la **experiencia** experience
el **gerente** manager
los **informes** information, data

inmediatamente immediately
la **maquinaria** machinery
la **novia** fiancée, sweetheart, girl friend
obtener (*like* **tener**) to obtain, get
la **persona** person
próximo, -a next
el **puesto** position, place, job
quien (*pl.* **quienes**) who, whom (*after prep.*)
recomendar (ie) to recommend
la **responsabilidad** responsibility
responsable responsible
sorprender to surprise
suponer (*like* **poner**) to suppose
telefonear to telephone
el **telegrama** (*note gender*) telegram
trabajador, -ora[1] industrious
traducir to translate
unos, -as about (*quantity*)
valer to be worth

darse cuenta de (que) to realize (that)
en vista de que in view of the fact that
estar para to be about to
los señores (Jones) Mr. and Mrs. (Jones)
llevar cuentas to keep accounts
poner un telegrama to send a telegram
por correo aéreo by air mail
por lo menos at least
¡por supuesto! of course! certainly!
traducir al inglés to translate into English
valer más to be better

---

[1]Adjectives which end in **-án, -ón, -or** (except comparative-superlatives as **mejor, peor, mayor, menor, superior,** and a few others) add **-a** to form the feminine: **trabajador, trabajadora.**

Conversación 3

En un hotel mexicano

Luis y Juan, dos estudiantes norteamericanos, están haciendo un viaje en coche por México. Llegan a la ciudad de Monterrey, donde deciden pasar la noche. Entran en un hotel y hablan con el empleado.

LUIS —¿Tienen Uds. un cuarto para dos personas?

EMPLEADO —¿Con baño o sin baño?

LUIS —¿Cuánto cuesta un cuarto con baño?

EMPLEADO —Para dos personas, sin comida, doscientos pesos, y, con comida, trescientos veinticinco pesos por persona.

LUIS —El hotel tiene garaje, ¿verdad?

EMPLEADO —Sí, señor; cobramos veinte pesos por el estacionamiento del coche.

JUAN —¿Nos permite ver el cuarto?

EMPLEADO —¡Cómo no! Pasen Uds. por aquí. (*Toman el ascensor al tercer piso y entran en un cuarto.*) Creo que este cuarto les gustará. Es grande y tiene dos ventanas que dan a las montañas. Tengo otro más pequeño; es un poco más barato, pero no tiene cuarto de baño.

JUAN —¿Son cómodas las camas?

EMPLEADO —Son muy cómodas. Y aquí está el cuarto de baño, con agua fría y caliente a todas horas. La criada traerá jabón y toallas en seguida.

LUIS —¿No te gusta este cuarto, Juan? Parece muy bueno por ese precio, ¿verdad?

JUAN —Sí, Luis; a mí también me gusta. Hay una vista magnífica desde la ventana.

EMPLEADO —Muy bien. Aquí tienen Uds. la llave. Pueden firmar el registro cuando bajen. Estoy seguro de que Uds. van a estar muy cómodos aquí. El botones subirá las maletas dentro de unos minutos.

JUAN —¿A qué hora se abre el comedor?

EMPLEADO —Aquí se come a las ocho, porque sabemos que a los turistas no les gusta esperar hasta más tarde. (*Los jóvenes descansan hasta las ocho y bajan al comedor. El mesero se acerca a su mesa y les pregunta qué desean.*)

LUIS —Deseamos una comida mexicana. ¿Qué recomienda Ud.?

MESERO —Primero deben tomar huevos rancheros. Son huevos fritos, con salsa de chile. Muchas personas los comen con tortillas.

JUAN —¿Qué son tortillas?

MESERO —Son tortas delgadas de maíz. Después pueden tomar tacos de pollo o mole de guajolote. Los tacos son tortillas tostadas, con pollo o carne y salsa de chile.

JUAN —Y, ¿mole de guajolote?

MESERO —El mole de guajolote es un guisado que se hace de guajolote, chile, cacahuetes, chocolate y otras cosas. Es uno de los platillos más famosos de México.

LUIS —El guacamole es un plato diferente, ¿verdad?

MESERO —¡Claro! Es una ensalada muy sabrosa. Se hace con aguacate, cebolla, jitomate y chile. Y a muchos mexicanos les gusta tomar frijoles con todas las comidas.

LUIS —Muy bien. Pues, tráiganos huevos rancheros, con tortillas, frijoles, tacos de pollo y guacamole.

MESERO —¿Desean Uds. una cerveza?

JUAN —No, gracias. Una botella de agua mineral, por favor. Después tomaremos café solo, con algún postre.

MESERO —Muy bien. Vuelvo en seguida.

Preguntas

Sobre la conversación

1. ¿A qué ciudad han llegado Luis y Juan en su viaje por México? 2. ¿Qué deciden hacer? 3. ¿Qué le pregunta Luis al empleado del hotel? 4. ¿Cuánto cuesta un cuarto con baño para dos personas? 5. ¿En qué piso está el cuarto que les enseña el empleado? 6. ¿Qué traerá la criada en seguida?

7. ¿A qué hora se come en el hotel? 8. ¿Qué recomienda el mesero que tomen primero? 9. ¿De qué se hacen las tortillas en México? 10. ¿De qué se preparan los tacos? 11. ¿De qué se hace el mole de guajolote? 12. ¿Qué es el guacamole?

Aplicación de la conversación

1. ¿Qué viajes largos en coche ha hecho Ud.? 2. ¿Le gustaría hacer un viaje en coche por México? 3. ¿Puede Ud. recomendar un buen hotel cerca de la universidad? 4. ¿Cuánto cuesta un cuarto en un buen hotel? 5. ¿Acostumbran los estudiantes celebrar sus fiestas en algún hotel? 6. ¿Qué hay en los hoteles para llegar a los pisos altos?

7. ¿Hay algún restaurante mexicano por aquí? 8. ¿Cuáles son algunos platos típicos de México? 9. ¿Qué plato mexicano le gusta a Ud. más? 10. ¿Cómo se preparan los huevos rancheros? 11. ¿En qué país toman mucha cerveza los estudiantes? 12. ¿Sabe Ud. si se toma mucha cerveza en los partidos de béisbol?

Prácticas orales

Groups of students will be selected to prepare a conversation of eight to ten exchanges, using vocabulary already given. (For fast learners a supplementary vocabulary is provided below.)

1. Groups of students ask for rooms in a hotel, with one acting as hotel clerk and others as travelers.

2. Groups of students order a Mexican meal, with one acting as waiter (**mesero,** in Mexico) and others as customers.

VOCABULARIO

el **aguacate** avocado, alligator pear
el **ascensor** elevator
el **baño** bath
 barato, -a cheap, inexpensive
el **cacahuete** peanut
 caliente *adj.* warm, hot
la **cebolla** onion
la **cerveza** beer
 cobrar to charge, collect
la **criada** maid
el **cuarto de baño** bathroom
el **chile** chili
 delgado, -a thin
 dentro de *prep.* within
el **estacionamiento** parking
 firmar to sign
el **frijol** kidney bean
el **garaje** garage
el **guacamole** guacamole (*salad*)
el **guajolote** turkey (*Mex.*)
el **guisado** stew

el **jabón** (*pl.* **jabones**) soap
el **jitomate** tomato (*Mex.*)
la **llave** key
el **maíz** maize, corn
la **maleta** suitcase
el **mesero** waiter (*Mex.*)
 mineral mineral
el **mole** mole (*a stew*)
el **peso** peso (*Spanish American monetary unit*)
el **piso** floor, story
el **platillo** dish (*food*)
el **registro** register
la **salsa** sauce
 subir to bring (take) up
el **taco** taco
la **toalla** towel
la **torta** flat pancake
la **tortilla** corn pancake (*Mex.*)
 tostado, -a toasted
el (la) **turista** tourist

 ¡cómo no! of course! certainly!
 dar a to face
 huevos rancheros eggs ranch style
 ¿nos permite (ver)? may we (see)? (*lit.*, do you permit us [to see]?)
 por persona per (for each) person

Vocabulario suplementario (*Supplementary vocabulary*)

(This list of words, not used in the active vocabularies nor in **Conversaciones I** and **II,** may be used for further drill. These words are not included in the general vocabulary unless they also appear in the **Lecturas.**)

LEGUMBRES

el **apio** celery
la **batata** sweet potato
el **betabel** beet (*Mex.*)
la **calabaza** squash, pumpkin
el **camote** sweet potato (*Am.*)
la **col** cabbage
la **coliflor** cauliflower
los **chícharos** green peas (*Am.*)
los **ejotes** string beans (*Am.*)
el **elote** ear of green corn (*Mex.*)
los **espárragos** asparagus

los **guisantes** green peas
las **habas** lima beans
las **judías verdes** string beans
la **lechuga** lettuce
el **nabo** turnip
la **papa** potato (*Am.*)
el **puré de patatas** mashed potatoes
el **rábano** radish
la **remolacha** beet
el **tomate** tomato
la **zanahoria** carrot

CARNES

la **carne de vaca (de res)**   beef
el **carnero**   mutton
la **chuleta**   chop, cutlet
los **fiambres**   cold cuts
el **filete**   tenderloin

el **pato**   duck
el **pavo**   turkey (*Spain*)
el **puerco (asado)**   (roast) pork
la **salchicha**   sausage
la **ternera**   veal

FRUTAS

el **albaricoque**   apricot
la **banana**   banana
la **cereza**   cherry
la **ciruela**   plum
el **chabacano**   apricot (*Am.*)
el **dátil**   date
el **durazno**   peach
la **frambuesa**   raspberry
el **higo**   fig
la **lima**   lime
la **pera**   pear

la **mandarina**   tangerine
el **mango**   mango
la **manzana**   apple
el **melocotón** (*pl.* **melocotones**)   peach
el **melón** (*pl.* **melones**)   melon
la **naranja**   orange
la **piña**   pineapple
el **plátano**   banana, plantain
la **sandía**   watermelon
la **toronja**   grapefruit
la **uva**   grape

MISCELÁNEA

el **aceite (de oliva)**   (olive) oil
la **aceituna**   olive
el **ajo**   garlic
asar   to roast
el **batido de leche**   milk shake
bien cocido, -a   well done
el **bollo**   roll
el **caldo**   broth
el **camarón** (*pl.* **camarones**)   shrimp
la **canela**   cinnamon
el **cangrejo**   crab
la **cocinera**   cook (*f.*)
el **cocinero**   cook (*m.*)
el **consomé**   consommé
la **crema de cacahuete**   peanut butter
el **emparedado**   sandwich

los **encurtidos**   relish, pickles
el **fósforo**   match
la **galleta**   cookie
la **galleta de soda**   soda cracker
la **hamburguesa**   hamburger
la **harina**   flour
el **jugo (de naranja)**   (orange) juice
la **mermelada**   marmalade
la **mostaza**   mustard
la **ostra**   oyster
el **pan dulce**   sweet bread, roll
el **panecillo**   hard roll
el **perro caliente**   hot dog
la **pimienta**   pepper
la **sal**   salt
el **vinagre**   vinegar

For use in making up a variety of shopping lists:

la **caja**   box
la **docena**   dozen
la **lata**   (tin) can
la **libra**   pound, lb.

media libra   half pound, $\frac{1}{2}$ lb.
medio kilo   half kilo
un **cuarto de kilo** $\frac{1}{4}$ kilogram
el **litro**   liter (*about 1.06 quarts*)

REPASO 4

A. Answer each question using a formal affirmative command and the correct object pronoun for the noun object; then compose a new sentence beginning with **Yo quiero que:**

MODEL: ¿Compro el traje?   *Sí, cómprelo Ud.*
   Yo quiero que Ud. lo compre.

1. ¿Busco un regalo?
2. ¿Pago la cuenta?
3. ¿Toco los discos ahora?
4. ¿Sirvo los refrescos?
5. ¿Me pongo la blusa?
6. ¿Me pruebo el traje?

B. Say after your teacher; when you hear the cue, compose a new sentence, following the model:

MODEL: Yo prefiero hacerlo.   *Yo prefiero hacerlo.*
   que Ud.   *Yo prefiero que Ud. lo haga.*

1. ¿Quiere Ud. jugar al tenis?   (que yo)
2. Nos alegramos de saber eso.   (de que tú)
3. ¿Se alegran Uds. de verlos?   (de que Luis)
4. Sentimos no poder ir al teatro.   (que Marta)
5. ¿Siente Ud. no entenderlo?   (que ellos)
6. Es importante estar seguro.   (que Tomás)
7. Me sorprende no encontrarlos.   (que Uds.)
8. Es lástima no conocerla bien.   (que tú)
9. Esperan llegar a tiempo.   (que nosotros)
10. Prefieren quitarse los zapatos.   (que Ud. y yo)
11. Carolina desea comenzar a leer.   (que yo)
12. ¿Quieres ir a la playa esta tarde?   (que nosotros)

C. Say after your teacher; when you hear the cue, compose a new sentence:

MODEL: Han ido al cine.   *Han ido al cine.*
   Dudo que   *Dudo que hayan ido al cine.*

1. Ricardo ha vuelto de España.   (Es posible que)
2. Nosotros hemos hecho una excursión.   (Ellos no creen que)
3. Los muchachos no han dicho nada.   (Yo tengo miedo de que)
4. Tú has visto a los señores Gómez.   (Nos alegramos de que)
5. Isabel no se ha puesto el sombrero.   (Es lástima que)
6. Yo no me he divertido mucho.   (Carlos siente que)
7. Ud. ha dormido la siesta.   (Me sorprende que)
8. Uds. han abierto la puerta.   (No estamos seguros de que)

D. Say after your teacher; then make a new sentence, using an indirect command and substituting the pronoun for the noun object:

MODEL: José quiere buscar un regalo.   *José quiere buscar un regalo.*
Que lo busque José.

1. Jorge quiere comprar una camisa.
2. Marta necesita traer unas flores.
3. Jaime va a poner un telegrama.
4. Roberto desea obtener un puesto.
5. Elena prefiere ponerse el vestido.
6. Luis quiere envolver los paquetes.

E. Say after your teacher; then give the alternate form affirmatively and negatively:

MODEL: Vamos a detenernos.   *Vamos a detenernos.*
Detengámonos.   No nos detengamos.

1. Vamos a sentarnos.
2. Vamos a levantarnos.
3. Vamos a lavarnos las manos.
4. Vamos a quitarnos las corbatas.
5. Vamos a ponernos los guantes.
6. Vamos a quedarnos aquí.

F. Repeat each question; then answer it, making the first clause negative:

MODEL: ¿Ve Ud. a alguien que sepa bailar?   *¿Ve Ud. a alguien que sepa bailar?*
No, no veo a nadie que sepa bailar.

1. ¿Conoce Ud. a alguien que juegue bien?
2. ¿Viene alguna joven que quiera cantar?
3. ¿Tiene Ud. algo que yo pueda comprar?
4. ¿Hay algo en el escaparate que le guste a Ana?
5. ¿Conoces a alguien que lo haya creído?
6. ¿Hay alguien que se haya desayunado?

G. Say after your teacher; then make two comparisons, following the model:

MODEL: Esta casa es grande.   *Esta casa es grande.   Es más grande que aquélla.*
Es la más grande de todas.

1. Esta playa es bonita.
2. Este paquete es pequeño.
3. Este jugador es bueno.
4. Esta película es mala.
5. Estos discos son populares.
6. Estas flores son hermosas.
7. Estos lagos son grandes.
8. Estas pulseras son caras.

H. Answer in Spanish, using complete sentences:

1. ¿Qué hora será?   2. ¿A qué hora empezó esta clase?   3. ¿Cuánto tiempo hace que estudia Ud. español?   4. ¿Le gustaría a Ud. pasar un verano en México?   5. ¿Habla Ud. mucho por teléfono?   6. ¿Conoce Ud. a alguien que haya hecho un viaje a México?   7. ¿Juega Ud. al tenis?   8. ¿Es Ud. aficionado al básquetbol?   9. ¿Qué otros

deportes tenemos en los Estados Unidos? 10. ¿Ha visto Ud. un partido de pelota vasca? 11. ¿Dónde se juega al *jai alai?* 12. ¿Se divierte Ud. mucho en los bailes? 13. ¿Le gusta a Ud. la música popular? 14. ¿Cómo se siente Ud. hoy? 15. ¿Tiene Ud. un resfriado? 16. ¿Le duele a Ud. la cabeza ahora? 17. ¿Duerme Ud. la siesta todas las tardes? 18. ¿Qué número de zapatos usa Ud.? 19. ¿A qué tienda vamos para comprar una pulsera? 20. Cuando nos acercamos a un dependiente en una tienda, ¿qué pregunta él? 21. Si Ud. decide comprar algo, ¿qué le dice al dependiente? 22. ¿Va Ud. de compras a menudo? 23. ¿A qué hora salió Ud. a la calle esta mañana? 24. ¿Ha traducido Ud. cartas españolas al inglés?

I. Give the Spanish for:

1. Let's go home. 2. Let's be going. 3. Let's not go yet. 4. Let's sit down here. 5. May you (*fam. sing.*) sleep well. 6. May you (*pl.*) have a good time. 7. They will leave at midnight. 8. I am pleased to meet you (*formal sing.*). 9. It is a great pleasure to be here. 10. We are very eager to see them. 11. Go (*pl.*) to the right, not to the left. 12. The suit fits me. 13. They are very lucky. 14. Send (*formal sing.*) the telegram at once. 15. I arrived at about ten o'clock. 16. Of course! (*Two ways*) 17. They must have spent most of the day downtown. 18. Two friends of mine have just arrived. 19. My brother fell in love with Jane. 20. I want my roommate (*m.*) to spend the weekend with me.

Verbs with changes in spelling • **The subjunctive in adverbial clauses** • **Spanish equivalents for** *to become* • *Pero* **and** *sino* • **Use of the infinitive after** *oír* **and** *ver*

LECCIÓN 21

Preparándose para el viaje

Tomás ve salir de un almacén a su amigo Ricardo. Sin que Ricardo se dé cuenta, Tomás se acerca y lo llama.

TOMÁS —¡Te felicito, Ricardo! Ven, sube al coche. Oí decir que conseguiste el puesto en México.

RICARDO —He tenido mucha suerte, Tomás. Siempre he oído decir que querer es poder.[1] Hacía mucho tiempo que trataba de encontrar un puesto como éste.

TOMÁS —¡Pues, espero que te hagas muy rico! ¿Cuándo piensas partir?

RICARDO —Quiero salir el sábado. Pero me queda poco tiempo para las mil cosas que tengo que hacer. Es posible que retrase la salida.

TOMÁS —Bueno, cálmate un poco. No te pongas nervioso. Ya sabes que mientras yo pueda ayudarte . . .

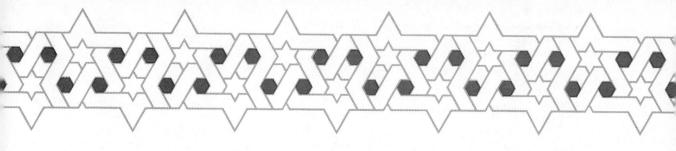

RICARDO —Gracias, Tomás. Ayer anduve[2] buscando unas maletas que sean ligeras. Me he vuelto loco y todavía no puedo encontrarlas. ¿Sabrías tú . . . ?

TOMÁS —Hombre, ya sé que las necesitarás para los muchos viajes de negocios en avión que tendrás que hacer. Con tal que las consigas en cuanto llegues a México . . . Pero, dime, ¿ya tienes tu boleto?

RICARDO —No pensaba comprarlo hoy, sino mañana, cuando reciba el dinero que mande la empresa.

TOMÁS —De todos modos, aunque no compres el boleto hoy, deberías[3] reservar tu asiento. En estos días hay mucha gente que viaja a México.

RICARDO —¡Tienes razón! ¿Por qué no me acompañas ahora mismo a la agencia de viajes? Sigue por esa calle a la derecha.

◆　◆　◆　◆　◆

RICARDO (*Al empleado.*)—Deseo salir el sábado para la ciudad de México y necesito reservar un asiento.

EMPLEADO —Hay dos vuelos diarios; el vuelo de la mañana es directo y el vuelo de la tarde hace una parada en Guadalajara.

RICARDO —Me gustaría tomar el directo, para llegar a México lo más pronto posible.

EMPLEADO (*Habla con el aeropuerto para preguntar si quedan asientos.*)—Lo siento, señor, pero no queda ningún asiento en el vuelo de la mañana, a menos que alguien cancele.

RICARDO —Pues, tendré que ir en el vuelo de la tarde. ¿Cuánto equipaje puedo llevar?

EMPLEADO —Veinte kilos. ¿Boleto sencillo o de ida y vuelta?

RICARDO —Boleto sencillo, por favor. Aceptan un cheque personal, ¿verdad?

EMPLEADO —Sí, señor. Son ciento veinte dólares. ¿Cuándo desea recoger su boleto?

RICARDO —Mi amigo me hará el favor de recogerlo a las dos, a menos que Ud. me diga otra hora.

EMPLEADO —Prepararé el boleto para que esté listo a las dos. ¡Que tenga Ud. buen viaje, Sr. Smith!

---

[1]This proverb is equivalent to "Where there's a will, there's a way."　　[2]**Andar**, *to go, walk* (often without definite destination), has a **u**-stem preterit: **anduve, anduviste, anduvo, anduvimos, anduvisteis, anduvieron.**　　[3]**deberías**, *you should.*

Conversación

A. Preguntas sobre el diálogo

1. ¿Qué le dice Tomás a Ricardo cuando lo ve salir del almacén? 2. ¿Qué ha conseguido Ricardo? 3. ¿Qué ha oído decir? 4. ¿Podrá Ricardo partir para México el sábado? ¿Qué le dice Tomás? 5. ¿Qué ha estado buscando Ricardo? ¿Qué piensa su amigo? 6. ¿Ya ha comprado Ricardo el boleto de avión? ¿Por qué es necesario que él reserve un asiento? 7. ¿Qué le pide Ricardo a Tomás? 8. ¿Por qué tiene Ricardo que tomar el vuelo de la tarde? ¿Por qué prefería el vuelo de la mañana? 9. ¿Cuánto equipaje puede llevar? 10. ¿A qué hora podrá Tomás recoger el boleto?

B. Aplicación del diálogo

1. ¿Viaja Ud. muy a menudo en avión? 2. ¿Se pone Ud. nervioso cuando tiene que viajar? 3. ¿Qué es necesario hacer para poder viajar en avión? 4. ¿Qué maletas hay que llevar? 5. Cuando Ud. vuelva a su casa este verano, ¿cómo hará el viaje? 6. ¿Comprará Ud. un boleto sencillo o un boleto de ida y vuelta? 7. ¿Dónde recoge Ud. el boleto, en el aeropuerto o en una agencia de viajes? 8. ¿Cuántos años le quedan a Ud. para terminar sus clases en esta universidad?

NOTAS GRAMATICALES

A. Verbs with changes in spelling

1. In verbs ending in **-ger (-gir)**, **g** changes to **j** before the endings beginning with **-o** or **-a,** that is, in the first person singular present indicative and in all six forms of the present subjunctive: **recoger,** *to pick up.*

Pres. Ind.	**recojo,** recoges, recoge, recogemos, recogéis, recogen
Pres. Subj.	**recoja, recojas, recoja, recojamos, recojáis, recojan**

2. In verbs ending in **-guir, u** is dropped after **g** before the endings **-o** and **-a,** that is, in the first person singular present indicative and in all six forms of the present subjunctive. The model verb for this change, **seguir,** *to follow, continue, go on,* is also a stem-changing verb, Class III, like **pedir.**

Pres. Part.	**siguiendo**
Pres. Ind.	**sigo, sigues, sigue,** seguimos, seguís, **siguen**
Pres. Subj.	**siga, sigas, siga, sigamos, sigáis, sigan**
Preterit	seguí, seguiste, **siguió,** seguimos, seguisteis, **siguieron**
Sing. Imper.	**sigue**

Seguir is followed by the present participle, like the English verb *to continue:* **Ellos siguen charlando,** *They continue chatting;* **Siga Ud. leyendo,** *Continue reading.*

3. In certain verbs whose stem ends in a vowel, unaccented **i** between vowels is written **y** (note the present participle and the third person singular and plural preterit forms below). Also note the additional forms which have written accent marks. **Creer** and **leer** are other verbs of this type. The model verb **oír,** *to hear,* also has an irregular first person singular present indicative, which affects all the present subjunctive forms.

Pres. Part.	**oyendo**	*Past Part.*	oído
Pres. Ind.	**oigo, oyes, oye,** oímos, oís, **oyen**		
Pres. Subj.	**oiga, oigas, oiga, oigamos, oigáis, oigan**		
Preterit	oí, oíste, **oyó,** oímos, oísteis, **oyeron**		
Sing. Imper.	**oye**		

B. The subjunctive in adverbial clauses

An adverbial clause, which modifies a verb and indicates *time, manner, purpose, condition,* and the like, is introduced by a conjunction, often a compound with **que** as the last element. The indicative mood is used in adverbial clauses if the act has taken place or is accepted as an accomplished fact; otherwise the subjunctive is normally used.

1. Time clauses:

> **Cuando yo lo veo, charlo con él.**   When I see him, I chat with him.
> **En cuanto lo vea yo, charlaré con él.**   As soon as I see him, I shall chat with him.
> **Vámonos antes (de) que vuelvan ellos.**   Let's go before they return.
> **Quédese Ud. hasta que lleguen los muchachos.**   Stay until the boys arrive.

The subjunctive is used after time conjunctions when the time referred to in the clause is *indefinite* and *future,* from the standpoint of the time of the main clause. When the clause expresses an accomplished fact in the present or past time, the indicative is used (first example). **Antes (de) que** is *always* followed by the subjunctive. Other common conjunctions (not all of which have been used in earlier lessons, but which will be used in the exercises) which introduce time clauses are:

antes (de) que	before	**después que**	after
cuando	when	**hasta que**	until
en cuanto	as soon as	**mientras (que)**	while, as long as

Así que and **luego que** are less common than **en cuanto** for *as soon as.* They will be found in reading, but they are not used in this text.

2. Concessive and result clauses:

> **Aunque está lloviendo, saldré.**   Even though it is raining, I shall leave.
> **Aunque llueva esta noche, saldré.**   Although it may rain (rains) tonight, I shall leave.

Aunque, *although, even though, even if,* is followed by the indicative mood if an accomplished fact is indicated, and by the subjunctive if the action is yet to happen. Compare the two examples above.

> **Yo hablo despacio de modo que ellos siempre me entienden.**
> I speak slowly so that (*as a result of which*) they always understand me.
> **Lea Ud. de manera que ellos lo entiendan.**
> Read so that they may understand you (it).

Two other conjunctions, **de modo que** and **de manera que,** both of which mean *so, so that,* may express result, in which case they are followed by the indicative mood. They may also express purpose, in which case the subjunctive is used. Compare the two examples, and also compare the use of **para que** in section 3.

3. Purpose, proviso, conditional, negative result clauses:

> **Prepararé el boleto para que esté listo a las dos.**
> I shall prepare the ticket so (in order) that it will be ready at two o'clock.
> **No queda ningún asiento, a menos que alguien cancele.**
> No seat is left, unless someone cancels.
> **Sin que Ricardo se dé cuenta, Tomás se acerca.**
> Without Richard's realizing it, Thomas approaches.
> **Con tal que las consigas en cuanto llegues a México . . .**
> Provided that you get them as soon as you reach México . . .

Certain conjunctions denoting *purpose, proviso, condition, negation,* and the like, *always* require the subjunctive, since they cannot introduce a statement of fact. In addition to **de manera que** and **de modo que,** *so that* (see section 2), which require the subjunctive when they express purpose, other conjunctions which always require the subjunctive are:

a menos que	unless	**para que**	in order (so) that
con tal que	provided that	**sin que**	without

C. Spanish equivalents for *to become*

> **Espero que te hagas muy rico.**   I hope that you become (get) very rich.
> **No te pongas nervioso.**   Don't become (get) nervous.
> **Me he vuelto loco.**   I have become (gone) crazy.

Hacerse plus a noun or a few adjectives like **rico** and **feliz,** *happy,* means *to become,* denoting conscious effort. **Llegar a ser** means approximately the same, indicating final result: **Él llegó a ser (se hizo) médico,** *He became a doctor.*
   Ponerse followed by an adjective or past participle, which agrees with the subject of

the verb, expresses a physical, mental, or emotional change. A violent change is expressed by **volverse.**

Se is used with many transitive verbs to express the idea of *become.* Contrast **Los calmé,** *I calmed them,* with **Se calmaron,** *They became calm (calmed themselves).* **Cálmate un poco** means *Calm yourself (Calm down) a little.*

D. **Pero** and **sino,** *but*

Lo siento, pero no queda ningún asiento. I'm sorry, but no seat is left.
Yo no voy en avión, sino en coche. I'm not going by plane, but by car.
(Yo) no pensaba comprarlo hoy, sino mañana. I didn't intend to buy it today, but tomorrow.

The English conjunction *but* is usually expressed by **pero** in Spanish. When *but* means *on the contrary, but instead,* **sino** is used in place of **pero** in an affirmative statement which is in direct contrast to a preceding negative statement. Usually no other verb— other than an infinitive—may be used after **sino: Yo no quiero estudiar, sino dormir,** *I don't want to study, but to sleep.*

If clauses containing different verbs are contrasted, **sino que** is used: **Juan no andaba, sino que corría,** *John wasn't walking, but (he was) running.* This construction is not used in the exercises.

E. Use of the infinitive after **oír** and **ver**

Tomás ve salir a su amigo. Tom sees his friend leave (leaving).
Oigo entrar a Juan. I hear John coming in (enter).
Oí decir que . . . I heard (it said *or* people say) that . . .

After **oír** and **ver** the infinitive is regularly used in Spanish, while the present participle is often used in English. Note the word order in the second example. A subject of the infinitive is considered the direct object of **oír** and **ver.**

EJERCICIOS

A. Substitution drill:

1. *Yo* los oigo hablar todos los días.
   (*Nosotros, Ana, Tú, Ud., Él y ella*)
2. *Tomás* recoge el boleto.
   (*Yo, Tú, Uds., Nosotros, Ellos*)
3. *Los muchachos* siguen charlando.
   (*Él, Uds., Nosotros, Tú, Yo*)
4. *Tomás y Ricardo* siguieron andando.
   (*Pablo, Nosotros, Yo, Ella, Uds.*)

B. Repeat the question after your teacher; then follow the same pattern in your replies to the other questions:

MODEL: ¿Lo hará Ud.? *¿Lo hará Ud.? Sí, aunque Carlos lo haga también.*

1. ¿La buscará Ud.?
2. ¿Los recogerá Ud.?
3. ¿Saldrá Ud. de la tienda?
4. ¿Seguirán Uds. trabajando?
5. ¿Vendrán Uds. temprano?
6. ¿Empezarán Uds. a leer?

C. Repeat the question after your teacher; when you hear the question again and the cue (an infinitive), use the inflected form of the verb in the adverbial clause after **para que,** following the model:

MODEL: ¿Trae Ud. los cuadros? *¿Trae Ud. los cuadros?*
¿Trae Ud. los cuadros? Ver. *Sí, los traigo para que Ud. los vea.*

1. Mirar. 2. Comprar. 3. Pagar. 4. Vender. 5. Conocer. 6. Llevar a casa.

D. After you repeat the question and answer, your teacher will give other conjunctions to be used in the adverbial clause of the answer:

1. ¿Va Ud. a tocar los discos? Sí, los tocaré en cuanto vuelvan ellos.
   (cuando, antes que, después que, aunque)
2. ¿Vas a seguir trabajando? Sí, seguiré trabajando con tal que me paguen.
   (para que, de manera que, hasta que, mientras)

E. Listen to the two sentences; when you hear the cue (a conjunction), combine the two sentences into one, following the model:

MODEL: Yo no saldré. Juan paga sus compras. *Yo no saldré hasta que*
(hasta que) *Juan pague sus compras.*

1. Yo te doy cinco dólares. Puedes comprar un regalo. (para que)
2. Comprará el boleto. La empresa le mandará un cheque. (en cuanto)
3. Los dos pasarán por aquí. Ella saldrá de la biblioteca. (después que)
4. Lean Uds. despacio. Podemos entenderlos. (de manera que)
5. No queremos irnos. Vienen nuestros amigos. (antes de que)
6. Tú no podrás llegar a tiempo. Sales ahora mismo. (aunque)

F. Repeat the question; then answer it, beginning with **Es posible que,** and substituting the correct object pronoun for the noun, following the model:

MODEL: ¿Oye él la música? *¿Oye él la música? Sí, es posible que él la oiga.*

1. ¿Busca él a su hermana?
2. ¿Consigue ella el puesto?
3. ¿Encuentra Carlos la maleta?
4. ¿Recoge él los boletos?
5. ¿Reserva Marta el asiento?
6. ¿Trae Luis el equipaje?

G. Give the Spanish equivalent, using the familiar forms for *you*:

1. "I congratulate you, Richard! I have heard that you got the position in Mexico. I hope that you will become rich." 2. "Thanks, Thomas. I am very lucky. I have been looking for a position like this one for several years. 3. Unless I finish the many (thousand) things that I have to do, I shall not be able to leave on Saturday. 4. It is possible that I may delay the departure, because I have very little time left. 5. Yesterday I went looking for a suitcase which is light. 6. I have almost gone crazy; it is important that I find one, because I shall need it for the many business trips that I shall have to take." 7. "Don't get (become) so nervous. Provided that you get it as soon as you reach Mexico . . . 8. Now it is urgent that you buy your ticket. Have you bought it yet?" 9. "I was not planning to buy it today, but tomorrow, when I receive a check from the company in Mexico." 10. "At any rate, it is better that you reserve a seat; there are many people who are traveling to Mexico these days." 11. "It is possible that you are right. Let's go right now to the travel agency." 12. Upon arriving at the agency, Richard asks for a one-way ticket for Saturday morning. 13. The employee calls the airport to ask whether there are [any] seats left. 14. Richard has to take the afternoon flight, which makes a stop in Guadalajara. 15. He pays with a personal check, and the employee tells him that he can carry twenty kilos of luggage. 16. The employee will prepare the ticket so that it will be ready at two o'clock. Thomas will pick it up.

H. **Composición**

Assuming that you are preparing to take a trip by plane, write a composition of about 150 words, telling of your plans and some of the problems involved in preparing for the trip.

Restaurante popular al aire libre, Ciudad de México.

VOCABULARIO

la **agencia** agency
andar to go, walk
el **asiento** seat
calmar to calm; *reflex.* to calm
  oneself, become calm, calm down
cancelar to cancel
conseguir (i, i) to get, obtain
el **cheque** check
diario, -a daily
directo, -a direct, non-stop
el **equipaje** baggage, luggage
felicitar to congratulate
la **ida** departure
el **kilo** (= el **kilogramo**) kilo(gram) (*about
  2.2 pounds*)
ligero, -a light
listo, -a ready
loco, -a crazy, wild
la **maleta** suitcase
la **manera** manner, way

el **modo** manner, means, way
los **negocios** business
nervioso, -a nervous
ningún (*used for* **ninguno** *before m. sing.
  nouns*) no, (not) . . . any
oír to hear, listen
la **parada** stop, stop over
partir (**de** + *obj.*) to depart, leave
  (from)
personal personal
recoger to pick up
reservar to reserve
retrasar to delay
la **salida** departure
seguir (i, i) to follow, continue, go on
sencillo, -a simple, one-way
subir (**a** + *obj.*) to get into, climb up
  (into)
la **vuelta** return

agencia de viajes travel agency
ahora mismo right now, right away
boleto sencillo (de ida y vuelta) one-way (round-trip) ticket
de todos modos at any rate, by all means
en estos días these days
hacer una parada to stop over, make a stop
hacerse + *noun* to become
lo siento (mucho) I'm (very) sorry
(me) queda (poco tiempo) (I) have (little time) left (*used like* **gustar**)
no queda ningún asiento no seat is left (remains), there isn't any seat left
oír decir que to hear that
ponerse + *adj.* to become
prepararse para to prepare oneself for, get ready for
viaje de negocios business trip
volverse (ue) loco, -a to become *or* go (crazy, wild)

*Dibujo a lápiz y tinta de Honoré Daumier (1808–1879),
que representa a Don Quijote y a Sancho Panza.*

Lectura 11

La cultura española a través de los siglos

La literatura española, una de las más ricas del mundo, es a la vez una de las manifestaciones más notables de la cultura española. Es importante no sólo por su valor intrínseco y por la creación de nuevos géneros[1] y de personajes universales, sino también por su influencia en otras literaturas modernas, especialmente en las de Inglaterra y de Francia. Desde el siglo doce hasta el siglo veinte la literatura ha expresado directamente el alma y el espíritu de los españoles en su larga y gloriosa historia.

El primer monumento literario de España es un poema épico, *El cantar de Mío Cid,*[2] compuesto hacia 1140. Este poema trata de las hazañas del Cid, el famoso héroe nacional, en las luchas de Castilla para reconquistar sus tierras de manos de los moros.

Una de las mayores glorias de los Reyes Católicos, Fernando e Isabel, fue el impulso que dieron a las letras y a la cultura en general a fines del siglo XV. Iniciaron el estudio de las humanidades y trajeron a España muchos humanistas de Italia, donde se originó la época de la cultura que se llama el Renacimiento. Los Reyes Católicos contribuyeron a la introducción de la imprenta[3] en España en 1474 y fundaron bibliotecas, escuelas y universidades, sobre todo la famosa Universidad de Alcalá de Henares en 1508. Durante su reinado aparecieron algunas de las mejores obras de la literatura española, entre ellas *La Celestina,* en 1499, una de las grandes obras de la literatura universal, y el *Amadís de Gaula,* publicado en 1508, que popularizó la novela de caballerías[4] en España. En 1492 se publicó la *Gramática castellana* de Nebrija, la primera gramática científica de una lengua moderna, y la víspera de Navidad del mismo año se representaron dos piezas dramáticas de Juan del Encina, llamado el padre del teatro español.

La Celestina, célebre novela dramática, relata la triste historia de los amantes Calisto y Melibea, que viven bajo la influencia de una perversa y astuta vieja, llamada Celestina. Esta obra refleja a la vez el espíritu de la Edad Media[5] y el del Renacimiento, y una de sus características más extraordinarias es que se mezclan por primera vez[6] en la prosa el

---

[1]**género,** *genre, literary type.*   [2]**El cantar de Mío Cid,** *The Song (Lay) of the Cid.*   [3]**imprenta,** *printing.*
[4]**novela de caballerías,** *novel (romance) of chivalry.*   [5]**Edad Media,** *Middle Ages.*   [6]**por primera vez,** *for the first time.*

idealismo puro y el realismo crudo. Después de *Don Quijote, La Celestina* ocupa el primer lugar en la literatura española.

Un género literario que había de gozar de[7] una gran popularidad durante el siglo XVI fue la novela de caballerías. El *Amadís de Gaula,* según Cervantes, fue «el mejor de todos los libros que de este género se han compuesto, y . . . único en su arte». Esta novela narra las aventuras de Amadís, el noble, generoso y valiente héroe, que siempre trata de hacerse digno[8] del amor de Oriana, la bella y fiel heroína. Ha influido poderosamente no sólo en la literatura española, especialmente en la obra de Cervantes, sino también, por sus numerosas traducciones, en la de todo el mundo.

El período comprendido entre mediados del siglo XVI y fines[9] del siglo XVII es llamado el Siglo de Oro.[10] Es la época de la conquista y la colonización del Nuevo Mundo; es la época en que España llegó a ser la nación más poderosa del mundo; es la época de nuevos géneros literarios, de grandes historiadores, filósofos y teólogos, de famosos artistas, escultores y arquitectos; en fin,[11] es la época en que España llegó a su apogeo[12] en todos los aspectos de la civilización y la cultura.

Aquí podemos mencionar solamente unos cuantos[13] nombres de gran importancia en la literatura del Siglo de Oro. El siglo XVII fue la época gloriosa del teatro español. En esta época Lope de Vega, llamado por los españoles el fénix de los ingenios,[14] fue el dramaturgo más popular de España y también uno de los más grandes del mundo. Fue el fundador del drama nacional de su país, además de ser un gran poeta lírico. Él mismo dice que

compuso unas mil quinientas comedias; de ellas se conservan hoy día sólo unas cuatrocientas veinticinco.

Otros dramaturgos famosos del mismo período son Ruiz de Alarcón, Tirso de Molina y Calderón de la Barca. En *El burlador de Sevilla,* Tirso de Molina presenta por primera vez en forma dramática el personaje de don Juan, una de las grandes creaciones de la literatura universal. Según algunos críticos, solamente don Quijote, Hamlet y Fausto[15] lo igualan en originalidad y profundidad.

En 1605 apareció la primera parte de *El ingenioso hidalgo[16] don Quijote de la Mancha,* de Miguel de Cervantes. Aunque la novela logró un éxito enorme, Cervantes ganó poco de su venta. Diez años después, en 1615, se publicó la segunda parte de la célebre novela. Un pobre hidalgo, Alonso Quijano *el Bueno,* se aficionó tanto a[17] la lectura de los libros de caballerías que llegó a perder el juicio. Por fin decidió «. . . así para el aumento de su honra, como[18] para el servicio de su república,[19] hacerse caballero andante,[20] e irse por todo el mundo con sus armas y caballo a buscar aventuras . . . , deshaciendo todo género de agravio,[21] y poniéndose en ocasiones y peligros donde, acabándolos, cobrase[22] eterno nombre y fama». Después de limpiar unas armas antiguas y de dar nombre a su caballo, se dio el nombre de don Quijote de la Mancha. Luego le persuadió a un labrador, vecino suyo, a salir con él y servirle de escudero.[23]

En la larga serie de aventuras de la novela, Cervantes presenta el eterno conflicto entre el espíritu idealista e imaginativo de don Quijote

---

[7]**gozar de,** *to enjoy.*   [8]**hacerse digno,** *to make himself (become) worthy.*   [9]**comprendido . . . fines,** *comprised between the middle of the . . . and the end.*   [10]**Siglo de Oro,** *Golden Age.*   [11]**en fin,** *in short.*   [12]**apogeo.** *apogee, highest point.*   [13]**unos cuantos,** *a few.*   [14]**fénix de los ingenios,** *phoenix (model) of geniuses.*   [15]**Fausto,** *Faust (created by the German writer Goethe, 1749–1832).*   [16]**hidalgo,** *nobleman.*   [17]**se aficionó tanto a,** *became so fond of.*   [18]**así para . . . como,** *as much for the increase in his honor, as (or both for . . . and).*   [19]**república,** *country.*   [20]**caballero andante,** *knight errant.*   [21]**deshaciendo . . . agravio,** *righting every type of wrong.*   [22]**cobrase** *(imp. subj. of* **cobrar***), he would gain.*   [23]**escudero,** *squire.*

y el sentido realista y práctico de su escudero Sancho Panza. Aunque la locura de don Quijote mueve a risa[24] en muchas ocasiones, no lo supera nadie en cortesía, dignidad, humildad, nobleza y generosidad. En cambio, Sancho Panza es un aldeano[25] crédulo, tímido, hablador, socarrón,[26] algo glotón,[27] y, además, una figura muy graciosa.[28] En vano Sancho trata de hacerle a su amo volver a la realidad; en vano trata de convencerle que no son gigantes los molinos de viento,[29] que no son ejércitos las manadas de ovejas, etcétera. A medida que[30] progresa la acción de la novela, especialmente en la segunda parte, las personalidades de caballero y de escudero se desarrollan hasta tal punto que el pobre escudero acaba por creer[31] en la existencia real de los caballeros andantes. Cuando muere su amo, ya en su cabal juicio,[32] a Sancho ya no le parece locura la vida de los caballeros andantes con todos sus nobles ideales.

En esta obra maestra[33] pasa ante nuestros ojos todo el rico panorama del siglo XVII en España. Ninguna obra literaria es más nacional y a la vez más universal, porque su fondo es la humanidad de todos los tiempos y de todos los países del mundo. El *Quijote*, síntesis de todos los géneros de ficción del Siglo de Oro, se ha llamado, y con razón, la novela más célebre del mundo.

---

[24]**mueve a risa,** *moves one to laughter.*   [25]**aldeano,** *villager.*   [26]**socarrón,** *crafty.*   [27]**algo glotón,** *something of a glutton.*
[28]**graciosa,** *witty, amusing.*   [29]**que no . . . viento,** *that the windmills are not giants.*   [30]**A medida que,** *As.*
[31]**acaba por creer,** *ends up by believing.*   [32]**cabal juicio,** *right mind.*   [33]**obra maestra,** *masterpiece.*

Reproducción de un grabado de la época que muestra un teatro al aire libre durante el Siglo de Oro.

Preguntas

1. ¿Cuál es una de las manifestaciones más notables de la cultura española?   2. ¿Ha tenido influencia en otras literaturas?   3. ¿Qué ha expresado a través de los siglos?   4. ¿Cuál es el primer monumento literario de España?   5. ¿De qué trata esa obra?

6. ¿Cuál fue una de las mayores glorias de los Reyes Católicos?   7. ¿Qué obra popularizó la novela de caballerías?   8. ¿En qué año se publicó la gramática de Nebrija?   9. ¿Quién fue el padre del teatro español?   10. ¿Qué relata *La Celestina*?   11. ¿Por qué es importante la obra?   12. ¿Qué narra el *Amadís de Gaula*?

13. ¿Qué período comprende el Siglo de Oro?   14. ¿Qué llegó a ser España durante aquella época?   15. ¿Quién fue Lope de Vega?   16. ¿Cuántas comedias compuso?   17. ¿Cuáles son los nombres de otros dramaturgos del mismo período?   18. ¿Qué personaje presentó Tirso de Molina por primera vez?   19. ¿Cuáles son otros grandes personajes de la literatura universal?

20. ¿En qué año publicó Cervantes la primera parte del *Quijote*?   21. ¿Ganó mucho en la venta de la novela?   22. ¿Cuándo apareció la segunda parte?   23. ¿Cómo llegó a perder el juicio don Quijote?   24. ¿Qué decidió hacer?

25. ¿Qué presenta Cervantes en la larga serie de aventuras de don Quijote?   26. ¿Cuáles son algunos de los ideales que representa don Quijote?   27. ¿Qué clase de persona es Sancho Panza?   28. ¿En qué acciones de Sancho podemos ver su sentido realista y práctico?   29. ¿En qué llega a creer Sancho a medida que progresa la acción de la novela?

30. ¿Qué interés social tiene la novela?   31. ¿Por qué puede decirse que ninguna obra literaria es más universal que esta novela?   32. ¿Qué más se ha dicho de esta novela?

Estudio de palabras

a. Approximate cognates. Many Spanish nouns ending in **-ista** end in *-ist* in English: artista, humanista, novelista, turista. The corresponding adjective presents two forms, as in English: **-ista** = English *-ist,* and **-ístico** = English *-istic.* The choice of ending, however, is not always the same in the two languages, and the correct form can be learned only by observation. The adjectives **idealista,** *idealistic,* and **realista,** *realistic* are especially troublesome for English speakers, who often tend to give them in Spanish the ending found, for example, in **característico,** *characteristic.*

b. Less approximate cognates. Pronounce the following words aloud, note the English cognates, and describe the variations: arquitecto, *architect;* aventura, *adventure;* científico, *scientific;* enorme, *enormous;* escultor, *sculptor;* espíritu, *spirit;* filósofo, *philosopher;* fundador, *founder;* igualar, *to equal;* intrínseco, *intrinsic;* lírico, *lyric;* personaje, *personage, character* (in literature); reflejar, *to reflect;* Renacimiento, *Renaissance;* teólogo, *theologian.*

c. Compare the meanings of: caballo, *horse,* caballero, *one who goes mounted, knight, and* caballerías, *chivalry;* conquista, *conquest, and* reconquista, *reconquest;* drama, *drama,* dramático, *dramatic, and* dramaturgo, *dramatist;* hablar, *to talk, speak, and* hablador, *talkative;* hacer, *to do, make, and* hazaña, *deed;* héroe, *hero, and* heroína, *heroine;* historia, *history,* histórico, *historical, and* historiador, *historian;* humanidad, *humanity,* humanidades, *humanities, and* humanista, *humanist;* ideal, *ideal,* idealismo, *idealism, and* idealista, *idealist;* mano, *hand, and* manada, *handful, flock;* mezcla, *mixture, and* mezclar, *to mix, mingle;* noble, *noble, and* nobleza, *nobility;* origen, *origin, and* originalidad, *originality;* persona, *person,* personaje, *personage, character* (in literature), *and* personalidad, *personality;* real, *real,* realista, *realistic, and* realidad, *reality.*

d. Deceptive cognates. Some words do not have the apparent meaning: **comedia** may mean *theater, play,* in addition to *comedy;* **éxito,** *success;* **historia,** *history,* also means *tale, story;* **valor,** *valor,* also means *value.*

De izquierda a derecha se ven Juan Ruiz de Alarcón, Lope de Vega y Santa Teresa de Jesús.

The imperfect subjunctive • The pluperfect subjunctive • Use of the
subjunctive tenses • Use of the infinitive after certain verbs • The
subjunctive in a polite or softened statement • Exclamations

LECCIÓN 22

Esposas jóvenes

Clara e[1] Isabel viven en una casa de apartamentos[2] cerca de la Universidad. Sus
esposos estudian en la Facultad de Derecho. El esposo de Isabel se llama Ramón;
tienen una niña, Juanita. Clara quisiera ir al cine y llama a Isabel para que la
acompañe.

CLARA — ¡Hola, Isabel! ¿Estás ocupada? ¿No te gustaría ir al cine?

ISABEL — Quisiera decirte que sí, Clara, pero prefiero quedarme en casa descansando. ¡Qué día he tenido! Primero Ramón me pidió que llevara un
traje a la tintorería para hacerlo limpiar, y luego, como él tenía clase, me
dijo que llevara a Juanita al dentista.

CLARA — Juanita acaba de decirme que también la llevaste al parque.

ISABEL — Sí, antes de volver a casa, me pidió que la llevara a ver los animales.

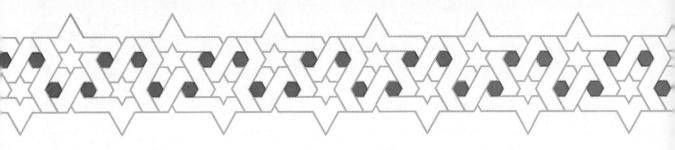

CLARA —Bueno, ¡se divertirían las dos!³ ¿Qué pasó luego?

ISABEL —Le permití jugar un rato, y aunque le aconsejé que tuviera cuidado, se cayó y se hizo daño. Me puse muy nerviosa y como te imaginarás, ahora estoy muy cansada.

CLARA —¡Cuánto siento que no puedas acompañarme!

◆ ◆ ◆ ◆ ◆

CLARA —A propósito, ¿te divertiste mucho el sábado en casa de Carolina?

ISABEL —Muchísimo. ¡Qué noche tan agradable pasamos! ¡Es lástima que tuvieras otro compromiso! ¿Te acuerdas de Margarita Brown, que se casó hace un mes?

CLARA —Sí, la recuerdo bien. ¡Cuánto me gustaría volver a verla!

ISABEL —Pues acabábamos de sentarnos a jugar a las cartas cuando llegaron Margarita y su esposo Roberto.

CLARA —¿De modo que han vuelto de su luna de miel en México?

ISABEL —Sí, hace unos días. Cuando supimos que Roberto traía las fotos y transparencias que había sacado en su viaje, le rogamos que nos las enseñara.

CLARA —¡Cuánto siento no haber estado con Uds.! ¡Ojalá que las hubiera visto! Y, ¿qué te parece Roberto? Quisiera conocerlo.

ISABEL —¡Qué guapo es! Es alto, simpático y muy cortés.

CLARA —¿Cuánto tiempo van a pasar aquí?

ISABEL —Es probable que ya se hayan marchado. Roberto telefoneó ayer a la oficina de su compañía, e insistieron en que volviera cuanto antes.

CLARA —¡Qué interesante! Bueno, Isabel, debiera dejarte dormir la siesta. Que descanses mucho.

ISABEL —Gracias por llamarme, Clara. ¡Que te diviertas!

---

¹Before words beginning with **i-, hi-,** Spanish uses **e,** *and,* for **y.**   ²In certain regions *apartment* is expressed by **el apartamiento or el departamento.**   ³¡**se divertirían las dos!** *you two must have had a very good time!* As you learned in Lesson 16, the conditional tense is used in Spanish to indicate probability or conjecture concerning an action or state in the past. Also note in this phrase that the subject pronoun **ustedes,** in apposition to **las dos,** need not be expressed.

Conversación

A. Preguntas sobre el diálogo

1. ¿Para qué llama Clara a Isabel?   2. ¿Le gustaría a Isabel ir al cine? ¿Por qué no irá?
3. ¿Qué ha hecho Isabel durante ese día?   4. ¿Qué le pidió Juanita a su madre?
5. ¿Qué pasó en el parque?   6. ¿Adónde fue Isabel el sábado? ¿Qué le contó ella a
Clara?   7. ¿Qué llevó Roberto a casa de Carolina? ¿Qué le pidieron los invitados?
8. ¿Es posible que Clara vea a Margarita y que conozca a Roberto?

B. Aplicación del diálogo

1. ¿Quién le aconsejó a Ud. que viniera a esta universidad?   2. ¿Le aconseja su familia
que Ud. viva en un apartamento?   3. ¿Dónde vive Ud. ahora? ¿Quisiera Ud. vivir en
una residencia de estudiantes?   4. ¿Qué es una tintorería? ¿Hay cerca de aquí una
tintorería que sea buena?   5. ¿Cuánto tiempo hace que Ud. fue al dentista? ¿Conoce Ud.
en esta ciudad un dentista que sea bueno?   6. ¿Quisiera Ud. casarse ahora o cree Ud. que
sería mejor esperar un poco? ¿Por qué?

NOTAS GRAMATICALES

A. The imperfect subjunctive

1. Regular verbs:

hablar		comer, vivir	
singular		*singular*	
hablara	hablase	comiera	viviese
hablaras	hablases	comieras	vivieses
hablara	hablase	comiera	viviese
plural		*plural*	
habláramos	hablásemos	comiéramos	viviésemos
hablarais	hablaseis	comierais	vivieseis
hablaran	hablasen	comieran	viviesen

The imperfect subjunctive in Spanish has two forms, often referred to as the **-ra** and the
-se forms, and the same two sets of endings are used for the three conjugations. To form
the imperfect subjunctive of *all* verbs, regular and irregular, drop **-ron** of the third
person plural preterit indicative and add **-ra, -ras, -ra, -́ramos, -rais, -ran** or **-se, -ses,
-se, -́semos, -seis, -sen.** Only the first person plural form has a written accent mark.

Except in softened statements (section E) and in conditional sentences (Lesson 24), the imperfect subjunctive tenses are interchangeable in Spanish. Just as the present subjunctive is often expressed with *may* as a part of its meaning, so the imperfect subjunctive is expressed with *might:* **que él hablara,** *that he might talk;* **que comiesen,** *that they might eat.*

2. Stem-changing verbs:

Stem-changing verbs, Class I, are regular in the imperfect subjunctive:

pensar:	pensara, pensaras, etc.	pensase, pensases, etc.
volver:	volviera, volvieras, etc.	volviese, volvieses, etc.

Since stem-changing verbs, Classes II and III, change **e** to **i** and **o** to **u** in the third person singular and plural of the preterit, this change also occurs throughout the imperfect subjunctive:

inf.	*3rd pl. pret.*	*imperfect subjunctive*	
sentir	**sintieron**	**sintiera, –ras,** etc.	**sintiese, –ses,** etc.
dormir	**durmieron**	**durmiera, –ras,** etc.	**durmiese, –ses,** etc.
pedir	**pidieron**	**pidiera, –ras,** etc.	**pidiese, –ses,** etc.

3. Irregular verbs:

inf.	3rd pl. pret.	imp. subj.	inf.	3rd pl. pret.	imp. subj.
andar	**anduvieron**	**anduviera, -se**	oír	**oyeron**	**oyera, -se**
caer	**cayeron**	**cayera, -se**	poder	**pudieron**	**pudiera, -se**
creer	**creyeron**	**creyera, -se**	poner	**pusieron**	**pusiera, -se**
dar	**dieron**	**diera, -se**	querer	**quisieron**	**quisiera, -se**
decir	**dijeron**	**dijera, -se**	saber	**supieron**	**supiera, -se**
estar	**estuvieron**	**estuviera, -se**	ser	**fueron**	**fuera, -se**
haber	**hubieron**[1]	**hubiera, -se**	tener	**tuvieron**	**tuviera, -se**
hacer	**hicieron**	**hiciera, -se**	traducir	**tradujeron**	**tradujera, -se**
ir	**fueron**	**fuera, -se**	traer	**trajeron**	**trajera, -se**
leer	**leyeron**	**leyera, -se**	venir	**vinieron**	**viniera, -se**

B. The pluperfect subjunctive

hubiera	**hubiese**	
hubieras	**hubieses**	
hubiera	**hubiese**	
		hablado, comido, vivido
hubiéramos	**hubiésemos**	
hubierais	**hubieseis**	
hubieran	**hubiesen**	

Él temía que yo no lo hubiera visto.   He feared that I had not seen him.

The pluperfect subjunctive is formed by using either form of the imperfect subjunctive of **haber** with the past participle. Its meaning is similar to that of the pluperfect indicative: **que hubiesen vivido,** *that they had lived;* sometimes the word *might* is a part of the meaning: *that they might have lived.*

C. Use of the subjunctive tenses

Yo espero que ella tenga cuidado.   I hope she will be careful.
Ella lo ha traído para que Ud. lo vea.   She has brought it so that you may see it.
Ella insistirá en que ellos lo limpien.   She will insist that they clean it.
Es probable que ya se hayan marchado.   It is probable that they have already left.

---

[1]See Appendix B for the preterit forms of **haber.**

When the main verb in a sentence requiring the subjunctive in the dependent clause is in the present, future, or present perfect tense, or is a command, the verb in the dependent clause is regularly in the *present* or *present perfect* subjunctive tense.

Le rogamos que nos las enseñara.   We begged him to show them to us.
No vimos a nadie que lo conociese.   We saw no one who knew him.
Ramón me dijo que llevara a Juanita al dentista.   Raymond told me to take Jane to the dentist.
La llevé al parque para que viera los animales.   I took her to the park so that she might see the animals.
Le aconsejé (a ella) que tuviera cuidado.   I advised her to be careful.
Yo sentía que ella se hubiera caído.   I was sorry that she had fallen down.

When the main verb is in the preterit, imperfect, conditional or pluperfect tense, the verb in the dependent clause is normally in the *imperfect* subjunctive, unless the English past perfect tense is used in the dependent clause, in which case the pluperfect subjunctive is used in Spanish (last example).

However, the imperfect subjunctive may follow the present, future, or present perfect tense when, as in English, the action of the dependent verb took place in the past:

¡Es (una) lástima que tuvieras otro compromiso!   It's a pity that you had another commitment.

D.   Use of the infinitive after certain verbs

1.   **Déjeme Ud.** *or* **Déjame (tú) mirar la foto.**   Let me look at the photo.
  Le permití (a ella) jugar un rato.   I permitted (allowed) her to play a while.
  Te dejaré dormir la siesta.   I shall let you take a nap.

By exception to the rule which requires a clause in Spanish after certain verbs when there is a change in subject, the infinitive is generally used after **dejar** and **permitir,** particularly when a personal pronoun is the object of the main verb. **Permítame Ud.** or **Permíteme (tú)** may be used in the first example for *Let me.*

For emphasis, or especially when a noun is the object of the main verb and also the subject of the following verb, the subjunctive is used after these verbs:

Permítale Ud. (Permítele tú) a Juan que haga eso.   Permit *or* Allow John to (Let John) do that.

2.   **Mamá me mandó (hizo) esperar.**   Mother ordered me to wait (made me wait).
  El médico le mandó descansar.   The doctor ordered him to rest.
  Llevé el vestido para mandarlo (hacerlo) limpiar.   I took the dress to have it cleaned.

The infinitive is also regularly used after **hacer** and **mandar** when a personal pronoun is the object of the main verb.

Often the infinitive is translated by the passive voice, especially if its subject is a noun referring to a thing (third example).

E. The subjunctive in a polite or softened statement

>   **Yo quiero jugar a las cartas.**   I want to play cards.
>   **Yo quisiera jugar a las cartas.**   I should like to play cards.
>   **Yo debo dejarte descansar un rato.**   I must let you rest a while.
>   **Yo debiera dejarte dormir la siesta.**   I should (ought to) let you take a nap.

It is considered polite to soften statements by using the **-ra** imperfect subjunctive of forms of **querer.** The **-ra** forms of **deber,** and occasionally **poder,** are also used to form a polite or softened statement. In the case of other verbs, the conditional (as in English) is used: **Me gustaría ir con Ud.,** *I should like to go with you.* (See Lesson 16.)

F. Exclamations

1. **¿Qué . . . !**   *What a (an) . . . !   How . . . !*

>   **¡Qué día he tenido!**   What a day I've had!
>   **¡Qué noche tan (más) agradable!**   What a pleasant evening!

¡Qué + a noun! means *What a (an) . . . !* When an adjective follows the noun, **tan** or **más** regularly precedes the adjective.

>   **¡Qué guapo es!**   How handsome he is!
>   **¡Qué bien juega Carlos!**   How well Charles plays!
>   **¡Qué suerte tienes!**   How lucky you are!

¡Qué + an adjective or adverb! means *How . . . !* In the last example **suerte** is a noun in Spanish but an adjective in English; the expression means literally: *What luck you have!*

2. **¡Cuánto!**   *How!*

>   **¡Cuánto me gustaría volver a verla!**   How glad I would be to see her again!
>   **¡Cuánto siento no haber estado con Uds.!**   How I regret not having been (How sorry I am not to have been) with you!

With verbs the adverb **¡cuánto!** means *how!* The adjective **¡cuánto, -a!** has its literal meaning: **¡Cuántos libros tienes!** *How many books you have!*

3. **¡Ojalá (que)!**   *Would that!*   *I wish that!*

¡Ojalá que ella venga pronto!   Would that she come soon!
¡Ojalá (que) él estuviera aquí   Would (I wish) that he were here!
¡Ojalá que yo las hubiera visto!   I wish that I had seen them!

In exclamatory wishes **¡Ojalá!,** with or without **que,** is followed by the subjunctive. The present subjunctive is used in an exclamatory wish which refers to something which may happen in the future (first example). The imperfect subjunctive is used to express a wish concerning something that is contrary to fact (that is, not true) in the present (second example), and the pluperfect subjunctive to express a wish concerning something that was contrary to fact in the past (third example).

EJERCICIOS

A. Substitution exercises:

1. Querían que *yo* limpiara el coche.
   (*Ud., tú, nosotros, Carlos, Uds.*)
2. Trajeron las fotos para que *Pepe* las viera.
   (*Ana y María, tú, Juan y yo, Ud., él*)
3. Margarita dudaba que *yo* fuera con ella.
   (*Roberto, Luis y Ana, tú, Uds., su esposo*)
4. Sería mejor que *Marta* durmiera la siesta.
   (*yo, nosotros, Juanita y María, tú, Ud.*)
5. Sentían que *Ricardo* no hubiera vuelto.
   (*tú, Pablo e Isabel, Uds., yo, Clara*)

Although only the **-ra** forms of the imperfect subjunctive are used in the drill exercises, your teacher may ask you to give the **-se** forms in this or in other exercises.

B. Read in Spanish, supplying the correct form of the verb in parentheses; give the **-ra** form when the imperfect subjunctive is required:

1. El jefe prefiere que ellos (salir) _____ a las cinco, pero hoy él insistió en que ellos (marcharse) _____ a las cuatro.   2. La madre no quiere que la niña (hacerse) _____ daño; siempre le aconseja que (tener) _____ cuidado.   3. Yo espero que mi novia (volver) _____ mañana, aunque su familia le pidió que (quedarse) _____ varios días más.   4. Me alegro de que Luis (estar) _____ contigo; yo le dije que te (acompañar) _____.   5. Sería mejor que Uds. (jugar) _____ a las cartas ahora; es lástima que Juan y yo (estar) _____ muy ocupados.   6. Valdrá más que tú no (casarse) _____ todavía; debes esperar hasta que (conseguir) _____ un buen puesto. 7. Margarita quería que tú la (llamar) _____ en cuanto (tú) (llegar) _____ a casa; es posible que tú no (acordarse) _____ de eso.   8. Juanita esperaba que tú la (visitar) _____ antes que ella (partir) _____ para México.

C. Say after your teacher; then, when you hear the cue, compose a new sentence, using the **-ra** form of the imperfect subjunctive in the clauses:

MODEL: Es mejor que salgan temprano. *Es mejor que salgan temprano.*
Fue mejor *Fue mejor que salieran temprano.*

1. Tomás insiste en que Ricardo recoja su boleto de avión. (Tomás insistió)
2. Ricardo le dice que lo haga inmediatamente. (Ricardo le dijo)
3. Quieren que Clara saque unas fotos. (Querían)
4. Te pido que no te pongas nerviosa. (Te pedí)
5. Ellos no creen que Margarita se sienta bien. (Ellos no creían)
6. Temo que Jorge no se siente con ella. (Temía)
7. Luis trae las transparencias para que Uds. las vean. (Luis trajo)
8. Ricardo anda buscando una maleta que sea ligera. (Ricardo anduvo)
9. No hay nadie aquí que sepa la verdad. (No había)
10. El médico le aconseja que siga descansando. (El médico le aconsejó)
11. Es probable que José no haya vuelto. (Era probable)
12. Marta duda que Luis haya oído decir eso. (Marta dudaba)

D. Say after your teacher; when you hear the cue, substitute it in the sentence:

1. *Quiero* ir al parque esta tarde. (Yo quisiera)
2. *Yo quisiera* conocer a Roberto. (Me gustaría)
3. *Debemos* volver a hablar con ella. (Debiéramos)
4. *Debo* descansar un rato. (Yo debiera)
5. *Mamá me hizo* limpiar el apartamento. (Mamá me mandó)
6. *Su papá le mandó* lavar el coche. (Su papá le hizo)
7. *Permítame Ud.* sacar una foto. (Déjeme Ud.)
8. *Déjame* ayudarte un poco. (Permíteme)
9. *¡Qué amable* es! (¡Qué simpático!)
10. *¡Cuánto me alegro de no* haber estado allí! (¡Cuánto siento no!)
11. *¡Qué día* tan agradable! (¡Qué noche!)
12. *¡Ojalá que* ella no se casara tan joven! (¡Cuánto me alegré de que!)

E. Give the Spanish equivalent, using familiar forms for *you:*

1. I should like to go to the movies with you, but I must (ought to) stay at home in order to rest. 2. This morning Raymond asked me to take Jane to the dentist's office. 3. Also he had me take a suit to the cleaning shop in order that they might clean it. 4. Before returning home, I allowed Jane to play with some friends of hers in the park. 5. Even though I asked her to be careful, she fell down and hurt herself; then I had to take her home. 6. Do you remember Mary Smith? She and Robert Brown were married two weeks ago. 7. They have just returned from their honeymoon in Mexico. 8. We were playing cards at Caroline's last night when they passed by there. 9. How glad we were to see them! Would (I wish) that you had been there too!

10. We insisted that Robert show us some photos and slides that he had taken on the trip.   11. Yesterday Robert telephoned the manager of his company, and the latter asked him to return to the office as soon as possible.   12. It is probable that they have already left. It is too bad that you could not see them.

F. **Composición**

Assuming that a friend or relative has come to visit you on some Saturday, write a composition of about 150 words telling how you spent the day and indicate some of the experiences you encountered.

VOCABULARIO

aconsejar (*requires indir. obj. of a person*)   to advise, warn
acordarse (ue) (de + obj.)   to remember, recall
el **animal**   animal
el **apartamento**   apartment
caer(se) (*like* **oír** *in certain forms*)   to fall, fall down
la **carta**   card (*playing*)
casarse   to marry, get married
Clara   Clara, Clare, Claire
el **compromiso**   engagement, commitment
cortés (*pl.* **corteses**)   courteous
el **cuidado**   care
el **daño**   harm, damage
el **dentista**   dentist
el **derecho**   law

e   and
el **esposo**   husband
la **Facultad**   School (*in a university*)
la **foto** (*for* **fotografía**)   photo
limpiar   to clean
la **luna de miel**   honeymoon
marcharse   to leave, go away
Margarita   Margaret, Marguerite
la **niña**   little girl
¡ojalá (que)!   would that! I wish that!
¿para qué?   why? for what purpose?
permitir   to permit, allow, let
probable   probable
Ramón   Raymond
la **tintorería**   cleaning shop
la **transparencia**   transparency, slide

casa de apartamentos   apartment house
cuanto antes   at once, immediately, as soon as possible
en casa de (Carolina)   at (Caroline's)
Facultad de Derecho   Law School
hacerse daño   to hurt oneself
jugar (ue) a las cartas   to play cards
¡que te diviertas!   have fun!
tener (mucho) cuidado (de)   to be (very) careful (to)
volver (ue) a (verla)   (to see her) again (*lit.*, to return to see her)

De izquierda a derecha aparecen
José Ortega y Gasset y Juan
Ramón Jiménez pintados por el
pintor Joaquín Sorolla y Bastida
(1863–1923). A continuación
aparece Miguel de Unamuno,
pintado por Ignacio Zuloaga y
Zamora (1870–1945). En la
página de enfrente aparece Ramón
Menéndez Pidal, pintado por
Sorolla.

Lectura 12

La literatura española moderna

Durante el siglo XVII España comenzó a perder su poderío político y militar. A la decadencia política la siguió la cultural, y en el siglo siguiente se produjeron pocas obras de valor literario. Solamente en el último tercio del siglo XVIII, con escritores como Gaspar Melchor de Jovellanos y Juan Meléndez Valdés, empezaron a renacer las actividades literarias, si bien[1] fueron interrumpidas otra vez por las guerras contra Napoleón y las represiones de Fernando VII.

Con el fin del reinado de Fernando VII en 1833 y la vuelta a España de los liberales que habían sido desterrados[2] o que se habían refugiado en tierras extranjeras, brotó[3] el romanticismo, especialmente en la poesía y en el drama. Por lo general,[4] este movimiento en España se caracteriza por su índole[5] nacional; los escritores empezaron de nuevo[6] a buscar inspiración en la historia nacional, en el paisaje, en el cristianismo y en la completa libertad artística. Para ellos el arte era individualista y les proporcionaba[7] oportunidad para la libre expresión de sus sentimientos y de su emoción personal.

Entre los escritores del período romántico en España se destacan José de Espronceda, poeta lírico, el Duque de Rivas y José Zorrilla, poetas también y autores de leyendas y dramas históricos basados en la historia nacional. El último de los grandes poetas románticos fue Gustavo Adolfo Bécquer, autor también de cuentos y leyendas en prosa. Sus famosas *Rimas* expresan su desilusión, su melancolía y su pesimismo, características de la obra romántica en general. Ejemplos de sus *Rimas* son:

Los suspiros son aire y van al aire.
Las lágrimas son agua y van al mar.
Dime, mujer: cuando el amor se olvida,
　¿Sabes tú adónde va?

❖　❖　❖

Hoy la tierra y los cielos me sonríen;[8]
Hoy llega al fondo de mi alma el sol;
Hoy la he visto . . . la he visto y me ha mirado . . .
　　¡Hoy creo en Dios!

❖　❖　❖

---

[1]**si bien,** *although.*　[2]**desterrados,** *exiled.*　[3]**brotó,** *burst forth.*　[4]**Por lo general,** *In general.*　[5]**índole,** *character, nature.*　[6]**de nuevo,** *again, anew.*　[7]**proporcionaba,** *it offered.*　[8]**me sonríen,** *smile at (upon) me.*

¿Qué es poesía? dices mientras clavas[9]
En mi pupila tu pupila azul;
¿Qué es poesía? ¿Y tú me lo preguntas?
    Poesía . . . eres tú.

En el mismo período había escritores que
comenzaron a cultivar el artículo de costumbres,[10] en que presentaban cuadros y tipos
realistas de la vida diaria, y en que a la vez
señalaban los defectos de los españoles de la
época. Los costumbristas prepararon el
terreno para la novela realista, que surgió en
el último tercio del siglo XIX. Entre los muchos novelistas ocupa el primer lugar Benito
Pérez Galdós (1843–1920), el maestro de la
novela española moderna. No fue un novelista regional, como Alarcón, Pereda, Palacio
Valdés, Blasco Ibáñez y otros escritores de la
época, sino el novelista de toda España. Presenta en su extensa obra todas las regiones y
todos los tipos—en fin, toda la historia española del siglo XIX. Ningún otro novelista español, con la excepción de Cervantes, lo
supera en el genio creador y en el conocimiento de la vida y del carácter humano. Es
el novelista más nacional y al mismo tiempo
el más universal de la España moderna. En
algunas de sus mejores novelas, como *Doña
Perfecta* y *Gloria,* se presenta el conflicto entre
lo antiguo y lo moderno, entre el fanatismo y
la tolerancia, y casi siempre el protagonista
trata de elevarse sobre el medio social en que
vive. Pérez Galdós luchó siempre por la
verdad, la justicia, la libertad y el progreso.

   El año de 1898 tuvo grandes consecuencias
en España, primero en la historia política y
después en la vida intelectual. Con la pérdida
de Cuba, de Puerto Rico y de las Islas Filipinas en la guerra con los Estados Unidos,
un grupo de escritores jóvenes, que se ha
llamado «la generación del 98», comenzó a
protestar contra el tradicionalismo, los defectos

*Fotografía de la época que muestra a
Jacinto Benavente en su juventud.*

---

[9]**clavas,** *you fix.*   [10]**artículo de costumbres,** *article of customs and manners.*

del gobierno español y la falta de ideas progresivas en el país. En su clamor por un nuevo espíritu nacional, ensayistas, novelistas, dramaturgos y poetas produjeron un notable renacimiento de las letras españolas que llegó a su apogeo en los primeros años del siglo veinte.

Algunas de las personalidades más importantes de este grupo fueron el gran pensador Miguel de Unamuno, que ha dejado una larga serie de ensayos, de novelas y de poesías; Azorín, ensayista y fino crítico literario; y Ortega y Gasset, filósofo y ensayista.

Otro movimiento literario que influyó mucho en la España de los primeros años del siglo actual fue el modernismo, contribución del Nuevo Mundo a la madre patria. El nicaragüense Rubén Darío fue el maestro reconocido de este movimiento, que realizó muchas innovaciones de metro, de forma, de lenguaje y de ideas. Enorme ha sido la influencia de Darío y de otros poetas hispanoamericanos sobre la poesía española del siglo XX. Con el tiempo los poetas españoles, como Juan Ramón Jiménez, que en 1956 recibió el premio Nobel de literatura, y Antonio Machado, reaccionaron contra el modernismo para buscar rutas más personales en su producción artística.

El dramaturgo más eminente del teatro contemporáneo es Jacinto Benavente, otro escritor español que recibió el premio Nobel de literatura en 1923. Aunque su teatro es muy diverso, sus mejores comedias se caracterizan por la ironía sutil, por la fina sátira, por la maestría en la estructura técnica y por la presentación exacta y artística de la sociedad contemporánea, con todos sus defectos e injusticias.

Las obras dramáticas más espontáneas del siglo actual son los sainetes[11] y las comedias de los hermanos Álvarez Quintero, que han dejado en sus producciones cuadros vivos de la vida andaluza, llenos de gracia, de emoción y de optimismo. Otro dramaturgo del siglo XX es Gregorio Martínez Sierra, autor de una larga serie de comedias en que interpreta de una manera optimista e idealista el carácter español, especialmente el alma femenina.

No se ha cultivado la novela tanto como el ensayo, la poesía y el teatro en el siglo XX. En la primera parte del siglo el vasco Pío Baroja fue uno de los novelistas más populares. Continúa en él el realismo de los novelistas anteriores, pero modificado por el fondo lírico y personal de su sensibilidad. Subjetivo, apasionado e impresionista, es un escritor típico de «la generación del 98».

Entre los novelistas que comenzaron a escribir después de la guerra civil española de 1936–1939 se ha distinguido especialmente don Camilo José Cela. La producción novelística de Cela muestra muchos rasgos de la novela europea contemporánea. Uno de sus rasgos principales es la nota personal; otros son la presencia de preocupaciones morales y sociales y su dominio del lenguaje.

Otras grandes figuras de la literatura española del siglo XX son el poeta y dramaturgo Federico García Lorca, autor del *Romancero gitano,*[12] y de tres tragedias rurales bien conocidas en nuestro país, *Bodas de sangre,*[13] *Yerma* y *La casa de Bernarda Alba,* y los dramaturgos Alejandro Casona y Antonio Buero Vallejo.

El filólogo más eminente de la España contemporánea ha sido don Ramón Menéndez Pidal, autor de *Orígenes del español, La España del Cid* y otros estudios.

En estos últimos años varios escritores y eruditos se han trasladado a las Américas. Algunos, como los poetas Jorge Guillén y Pedro Salinas y los eruditos Américo Castro y Tomás Navarro, han trabajado como profesores en nuestro país.

---

[11]**sainete,** *one-act farce.* [12]**Romancero gitano,** *Gypsy Ballad Book.* [13]**Bodas de sangre,** *Blood Wedding.*

Preguntas

1. ¿Cuándo empezó España a perder su poderío político y militar?   2. ¿Qué puede decirse de la literatura en el siglo XVIII?   3. ¿Cuándo brotó el romanticismo?   4. ¿En qué géneros se vio especialmente?   5. ¿Dónde empezaron a buscar inspiración los escritores?   6. ¿Cuáles son los nombres de tres escritores románticos?   7. ¿Qué escribió Bécquer?   8. ¿Qué expresan sus *Rimas?*

9. ¿Qué comenzaron a cultivar otros escritores del mismo período?   10. ¿Qué presentaban en los artículos de costumbres?   11. ¿Quién fue el maestro de la novela moderna?   12. ¿Cuáles son los nombres de algunos novelistas regionales?   13. ¿Qué presentó Pérez Galdós en su obra?   14. ¿Qué conflictos se presentan en algunas de sus novelas?   15. ¿Qué ideales defendió siempre?

16. ¿Qué perdió España en 1898?   17. ¿Qué nombre se ha dado al grupo de escritores jóvenes de este período?   18. ¿Contra qué comenzaron a protestar?   19. ¿Quiénes son algunos escritores de este grupo?   20. ¿Quién fue el maestro del modernismo?

21. ¿Quién es el autor más eminente del teatro contemporáneo español?   22. ¿Qué escribieron los hermanos Álvarez Quintero?   23. ¿Quién es otro dramaturgo contemporáneo?   24. ¿Quién es Pío Baroja?   25. ¿Qué rasgos muestra Camilo José Cela en su producción novelística?   26. ¿Quiénes son otras grandes figuras de la literatura española del siglo XX?   27. ¿Cuáles son algunas de las obras de García Lorca?

A la izquierda aparece Ramón Pérez de Ayala pintado por López Mezquita. A la derecha, una foto de Federico García Lorca, tomada en Buenos Aires.

Estudio de palabras

a. Less approximate cognates. Pronounce the following words aloud, note the English cognates, and describe the variations: consecuencia, *consequence;* contemporáneo, *contemporary;* desilusión, *disillusion;* espontáneo, *spontaneous;* genio, *genius;* interrumpir, *to interrupt;* maestría, *mastery, skill;* melancolía, *melancholy;* modificado, *modified;* reaccionar, *to react;* ruta, *route, direction;* sutil, *subtle;* técnico, *technical.*

b. Compare the meanings of: carácter, *character,* característica, *characteristic, trait, and* caracterizar, *to characterize;* conocer, *to know, and* conocimiento, *knowledge;* dominio, *domination,* dominar, *to dominate, and* predominar, *to predominate;* ensayo, *essay, and* ensayista, *essayist;* libre, *free,* libertad, *liberty, freedom, and* liberal, *liberal;* país, *country, and* paisaje, *countryside, landscape;* pensar, *to think, and* pensador, *thinker;* perder, *to lose, and* pérdida, loss; presentar, *to present, and* presentación, *presentation, introduction;* producir, *to produce, and* producción, *production;* sentir, *to feel, and* sentimiento, *sentiment, feeling.*

c. Deceptive cognates. **Actual** means *present, present-day.* **Diverso,** as in the case of English *diverse,* means both *different* and *varied.*

Possessive pronouns • **The definite article used as a demonstrative** • **The passive voice** • **The subjunctive after** *tal vez,* *quizá(s)* • **The neuter** *lo* • **Forms of verbs in** *-uir*

LECCIÓN 23

Buscando un apartamento

Dos estudiantes, Carlos Guzmán y Juan Martínez, están buscando un apartamento que sea más cómodo que el que ocupan ahora. Se encuentran frente a una casa de apartamentos que les ha sido recomendada por un profesor suyo.

CARLOS —Ésta parece ser la casa de apartamentos que recomienda el profesor Gómez. La calle es ancha y bonita.

JUAN —Además, no parece haber[1] mucho tránsito. ¿De quién será este edificio?

CARLOS —Pronto lo sabremos. (*Tocan el timbre y abre la puerta un señor.*)

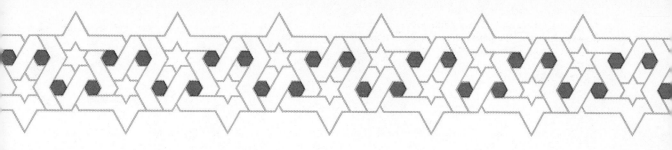

JUAN —Buenos días. Nos ha dicho un amigo nuestro, el profesor Gómez, que Ud. alquila apartamentos. ¿Es Ud. el dueño?

SR. BROWN —Sí, señor, lo soy. Pasen Uds. Me llamo José Brown, a sus órdenes.

JUAN —Mucho gusto en conocerlo, Sr. Brown. Yo me llamo Juan Martínez. Quiero presentarle a mi compañero, Carlos Guzmán. ¿Tiene Ud. algún apartamento vacante?

SR. BROWN —Sí, señor. Acaban de marcharse dos estudiantes extranjeros que lo ocupaban.

CARLOS —¿Cuántas habitaciones tiene?

SR. BROWN —Tiene cuatro, sin contar el cuarto de baño: la sala, con espacio para poner una mesa de comer, la cocina y dos alcobas. Está en el piso bajo. Me gustaría enseñárselo. (*Examinan con cuidado el apartamento.*)

◆ ◆ ◆ ◆

JUAN —El apartamento parece nuevo, Sr. Brown. ¿Cuándo se construyó el edificio?

SR. BROWN —Hace cinco años. Fue construido por un buen amigo mío. El que está allí enfrente, con el tejado de tejas, es mío también, pero todos los apartamentos están ocupados.

JUAN —Veo que hay familias con niños en el edificio.

SR. BROWN —Solamente la mía. De las tres niñas que están jugando en el jardín, dos son hijas nuestras. Son las que tienen el pelo castaño; la del pelo rubio es una amiguita suya.

CARLOS —A mí me gusta el apartamento. Los muebles son mejores que en el nuestro—es decir, el que estamos alquilando.

JUAN —Y éste tiene un jardín bonito y una piscina, donde podremos bañarnos.

CARLOS —Lo malo es que tal vez sea muy caro.

SR. BROWN —Como vienen recomendados por el Sr. Gómez, puedo alquilárselo por ciento cincuenta dólares al mes, sin la electricidad.

CARLOS —Agradecemos mucho su amabilidad. Quisiéramos pensarlo un poco antes de llegar a una decisión. Quizás lo sabremos mañana.

SR. BROWN —Muy bien. Pero si deciden Uds. alquilarlo, no dejen de avisarme lo más pronto posible.

---

[1]**no parece haber,** *there doesn't seem to be.*

Conversación

A. Preguntas sobre el diálogo

1. ¿Qué están buscando los dos estudiantes? 2. ¿Quién les ha recomendado la casa de apartamentos que están visitando? 3. ¿Cómo se llama el dueño del edificio? 4. ¿Cuántas habitaciones tiene el apartamento? 5. ¿Cuándo se construyó el edificio? ¿Quién lo construyó? 6. ¿Cuántas hijas tienen los señores Brown? 7. ¿Por qué le interesa a Juan el apartamento? 8. ¿Por cuánto puede alquilarles el apartamento el Sr. Brown? 9. ¿Qué les pide el Sr. Brown?

B. Aplicación del diálogo

1. ¿Cuáles son las habitaciones de una casa? 2. ¿Se ven muchos techos de tejas en esta parte del país? 3. ¿Viven sus padres en una casa o en un apartamento? 4. ¿Cuántas alcobas tiene la casa en que Ud. vive? 5. ¿En qué casas hay más espacio, en las casas modernas o en las antiguas? 6. ¿Les gustan a los estudiantes los apartamentos con mucho espacio? 7. ¿Tiene Ud. el pelo rubio, castaño o negro? 8. ¿Conoce Ud. a alguien que tenga el pelo rubio?

NOTAS GRAMATICALES

A. Possessive pronouns

el mío	la mía	los míos	las mías	mine
el tuyo	la tuya	los tuyos	las tuyas	yours (*fam.*)
el nuestro	la nuestra	los nuestros	las nuestras	ours
el vuestro	la vuestra	los vuestros	las vuestras	yours (*fam.*)
el suyo	la suya	los suyos	las suyas	his, hers, its, yours (*formal*), theirs

1. **mi coche, nuestro coche; el mío, el nuestro**   my car, our car; mine, ours
nuestra casa, mi casa; la nuestra, la mía   our house, my house; ours, mine
sus flores; las suyas   his (her, its, your, their) flowers; his (hers, its, yours, theirs)

¿Tiene Ud. el suyo?   Do you have yours?
Alquilaron la suya.   They rented theirs.
Este jardín es nuestro.   This garden is ours.
El coche es de Juan (suyo).   The car is John's (his).

The possessive pronouns are formed by using the definite article **el (la, los, las)** with the long forms of the possessive adjectives (Lesson 17). After **ser** the article is usually omitted (last two examples).

2. **mi madre y la de ella**   my mother and hers

nuestros padres y los de él   our parents and his
el coche de ellos y el de Ud.   their car and yours

Since **el suyo (la suya, los suyos, las suyas)** may mean *his, hers, its, yours* (formal), *theirs,* these pronouns may be clarified by substituting **el de él, el de ella, el de Ud(s)., el de ellos (ellas).** The article agrees with the thing possessed.

B. The definite article used as a demonstrative

1. **mi habitación y la de Juan**   my room and that of John (John's)
   este apartamento y el del Sr. Gómez   this apartment and that of Mr. Gómez
   la del sombrero rojo   the one in (with) the red hat
   las del pelo rubio   the ones with the blond hair

Before a phrase beginning with **de,** Spanish uses the definite article (which originated from the Latin demonstrative), instead of the demonstrative pronoun. **El (la, los, las) de** is translated *that (those) of, the one(s) of (with, in)*, and occasionally by an English possessive (first example).

2. **La que está allí es mía también.**   The one which is there is mine also.
   Son las que tienen el pelo castaño.   They are the ones who have dark hair.
   El que salió es un amigo suyo.   The one who left is a friend of his.

Spanish also regularly uses the definite article before a relative clause introduced by **que,** instead of the demonstrative pronoun. **El (la, los, las) que** corresponds to *he who, the one(s) who (that, which), those who (which)*. These forms, which may refer to persons or things, are often called compound relatives because the article serves as the antecedent of the **que**-clause. (Do *not* use **el cual** in this construction.)

Quien (*pl.* **quienes**), which refers to persons only, sometimes means *he (those) who, the one(s) who,* particularly in proverbs:

Quien busca, halla.   He (The one) who seeks, finds.
Quienes (Los que) estudian, aprenden.   Those who study, learn.

Lo que is the neuter form of **el que** and means *what, that which:*

Lo que dicen es verdad.   What they say is true.
Agradezco mucho lo que ha hecho Ud.   I am very grateful for what you have done.

C. The passive voice

La casa fue construida por un amigo mío.   The house was built by a friend of mine.

El boleto fue enviado por la empresa.   The ticket was sent by the company.
La película les ha sido recomendada por un profesor suyo.   The film has been recommended to them by a professor of theirs.

The true passive voice in Spanish is formed as in English.   When an action is performed by an agent, Spanish uses **ser** and the past participle.   The past participle agrees with the subject in gender and number, and the agent is usually expressed by **por.**   (In the second example note that **sido** completes the compound tense with **haber** and is invariable, whereas **recomendada** agrees with the subject.)   In the spoken language the passive is often avoided, in Spanish as in English, by changing the sentence to active voice.

Remember that when the agent is not expressed, and the subject is a thing, the reflexive substitute for the passive is regularly used (Lesson 7): **Aquí se habla español,** *Spanish is spoken here.*

Do not confuse the true passive, which expresses *action,* with the use of **estar** plus a past participle to express the *state* which results from the action of a verb (see Lesson 15):

La casa está bien construida.   The house is well built.
Esta carta está escrita en español.   This letter is written in Spanish.

D. The subjunctive after **tal vez, quizá(s),** *perhaps*

Tal vez (Quizás) sea muy caro.   Perhaps it may be very expensive.
Quizá(s) lo sabremos mañana.   Perhaps we shall know tomorrow.

The indicative mood is used after **tal vez, quizá(s),** *perhaps,* when certainty is expressed or implied.   The subjunctive, however, is used when doubt or uncertainty is implied.

E. The neuter **lo**

1. **Él siempre prefiere lo bueno.**   He always prefers the good (what is good).
Lo malo es que hay mucho tránsito.   What is bad (The bad thing) is that there is much traffic.

The neuter article **lo** is used with masculine singular adjectives to form an expression almost equivalent to an abstract noun.   The word *thing* or *part* is often a part of the meaning.

Recall that the neuter article **lo** is also used with an adverb when an expression of possibility is used (Lesson 17): **No dejen de avisarme lo más pronto posible,** *Don't fail to inform me the soonest (as soon as) possible.*

2. **—¿Es Ud. el dueño? —Lo soy.**   "Are you the owner?" "I am."

The neuter pronoun **lo** is used with **ser** and a few other verbs to represent a previously expressed idea.   In the example, **lo** stands for **el dueño.**

F. Forms of verbs in **-uir: construir,** *to construct*

Pres. Part.	**construyendo**
Pres. Ind.	**construyo, construyes, construye,** construimos, construís, **construyen**
Pres. Subj.	**construya, construyas, construya, construyamos, construyáis, construyan**
Preterit	construí, construiste, **construyó,** construimos, construisteis, **construyeron**
Imp. Subj.	**construyera,** etc. **construyese,** etc.
Sing. Imper.	**construye**

Verbs ending in **-uir** insert **y** except before the endings beginning with **i,** and change unaccented **i** between vowels to **y.**

EJERCICIOS

A. Substitution drill:

1. *Esa empresa* construye edificios modernos.
   (*Ellos, Uds., Nosotros, Yo, Tú*)
2. *Luis* sigue buscando trabajo.
   (*Mis amigos, Yo, Nosotros, Tú, Uds.*)
3. *Ella* agradece lo que Tomás ha hecho.
   (*Yo, Nosotros, Sus amigos, Tú, Uds.*)
4. Tal vez *ellos* alquilen un apartamento cerca de aquí.
   (*yo, Uds., su familia, nosotros, tú*)

B. Say the question or sentence after your teacher; then repeat it, using a possessive pronoun:

MODELS: ¿Vio Ud. su libro?   *¿Vio Ud. su libro? ¿Vio Ud. el suyo?*
          No he visto el libro   *No he visto el libro de Ana. No he visto*
          de Ana.   *el suyo.*

1. ¿Tiene Marta su boleto?
2. ¿Tienen ellos sus boletos?
3. ¿Dejó Carlos su maleta?
4. ¿Mandó Juan sus cartas?
5. No dejes tus transparencias allí.
6. Paga (tú) tus cuentas pronto.
7. Quizás yo le preste mis discos.
8. Quizás me ponga los zapatos.
9. Tal vez vengan nuestros padres.
10. Tal vez él trae nuestro equipaje.
11. Nuestras flores son más hermosas este año.
12. Nuestro apartamento es más cómodo que el tuyo.

C. Listen to the sentence; then repeat, following the models:

MODELS: Quiero ese vaso y el vaso de Ana.   *Quiero ese vaso y el de Ana..*
         Esa foto y las fotos que tengo   *Esa foto y las que tengo son*
           son bonitas.   *bonitas.*

1. Me gustan este jardín y el jardín de su casa.
2. Esta alcoba y la alcoba de Marta son cómodas.
3. ¿Te gustan estas flores y las flores que ella trajo?
4. Aquella niña y la niña del pelo rubio son primas mías.
5. Este joven y el joven que se acerca son estudiantes.
6. Este disco y los discos que compraste ayer son buenos.
7. Aquel coche y el coche que pasa por la calle son nuevos.
8. Este edificio y el edificio del Sr. López son modernos.

D. Say after your teacher; then repeat, using the reflexive substitute for the passive (see Lesson 7):

MODELS: Allí hablan español.   *Allí hablan español.*   *Allí se habla español.*
         Aquí venden zapatos.   *Aquí venden zapatos.*   *Aquí se venden zapatos.*

1. Cierran la puerta a las cinco.
2. Abren las tiendas a las diez.
3. En México oímos mucha música popular.
4. No venden libros en la biblioteca.
5. Exhiben muchas cosas en el escaparate.
6. ¿Cómo dicen eso en español?
7. Aquí construyen muchas casas nuevas.
8. ¿Dónde limpian los trajes?

E. Say after your teacher; then repeat, using the passive voice. Watch the agreement of the verb and the past participle:

MODEL: Otro profesor preparó los   *Los exámenes fueron preparados por otro*
          exámenes.   *profesor.*

1. El Sr. Carter recomendó a Ricardo.
2. Una empresa peruana construyó estos edificios.
3. El mal tiempo retrasó la salida del avión.
4. La compañía pagó todas sus cuentas.
5. Dos estudiantes alquilaron el apartamento.
6. Una agencia mandó todos esos paquetes.
7. Unos amigos nuestros celebraron la fiesta.
8. Tomás sacó todas esas fotos el mes pasado.

F. Answer in Spanish, using a sentence which expresses the resultant state of the action mentioned:

MODEL: ¿Ha cerrado Ud. la puerta?   *Sí, ya está cerrada.*

1. ¿Ha lavado Ud. los coches?   3. ¿Ha decidido Ud. el asunto?
2. ¿Ha preparado Ud. el desayuno?   4. ¿Ha escrito Ud. la tarjeta?

MODEL: ¿Abrió Ud. el edificio?   *No, ya estaba abierto.*

5. ¿Terminó ella el vestido?   7. ¿Reservaste el asiento?
6. ¿Pusiste las flores allí?   8. ¿Alquilaron Uds. el apartamento?

G. Repeat the sentence; when you hear the cue, compose a new sentence, using the **–ra** imperfect subjunctive in the dependent clause:

MODEL: Quieren una casa que tenga patio.   *Quieren una casa que tenga patio.*
         Querían una casa   *Querían una casa que tuviera patio.*

1. Buscan un apartamento que sea más grande.   (Buscaban un apartamento)
2. Quieren mucho espacio para que jueguen las niñas.   (Querían mucho espacio)
3. Prefieren una casa que tenga dos pisos.   (Preferían una casa)
4. Yo les recomiendo que alquilen la del Sr. López.   (Yo les recomendé)
5. Temo que no encuentren otra más cómoda.   (Yo temía)
6. Será mejor que la examinen con cuidado.   (Sería mejor)
7. Les aconsejaré que vayan a verla lo más pronto posible.   (Yo les aconsejaría)
8. Me prometen ir en cuanto puedan.   (Me prometieron ir)

H. Give the Spanish equivalent:

1. Charles and John want to find an apartment that is larger than the one (that) they are occupying.   2. They go to see an apartment house which was recommended to them by Professor Gómez, a friend of theirs.   3. They approach the building, and, after they ring the doorbell, a gentleman opens the door.   4. When John asks him whether he is the owner, the latter replies (to them) that he is and that his name is Joseph Brown.   5. The apartment has four rooms, without counting the bathroom: a **(la)** living room, with space to put a dining table, a **(la)** kitchen, and two bedrooms. 6. The building has four floors, but the apartment is on the first floor.   7. Mr. Brown tells them that the apartment house was built three years ago.   8. It was built by a good friend of his, who has been building houses for many years.   9. Mr. Brown also tells them that the one that is opposite is his, but all the apartments are occupied.   10. The two young men like the apartment house very much, because it has a garden and a swimming pool where they can take a swim.   11. Also, it seems to them that there is little traffic on the street even though it is very wide.   12. When the owner says that he can rent the apartment to them for one hundred fifty dollars a month, they decide to take it.

I. **Composición**

Assuming that you are one of the two students (John or Charles), who went to look for an apartment, write a composition telling what happened. Use the dialogue and Exercise H as your reference, but keep in mind that it is you who will be giving the account in the first person.

J. Proverbs

Repeat the following proverbs after your teacher, and learn them for future use:

1. Poco a poco (*Little by little*) se va lejos.
2. Quien mal (*evil*) dice, peor oye.
3. Lo que mucho vale, mucho cuesta.
4. Lo que no se empieza, no se termina.
5. Más vale tarde que nunca.
6. Más vale algo que nada.
7. Quien mucho duerme, poco aprende.
8. Mañana será otro día.
9. Nunca lo bueno fue mucho.
10. La mejor salsa (*sauce*) es el hambre.

VOCABULARIO

agradecer (*like* **conocer**) to be grateful, (thank) for
la **alcoba** bedroom
alquilar to rent
la **amabilidad** kindness
la **amiguita** little (girl) friend
ancho, -a broad, wide
avisar to advise, inform
bajo, -a low, lower
bañarse to take a swim (dip)
castaño, -a dark, brown, brunet(te)
la **cocina** kitchen
construir to construct, build
contar (ue) to count
el **cuarto de baño** bathroom
la **decisión** (*pl.* **decisiones**) decision
el **dueño** owner
la **electricidad** electricity

enfrente *adv.* in front, opposite
el **espacio** space, room
examinar to examine
la **habitación** (*pl.* **habitaciones**) room
el **jardín** (*pl.* **jardines**) garden
la **mesa de comer** dining table
los **muebles** furniture
el **niño** little boy, child; *pl.* children
ocupar to occupy
la **orden** (*pl.* **órdenes**) order, command
el **pelo** hair
el **piso** floor, story
quizá(s) perhaps
rubio, -a fair, blond(e)
la **teja** tile
el **tejado** roof (*of tiles*)
el **tránsito** traffic
vacante vacant, empty

a sus órdenes at your service
con cuidado carefully
es decir that is (to say)
llegar a una decisión to reach (make) a decision
no dejar de + *inf.* not to fail to + *verb*
pensarlo (ie) to think about it, think it over
piso bajo first (lower) floor
por . . . al mes for . . . a month
tal vez perhaps
tener el pelo (castaño) to have (dark) hair

Quinta de Simón Bolívar, hoy museo dedicado a su memoria, Bogotá, Colombia.

LA CARRETERA PANAMERICANA

Cosmopolitan cities of over one million inhabitants

Important pre-Columbian archaeological sites

Urban centers of historical and artistic interest; important colonial buildings

Scenic areas, lakes, mountains and volcanic regions

Areas rich in folk arts and festivals

Great waterfalls

Winter sports centers

Beaches and water sports centers

1. Guadalajara **(Mexico)**
2. Mexico City; Toluca, Cuernavaca, Puebla, Taxco, Teotihuacán, San Miguel Allende, Morelia, Guanajuato, Pátzcuaro, Querétaro **(Mexico)**
3. Veracruz, Jalapa **(Mexico)**
4. Acapulco **(Mexico)**
5. Oaxaca; ruins of Monte Albán and Mitla **(Mexico)**
6. Mérida; ruins of Uxmal and Chichén-Itzá **(Mexico)**
7. Guatemala City; Antigua, Lake Atitlán, Chichicastenango, ruins of Tikal* **(Guatemala)**
8. San Salvador and surroundings; ruins of Tazumal, Izalco Volcano National Park **(El Salvador)**
9. Tegucigalpa; ruins of Copán* **(Honduras)**
10. Managua; León, Lake Nicaragua **(Nicaragua)**
11. San José; Irazú and Poás Volcanoes, Cartago **(Costa Rica)**
12. Canal Zone; Panama City, Portobelo, San Blas Islands* **(Panama)**
13. Cartagena and surroundings **(Colombia)**
14. Caracas and surroundings; Maracay, Angel Falls*, Margarita Island* **(Venezuela)**
15. Mérida, Trujillo, Lake Maracaibo **(Venezuela)**
16. Bogotá; Tequendama Falls, Tunja **(Colombia)**
17. Cali and Popayán in the Cauca Valley **(Colombia)**
18. Route of the Incas; Otavalo, Quito, Ambato, Cuenca, ruins of Incapirca, Mt. Cotopaxi and Mt. Chimborazo **(Ecuador)**
19. Guayaquil; Galápagos Islands* **(Ecuador)**
20. Trujillo; ruins of Chavín, Callejón de Huaylas, Cajamarca **(Peru)**
21. Lima; Callao **(Peru)**
22. Cuzco area; Chincheros, Ayacucho, Machu Picchu* **(Peru)**
23. Lake Titicaca Region: Arequipa and Puno **(Peru)**; La Paz, Copacabana, and ruins of Tiahuanaco **(Bolivia)**
24. Sucre and Potosí **(Bolivia)**
25. Asunción and surroundings **(Paraguay)**
26. Iguazú Falls and surroundings; Jesuit mission ruins **(Argentina, Paraguay, Brazil)**
27. São Paulo **(Brazil)**
28. Río de Janeiro and surroundings **(Brazil)**
29. Belo Horizonte; Ouro Prêto **(Brazil)**
30. Brasilia **(Brazil)**
31. Brasilia-Belém Highway; Araguia National Park, Belém **(Brazil)**
32. Salvador (Pelourinho) **(Brazil)**
33. Recife (Pernambuco) **(Brazil)**
34. Fortaleza **(Brazil)**
35. River Plate Region: Greater Buenos Aires **(Argentina)**; Montevideo **(Uruguay)**
36. Córdoba, Rosario, Santa Fe **(Argentina)**
37. Bariloche **(Argentina)**
38. Santiago de Chile; Valparaíso, Viña del Mar, Portillo, Farellones, Juan Fernández Archipelago* **(Chile)**
39. Tierra del Fuego: Punta Arenas **(Chile)**; Ushuaia **(Argentina)**

*Reached by train, boat, or plane.

Drawn by OAS Graphic Services Unit, 1973

Conversación 4

En la Carretera Panamericana

Luis y Juan se desayunan temprano en el hotel y, después de pagar su cuenta, van al garaje, donde han guardado su coche. El botones baja el equipaje y lo mete en la cajuela del coche.

JUAN —Luis, ayer manejé yo casi todo el día, de manera que te toca a ti manejar un rato esta mañana.

LUIS —Está bien. (*Entra en el coche y pone en marcha el motor.*) Parece que necesitamos gasolina, ¿no?

JUAN —No falta mucha, pero es mejor estar seguros. Vamos a pararnos en una de las estaciones que vimos anoche al llegar a la ciudad. (*Quince minutos más tarde se paran en una gasolinera que encuentran en la Carretera Panamericana.*)

EMPLEADO —Buenos días, señores. ¿En qué puedo servirles? ¿Gasolina? ¿Aceite?

LUIS —Necesitamos gasolina.

EMPLEADO —¿Desean llenar el tanque?

LUIS —Sí, llénelo, por favor. Siempre es bueno llevar suficiente gasolina. Habrá muchas estaciones de gasolina por la carretera, ¿verdad?

EMPLEADO —Pues, sí, señor, si van por esta carretera. Hasta en los pueblos pequeños las[1] hay . . . Puse (Eché) treinta y un litros de gasolina. ¿Qué tal el aceite? ¿Quieren que lo mire?

LUIS —Lo cambiamos ayer en San Antonio, pero es posible que necesitemos un poco. El coche ya no es nuevo y gasta bastante.

EMPLEADO —Pues, vale más mirarlo . . . Sí, necesita un litro. ¿Qué marca?

LUIS —Es igual. Uno que sea bueno. Y, ¿quiere ver si el radiador tiene bastante agua?

EMPLEADO —Está lleno. Y la batería tiene agua también. ¿Ponemos (Echamos) aire en los neumáticos?

LUIS —Sí, veinte y ocho libras; y en el neumático de repuesto también, por favor. Aquí tiene la llave de la cajuela.

EMPLEADO —Ya está hecho. No necesitan aire. El parabrisas está muy sucio. Lo limpio en un momento . . . Bueno, todo está listo.

LUIS —¿Cuánto es?

---

[1]Used with impersonal forms of **haber** the direct object pronouns **lo, la, los, las** usually mean *one, some,* expressed or understood: **Hasta en los pueblos pequeños las hay,** *Even in the small towns there are* (*some*). Also see page 354, line 16: **Los hay muy buenos,** *There are some very good ones.* In negative sentences, these object pronouns may mean *any* (*one*):—**¿Hay estación allí? No, no la hay.** *"Is there a station there?" "No, there isn't any."*

EMPLEADO   —Ciento dieciséis²

LUIS   —Aquí tiene Ud. ciento cincuenta pesos.

EMPLEADO   —Y aquí tiene Ud. el cambio, señor.

JUAN   —¿Está la carretera en buenas condiciones?

EMPLEADO   —Hay algunos puentes angostos y algunos tramos en reparación, pero, en general, está en muy buenas condiciones. Pero les advierto una cosa, señores; no excedan la velocidad máxima o los detiene la policía.

JUAN   —Muchas gracias por la advertencia. Tendremos mucho cuidado, si bien no tenemos mucha prisa. Pensamos pararnos de vez en cuando para sacar fotografías y para mirar el paisaje. ¿Qué distancia hay de aquí a la capital?

EMPLEADO   —Unos mil ciento cincuenta kilómetros. No tratarán de hacer el viaje en un día, ¿verdad? Les aconsejo que pasen la noche en Valles o en Tamazunchale.

LUIS   —Eso pensamos hacer. Así no tendremos que viajar de noche y podremos cruzar las montañas mañana por la mañana.

JUAN   —Hay buenos hoteles en esos lugares, ¿verdad?

EMPLEADO   —¡Ya lo creo! Los hay muy buenos. También hay campos de turismo (moteles), como en su país.

JUAN   —Muchísimas gracias.

EMPLEADO   —De nada. ¡Que les vaya bien! ¡Buen viaje!

Preguntas

Sobre la conversación

1. ¿Qué hacen Luis y Juan después de desayunarse?   2. ¿Qué hace el botones?   3. ¿Quién va a manejar un rato?   4. ¿Qué van a hacer antes de salir de la ciudad?   5. ¿Por qué prefieren llenar el tanque?   6. ¿Qué le pregunta Luis al empleado?

7. ¿Cuántos litros de gasolina puso en el tanque?   8. ¿Por qué dice Luis que es posible que el coche necesite aceite?   9. ¿Qué tiene que limpiar el empleado?   10. ¿Qué dice el empleado de la carretera?   11. ¿Qué distancia hay de Monterrey a la capital?   12. ¿Dónde van a pasar la noche?

Aplicación de la conversación

1. ¿Qué le damos al botones cuando nos ayuda con nuestro equipaje?   2. ¿Le gusta a Ud. manejar de noche?   3. ¿Cuántos años tenía Ud. cuando aprendió a manejar?   4. ¿Dónde guarda Ud. su coche?   5. ¿Qué es una gasolinera?   6. ¿Hay muchas gasolineras cerca de la universidad?

7. ¿Cuántas libras de aire pone Ud. en los neumáticos de su coche?   8. ¿Por qué es importante que esté en buenas condiciones el neumático de repuesto?   9. ¿Qué pasa algunas veces cuando excedemos la velocidad máxima?   10. ¿Qué distancia hay desde esta ciudad

---

²That is, **Ciento dieciséis pesos, sesenta centavos.**

hasta la capital del estado? 11. ¿Sabe Ud. si hay buenos moteles por aquí? 12. ¿Hay que tener mucho cuidado al manejar en las carreteras de este país?

Prácticas orales

Groups of students will be selected to prepare a conversation of eight to ten exchanges, using vocabulary already given, on:

1. Servicing a car at a filling station.
2. Paying a hotel bill, loading luggage into the car, and departing.
3. Asking for directions and about road conditions.

Estación de gasolina, Asunción, Paraguay.

VOCABULARIO

el **aceite** oil
la **advertencia** warning
 advertir (ie, i) to advise, point out, warn
 angosto, -a narrow
 bajar to bring down
la **batería** battery
la **cajuela** auto trunk
 cambiar to change
el **cambio** change
el **campo de turismo** tourist camp, motel
la **carretera** highway
la **condición** (*pl.* **condiciones**) condition
 cruzar to cross, pass (go) across
la **distancia** distance
 echar to throw, put (in)
la **estación** (*pl.* **estaciones**) station
 exceder to exceed
la **gasolina** gasoline
la **gasolinera** filling (gas) station
 gastar to waste, use (up)
 guardar to keep, guard
 hasta *adv.* even
 igual equal
el **kilómetro** kilometer (⅝ *mile*)
la **libra** pound

el **lugar** place
el **neumático (de repuesto)** (spare) tire
 llenar to fill
 lleno, -a full
 manejar to drive (*Mex.*)
la **marca** brand, kind, make
 máximo, -a maximum
 meter to put (in)
el **motel** motel
el **motor** motor
el **paisaje** landscape, countryside
 panamericano, -a Pan American
el **parabrisas** windshield
 pararse to stop
la **policía** police
la **prisa** haste, hurry
el **pueblo** village, town
el **puente** bridge
el **radiador** radiator
la **reparación** (*pl.* **reparaciones**) repairing, repair
 sucio, -a dirty
 suficiente sufficient, enough
el **tanque** tank
el **tramo** stretch, section
la **velocidad** speed

 ¡buen viaje! (have) a good trip!
 de noche at night
 en buenas condiciones in good condition
 es igual it's all the same, it doesn't matter
 estación de gasolina gasoline station
 poner en marcha to start
 ¡que les vaya bien! good luck (*lit.*, may it go well with you)!
 ¿qué distancia hay? how far is it?
 si bien though, while
 te toca a ti it's your turn
 tener mucha prisa to be in a big hurry
 tramo en reparación section under repair
 ya no no longer

Barca usada para el transporte de vehículos y carga en el lago Titicaca, Bolivia.

Familiar commands • *Si*-clauses • Special use of plural reflexive pronouns • Forms of *enviar* and *continuar* • Summary of uses of *para* • Summary of uses of *por*

LECCIÓN 24

«Los que tienen buenos amigos son ricos.»

Ricardo Smith vive en un apartamento con dos compañeros, Miguel Cruz y Luis Hernández. Suena el despertador en el cuarto que ocupan Miguel y Ricardo. Éstos no dan señales de vida; por eso, Luis llama a la puerta. Esta semana le toca a Luis preparar el desayuno para los tres. Luis es español y emplea formas peninsulares.

LUIS —¡Despertaos, muchachos! ¡Ya son casi las ocho! No os olvidéis de que Ricardo tiene que estar en la oficina del Sr. Ortiz a las nueve. ¡Daos prisa!

RICARDO (*Desperezándose.*)—¿De veras son las ocho? Dime la verdad, Miguel.

MIGUEL (*Bostezando.*)—Luis está llamando, y está sonando el despertador.

RICARDO —¡Ay, si pudiera dormir un poco más, sería el hombre más feliz del mundo!

LUIS —¡Levantaos y vestíos, dormilones! El desayuno estará listo dentro de diez minutos. (*Los dos jóvenes se levantan, se afeitan y se visten. Pasan al comedor, donde se desayunan despacio, charlando como si no tuviesen nada que hacer.*)

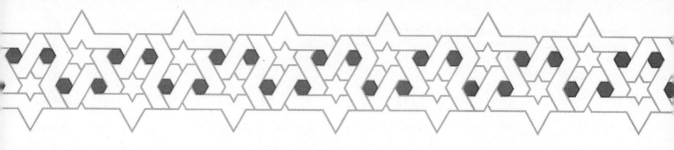

LUIS —Oíd, si continuáis charlando, vais a perder el autobús. Apenas tenéis tiempo. (*Ricardo y Miguel se miran sorprendidos.*) No me digáis que no os desperté a tiempo. Poneos el abrigo, porque hace fresco. ¡Hala, idos ahora mismo!

◆ ◆ ◆ ◆ ◆

Media hora más tarde Ricardo entra en la oficina del Sr. Ortiz.

SR. ORTIZ —Pase Ud., Ricardo. He oído decir que Ud. ha conseguido el puesto en México. Lo felicito muy cordialmente.

RICARDO —Muchas gracias, Sr. Ortiz. Sé por el Sr. Carter que sin la ayuda de Ud. me habría sido difícil conseguirlo. Le agradezco mucho cuanto[1] ha hecho por mí.

SR. ORTIZ —He enviado por Ud. porque quisiera darle algunas cartas de presentación para varios amigos míos que viven en México. Si lo hubiera sabido antes, les habría escrito directamente.

RICARDO —¡Es Ud. muy amable! ¿Viven los señores en la ciudad de México?

SR. ORTIZ —Sí; son abogados, médicos, ingenieros, comerciantes . . . Si yo estuviera en su lugar, iría a hablar con esos señores en cuanto llegara. Todos se pondrán a su disposición y harán todo lo que puedan para hacer más agradable su estancia en México.

RICARDO —Esto me recuerda el viejo refrán que dice: «Los que tienen buenos amigos son ricos.»

SR. ORTIZ —Pues, ¿para qué sirven los amigos? Me gustaría charlar más con Ud., pero sé que tendrá mucho que hacer antes de salir para México. Para norteamericano, Ud. habla muy bien el español.

RICARDO —Hace muchos años que lo estudio.

SR. ORTIZ —Podría uno tomarlo por mexicano. Los que saben español como Ud. pueden hacer mucho para mejorar las relaciones entre nuestros dos países.

RICARDO —Quisiera poder colaborar en la labor de estrechar las relaciones entre los dos pueblos. Mil gracias por todo, Sr. Ortiz.

SR. ORTIZ —No hay de qué, Ricardo. ¡Que tenga mucha suerte! Envíeme una tarjeta de vez en cuando.

---

[1]**Cuanto,** *All that,* is often used instead of **todo lo que.**

Conversación

A. Preguntas sobre el diálogo

1. ¿Se despiertan Ricardo y Miguel al sonar el despertador? ¿Quién llama a la puerta?
2. ¿A quién le toca esa semana preparar el desayuno? 3. ¿Dónde tiene que estar Ricardo a las nueve de la mañana? ¿Cuándo estará listo el desayuno? 4. ¿Qué hacen Ricardo y Miguel antes de desayunarse? 5. ¿Por qué les aconseja Luis a sus compañeros que se pongan el abrigo? 6. ¿Por qué ha enviado el Sr. Ortiz por Ricardo? 7. ¿Qué haría el Sr. Ortiz si estuviera en el lugar de Ricardo? 8. ¿De qué refrán se acuerda Ricardo?

B. Aplicación del diálogo

1. ¿Se levanta Ud. en seguida cuando suena el despertador? 2. ¿Le gusta a Ud. desayunarse rápidamente? 3. ¿Lee Ud. el periódico durante el desayuno? 4. ¿Lo despierta alguien cuando Ud. tiene que salir de casa temprano? 5. ¿Qué lenguas debe uno saber si desea trabajar en Suramérica? 6. ¿Envía Ud. tarjetas cuando viaja? ¿A quiénes? 7. ¿Lo tomarían a Ud. por español en España? 8. ¿Continuará Ud. estudiando español el próximo año? ¿Por qué? (¿Por qué no?)

NOTAS GRAMATICALES

A. Familiar commands

Recall that the form of the affirmative familiar singular command is the same as the third person singular of the present indicative tense of all but a few irregular verbs (see Lessons 9 and 17). Recall that this form is often called the singular imperative.

Also, remember that the negative familiar singular command form is the same as the second person singular of the present subjunctive. Examples: **hablar, habla (tú), no hables; hacer, haz (tú), no hagas.**

1. Familiar plural commands:

hablar:	hablad	no habléis	dormir:	dormid	no **durmáis**
comer:	comed	no comáis	pedir:	pedid	no **pidáis**
escribir:	escribid	no escribáis	venir:	venid	no **vengáis**

To form the affirmative familiar plural commands (the plural imperative) of *all* verbs, drop **-r** of the infinitive and add **-d.** For the negative familiar plural commands, use the second person plural of the present subjunctive.

In this text we have followed the practice, which is common in Spanish America, of using **Uds.** with the third person plural present subjunctive in familiar plural commands: **Hablen Uds.; Vengan Uds.** The familiar plural forms used in this lesson will, however, be needed for recognition in reading.

2. Familiar commands of reflexive verbs:

	singular			*plural*	
levantarse:	levántate	no te levantes		levantaos	no os levantéis
despertarse:	**despiérta**te	no te **despiertes**		despertaos	no os **despertéis**
ponerse:	**pon**te	no te **pongas**		poneos	no os **pongáis**
vestirse:	**víste**te	no te **vistas**		vestíos	no os **vistáis**
irse:	**ve**te	no te **vayas**		**id**os	no os **vayáis**

Remember: (*a*) that the second person reflexive object pronouns are **te** and **os,** and (*b*) that all object pronouns are attached to affirmative commands, while they precede in negative commands. An accent mark must be written when **te** is added to a singular command form of more than one syllable; also, when **os** is added to an **-ir** reflexive verb, except for **idos,** an accent mark must be written: **vestíos.**

In forming the affirmative plural familiar commands of reflexive verbs, final **-d** is dropped before **os** in all forms except **idos.**

B. **Si-**clauses

In earlier lessons we have had simple conditions in which the present indicative tense is used in the English *if*-clause, and the same tense in the Spanish **si-**clause:

Si él tiene el dinero, me lo dará.
If he has the money, he will give it to me.

Si continuáis charlando, vais a perder el autobús.
If you continue chatting, you are going to miss the bus.

Now contrast these sentences with the following:

Si él tuviera (tuviese) el dinero, me lo daría.
If he had the money (*but he doesn't*), he would give it to me.

Si yo estuviera (estuviese) en su lugar, iría a hablar con esos señores.
If I were in your place (*but I'm not*), I would go to talk with those gentlemen.

Si yo lo hubiera (hubiese) sabido antes, les habría escrito.
If I had known it before (*but I didn't*), I would have written to them.

Si ellos vinieran (viniesen) mañana, lo harían.
If they should (were to) come tomorrow, they would do it.

Continúan charlando como si no tuviesen (tuvieran) nada que hacer.
They continue chatting as if they had nothing to do.

To express something that is contrary to fact (*i.e.,* not true) at the *present* time (first two examples), or something that was contrary to fact in the past (third example), Spanish uses either form of the imperfect or pluperfect subjunctive respectively. The result or main clause is usually expressed by the conditional (or conditional perfect), as in English. (In reading you will also find the **-ra** form of the imperfect subjunctive in the result clause, but not in this text.) **Como si** also expresses a contrary-to-fact condition (last example).

Likewise, either form of the imperfect subjunctive is used in the **si**-clause to express something that is not expected to happen, but which *might* happen in the future (fourth) example). Whenever the English sentence has *should, were to,* in the *if*-clause, the imperfect subjunctive is used in Spanish.

The future indicative, the conditional, and the present subjunctive tenses are not used after **si** meaning *if* in conditional sentences. Also see page 233, section E, Note.

C. Special use of plural reflexive pronouns

Se miraron sorprendidos.   They looked at each other surprised.
Nos vemos mañana.   We'll be seeing one another (each other) tomorrow.

The plural forms of the reflexive pronouns **(nos, os, se)** may be used with verbs to translate *each other, one another.*

D. Forms of **enviar,** *to send;* **continuar,** *to continue*

Pres. Ind.	**envío, envías, envía,** enviamos, enviáis, **envían**
Pres. Subj.	**envíe, envíes, envíe,** enviemos, enviéis, **envíen**
Sing. Imper.	**envía**

Pres. Ind.	**continúo, continúas, continúa,** continuamos, continuáis, **continúan**
Pres. Subj.	**continúe, continúes, continúe,** continuemos, continuéis, **continúen**
Sing. Imper.	**continúa**

A few verbs ending in **-iar** and **-uar** require an accent mark on the final stem vowels **i** and **u** in the singular and third person plural of the present indicative tense, in the same forms of the present subjunctive, and in the singular familiar command. All other forms are regular.

E. Summary of uses of **para**

Para and **por** are not interchangeable, even though both often mean *for.*

Para is used:

1. To express the purpose, the use, the person, or the destination for which something is intended:

Él trajo los boletos para el partido.   He brought the tickets for the game.

Los muebles son para la sala.　The furniture is for the living room.
La carta es para mí.　The letter is for me.
Ellos partieron para México.　They left for Mexico.

2. To express a point or farthest limit of time in the future, often meaning *by:*

La lección es para mañana.　The lesson is for tomorrow.
Estén Uds. aquí para las seis.　Be here by six o'clock.

3. With an infinitive to express purpose, meaning *to, in order to:*

Pueden hacer mucho para mejorar las relaciones entre nuestros dos países.　They can do much (in order) to improve relations between our two countries.

4. To express *for* in comparisons which are understood:

Para norteamericano, Ud. habla muy bien el español.
For a North American, you speak Spanish very well.

F. Summary of uses of **por**

Por is used:

1. To express *for* in the sense of *because of, on account of, for the sake of, in behalf of, in exchange for,* as:

Por eso te llamé.　Because of that (Therefore), I called you.
Ella lo ha hecho por mí.　She has done it for me (for my sake).
Podría uno tomarlo por mexicano.　One could take him for (as) a Mexican.
Él lo vendió por cinco dólares.　He sold it for five dollars.
¡Por Dios!　For heaven's sake!
por ejemplo　for example

2. To express the space of time during which an action continues, *for, during:*

Beatriz estudia por la noche.　Beatrice studies in (during) the evening.
Miguel estuvo allí por tres días.　Michael was there for three days.

3. To express the place *through, along,* or *around* which motion takes place:

Pensamos viajar por México.　We intend to travel through Mexico.
por aquí　this way, around here

4. To express the agent by which something is done, *by:*

El edificio fue construido por una compañía de ingenieros.   The building was built by a company of engineers.
Luis me llamó por teléfono.   Louis called me by telephone.
Yo la envié por correo aéreo.   I sent it (by) air mail.

5. To express *for* (the object of an errand or search) after verbs such as **ir, mandar, enviar, venir, preguntar:**

He enviado (venido) por Ud.   I have sent (come) for you.
Ellos preguntaban por él.   They were asking for (about) him.

6. To form certain idiomatic expressions:

por ahora for now (the present)	**por fin** finally, at last
por eso therefore, because of that	**por lo menos** at least
por favor please	**¡por supuesto!** of course! certainly!

EJERCICIOS

A. Say after your teacher; then make negative formal and negative familiar singular commands:

MODEL: Juan se cae. *Juan se cae. Juan, no se caiga Ud. Juan, no te caigas.*

1. Tomás se olvida de llamar.
2. Ricardo se levanta ahora.
3. Marta se pone nerviosa.
4. Elena se da prisa.
5. Enrique se sienta a la derecha.
6. Isabel se hace daño.
7. Pablo se va temprano.
8. Carlos se viste despacio.

B. Say after your teacher; then make each familiar plural command negative:

MODEL: Buscad a vuestra tía. *Buscad a vuestra tía. No busquéis a vuestra tía.*

1. Id por vuestra hermana.
2. Enviad por vuestro coche.
3. Hacedlo como dice Marta.
4. Sentaos aquí cerca de mí.
5. Poneos los guantes ahora.
6. Daos prisa, por favor.
7. Vestíos ahora mismo.
8. Dormíos antes que vuelva ella.

C. Say these sentences after your teacher, and explain briefly the differences in meaning in each series:

1. Si yo veo a Tomás en la calle, hablo con él.
    Si yo viera a Tomás en la calle, hablaría con él.

Si yo hubiera visto a Tomás en la calle, habría hablado con él.
2. Si ellos tienen tiempo, vendrán a vernos.
   Si ellos tuviesen tiempo, vendrían a vernos.
   Si ellos hubiesen tenido tiempo, habrían venido a vernos.
3. Si Luis va a México, verá muchas cosas interesantes.
   Si Luis fuera a México, vería muchas cosas interesantes.
   Si Luis hubiera ido a México, habría visto muchas cosas interesantes.

Your teacher may repeat the first sentence in each series, then follow with the two **si-**clauses and ask you to complete the sentences.

D. Say after your teacher; then repeat, substituting the **-ra** form of the imperfect subjunctive for the present indicative tense in the **si-**clause, and the conditional for the future tense in the main clause:

1. Si Carlos está en su cuarto, escribirá la carta.
2. Si ellos se dan prisa, no perderán el autobús.
3. Si Marta no puede salir, me lo dirá.
4. Beatriz vendrá a verte si la llamas por teléfono.
5. Felipe no tendrá frío si se pone el abrigo.
6. Si él va a México, me enviará varias tarjetas.
7. Si suena el despertador, Juan se despertará.
8. Si él escribe la composición, irá al cine.
9. Si Luis trae el dinero, se lo dará a Miguel.
10. Si Juan compra el regalo, se lo enviará a su novia.

Say sentences 6–10 again after your teacher; then compose new sentences substituting the **-ra** form of the pluperfect subjunctive in the **si-**clause and the conditional perfect for the future tense in the main clause.

E. Give in Spanish, using both the **-ra** and the **-se** forms of the imperfect subjunctive when that tense is required:

1. If Richard is in Mexico, he will send me a card. 2. If Richard were in Mexico, he would send me a card. 3. If Richard had been in Mexico, he would have sent me a card. 4. If the boys come tonight, they will bring us the tickets. 5. If the boys should come tonight, they would bring us the tickets. 6. If the boys had come last night, they would have brought us the tickets. 7. If Richard should spend the night with us, we would talk about the trip. 8. That young man talks as if he were from Spain.

F. Read in Spanish, supplying **para** or **por,** as required:

1. Se dice que comemos _____ vivir. 2. Mis amigos saldrán _____ México el lunes. 3. Yo quisiera darle a Ud. una carta de presentación _____ un amigo mío. 4. Ricardo compró un boleto _____ el sábado. 5. ¿Cuánto tuvo que pagar _____ el

boleto?   6. Mi madre estuvo en el centro _____ tres horas.   7. ¿Comprará Ud. algunas flores _____ su amiga?   8. Juan vendrá _____ mí al mediodía.   9. Cuando conocí a Carlos Molina, lo tomé _____ argentino.   10. Ellos tomaron un autobús _____ ir a casa de Vicente.   11. Carlos no se despertó; _____ eso perdió el autobús.   12. Tenemos que estar en casa _____ las seis.   13. Clara hizo este vestido _____ ti (*i.e., for your use*).   14. Carolina es muy alta _____ una muchacha de quince años.   15. ¿No sabe Ud. _____ qué sirven los amigos?   16. Nuestra casa fue construida _____ un amigo nuestro.   17. Será mejor enviar esta carta _____ correo aéreo.   18. Mis padres piensan viajar _____ Suramérica.   19. Mil gracias _____ cuanto has hecho.   20. _____ norteamericanos, ellos conocen muchas costumbres mexicanas.

G. Say after your teacher; then compose a new sentence, using **nos** or **se,** following the models:

MODELS: Ricardo vio a Tomás anoche.   *Ricardo vio a Tomás anoche.*
                                                  Ricardo y Tomás se vieron anoche.
          Yo veo a Tomás a menudo.   *Yo veo a Tomás a menudo.*
                                                  Tomás y yo nos vemos a menudo.

1. Ud. entiende bien al señor Díaz.   4. Yo le escribo a Luis de vez en cuando.
2. Elena mira a Carlos a menudo.   5. Ana encontró a María en el centro.
3. ¿Veían Uds. a Pablo todos los días?   6. ¿Envía él muchas cartas a Juanita?

H. Give the Spanish equivalent, using the familiar forms for the verbs in sentences 2, 3, 7:

1. Richard and Michael do not show [any] signs of life when the alarm clock sounds.
2. Louis awakens them, saying: "Get up, sleepyheads! Shave and get dressed at once!
3. Don't forget that Richard has to (must) be at Mr. Ortiz's office at nine o'clock."
4. Richard says that he would be the happiest man in the world if he could sleep until noon.   5. Finally the two young men go downstairs to the dining room and they begin to eat breakfast slowly, chatting as if they had nothing to do.   6. When Louis tells them that they will miss the bus if they don't hurry, they look at each other surprised. 7. Then he continues: "Get going, boys! Don't delay [any] longer! Put on your topcoats, because it is very cool this morning."   8. Mr. Ortiz had sent for Richard in order to give him some letters of introduction.   9. The letters were for some friends of his—engineers, lawyers, and merchants—who lived in Mexico City.   10. He says that if he were in Richard's place, he would present them to those gentlemen as soon as he arrived.   11. Richard is very grateful to Mr. Ortiz for all that he has done for him, and he says to him: "Many thanks for everything."   12. The latter answers: "You are welcome. Good luck to you (May you have much luck)! Don't fail to send me a card from time to time."

I. **Composición**

Write a short composition in Spanish on one of the following topics:

1. Mi familia
2. Una experiencia importante
3. Mis próximas vacaciones de verano
4. Mis deseos por saber español
5. Mi primer año en la universidad

VOCABULARIO

el **abogado**   lawyer
el **abrigo**   topcoat, overcoat
   afeitarse   to shave (oneself)
   apenas   *conj.* hardly, scarcely
   bostezar   to yawn
   colaborar   to collaborate
el **comerciante**   merchant, tradesman, businessman
   como si   as if
   continuar   to continue
   cordialmente   cordially
   cuanto   all that
   dentro de   *prep.* within
   desperezarse   to stretch (one's arms and legs)
el **despertador**   alarm clock
la **disposición**   (*pl.* **disposiciones**) disposition, service
el **dormilón** (*pl.* **dormilones**)   sleepyhead
   emplear   to employ, use
   enviar   to send

la **estancia**   stay
   estrechar   to tighten, bring closer together
   feliz (*pl.* **felices**)   happy
la **forma**   form
   ¡hala!   come on! get going! hurry up!
el **ingeniero**   engineer
la **labor**   work, labor
el **lugar**   place
   mejorar   to better, improve
   Miguel   Michael, Mike
   olvidarse (**de** + *obj.*)   to forget
   peninsular   peninsular (*of Spain*)
   perder (ie)   to lose, miss
la **prisa**   haste
el **pueblo**   people, nation
el **refrán** (*pl.* **refranes**)   proverb
la **relación** (*pl.* **relaciones**)   relation
la **señal**   sign
   vestir (i, i)   to dress; *reflex.* to dress (oneself), get dressed

a su disposición   at your service
carta de presentación   letter of introduction
dar señales de   to show signs of
darse prisa   to hurry up
estrechar las relaciones   to establish closer relations
(no) tener (nada) que (hacer)   to have (nothing) to (do), (not) to have (anything) to (do)
¿para qué sirven los amigos?   what are friends (good) for?
por eso   therefore, because of that
¡que tenga mucha suerte!   good luck (may you have much luck)!
tocar a (uno) (*used like* **gustar**)   to be (one's) turn

Virgen con el Niño,
imagen española del siglo XIII.

La Pintura Española

LA TRINIDAD ADORADA POR TODOS LOS SANTOS
Retablo, pintado al temple, en madera, por un
pintor valenciano anónimo de la primera mitad del
siglo XV
Cortesía, The Metropolitan Museum of Art, New York

SÁNCHEZ COELLO

A la izquierda:
RETRATO DE FELIPE II
Cortesía, Museo del Prado, Madrid

Debajo, a la izquierda:
RETRATO DE LA PRINCESA DE ÉBOLI
Cortesía, Museo del Prado, Madrid

Debajo, a la derecha:
Anónimo (hacia 1475).
RETRATO DE UN MENDOZA, (Sin duda, el
primer duque del Infantado.)
Cortesía, Museo del Prado, Madrid

EL GRECO

EL ENTIERRO DEL CONDE DE ORGAZ
Cortesía, Iglesia de Santo Tomé, Toledo
Fotografía de Mas

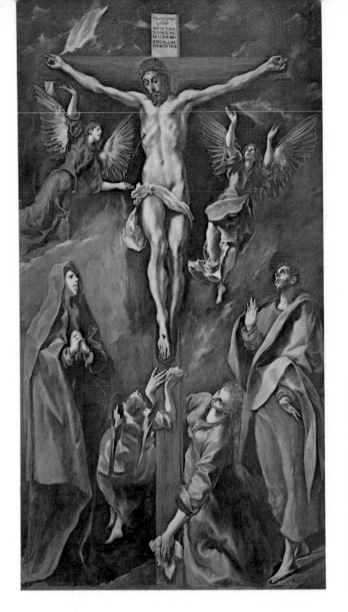

EL GRECO

Arriba:
LA CRUCIFIXIÓN
Cortesía, Museo del Prado, Madrid

A la derecha:
JULIÁN ROMERO DE LAS AZAÑAS
Cortesía, Museo del Prado, Madrid

EL GRECO

VISTA DE TOLEDO
Cortesía, The Metropolitan Museum of Art, New York

Lectura 13

Las artes españolas

No solamente la literatura sino todas las artes han florecido en España: la pintura, la música, el baile, la arquitectura, la escultura y las artes manuales. En las páginas siguientes se harán algunas observaciones sobre la pintura en España, especialmente a partir del siglo XV, y se dedicarán algunos párrafos a la música en la época moderna.

En la Edad Media las manifestaciones más notables del arte de pintar son la pintura sobre pergamino,[1] en las miniaturas con que se adornaban los libros, y la pintura sobre vidrio,[2] que produjo las magníficas vidrieras de colores[3] de los siglos XIII, XIV y XV. En el siglo XIII las pinturas murales son frecuentes y en el siglo siguiente se desarrolla la pintura sobre tabla,[4] especialmente en los retablos[5] e imágenes de las iglesias.

En el desarrollo de la pintura española en aquella época, se observan dos influencias importantes: la italiana y la flamenca.[6] Como los catalanes y los aragoneses tenían relaciones políticas muy estrechas con Italia y el comercio del norte de España con Flandes era muy activo, los artistas españoles iban a aquellos países a estudiar y los flamencos y los italianos venían a España a trabajar. Gracias a este intercambio llegaban a España las ideas y métodos de afuera. Sin embargo,[7] el espíritu nacional era tan fuerte que en general el arte de los españoles nunca se sometió mucho a las influencias extranjeras.

Ejemplo de la pintura en tabla, típica de aquella época, es el hermoso retablo, «La Trinidad adorada por todos los santos»,[8] pintado al temple[9] por un pintor valenciano anónimo de la primera parte de siglo XV.

En la segunda mitad del siglo XVI Alonso Sánchez Coello (1531-1588), discípulo del holandés Antonio Moro, crea el tipo del nuevo retrato cortesano,[10] como en los retratos de Felipe II y de la princesa de Éboli. Para apreciar la maestría de Coello en el arte del retrato es interesante comparar estas obras con la de un pintor anónimo del siglo anterior, el «Retrato de un Mendoza» (sin duda, el primer duque del Infantado[11]), pintado hacia 1475.

---

[1]**pergamino,** *parchment.* [2]**vidrio,** *glass.* [3]**vidrieras de colores,** *stained-glass windows.* [4]**tabla,** *board, wood.* [5]**retablos,** *altarpieces.* [6]**flamenca,** *Flemish.* [7]**Sin embargo,** *Nevertheless.* [8]For this painting and others mentioned in this Lectura, see art section between pages 368-369. [9]**al temple,** *in distemper (tempera).* [10]**cortesano,** *courtly.* [11]This noble title, one of the most distinguished in Spanish history, was created by Ferdinand and Isabella in 1475.

El Greco, retrato de un hombre que se supone es el pintor.

1665), presentó en sus lienzos[14] todos los aspectos de la vida y la sociedad de su tiempo, todo ello con una claridad y una precisión no conocidas antes. Para ver las obras maestras de Velázquez hay que visitar el Museo del Prado en Madrid, uno de los museos más importantes de Europa. Algunas de sus mejores obras son «La Infanta[15] Margarita», «La Reina Isabel de Borbón a caballo» (primera mujer de Felipe IV), «Las hilanderas»,[16] y «Las meninas».[17]

"Los Borrachos", Diego Velázquez

El primer gran pintor del Siglo de Oro fue El Greco (¿1548?-1614). Desde la isla de Creta, donde nació, fue a Venecia, como tantos otros artistas, para estudiar con los maestros italianos. Hacia el año 1577 llegó a Toledo, no lejos de Madrid, donde desarrolló y perfeccionó su arte, llegando a ser uno de los pintores más originales e individualistas del mundo. Gran parte de su obra artística consta de una larga serie de retratos y cuadros religiosos, en que demuestra su sentido místico y su maestría en el uso del colorido. Su obra maestra, «El entierro[12] del Conde de Orgaz», que encierra muchos aspectos del alma española, fue pintada para la pequeña iglesia de Santo Tomé de Toledo, donde puede admirarse hoy día. Otro aspecto importante del arte de El Greco es su interés por el paisaje de Toledo. La gran composición en que aparece la ciudad bajo un cielo tormentoso[13] se considera como el paisaje español más impresionante que se ha producido hasta la actualidad.

Diego Velázquez (1599–1660), de Sevilla, tiene el honor de ser el genio más ilustre de la pintura de su época. Gran realista, este pintor de la corte del rey Felipe IV (1621-

En el cuadro «Las meninas», considerado por muchos como la obra maestra de Velázquez, vemos a la infanta Margarita rodeada de su corte de meninas y enanos.[18] Detrás de ellos aparecen una dueña[19] y un cortesano,[20] y al lado de ellos se halla el pintor mismo,[21] ocupado en dibujar al rey y a la reina, quienes se supone están parados donde se halla el espectador y se reflejan en un espejo que está en la pared del fondo.

Realista también fue José de Ribera (1591–1652), que muy joven pasó a Italia para perfeccionar su arte. El dominio de los

---

[12]**entierro,** *burial.*   [13]**tormentoso,** *stormy.*   [14]**lienzos,** *canvases.*   [15]**Infanta,** *Princess.*   [16]**hilanderas,** *Spinning Girls.*
[17]**meninas,** *Little Ladies in Waiting.*   [18]**enanos,** *dwarfs.*   [19]**dueña,** *chaperone.*   [20]**cortesano,** *courtier.*
[21]**el pintor mismo,** *the painter himself.*

efectos de luz, forma y color, el naturalismo y la nota dramática y apasionada caracterizan la obra de este gran pintor, que halló su inspiración en los motivos[22] religiosos.

La fusión del realismo con el idealismo espiritual se realiza en Francisco de Zurbarán (1598-1664) y en Bartolomé Esteban Murillo (1618-1682). Continuaron con éxito las excelencias del arte naturalista de Ribera, pero se distinguen de éste por su manera de serenar y simplificar la realidad. Zurbarán es considerado como el más fiel intérprete de la vida religiosa. Los dos saben producir también maravillosas figuras femeninas, en que realzan[23] la belleza y elegancia de la mujer andaluza.

"Naturaleza muerta con objectos de metal", Zurbarán

A fines del siglo XVIII aparecieron las primeras obras de Francisco de Goya (1746-1828), uno de los pintores más originales del mundo moderno. Aunque de familia humilde, Goya llegó a ser el pintor de la corte de Carlos IV y de Fernando VII. Produjo una gran cantidad de retratos de las dos familias reales, pintados con un realismo y una franqueza que asombran.[24] En su extensa y variada obra vemos, en realidad, toda la historia de su

época. Al lado de los cuadros que representan claramente la brutalidad de la guerra de la independencia, después de la invasión de Napoleón en 1808, hay una larga serie de cartones[25] o modelos para tapices,[26] en que pinta escenas y tipos del pueblo, fiestas, bailes populares y otros aspectos de la vida diaria de la época. Por su realismo, su maestría en la técnica, su espontaneidad, su espíritu crítico, su individualismo y su conocimiento de la época en que vivía, Goya es considerado como uno de los genios de la pintura moderna.

Retrato de la señora Sabasa García pintado por Goya.

Durante el período romántico la pintura española se vuelve convencional y los artistas buscan inspiración en obras extranjeras. Sin

---

[22]**motivos,** *motifs, themes.*   [23]**realzan,** *they enhance.*   [24]**asombran,** *are amazing.*   [25]**cartón:** a painting or drawing on strong paper or cardboard   [26]**tapices,** *tapestries.*

embargo, hacia fines del siglo XIX, cuando el realismo reina en la literatura y en las artes, la pintura tiene su mejor representante en el valenciano Joaquín Sorolla (1863–1923), que se ha distinguido por la luz y el colorido de sus hermosos cuadros de la vida y las costumbres de su región. Algunos de sus mejores lienzos se encuentran en el museo de la Sociedad Hispánica de Nueva York y en el Museo Metropolitano de la misma ciudad. La obra vigorosa y dramática de Ignacio Zuloaga (1870–1945), gran pintor de la España vieja y tradicional, contrasta fuertemente con la de Sorolla.

cípulo de Picasso, superó a su maestro en el estilo cubista. Juan Miró (1893–   ) es uno de los más grandes pintores de la escuela surrealista. Las obras cubistas y surrealistas del gran dibujante y colorista Salvador Dalí (1904–   ) representan el triunfo de la interpretación libre de la realidad, típica del arte actual. Antonio Tapies (1923–   ), el pintor más joven de este grupo, ha creado cuadros de intenso dramatismo.[28] Su obra, que se caracteriza por una inmensa variedad y riqueza de recursos, aspira a expresar una nueva comprensión de la angustia de nuestro tiempo.

◆ ◆ ◆

"La familia del pintor Zuloaga", Zuloaga

La influencia de los pintores españoles en el arte de nuestro tiempo es incalculable. Pablo Picasso (1881–1973), que pasó muchos años en Francia, ha sido, sin duda, el artista que ha ejercido mayor influencia sobre la pintura contemporánea. Su arte ha atravesado distintas etapas, desde su período azul y período rosa,[27] a través del cubismo, el surrealismo y las composiciones abstractas y el expresionismo.

Juan Gris (1887–1927), compañero y dis-

"El viejo guitarrista", Pablo Picasso

---

[27] **rosa,** *pink.*   [28] **dramatismo,** *dramatic effect.*

Fotografía de Pablo Picasso en su taller, al lado de una de sus obras

Puede decirse que la música siempre ha sido muy popular en España entre todas las clases sociales. Gracias a las composiciones de los grandes artistas Albéniz y Granados, la música española moderna ya es conocida en todo el mundo. Isaac Albéniz (1860–1909), notable pianista y compositor, ha dado a conocer[29] una gran variedad de ritmos, especialmente melodías andaluzas. Las escenas del

pintor Goya han servido de inspiración para *Goyescas,* seis famosas piezas para piano, compuestas por Enrique Granados (1867–1916).

Según muchos músicos, Manuel de Falla (1876–1946) es el mejor compositor español moderno. Natural de Andalucía, compuso las encantadoras melodías llamadas *Noches en los jardines de España.* Se oye mucho en los Estados Unidos su *Danza del fuego,*[30] del famoso ballet *El amor brujo.*[31] Para conocer la pasión, la fuerza y la gran variedad de la música española, uno debe escuchar la música de Manuel de Falla.

Manuel de Falla y Matheu, pintado por López Mezquita

---

[29] **ha dado a conocer,** *has made known.*   [30] **Danza del fuego,** *Fire Dance.*   [31] **El amor brujo,** *Wedded by Witchcraft.*

Otras grandes figuras españolas del mundo musical contemporáneo son Pablo Casals (1876–1973), célebre violoncelista, Andrés Segovia, guitarrista sin igual, y José Iturbi, eminente pianista, compositor y director de orquesta.

Gracias a *la Argentina,* célebre intérprete del baile español en la primera parte del siglo actual, conocemos mejor no sólo el antiguo arte del baile español, sino también la música de Albéniz, Granados, Falla y otros compositores.

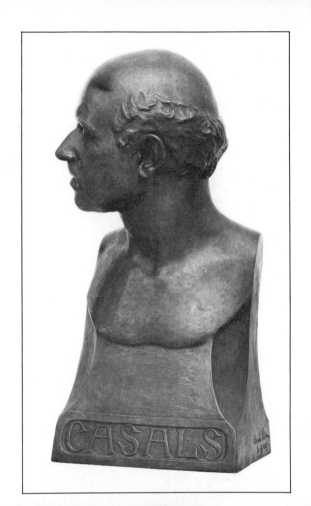

De izquierda a derecha aparecen, La Argentina, escultura de Paul Troubetzkoy (1866–1938), Pablo Casals, escultura de Brenda Putnam (1890–   ) y Andrés Segovia, en una fotografía tomada en su casa.

Preguntas

1. ¿Qué artes han florecido en España?   2. ¿Qué tipo de pintura se desarrolla en el siglo XIV?   3. ¿Qué influencias extranjeras se observan en la pintura española de aquella época? 4. ¿Puede decirse que el arte de los españoles se sometió mucho a las influencias extranjeras?

5. ¿Qué tipo de arte crea Sánchez Coello?   6. ¿Quién fue El Greco?   7. ¿Dónde estudió El Greco?   8. ¿A qué ciudad de España llegó?   9. ¿Qué clase de obras pintó?   10. ¿Cuál es su obra maestra?

11. ¿Quién fue el genio más ilustre de la pintura del Siglo de Oro?   12. ¿Qué presentó en sus lienzos?   13. ¿Dónde se encuentran sus obras maestras?   14. ¿Cuáles son algunas de sus mejores obras?   15. ¿Quiénes rodean a la infanta Margarita en «Las meninas»?

16. ¿Qué rasgos caracterizan la pintura de Ribera?   17. ¿Qué se realiza en el arte de Zurbarán y de Murillo?   18. ¿Qué puede decirse de sus figuras femeninas?

19. ¿Cuándo aparecieron las primeras obras de Francisco de Goya?   20. ¿Qué llegó a ser? 21. ¿Qué vemos en su extensa y variada obra?   22. ¿Cuándo reinó el realismo en la literatura y en las artes?   23. ¿Quién es el mejor representante del realismo en la pintura? 24. ¿Dónde se encuentran algunos de sus mejores lienzos?   25. ¿Qué pintor contemporáneo buscó inspiración en la España vieja y tradicional?

26. ¿Qué etapas pueden señalarse en el arte de Picasso?   27. ¿Supera Picasso a Juan Gris en el estilo cubista?   28. ¿Qué escuela representa Juan Miró?   29. ¿Qué representan las obras de Salvador Dalí?   30. ¿Qué aspira a expresar la obra de Antonio Tapies?

31. ¿Quién fue Albéniz?   32. ¿Quiénes son otros compositores modernos?   33. ¿Cuáles son algunas de las obras de Falla?   34. ¿Quién fue Pablo Casals?   35. ¿Quiénes son otras grandes figuras del mundo musical contemporáneo?   36. ¿Quién ha sido la intérprete más célebre del baile español?

Estudio de palabras

1. Less approximate cognates. Pronounce the following words aloud, note the English cognates, and describe the variations: anónimo, *anonymous;* detalle, *detail;* discípulo, *disciple, pupil;* escena, *scene;* espontaneidad, *spontaneity;* melodía, *melody;* método, *method;* místico, *mystic;* perfeccionar, *to perfect;* simplificar, *to simplify.*

2. *Compare the meanings of:* color, *color,* colorido, *coloring,* and colorista, *colorist;* componer, *to compose,* composición, *composition,* and compositor, *composer;* dibujar, *to draw, paint,* dibujo, *drawing,* and dibujante, *draftsman;* drama, *drama,* dramático, *dramatic,* and dramatismo, *dramatic effect;* flor, *flower,* and florecer, *to flourish;* fuerte, *strong,* fuertemente, *strongly,* and fuerza, *strength;* interpretar, *to interpret,* intérprete, *interpreter,* and interpretación, *interpretation;* música, *music,* músico, *musician,* and musical, *musical;* pintor, *painter,* pintar, *to paint, and* pintura, *painting;* rey, *king,* reina, *queen,* reinar, *to reign,* and reinado, *reign;* varios, *various, several,* variado, *varied,* and variedad, *variety;* vidrio, *glass,* and vidriera, *glass window.*

3. Deceptive cognates. Note the following: **actual,** *present, present-day;* **la actualidad,** *present time;* **realizarse,** *to be carried out;* **el representante,** *representative* (*noun*); **el sentido,** *sense, feeling,* and, also, *meaning;* **la tabla,** *board,* as well as *table* (= *list, contents*).

REPASO 5

A. Answer in Spanish, following the models:

MODEL: ¿Quiere Ud. ese sombrero?   *No, quiero el que Ud. tiene.*

1. ¿Quiere Ud. esos guantes?
2. ¿Le gusta a Ud. esa blusa?
3. ¿Vas a comprar esas camisas?
4. ¿Te gusta ese abrigo?

MODEL: ¿Llegó ese joven ayer?   *Sí, es el que llegó ayer.*

5. ¿Vino esa joven anoche?
6. ¿Vinieron esas muchachas ayer?
7. ¿Llamó ese señor por teléfono?
8. ¿Enviaron esos jóvenes las flores?

B. Say after your teacher; then repeat, using a possessive pronoun for the noun or prepositional phrase:

MODELS: Tengo la maleta de Juan.   *Tengo la maleta de Juan. Tengo la suya.*
Nuestro coche es viejo.   *Nuestro coche es viejo. El nuestro es viejo.*

1. No examine Ud. la maleta.
2. Yo traigo el equipaje de Marta.
3. Póngase Ud. el abrigo.
4. Deja tú aquí nuestras flores.
5. Fui por mi boleto.
6. Mis amigos me felicitaban.
7. Dame tú tus paquetes.
8. El jardín de mi mamá es bonito.

C. Listen to the question; then reply affirmatively, using the correct possessive pronoun:

MODEL: ¿Es de Ud. este reloj?   *Sí, es mío.*

1. ¿Es de Ud. este abrigo?
2. ¿Es de ellos este coche?
3. ¿Es tuya esa blusa?
4. ¿Es mía esta pulsera?
5. ¿Son de Ramón estas corbatas?
6. ¿Son de ella estas maletas?
7. ¿Son nuestros esos muebles?
8. ¿Son de Uds. esas cartas?

D. Say after your teacher; then repeat, using the passive voice and making the past participle agree with the subject of the verb:

MODEL: Juan escribió la tarjeta.   *La tarjeta fue escrita por Juan.*

1. Ana hizo el vestido blanco.
2. Nuestro profesor de español recomendó a Marta para el puesto.
3. Elena pagó las cuentas.
4. Una compañía extranjera construyó los parques.
5. Tomás tradujo las cartas al inglés.
6. La agencia compró todos los boletos.

E. Repeat the sentence; when you hear the cue, compose a new sentence:

MODEL: Yo hablé con él cuando lo vi.   *Yo hablé con él cuando lo vi.*
             Yo hablaré con él.   *Yo hablaré con él cuando lo vea.*

1. Ellos volvieron a casa en cuanto yo los llamé.   (Ellos volverán a casa)
2. Nosotros tuvimos que salir aunque llovía.   (Nosotros tendremos que salir)
3. Yo hablaba despacio de modo que ellos me entendían.   (Yo hablaré despacio)
4. Nos quedamos en casa hasta que llegaron ellos.   (Nos quedaremos en casa)
5. Yo le pagué a él cuando me trajo el paquete.   (Yo le pagaré a él)
6. Juan no pudo irse aunque consiguió el puesto.   (Juan no podrá irse)
7. Ella y yo fuimos a verlos en cuanto fue posible.   (Ella y yo iremos a verlos)
8. Yo charlaba con ellas cuando estaban aquí.   (Yo charlaré con ellas)

F. Listen carefully to the sentence; then compose a conditional sentence. Use the **-ra** imperfect subjunctive in the first three sentences, and the **-se** form in the last three:

MODEL: Juan escribiría la carta,   *Si Juan estuviera aquí, escri-*
            pero no está aquí.   *biría la carta.*

1. Ellos irían al parque hoy, pero no tienen tiempo.
2. Carolina les daría el paquete, pero no los ve.
3. Nosotros saldríamos con Uds., pero no estamos listos.
4. Yo compraría la maleta, pero no voy a hacer el viaje.
5. Ana podría llegar a tiempo, pero no se da prisa.
6. Me gustaría ir al cine, pero la película no es buena.

G. Read in Spanish, supplying the correct form of the infinitive in parentheses:

1. Mi hermanito corría como si (tener) miedo.
2. ¡Ojalá que ellos (haber) llegado a tiempo anoche!
3. Los padres de él buscan un apartamento que (ser) más grande.
4. Yo no conozco a nadie que (construir) casas tan bien como el Sr. Smith.
5. No había nadie que (querer) jugar a las cartas.
6. Déjame el coche, por favor, para que yo lo (usar) esta tarde.
7. Juan dijo que se iría mañana aunque (hacer) mucho frío.
8. Yo insistí en que los dos (seguir) andando por el parque.
9. Mi hermana no pudo hallar ninguna cartera que le (gustar).
10. Ellos me llamaron en cuanto (volver) a casa.
11. Aunque (llover) mucho anoche, fuimos al cine.
12. Aunque ellas (vestirse) pronto, van a perder el autobús.
13. Les aconsejé a ellos que (tener) cuidado.
14. Diles a las niñas que (ponerse) los zapatos.
15. No creo que Eduardo (olvidarse) del asunto.
16. ¿Duda Ud. que Elena (haber) oído decir eso?
17. Yo sentía mucho que las muchachas no (haber) limpiado su habitación.

18. ¿Fue preciso que ellas (volver) a la universidad?
19. Será mejor que Carlos (buscar) un regalo para su novia esta tarde.
20. ¿Se alegra Ud. de que ésta (ser) la última lección del libro?

H. Listen carefully to each sentence; then answer, with a complete sentence, the question based on it:

1. Roberto partió ayer y fue a México.
   ¿Para dónde partió Roberto?
2. El señor Gómez escribió una carta de presentación.
   ¿Por quién fue escrita la carta de presentación?
3. Vicente le vendió un libro a Luis y éste le pagó cinco dólares por él.
   ¿Cuánto le pagó Luis a Vicente por el libro?
4. Ricardo estuvo aquí por tres días antes de salir para California.
   ¿Por cuántos días estuvo aquí Ricardo?
5. Los jóvenes tomaron un autobús para ir a casa de Margarita.
   ¿Qué tomaron los jóvenes para ir a casa de Margarita?
6. Yo tengo un regalo y se lo voy a dar a Eduardo.
   ¿Para quién es el regalo?
7. Ramón y Luis pasaron por la casa de Tomás para hablar con él.
   ¿Para qué pasaron los dos por la casa de Tomás?
8. Como llegaron tarde al aeropuerto, tuvieron que darse prisa para subir al avión.
   ¿Por qué tuvieron que darse prisa para subir al avión?

I. Give in Spanish:

1. At your service.   2. Tell them (*formal and fam. sing.*) to be careful.   3. Don't fail (*fam. sing.*) to write to me.   4. We have to hurry.   5. Jane has blond hair.   6. Paul has nothing to do.   7. What are friends good for?   8. Send (*pl.*) her a card today.   9. Get dressed at once (*formal and fam. sing.*).   10. Let's sit down near the window.   11. Let's not eat breakfast yet.   12. Henry forgot to reserve a seat.   13. He bought a round-trip ticket.   14. Perhaps Ann may not come. I doubt it.   15. Jane's little brother hurt himself.   16. Mike's mother became very ill.

J. Answer in Spanish using complete sentences:

1. Cuando Ud. tiene que hacer un viaje largo, ¿prefiere hacerlo en coche o en avión?   2. Si Ud. tuviera dinero, ¿qué país hispanoamericano le gustaría visitar?   3. ¿Qué les enviamos a nuestros amigos cuando viajamos?   4. ¿Qué les decimos a los amigos cuando nos despedimos de ellos?   5. ¿Dónde conseguimos informes acerca de los viajes en avión?   6. ¿Qué les pedimos a los amigos cuando buscamos un puesto?

7. ¿Hay mucho tránsito en la calle en que vive Ud.?   8. ¿Cuándo fue construida la casa en que viven sus padres?   9. ¿Es su casa más grande o más pequeña que las otras de la misma calle?   10. ¿Cuántas habitaciones tiene su casa en el piso bajo?

11. ¿Qué hacemos cuando creemos que no vamos a llegar a tiempo a algún sitio?

12. ¿A quién llamamos cuando una persona está muy enferma? 13. ¿Adónde llevamos los trajes y los vestidos para hacerlos limpiar? 14. ¿Se levanta Ud. temprano los domingos? 15. ¿Qué hizo Ud. ayer después de almorzar?

16. ¿Juega Ud. a menudo a las cartas? 17. ¿Con quiénes juega Ud. a las cartas? 18. ¿Cómo termina el refrán que comienza, «Lo que no se empieza...»? 19. ¿Qué otros refranes españoles sabe Ud.? 20. ¿Cuánto tiempo hace que estudia Ud. español?

Cartas españolas

In the following pages will be given some of the essential principles for personal and business letters in Spanish. Even though many formulas used in Spanish letters are less formal and flowery than formerly, in general they are still less brief and direct than in English letters, and at times they may seem rather stilted. There is no attempt to give a complete treatment of Spanish correspondence, but careful study of the material included should serve for ordinary purposes.

The new words and expressions whose English equivalents are given throughout this section are not included in the Spanish-English vocabulary, unless used elsewhere in the text.

A. Professional titles

Professional titles are more widely used in the Spanish-speaking countries than in the United States. Three masculine titles are:

Doctor (Dr.)   Doctor
Licenciado (Lic.)   Licentiate (lawyer, or person who has a permit to practice a profession)
Ingeniero (Ing.)   Engineer

Normally these professional titles are accompanied by **señor / señora** (abbreviated **Sr. / Sra.**) and followed by **don / doña** (abbreviated **D. / Dª.**):

Dr. D. Carlos Estrada   **Lic. D. Ramón Gómez**

B. Address on the envelope

The title of the addressee begins with **señor (Sr.) señora (Sra.),** or **señorita (Srta.).** **Sr. don (Sr. D.)** may be used for a man, **Sra. doña (Sra. Dª.)** for a married woman, and **Srta.** for an unmarried woman:

Señor don Carlos Morelos   **Sr. D. Pedro Ortega y Moreno**
Srta. Carmen Alcalá   **Sra. Dª. María López de Martín**

In the third example note that Spanish surnames often include the name of the father **(Ortega),** followed by that of the mother **(Moreno).**[1] Often the mother's name is dropped (first two examples). A woman's married name is her maiden name followed by **de** and the surname of her husband (fourth example).

The definite article is not used with the titles **don** and **doña,** which have no English equivalents.

Two complete addresses follow:

Sr. D. Luis Montoya   **Srta. Elena Pérez**
Calle de San Martín, 25   **Avenida Bolívar, 245**
Santiago, Chile   **Caracas, Venezuela**

Business letters are addressed to a firm:

Suárez Hermanos (Hnos.)   **Señores (Sres.) López Díaz y Cía., S. A.**
Apartado (Postal) 867   **Paseo de la Reforma, 12**
Buenos Aires, Argentina   **México, D. F., México**

---

[1]The conjunction **y** is often not used between the surnames; the person named might prefer to be known as **D. Pedro Ortega Moreno.**

In an address in Spanish one writes first **Calle** (**Avenida,** *Avenue;* **Paseo,** *Boulevard;* **Camino,** *Road;* **Plaza,** *Square*), then the house number. **Apartado (Postal),** *Post Office Box,* may be abbreviated to **Apdo. (Postal).** The abbreviation **Cía. = Compañía; S. A. = Sociedad Anónima,** equivalent to English *Inc.* (*Incorporated*); and **D. F. = Distrito Federal,** *Federal District.*

Air mail letters are marked **Vía aérea, Correo aéreo,** or **Por avión.** Special delivery letters are marked **Urgente,** or **Entrega inmediata,** and registered letters, **Certificada.**

C. Heading of the letter

The usual form of the date line is:

México, D. F., 27 de enero de 1979

The month is usually not capitalized unless it is given first in the date. For the first day of the month 1° **(primero)** is commonly used; the other days are written 2, 3, 4, etc. Other less common forms for the date line are:

Lima, junio 15 de 1968
Bogotá, 1° agosto 1977

The address which precedes the salutation of the business and formal social letter is the same as that on the envelope. In familiar letters only the salutation need be used.

D. Salutations and conclusions for familiar letters

Forms used in addressing relatives or close friends are:

Querido hermano:	**Querida Beatriz:**
(Mi) Querida amiga:	**(Mi) Querida hija:**
Querido Luis:	**Queridísima**[1] **mamá:**

In conclusions of familiar letters a great variety of formulas may be used. Some commonly used endings for letters in the family are:

(Un abrazo de) tu hijo, (*one boy signs*)
Tu hijo (hija), que te quiere,[2] (*one boy or girl signs*)
Con todo el cariño[3] **de tu hermano (hermana),** (*one boy or girl signs*)
Con todo el amor[4] **(cariño) de tu hijo (hija),** (*one boy or girl signs*)
Recibe todo mi cariño (amor), (*one boy or girl signs*)

---

[1] **Queridísima,** *Dearest.*   [2] When **querer** has a personal object, it means *to love.*   [3] **cariño,** *affection.*
[4] **amor,** *love.*

For friends (also for the family) the following, with many possible variations, are suitable:

> **Un abrazo de tu (su) amiga, que te (la, lo) quiere,**
> **Tuyo (Suyo) afectísimo (afmo.),**[1] *or* **Tuya (Suya)**
>   **afectísima (afma.),**
> **Cariñosos saludos**[2] **de tu amigo (amiga),**
> **(Con el cariño de) tu buen amigo (buena amiga),**
> **Con el cariño de siempre,**
> **Sinceramente, Cariñosamente,** *or* **Afectuosamente,**[3]

E. Salutations for business letters or those addressed to strangers

Appropriate salutations, equivalent to "My dear Sir," "Dear Sir," "Dear Madam," "Gentlemen," etc., are:

> **Muy señor (Sr.) mío:** (*from one person to one gentleman*)
> **Muy señor nuestro:** (*from a firm to one gentleman*)
> **Muy señores (Sres.) míos:** (*from one person to a firm*)
> **Muy señores nuestros:** (*from one firm to another firm*)
> **Muy señora (Sra.) mía:** (*from one person to a woman*)

Formulas which may be used in less formal letters are:

> **Muy estimado Sr. Salas:** Dear Mr. Salas:
> **Estimada amiga (Isabel):** Dear friend (Betty):
> **Mi distinguido amigo (colega):** Dear Friend (Colleague):
> **Estimado profesor:** Dear Professor:
> **Muy distinguido señor (colega):** Dear Sir (Colleague):
> **(Muy) estimado señor (colega):** Dear Sir (Colleague):
> **(Muy) apreciado señor (amigo):** Dear Sir (Friend):

F. Conclusions for informal social and business letters

Common forms equivalent to "Sincerely yours," "Cordially yours," "Affectionately yours," are:

> **Suyo afectísimo (afmo.),** *or* **Suyos afectísimos (afmos.),**
> **Queda**[4] **(Quedo) suyo afmo. (suya afma.),**
> **Lo saluda (muy) atentamente,**
> **Se despide afectuosamente tu amigo,**
> **Cordialmente,**

---

[1] **Tuyo (Suyo) afectísimo,** *Affectionately yours.*   [2] **Cariñosos saludos,** *Affectionate greetings.*
[3] **Afectuosamente,** *Affectionately, Sincerely.*   [4] **Queda** is in the third person if the signee is the subject. Also note the next example.

G. The body of business letters

The Spanish business letter usually begins with a brief sentence which indicates the purpose of the letter. A few examples, with English translations, follow. Note that the sentences cannot always be translated word for word:

Acabo (Acabamos) de recibir su carta del 10 de septiembre.
I (We) have just received your letter of September 10.

Le doy a Ud. las gracias por el pedido que se sirvió hacerme . . .
Thank you for the order which you kindly placed with me . . .

He recibido con mucho agrado su amable carta . . .
I was very glad to receive your (kind) letter . . .

Le acusamos recibo de su atenta[1] del 2 del corriente . . .
We acknowledge receipt of your letter of the 2nd (of this month) . . .

Mucho agradeceré a Ud.[2] el mandarme . . .
I shall thank you if you will send me . . .

Le envío giro postal por $3.00 . . .
I am sending you a postal money order for $3.00 . . .

Con fecha 8 del actual me permití escribir a Ud., informándole . . .
On the 8th (of this month) I took the liberty of writing to you, informing you . . .

Some proper conclusions which might accompany such salutations are:

Muy agradecidos por la buena atención que se dignará Ud. prestar a la presente, saludamos a Ud. con nuestro mayor aprecio y consideración,
Thanking you for your kind attention to this letter, we remain,
Very truly yours,

En espera de su envío y con gracias anticipadas, quedo de Ud. atto. S.S.,[3]
Awaiting the shipment and thanking you in advance, I remain,
Sincerely yours,

Aprovechamos esta ocasión para ofrecernos sus attos., y ss. ss.,
We take advantage of this opportunity to remain,
Yours truly,

Quedamos de ustedes afmos. y Ss. Ss.,
We remain,
Very truly yours,

---

[1] **Carta** is often replaced with **favor, grata, atenta.**   [2] Since **usted** is technically a noun (coming from **vuestra merced**), the indirect object pronoun **le** may be omitted before the verb. This practice is noted particularly in letter writing.   [3] **Seguro servidor** (*sing.*) may be abbreviated to **S.S.** or **s.s.; seguros servidores** (*pl.*) to **SS. SS., Ss. Ss.,** or **ss. ss. Atto. = atento; attos. = atentos.**

Me repito[1] su afmo. s. s., *or* **Nos repetimos sus afmos. ss. ss.,**
    I (We) remain,
                Sincerely,

As noted above, the Spanish conclusion usually requires more than a mere "Very truly yours," or "Sincerely yours." However, there is a tendency nowadays to shorten conclusions of business letters, particularly as correspondence continues with an individual or firm.

    Great care must be taken to be consistent in the agreement of salutations and conclusions of letters, keeping in mind whether the letters are addressed to a man or a woman, or to a firm, and whether the letters are signed by one person or by an individual for a firm.

H. Sample letters

The following letters translated freely from Spanish to English will show how natural, idiomatic phrases in one language convey the same idea in another. Read the following letters aloud for practice, and be able to write either one from dictation. The teacher may want to test comprehension by asking questions in Spanish on the content of the letters. At the end of this section are listed some words and phrases, not all of which are used in the sample letters, which should be useful in composing original letters.

1

12 de marzo de 1978

Librería de Porrúa Hnos. y Cía.
Apartado 7990
México, D. F., México

Muy señores míos:

    Tengo el gusto de avisarles a ustedes que acabo de recibir su atenta del 8 del actual y el ejemplar de su catálogo con la lista de precios que se sirvieron remitirme por separado.
    Sírvanse enviarme a la mayor brevedad posible la lista de libros que envío anexa. También hallarán adjunto un cheque por pesos 596,40[2] en pago de la factura del 20 del pasado.
    Quedo de ustedes su atto. y S. S.,

---

[1] After the first letter (where the verb **aprovechar** may have been used) **Me repito** is a good follow-up.   [2] Read **quinientos noventa y seis pesos, cuarenta centavos.** While the comma between the **pesos** and **centavos** has largely been replaced in Spanish by a period, it is still used. The English comma is often written as a period in Spanish: **pesos** 1.250,35.

March 12, 1978

Porrúa Brothers and Co., Bookstore
Post Office Box 7990
Mexico City, Mexico

Gentlemen:

I am glad to inform you that I have just received your letter of March 8 and the copy of your catalogue with the list of prices which you kindly sent me under separate cover.

Please send me as soon as possible the list of books which I am including (in this letter). Also you will find enclosed a check for $596.40 (596.40 pesos) in payment of your bill of February 20 (of the 20th of last month).

Sincerely yours,

2

19 de mayo de 1979

Señor Director
Programa de Estudiantes Extranjeros
Instituto Caro y Cuervo
Apartado Postal 6411
Bogotá, Colombia

Estimado señor Director:

Me dirijo a Ud. con el fin de solicitar su amable cooperación respecto del siguiente asunto. Actualmente estudio lengua y literatura españolas en la Universidad de Cali-

fornia en Santa Bárbara, pero tengo interés en poder estudiar, por lo menos durante un semestre, en una universidad hispanoamericana.

Mucho se lo agradecería si pudiera Ud. enviarme a la mayor brevedad posible la descripción del nuevo programa de estudios para estudiantes extranjeros que ha establecido su Instituto. Le pido, además, que me mande informes sobre el procedimiento de admisión (ingreso) y sobre cualquier otro detalle que Ud. considere pertinente al caso.

En espera de sus gratas noticias, lo saludo muy atentamente,

Ricardo Smith

May 19, 1979

Director, Program of Foreign Studies
Caro y Cuervo Institute
P. O. Box 6411
Bogotá, Colombia

Dear Sir:

My purpose in writing you is to ask for your kind cooperation concerning the following matter. At present I am studying Spanish language and literature at the University of California, Santa Barbara, but I am interested in being able to study, for at least one semester, in a Spanish American university.

I would be very grateful if you could send me as soon as possible the description of the new schedule of courses for foreign students which your Institute has established. Furthermore, I am asking you to send me information about entrance procedures and any other detail which you may consider relevant to my situation.

Awaiting your kind reply, I remain,

Sincerely yours,
Richard Smith

EJERCICIO

1. Write to a foreign student, describing some of your daily activities. Try to use words which you have had in this text.
2. Write to a member of your family, describing some shopping you have done.
3. Assume that you are the Spanish secretary for an American exporting firm. Write a reply to a Spanish American firm which has asked for a recent catalogue and prices.

VOCABULARIO ÚTIL

abonar to credit, to pay
adjunto, -a enclosed, attached
anexo, -a enclosed, attached
el **buzón** mailbox
la **cantidad** quantity, amount
cargar to charge
la **casa (oficina) de correos** post office
el **catálogo** catalogue
certificar to register
comunicar to inform, tell
dirigir to address, direct; *reflex.* to address (*a person*), direct oneself (to)
el **ejemplar** copy
el **envío** shipment, remittance
la **estampilla** (postage) stamp (*Am.*)
la **factura** bill, invoice
la **firma** signature
el **folleto** folder, pamphlet
el **franqueo** postage
el **giro** draft

grato, -a kind, pleased
el **importe** cost, amount
la **muestra** sample
las **noticias** news, information
ofrecer(se) to offer, be, offer one's services
el **pago** payment
el **pasado** last (month)
el **pedido** order
permitirse to take the liberty (to)
el **recibo** receipt
referirse (ie, i) a to refer to
remitir to remit, send
el **saldo** balance
el **sello** (postage) stamp (*Spain*)
servirse (i, i) + *inf.* to be so kind as to + *inf.*
el **sobre** envelope
la **solicitud** request
suplicar to beg, ask
el **timbre** (postage) stamp (*Am.*)

a la mayor brevedad posible as soon as possible
a vuelta de correo by return mail
acusar recibo de to acknowledge receipt of
anticipar las gracias to thank in advance
dar las gracias (a) to thank
de acuerdo con in compliance with
del corriente (actual) of the present month
echar al correo to mail
en contestación a in reply to
en espera de awaiting
en pago de in payment of
en su cuenta to one's account
estar encargado, -a de to be in charge of
giro postal money order
hacer un pedido to place (give) an order
lista de precios price list
(nos) es grato (we) are pleased
nos place we are pleased
paquete postal parcel post
por separado under separate cover
sírva(n)se + *inf.* please + *verb,* be pleased to + *inf.*
tener el agrado (gusto) de + *inf.* to be pleased to + *inf.*
tener la bondad de + *inf.* to have the kindness to + *inf.,* please + *verb*

Appendices

Vocabularies

Index

APPENDIX A

El alfabeto español (*The Spanish alphabet*)

Letter	Name	Letter	Name	Letter	Name
a	a	j	jota	r	ere
b	be	k	ka	rr	erre
c	ce	l	ele	s	ese
ch	che	ll	elle	t	te
d	de	m	eme	u	u
e	e	n	ene	v	ve, uve
f	efe	ñ	eñe	w	doble ve
g	ge	o	o	x	equis
h	hache	p	pe	y	i griega
i	i	q	cu	z	zeta

In addition to the letters used in the English alphabet, **ch, ll, ñ,** and **rr** represent single sounds in Spanish and are considered single letters. In dictionaries and vocabularies words or syllables which begin with **ch, ll,** and **ñ** follow words or syllables that begin with **c, l,** and **n,** while **rr,** which never begins a word, is alphabetized as in English. **K** and **w** are used only in words of foreign origin. The names of the letters are feminine: **la be,** (*the*) *b;* **la jota,** (*the*) *j.*

Frases para la clase (*Classroom expressions*)

A number of expressions and grammatical terms which may be used in the classroom and laboratory are listed below. They are not included in the end vocabularies unless they are used in the preceding lessons. Other common expressions are used in the text.

Voy a pasar lista.	I am going to call the roll.
Presente.	Present.
¿Qué lección tenemos hoy?	What lesson do we have today?
Tenemos la Lección primera (dos).	We have Lesson One (Two).
¿En qué página empieza?	On what page does it begin?
¿Qué línea (renglón)?	What line?
(La lectura) empieza en la página . . .	(The reading) begins on page . . .
Al principio de la página.	At the beginning of the page.
En el medio (Al pie) de la página.	In the middle (At the bottom) of the page.
Abra(n) Ud(s). su(s) libro(s).	Open your book(s).
Cierre(n) Ud(s). su(s) libro(s).	Close your book(s).

Lea Ud. en español.	Read in Spanish.
Empiece Ud. a leer.	Begin to read.
Siga Ud. leyendo.	Continue (Go on) reading.
Traduzca Ud. al español (inglés).	Translate into Spanish (English).
Repítalo Ud.	Repeat it.
Pronuncie Ud.	Pronounce.
Basta.	That is enough, That will do.
Vayan (Pasen) Uds. a la pizarra.	Go (Pass) to the blackboard.
Escriban Uds. (al dictado).	Write (at dictation).
Corrijan Uds. las oraciones (frases).	Correct the sentences.
Vuelva(n) Ud(s). a su(s) asiento(s).	Return to your seat(s).
Siénte(n)se Ud(s).	Sit down.
Haga(n) Ud(s). el favor de (+*inf.*) . . .	Please (+*inf.*) . . .
Está bien.	All right, That's fine.
¿Qué significa la palabra . . . ?	What does the word . . . mean?
¿Cómo se dice . . . ?	How does one say . . . ?
¿Quién quiere hacer una pregunta?	Who wants to ask a question?
Escuchen Uds. bien.	Listen carefully.
Preparen Uds. para mañana . . .	Prepare for tomorrow . . .
Ha sonado el timbre.	The bell has rung.
La clase ha terminado.	The class has ended.
Uds. pueden marcharse.	You may leave (You are excused).

Palabras y expresiones para el laboratorio *(Words and expressions for the laboratory)*

el **alto parlante**   loud speaker
los **auriculares (audífonos)**   ear(head)phones
la **cabina**   booth
el **carrete**   reel
la **cinta (magnetofónica)**   (magnetic) tape
la **cinta maestra (matriz)**   master tape
la **corriente (eléctrica)**   power; (electric) current
el **disco (fonográfico)**   disc, (phonograph) record
   empalmar   to splice
el **enchufe**   plug
la **entrada**   input
   externo, -a   external
la **grabadora (de cinta)**   (tape) recorder
   grabar   to record
el **interruptor**   switch
el **micrófono**   microphone
la **perilla**   knob
   reparar   to repair
la **salida**   output

el **sonido**　sound

el **volumen**　volume

Acérquese más al micrófono.　Get closer to the microphone.

Aleje más el micrófono.　Move the microphone away from you.

Apriete el botón.　Push the button.

Aumente el volumen.　Turn it louder (Increase the volume).

Escuche la grabación.　Listen to the recording.

Hable en voz más alta (más baja, natural).　Speak in a louder (lower, natural) voice.

Hable más rápido (despacio).　Speak faster (slower).

Imite lo que oiga.　Imitate what you hear.

Mi máquina no funciona.　My machine does not work.

Pare (Apague) su máquina.　Stop (Turn off) your machine.

Ponga en marcha (Encienda) . . .　Start, turn on . . .

Póngase (Quítese) los audífonos.　Put on (Take off) your headphones.

Repita la respuesta.　Repeat the answer.

Se oirá (Ud. oirá) cada frase una vez (dos veces), seguida de una pausa.　You will hear each sentence once (twice), followed by a pause.

Se oirá (Ud. oirá) luego la respuesta (correcta).
　You will hear the (correct) answer later.

¿Se oye claramente la señal?　Is the signal clear?

Vuelva a enrollar la cinta.　Rewind the tape.

Términos gramaticales (*Grammatical terms*)

el **adjetivo**	adjective
demostrativo	demonstrative
posesivo	possessive
el **adverbio**	adverb
el **artículo**	article
definido	definite
indefinido	indefinite
el **cambio ortográfico**	change in spelling
la **capitalización**	capitalization
la **cláusula**	clause
la **comparación**	comparison
el **comparativo**	comparative
el **complemento**	object
directo	direct
indirecto	indirect
la **composición**	composition
la **concordancia**	agreement
la **conjugación**	conjugation
la **conjunción**	conjunction
la **consonante**	consonant

el **diptongo**	diphthong
el **género**	gender
masculino	masculine
femenino	feminine
el **gerundio**	gerund, present participle
el **infinitivo**	infinitive
la **interjección**	interjection
la **interrogación**	interrogation, question (mark)
la **letra**	letter (of the alphabet)
mayúscula	capital
minúscula	small
el **modo indicativo (subjuntivo)**	indicative (subjunctive) mood
el **nombre (substantivo)**	noun, substantive
el **nombre propio**	proper noun
el **número**	number, numeral
cardinal (ordinal)	cardinal (ordinal)
el **objeto**	object
la **palabra (negativa)**	(negative) word
las **partes de la oración**	parts of speech
el **participio pasado (presente)**	past (present) participle
la **persona**	person
primera	first
segunda	second
tercera	third
el **plural**	plural
la **posición**	position
el **predicado**	predicate
la **preposición**	preposition
el **pronombre**	pronoun
interrogativo	interrogative
personal	personal
reflexivo	reflexive
relativo	relative
la **puntuación**	punctuation
el **radical (la raíz)**	stem
el **significado**	meaning
la **sílaba**	syllable
última	last
penúltima	next to the last
el **singular**	singular
el **subjuntivo**	subjunctive
el **sujeto**	subject
el **superlativo (absoluto)**	(absolute) superlative
la **terminación**	ending
el **tiempo**	tense

el **tiempo simple (compuesto)**	simple (compound) tense
presente	present
imperfecto	imperfect
pretérito	preterit
futuro	future
condicional	conditional
perfecto	perfect (present perfect)
pluscuamperfecto	pluperfect
futuro perfecto	future perfect
condicional perfecto	conditional perfect
el **triptongo**	triphthong
el **verbo**	verb
auxiliar	auxiliary
impersonal	impersonal
irregular	irregular
reflexivo	reflexive
regular	regular
(in) transitivo	(in) transitive
la **vocal**	vowel
la **voz**	voice
activa	active
pasiva	passive

Signos de puntuación (*Punctuation marks*)

,	coma	( )	(los) paréntesis
;	punto y coma	« »	comillas
:	dos puntos	´	acento escrito
.	punto final	¨	(la) diéresis
. . .	puntos suspensivos	˜	(la) tilde
¿ ?	signo(s) de interrogación	¯	(el) guión
¡ !	signo(s) de admiración	—	raya

Abreviaturas y signos (*Abbreviations and signs*)

adj.	adjective	*m.*	masculine
adv.	adverb	*masc.*	masculine
Am.	American	*Mex.*	Mexican
cond.	conditional	*n.*	noun
conj.	conjunction	*obj.*	object
dir.	direct	*p.*	page
e.g.	for example	*p.p.*	past participle

etc.	and so forth	*part.*	participle
f.	feminine	*pl.*	plural
fem.	feminine	*prep.*	preposition
fam.	familiar	*pres.*	present
i.e.	that is	*pret.*	preterit
imp.	imperfect	*pron.*	pronoun
imper.	imperative	*reflex.*	reflexive
ind.	indicative	*sing./s.*	singular
indef.	indefinite	*subj.*	subjunctive
indir.	indirect	*trans.*	transitive
inf.	infinitive	*U.S.*	United States
lit.	literally		

( ) Words in parentheses are explanatory or they are to be translated in the exercises.

[ ] Words in brackets in the exercises are not to be translated.

— In the general vocabularies a dash indicates a word repeated, while in the exercises it usually is to be supplied by some grammatical form.

+ = followed by.

APPENDIX B

Regular verbs

hablar, *to speak*   **comer,** *to eat*   **vivir,** *to live*

PRESENT PARTICIPLE

hablando, *speaking*   **comiendo,** *eating*   **viviendo,** *living*

PAST PARTICIPLE

hablado, *spoken*   **comido,** *eaten*   **vivido,** *lived*

The simple tenses

Indicative mood

PRESENT

I speak, do speak, am speaking, etc.	*I eat, do eat, am eating, etc.*	*I live, do live, am living, etc.*
hablo	como	vivo
hablas	comes	vives
habla	come	vive
hablamos	comemos	vivimos
habláis	coméis	vivís
hablan	comen	viven

IMPERFECT

I was speaking, used to speak, spoke, etc.	*I was eating, used to eat, ate, etc.*	*I was living, used to live, lived, etc.*
hablaba	comía	vivía
hablabas	comías	vivías
hablaba	comía	vivía
hablábamos	comíamos	vivíamos
hablabais	comíais	vivíais
hablaban	comían	vivían

PRETERIT

I spoke, did speak, etc.	*I ate, did eat, etc.*	*I lived, did live, etc.*
hablé	comí	viví
hablaste	comiste	viviste
habló	comió	vivió
hablamos	comimos	vivimos
hablasteis	comisteis	vivisteis
hablaron	comieron	vivieron

FUTURE

I shall (will) speak, etc.	*I shall (will) eat, etc.*	*I shall (will) live, etc.*
hablaré	comeré	viviré
hablarás	comerás	vivirás
hablará	comerá	vivirá
hablaremos	comeremos	viviremos
hablaréis	comeréis	viviréis
hablarán	comerán	vivirán

CONDITIONAL

I should (would) speak, etc.	*I should (would) eat, etc.*	*I should (would) live, etc.*
hablaría	comería	viviría
hablarías	comerías	vivirías
hablaría	comería	viviría
hablaríamos	comeríamos	viviríamos
hablaríais	comeríais	viviríais
hablarían	comerían	vivirían

Subjunctive mood

PRESENT

(that) I may speak, etc.	*(that) I may eat, etc.*	*(that) I may live, etc.*
hable	coma	viva
hables	comas	vivas
hable	coma	viva
hablemos	comamos	vivamos
habléis	comáis	viváis
hablen	coman	vivan

-ra IMPERFECT

(that) I might speak, etc.	(that) I might eat, etc.	(that) I might live, etc.
hablara	comiera	viviera
hablaras	comieras	vivieras
hablara	comiera	viviera
habláramos	comiéramos	viviéramos
hablarais	comierais	vivierais
hablaran	comieran	vivieran

-se IMPERFECT

(that) I might speak, etc.	(that) I might eat, etc.	(that) I might live, etc.
hablase	comiese	viviese
hablases	comieses	vivieses
hablase	comiese	viviese
hablásemos	comiésemos	viviésemos
hablaseis	comieseis	vivieseis
hablasen	comiesen	viviesen

Imperative

speak	eat	live
habla (tú)	come (tú)	vive (tú)
hablad (vosotros)	comed (vosotros)	vivid (vosotros)

The compound tenses

PERFECT INFINITIVE

haber hablado (comido, vivido) *to have spoken (eaten, lived)*

PERFECT PARTICIPLE

habiendo hablado (comido, vivido) *having spoken (eaten, lived)*

Indicative mood

PRESENT PERFECT	PLUPERFECT	PRETERIT PERFECT[1]
I have spoken, eaten, lived, etc.	*I had spoken, eaten, lived, etc.*	*I had spoken, eaten, lived, etc.*

---

[1]The preterit perfect tense is used only after conjunctions such as **cuando, en cuanto, después que, apenas.** In spoken Spanish the pluperfect or the simple preterit often replaces the preterit perfect.

he		había			hube	
has		habías			hubiste	
ha	hablado	había		hablado	hubo	hablado
	comido			comido		comido
hemos	vivido	habíamos		vivido	hubimos	vivido
habéis		habíais			hubisteis	
han		habían			hubieron	

FUTURE PERFECT

I shall (will) have spoken, etc.

habré	
habrás	
habrá	hablado
	comido
habremos	vivido
habréis	
habrán	

CONDITIONAL PERFECT

I should (would) have spoken, etc.

habría	
habrías	
habría	hablado
	comido
habríamos	vivido
habríais	
habrían	

Subjunctive mood

PRESENT PERFECT

(that) I may have spoken, etc.

haya	
hayas	
haya	hablado
	comido
hayamos	vivido
hayáis	
hayan	

-ra AND -se PLUPERFECT

(that) I might have spoken, etc.

hubiera *or* hubiese	
hubieras *or* hubieses	
hubiera *or* hubiese	hablado
	comido
hubiéramos *or* hubiésemos	vivido
hubierais *or* hubieseis	
hubieran *or* hubiesen	

Irregular past participles of regular and stem-changing verbs

abrir:	**abierto**	envolver:	**envuelto**
componer:	**compuesto**	escribir:	**escrito**
cubrir:	**cubierto**	morir:	**muerto**
descubrir:	**descubierto**	romper:	**roto**
devolver:	**devuelto**	volver:	**vuelto**

Comments concerning forms of verbs

a. From five forms (infinitive, present participle, past participle, first person singular present indicative, and third person plural preterit) all other forms may be derived.

INFINITIVE decir	PRES. PART. **diciendo**	PAST PART. **dicho**	PRES. IND. **digo**	PRETERIT **dijeron**
IMP. IND. decía	PROGRESSIVE TENSES **estoy,** etc. **diciendo**	COMPOUND TENSES **he,** etc. **dicho**	PRES. SUBJ. **diga**	IMP. SUBJ. **dijera** **dijese**
FUTURE **diré**			IMPERATIVE **di** decid	
CONDITIONAL **diría**				

b. The first and second persons plural of the present indicative of all verbs are regular, except in the cases of **haber, ir, ser.**

c. The third person plural is formed by adding **-n** to the third person singular in all tenses, except the preterit and in the present indicative of **ser.**

d. All familiar forms (second person singular and plural) end in **-s,** except the second person singular preterit and the imperative.

e. The imperfect indicative is regular in all verbs, except **ir (iba), ser (era), ver (veía).**

f. If the first person singular preterit ends in unaccented **-e,** the third person singular ends in unaccented **-o;** the other endings are regular, except that after **j** the ending for the third person plural is **-eron.** Eight verbs of this group, in addition to those which end in **-ducir,** have a **u**-stem preterit **(andar, caber, estar, haber, poder, poner, saber, tener);** four have an **i**-stem **(decir, hacer, querer, venir); traer** has a regular stem with the above endings. (The third person plural preterit forms of **decir** and **traer** are **dijeron** and **trajeron,** respectively. The third person singular form of **hacer** is **hizo**). **Ir** and **ser** have the same preterit, while **dar** has second-conjugation endings in this tense.

g. The conditional always has the same stem as the future. Only twelve verbs have irregular stems in these tenses. Five drop **e** of the infinitive ending **(caber, haber, poder, querer, saber);** five drop **e** or **i** and insert **d (poner, salir, tener, valer, venir);** and two **(decir, hacer)** retain the Old Spanish stems **dir-, har- (far-).**

h. The stem of the present subjunctive of all verbs is the same as that of the first person singular present indicative, except for **dar, estar, haber, ir, saber, ser.**

i. The imperfect subjunctive of all verbs is formed by dropping **-ron** of the third person plural preterit and adding the **-ra** or **-se** endings.

j. The singular imperative is the same in form as the third person singular present indicative, except in the case of ten verbs **(decir, di; haber, he; hacer, haz; ir, ve; poner, pon; salir, sal; ser, sé; tener, ten; valer, val** *or* **vale; venir, ven).** The plural imperative is always formed by dropping final **-r** of the infinitive and adding **-d.** (Remember that the imperative is used only for familiar affirmative commands.)

k. The compound tenses of all verbs are formed by using the various tenses of the auxiliary verb **haber** with the past participle.

Irregular verbs

(Participles are given with the infinitive; tenses not listed are regular.)

1. **andar,** andando, andado, *to go, walk*

PRETERIT	**anduve**	**anduviste**	**anduvo**	**anduvimos**	**anduvisteis**	**anduvieron**
IMP. SUBJ.	**anduviera,** etc.		**anduviese,** etc.			

2. **caber,** cabiendo, cabido, *to fit, be contained in*

PRES. IND.	**quepo**	cabes	cabe	cabemos	cabéis	caben
PRES. SUBJ.	**quepa**	**quepas**	**quepa**	**quepamos**	**quepáis**	**quepan**
FUTURE	**cabré**	**cabrás,** etc.		COND.	**cabría**	**cabrías,** etc.
PRETERIT	**cupe**	**cupiste**	**cupo**	**cupimos**	**cupisteis**	**cupieron**
IMP. SUBJ.	**cupiera,** etc.		**cupiese,** etc.			

3. **caer, cayendo, caído,** *to fall*

PRES. IND.	**caigo**	caes	cae	caemos	caéis	caen
PRES. SUBJ.	**caiga**	**caigas**	**caiga**	**caigamos**	**caigáis**	**caigan**
PRETERIT	caí	**caíste**	**cayó**	**caímos**	**caísteis**	**cayeron**
IMP. SUBJ.	**cayera, etc.**		**cayese,** etc.			

4. **dar,** dando, dado, *to give*

PRES. IND.	**doy**	das	da	damos	dais	dan
PRES. SUBJ.	**dé**	des	**dé**	demos	deis	den
PRETERIT	**di**	**diste**	**dio**	**dimos**	**disteis**	**dieron**
IMP. SUBJ.	**diera,** etc.		**diese,** etc.			

5. **decir, diciendo, dicho,** *to say, tell*

PRES. IND.	**digo**	**dices**	**dice**	decimos	decís	**dicen**
PRES. SUBJ.	**diga**	**digas**	**diga**	**digamos**	**digáis**	**digan**
IMPERATIVE	**di**				decid	
FUTURE	**diré**	**dirás,** etc.		COND.	**diría**	**dirías,** etc.
PRETERIT	**dije**	**dijiste**	**dijo**	**dijimos**	**dijisteis**	**dijeron**
IMP. SUBJ.	**dijera,** etc.		**dijese,** etc.			

6. **estar,** estando, estado, *to be*

PRES. IND.	**estoy**	**estás**	**está**	estamos	estáis	**están**
PRES. SUBJ.	**esté**	**estés**	**esté**	estemos	estéis	**estén**
PRETERIT	**estuve**	**estuviste**	**estuvo**	**estuvimos**	**estuvisteis**	**estuvieron**
IMP. SUBJ.	**estuviera,** etc.		**estuviese,** etc.			

7. **haber,** habiendo, habido, *to have* (auxiliary)

PRES. IND.	**he**	**has**	**ha**	**hemos**	habéis	**han**
PRES. SUBJ.	**haya**	**hayas**	**haya**	**hayamos**	**hayáis**	**hayan**
IMPERATIVE	**he**				habed	
FUTURE	**habré**	**habrás,** etc.			COND. **habría**	**habrías,** etc.
PRETERIT	**hube**	**hubiste**	**hubo**	**hubimos**	**hubisteis**	**hubieron**
IMP. SUBJ.	**hubiera,** etc.		**hubiese,** etc.			

8. **hacer,** haciendo, **hecho,** *to do, make*

PRES. IND.	**hago**	haces	hace	hacemos	hacéis	hacen
PRES. SUBJ.	**haga**	**hagas**	**haga**	**hagamos**	**hagáis**	**hagan**
IMPERATIVE	**haz**				haced	
FUTURE	**haré**	**harás,** etc.			COND. **haría**	**harías,** etc.
PRETERIT	**hice**	**hiciste**	**hizo**	**hicimos**	**hicisteis**	**hicieron**
IMP. SUBJ.	**hiciera,** etc.		**hiciese,** etc.			

9. **ir, yendo, ido,** *to go*

PRES. IND.	**voy**	**vas**	**va**	**vamos**	**vais**	**van**
PRES. SUBJ.	**vaya**	**vayas**	**vaya**	**vayamos**	**vayáis**	**vayan**
IMPERATIVE	**ve**				id	
IMP. IND.	**iba**	**ibas**	**iba**	**íbamos**	**ibais**	**iban**
PRETERIT	**fui**	**fuiste**	**fue**	**fuimos**	**fuisteis**	**fueron**
IMP. SUBJ.	**fuera,** etc.		**fuese,** etc.			

10. **oír, oyendo,** *oído, to hear*

PRES. IND.	**oigo**	**oyes**	**oye**	oímos	oís	**oyen**
PRES. SUBJ.	**oiga**	**oigas**	**oiga**	**oigamos**	**oigáis**	**oigan**
IMPERATIVE	**oye**				oíd	
PRETERIT	oí	oíste	**oyó**	oímos	oísteis	**oyeron**
IMP. SUBJ.	**oyera,** etc.		**oyese,** etc.			

11. **poder, pudiendo,** podido, *to be able*

PRES. IND.	**puedo**	**puedes**	**puede**	podemos	podéis	**pueden**
PRES. SUBJ.	**pueda**	**puedas**	**pueda**	podamos	podáis	**puedan**
FUTURE	**podré**	**podrás,** etc.			COND. **podría**	**podrías,** etc.
PRETERIT	**pude**	**pudiste**	**pudo**	**pudimos**	**pudisteis**	**pudieron**
IMP. SUBJ.	**pudiera,** etc.		**pudiese,** etc.			

12. **poner,** poniendo, **puesto,** *to put, place*

PRES. IND.	**pongo**	pones	pone	ponemos	ponéis	ponen
PRES. SUBJ.	**ponga**	**pongas**	**ponga**	**pongamos**	**pongáis**	**pongan**
IMPERATIVE	**pon**				poned	

FUTURE	**pondré**	**pondrás,** etc.			COND.	**pondría**	**pondrías,** etc.
PRETERIT	**puse**	**pusiste**	**puso**	**pusimos**	**pusisteis**	**pusieron**
IMP. SUBJ.	**pusiera,** etc.		**pusiese,** etc.			

Like **poner:** componer, *to compose;* oponerse a, *to oppose;* suponer, *to suppose.*

13. **querer,** queriendo, querido, *to wish, want*

PRES. IND.	**quiero**	**quieres**	**quiere**	queremos	queréis	**quieren**
PRES. SUBJ.	**quiera**	**quieras**	**quiera**	queramos	queráis	**quieran**
FUTURE	**querré**	**querrás,** etc.			COND.	**querría**	**querrías,** etc.
PRETERIT	**quise**	**quisiste**	**quiso**	**quisimos**	**quisisteis**	**quisieron**
IMP. SUBJ.	**quisiera,** etc.		**quisiese,** etc.			

14. **saber,** sabiendo, sabido, *to know*

PRES. IND.	**sé**	sabes	sabe	sabemos	sabéis	saben
PRES. SUBJ.	**sepa**	**sepas**	**sepa**	**sepamos**	**sepáis**	**sepan**
FUTURE	**sabré**	**sabrás,** etc.			COND.	**sabría**	**sabrías,** etc.
PRETERIT	**supe**	**supiste**	**supo**	**supimos**	**supisteis**	**supieron**
IMP. SUBJ.	**supiera,** etc.		**supiese,** etc.			

15. **salir,** saliendo, salido, *to go out, leave*

PRES. IND.	**salgo**	sales	sale	salimos	salís	salen
PRES. SUBJ.	**salga**	**salgas**	**salga**	**salgamos**	**salgáis**	**salgan**
IMPERATIVE	**sal**				salid	
FUTURE	**saldré**	**saldrás,** etc.			COND.	**saldría**	**saldrías,** etc.

16. **ser,** siendo, sido, *to be*

PRES. IND.	**soy**	**eres**	**es**	**somos**	**sois**	**son**
PRES. SUBJ.	**sea**	**seas**	**sea**	**seamos**	**seáis**	**sean**
IMPERATIVE	**sé**				sed	
IMP. IND.	**era**	**eras**	**era**	**éramos**	**erais**	**eran**
PRETERIT	**fui**	**fuiste**	**fue**	**fuimos**	**fuisteis**	**fueron**
IMP. SUBJ.	**fuera,** etc.		**fuese,** etc.			

17. **tener,** teniendo, tenido, *to have*

PRES. IND.	**tengo**	**tienes**	**tiene**	tenemos	tenéis	**tienen**
PRES. SUBJ.	**tenga**	**tengas**	**tenga**	**tengamos**	**tengáis**	**tengan**
IMPERATIVE	**ten**				tened	
FUTURE	**tendré**	**tendrás,** etc.			COND.	**tendría**	**tendrías,** etc.
PRETERIT	**tuve**	**tuviste**	**tuvo**	**tuvimos**	**tuvisteis**	**tuvieron**
IMP. SUBJ.	**tuviera,** etc.		**tuviese,** etc.			

Like **tener:** contener, *to contain;* detener, *to stop;* mantener, *to maintain;* obtener, *to obtain.*

18. **traer, trayendo, traído,** *to bring*

PRES. IND.	**traigo**	traes	trae	traemos	traéis	traen
PRES. SUBJ.	**traiga**	**traigas**	**traiga**	**traigamos**	**traigáis**	**traigan**
PRETERIT	**traje**	**trajiste**	**trajo**	**trajimos**	**trajisteis**	**trajeron**
IMP. SUBJ.	**trajera,** etc.		**trajese,** etc.			

Like **traer:** atraer, *to attract.*

19. **valer,** valiendo, valido, *to be worth*

PRES. IND.	**valgo**	vales	vale	valemos	valéis	valen
PRES. SUBJ.	**valga**	**valgas**	**valga**	**valgamos**	**valgáis**	**valgan**
IMPERATIVE	**val**(vale)				valed	
FUTURE	**valdré**	**valdrás,** etc.		COND.	**valdria**	**valdrías,** etc.

20. **venir, viniendo,** venido, *to come*

PRES. IND.	**vengo**	**vienes**	**viene**	venimos	venís	**vienen**
PRES. SUBJ.	**venga**	**vengas**	**venga**	**vengamos**	**vengáis**	**vengan**
IMPERATIVE	**ven**				venid	
FUTURE	**vendré**	**vendrás,** etc.		COND.	**vendría**	**vendrías,** etc.
PRETERIT	**vine**	**viniste**	**vino**	**vinimos**	**vinisteis**	**vinieron**
IMP. SUBJ.	**viniera,** etc.		**viniese,** etc.			

21. **ver,** viendo, **visto,** *to see*

PRES. IND.	**veo**	ves	ve	vemos	veis	ven
PRES. SUBJ.	**vea**	**veas**	**vea**	**veamos**	**veáis**	**vean**
PRETERIT	**vi**	viste	**vio**	vimos	visteis	vieron
IMP. IND.	**veía**	**veías**	**veía**	**veíamos**	**veíais**	**veían**

Verbs with changes in spelling

Changes in spelling are required in certain verbs in order to preserve the sound of the final consonant of the stem. The changes occur in only seven forms: in the first four types given on page 405 the change is in the first person singular preterit, and in the remaining types in the first person singular present indicative, while all types change throughout the present subjunctive.

	before a	before o	before u	before e	before i
Sound of *k*	ca	co	cu	que	qui
Sound of *g*	ga	go	gu	gue	gui
Sound of *th* (*s*)	za	zo	zu	ce	ci
Sound of *h*	ja	jo	ju	ge, je	gi, ji
Sound of *gw*	gua	guo		güe	güi

1. Verbs ending in **-car** change to **c** to **qu** before **e: buscar,** *to look for.*

PRETERIT **busqué** buscaste buscó, etc.
PRES. SUBJ. **busque** **busques** **busque** **busquemos** **busquéis** **busquen**

Like **buscar:** acercarse, *to approach;* colocar, *to place;* comunicar, *to communicate;* dedicar, *to dedicate;* desembarcar, *to disembark;* desembocar, *to empty;* destacarse, *to stand out;* indicar, *to indicate;* mascar, *to chew;* pescar, *to fish;* practicar, *to practice;* predicar, *to preach;* publicar, *to publish;* sacar, *to take out;* significar, *to mean;* simplificar, *to simplify;* tocar, *to play* (music).

2. Verbs ending in **-gar** change **g** to **gu** before **e: llegar,** *to arrive.*

PRETERIT **llegué** llegaste llegó, etc.
PRES. SUBJ. **llegue** **llegues** **llegue** **lleguemos** **lleguéis** **lleguen**

Like **llegar:** agregar, *to add;* colgar (ue),[1] *to hang;* entregar, *to hand* (over); jugar (ue), *to play* (a game); navegar, *to sail;* negar (ie), *to deny;* pagar, *to pay;* pegar, *to beat;* rogar (ue), *to beg, ask.*

3. Verbs ending in **-zar** change **z** to **c** before **e: gozar,** *to enjoy.*

PRETERIT **gocé** gozaste gozó, etc.
PRES. SUBJ. **goce** **goces** **goce** **gocemos** **gocéis** **gocen**

Like **gozar:** abrazar, *to embrace;* alcanzar, *to reach;* almorzar (ue), *to take lunch;* bautizar, *to baptize;* bostezar, *to yawn;* caracterizar, *to characterize;* comenzar (ie), *to commence, begin;* cruzar, *to cross;* desperezarse, *to stretch;* empezar (ie), *to begin;* gozar, *to enjoy;* lanzar, *to hurl;* organizar, *to organize;* realizar, *to realize, carry out;* realzar, *to enhance.*

4. Verbs ending in **-guar** change **gu** to **gü** before **e: averiguar,** *to find out.*

PRETERIT **averigüé** averiguaste averiguó, etc.
PRES. SUBJ. **averigüe** **averigües** **averigüe** **averigüemos** **averigüéis** **averigüen**

5. Verbs ending in **-ger** or **-gir** change **g** to **j** before **a** and **o: escoger,** *to choose.*

PRES. IND. **escojo** escoges escoge, etc.
PRES. SUBJ. **escoja** **escojas** **escoja** **escojamos** **escojáis** **escojan**

Like **escoger:** proteger, *to protect;* recoger, *to pick up;* surgir, *to surge, appear.*

6. Verbs in **-guir** change **gu** to **g** before **a** and **o: distinguir,** *to distinguish.*

PRES. IND. **distingo** distingues distingue, etc.
PRES. SUBJ. **distinga** **distingas** **distinga** **distingamos** **distingáis** **distingan**

Like **distinguir:** conseguir (i,i), *to get;* seguir (i,i), *to follow.*

7. Verbs ending in **-cer** or **-cir** preceded by a consonant change **c** to **z** before **a** and **o:** **vencer,** *to overcome.*

---

[1]See pages 407–409 for stem changes.

PRES. IND.	**venzo**	vences	vence, etc.			
PRES. SUBJ.	**venza**	**venzas**	**venza**	**venzamos**	**venzáis**	**venzan**

Like **vencer:** convencer, *to convince;* ejercer, *to exert.*

8. Verbs ending in **-quir** change **qu** to **c** before **a** and **o: delinquir,** *to be guilty.*

PRES. IND.	**delinco**	delinques	delinque, etc.			
PRES. SUBJ.	**delinca**	**delincas**	**delinca**	**delincamos**	**delincáis**	**delincan**

Verbs with special endings

1. Verbs ending in **-cer** or **-cir** following a vowel insert **z** before **c** in the first person singular present indicative and throughout the present subjunctive: **conocer,** *to know, be acquainted with.*

PRES. IND.	**conozco**	conoces	conoce, etc.			
PRES. SUBJ.	**conozca**	**conozcas**	**conozca**	**conozcamos**	**conozcáis**	**conozcan**

Like **conocer:** agradecer, *to be thankful for;* aparecer, *to appear;* crecer, *to grow;* desaparecer, *to disappear;* establecer, *to establish;* florecer, *to flourish;* nacer, *to be born;* ofrecer, *to offer;* parecer, *to seem;* pertenecer, *to belong;* prevalecer, *to prevail;* reconocer, *to recognize;* renacer, *to be revived.*

2. Verbs ending in **-ducir** have the same changes as **conocer,** with additional changes in the preterit and imperfect subjunctive: **traducir,** *to translate.*

PRES. IND.	**traduzco**	traduces	traduce, etc.			
PRES. SUBJ.	**traduzca**	**traduzcas**	**traduzca**	**traduzcamos**	**traduzcáis**	**traduzcan**
PRETERIT	**traduje**	**tradujiste**	**tradujo**	**tradujimos**	**tradujisteis**	**tradujeron**
IMP. SUBJ.	**tradujera,** etc.		**tradujese,** etc.			

Like **traducir:** conducir, *to conduct, lead;* producir, *to produce.*

3. Verbs ending in **-uir** (except **-guir**) insert **y** except before **i,** and change unaccented **i** between vowels to **y: construir,** *to construct.*

PARTICIPLES	**construyendo**		construido		
PRES. IND.	**construyo**	**construyes**	**construye**	construimos	construís
	construyen				
PRES. SUBJ.	**construya**	**construyas**	**construya**	**construyamos**	**construyáis**
	construyan				**construid**
IMPERATIVE	**construye**				
PRETERIT	construí	construiste	**construyó**	construimos	construisteis
	construyeron				
IMP. SUBJ.	**construyera,** etc.		**construyese,** etc.		

Like **construir:** constituir, *to constitute;* contribuir, *to contribute;* destruir, *to destroy;* incluir, *to include;* influir, *to influence.*

4. Certain verbs ending in **-er** preceded by a vowel replace unaccented **i** of the ending by **y: creer,** *to believe.*

PARTICIPLES	**creyendo**		**creído**			
PRETERIT	creí	**creíste**	creyó	**creímos**	**creísteis**	**creyeron**
IMP. SUBJ.	**creyera,** etc.		**creyese,** etc.			

Like **creer:** leer, *to read.*

5. Some verbs ending in **-iar** require a written accent on the **i** in the singular and third person plural in the present indicative and present subjunctive and in the singular imperative: **enviar,** *to send.*

PRES. IND.	**envío**	**envías**	**envía**	enviamos	enviáis	**envían**
PRES. SUBJ.	**envíe**	**envíes**	**envíe**	**enviemos**	**enviéis**	**envíen**
IMPERATIVE	**envía**			enviad		

Like **enviar:** criar, *to grow;* variar, *to vary.*

However, such common verbs as **anunciar,** *to announce;* **apreciar,** *to appreciate;* **cambiar,** *to change;* **estudiar,** *to study;* **iniciar,** *to initiate;* **limpiar,** *to clean;* **pronunciar,** *to pronounce,* **refugiarse,** *to take refuge,* do not have the accented **i.**

6. Verbs ending in **-uar** have a written accent on the **u** in the same forms as verbs in section **5:**[1] **continuar,** *to continue.*

PRES. IND.	**continúo**	**continúas**	**continúa**	continuamos	continuáis	**continúan**
PRES. SUBJ.	**continúe**	**continúes**	**continúe**	continuemos	continuéis	**continúen**
IMPERATIVE	**continúa**			continuad		

Stem-changing verbs

CLASS I (-ar, -er)

Many verbs of the first and second conjugations change the stem vowel **e** to **ie** and **o** to **ue** when the vowels **e** and **o** are stressed, *i.e.,* in the singular and third person plural of the present indicative and present subjunctive and in the singular imperative. Class I verbs are designated: **cerrar (ie), volver (ue).**

cerrar, *to close*

PRES. IND.	**cierro**	**cierras**	**cierra**	cerramos	cerráis	**cierran**
PRES. SUBJ.	**cierre**	**cierres**	**cierre**	cerremos	cerréis	**cierren**
IMPERATIVE	**cierra**					

Like **cerrar:** atravesar, *to cross;* comenzar, *to commence;* despertar, *to awaken;* empezar, *to begin;* encerrar, *to enclose;* negar, *to deny;* pensar, *to think;* recomendar, *to recommend;* sentarse, *to sit down.*

---

[1]**Reunir (se),** *to gather,* has a written accent on the **u** in the same forms as **continuar:**

PRES. IND.	reúno, reúnes, reúne . . . reúnen
PRES. SUBJ.	reúna, reúnas, reúna . . . reúnan
IMPERATIVE	reúne

perder, *to lose*

PRES. IND.	**pierdo**	**pierdes**	**pierde**	perdemos	perdéis	**pierden**
PRES. SUBJ.	**pierda**	**pierdas**	**pierda**	perdamos	perdáis	**pierdan**
IMPERATIVE	**pierde**				perded	

Like **perder:** defender, *to defend;* entender, *to understand;* extenderse, *to extend.*

contar, *to count*

PRES. IND.	**cuento**	**cuentas**	**cuenta**	contamos	contáis	**cuentan**
PRES. SUBJ.	**cuente**	**cuentes**	**cuente**	contemos	contéis	**cuenten**
IMPERATIVE	**cuenta**				contad	

Like **contar:** acordarse, *to remember;* acostarse, *to go to bed;* almorzar, *to take lunch;* colgar, *to hang;* costar, *to cost;* demostrar, *to demonstrate;* encontrar, *to find;* mostrar, *to show;* probarse, *to try on;* recordar, *to remember;* rogar, *to beg, ask;* sonar, *to sound, ring;* volar, *to fly.*

volver,[1] *to return*

PRES. IND.	**vuelvo**	**vuelves**	**vuelve**	volvemos	volvéis	**vuelven**
PRES. SUBJ.	**vuelva**	**vuelvas**	**vuelva**	volvamos	volváis	**vuelvan**
IMPERATIVE	**vuelve**				volved	

Like **volver:** devolver, *to give back;* doler, *to ache;* envolver, *to wrap up;* llover, *to rain;* mover, *to move;* resolver, *to resolve.*

jugar, *to play* (a game)

PRES. IND.	**juego**	**juegas**	**juega**	jugamos	jugáis	**juegan**
PRES. SUBJ.	**juegue**	**juegues**	**juegue**	juguemos	juguéis	**jueguen**
IMPERATIVE	**juega**				jugad	

CLASS II (-ir)

Certain verbs of the third conjugation have the changes in the stem indicated below. Class II verbs are designated: **sentir (ie,i), dormir (ue,u).**

PRES. IND.	I, 2, 3, 6	} e > ie	PRES. PART.			} e > i
PRES. SUBJ.	I, 2, 3, 6	o > ue	PRETERIT	3, 6		o > u
IMPERATIVE	Sing.		PRES. SUBJ.	4, 5		
			IMP. SUBJ.	I, 2, 3, 4, 5, 6		

sentir, *to feel*

PRES. PART.	**sintiendo**					
PRES. IND.	**siento**	**sientes**	**siente**	sentimos	sentís	**sienten**
PRES. SUBJ.	**sienta**	**sientas**	**sienta**	**sintamos**	**sintáis**	sientan
IMPERATIVE	**siente**				sentid	
PRETERIT	sentí	sentiste	**sintió**	sentimos	sentisteis	**sintieron**
IMP. SUBJ.	**sintiera**, etc.		**sintiese**, etc.			

Like **sentir:** advertir, *to advise;* convertir, *to convert;* divertirse, *to amuse oneself;* preferir, *to prefer.*

---

[1] The past participles of **volver, devolver, envolver, resolver** are: **vuelto, devuelto, envuelto, resuelto.**

dormir, *to sleep*

PRES. PART.	**durmiendo**					
PRES. IND.	**duermo**	**duermes**	**duerme**	dormimos	dormís	**duermen**
PRES. SUBJ.	**duerma**	**duermas**	**duerma**	**durmamos**	**durmáis**	**duerman**
IMPERATIVE	**duerme**				dormid	
PRETERIT	dormí	dormiste	**durmió**	dormimos	dormisteis	**durmieron**
IMP. SUBJ.	**durmiera,** etc.		**durmiese,** etc.			

Like **dormir:** morir,[1] *to die.*

CLASS III (-ir)

Certain verbs in the third conjugation change **e** to **i** in all forms in which changes occur in Class II verbs. These verbs are designated: **pedir (i,i).**

pedir, *to ask*

PRES. PART.	**pidiendo**					
PRES. IND.	**pido**	**pides**	**pide**	pedimos	pedís	**piden**
PRES. SUBJ.	**pida**	**pidas**	**pida**	**pidamos**	**pidáis**	**pidan**
IMPERATIVE	**pide**				pedid	
PRETERIT	pedí	pediste	**pidió**	pedimos	pedisteis	**pidieron**
IMP. SUBJ.	**pidiera,** etc.		**pidiese,** etc.			

Like **pedir:** competir, *to compete;* conseguir, *to get;* despedirse, *to take leave;* repetir, *to repeat;* seguir, *to follow;* servir, *to serve;* vestir, *to dress.*

reír, *to laugh*

PARTICIPLES	**riendo**		reído			
PRES. IND.	**río**	**ríes**	**ríe**	reímos	reís	**ríen**
PRES. SUBJ.	**ría**	**rías**	**ría**	**riamos**	**riáis**	**rían**
IMPERATIVE	**ríe**				reíd	
PRETERIT	reí	reíste	**rió**	reímos	reísteis	**rieron**
IMP. SUBJ.	**riera,** etc.		**riese,** etc.			

Like **reír: sonreír,** *to smile.*

---

[1]Past participle: **muerto.**

VOCABULARY

Spanish-English

A

a to, at, in, from, by, *etc.*
a caballo on horseback
a casa de (María) to (Mary's)
a causa de *prep.* because of
¿a cuántos estamos? what is the date?
a eso de at about (*time*)
a fines de at the end of
a la iglesia to church
a la medianoche at midnight
a lo largo de along
a lo lejos in the distance
a medida que as
a menos que *conj.* unless
a menudo often, frequently
a partir de since the end of
a principios de at the beginning of
a propósito by the way
¿a qué hora? at what time?
a su disposición at your service
a tiempo in (on) time
a veces at times
abajo *adv.* below
de abajo below
más abajo farther down
abandonado, -a abandoned
abandonar to abandon, leave
abierto, -a *p.p. of* **abrir** *and adj.* open, opened
el **abogado** lawyer
la **abreviatura** abbreviation
el **abrigo** topcoat, overcoat

abril April
abrir to open
absolutamente absolutely
abstracto, -a abstract
abundante abundant
abundar to abound, be abundant
acabar to end, finish, complete
acabar de + *inf.* to have just + *p.p.*
acabar por + *inf.* to end up by + *pres. part.*
la **academia** academy
acarrear to cart, haul, transport
la **acción** (*pl.* **acciones**) action
Día de Acción de Gracias Thanksgiving Day
el **aceite** oil, olive oil
la **aceituna** olive
aceptar to accept
acerca de *prep.* about, concerning
acercarse (a + *obj.)* to approach
acometer to attack
acompañar to accompany, go with
aconsejar to advise, warn
acordarse (ue) (de + *obj.)* to remember, recall
acostarse (ue) to go to bed, lie down
acostumbrar to be accustomed to, be in the habit of
la **actividad** activity
en actividad active
activo, -a active
actual *adj.* present, present-day

la **actualidad** present time
el **acueducto** aqueduct
acumular to accumulate, gather
el **adelanto** advance, progress
además *adv.* besides, furthermore
además de *prep.* besides, in addition to
adiós goodbye
el **adjetivo** adjective
admirado, -a admired
admirar to admire
puede admirarse it can be admired
el **adobe** *brick made of clay and straw*
¿adónde? where? (*with verbs of motion*)
adoptar to adopt
la **adoración** adoration
adorar to adore, worship
adornado, -a (de *or* **con)** adorned (with), decorated (with)
adornar (de, con) to adorn (with), decorate (with)
el **adorno** adornment
el **adversario** adversary, opponent
la **advertencia** warning
advertir (ie, i) to advise, point out, warn (of)
aéreo, -a air (*adj.*) aerial
por correo aéreo by air mail
el **aeropuerto** airport
en el aeropuerto at (in) the airport
afectar to affect
afeitarse to shave (oneself)

la **afición** fondness
aficionado, -a (a) fond (of)
  ser aficionado, -a (a) to be fond (of)
el **aficionado** fan
  aficionado, -a a los deportes sports fan
aficionarse (tanto) a to become (so) fond of
África Africa
africano, -a Africa(n)
afuera *adv.* outside, abroad
la **agencia** agency
  agencia de viajes travel agency
el **agente** agent
ágil agile
agosto August
agradable pleasant, agreeable
agradecer to be grateful (thankful) for
el **agravio** wrong
agrícola (*m. and f.*) agricultural, farm (*adj.*)
  las agrícolas the agricultural ones (*f.*)
el **agricultor** agriculturist, farmer
la **agricultura** agriculture
el **agua** (*f.*) water
el **aguacate** avocado, alligator pear
Agustín Augustine
¡ah! ah! oh!
ahí there (*near person addressed*)
ahora now
  ahora mismo right now, right away
  ahora vuelvo I'll be right back
  por ahora for now, for the present
el **aire** air
  al aire libre outdoor, (in the) open air
aislado, -a isolated
al = a + el to the

al + *inf.* on (upon) + *pres. part.*
al día siguiente on the following day
al fondo in the background
al lado de beside, at the side of
al mediodía at noon
al mes a month
al mismo tiempo at the same time
al poco tiempo after (in) a short time
al principio at first, in the beginning
al servicio de in the service of
la **albóndiga** meat ball
alcanzar to attain, reach
el **alcázar** alcazar, fortress, castle
la **alcoba** bedroom
alcohólico, -a alcoholic
la **aldea** village, town
el **aldeano** villager
alegórico, -a allegorical
alegrarse (de + *inf.*) to be glad (to)
  ¡cuánto me alegro (de)! how glad I am (to)!
  ¡cuánto me alegro de que! how glad I am that!
  me alegro (mucho) (de) I am (very) glad (to)
alegre cheerful, joyful, lively
la **alegría** joy, happiness
  ¡qué alegría me da verte! how happy I am to see you!
el **alemán** German (*language*)
Alemania Germany
el **alfabeto** alphabet
algo *pron.* something, anything; *adv.* somewhat
  algo de comer something to eat
  algo glotón somewhat gluttonous, something of a glutton

algo más something (anything) else
el **algodón** cotton
alguien someone, somebody, anybody, anyone
algún (*used for* **alguno** *before m. sing. nouns*)
alguno, -a *adj. and pron.* some, any, someone; *pl.* some, a few
la **Alhambra** *Palace of the Moorish Kings of Granada*
el **alimento** food
el **alma** (*f.*) soul, heart, spirit
el **almacén** (*pl.* **almacenes**) department store
el **almíbar** syrup; *pl.* fruit preserves
el **almirante** admiral
almorzar (ue) to take (have, eat) lunch
el **almuerzo** lunch
  para el almuerzo for lunch
  tomar el almuerzo to take (have, eat) lunch
Alonso Alphonsus
el **alpinismo** mountain climbing
alquilar to rent
alrededorde about, around
los **alrededores** environs, outskirts
el **altar** altar
el **altiplano** high plateau
la **altitud** altitude
alto, -a tall, high, upper
  en lo alto de on the top of
  la Alta California Upper California
  una alta a tall one (*f.*)
la **altura** height, altitude
el **aluminio** aluminum
la **alumna** pupil, student (*girl*)
el **alumno** pupil, student (*boy*)
el **alza** (*f.*) increase, advance
allí there (*distant*)
la **amabilidad** kindness
amable kind
Amalia Amalia

el **amante** lover
amarillo, -a yellow
el **Amazonas** Amazon (River)
ambos, -as both
América America
  la América Central
    Central America
  la América española
    Spanish America
  la América del Norte
    (Sur) North (South)
    America
  la América hispana
    Spanish America
americano, -a American (*of North and South America*)
la **amiga** friend (*f.*)
el **amigo** friend (*m.*)
la **amiguita** little (girl) friend
el **amo** master
el **amor** love
Ana Ann, Anne, Anna
el **ananá** (*pl.* **ananaes**) pineapple
ancho, -a broad, wide
  tiene . . . (millas) de ancho (it) is . . . (miles) wide
Andalucía Andalusia (*territory of southern Spain*)
andaluz, -uza Andalusian
andante: caballero—, knight errant
andar to go, walk; to run (*said of a watch*)
los **Andes** Andes
Andrés Andrew
el **ángel** angel
angosto, -a narrow
la **angustia** anguish
el **anillo** ring
el **animal** animal
  animal de carga beast of burden
el **aniversario** anniversary
anoche last night
anónimo, -a anonymous
anterior earlier, preceding
  anterior a previous to,

earlier than
antes *adv.* before, formerly, sooner
antes de *prep.* before (*time*)
antes (de) que *conj.* before
cuanto antes at once, immediately, as soon as possible
antiguamente formerly, in ancient times
antiguo, -a old, ancient; former
lo antiguo the old
Antillas Mayores Greater Antilles
Antonio Anthony, Tony
antropológico anthropological
anunciar to announce, advertise
el **anuncio** ad(vertisement)
el **año** year
  a los dos años after two years
  al año siguiente (in) the next *or* following year
  ¿cuántos años tiene (ella)? how old is (she)?
  ¿cuántos años (va a cumplir)? how old is (she) going to be?
  ¡Feliz Año Nuevo! (Have a) Happy New Year!
  ¡Próspero Año Nuevo! (Have a) Prosperous New Year!
  tener . . . años to be . . . years old
aparecer to appear
el **apartamento** apartment
  casa de apartamentos apartment house
el **apartamiento** apartment
apasionado, -a passionate
apenas *conj.* scarcely, hardly
aplaudir to applaud
la **aplicación** application
el **apogeo** apogee, highest point
el **aporte** contribution

el **apóstol** apostle
apreciar to appreciate
aprender (**a** + *inf.*) to learn (to)
aquel, aquella (-os, -as) *adj.* that, those (*distant*)
aquél, aquélla (-os, -as) *pron.* that (one), those
aquello *neuter pron.* that
aquí here
  pasar por aquí to pass (come) this way
  por aquí around (by) here
árabe (*m. and f.*) (*also noun*) Arab, Arabic
Aragón Aragon (*region and former kingdom in northeastern Spain*)
el **aragonés** (*pl* **aragoneses**) Aragonese
araucano, -a Araucanian
el **árbol** tree
la **arcada** arcade
el **arco** arch
el **Archipiélago** Archipielago
el **área** area
la **arena** sand
la **argamasa** mortar
la **Argentina** Argentina
argentino, -a Argentine
árido, -a arid, dry
aristocrático, -a aristocratic
las **armas** arms, weapons
  Armas: Plaza de public square
la **armonía** harmony
el **arquitecto** architect
arquitectónico, -a architectural
la **arquitectura** architecture
arriba *adv.* above
  de arriba above
arrojarse to throw oneself
el **arroz** rice
  arroz con leche rice pudding
el **arte** art; craft, skill, artifice
  Bellas Artes Fine Arts
  clase de arte art class

las artes arts, crafts
la **artesanía** craftsmanship
trabajos de artesanía work (labor) of craftsmen
el **artesano, -a** artisan
el **artículo** article
artículo de costumbres article of customs and manners
el **(la) artista** artist
artístico, -a artistic
Arturo Arthur
asado, -a roast(ed)
el **ascensor** elevator
así so, thus, that way
así, así so-so
así . . . como as much . . . as, both . . . and
el **asiento** seat
asociado, -a associated; associate
Estado Libre Asociado Commonwealth (Associated Free State)
asombrar to amaze (one), be amazing
el **aspecto** aspect
aspirar aspire
el **astillero** shipyard
astuto, -a astute, clever
el **asunto** matter, affair
el **ataque** attack
atardecer: al —, drawing towards evening
la **atención** attention
con atención attentively, carefully
Atlántico, -a Atlantic
la **atracción** attraction
atraer to attract
atravesar (ie) to cross; to pass through
atreverse (a + *inf.*) to dare (to)
el **auge** boom, vogue
el **aumento** increase
aun even
aunque *conj.* although, even though

ausentarse to be absent
el **autobús** (*pl.* **autobuses**) bus
el **automóvil** automobile
la **autonomía** autonomy
el **autor** author
la **autoridad** authority
avanzado, -a advanced
la **avenida** avenue
la **aventura** adventure
aventurarse a to venture to
Avila *City in west central Spain*
el **avión** (*pl.* **aviones**) (air)plane
avión de las cinco y media 5:30 plane
en avión by plane, in a plane
avisar to advise, inform
¡ay! oh; alas! ah!
ayer yesterday
la **ayuda** aid, help
ayudar (a + *inf.*) to help (to), aid (to)
el **(la) azteca** Aztec
el **(la) azúcar** sugar
(caña) de azúcar sugar (cane)
Industria del azúcar sugar industry
azucarero (*adj.*) sugar
central azucarero sugar mill
azul blue

B

bailar to dance
el **baile** dance
número de baile dance number
bajar to go *or* come down(stairs), bring down
bajar (a + *inf.*) to go down(stairs) (to)
bajar (de + *obj.*) to get off (out of)
bajo *prep.* under, beneath, below
bajo, -a low, lower
Baja California Lower California
piso bajo first (lower) floor

el **balcón** (*pl.* **balcones**) balcony
Baleares: Islas —, Balearic Islands
el **balompié** football
Baltasar Balthasar (*one of the Three Wise Men*)
el **ballet** ballet
la **banana** banana
bañarse to take a swim (dip); bathe, take a bath
el **baño** bath
cuarto de baño bathroom
traje de baño bathing suit
barato, -a inexpensive, cheap
barbaridad: ¡qué —! how terrible! what nonsense!
el **barco** boat; **barca,** barge
el **barrio** district
el **barro** clay
(olla) de barro clay (jar)
el **barroco** baroque
basado, -a based
la **base** base, basis
básicamente basically
básico, -a basic
la **basílica** basilica
el **básquetbol** basketball
bastante *adj.* enough, sufficient; *adv.* quite, quite a bit, rather
bastar to be enough, be sufficient
la **batalla** battle
la **batería** battery
bautizar baptize
se bautiza a un niño a child is baptized
Beatriz Beatrice
beber to drink
la **bebida** drink
el **béisbol** baseball
Belén Bethlehem
la **belleza** beauty
bello, -a pretty, beautiful
la **biblioteca** library
bien *adv.* well, fine
está bien it is all right

(O.K.), fine, very well,
excellent

más bien que rather than

muy bien! very well!

¡qué bien! how fine
(nice)!

si bien (al)though, while

bienvenido, -a welcome

el **biftec** steak

el **billete** bill, bank note; ticket

billete de (veinte) dólares
(twenty) dollar bill

el **bisté (bistec)** steak

el **bizcocho borracho** tipsy
(rum) cake

blanco, -a white

la **blusa** blouse

la **boca** mouth

la **boda** wedding

aniversario de bodas
wedding anniversary

el **bogotano** resident of
Bogotá (Colombia)

las **boleadoras** *lariat with balls at
one end, thrown so as to twist
around an animal's legs*

el **boleto** ticket (*Mex.*)

boleto de ida y vuelta
round-trip ticket

boleto sencillo one-way
ticket

despacho de boletos
ticket office

Bolívar, Simón (1783–1830)
*Venezuelan liberator of
Northwest South America*

bondadoso, -a kind

bonito, -a pretty, beautiful

el **borracho** drinker

el **bosque** woods, forest

bostezar to yawn

la **botella** bottle

el **botones** bellboy

el **boxeo** boxing

el **Brasil** Brazil

el **brazo** arm

breve brief, short

la **broma** trick, joke

dar bromas a to play
tricks on

brotar to burst forth

la **brutalidad** brutality

buen *used for* **bueno** *before
m. sing. nouns*

bueno *adv.* well, well now,
all right

bueno, -a good

lo bueno the (what is)
good

el **buey** ox (*pl.* ox, oxen)

carro de bueyes ox cart

bullicioso, -a bustling

el **burlador** deceiver

la **busca** search

en busca de in search of

buscar to look for, seek,
get, call for, pick up

buscar a uno to come
(go) for one

C

cabal complete, right

**caballerías: novela (libro)
de —,** novel *or* romance
(book) of chivalry

el **caballero** knight, one who
goes mounted

caballero andante knight
errant

el **caballo** horse

a caballo on horseback

carrera de caballos horse
race

(carro) de caballos
horsedrawn (cart)

montar a caballo to ride
horseback

la **cabeza** head

me duele la cabeza I
have a headache, my
head aches

**Cabeza de Vaca: (Álvar
Núñez)** *Spanish explorer of
the southwestern U.S. in the
early 16th century*

el **cabildo** city hall

**Cabrillo: (Juan
Rodríguez)** *Portuguese-*

*born navigator and explorer,
discoveror of California, 1542*

el **cacahuete** peanut

el **cacao** cacao (*plant*)

cada (*invariable*) each, every

caer(se) to fall, fall down

el **café** café; coffee

(árbol) de café coffee
(tree)

café solo black coffee

la **cafetería** cafeteria

la **caída** fall

la **cajuela** auto trunk

la **calabaza** pumpkin, squash,
gourd

el **calcetín** (*pl.* **calcetines**)
sock

la **calidad** quality

caliente *adj.* warm, hot

el **califato** caliphate

calmar to calm; *reflex.* to
calm oneself, become calm,
calm down

el **calor** heat, warmth

hacer (mucho) calor to
be (very) warm (*weather*)

tener (mucho) calor to
be (very) warm (*living
beings*)

calzado: de—, shoes,
footwear (*adj.*)

la **calle** street

salir a la calle to go out
into the street

callejero, -a street (*adj.*)

la **cama** bed

la **camarera** waitress

el **camarero** waiter

cambiar to change

el **cambio** change

en cambio on the other
hand

caminar to walk, go, travel

caminar por to walk in
(through)

el **camino** road, way

Camino Real King's
(Royal) Highway

el **camión** (*pl.* **camiones**)
truck

la **camisa** shirt
el **camote** sweet potato
la **campana** bell
la **campanada** stroke (*of bell*)
el **campeonato** championship
el **campesino** farmer
campestre (*m. and f.*) rural, country (*adj.*)
el **campo** country, field
    campo de turismo tourist camp
    casa de campo country house (home)
el **canal** canal
    Canarias: Islas —, Canary Islands
cancelar to cancel
la **canción** (*pl.* **canciones**) song
cansado, -a tired
Cantábrico, -a Cantabrian
cantar to sing
el **cantar** song
    Cantar de Mío Cid Song (Lay) of the Cid
la **cantidad** quantity
la **caña** cane
    campo de caña cane field
    caña de azúcar sugar cane
el **cañón** canyon
la **capacidad** capacity
la **capilla** chapel
la **capital** capital (*city*)
el **capitán** captain
el **Capitolio** Capitol
Capricornio Capricorn
la **cara** face
la **carabela** caravel, boat
el **caracol** snail
el **carácter** (*pl.* **caracteres**) character
la **característica** characteristic
característico, -a characteristic
caracterizar to characterize
¡caramba! gosh! dear me! good gracious! goodness!
el **carbón** coal
la **carga** freight, cargo
    animal de carga beast of burden

caribe *adj.* Caribbean
    Mar Caribe Caribbean Sea
el **Caribe** Caribbean (Sea)
la **caricatura** caricature
Carlos Charles
Carmen Carmen
la **carne** meat
caro, -a expensive, dear
Carolina Caroline
la **carrera** career; race
    carrera de caballos horse race
la **carretera** highway
    Carretera Panamericana Pan American Highway
el **carro** cart
    carro de bueyes ox cart
la **carta** letter; card (*playing*)
    carta de presentación letter of introduction
    jugar (ue) a las cartas to play cards
el **cartaginés** (*pl.* **cartagineses**) Carthaginian
la **cartera** purse
el **cartón** (*pl.* **cartones**) *painting or drawing on strong paper*
la **casa** house, home
    a casa de (María) to (Mary's)
    casa de apartamentos apartment house
    casa de campo country house (home)
    casa de la ciudad city house (home)
    en casa at home
    en casa de (Carolina) at (Caroline's)
    salir de casa to leave home
    venir a casa to come to (our) house
casarse get married
la **cascada** cascade, waterfall
casi almost
castaño, -a dark, brown, brunet(te)
castellano, -a Castilian, of Castile
el **castellano** Castilian (*language*)

Castilla Castile
    Castilla la Nueva New Castile
    Castilla la Vieja Old Castile
el **castillo** castle
casualidad: ¡qué —! what a coincidence!
catalán, -ana Catalonian
el **catalán** Catalan (*language*)
Cataluña Catalonia (*region in northeastern Spain*)
la **catarata** cataract
la **catedral** cathedral
católico, -a Catholic
catorce fourteen
la **causa** cause
    a causa de *prep.* because of
la **caza** hunting
la **cebolla** onion
ceder to cede, grant
celebrar to celebrate
célebre celebrated, famous
el **celta** Celt
cenar to eat supper
el **centavo** cent (*U.S.*)
central central
    la América Central Central America
el **central** sugar mill
el **centro** center (of town), downtown
    (estar) en el centro (to be) downtown
    (ir) al centro (to go) downtown
la **céramica** ceramics
cerca *adv.* near, close by
    cerca de *prep.* near
el **cerdo** pork, pig
la **ceremonia** ceremony
cerrar (ie) to close
la **cerveza** beer
la **cesta** basket; wickerwork racket
Cíbola: Siete Ciudades de —, *supposed cities in southwestern U.S. for which the Spaniards searched in vain in the 16th century*

el **Cid**   *Spain's national hero*
el **cielo**   sky
la **ciencia**   science
   científico, -a   scientific
   ciento (cien)   one (a)
      hundred
      ciento (dos)   one
         hundred (two)
   cierto, -a   (a) certain, true
el **cinc**   zinc
   cinco   five
   cincuenta   fifty
      ciento cincuenta   one
         hundred fifty
el **cine**   movie(s)
la **cita**   date, appointment
la **ciudad**   city
   casa de la ciudad   city
      house (home)
   la ciudad de México
      Mexico City
el **ciudadano**   citizen
la **ciudadanía**   citizenship
   civil   civil
la **civilización** (*pl.* **civilizaciones**)
   civilization
el **clamor**   clamor, outcry
   Clara   Clara, Clare, Claire
   claramente   clearly
la **claridad**   clarity, clearness
   claro   *adv.* clearly, naturally,
      of course
      ¡claro!   of course!
         certainly!
la **clase**   class, classroom; kind
   clase (de español)
      (Spanish) class
   dar clases   to teach
   de toda clase   of all kinds
   en clase   in (the) class
   frase para la clase
      classroom expression
   (no) . . . de ninguna clase
      (not) . . . of any kind
   sala de clase   classroom
   clavar   to fix
el **clima**   climate
   cobrar   to charge, collect
el **cobre**   copper

el **cocido**   Spanish stew
la **cocina**   kitchen
el **coche**   car
   en coche   by car, in a car
la **cofradía**   brotherhood,
      sisterhood
   colaborar   to collaborate
la **colección** (*pl.* **colecciones**)
      collection
   colgar (ue)   to hang
   colocar   to place, put
   colombiano, -a   Colombian
   Colón   Columbus
      Día de Colón   Columbus
         Day
la **colonia**   colony, district
   colonial   colonial
la **colonización**   colonization
   colonizador, -ora   colonizer
el **color**   color
   ¿de qué color es?   what
      color is (it)?
   colorado, -a   red
   colorido, -a   colorful
el **colorido**   coloring, color
el (la) **colorista**   colorist
el **collar**   necklace
   combatir (contra)   to
      combat, fight against
la **comedia**   comedy, play;
      theater
el **comedor**   dining room
   comenzar (ie) (**a** + *inf.*)
      to begin (to), commence
      (to)
   comer   to eat, dine, have
      (eat) dinner
      algo de comer   something
         to eat
      mesa de comer   dining
         table
      se come muy bien aquí
         the food is very good
         here
   comercial   commercial,
      business
el **comerciante**   merchant,
      tradesman, businessman
el **comercio**   commerce, trade

la **comida**   meal, dinner, food
   como   as, like; since
      así . . . como   as much
         . . . as, both . . . and
      como si   as if
      tan   + *adj. or adv.* +
         como as . . . as
      tanto . . . como   both
         . . . and
      **tanto, -a (os, -as) . . .
         como** as (so) much
         (many) . . . as
   ¿cómo?   how?
      ¿cómo es (la ciudad)?
         how is (the city)? what
         is (the city) like?
   ¡cómo!   what (are you
      saying)! how!
   ¡cómo no!   certainly! of
      course!
   cómodo, -a   comfortable
la **compañera**   companion (*f.*)
      compañera de cuarto
         roommate (*f.*)
el **compañero**   companion
      compañero de cuarto
         roommate (*m.*)
      compañero de viaje
         traveling companion
la **compañía**   company
   La Compañía   *Jesuit church
      in Quito, Ecuador*
   comparar   to compare
   competir (i,i)   to compete
   completo, -a   complete
   componer   to compose
la **composición**
      (*pl.* **composiciones**)
      composition
el **compositor**   composer
la **compra**   purchase
      ir de compras   to go
         shopping
   comprar   to buy, purchase
   comprender   to
      comprehend, understand;
      to comprise, include
la **comprensión**   comprehension,
      understanding

el **compromiso** engagement, commitment

compuesto, -a *p.p. of* **componer** *and adj.* composed

compuso *pret. of* **componer**

común (*pl.* **comunes**) common, usual, ordinary

los comunes the ordinary (common) ones

por lo común commonly, generally

comunicar communicate

con with

con tal que *conj.* provided that

lindar con to border on

la **concepción** conception

el (la) **concertista** performer (*musical*)

el **concurso** contest, competition

la **concha** shell

el **conde** count

la **condición** (*pl.* **condiciones**) condition

en buenas condiciones in good condition

conducir to conduct, lead

el **conflicto** conflict

conmemorar commemorate

conmigo with me

conocer to know, be acquainted with, meet

dar a conocer to make known

lo conocimos we came to know it

conocido, -a well known, recognized

la más conocida the best known (*f.*)

el **conocimiento** knowledge

la **conquista** conquest

conquistado, -a conquered

el **conquistador** conqueror

conquistar to conquer

la **consecuencia** consequence

conseguir (i,i) to get, obtain, attain

la **conservación** conservation, preservation

conservado, -a kept, preserved

conservar to conserve, keep, preserve, hold

considerar to consider; *reflex.* to be considered

consigo with himself (herself, *etc.*)

consiguió *pret. of* **conseguir**

constantemente constantly

constar de to consist of, be composed of

constitucional constitutional

constituir to constitute, make up

constituyen *pres. ind. of* **constituir**

la **construcción** (*pl.* **construcciones**) construction, building

construido, -a constructed, built

construir to construct, build

construyeron, construyó *pret. of* **construir**

consumir consume

contar(ue) to count; to tell

contar con to count on; to have

contemporáneo, -a contemporary

contener to contain

contentísimo, -a very happy

contento, -a happy, pleased, glad

la **contestación** (*pl.* **contestaciones**) answer

contestar to answer, reply

contigo with you (*fam.*)

el **continente** continent

continúa *pres. ind. of* **continuar**

continuación: a—, immediately afterward(s)

continuar to continue

contra *prep.* against

contrario: por lo —, on the contrary

contrastar to contrast

el **contraste** contrast

la **contribución** (*pl.* **contribuciones**) contribution

contribuir to contribute

contribuyeron *pret. of* **contribuir**

convencer to convince

convencional conventional

el **convenio** covenant, pact

la **conversación** (*pl.* **conversaciones**) conversation

conversar to converse, talk

convertir (ie,i) to convert; *reflex.* to be converted

convirtieron *pret. of* convertir

el **coraje** mettle, spirit

el **corazón** heart

la **corbata** necktie

el **cordero** lamb

cordialmente cordially

la **cordillera** cordillera, mountain range

Coronado: (Francisco Vásquez de) *Spanish explorer of the southwestern U.S., 1540–42*

el **corredor** corridor

el **correo** mail

oficina de correos post office

por correo aéreo by air mail

correr to run

la **correspondencia** correspondence

corresponder to correspond

la **corrida (de toros)** bullfight, bullfighting

cortar to cut

la **corte** court

cortés (*pl.* **corteses**) courteous

Cortés: (Hernán) *conqueror of Mexico*

cortesano, -a courtly

el **cortesano** courtier

la **cortesía** courtesy

cosa thing

cosechar to harvest

la **costa** coast

costa del sur southern coast

Costa del Sol Sunny Coast (*coastal area in Andalusia, between Marbella and Málaga*)

costar (ue) to cost

el **costo** cost

la **costumbre** custom

artículo de costumbres article of customs and manners

el (la) **costumbrista** writer of articles of customs and manners

la **creación** (*pl.* **creaciones**) creation

creador, -ora creative

crear to create

crecer to grow, increase

crédulo, -a credulous

creer to believe, think

creer que (sí) to think *or* believe (so)

¡ya lo creo! of course! certainly!

la **crema** cream

Creta Crete (*Greek island*)

creyó *pret. of* **creer**

la **criada** maid

criar to grow; *reflex.* to be raised

el **cristianismo** Christianity

cristiano, -a Christian

Cristo Christ

Cristóbal Christopher

crítico, -a critical

el **crítico** · critic

la **crónica** chronicle

crudo, -a crude, stark

la **cruz** (*pl.* **cruces**) cross

cruzado, -a crossed

cruzar to cross, pass (go) across

el **cuaderno** notebook

el **cuadro** picture, scene, vivid description

cual: el —, la — (los, las cuales) that, which, who, whom

lo cual which (fact)

por lo cual for which reason

¿cuál (*pl.* **cuáles**)? which one (ones)? what?

cuando when

de vez en cuando from time to time, occasionally

¿cuándo? when?

cuanto *neuter pron.* all that

cuanto: en—, *conj.* as soon as

cuanto antes at once, immediately, as soon as possible

cuanto, -a all that (who)

unos (-as) cuantos (-as) some, a few

¿cuánto, -a (-os, -as)? how much (many)?

¿a cuántos estamos? what is the date?

¿cuánto tiempo? how much time? how long?

¡cuánto + *verb!* how!

cuarenta forty

la **Cuaresma** Lent

cuarto, -a fourth

el **cuarto** quarter; room

compañero (compañera) de cuarto roommate

cuarto de baño bathroom

es la una y cuarto it is a quarter after one, it is 1:15

son las diez menos cuarto it is a quarter to ten

cuatro four

cuatrocientos, -as four hundred

Cuba Cuba

Cuculcán *Maya name of Quetzalcóath, a Toltec god*

cubano, -a Cuban

cubierto, -a (de) covered (with)

el **cubismo** cubism

cubista (*m. and f.*) cubist, of the cubist school

la **cuenta** account, bill

darse cuenta de (que) to realize (that)

llevar cuentas to keep accounts

por su cuenta on their own (account)

el **cuento** short story, tale

el **cuero** leather

la **cueva** cave

el **cuidado** care

con cuidado carefully

tener (mucho) cuidado (de) to be (very) careful (to)

cuidar (de + *obj.*) to look after, care for, take care of

cultivable cultivable

cultivar to cultivate

el **cultivo** cultivation, crops

campo de cultivo cultivated field

la **cultura** culture

cultural cultural

la cultural the cultural one (*f.*)

la **cumbia** *popular Colombian dance*

el **cumpleaños** birthday

cumplir to fulfill, keep (one's word); to reach (one's birthday), be (years old)

¿cuántos años va a cumplir? how old is (she) going to be?

cumplir (dieciocho) años to reach one's (eighteenth) birthday, be (eighteen) years old

el **curandero** medicine man

curvo, -a curved

cuyo, -a whose, of whom (which)
el **Cuzco** Cuzco

Ch

charlar to chat
la **charola** tray
el **cheque** check
la **chica** girl
el **chicle** chicle (*used for making chewing gum*)
Chichén Itzá *ancient Maya city in Yucatán*
Chichicastenango *town in Guatemala*
el **chile** chili
chileno, -a (*also noun*) Chilean
la **chimenea** chimney, fireplace
el **chocolate** chocolate
el **chorizo** smoked pork sausage

D

las **damas** checkers
la **danza** dance
el **daño** harm
hacerse daño to hurt oneself
dar to give, look out on
dar a to face
dar a conocer to make known
dar bromas a to play tricks on
dar clases to teach
dar nombre a to name
dar permiso para to give permission to
dar señales de to show signs of
dar un paseo to take a walk (ride)
darse cuenta de (que) to realize (that)
darse prisa to hurry
lo damos a we are offering (selling) it for

¡qué alegría me da verte! how happy I am to see you!
datar to date
el **dáti** date (*fruit*)
de of, from, about, by, to, with, as; in (*after a superlative*); than (*before numerals*)
de mi parte for me, on my part
de nada don't mention it, you're welcome
de una manera (solemne) in a (solemn) manner
de vez en cuando from time to time, occasionally
debajo *adv.* below
debajo de *prep.* below, under, beneath
deber to owe; must, should, ought to
debido a due to
debiera (I) ought to, should
la **década** decade
la **decadencia** decadence
decidir to decide
décimo, -a tenth
decir to say, tell
decir que (sí) to say (so *or* yes)
es decir that is (to say)
oír decir que to hear that
la **decisión** (*pl.* **decisiones**) decision
llegar a una decisión to reach (make) a decision
decisivo, -a decisive
la **decoración** decoration
decorado, -a decorated
dedicar to dedicate, devote
dedicarse to dedicate (devote) oneself to, be dedicated (devoted) to
el **defecto** defect
defender (ie) defend
la **defensa** defense

dejar to leave (behind), abandon; to let, allow
no dejar de + *inf.* not to fail to + *verb*
del = de + el of (from) the
delante de *prep.* in front of
delgado, -a thin
demás *adj. and pron.* (the) rest, other(s)
demasiado *adv.* too, too much
demasiado, -a *adj. and pron.* too much (many)
demostrar (ue) to demonstrate, show
densamente densely
el **dentista** dentist
dentro de *prep.* within
el **departamento** apartment
el **dependiente** clerk
el **deporte** sport
aficionado, -a a los deportes sports fan
sección de deportes sports section
derecho, -a right
a la derecha to (on, at) the right
el **derecho** law; right
Facultad de Derecho Law School
desaparecer to disappear
desarrollar to develop; *reflex.* to be developed
el **desarrollo** development
desayunarse to take, have, (eat) breakfast
el **desayuno** breakfast
tomar el desayuno to take (have, eat) breakfast
descansar to rest
el **descanso** rest
desconocido, -a unknown
descubierto, -a *p.p. of* **descubrir** *and adj.* discovered
el **descubridor** discoverer
el **descubrimiento** discovery
descubrir to discover
desde from, since (*time*); for (*time*)
desde . . . hasta from . . . to

desear to desire, wish, want

desembarcar to disembark, land

desembocar to empty

el **desempleo** unemployment

el **deseo** desire, wish

tener muchos deseos de to be very eager (wish very much) to

la **desgracia** misfortune

por desgracia unfortunately

deshacer to right, undo

el **desierto** desert

designar to designate, call

la **desilusión** disillusion

desilusionado, -a disillusioned

despacio slowly

el **despacho** office

despacho de boletos ticket office

la **despedida** farewell

despedirse (i,i) (de + obj.) to say goodbye (to), take leave (of)

desperezarse to stretch (one's arms and legs)

el **despertador** alarm clock

despertar (ie) to wake up, awaken; *reflex.* to wake up (oneself)

después *adv.* afterwards, later

después de *prep.* after

después que *conj.* after

poco después shortly afterward

destacarse to stand out

desterrado, -a exiled, banished

destilar to distill

destinado, -a destined

destinar to destine

la **destrucción** destruction

destruir to destroy

destruyó *pret. of* **destruir**

el **detalle** detail

detener to detain, stop;

reflex. to stop (oneself)

detrás *adv.* behind

devolver (ue) to return, give back

te lo devuelvo I'll return it to you

el **día** day

al día siguiente (on) the following *or* next day

buenos días good morning (day)

Día de Acción de Gracias Thanksgiving Day

Día de la Navidad Christmas Day

Día de los Inocentes Day of the Holy Innocents (*December 28, equivalent to April Fool's Day*)

Día (de San Patricio) (St. Patrick's) Day

en estos días these days

hoy día nowadays

todo el día all day, the entire (whole) day

todos los días every day

el **dialecto** dialect

el **diálogo** dialogue

Diana Diana, Diane

diario, -a daily

el **diario** diary

el (la) **dibujante** draftsman; illustrator, master in the art of drawing

dibujar to draw, paint

el **dibujo** drawing

el **diccionario** dictionary

diciembre December

el **dictado** dictation

diecinueve nineteen

dieciocho eighteen

dieciséis sixteen

diecisiete seventeen

Diego James

diez ten

diez (y seis) (six)teen

la **diferencia** difference

diferente different

difícil *adj.* difficult, hard

la **dignidad** dignity

digno, -a worthy

dime = di + me tell me

el **dinero** money

el **dios** god

Dios God

¡Dios mío! heavens!

directamente directly

directo, -a direct, non-stop

el **director** director

el **discípulo** disciple, pupil

el **disco** record (*phonograph*)

el **diseño** design

disfrutar (de + obj.) to enjoy

la **disposición** (*pl.* **disposiciones**) disposition, service

a su disposición at your service

la **distancia** distance

¿qué distancia hay? how far is it?

distinguir to distinguish; *reflex.* to distinguish oneself, be (become) distinguished

distinto, -a distinct, different

la **distribución** distribution

el **distrito** district

la **diversión** diversion, amusement

diverso, -a diverse, varied, different

divertido, -a entertaining, enjoyable

divertir (ie,i) to divert, amuse; *reflex.* to have a good time, amuse oneself

divertirse (ie,i) mucho (muchísimo) to have a very good time

divertirse (ie,i) tanto to have such a good time

¡que te diviertas! have fun!

dividir to divide

divino, -a divine

la **división** (*pl.* **divisiones**) division

doce twelve

la **docena (de)** dozen (of)

el **dólar** dollar (*U.S.*)

doler(ue) to ache, pain

me duele la cabeza my head aches, I have a headache

el **dolor** sorrow

Virgen de los Dolores Virgin of Sorrows

doméstico, -a domestic

la **dominación** domination

dominar to dominate, control, subdue

Domingo Dominic

el **domingo** (on) Sunday

Domingo de Ramos Palm Sunday

Domingo de Resurrección Easter Sunday

domingo por la mañana Sunday morning

los domingos (on) Sundays

dominicano, -a Dominican

la República Dominicana Dominican Republic

el **dominico** Dominican (*of religious order*)

el **dominio** dominion, domination, control

don Don (*title used before first names of men*)

donde where, in which

¿dónde? where?

el **dormilón** (*pl.* **dormilones**) sleepyhead

dormir (ue, u) to sleep; *reflex.* to fall asleep, go to sleep

dos two

los (las) dos the two, both

doscientos, -as two hundred

el **drama** drama

dramático, -a dramatic

el **duque** duke

la **duquesa** duchess

el **dramatismo** dramatic effect

el **dramaturgo** dramatist

la **duda** doubt

sin duda doubtless, without a doubt

dudar to doubt

dudoso, -a doubtful

la **dueña** chaperone

el **dueño** owner

los **dulces** sweets, candy

durante during

durar to last

duro, -a hard, rigorous

E

e and (*used for* **y** *before* **i-**, **hi-**, *but not* **hie-**)

Éboli: La princesa de- Princess of Eboli (1540–1591), *wife of a councilor of Philip II, banished because of her political intrigues*

la **economía** economy

económico, -a economic

el **ecuador** equator

el **Ecuador** Ecuador

echar to throw, put (in)

echar por tierra (a) to throw to the ground

la **edad** age

Edad Media Middle Ages

el **edificio** building, edifice

Eduardo Edward

la **educación** education

el **efecto** effect

llevar a efecto to carry out

¿eh? eh? right?

el **ejemplo** example

por ejemplo for example, for instance

ejercer to exert, exercise

el **ejercicio** exercise

ejercitar to exercise; to practice

el **ejército** army

el (*pl.* **los**) the (*m.*)

el (los) de that (those) of, the one(s) of (with, in)

el (los) que that, who,

which, he (those) who (whom), the one(s) who (that, which)

él he, him (*after prep.*)

la **electricidad** electricity

eléctrico, -a electric

la **elegancia** elegance

elegante elegant

el **elemento** element, ingredient

Elena Helen, Ellen

elevarse to rise, raise oneself

ella she, her (*after prep.*)

ello *neuter pron.* it

todo ello all of it

ellos, -as they, them (*after prep.*)

la **embarcación** (*pl.* **embarcaciones**) boat

embargo: sin —, nevertheless

eminente eminent, prominent

la **emoción** emotion

el **emperador** emperor

empezar (ie) (a + *inf.*) to begin (to)

el **empleado** employee

emplear to employ, use

la **empresa** company, firm

en in, on, at, into, of, by

en avión (coche) by plane (car)

en casa at home

en cuanto *conj.* as soon as

en (el aeropuerto) at *or* in (the airport)

en el centro downtown

en estos días these days

en punto sharp (*time*)

en seguida at once, immediately

en todas partes everywhere

en vista de que in view of the fact that

enamorado, -a enamored, in love

estar (muy) enamorado, -a to be (very much) in love

enamorarse (**de** + *obj.*) to fall in love (with)

el **enano** dwarf

encantado, -a delighted (to)

encantado, -a de conocerte delighted (pleased) to meet you

encantador, -ora enchanting, delightful

encantar to enchant, delight, fascinate, love

encerrar (ie) to enclose, include

encontrar (ue) to meet, encounter, find; *reflex.* to find oneself, be found, be reciprocal, to meet (each other)

encontrarse (ue) con to meet, run across

el **encuentro** encounter, meeting

enérgico, -a energetic

enero January

enfermo, -a ill, sick

enfrente *adv.* in front, opposite

de enfrente *adj.* opposite

enfrente de *prep.* in front of

engomado, -a gummed, glued

enorme enormous, great

Enrique Henry

la **ensalada** salad

el **ensayista** essayist

el **ensayo** essay

enseñar to teach, show

enseñar a + *inf.* to teach (show) how to

entender (ie) to understand

enterrado, -a buried

el **entierro** burial

entonces then, at that time

la **entrada** entrance

entrar (**en** + *obj.*) to enter, go *or* come in (into)

entre *prep.* among, between

entregar to hand (over), give

el **entremés** (*pl.* **entremeses**) side dish, hors d'oeuvre

el **entusiasmo** enthusiasm

envasar to package, pack

enviar to send

envolver (ue) to wrap (up)

épico, -a epic

la **Epifanía** Epiphany (*January 6*)

la **época** epoch, period

el **equipaje** baggage, luggage

el **equipo** team

el **erudito** scholar

el **escaparate** show window

la **escasez** scarcity

la **escena** scene

la **esclavitud** slavery

el **esclavo** slave

la **esclusa** lock

escoger to choose, select

escribir to write

escrito, -a *p.p. of* **escribir** *and adj.* written

el **escritor** writer

escuchar to listen (to)

el **escudero** squire

la **escuela** school

Escuela de (Agricultura) School of (Agriculture)

escuela superior high school

el **escultor** sculptor

la **escultura** sculpture

ese, esa (-os, -as) *adj.* that, those (*nearby*)

ése, ésa (-os, -as) *pron.* that (one), those

eso *neuter pron.* that

a eso de at about (*time*)

por eso therefore, that's why, because of that

el **espacio** space, room

España Spain

Nueva España New Spain (= Mexico)

español, -ola Spanish, (*noun*) Spaniard

el **español** Spanish (*language*)

(clase) de español Spanish (class)

la **Española** Hispaniola

especial special

a precio especial on sale, at a special price

la **especialidad** specialty

especialmente especially

el **espectáculo** spectacle, show, event

el **espectador** spectator

el **espejo** mirror

esperar to wait, wait for; to hope, expect

esperar que (sí) to hope (so)

el **espíritu** spirit

espiritual spiritual

espléndido, -a splendid

el **esplendor** splendor

la **espontaneidad** spontaneity

espontáneo, -a spontaneous

la **esposa** wife

el **esposo** husband

establecer to establish, to settle; *reflex.* to settle, establish oneself

establecido, -a established, settled

el **establecimiento** establishment, settlement

el **establo** stable

la **estación** (*pl.* **estaciones**) season; station

el **estacionamiento** parking

el **estadio** stadium

el **estado** state

Estado Libre Asociado Commonwealth (Associated Free State)

los Estados Unidos United States

la **estancia** stay

estar to be

¿a cuántos estamos? what is the date?

está bien it is all right (O.K.), fine, very well, excellent

estamos a (ocho de noviembre) it is (November 8)

estar de visita to be visiting, be on a visit

estar en (la oficina) to be at (the office)

estar para to be about to

la **estatua** statue

este, esta (-os, -as) *adj.* this, those

el **este** east

éste, ésta (-os, -as) *pron.* this (one), these; the latter

la **estela** stele (*upright sculptured tablet of stone*)

el **estilo** style

estimar to esteem

esto *neuter pron.* this

estratégico, -a strategic

estrechar to tighten, bring closer together

estrechar las relaciones to establish closer relations

estrecho, -a narrow, tight, close

el **estrecho** strait

la **estrella** star

la **estructura** structure

el (la) **estudiante** student

comedor de estudiantes student dining room

residencia de estudiantes student residence hall

estudiar to study

el **estudio** study

estudio de palabras word study

estupendo, -a stupendous, great, wonderful

la **etapa** stage, period

etcétera and so forth, etc.

eterno, -a eternal, everlasting

Europa Europe

europeo, -a (*also noun*) European

evidente evident

exactamente exactly

exacto, -a exact

el **examen** (*pl.* **exámenes**) examination, exam, test

examinar to examine

exceder to exceed

la **excelencia** excellence, superiority, refinement

excelente excellent

la **excepción** exception

la **excursión** (*pl.* **excursiones**) excursion, trip

hacer una excursión to take (make) an excursion (trip)

exhibir to exhibit, show, display

la **existencia** existence

existir to exist, be

el **éxito** success

con éxito successfully

la **expansión** expansion

la **expedición** expedition

la **experiencia** experience

la **exploración** (*pl.* **exploraciones**) exploration

el **explorador** explorer

explorar to explore

la **explotación** exploitation

la **exportación** export, exportation

el **exportador** exporter

expresar to express

la **expresión** (*pl.* **expresiones**) expression

el **expresionismo** expressionism

expulsar to expel, drive out

extenderse (ie) to extend

la **extensión** extension; size

extenso, -a extensive, vast, widely spread

extranjero, -a foreign

extraño, -a strange, foreign; unusual

extraordinario, -a extraordinary

el **extremo** end

extremo (sur) (southern) end

F

la **fábrica** factory

fabricar to fabricate, make,

manufacture

fabuloso, -a fabulous

fácil easy

la **Facultad** School (*in a university*)

Facultad de Derecho Law School

la **faja** band, zone

la **falta** lack

faltar to lack, be lacking

falta mucho tiempo para las seis it is a long time before six o'clock

la **falla** *image burned in street of Valencia on St. Joseph's Day, March 19*

la **fama** fame, renown, name, reputation

tener fama (de) to have the (a) reputation (of, as)

tener fama por to have a reputation for, be known for

la **familia** family

famoso, -a famous

el **fanatismo** fanaticism

farmacéutico, -a pharmaceutical

Fausto Faust

el **favor** favor

hacer un favor (favores) a to do a favor (favors) for

hága(n)me Ud(s). el favor de + *inf.* please + *verb*

por favor please (*usually at end of statement*)

si me hace el favor (if you will) please

favorito, -a favorite

la **fe** faith

febrero February

la **fecha** date

Federico Frederick

felicitar to congratulate

Felipe Philip

feliz (*pl.* **felices**) happy

¡Feliz Año Nuevo! (Have a) Happy New Year!

femenino, -a feminine

el **fenicio** Phoenician
el **fénix** phoenix, model
el **fenómeno** phenomenon
la **feria** fair
Fernando Ferdinand
fértil fertile
el **festival** festival
la **ficción** fiction
la **fiebre** fever
fiel faithful
la **fiesta** fiesta, festival, holiday, feast
la **figura** figure, person
la **figurita** small figure
las **Filipinas** Philippine Islands
filipino, -a Philippine
Islas Filipinas Philippine Islands
el **filólogo** philologist
el **filósofo** philosopher
el **fin** end
a fines de at the end of
en fin in short
fin de semana weekend
hacia fines de towards the end of
por fin finally, at last
y fines de and the end of
el **final** end
la **finca** ranch, farm
fino, -a fine, nice, perfect
firmar to sign
fiscal fiscal
flamenco, -a (*also noun*) Flemish, from Flanders
el **flan** custard
Flandes Flanders (*in Belgium*)
la **flor** flower
florecer to flourish
la **Florida** Florida
florido, -a flowery
Pascua Florida Easter
el **folklore** folklore
folklórico, -a folklore (*adj.*)
el **fondo** background, depth, bottom, substance
al fondo in the background

forjado, -a forged
la **forma** form, shape
en forma (impresionante) in an (impressive) form
la **formación** formation
formar to form
la **fortaleza** fortress
la **fortificación** (*pl.* **fortificaciones**) fortification
la **foto** (*for* **fotografía**) photo
la **fotografía** photograph
sacar fotografías to take photographs
el **fragmento** fragment
el **fraile** friar
francés, -esa French; *pl. noun* French, Frenchmen
el **francés** French (*language*)
Francia France
franciscano, -a (*also noun*) Franciscan
Francisco Francis
la **franqueza** frankness
la **frase** sentence, expression
frase para la clase classroom expression
Fray Friar (*title*)
frecuente frequent
la **frente** forehead
frente a *prep.* in front of, facing, opposite
la **fresa** strawberry
helado de fresa strawberry ice cream
fresco, -a cool, fresh
el **fresco** coolness
hacer fresco to be cool (*weather*)
el **fresno** ash (tree)
el **frijol** kidney bean
frío, -a cold
el **frío** cold
hacer (mucho) frío to be (very) cold (*weather*)
tener (mucho) frío to be (very) cold (*living beings*)
frito, -a fried

la **frontera** frontier
el **frontón** (*pl.* **frontones**) (*jai alai*) court
frutal *adj.* fruit
las **frutas** fruit(s)
el **fuego** fire
la **fuente** fountain; source
Fuente de la Juventud Fountain of Youth
fuera de *prep.* outside of
fuerte strong
fuertemente strongly
la **fuerza** force, strength
la **función** show, performance
fundado, -a founded
el **fundador** founder
fundar to found, settle
la **fusión** fusion
el **fútbol** football
partido de fútbol football game

G

las **gafas** spectacles, (eye) glasses
gala: de —, gala, state (*adj.*)
Galicia Galicia (*in northwestern Spain*)
el **gallego** Galician (*language*)
la **gana** desire
tener (muchas) ganas de to be (very) eager *or* wish (very much) to
la **ganadería** cattle (livestock) raising
el **ganado** cattle, livestock
ganar to gain, earn, win
el **garaje** garage
el **garbanzo** chickpea
la **gasolina** gasoline
de gasolina gasoline
la **gasolinera** filling (gas) station
Gaspar Jasper (*one of the Three Wise Men*)
gastar to waste, use (up)
el **gaucho** gaucho, South American cowboy

el **gazpacho**   cold vegetable
   soup
la **generación**   generation
  general   general
    por lo general   in general
  generalmente   generally
el **género**   genre, literary type;
   sort, kind, type
la **generosidad**   generosity
  generoso, -a   generous
el **genio**   genius
la **gente**   people
  geográfico, -a
   geographic(al)
el **gerente**   manager
  germánico, -a   Germanic
el **gigante**   giant
la **Giralda**   *Moorish tower of the*
   cathedral of Seville
el **gitano**   gypsy
la **gloria**   glory
   Sábado de Gloria   Holy
    Saturday
  glorioso, -a   glorious
  glotón, -ona   gluttonous
   algo glotón   somewhat
    gluttonous, something of
    a glutton
el **gobernador**   governor
el **gobierno**   government
el **golf**   golf
el **golfo**   gulf
la **goma de mascar**   chewing
   gum
  gótico, -a   Gothic
  gozar (de + *obj.***)**   to enjoy
el **grabado**   engraving, print
la **gracia**   grace, charm
  gracias   thanks, thank you
   Día de Acción de Gracias
    Thanksgiving Day
   gracias a ustedes (ellos)
    thanks to you (them)
   gracias por (la visita)
    thanks for (the call)
   mil gracias   many (a
    thousand) thanks
   muchas gracias   many
    thanks, thanks a lot

gracioso, -a   witty, amusing
la **gramática**   grammar
  gramatical   grammatical
  gran   *adj.* large, great (*used*
   for **grande** *before a sing.*
   noun)
  grande   large, big, great
  grandioso, -a   grandiose,
   magnificent
el **grano**   grain
  grave   grave, serious
el **griego**   Greek
  gritar   to shout
el **grupo**   group
el **guacamole**   guacamole (*a*
   salad)
  Guadalupe: Nuestra Señora
   de —,   Our Lady of
   Guadalupe
el **guajolote**   turkey (*Mex.*)
el **guante**   glove
  guapo, -a   handsome,
   good-looking
el **guaraní**   *Indian language of*
   Paraguay
  guardar   to keep, guard
  Guayana   Guiana
la **guerra**   war
  guerrero, -a   warlike
el **guerrero**   warrior
el **guisado**   stew
la **guitarra**   guitar
el **guitarrista**   guitar player
  gustar   to be pleasing (to),
   like
   gustar más   to like better
    (more, most), prefer
el **gusto**   pleasure, delight; taste
   con mucho gusto   gladly,
    with great pleasure
   de su gusto   to his (her,
    your, their) liking
   el gusto es mío   the
    pleasure is mine
   mucho gusto   (I am)
    pleased *or* glad to know you
   mucho gusto en conocerte
    (I am) very pleased (glad)
    to know (meet) you

  ¡qué gusto!   what a
   pleasure (delight)!
  tener (mucho) gusto en
   to be (very) glad to

H

la **Habana**   Havana
  haber   to have (*auxiliary*);
   to be (*impersonal*)
  ha habido   there has
   (have) been
  haber de + *inf.*   to be to,
   be supposed to
  había   there was (were)
  habrá   there will be
  habría   there would be
  hay   there is (are)
  hay (había) que + *inf.*
   it is (was) necessary to,
   one must (should)
  hay (había) sol   the sun
   is (was) shining, it is
   (was) sunny
  hubo (*pret.*)   there was
   (were)
  los (las) hay   there are
   some
  no hay de qué   you're
   welcome, don't mention
   it
  ¿qué hay de nuevo?
   what's new? what do
   you know?
la **habitación** (*pl.* **habitaciones**)
   room
el **habitante**   inhabitant
  habitar   to inhabit, live in
  habla: de — española
   Spanish-speaking
  hablado, -a   spoken
  hablador, -ora   talkative
  hablar   to speak, talk
   se habla   one talks, people
   talk
   te habla (Carmen)
    (Carmen) is talking to
    you, this is (Carmen)
    talking (speaking)

hacer to do, make; to be (*weather*)

¿cuánto tiempo hace? how long (much time) has it been?

desde hace tres horas (for) three hours

hace (dos semanas) (two weeks) ago

hacer buen (mal) tiempo to be good (bad) weather

hacer calor (frío, fresco, viento) to be warm (cold, cool, windy)

hacer un favor (favores) a to do a favor (favors) for

hacer un (el) viaje to take *or* make a (the) trip

hacer una excursión to take (make) an excursion (trip)

hacer una parada to make a stop, stop over

hacer una pregunta (a) to ask a question (of)

hacerse + *noun* to become

hacerse daño to hurt oneself

hacerse (digno) to make oneself *or* become (worthy)

hága(n)me Ud(s). el favor de + *inf.* please + *verb*

¿qué tiempo hace? what kind of weather is it?

si me hace el favor (if you will) please

hacia toward(s); about (*time*)

la **hacienda** hacienda, plantation

¡hala! come on! get going!

hallar to find; *reflex.* to find oneself, be found, be

el **hambre** (*f.*) hunger

tener (mucha) hambre to be (very) hungry

hasta *prep.* until, to, up to, as far as; *adv.* even

desde . . . hasta from . . . to

hasta fines de up to the end of

hasta la vista until (I'll see you) later, so long

hasta luego until (I'll) see you later, until later

hasta que *conj.* until

hay there is (are)

hay que + *inf.* it is necessary to, one must

los (las) hay there are some

no hay de qué you're welcome, don't mention it

¿qué hay de nuevo? what's new? what do you know?

la **hazaña** deed

hecho, -a (de) *p.p. of* **hacer** *and adj.* done, made (of)

el **hecho** event, deed

el **helado** ice cream

el **hemisferio** hemisphere

la **herencia** heritage, inheritance

la **hermana** sister

la **hermandad** brotherhood, guild

el **hermanito** little brother

el **hermano** brother

hermoso, -a beautiful, pretty

Hernán, Hernando Ferdinand

Hernando de Soto *Spanish explorer in the Americas, and discoverer of the Mississippi River, 1541*

el **héroe** hero

la **heroína** heroine

la **herradura** horseshoe

arco de herradura horseshoe arch

el **hidalgo** nobleman

el **hielo** ice

el **hierro** iron

reja de hierro iron grill (grating)

la **hija** daughter

el **hijo** son; *pl.* children

la **hilandera** spinning girl

hispánico, -a Hispanic

la **Hispanidad** Spanish Solidarity (Union)

Hispano, -a Spanish

la América hispana Spanish America

Hispanoamérica Spanish America

hispanoamericano, -a (*also noun*) Spanish American

hispanoparlante *adj.* Spanish-speaking; (*also noun*) Spanish-speaking person

la **historia** history; story, tale

el **historiador** historian

histórico, -a historical

hojear to turn the pages of

¡hola! hello! hi!

holandés, -esa (*also noun*) Dutch; *pl.* Dutch, Dutchmen

el **hombre** man

¡hombre! man (man alive)!

el **honor** honor

la **honra** honor

honrar to honor

la **hora** hour, time (*of day*)

es hora de it is time to

hora en que the time (hour) when

media hora a half hour, half an hour

¿qué hora es? what time is it?

ya es la hora the hour is over

el **hotel** hotel

hoy today

hoy día nowadays

hoy no not today

periódico de hoy today's (news)paper

hubo *pret. of* **haber** there was (were)

el **huevo**   egg
  huevos rancheros   eggs
    ranch style
el **hule**   rubber
  pelota de hule   rubber
    ball
la **humanidad**   humanity (*pl.*
  humanities)
el **humanista**   humanist
  humano, -a   human
la **humildad**   humility
  humilde   humble

I

  ibérico, -a   Iberian
  la Península Ibérica
    Iberian Peninsula
  ibero, -a   (*also noun*) Iberian
la **ida**   departure
  (boleto) de ida y
    vuelta   round-trip
    (ticket)
la **idea**   idea, thought
  ideal   *adj.* ideal
el **ideal**   ideal
el **idealismo**   idealism
  idealista   (*m. and f.*)   idealistic
la **iglesia**   church
  a la iglesia   to church
  igual   equal
    es igual   it's all the same,
      it doesn't matter
    igual que   the same as
    sin igual   matchless,
      without equal
  igualar   to equal
el **Iguazú**   Iguazú Falls
  ilustrar   to illustrate
la **imagen** (*pl.* **imagénes**)
  image
  ilustre   illustrious, famous
  imaginado, -a   imagined
  imaginarse   to imagine
  imaginativo, -a   imaginative
el **imperio**   empire
la **importancia**   importance
  importante   important
la **imprenta**   printing

  impresionante   impressive
  impresionista (*m. and f.*)
    impressionistic
el **impulso**   impulse, impetus
  inacabado, -a   unfinished
  inca   (*m. and f.*) (*also m.*
    noun) Inca
  incalculable   incalculable,
    inestimable
el **incienso**   incense
  incluir   to include
la **independencia**   independence
la **India**   India
  indicar   indicate
  indígena (*m. and f.*)
    indigenous, native
el (la) **indígena**   native, Indian
  indio, -a (*also noun*)   Indian
el **individualismo**   individualism
  individualista (*m. and f.*)
    individualistic
la **índole**   character, nature
la **industria**   industry, trade
  industrial   industrial (*m. n.*)
    industrialist
  industrioso, -a   industrious;
  Inés. Inez, Agnes
  inesperado, -a   unexpected
la **infanta**   royal princess
el **infantado**   *territory given by*
    royalty to a prince
la **influencia**   influence
  influir (en)   to influence,
    have influence (on)
os **informes**   information, data
la **ingeniería**   engineering
  Escuela de Ingeniería
    Engineering School
el **ingeniero**   engineer
el **ingenio**   genius, sugar mill
  (*Am.*)
  ingenioso, -a   ingenious
  Inglaterra   England
  inglés, -esa   English; *pl. noun*
    English, Englishmen
el **inglés**   English (*language*)
  clase de inglés   English class
  ingresar (en + *obj.*)   to
    enter, become a member of

los **ingresos**   income, revenue
  iniciar   to initiate, begin
la **injusticia**   injustice
  inmaculado, -a
    immaculate, without stain
  Inmaculada Concepción
    Immaculate Conception
  inmediatamente   immediately
  inmenso, -a   immense, great
la **innovación** (*pl.* **innovaciones**)
  innovation
  innumerable   innumerable,
    numberless
el **inocente**   person easily duped
  Día de los Inocentes
    Day of the Holy
    Innocents (*December 28,*
    equivalent to April Fool's
    Day)
  insistir (**en** + *obj.*)   to insist
    (on)
  inspeccionar   to inspect
la **inspiración**   inspiration
  inspirarse   to be inspired
el **instituto**   institute
la **integración**   integration
  intelectual   intellectual
  intenso, -a   intense
  interamericano, -a   inter-
    American
el **intercambio**   interchange,
    exchange
el **interés** (*pl.* **intereses**)
    interest
  interés por   interest in
  interesante   interesting
  interesar   to interest
    interesarse en   to be
      interested in, be
      concerned with
    nos interesó mucho (la
      ciudad)   we were
      (became) much
      interested in (the city)
el **interior**   interior
  internacional   international
la **interpretación**   interpretation
  interpretar   interpret
el (la) **intérprete**   interpreter

interrumpir to interrupt
intrínseco, -a intrinsic
la **introducción** introduction
invadir to invade
la **invasión** invasion
el **invasor** invader
el **invierno** winter
la **invitación** (*pl.*
 invitaciones) invitation
el **invitado** guest
invitar (**a** + *inf.*) to invite
 (to)
ir (**a** + *inf.*) to go (to);
 reflex. to go (away),
 leave
 ir al centro to go
  downtown
 ir de compras to go
  shopping
 irse por to go (set out)
  through
 ¡que le(s) vaya bien!
  good luck (may it go
  well with you)!
 vámonos let's be going
 vamos a (ver) let's (see)
la **ironía** irony
Isabel Isabel, Betty,
 Elizabeth
la **isla** island
 Islas Baleares Balearic
  Islands
 Islas Filipinas Philippine
  Islands
el **istmo** isthmus
Italia Italy
italiano, -a (*also noun*)
 Italian
el **italiano** Italian (*language*)
izquierdo, -a left
 a la izquierda to (on,
  at) the left

J

el **jabón** (*pl.* **jabones**) soap
Jaime James, Jim
el **jamón** (*pl.* **jamones**) ham
el **jardín** (*pl.* **jardines**) garden

el **jefe** boss
Jesucristo: antes de —, B.C.
jesuita (*m. and f.*) (*also
 noun*) Jesuit
Jesús Jesus
la **jícara** cup
el **jinete** horseman, rider
la **jira** swing, trip, tour (*Am.*)
el **jitomate** tomato (*Mex.*)
Joaquín Joachim
Jorge George
José Joseph, Joe
joven (*pl.* **jóvenes**) young
 la **joven** young woman
 las **jóvenes** the young
  women (girls)
 (los) dos jóvenes (the)
  two *or* both young men
 los **jóvenes** the young
  people (men)
la **joyería** jewelry shop (store)
Juan John
Juanita Juanita, Jane
el **juego** game
el **jueves** (on) Thursday
el **jugador** player
jugar (**ue**) (**a** + *obj.*) to
 play (*a game*)
 jugar (**ue**) **a las cartas** to
  play cards
el **jugo** juice
el **juguete** toy, plaything
el **juicio** judgment, mind
Julia Julia
julio July
junio June
junto con *prep.* along with
juntos, -as together
la **justicia** justice
la **juventud** youth

K

el **kilo(gramo)** kilo(gram)
 (*about 2.2 pounds*)
el **kilómetro** kilometer (5/8
 mile)
 a muchos kilómetros unos

de otros at many
 kilometers from one
 another

L

la (*pl.* **las**) the (*f.*)
 la(s) de that (those) of,
  the one(s) of (with, in)
 la(s) que who, that,
  which, she who, the
  one(s) who (that, whom,
  which), those who
  (which, whom)
la *obj. pron.* her, it (*f.*), you
 (*formal f.*)
la **labor** labor, work
el **laboratorio** laboratory
el **labrador** farmer, peasant
el **lado** side
 al lado de beside, at the
  side of
 del lado de beside, on
  the side of
el **lago** lake
la **lágrima** tear
lanzar to throw, hurl
el **lápiz** (*pl.* **lápices**) pencil
 a lápiz y tinta pen-
  and-ink
largo, -a long
 a lo largo de along
 **tiene . . . millas de
  largo** (it) is . . . miles
  long
larguísimo, -a very long
las *obj. pron.* them (*f.*), you
 (*formal f.*) (*also see* **la**)
la **lástima** pity, shame
 es (una) lástima it's a
  pity (too bad)
 ¡qué lástima! what a pity
  (shame)!
el **látigo** whip
el **latín** Latin (*language*)
Latinoamérica Latin
 America
lavar to wash; *reflex.* to
 wash (oneself)

le *obj. pron.* him, you (*formal m.*); to him, her, it, you

la **lección** (*pl.* **lecciones**) lesson

lección (de español) (Spanish) lesson

Lección primera Lesson One

la **lectura** reading

la **leche** milk; milky juice

arroz con leche rice pudding

lechero, -a milk, dairy

el **lechón** (*pl.* **lechones**) suckling pig

leer to read

la **legumbre** vegetable

lejos *adv.* far, distant

a lo lejos in the distance

lejos de *prep.* far from

la **lengua** language, tongue

el **lenguaje** language, style

León *province and former kingdom, in northern Spain*

el **león** (*pl.* **leones**) lion

les *obj. pron.* to them, you (*pl.*)

las **letras** letters, learning

levantar to raise, lift; *reflex.* get up, rise

la **ley** law

la **leyenda** legend

el **liberal** liberal (*person*)

la **libertad** liberty, freedom

la **libra** pound

libre free

al aire libre outdoor, (in the) open air

el **libro** book

libro de español Spanish book

puesto de libros bookstall

el **lienzo** canvas

ligero, -a light

el **limón** (*pl.* **limones**) lemon

limpiar to clean

lindar con to border on

el **lino** flax

lírico, -a lyrical

la **lista** roll; menu

pasar lista to call the roll

listo, -a ready

literario, -a literary

la **literatura** literature

el **litro** liter (*about 1.06 quarts*)

lo *neuter article* the

de lo que (yo esperaba) than (I expected)

lo (bueno) what is (good), the (good part)

lo que what, that which, which (fact)

todo lo que all that (which)

lo *obj. pron.* him, it (*m. and neuter*), you (*formal m.*)

lo soy I am

los **locales** site, location, premises

loco, -a crazy, wild

la **locura** madness

lograr to attain, obtain, succeed in

el **lomo (de cerdo)** (pork) loin

los the (*m. pl.*)

los de those of, the ones of (with, in)

los dos the two, both

los que who, that, which, the ones *or* those who (that, which, whom)

los *obj. pron.* them, you (*m. pl.*)

los hay there are some

Los Ángeles Los Angeles

la **lucha** struggle

luchar to struggle, fight

luego then, later, next

hasta luego (I'll) see you later, until later

el **lugar** place

en lugar de instead of, in place of

Luis Louis

Luisa Louise

lujo: de —, de luxe

lujoso, -a luxurious

la **luna** moon

a la luz de la luna in the moonlight

luna de miel honeymoon

el **lunes** (on) Monday

la **luz** (*pl.* **luces**) light

Ll

la **llama** llama (*animal of the Andes*)

llamado, -a called, named

llamar to call; knock; *reflex.* to be called, be named, call (name) oneself

¿cómo se llama (Ud.)? what is (your) name?

llamar por teléfono to telephone, call by telephone

se llama (Felipe) his name is (Philip)

la **llanta (de repuesto)** (spare) tire

la **llanura** plain

la **llave** key

la **llegada** arrival

llegar (a) to arrive (at), reach, come (to)

llegar a ser to become, come to be

llegar a una decisión to reach (make) a decision

llenar to fill

lleno, -a full

llevado, -a taken, carried

llevar to take, carry; to bear; *reflex.* to take away, take with oneself

llevar a efecto to carry out

llover (ue) to rain

la **lluvia** rain

M

Machu Picchu *"lost city of the Incas," near Cuzco, Peru*

la **madera** wood
la **madre** mother
  madre patria motherland
  madrileño, -a of Madrid,
    (native of) Madrid,
    Madrid type
  maestra: obra —,
    masterpiece
la **maestría** mastery, skill
el **maestro** master, teacher
  Magallanes Magellan
la **magnificencia** magnificence
  magnífico, -a magnificent,
    fine
  Magos: Reyes —, Wise
    Men (Kings), Magi
el **maguey** maguey, century
    plant
el **maíz** maize, corn
la **maja** belle
  mal *adv.* badly
  mal *used for* **malo** *before m.*
    sing. nouns
el **mal** evil
la **maleta** suitcase
  malo, -a bad
    lo malo what is bad, the
      bad thing
  Mallorca Majorca
la **mamá** mama, mom, mother
la **manada** handful; flock
la **Mancha** *region in southern*
    New Castile
  mandar to send, order
  manejar to drive (*Mex.*)
la **manera** manner, way
  de manera que *conj.* so,
    so that
  de una manera
    (solemne) in a
    (solemn) manner
el **mango** handle
la **manifestación** (*pl.* **manifes-**
  taciones) manifestation
la **mano** hand
  a manos de into the
    hands of
  de manos de from the
    hands of

  mantener maintain
la **mantequilla** butter
  manual manual
  mañana *adv.* tomorrow
  hasta mañana until (see
    you) tomorrow
  mañana (por la tarde)
    tomorrow (afternoon)
la **mañana** morning
  (ayer) por la mañana
    (yesterday) morning
  el domingo por la
    mañana Sunday
    morning
  por (de) la mañana in
    the morning
  toda la mañana all
    morning, the whole
    (entire) morning
  vuelo de la mañana
    morning flight
el **mapa** map
la **maqueta** mock-up
la **maquinaria** machinery
el **mar** sea
la **maravilla** marvel, wonder
  maravilloso, -a marvelous,
    wonderful
la **marca** brand, kind, make
  Marcos de Niza, *see* **Niza**
  marcha: poner en —, to
    start
  marchar to go; march;
    reflex. to leave, go away
  Margarita Margaret,
    Marguerite
  María Mary
el **marido** husband
  marítimo, -a maritime, sea
    (*adj.*)
  Marruecos Morocco
  Marta Martha
el **martes** (on) Tuesday
  Martín Martin
  marzo March
  más more, most; and
  algo más something
    (anything) else
  más bien que rather than

  más o menos more or
    less, approximately
  (no) . . . nada más (not)
    . . . anything else
  no (tomar) más que (to
    take) only, (to take)
    nothing but
  ¿qué más? what else?
  un día más one (a) day
    longer, one more day
  un rato más a while
    longer
  valer más to be better
  mascar to chew
  goma de mascar
    chewing gum
el **material** material
  materno, -a maternal,
    mother (*e.g.,* tongue)
la **matrícula** registration fee
el **matrimonio** marriage
  máximo, -a maximum
  maya (*m. and f.*) (*also*
    noun) Maya, Mayan
  mayo May
la **mayonesa** mayonnaise
  mayor greater, greatest;
    older, oldest
  Antillas Mayores Greater
    Antilles
  la mayor parte de most
    (of), the greater part of
  Plaza Mayor Main
    Square (*in center of Old*
    Madrid)
  me *obj. pron.* me, to me,
    (to) myself
la **media** stocking; *pl.*
    stockings, hose
  mediados: entre — de
    between the middle of
la **medianoche** midnight
  a la medianoche at
    midnight
la **medicina** medicine
  Escuela de Medicina
    School of Medicine,
    Medical School
el **médico** doctor, physician

medida: a — que as
medio, -a half, a half
  a media milla (at) a half
  mile
  Edad Media Middle Ages
  media hora a half hour,
  half an hour
  (son las siete) y media
  (it is) half past (seven)
el **medio** means; middle
  medium, environment
  en medio de between
  por medio de by means
  of
mediodía: al —, at noon
Mediterráneo, -a
  Mediterranean
mejor better, best; rather
mejorar to better, improve
la **melancolía** melancholy
Melchor Melchior (*one of
  the Three Wise Men*)
la **melodía** melody
el **membrillo** quince (*fruit and
  paste*)
la **memoria** memory
mencionar to mention
Menéndez de Avilés
  *Spanish founder of St.
  Augustine, Florida, 1565*
la **menina** little lady in waiting
menor smaller, younger,
  lesser, smallest, youngest
menos less, least, fewer
  a menos que *conj.* unless
  más o menos more or
  less, approximately
  por lo menos at least
el **menú** menu
menudo: a —, often,
  frequently
el **mercader** merchant
el **mercado** market
el **mercurio** mercury
el **merengue** *Caribbean dance*
la **merluza** hake
el **mes** month
  el mes que viene next
  month

  por . . . al mes for . . . a
  month
la **mesa** table, desk
  mesa de comer dining
  table
el **mesero** waiter (*Mex.*)
la **meseta** tableland, plateau
la **mesita** small table
  mesita de noche night
  table (stand)
el **mestizo** mestizo (*person of
  white and Indian blood*)
el **metal** metal
la **metalurgía** metallurgy
meter to put (in)
el **método** method
el **metro** meter (*39.3 inches*);
  meter (*verse*); subway
metropolitano, -a
  metropolitan
mexicano, -a Mexican
  la mexicana Mexican girl
México Mexico, Mexico City
  la ciudad de México
  Mexico City
  Nuevo México New
  Mexico
la **mezcla** mixture
mezclar to mix, mingle
la **mezquita** mosque
mi my
mí *pron.* me, myself (*after prep.*)
Michoacán *state in west
  central Mexico*
el **miedo** fear
  por miedo de for fear of
  tener miedo (de +
  obj.) to be afraid (of)
  tener miedo de que to
  be afraid that
el **miembro** member
mientras (que) *conj.* while,
  as long as
el **miércoles** (on) Wednesday
Miguel Michael, Mike
mil a (one) thousand; *pl.*
  thousands, many
  mil gracias por many (a
  thousand) thanks for

militar *adj.* military
la **milla** mile
el **millón** (*pl.* **millones**)
  million
la **mina** mine
mineral *adj.* mineral
el **mineral** mineral
minero, -a mining, mineral
  (*adj.*)
el **minero** miner
la **miniatura** miniature
la **minoría** minority
el **minuto** minute
mío, -a *adj.* my, of mine
  (el) mío, (la) mía, (los)
  míos, (las) mías *pron.*
  mine
el **mirador** balcony,
  watchtower
mirar to look at, watch
  mirar la televisión to
  watch television
la **mirra** myrrh
la **miscelánea** miscellany
la **misión** (*pl.* **misiones**)
  mission
el **misionero** missionary
mismo, -a same
  ahora mismo right now,
  right away
  (él) mismo (he) himself
  el pintor mismo the
  painter himself
  la misma the same
  (type) (*f.*)
místico, -a mystic
la **mitad** half
Moctezuma Montezuma
la **moda** style, fashion
  estar (muy) de moda to
  be (very) stylish, be
  (very) fashionable
el **modelo** model
el **modernismo** modernism
moderno, -a modern
  lo moderno the (what
  is) modern
modificado, -a modified
el **modo** manner, means, way

de modo que *conj.* so (that)
de todos modos at any
rate, by all means
el **mole** mole (*a sauce*)
molestar to bother, molest
el **molino de viento** windmill
el **momento** moment
en buen momento llegas
you arrive just at the
right time (moment)
por un momento for a
moment
el **monarca** monarch
la **monarquía** monarchy
el **monasterio** monastery
la **moneda** coin, currency
la **montaña** mountain
montañoso, -a
mountainous
montar to mount, ride
montados a caballo
riding horseback
montar a caballo to ride
horseback
el **monte** mountain
el **monumento** monument
moral *adj.* moral
morir (ue,u) to die
moro, -a (*adj.*) Moorish
el **moro** Moor
el **Morro** *fortress, San Juan,*
Puerto Rico and Havana, Cuba
el **mosaico** mosaic, tile
el **mostrador** counter,
showcase
mostrar (ue) to show
el **motel** motel
el **motivo** motif, theme
el **motor** motor
mover (ue) move
mueve a risa (it) moves
one to laughter
el **movimiento** movement
la **muchacha** girl
el **muchacho** boy
muchísimo *adv.* very much
muchísimo, -a (-os, -as)
very much (many)
mucho *adv.* (very) much,
hard, a great deal, a lot

mucho, -a (-os, -as) much,
(many); very
mudar to change
mudarse de ropa to
change clothes (clothing)
Mudéjar *adj. and m. noun.*
Mudejar (*architectural style*
with Moorish elements
originating in Christian Spain
in the 12th century.)
los **muebles** furniture
fábrica de muebles
furniture factory, factory
of furniture
muere *pres. ind. of* **morir**
muerto, -a *p.p. of* **morir**
and adj.
naturaleza muerta still
life (*art*)
la **muestra** sample
la **mujer** woman, wife, "dear"
la **mula** mule
mundial *adj.* world
el **mundo** world
Nuevo Mundo New
World
todo el mundo
everybody, the whole
(entire) world
el **municipio** municipality
mural *adj.* mural
el **mural** mural (*painting*)
el **muralista** mural painter
la **muralla** wall
murió *pret. of* **morir**
el **museo** museum
la **música** music
musical musical
el **músico** musician
musulmán, -ana (*also*
noun) Moslem, Musselman
muy very; greatly

N

nacer to be born
el **nacimiento** birth; manger
scene
la **nación** (*pl.* **naciones**) nation
nacional national

nada nothing
de nada don't mention it,
you're welcome, not at all
nada de particular
nothing special
(no) . . . nada más (not)
. . . anything else
nadar to swim
nadie no one, nobody,
(not) . . . anybody (anyone)
Napoleón Napoleon
la **naranja** orange
el **naranjo** orange tree
narrar to narrate, relate
Narváez: Pánfilo de —,
early Spanish explorer
la **natación** swimming
natural natural
el (la) **natural** native
la **naturaleza** nature
naturaleza muerta still
life (*art*)
el **naturalismo** naturalism
naturalista (*m. and f.*)
naturalistic
naturalmente naturally, of
course
Navarra Navarre (*province,*
and former kingdom, in
northern Spain)
navegar to sail
la **Navidad** Christmas
Día de la Navidad
Christmas Day
(fiesta) de Navidad
Christmas (festival)
necesario, -a necessary
la **necesidad** necessity
necesitar to need
se necesita un
compañero needed
(wanted), a companion
negar (ie) to deny
los **negocios** business
viaje de negocios
business trip
negro, -a black
neoclásico, -a neoclassic
nervioso, -a nervous
la **nevada** snowfall

nevado, -a snow-covered

ni neither, nor, (not) . . . or

ni . . . ni neither . . . nor, (not) . . . either . . . or

el **Niágara** Niagara Falls

el **nicaragüense** Nicaraguan

la **niebla** fog

la **nieve** snow

ningún (*used for* **ninguno** *before m. sing. nouns*)

ninguno, -a no, none, (not) . . . any

de ninguna clase of any kind (*after negative*)

la **niña** little girl

el **niño** little boy, child; *pl.* children

el **Niño (Jesús)** Christ Child, Child Jesús

Niza: Fray Marcos de —, *Franciscan friar, sent from Mexico in 1539 to search for the Seven Cities of Cíbola*

no no, not

no romance non-Romance (*language*)

noble noble

la **nobleza** nobility

nocturno, -a night (*adj.*)

la **noche** night, evening

buenas noches good evening (night)

de noche at night

el sábado (los sábados) por la noche (on) Saturday night (nights)

esta noche tonight

mesita de noche night table (stand)

pasar una noche to spend an evening

por (de) la noche in the evening

todas las noches every night (evening)

la **Nochebuena** Christmas Eve

nombrar to name, appoint

el **nombre** name

dar nombre a to name

en nombre de in the name of

el **nordeste** *adj.* northeast

el **noroeste** northwest

norte *adj.* north, northern

el **norte** north

la **América del Norte** North America

norteamericano, -a (North) American (*of the U.S.*)

nos *obj. pron.* us, to us, (to) ourselves

nosotros, -as we, us, ourselves (*after prep.*)

la **nota** note

notable notable, noteworthy

notar to note, observe

novecientos, -as nine hundred

la **novela** novel, romance

novela de caballerías novel (romance) of chivalry

el **novelista** novelist

novelístico, -a novelistic

noveno, -a ninth

noventa ninety

noventa y nueve ninety-nine

la **novia** fiancée, sweetheart, girl friend

noviembre November

el **novio** sweetheart, fiancé, boy friend

la **nube** cloud

nuestro, -a *adj.* our, of ours

(el) nuestro, (la) nuestra, (los) nuestros, (las) nuestras *pron.* ours

Nueva York New York

nueve nine

nuevo, -a new

de nuevo again, anew

Nueva España New Spain (= Mexico)

Nueva York New York

Nuevo México New Mexico

¿qué hay de nuevo? what's new? what do you know?

la **nuez** (*pl.* **nueces**) nut

el **número** number, size (*of shoes*)

número de baile dance number

numeroso, -a numerous, many, large

nunca never, (not) . . . ever

O

o or, either

el **objeto** object

la **obra** work

obra maestra masterpiece

el **obrero** workman

la **observación** (*pl.* **observaciones**) observation

observar to observe; *reflex.* to be observed, be seen

obtener to obtain, get

la **ocasión** (*pl.* **ocasiones**) occasion, opportunity, chance

occidental occidental, western

el **océano** ocean

Océano Pacífico Pacific Ocean

octavo, -a eighth

octubre October

ocupado, -a busy, occupied

ocupar to occupy

ocurrir to occur

ochenta eighty

ocho eight

ochocientos, -as eight hundred

el **oeste** west

al oeste to (on) the west

oficial *adj.* official

la **oficina** office

oficina de correos post office

el **oficio** craft, trade
ofrecer to offer
la **ofrenda** offering
oír to hear, listen
   oír decir que to hear that
   ¡oye! listen! hey! (*fam. sing.*)
   ¡ojalá (que)! would that! I wish that!
la **ojeada** glance
el **ojo** eye
la **oliva** olive (*tree and fruit*)
   aceite de oliva olive oil
el **olivar** olive grove
olvidar to forget
   olvidarse (de + *obj.*) to forget
la **olla** jar
once eleven
oponerse a to oppose, face
la **oportunidad** opportunity
   tener la oportunidad de + *inf.* to have the opportunity to + *verb*
el **optimismo** optimism
optimista (*m. and f.*) optimistic
oral oral
el **orden** (*pl.* **órdenes**) order, arrangement
la **orden** (*pl.* **órdenes**) order, command; religious order
   a sus órdenes at your service
ordenar to ordain
   ordenarse de to be ordained as, take orders as
el **organismo** organism
la **organización** organization
organizar to organize
oriental oriental, eastern
   la (más) oriental the (most) eastern one (*f.*)
el **Oriente** Orient, East
el **origen** (*pl.* **orígenes**) origin
   dar origen a to begin, start, originate
original original

la **originalidad** originality
originar to originate, create; *reflex.* to originate
la **orilla** shore
   a orillas de on the shores (banks) of
el **oro** gold
   (reloj) de oro gold (watch)
   Siglo de Oro Golden Age
la **orquesta** orchestra
   director de orquesta orchestra director
os *obj. pron.* you (*fam. pl.*), to you, (to) yourselves
Otavalo *town in Ecuador*
el **otoño** fall, autumn
   día de otoño fall day
otro, -a other, another; *pl.* other(s)
   a muchos (. . .) de otros at many (. . .) from one another
la **oveja** sheep
oye *pres. ind. of and fam. command of* **oír**
   ¡oye! listen! hey!

P

Pablo Paul
pacífico, -a pacific, peaceful
   Océano Pacífico Pacific Ocean
el **Pacífico** Pacific (Ocean)
el **padre** father; priest; *pl.* parents
la **paella** *a rice dish, containing meat, vegetables, and shellfish*
pagar to pay, pay for
la **página** page
el **país** country (*nation*)
el **paisaje** landscape
la **paja** straw
el **pájaro** bird
la **palabra** word
   con la pluma y con la palabra writing and talking

el **palacio** palace
el **palo** stick
la **pampa** pampa, plain (*of Argentina*)
el **pan** bread
Panamá Panama
panamericano, -a Pan American
Pánfilo de Narváez *see* **Narváez**
el **panorama** panorama
la **papa** potato (*Am.*)
el **papá** papa, dad, father
el **papel** paper
el **paquete** package
el **par** pair, couple
para *prep.* for, in order to, to, by (*future time*)
   estar para to be about to
   para que *conj.* in order that, so that
   ¿para qué? why? for what purpose?
el **parabrisas** windshield
la **parada** stop, stop over
   hacer una parada to make a stop, stop over
parado, -a standing
el **Paraguay** Paraguay
el **paraguayo** native of Paraguay, Paraguayan
paralelo, -a parallel
pararse to stop
parcial partial
parecer to appear, seem, like
   ¿no (te) parece? don't (you) think so?
   parecerse a to resemble
   ¿qué (te) parece? what do (you) think of?
parecido, -a similar
la **pared** wall
la **pareja** pair, couple
el **parque** park
el **párrafo** paragraph
la **parte** part, place; area, district
   de mi parte for me, on my part

en gran parte largely
en la parte norte (sur) in the northern (southern) part
en (por) todas partes everywhere
gran parte de a great part of
la mayor parte de most (of), the greater part of
la (tercera) parte one *or* a (third)
por la mayor parte for the most part
particular particular, special
nada de particular nothing special
la **partida** match, game
el **partido** match, game
partido de fútbol football game
partir (de + *obj.*) to leave, depart (from)
a partir de since the end of, starting with
pasado, -a past, last
el **pasado** past
pasar to pass *or* come (by), come in, spend (*time*); to happen, be the matter with
pasa (tú) come in
pasar lista to call the roll
pasar por aquí to pass (come) this way *or* by here
¿qué (te) pasa? what's the matter *or* what's wrong with (you)?
la **Pascua Florida** Easter
pasearse to walk, stroll
el **paseo** walk, stroll, ride; boulevard, outing, excursion
dar un paseo to take a walk (ride)
la **pasión** passion
el **paso** step; float; pass
el **pastel** pastry, pie

el **pastor** shepherd
la **patata** potato
el **patio** patio, courtyard
el **pato** duck
patria fatherland, native country
madre patria motherland
el **patriota** patriot
la **paz** peace
pedir (i,i) to ask, ask for, request
Pedro Peter
pegar to beat, lash
la **película** film
el **peligro** danger
peligroso, -a dangerous
el **pelo** hair
tener el pelo (castaño) to have (dark) hair
la **pelota** ball, *jai alai*
la **península** peninsula
peninsular peninsular (*of Spain*)
el **pensador** thinker
pensar (ie) to think; **+ *inf.*** to intend
pensarlo (ie) to think about it; to think it over
la **pensión** (*pl.* **pensiones**) boardinghouse
peor worse, worst
Pepe Joe
pequeño, -a small, little (*size*)
perder (ie) to lose, miss
comenzó a perderse (it) began to fade
la **pérdida** loss
perdido, -a lost
perfeccionar to perfect
perfectamente perfectly, fine
perfecto, -a perfect
el **pergamino** parchment
el **periódico** newspaper, paper
periódico de hoy today's (news)paper
periódico de la universidad university (news)paper

el **período** period
permanente permanent
el **permiso** permission
dar permiso para (usar) to give permission to (use)
permitir to permit, allow, let
¿nos permite (ver)? may we (see)?
pero but
la **persona** person
por persona per (for each) person
el **personaje** personage, character (*in literature*)
personal personal
la **personalidad** personality
persuadir to persuade
pertenecer a to belong to
el **Perú** Peru
peruano, -a (*also noun*) Peruvian
perverso, -a perverse, evil
pesado, -a heavy
pesar: a — de *prep.* in spite of, despite
la **pesca** fishing
barco de pesca fishing boat
el **pescado** fish
el **pescador** fisherman
pescar to fish
el **pesimismo** pessimism
el **peso** peso (*Spanish American monetary unit*)
pesquero, -a (*adj.*) fishing
el **petróleo** petroleum, oil
petrolero, -a oil, petroleum (*adj.*)
el **(la) pianista** pianist
el **piano** piano
el **pico** peak
pidió *pret. of* **pedir**
el **pie** foot
la **piedra** stone
la **pieza** piece (*of music*), play
pintar to paint
el arte de pintar the art of painting
el **pintor** painter

el pintor mismo the painter himself

pintoresco, -a picturesque

la **pintura** painting

la **piña** pineapple

la **piñata** *jar filled with sweets and toys*

la **pirámide** pyramid

el **pirata** pirate

los **Pirineos** Pyrenees

la **piscina** swimming pool

el **piso** floor, story

    piso bajo first (lower) floor

la **pizarra** (black)board

el **placer** pleasure

la **planta** plant

la **plantación** plantation

Plata: Río de la —, La Plata river

la **plata** silver

    (prendedor) de plata silver (pin)

el **plátano** plantain, banana

plateresco, -a Plateresque

el **platillo** dish (*food*)

el **plato** plate, dish, course (*at meals*)

la **playa** beach

la **plaza** plaza, square

    Plaza de Armas public square

    Plaza Mayor Main Square (*in center of Old Madrid*)

el **plomo** lead

la **pluma** pen

    con la pluma y con la palabra writing and talking

la **población** population; town, village

poblado, -a populated

el **poblador** populator, settler

pobre poor

    el pobre the poor (fellow)

poco, -a *adj., pron., and adj.* little (*quantity*); *pl.* (a) few

    poco a poco little by little

poco después shortly afterward

un poco (de) a little (of)

poder to be able, can

¿podemos (escribirlo)? may *or* can we (write it)?

el **poder** power, hands

el **poderío** power, dominion

poderosamente powerfully

poderoso, -a powerful

el **poema** poem

la **poesía** (*also pl.*) poetry

el **poeta** poet

la **policía** police

la **política** politics

político, -a political

el **polo** polo

el **pollo** chicken

Ponce de León: (Juan) *Spanish explorer, early 16th century, discoverer of Florida*

poner to put, put on, place, turn on, set (put) up; *reflex.* to put on (oneself)

    poner en marcha to start

    poner un telegrama to send a telegram

    ponerse + *adj.* to become, get

popular popular

la **popularidad** popularity

popularizar to popularize, make popular

populoso, -a populous

por for, during, in, through, along, by, around, in behalf of, for the sake of, on account of, about, because of, per, as (a), in exchange for

    por . . . al mes for . . . a month

    por aquí by (around) here, this way

    por ejemplo for example

    por eso therefore, because of that, that's why

    por estas razones for (because of) these reasons

    por favor please

    por la mañana (tarde, noche) in the morning (afternoon, evening)

    por lo contrario on the contrary

    por lo general in general

    por lo menos at least

    por medio de by means of

    por miedo de for fear of

    por persona for each (per) person

    por primera vez for the first time

    ¿por qué? why? for what reason?

    ¡por supuesto! of course! certainly!

    por todas partes everywhere

porque because, for

el **portal** doorway

Portugal Portugal

portugués, -esa (*also noun*) Portuguese

el **portugués** Portuguese (*language*)

la **posada** inn, lodging; *religious celebration* (*Mex.*)

la **posesión** (*pl.* **posesiones**) possession

posible possible

    lo más pronto posible as soon as possible

la **posición** position

el **postre** dessert

la **práctica** practice

practicar to practice

    practicar deportes to practice (go in for) sports

práctico, -a practical

Prado: Museo del —, Prado Museum

el **precio** price

    a precio especial on sale, at a special price

¿qué precio tiene? what is the price of (it)?

precioso, -a precious, darling, beatiful

precisamente precisely, exactly

la **precisión** precision

preciso, -a necessary, precise

precolombino, -a pre-Columbian (*before the arrival of Columbus*)

predicar to preach

predominantemente predominantly

preferible *adj.* preferable

preferir (ie,i) to prefer

la **pregunta** question

hacer una pregunta (a) to ask a question (of)

preguntar to ask (*a question*), inquire

preguntar por to ask (inquire) about

el **premio** prize

el **prendedor** pin, brooch

la **preocupación** (*pl.* **preocupaciones**) preoccupation

preparar to prepare, prepare for

prepararse para to prepare oneself for, get ready for

la **presencia** presence

la **presentación** (*pl.* **presentaciones**) presentation, introduction

carta de presentación letter of introduction

presentar to present, introduce; to give (*a performance*); *reflex.* to present oneself, appear

presente *adj.* present

el **presente** present (*time*)

presidencial presidential

el **presidente** president

prestar to lend

el **presupuesto** budget

prevalecer to prevail

la **prima** cousin (*f.*)

primario, -a primary, elementary

la **primavera** spring

primer *used for* **primero** *before m. sing. nouns*

primero *adv.* first

primero, -a first; early

Lección primera Lesson One

el **primo** cousin (*m.*)

la **princesa** princess

principal principal, main

principalmente principally, mainly

el **principio** beginning

a principios de at the beginning of

al principio at first, at the beginning

la **prisa** haste

darse prisa to hurry

tener mucha prisa to be in a big hurry

probable probable

probar (ue) to try, sample, taste; *reflex.* try on

el **problema** problem

la **procesión** (*pl.* **procesiones**) procession

proclamar to proclaim

la **producción** production

producir to produce, yield

se ha producido has been produced

el **producto** product

produjeron, produjo *pret. of* **producir**

profesional *adj.* professional

el **profesor** teacher, professor (*man*)

profesor *or* **profesora de inglés (español)** English (Spanish) teacher *or* professor

la **profesora** teacher, professor (*woman*)

la **profundidad** depth

profundo, -a deep

el **programa** program

progresar to progress, move forward

progresivo, -a progressive

el **progreso** progress

prohibir to prohibit, forbid

prometer to promise

pronto soon, quickly

lo más pronto posible as soon as possible

la **pronunciación** pronunciation

pronunciar to pronounce

la **propina** tip

propio, -a (one's) own

proporcionar to offer

propósito: a —, by the way

la **prosa** prose

la **prosperidad** prosperity

próspero, -a prosperous

¡Próspero Año Nuevo! (Have a) Prosperous New Year!

el **protagonista** protagonist, central figure

el **protector** protector

proteger to protect

protestar to protest

la **provincia** province

Provincias Vascongadas Basque Provinces

próximo, -a next

publicar to publish

público, -a public

el **pueblo** town, village; people, nation

de pueblo en pueblo from village to village

el **puente** bridge

la **puerta** door

de puerta en puerta from door to door

el **puerto** port

Puerto Rico Puerto Rico

puertorriqueño, -a Puerto Rican

pues well, well then, then

puesto, -a *p.p. of* **poner** *and adj.* put, placed

el **puesto** position, place, job; stand

puesto de libros bookstall

puesto que *conj.* for, since

la **pulsera** bracelet

el **punto** point

en punto sharp (*time*)

la **puntuación** punctuation

signo de puntuación punctuation mark

la **pupila** pupil (*of eye*)

purísimo, -a immaculate, very pure

Purísima Concepción Immaculate Conception

puro, -a pure

Q

que that, which, who, whom; than; *indirect command* have, let, may, I wish (hope)

de lo que (yo esperaba) than (I expected)

el (la, los, las) que that, which, who, whom, he (she, those) who (*etc.*), the one(s) who (*etc.*)

lo que what, that which, which (fact)

tener que + *inf.* to have to, must + *verb*

todo lo que all that

¿qué? what? which?

¿para qué? why? for what purpose?

¿por qué? why? for what reason?

¿qué tal? how goes it? how are you?

¿qué tal . . . ? how about . . . ? how is *or* are (was, were) . . . ?

¡qué! how! what (a)!

¡qué barbaridad! how terrible! what nonsense!

¡qué suerte! what luck! how lucky (fortunate)!

quedar(se) to stay, remain; to be

(me) queda (poco tiempo) (I) have (little time) left

me quedo con (ellos) I'll take (them)

no queda ningún asiento no seat is left (remains), there isn't any seat left

querer to wish, want

¿no quieren (Uds.) pasar? won't you come in?

¿quiere Ud. (decirle)? will you (tell him)?

el **queso** cheese

fábrica de quesos cheese factory

Quetzalcóatl *Toltec god*

quien (*pl.* **quienes**) who, whom, he (those) who, the one(s) who

¿quién? (*pl.* **¿quiénes?**) who? whom?

¿de quién es el libro? whose book is it?

químico, -a chemical

quince fifteen

quinientos, -as five hundred

la **quinta** villa, country house

quinto, -a fifth

una quinta parte one fifth

quisiera (I) should like

quitar to remove, take off; *reflex.* to take off (oneself)

quizá(s) perhaps

R

racial racial

el **radiador** radiator

la **rama** branch, limb

el **ramal** branch, strand

las **Ramblas** avenues (*in Barcelona, Spain*)

Ramón Raymond

Ramos: Domingo de—, Palm Sunday

rancheros: huevos —, eggs ranch style

rápidamente rapidly

rápido, -a rapid, fast

el (los) **rascacielos** skyscraper(s)

el **rasgo** trait, characteristic; *pl.* features, characteristics

el **rato** short time, while

un rato más a while longer

la **raza** race

la **razón** (*pl.* **razones**) reason

con razón rightly

tener razón to be right

reaccionar to react

real real, actual; royal

Camino Real King's (Royal) Highway

la **realidad** reality

en realidad in reality, in fact

el **realismo** realism

realista (*m. and f.*) realistic

realizar to realize, carry out

realzar to enhance

recetar to prescribe

recibir to receive

recoger to pick up

la **recolección** harvest

recolectar to gather

recomendar (ie) to recommend

reconocer to recognize

la **reconquista** reconquest

reconquistar to reconquer

recordar (ue) to recall, remember; to recall (to one), remind (one) of

recreo: sala de—, recreation room

rectangular rectangular

los **recursos** resources, means

la **refinería** refinery

reflejar reflect

la **reforma** reform

el **refrán** (*pl.* **refranes**) proverb

el **refresco** refreshment, cold (soft) drink
refugiarse to take refuge
regalar to give (*as a gift*)
el **regalo** gift
la **región** (*pl.* **regiones**) region
regional regional
el **registro** register
regresar to return
regreso: de —, back
regularidad: con —, with regularity, regularly
la **reina** queen
el **reinado** reign
reinar to reign, rule
el **reino** kingdom
la **reja** grill(e), grating
el **rejoneador** *mounted bullfighter who breaks lance in neck of bull*
la **relación** (*pl.* **relaciones**) relation
relatar to relate, tell
el **relato** tale, story
la **religión** religion
religioso, -a religious
el **reloj** watch, clock
renacer to be born again, be revived, spring up again
el **renacimiento** rebirth, revival, renaissance
el **Renacimiento** Renaissance
de estilo Renacimiento of Renaissance style
la **reparación** (*pl.* **reparaciones**) repairing, repair
tramo en reparación section under repair
el **repaso** review
repasar to review
repetido, -a repeated
repetir (i,i) to repeat
repita(n) usted(es) repeat
el **representante** representative
representar to represent
la **represión** (*pl.* **represiones**) repression
la **reprodución** reproduction

la **república** republic; country
la **República Dominicana** Dominican Republic
repuesto: llanta de —, spare tire
reservar to reserve
el **resfriado** cold (*disease*)
la **residencia** residence, residence hall
residencia de estudiantes student residence hall
resolver (ue) to resolve, solve, settle
respectivamente respectively
responsable responsible
el **restaurante** restaurant
el **resto** rest; *pl.* remains
resultar to result, be, turn out (to be)
Resurrección: Domingo de —, Easter Sunday
el **retablo** altarpiece
retrasar to delay, put off
el **retrato** portrait, picture
reunirse to meet, gather
la **revista** magazine, journal
revolucionario, -a revolutionary
el **rey** king; *pl.* king(s) and queen(s)
Reyes Católicos Catholic King and Queen
Reyes Magos Wise Men (Kings), Magi
Ricardo Richard
rico, -a rich
el **río** river
la **Rioja** *part of province of Logroño in northern Old Castile, famous for its wines*
la **riqueza** (*also pl.*) riches, wealth, richness
la **risa** laughter
el **ritmo** rhythm
riquísimo, -a very rich
Roberto Robert
rodeado, -a (de) surrounded (by)

rodear to surround
rogar (ue) to ask, beg
rojo, -a red
romance *adj.* Romance (*language*)
no romance non-Romance
el **romance** ballad
el **romancero** ballad book, collection of ballads
romano, -a (*also noun*) Roman
el **romanticismo** romanticism
romántico, -a romantic
romper to break
la **ropa** clothes, clothing
mudarse de ropa to change clothes (clothing)
rosa (*m. and f.*) pink, rose (*color*)
rubio, -a fair, blond(e)
la **rueda** wheel
las **ruinas** ruins
rural rural
la **ruta** route, direction

S

el **sábado** (on) Saturday
el sábado (los sábados) por la noche (on) Saturday night (nights)
Sábado de Gloria Holy Saturday
saber to know, know how; *in pret.* to learn, find out
sabroso, -a delicious, tasty
sacar to take, take out
sacar fotografías to take photographs
el **sacerdote** priest
sagrado, -a holy
la Sagrada Familia The Holy Family
el **sainete** one-act farce
la **sal** salt
mina de sal salt mine
la **sala** (living) room

sala de clase classroom

sala de recreo recreation room

Salamanca *city in western Spain*

la **salida** departure

salir (de + *obj.*) to leave, go (come) out

salir a la calle to go out into the street

salir de casa to leave home

salir para to leave for

el **salón** (*pl.* **salones**) salon, (meeting) room, large hall

Salón del Trono Throne Room

la **salsa** sauce

saludar to greet, speak to, say hello to

el **saludo** greeting

El **Salvador** El Salvador

San Salvador Saint (Holy) Savior

san *used for* **santo** *before m. name of saints not beginning with* **To-, Do-**

San Agustín St. Augustine

San Marcos St. Mark

San Patricio St. Patrick

San Quintín St. Quentin (*city in northern France, site of battle in 1557 between France and Spain*)

San Valentín St. Valentine

la **sangre** blood

santo, -a saint, holy

Semana Santa Holy Week

Viernes Santo Holy Friday

el **santo** saint

día de su santo his saint's day

el **Santuario** Sanctuary

la **sátira** satire

se *pron. used for* **le, les** to him, her, it, them, you (*formal*); *reflex.* (to) himself, herself, *etc.*; *indef. subject* one, people, you, *etc.*

secar to dry

la **sección** (*pl.* **secciones**) section

sección de deportes sports section

la **secretaria** secretary

la **sed** thirst

tener (mucha) sed to be (very) thirsty

la **seda** silk

la **sede** seat, headquarters

seguida: en —, at once, immediately

seguir (i,i) to follow, continue, go on

según *prep.* according to

segundo, -a second

seguro, -a sure, certain

estar seguro, -a (de) to be sure (of)

estar seguro, -a de que to be sure that

el **Seguro Social** Social Security

seis six

seiscientos, -as six hundred

la **selección** (*pl.* **selecciones**) selection

seleccionar to select, choose

la **selva** forest

la **semana** week

fin de semana weekend

Semana Santa Holy Week

todas las semanas every week

semejante similar

el **semestre** semester

la **semilla** seed

sencillo, -a simple

boleto sencillo one-way ticket

la **sensibilidad** sensibility, sensitivity

sentado, -a seated

sentar (ie) to seat, set; *reflex.* to sit down

¿nos sentamos? shall we sit down?

sentar (ie) bien a

(uno) to fit (one)

el **sentido** sense, feeling, meaning, judgment, reason

el **sentimiento** feeling

sentir (ie,i) to feel, regret, be sorry

lo siento (mucho) I'm (very) sorry

sentirse (ie,i) (bien) to feel (well)

la **señal** sign

dar señales de to show signs of

señalar to point at (out), indicate

señor sir, Mr.

el **señor** gentleman; *pl.* gentlemen, ladies and gentlemen

los señores (Jones) Mr. and Mrs. (Jones)

señora madam, ma'am, Mrs.

la **señora** woman, lady, mistress

Nuestra Señora Our Lady

señorita Miss

la **señorita** Miss, young lady (woman)

separado, -a separated

septiembre September

séptimo, -a seventh

ser to be

¿cómo es (la ciudad)? how is (the city)? what is (the city) like?

continúa (sigue) siendo (it) continues to be

es decir that is (to say)

es que the fact is (that)

serenar to calm down, make serene

la **serie** series

serio, -a serious

el **servicio** service

al servicio de in the service of

servir (i,i) to serve

¿en qué puedo servirle(s)? what can I do for you?

¿para qué sirven los
  amigos? what are
  friends (good) for?
servir de to serve as
sesenta sixty
setecientos, -as seven
  hundred
setenta seventy
Sevilla Seville
sexto, -a sixth
si if, whether
  si bien (al)though, while
sí yes
  decir (esperar, creer) que
    sí to say (hope,
    believe) so
sí *reflex. pron.* himself,
  herself, yourself (*formal*),
  themselves, yourselves
siempre always
la sierra mountains, mountain
  range
la siesta nap
  dormir (ue,u) la (una)
    siesta to take a nap
siete seven
el siglo century
  Siglo de Oro Golden
    Age
significar to signify, mean
el signo sign, mark
siguiente next, following
  al (día) siguiente (on)
    the next *or* following
    (day)
siguieron *pret. of* seguir
la sílaba syllable
silvestre wild
la silla chair
  simpático, -a charming,
    likeable, nice
simplificar to simplify
sin *prep.* without
  sin embargo nevertheless
  sin que *conj.* without
sino but
  no sólo . . . sino
    (también) not only
    . . . but (also)

sino que *conj.* but
la síntesis synthesis
sinuoso, -a wavy, sinuous
sirve, sirven *pres. ind. of*
  servir
el sistema system
el sitio site, place
la situación (*pl.*
  situaciones) situation
situado, -a situated, located
sobre on, upon, about,
  concerning
  sobre todo above all,
    especially
socarrón, -ona crafty
social social
  Seguro Social Social
    Security
la sociedad society
el sol sun
  Costa del Sol Sunny
    Coast (*coastal area in
    Andalusia, between
    Marbella and Málaga*)
  hace (hacía) sol *or* hay
    (había) sol it is (was)
    sunny, the sun is (was)
    shining
  tomar el sol to take a
    sun bath
solamente *adv.* only
el soldado soldier
solemne solemn
solo, -a alone
  café solo black coffee
sólo *adv.* only
  no sólo . . . sino
    (también) not only
    . . . but (also)
la sombra shade, shadow
el sombrero hat
someterse to submit, be
  subjected
sonar (ue) to sound, ring
sonreír (i,i) to smile (at)
sonríen *pres. ind. of* sonreír
la sopa soup
sorprender to surprise
la sorpresa surprise

¡qué sorpresa! what a
  surprise!
¡qué sorpresa más
  agradable! what a
  pleasant surprise!
Soto: Hernando de —, *see*
  Hernando
Sr. = señor
Sra. = señora
Srta. = señorita
su his, her, its, your
  (*formal*), their
subir to bring (take, carry)
  up
  subir (a + *obj.*) to get
    into, climb up (into)
subjetivo, -a subjective
sucio, -a dirty
Sudamérica South America
sudamericano, -a South
  American
el sudeste southeast
el suelo soil
el sueño sleep; dream
  tener (mucho) sueño to
    be (very) sleepy
la suerte luck
  ¡qué suerte (tienes)!
    what luck (you have)!
    how lucky *or* fortunate
    (you are)!
  ¡que tenga mucha
    suerte! good luck (may
    you have much luck)!
  tener (mucha) suerte to
    be (very) lucky *or*
    fortunate
suficiente sufficient
superar to surpass, excel
la superficie surface
  superior: escuela —, high
    school
la superposición superposition
suplementario, -a
  supplementary
suponer to suppose
supuesto: por —, of
  course, certainly
el sur south

(costa) del sur southern (coast)

en la parte sur in the southern part

extremo sur southern end

la América del Sur South America

Suramérica South America

suramericano, -a South American

surgir to appear, surge, arise

el **suroeste** southwest

el **surrealismo** surrealism

surrealista (*m. and f.*) surrealist(ic)

el **suspiro** sigh

sutil subtle

suyo, -a *adj.* his, her, your (*formal*), its, their, of his, of hers, of yours, of theirs

(el) suyo, (la) suya, (los) suyos, (las) suyas *pron.* his, hers, theirs, yours (*formal*)

T

el **tabaco** tobacco

la **tabla** board, wood

el **taco** taco

tal such, such a

con tal que *conj.* provided that

¿qué tal? how goes it? how are you?

¿qué tal? how about . . . ? how is *or* are (was, were) . . . ?

tal vez perhaps

la **talla** size (*of a dress*)

el **taller** shop

también also, too

tampoco neither, (not) . . . either

tan *adv.* so, as

tan + *adj. or adv.* + **como** as . . . as

el **tango** tango

el **tanque** tank

tanto, -a (-os, -as) *adj. and pron.* as (so) much; *pl.* as (so) many; *adv.* as (so) much

tanto . . . como both . . . and

tanto, -a (-os, -as) . . . como as (so) much (many) . . . as

divertirse (ie,i) tanto to have such a good time

la **tapioca** tapioca

el **tapiz** (*pl.* **tapices**) tapestry

tardar to delay, be long

tardar mucho to take long (a long time)

tardar tanto to take so long, delay so much (long)

tarde late

más tarde later

la **tarde** afternoon

ayer por la tarde yesterday afternoon

buenas tardes good afternoon

(mañana) por la tarde (tomorrow) afternoon

por (de) la tarde in the afternoon, p.m.

toda la tarde all afternoon, the whole (entire) afternoon

todas las tardes every afternoon

vuelo de la tarde afternoon flight

la **tarjeta** card (*postal, birthday, etc.*)

el **taxi** taxi

la **taza** cup

te *obj. pron.* you (*fam.*), to you, (to) yourself

el **té** tea

el **teatro** theater

compañía de teatro theatrical company

la **técnica** technique

técnico, -a technical

la **teja** tile

el **tejado** roof (*of tiles*)

el **tejido** textile, weaving

(fábrica) de tejidos textile (factory)

el **telar** loom

telefonear to telephone

el **teléfono** telephone

llamar por teléfono to telephone (call)

el **telegrama** telegram

poner un telegrama to send a telegram

la **televisión** television, TV

programa de televisión television program

el **tema** theme, topic, subject

temer to fear

la **tempestad** storm, tempest

temple: al —, in distemper (tempera)

el **templo** temple

temprano early

tener to have (*possess*); *in pret.* to get, receive

aquí (lo) tienes here (it) is

¿cuántos años tiene (ella)? how old is (she)?

(no) tener (nada) que (hacer) to have (nothing) to (do), (not) to have (anything) to (do)

¿qué precio tiene? what is the price of (it)?

¡que tenga mucha suerte! good luck (may you have much luck)!

tener . . . años to be . . . years old

tener calor (frío, *etc.*) to be warm (cold, etc.) (*living beings*)

tener mucha prisa to be in a big hurry

tener (mucha) suerte to be (very) lucky *or* fortunate

tener muchas ganas

(muchos deseos) de to be very eager (wish very much) to

tener (mucho) cuidado de to be (very) careful to

tener por to consider as

tener que + *inf.* to have to (must) + *inf.*

tener razón to be right

tener tiempo para to have time to (for)

el **tenis** tennis

Tenochtitlán *Indian name of Mexico City when capital of the Aztec empire*

el **teólogo** theologian

la **tequila** tequila (*Mexican liquor*)

tercer *used for* **tercero** *before m. sing. nouns*

tercero, -a third

el **tercio** third

terminar to end, finish

el **término** term

en primer término in the foreground

la **terraza** terrace

el **terremoto** earthquake

el **terreno** ground, land, terrain

terrible terrible

el **territorio** territory

la **tertulia** party, social gathering

el **testimonio** testimony, evidence

ti *pron.* you (*fam.*), yourself (*after prep.*)

la **tía** aunt

el **tiempo** time (*in general sense*); weather

a tiempo in (on) time

al mismo tiempo at the same time

al poco tiempo after (in) a short time

con el tiempo in (the course of) time

¿cuánto tiempo? how much time? how long?

falta mucho tiempo para

it is a long time before

hacer buen (mal) tiempo to be good (bad) weather

mucho tiempo long, a long time

¿qué tiempo hace (hacía)? what kind of weather is (was) it?

tener tiempo para to have time to (for)

la **tienda** store, shop

la **tierra** land

echar por tierra (a) to throw to the ground

el **timbre** doorbell

tímido, -a timid

la **tinta** ink

tinto, -a deep red; **el tinto** red wine

la **tintorería** cleaning shop

el **tío** uncle; *pl.* uncle(s) and aunt(s)

típico, -a typical

el **tipo** type

titular title

la **toalla** towel

el (los) **tocadiscos** record player(s)

tocar to play (*music*), touch; ring

tocar a (uno) to be (one's) turn

el **tocino** bacon

todavía still, yet

todavía no not yet

todo, -a all, every, entire, whole; *pron.* everything

por todas partes everywhere

sobre todo above all, especially

toda la (mañana) all (morning), the whole *or* entire (morning)

todas ellas all of them

todas las tardes (noches) every afternoon (night, evening)

todo el mundo

everybody

todo ello all of it

todo lo que all that (which)

todos los días every day

la **tolerancia** tolerance

el **tolteca** Toltec

tomar to take, eat, drink

tomar el desayuno (almuerzo) to take (have, eat) breakfast (lunch)

tomar el sol to take a sun bath

Tomás Thomas, Tom

el **tomate** tomato

el **torero** bullfighter

tormentoso, -a stormy

el **toro** bull; *pl.* bulls, bullfighting

corrida de toros bullfight

la **torre** tower

la **torta** flat pancake

la **tortilla** omelet (*Spain*); corn pancake (*Mex.*)

tostado, -a toasted

total *adj.* total

totalmente totally

trabajador, -ora industrious

el **trabajador** workman, worker

trabajar to work

el **trabajo** work, employment, job, position; *pl.* work, labor

trabajos de artesanía work (labor) of craftsmen

la **tradición** (*pl.* **tradiciones**) tradition

tradicional traditional

el **tradicionalismo** traditionalism

la **traducción** (*pl.* **traducciones**) translation

traducir to translate

traducir al inglés to translate into English

traer to bring

el **traficante** dealer, trader

la **tragedia** tragedy

el **traje** suit

traje de baño bathing
  suit
el **tramo** section, stretch
  tramo en reparación
    section under repair
el **tránsito** traffic
la **transparencia** transparency,
  slide
el **transporte** transportation
el **trapiche** sugar mill (*Am.*)
  trasladar to move
    trasladarse a to move to
  tratar (de + *obj.*) to treat,
    deal (with)
    tratar de + *inf.* to try to
      + *verb*
  través: a — de across,
    through
  trece thirteen
  treinta thirty
    treinta y un(o) thirty-one
    treinta y nueve thirty-
      nine
  tremendo, -a tremendous
  tres three
  trescientos, -as three
    hundred
la **tribu** tribe
el **tributo** tribute
el **trigo** wheat
la **Trinidad** Trinity
  triste sad
el **triunfo** triumph
el **trono** throne
  tropical tropical
el **trópico** tropics
  tu your (*fam.*)
  tú you (*fam.*)
la **tumba** tomb
  turismo: campo de —,
    tourist camp
el **(la) turista** tourist
  turístico, -a *adj.* tourist
el **turrón** (*pl.* **turrones**)
    nougat, almond candy
  tuyo, -a *adj.* your (*fam.*), of
    yours
    **(el tuyo, (la) tuya, (los)
      tuyos, (las) tuyas** *pron.*
      yours

U

Ud(s). = usted(es)
último, -a last (*in a series*)
  en estos últimos años in
    recent years
  por último finally, at last
un, una, uno a, an, one
único, -a only, unique
la **unidad** unity
  unido, -a united
    los Estados Unidos the
      United States
la **unificación** unification
  uniforme uniform
  universal universal
la **universidad** university
    **periódico de la
      universidad** university
      (news)paper
  universitario, -a
    adj. university
  unos, -as some, a few,
    several, about (*quantity*)
    a . . . unos de otros at
      . . . from one another
  urgente urgent
el **Uruguay** Uruguay
  Uruguayo, -a Uruguayan
  usar to use, wear
el **uso** use
  usted you (*formal*)
  útil useful
la **uva** grape

V

la **vaca** cow
las **vacaciones** vacation
    estar de vacaciones to be
      on vacation
  vacante vacant, empty
la **vainilla** vanilla
  Valencia Valencia
  valenciano, -a (*also noun*)
    Valencian, of Valencia
  Valentín: San —, St.
    Valentine
  valer to be worth
    valer más to be better

  valiente valiant, brave
el **valor** valor; value
el **valle** valley
  vamos we are going
    vamos a (hablar) we are
      going to (talk), let's
      (talk)
  vano, -a vain
la **vaquería** dairy
  variado, -a varied
  variar to vary
    varía it varies
la **variedad** variety
  varios, -as various, several
  vasco, -a Basque
  vascongado, -a Basque
    **Provincias
      Vascongadas** Basque
      Provinces
el **vascuence** Basque (*language*)
la **vasija** vessel
el **vaso** glass
Vd(s). = usted(es)
el **vecino** neighbor
la **vegetación** vegetation
el **vehículo** vehicle
  veinte twenty
    **veinte (y un, una,
      uno)** twenty (-one)
    veintidós twenty-two
    veintiocho twenty-eight
    veintiséis twenty-six
    veintitrés twenty-three
    **veintiuno (veintiún,
      veintiuna)** twenty-one
la **velocidad** speed
  vendado, -a bandaged
    con los ojos vendados
      blindfolded
el **vendedor** vendor, seller
la **vendedora** clerk (*f.*),
    saleslady
  vender to sell
la **vendimia** vintage
  Venecia Venice
  venezolano, -a Venezuelan
  venir (a + *inf.*) to come
    (to)
    (el mes) que viene next
      (month)

la **venta** sale

la **ventana** window

ver to see; *reflex.* to be, be seen

  (vamos) a ver let's see

veraniego, -a summer (*adj.*)

el **verano** summer

  (vacaciones) de verano summer (vacation)

veras: de —, really, truly

la **verdad** truth

  es verdad it is true, that's true

  ¿(no es) verdad? isn't it (true)? don't you? *etc.*

  ¿verdad? is it true? do (did) you? aren't you? will (he)? *etc.*

verdaderamente truly, really

verdadero, -a true, real

verde green

las **verduras** vegetables

el **vestíbulo** vestibule, lobby

el **vestido** dress

vestir (i,i) to dress; *reflex.* to dress (oneself), get dressed

la **vez** (*pl.* **veces**) time (*in a series*), occasion

  a la vez at the same time

  a veces at times

  de vez en cuando from time to time, occasionally

  en vez de instead of, in place of

  muchas veces many times, often

  otra vez again, another time

  por primera vez for the first time

  tal vez perhaps

  una vez once, one time

viajar to travel

el **viaje** trip, journey

  agencia de viajes travel agency

  ¡buen viaje! (have) a good trip!

compañero de viaje traveling companion

hacer un (el) viaje to take *or* make a (the) trip

viaje de negocios business trip

Vicente Vincent

la **victoria** victory

la **vida** life

la **vidriera de colores** stained-glass window

el **vidio** glass

viejo, -a old

  la **vieja** old woman

el **viento** wind

  hacer (mucho) viento to be (very) windy

  molino de viento windmill

el **viernes** (on) Friday

  Viernes Santo Holy Friday

vigoroso, -a vigorous

el **vino** wine

la **viñeta** vignette

el **violoncelista** cellist

la **Virgen** Blessed Virgin (Mary)

el **visigodo** Visigoth

la **visita** visit, call

  estar de visita to visit, be visiting

visitar to visit, call on

la **víspera** eve

  víspera de Navidad Christmas Eve

  víspera del Año Nuevo New Year's Eve

la **vista** sight, view

  en vista de que in view of the fact that

  hasta la vista until (I'll) see you later, so long

la **vivienda** dwelling, home

vivir to live

vivo, -a alive, live, living

Vizcaya Biscay (*one of the Basque Provinces in Northern Spain.*)

el **vocabulario** vocabulary

volar (ue) to fly

que ciento volando than one (a) hundred on the wing

el **volcán** (*pl.* **volcanes**) volcano

volver (ue) to return, come back; *reflex.* to become

  ahora vuelvo I'll be right back

  volver a (verla) (to see her) again

  volverse (loco) to become *or* go (crazy, wild)

  vuelvo en seguida I'll be right back, I'll return at once

vosotros, -as you (*fam. pl.*), yourselves

la **voz** (*pl.* **voces**) voice

el **vuelo** flight

  vuelo de la mañana (tarde) morning (afternoon) flight

la **vuelta** return; change (*money*)

  boleto de ida y vuelta round-trip ticket

vuestro, -a *adj.* your (*fam. pl.*), of yours

  (el) vuestro, (la) vuestra, (los) vuestros, (las) vuestras *pron.* yours

Y

y and

  (a la una) y (diez) (at ten minutes) after (one)

ya already, now

  ¡ya lo creo! of course! certainly!

  ya no no longer

yo I

la **yuca** yucca

Z

la **zapatería** shoe store

el **zapato** shoe

la **zona** zone

VOCABULARY
English-Spanish

A

a, an un, una; *often untranslated*
able: be —, poder
about *prep.* de, sobre, acerca de, en; (*probability*) *use future tense*
  at about (*time*) a eso de
  be about to estar para
above *prep.* sobre
  above all sobre todo
accompany acompañar
ache doler(ue)
  my head aches me duele la cabeza
across: run—, encontrarse (ue) con
ad el anuncio
afraid: be — (of, that) tener miedo (de, de que)
after *prep.* después de; *conj.* después que; (*in giving time*) y
afternoon la tarde
  afternoon flight vuelo de la tarde
  all afternoon toda la tarde
  every afternoon todas las tardes
  good afternoon buenas tardes
  in the afternoon por la tarde; (*when the hour is given*) de la tarde
  (tomorrow) afternoon (mañana) por la tarde
afterward(s) *adv.* después
again volver a (+ *inf.*)
against *prep.* contra
agency la agencia
  travel agency agencia de viajes
agent el agente
ago: (an hour)—, hace (una hora)

agriculture la agricultura
air: by—mail por correo aéreo
airport el aeropuerto
  at the airport en el aeropuerto
alarm clock el despertador
all todo, -a; *pl.* todos, -as
  above all sobre todo
  all that cuanto, todo lo que
allow dejar, permitir
almost casi
along *prep.* por
  pass along pasar por
already ya
also también
although aunque
always siempre
A.M. de la mañana
America América
  South America Suramérica
  Spanish America Hispanoamérica
American *adj. and noun* norteamericano, -a
  Spanish American hispanoamericano, -a
and y
Ann Ana
anniversary el aniversario
  wedding anniversary aniversario de bodas
another otro, -a
answer contestar
any *adj. and pron.* alguno, -a, (*before m. sing. nouns*) algún (*after negative*) ninguno, -a (ningún); *often not translated*
  at any rate de todos modos
anyone alguien, (*after negative or comparative*) nadie
anything algo, (*after negative*) nada
  anything else algo más

apartment el apartamento
  apartment house casa de apartamentos
approach acercarse (a + *obj.* or *inf.*)
April abril
aren't they? ¿(no es) verdad?
Argentina la Argentina
arrive llegar (a + *obj.*)
  arrive downtown llegar al centro
  arrive home llegar a casa
Arthur Arturo
as tan, como
  as + *adj. or adv.* + as tan . . . como
  as if como si
ask (*question*) preguntar; (*request*) pedir (i,i)
  ask a question (of) hacer una pregunta (a)
  ask about preguntar por
  ask for (*request*) pedir (i,i)
  (he) asks us questions (él) nos hace preguntas
aspect el aspecto
at a, en, de
  at about (*time*) a eso de
  at (Caroline's) en casa de (Carolina)
  at home en casa
  at noon al mediodía
  at (the university) en (la universidad)
August agosto
aunt la tía
awaken (*trans.*) despertar (ie)

B

bad malo, -a, (*before m. sing. nouns*) mal
  it is too bad es (una) lástima

baseball el béisbol
basketball el básquetbol
Basque vasco, -a
bath: take a sun— tomar el
 sol
bathing suit el traje de baño
bathroom el cuarto de baño
be estar, ser; encontrarse (ue),
 (*remain*) quedarse
  aren't they? isn't it, *etc.?*
   ¿(no es) verdad?
  be able poder
  be about to estar para
  be careful tener cuidado
  be fine (*health*) estar bien
  be on vacation estar de
   vacaciones
  be right tener razón
  be sleepy tener sueño
  be sorry sentir (ie,i)
  be true ser verdad (cierto)
  be (very) cold (warm) (*living
   beings*) tener (mucho) frío
   (calor)
  be (very) glad to tener
   (mucho) gusto en, alegrarse
   (mucho) de
  **be (very) grateful
   to** agradecer (mucho) a
  be (very) warm
   (*weather*) hacer (mucho)
   calor
  be (very) windy hacer
   (mucho) viento
  here (it) is aquí (lo) tienes
   (tiene Ud.)
  how are you? ¿cómo estás
   (está Ud.)?
  **how old is he going to
   be?** ¿cuántos años va a
   tener (cumplir)?
  there is (are) hay
  there was (were) había
  there will be habrá
  what time is it? ¿qué hora
   es?
  you're welcome no hay de
   qué, de nada
beach la playa

Beatrice Beatriz
beautiful hermoso -a,
 bonito, -a
because porque
become + *adj.* ponerse; + *noun
 or* rico hacerse, llegar a ser
bed la cama
  go to bed acostarse (ue)
bedroom la alcoba
before *prep.* antes de; *conj.* antes
 (de) que
beg rogar (ue)
begin (to) comenzar (ie)
 (a + *inf.*), empezar (ie)
 (a + *inf.*)
believe creer
bellboy el botones
besides *adv.* además
best, better mejor
  it is better es mejor, vale
   más
Betty Isabel
bill el billete
  (twenty-dollar) bill billete
   (de veinte dólares)
birth el nacimiento
birthday el cumpleaños
bit: quite a—, bastante
black negro, -a
blouse la blusa
blue azul
  the blue one (*m.*) el azul
book el libro
  Spanish book libro de
   español
boy el muchacho
bracelet la pulsera
breakfast el desayuno
  eat (take) breakfast
   desayunarse, tomar el
   desayuno
bring traer
brother el hermano
  little brother el hermanito
build construir
building el edificio
bus el autobús (*pl.* autobuses)
  the ten-o'clock bus el
   autobús de las diez

business los negocios; *adj.*
 comercial
  business trip viaje de
   negocios
busy ocupado, -a
but pero, (*after negative*) sino
buy comprar
by por
  by car (plane) en coche
   (avión)
  by the way a propósito

C

call llamar, (*telephone*) llamar
 (por teléfono)
can poder, (*know how*) saber;
 for conjecture use future tense
capital (*city*) la capital
car el coche
  by car en coche
card (*playing*) la carta; (*postal,
 birthday, etc.*) la tarjeta
  play cards jugar (ue) a las
   cartas
careful: be—, tener cuidado
Carmen Carmen
Caroline Carolina
  at Caroline's en casa de
   Carolina
carry llevar
celebrate celebrar
century el siglo
Charles Carlos
charming simpático, -a
  very charming (*m.*) muy
   simpático, simpatiquísimo
chat charlar
check el cheque
Christopher Cristóbal
church la iglesia
  to church a la iglesia
city la ciudad
  Mexico City México, la
   ciudad de México
class la clase
  (come) to class (venir) a
   clase

(French) class clase (de francés)

in class en clase

classroom la sala de clase

clean limpiar

cleaning shop la tintorería

clerk el dependiente, (*f.*) la vendedora

clock: alarm—, el despertador

close cerrar (ie)

cloud la nube

coffee el café

cold el frío, (*disease*) el resfriado

be (very) cold (*living beings*) tener (mucho) frío

Colombian colombiano, -a

colonial colonial

color el color

what color is (it)? ¿de qué color es . . . ?

Columbus Colón

Columbus Day Día de Colón

come venir

come by pasar

come in pasar, entrar

come to know conocer

won't you come in? ¿no quieren (Uds.) pasar (entrar)?

comfortable cómodo, -a

companion (*m.*) el compañero

traveling companion compañero de viaje

company la empresa, la compañía

congratulate felicitar

continue seguir (i,i), continuar

contribution la contribución (*pl.* contribuciones)

cool fresco, -a; (*noun with* hacer) el fresco

be (very) cool (*weather*) hacer (mucho) fresco

correspond corresponder

could *imp., pret., cond. ind., or imp. subj. of* poder

count contar (ue)

counter el mostrador

country el campo, (*nation*) el país

country home casa de campo

couple el par

course: of —! ¡claro! ¡ya lo creo! ¡por supuesto!

court (*jai alai*) el frontón

cousin el primo, la prima

covered (with) cubierto, -a (de)

crazy loco, -a

go crazy volverse (ue) loco, -a

culture la cultura

cumbia la cumbia

Cuzco el Cuzco

D

dad (el) papá

dance el baile; bailar

dance number número de baile

darling precioso, -a

date la fecha, (*appointment*) la cita

daughter la hija

day el día

Columbus Day Día de Colón

every day todos los días

Thanksgiving Day Día de Acción de Gracias

these days en estos días

deal: a great —, mucho

December diciembre

decide decidir

decision la decisión

make (reach) a decision llegar a una decisión

delay tardar; (*set back*) retrasar

delighted to encantado, -a de

dentist el dentista

department store el almacén

departure la salida

desire desear

desk la mesa

Diane Diana

different diferente

difficult difícil

dining room el comedor

dining table la mesa de comer

dinner: eat (have) —, comer

directly directamente

discover descubrir

display exhibir

district el barrio

do hacer; *not translated as an auxiliary*

do a favor to hacer un favor a

don't *or* **didn't (they)?, does he?** ¿(no es) verdad?

what can I do for you? ¿en qué puedo servirle(s)?

doctor el médico

dollar (*U.S.*) el dólar

(twenty)-dollar bill billete de (veinte) dólares

door la puerta

doorbell el timbre

down: go — (to) bajar (a)

fall down caerse

lie down acostarse (ue)

sit down sentarse (ie)

downstairs: go —, bajar

downtown el centro

(be) downtown (estar) en el centro

(go) downtown (ir) al centro

dress el vestido

dress (*oneself*), **get dressed** vestirse (i,i)

during durante

E

each cada (*invariable*)

(look at) each other (mirar)se

eager: be (very) — to tener (muchos) deseos de (+ *inf.*), tener (muchas) ganas de (+ *inf.*)

early temprano

easy fácil
eat comer
  eat breakfast tomar el desayuno, desayunarse
  eat lunch tomar el almuerzo, almorzar (ue)
  eat supper cenar
  something to eat algo de comer
Edward Eduardo
eh? ¿eh?
eight ocho
  at eight o'clock a las ocho
  at half past eight a las ocho y media
eleven once
  at eleven o'clock a las once
else: anything —, algo más
employee el empleado
engineer el ingeniero
English *adj.* inglés, -esa; (*language*) el inglés
  English (class) (clase) de inglés
enjoy disfrutar (de + *obj.*)
enough *adj.* bastante
enter entrar (en + *obj.*)
especially especialmente
even though aunque
evening la noche
  in the evening por la noche
  spend an evening pasar una noche
every todo, -a
  every afternoon (night) todas las tardes (noches)
  every day todos los días
everybody todo el mundo, todos
everything *pron.* todo
  he has probably prepared everything already ya lo habrá preparado todo
everywhere por todas partes
examination el examen (*pl.* exámenes)
example ejemplo
  for example por ejemplo
excellent excelente

excursion la excursión
  make an excursion hacer una excursión
exercise el ejercicio
expect esperar
expensive caro, -a
experience la experiencia

F

factory la fábrica
fail: not to — to no dejar de (+ *inf.*)
fall el otoño
  fall day día de otoño
  in fall en el otoño
fall down caerse
fall in love (with) enamorarse (de)
family la familia
famous famoso, -a
far (away) *adv.* lejos
farm *adj.* agrícola (*m. and f.*)
fascinate encantar
fast rápido, -a
father el padre, el papá
favor el favor
  do a favor to hacer un favor a
fear temer
February febrero
feel sentirse (ie,i)
  feel well (better) sentirse (ie, i) bien (mejor)
  how do you feel? ¿cómo te sientes (se siente Ud.)?
fever la fiebre
  (she) has a fever (ella) tiene fiebre
fifteen quince
fifty cincuenta
film la película
finally por fin
find encontrar (ue), hallar
  find out (*in pret.*) saber
fine fino, -a
  be fine (*health*) estar bien
finish terminar
firm la empresa

first *adj.* primero, -a, (*before m. sing. nouns*) primer; *adv.* primero
  at first al principio
  first floor piso bajo
fit (one) sentar (ie) bien a (uno)
five cinco
flight el vuelo
  afternoon flight vuelo de la tarde
floor el piso
  first floor piso bajo
Florida la Florida
flower la flor
fly volar (ue)
following siguiente
fond (of) aficionado, -a (a)
  be fond of ser aficionado, -a a
football el fútbol
  football game partido de fútbol
for para, por
  for (several years) desde hace (varios años) *or* hace (varios años) que (+ *verb*)
forehead la frente
foreign extranjero, -a
forest el bosque
forget (to) olvidarse (de + *obj.*)
  forget that olvidarse de que
four cuatro
  at four o'clock a las cuatro
  four hundred cuatrocientos, -as
  on the (four-o'clock) plane en el avión (de las cuatro)
fourteen catorce
fourth: the — of July el cuatro de julio
free libre
French *adj.* francés, -esa; (*language*) el francés
  French (class) (clase) de francés
friend el amigo, la amiga

girl friend la novia, la amiga
from de, desde
  from ... to desde ... hasta
front: in — of *prep.* frente a
furniture los muebles

G

game el juego, (*match*) el partido
garden el jardín (*pl.* jardines)
generally generalmente
gentleman el señor
  gentlemen señores
George Jorge
German (*language*) el alemán
get obtener, conseguir (i,i); (*after search*) buscar
  get *or* **become (nervous)** ponerse (nervioso, -a)
  get dressed vestirse (i,i)
  get going! ¡hala!
  get up levantarse
  let's get up vamos a levantarnos, levantémonos
gift el regalo
girl la muchacha, la chica
  girl friend la novia, la amiga
give dar, (*as a gift*) regalar
glad: be — that alegrarse de que
  be (very) glad (to) alegrarse (mucho) (de), tener (mucho) gusto en
gladly con mucho gusto
glass el vaso
glasses (*spectacles*) las gafas
glove el guante
go ir (a + *obj.*)
  get going! ¡hala!
  go crazy volverse (ue) loco, -a
  go down(stairs) (to) bajar (a)
  go looking for andar (ir) buscando

go shopping ir de compras
go to bed acostarse (ue)
go (to Mary's) ir (a casa de María)
go to sleep dormirse (ue,u)
go with ir con, acompañar
let's be going vámonos
let's go vamos (a + *obj.*)
let's not go no vayamos
we are going (to) vamos (a)
gold el oro
  gold (watch) (reloj) de oro
golf el golf
good bueno, -a, (*before m. sing. nouns*) buen
  good afternoon buenas tardes
  good morning buenos días
  have a very good time divertirse (ie,i) mucho (muchísimo)
grateful: be (very) — to agradecer (mucho) a
great (*before sing. nouns*) gran
  a great deal mucho
green verde
  the green one (*m.*) el verde
group el grupo
Guadalupe Guadalupe
guest el invitado

H

hair el pelo
half medio, -a
  a half hour later media hora más tarde
  at half past (twelve) a (las doce) y media
hall: residence —, la residencia
hand la mano
hand (over) entregar
handsome guapo, -a
  very handsome (*m.*) muy guapo, guapísimo
happy contento, -a, feliz (*pl.* felices)

how happy I am to see you! ¡qué alegría *or* gusto me da (¡cuánto me alegro de) verte!
  she is very happy (ella) está muy contenta (contentísima)
hard *adv.* mucho
  (study) hard (estudiar) mucho
hat el sombrero
have tener; (*auxiliary*) haber
  have (*causative*) hacer *or* mandar + *inf.*
  have (*indir. command*) que + *pres. subj.*
  have a (very) good time divertirse (ie,i) (mucho *or* muchísimo)
  have dinner comer
  have just acabar de (+ *inf.*)
  have little time left quedar poco tiempo a (uno)
  have lunch almorzar (ue), tomar el almuerzo
  have nothing to do no tener nada que hacer
  have time to tener tiempo para
  have to tener que (+ *inf.*)
he él, (*the latter*) éste
head la cabeza
  my head aches me duele la cabeza
hear oír
  hear that oír decir que
heavens! ¡Dios mío!
Helen Elena
hello hola
Henry Enrique
her *adj.* su(s); su(s) *or* el (la, los, las) ... de ella
her *dir. obj.* la; *indir. obj.* le; *after prep.* ella
here aquí
  here (it) is aquí (lo) tienes (tiene Ud.)
hers *pron.* (el) suyo, (la) suya, *etc.,* (el, la, los, las) de ella
  of hers *adj.* suyo, -a, de ella

him *dir. obj.* lo, le; *indir. obj.* le; *after prep.* él

his *adj.* su(s); su(s) *or* el (la, los, las) . . . de él; *pron.* (el) suyo, (la) suya, *etc.,* (el, la, los, las) de él

  of his *adj.* suyo, -a, de él

holiday la fiesta

home la casa

  (arrive) home (llegar) a casa

  at home en casa

  country home casa de campo

  leave home salir de casa

  take home llevar a casa

honeymoon la luna de miel

hope esperar

  hope so esperar que sí

horseback: ride —, montar a caballo

hot (*noun with* hacer) el calor

  be hot (*weather*) hacer calor

hotel el hotel

hour la hora

  a half hour media hora

house la casa

  apartment house casa de apartamentos

how: know — to saber (+ *inf.*)

how? ¿cómo?

  how are you? ¿cómo estás (está Ud.)? ¿qué tal?

  how long? ¿cuánto tiempo?

  how much (many)? ¿cuánto, -a (-os), -as)?

how + *adj. or adv.!* ¡qué . . . !

  how + *verb!* ¡cómo . . . ! ¡cuánto . . . !

  how glad we were to see them! ¡cuánto nos gustó (nos alegramos de) verlos!

  how (lucky)! ¡qué (suerte)!

  how I would like to meet him! ¡cómo (cuánto) me gustaría conocerlo!

hundred: a (one) —, ciento, (*before nouns and* mil) cien

  five hundred quinientos, -as

(four) hundred (cuatro-) cientos, -as

  one hundred (twenty-five) ciento (veinticinco *or* veinte y cinco)

hungry: be (very) —, tener (mucha) hambre

hurry darse prisa

hurt oneself hacerse daño

husband el marido, el esposo

I

I yo

idea la idea

if si

ill enfermo, -a

important importante

in en, por, de, a; (*after a superlative*) de

Inca el inca

independence la independencia

information los informes

inhabitant el habitante

insist (on) insistir (en + *obj.*)

intend pensar (ie) (+ *inf.*)

interesting interesante

introduce presentar

introduction la presentación (*pl.* presentaciones)

  letter of introduction carta de presentación

invite invitar (a + *inf.*)

it *dir. obj.* lo (*m. and neuter*), la (*f.*); *indir. obj.* le; (*usually omitted as subject*) él (*m.*), ella (*f.*); *after prep.* él (*m.*), ella (*f.*)

Italian italiano, -a

J

Jane Juanita

January enero

jewelry store (shop) la joyería

Jim Jaime

Joe Pepe, José

John Juan

Joseph José

Julia Julia

July julio

June junio

just: have —, acabar de (+ *inf.*)

K

kilo el kilo

kind: what — of weather is it? ¿qué tiempo hace?

kitchen la cocina

knock (on) llamar (a)

know (*facts*) saber, (*be acquainted with*) conocer

  come to know conocer

  know how to saber (+ *inf.*)

L

lake el lago

language la lengua

large grande

last pasado, -a, (*in a series*) último, -a

  last night anoche

  last week la semana pasada

  last year el año pasado

late tarde

  later más tarde, después

latter: the —, éste, ésta (-os, -as)

lawyer el abogado

learn aprender

least menos

  at least por lo menos

leave salir (de + *obj.*)., partir (de + *obj.*), irse, marcharse; (*trans.*) dejar

  leave for salir (partir) para

  leave home salir de casa

  take leave (of) despedirse (i,i) (de)

left izquierdo, -a

  to (on) the left a la izquierda

left: have (be) —, quedar (a)

  have (little time) left quedar (poco tiempo) a (uno)

**whether there are any seats
left** si quedan asientos
lend prestar
less menos
lesson la lección (*pl.* lecciones)
(Spanish) lesson lección (de
español)
let dejar, permitir
let me (*pl.*) + *verb* déjenme
Uds. (permítanme Uds.) *or*
dejadme (permitidme)
+ *inf.*
let's (let us) + *verb* vamos
a + *inf. or first pl. pres. subj.*
let's go (home) vamos (a
casa)
letter la carta
library la biblioteca
lie down acostarse (ue)
life la vida
light ligero, -a
like como; gustar
**Charles and Mary would
like to think about it**
Carlos y María quisieran (a
Carlos y a María les
gustaría) pensarlo
(he) would like (le)
gustaría, (él) quisiera
how do you like him? ¿qué
te (le) parece él?
**how I would like to meet
him!** ¡cómo (cuánto) me
gustaría conocerlo!
I should like me gustaría,
yo quisiera
like better (more) gustar
más (a uno)
would you like? ¿le gustaría
a Ud.? (¿te gustaría?)
listen (to) escuchar
listen! (*fam. sing. command*)
¡oye (tú)! ¡escucha!; (*fam.
pl.*) ¡oíd! ¡escuchad¡
little *adj.* (*quantity*) poco, -a;
adv. poco
a little un poco
little brother el hermanito
live vivir
living room la sala

lobby el vestíbulo
long largo, -a
how long? ¿cuánto tiempo?
longer más (tiempo)
one day longer un día más
look at mirar
by looking at mirando
look at each other mirarse
look for buscar
go looking for ir (andar)
buscando
Louis Luis
Louise Luisa
love: be in —, estar
enamorado, -a
**fall in love
(with)** enamorarse (de)
she must be in love! ¡estará
or debe (de) estar
enamorada!
luck: good — to you (*formal s.*)
**(may you have good
luck)!** ¡que tenga mucha
suerte!
lucky: be (very) —, tener
(mucha) suerte
luggage el equipaje
lunch el almuerzo
**eat (have, take)
lunch** tomar el almuerzo,
almorzar (ue)

M

machinery la maquinaria
magazine la revista
mail: by air —, por correo
aéreo
make hacer
make a decision llegar a
una decisión
**make a trip (an
excursión)** hacer un viaje
(una excursión)
man el hombre
man! ¡hombre!
the two young men los dos
jóvenes
manager el gerente
many muchos, -as; mil

how many? ¿cuántos, -as?
**many (a thousand)
things** mil cosas
many people mucha gente
many thanks muchas
(muchísimas) gracias
so many people tanta gente
map el mapa
March marzo
market el mercado
married: be —, casarse
Martha Marta
to Martha's a casa de Marta
Mary María
may (*wish, indir. command*)
que + *subj.; sign of pres. subj.*
May mayo
me *dir. and indir. obj.* me; *after
prep.* mí
with me conmigo
medicine la medicina
School of Medicine Escuela
de Medicina
meet (*a person for the first time*)
conocer
merchant el comerciante
merengue el merengue
Mexican mexicano, -a
Mexico México
Mexico City México, la
ciudad de México
Michael Miguel
midnight la medianoche
at midnight a la
medianoche
might *sign of the imp. subj.*
milk la leche
million el millón (*pl.* millones)
a (one) million un millón
de
mine *pron.* (el) mío, (la) mía,
etc.
of mine *adj.* mío, -a
minute el minuto
miss perder (ie)
Miss (la) señorita, (la) Srta.
modern moderno, -a
moment el momento
for a moment por un
momento

money el dinero
month el mes
  a (per) month por (al) mes
  next month el mes que
  viene
more más
morning la mañana
  all morning toda la mañana
  for Saturday morning para
  el sábado por la mañana
  good morning buenos días
  in the morning por la
  mañana
  (yesterday) morning (ayer)
  por la mañana
most más
  most of la mayor parte de
mother la madre, la mamá
mountain la montaña; *pl.* las
  montañas, la sierra
movie(s) el cine
Mr. (el) señor, (el) Sr.
  Mr. and Mrs. (Brown) los
  señores (Brown)
much *adj.* mucho, -a; *adv.*
  mucho, muy
  not so much as no tanto
  como
  too much *adv.* demasiado
  very much *adv.* mucho,
  muchísimo
must deber, tener que (+ *inf.*);
  for probability use future tense
  one must hay que *or* uno
  tiene que (+ *inf.*)

N

name: one's — is, be named
  llamarse
  his name is él se llama
  what's (his) name? ¿cómo se
  llama (él)?
nap la siesta
  take a nap dormir (ue,u) la
  (una) siesta
national nacional
near *prep.* cerca de
nearby *adv.* cerca

nearly casi
necessary necesario, -a,
  preciso, -a
  it is necessary to es
  necesario (preciso) *or* hay
  que (+ *inf.*)
necktie la corbata
need necesitar
nervous nervioso, -a
  become (get) nervous
  ponerse nervioso, -a
never nunca
new nuevo, -a
  New World Nuevo Mundo
  New York Nueva York
  what's new? ¿qué hay de
  nuevo?
newspaper el periódico
  university newspaper
  periódico de la universidad
next (month) (el mes) que
  viene
night la noche
  every night todas las noches
  last night anoche
  (on) Saturday nights los
  sábados por la noche
  Saturday night el sábado
  por la noche
nine nueve
  at (until) nine (o'clock) a
  (hasta) las nueve
  the nine-o'clock plane el
  avión de las nueve
ninety noventa
  ninety-two noventa y dos
no *adv.* no; *adj.* ninguno, -a,
  (*before m. sing. nouns*) ningún
  no one nadie
noon el mediodía
  at noon al mediodía
  until noon hasta el mediodía
not no
  not today hoy no
  not yet todavía no
note notar
notebook el cuaderno
nothing nada
  have nothing to do no
  tener nada que hacer

nothing special nada de
  particular
November noviembre
now ahora, ya
  right now ahora mismo
nowadays hoy día
number el número
  dance number número de
  baile

O

occupied ocupado, -a
occupy ocupar
o'clock: at (eleven) —, a las
  (once)
  before five o'clock antes de
  las cinco
  it is (six) o'clock son las
  (seis)
  the nine-o'clock plane el
  avión de las nueve
  until (ten) o'clock hasta las
  (diez)
October octubre
of de, a
office la oficina
  ticket office despacho de
  boletos
often a menudo
old antiguo, -a, viejo, -a
  **how old is he going to
  be?** ¿cuántos años va a
  tener (cumplir) él?
older mayor
on a, en, sobre
  on (Saturday) el (sábado)
  on time a tiempo
once: at —, en seguida, cuanto
  antes
one un, una, uno; *indef, subject*
  se, uno
  at one o'clock a la una
  no one nadie
  one must hay que *or* uno
  tiene que (+ *inf.*)
  one-way sencillo, -a
  the (blue) one el (azul), la
  (azul)

the one(s) that (who, which)
el (la) que, *pl.* los (las) que,
(*persons only*) quien(es)
only *adv.* solamente, sólo,
no . . . más que
open abrir
opportunity la oportunidad
have the opportunity
to tener la oportunidad de
opposite *adv.* enfrente
or o
orchestra la orquesta
order: in — that *conj.* para
que, de manera (modo) que
in order to *prep.* para
origin el origen (*pl.* orígenes)
other otro, -a
(look at) each other (mirar-)
se
ought to deber
our *adj.* nuestro, -a
ours *pron.* (el) nuestro, (la)
nuestra, *etc.*
of ours *adj.* nuestro, -a
out: find —, (*in pret.*) saber
owner el dueño

P

pair el par
paper el papel
parents los padres
park el parque
part la parte
party la fiesta
pass pasar
pass along (by) pasar por
past: (at) half — (twelve) (a)
(las doce) y media
Paul Pablo
pay (for) pagar
pencil el lápiz (*pl.* lápices)
people la gente (*requires sing.*
verb); *indef. subject* se
many people mucha gente
so many people tanta gente
perfectly perfectamente
perhaps tal vez, quizá(s)
permission el permiso

give permission to dar
permiso para
person la persona
personal personal
Peru el Perú
Peruvian peruano, -a
Philip Felipe
photo la foto
photograph la fotografía
take photographs sacar
fotografías
pick up buscar, recoger
picture el cuadro
picturesque pintoresco, -a
pin el prendedor
silver pin prendedor de
plata
pity la lástima
it is a pity es (una) lástima
what a pity! ¡qué lástima!
place el sitio, el lugar
plan pensar (ie) (+ *inf.*)
plane el avión (*pl.* aviones)
by plane en avión
(on) the (nine-o'clock)
plane (en) el avión (de las
nueve)
play (*game*) jugar (ue)
(a + *obj.*); (*music*) tocar
player el jugador
player: record —, el tocadiscos
pleasant agradable
please + *verb* hága(n)me
Ud(s). el favor de + *inf.;*
(*after request*) por favor
pleased contento, -a
I am pleased to meet
you mucho gusto en
conocerlo (-la) a Ud. *or* . . .
en conocerte
pleasure el gusto, el placer
what a pleasure! ¡qué gusto!
P.M. de la tarde (noche)
at (nine) P.M. a las (nueve)
de la noche
pool: (swimming) —, la
piscina
popular popular
position el puesto, el trabajo

possible posible
as soon as possible cuanto
antes, lo más pronto
posible, tan pronto como
posible
prefer preferir (ie,i)
prepare preparar
he has probably prepared
everything already ya lo
habrá preparado todo
prescribe recetar
present presentar
president el presidente
pretty bonito, -a, hermoso, -a
probable probable
probably *use future, future*
perfect, or cond. tense
professor el profesor, la
profesora
program el programa
pronounce pronunciar
provided that *conj.* con tal que
pupil el alumno, la alumna
purse la cartera
put poner
put on (*oneself*) ponerse
put on (*record*) poner

Q

quarter el cuarto
at a quarter to (ten) a las
(diez) menos cuarto
it is a quarter to (seven)
son las (siete) menos cuarto
question la pregunta
(he) asks us questions (él)
nos hace preguntas
quite bastante
quite a bit bastante

R

rain llover (ue)
rate: at any —, de todos
modos
Raymond Ramón
reach llegar (a + *obj.*), (*an*
anniversary) cumplir

reach a decision llegar a
  una decisión
read leer
ready listo, -a
really de veras
recall recordar (ue)
receive recibir
recommend recomendar (ie)
record el disco
  record player el tocadiscos
recreation room la sala de
  recreo
red rojo, -a
  the red one (*m.*) el rojo
religion la religión
religious religioso, -a
remember recordar (ue),
  acordarse (ue) (de + *obj.*)
rent alquilar
reply contestar
reserve reservar
residence hall la residencia
  student residence hall
  residencia de estudiantes
rest descansar
restaurant el restaurante
return volver (ue), (*give back*)
  devolver (ue)
  I'll return at once vuelvo
  en seguida
  return home volver (ue) a
  casa
rich rico, -a
Richard Ricardo
ride: take a —, dar un paseo
  ride horseback montar a
  caballo
right derecho, -a
  be right tener razón
  on (to) the right a la
  derecha
  right now ahora mismo
ring (*doorbell*) tocar, (*telephone*)
  sonar (ue)
road el camino
Robert Roberto
room el cuarto, la habitación
  (*pl.* habitaciones)
  dining room el comedor

living room la sala
recreation room la sala de
  recreo
roommate el compañero (la
  compañera) de cuarto
ruins las ruinas
run correr
  run across encontrarse (ue)
  con

S

sale: on —, a precio especial
saleslady la vendedora
sand la arena
Saturday el sábado
  for Saturday morning para
  el sábado por la mañana
  on Saturday el sábado
  (on) Saturday nights los
  sábados por la noche
  Saturday night el sábado
  por la noche
say decir
school la escuela
  School of Medicine Escuela
  de Medicina
seat el asiento
seated sentado, -a
second segundo, -a
  Philip the Second Felipe
  Segundo
secretary la secretaria
section la sección
see ver
  I'll see you lo (te) veo
  let's see (vamos) a ver
  see you tomorrow hasta
  mañana
seem parecer
sell vender
send mandar, enviar
  send for mandar (enviar)
  por
  send the telegram poner
  (enviar) el telegrama
sentence la frase
September septiembre
serve servir (i,i)

seven siete
several varios, -as
shade la sombra
shall *sign of future tense;*
  occasionally translated by the
  present tense
  shall I show you
  (*pl.*)? ¿les enseño (a Uds.)?
sharp (*time*) en punto
shave (*oneself*) afeitarse
she ella
shining: the sun was —, hacía
  (había) sol
shirt la camisa
shoe el zapato
  shoe store la zapatería
shop cleaning —, la tintorería
  jewelry shop la joyería
shopping: go —, ir de compras
should *sign of cond. ind. and imp.*
  subj.; deber
  I should like me gustaría,
  yo quisiera
show enseñar
  shall I show you (*pl.*)? ¿les
  enseño (a Uds.)?
  show signs of dar señales de
show window el escaparate
sick enfermo, -a
sign la señal
  show signs of dar señales de
silver la plata
  silver (pin) (prendedor) de
  plata
since como, pues
sing cantar
sister la hermana
sit down sentarse (ie)
  let's sit down sentémonos,
  vamos a sentarnos
six seis
  it is (was) six o'clock son
  (eran) las seis
sixteen dieciséis, diez y seis
size (*shoes*) el número, (*dress*) la
  talla
sky el cielo
sleep dormir (ue,u)
  go to sleep dormirse (ue,u)

sleepy: be (very) —, tener (mucho) sueño
sleepyhead el dormilón (*pl.* dormilones)
slide la transparencia
slowly despacio
small pequeño, -a
　small table mesita, mesa pequeña
snow la nieve
so tan
　(hope) so (esperar) que sí
　so many tantos, -as
　so many people tanta gente
　so that *conj.* para que, de manera (modo) que
some *adj. and pron.* alguno, -a, (*before m. sing. nouns*) algún; *pl.* algunos, -as; unos, -as; *often not translated*
someone alguien
something algo
　something to eat algo de comer
soon pronto
　as soon as *conj.* en cuanto
　as soon as possible tan pronto como posible, lo más pronto posible, cuanto antes
sooner antes
sorry: be (very) —, sentir (ie,i) (mucho)
sound sonar (ue)
south el sur
　South America Suramérica
space el espacio
Spain España
Spanish *adj.* español, -ola; (*language*) el español
　Spanish America Hispanoamérica
　Spanish American hispanoamericano, -a
　Spanish (lesson) (lección) de español
speak hablar
special: nothing —, nada de particular
spend (*time*) pasar
sport el deporte

sports section la sección de deportes
spring la primavera
　spring day día de primavera
States: (the) United —, los Estados Unidos
stay quedarse
still todavía
stop la parada; detenerse
　make a stop hacer una parada
store la tienda
　department store el almacén
　jewelry store (shop) la joyería
　shoe store la zapatería
street la calle
stroll pasearse
student el alumno, la alumna, el (la) estudiante
　student residence hall residencia de estudiantes
study estudiar
　study hard estudiar mucho
style el estilo
stylish: be (very) —, estar (muy) de moda
suit el traje
　bathing suit traje de baño
suitcase la maleta
summer el verano
　in summer en el verano
　summer vacation las vacaciones de verano
sun el sol
　take a sun bath tomar el sol
　the sun was shining hacía (había) sol
Sunday el domingo
　on Sunday el domingo
　on Sundays los domingos
supper: eat —, cenar
sure seguro, -a
　be sure that estar seguro, -a de que
surprise la sorpresa
　what a surprise! ¡qué sorpresa!
surprised sorprendido, -a
swim nadar

take a swim bañarse
swimming pool la piscina

T

table la mesa
　dining table mesa de comer
　small table mesita, mesa pequeña
take tomar, (*carry*) llevar, (*photos*) sacar
　I'll take it (*m.*) lo tomo
　I'll take it with me me lo llevo
　I'll take them (*m.*) me quedo con ellos, me los llevo, los tomo
　take a nap dormir (ue,u) la (una) siesta
　take a ride (walk) dar un paseo
　take a sun bath tomar el sol
　take a trip hacer un viaje (una excursión)
　take breakfast desayunarse, tomar el desayuno
　take leave (of) despedirse (i,i) (de)
　take lunch almorzar (ue), tomar el almuerzo
　take off (*oneself*) quitarse
talk hablar
　Mary is talking habla María
tall alto, -a
teach enseñar (a + *inf.*)
teacher el profesor, la profesora
　(English) teacher profesor *or* profesora (de inglés)
telegram el telegrama
　send the telegram poner (enviar) el telegrama
telephone el teléfono; telefonear, llamar por teléfono
　by telephone por teléfono
television la televisión
　television program programa de televisión
tell decir, contar (ue)
ten diez

at a quarter to ten a las diez menos cuarto

until ten o'clock hasta las diez

tennis el tenis

than que, (*before numerals*) de

than (I) expected de lo que (yo) esperaba

thank you, thanks gracias

many thanks muchas (mil) gracias

Thanksgiving Day Día de Acción de Gracias

that *adj.* (*near person addressed*) ese, esa (-os, -as), (*distant*) aquel, aquella (-os, -as); *pron.* ése, ésa (-os, -as), aquél, aquélla (-os, -as), (*neuter*) eso, aquello; *relative pron.* que

all that cuanto, todo lo que

provided that *conj.* con tal que

so that *conj.* para que, de manera (modo) que

the el, la, los, las

their *adj.* su(s), de ellos (-as)

theirs *pron.* (el) suyo, (la) suya, *etc.;* (el, la, los, las) de ellos (-as)

of theirs *adj.* suyo, -a, de ellos (-as)

them *dir. obj.* los, las; *indir. obj.* les, se; *after prep.* ellos (-as)

then luego, entonces

there (*near person addressed*) ahí, (*distant*) allí

there is (are) hay

there was (were) había

there will be habrá

these *adj.* estos, estas; *pron.* éstos, éstas

they ellos, ellas

thing la cosa

think creer, pensar (ie)

Charles and Mary would like to think about it Carlos y María quisieran (a Carlos y a María les gustaría) pensarlo

third tercero, -a, (*before m. sing. nouns*) tercer

the third of October el tres de octubre

thirsty: be —, tener sed

thirty treinta

thirty-one treinta y un(o), -a

this *adj.* este, esta; *pron.* this (one) éste, ésta

those *adj.* (*near person addressed*) esos (-as), (*distant*) aquellos (-as); *pron.* ésos (-as), aquéllos (-as)

though: even —, aunque

thousand: a (one) —, mil

thousands miles

three tres

it is 3:15 son las tres y cuarto

through por

Thursday el jueves

ticket el boleto, el billete

one-way ticket boleto sencillo

ticket office despacho de boletos

tight estrecho, -a

time (*in general sense*) el tiempo; (*of day*) la hora; (*series*) la vez (*pl.* veces)

about what time is it? ¿qué hora será?

at times a veces

at what time? ¿a qué hora?

from time to time de vez en cuando

have a (very) good time divertirse (ie,i) (mucho *or* muchísimo)

have time to tener tiempo para

it is time to es hora de (+ *inf.*)

most of the time la mayor parte del tiempo

on time a tiempo

the first time la primera vez

what time is it? ¿qué hora es?

tired cansado, -a

be tired of + *pres. part.* estar cansado, -a de + *inf.*

to a, de, para, que, (*in time*) menos

from . . . to desde . . . hasta

have to + *verb* tener que + *inf.*

to (Mary's) a casa de (María)

today hoy

not today hoy no

together juntos, -as

Tom Tomás

tomorrow mañana

see you tomorrow hasta mañana

tomorrow (afternoon) mañana (por la tarde)

tonight esta noche

Tony Antonio

too *adv.* también, demasiado

too much *adv.* demasiado

topcoat el abrigo

touch tocar

traffic el tránsito

travel viajar

travel agency agencia de viajes

traveling companion el compañero de viaje

tree el árbol

trip el viaje, la excursión (*pl.* excursiones)

business trip viaje de negocios

make *or* **take the (a) trip** hacer el (un) viaje

true: be —, ser verdad (cierto)

truth la verdad

try on probarse (ue)

try to tratar de (+ *inf.*)

Tuesday el martes

turn out (to be) resultar

twelve doce

half past twelve las doce y media

twenty veinte

twenty-one veintiún, veintiuno (-a) *or* veinte y un (una, uno)

twenty-five veinticinco
   (veinte y cinco)
two dos
   the two los (las) dos
typical típico, -a

U

uncle el tío
under *prep.* bajo
understand comprender
United States los Estados
   Unidos
university la universidad
   university newspaper
      periódico de la universidad
   University of Mexico
      Universidad de México
unless *conj.* a menos que
until *prep.* hasta
up: get —, levantarse
   pick up buscar, recoger
   wake up despertar (ie)
upon + *pres. part.* al + *inf.*
urgent urgente
Uruguay el Uruguay
us *dir. and indir. obj.* nos; *after*
   prep. nosotros, -as
use usar
used to *sign of the imp. ind. tense*

V

vacant vacante
vacation las vacaciones
   be on vacation estar de
      vacaciones
   summer vacation vacaciones
      de verano
Venezuelan venezolano, -a
very *adv.* muy; *adj.* mucho, -a
   very much *adv.* mucho,
      muchísimo
   very well muy bien, está
      bien
Vincent Vicente
visit visitar
   be visiting estar de visita

W

wait (for) esperar
wake up (*someone*) despertar
   (ie), (*oneself*) despertarse (ie)
walk el paseo; pasearse
   take a walk dar un paseo
wall la pared
want querer, desear
warm (*noun with* hacer *and*
   tener) el calor
   be (very) warm (*living*
      beings) tener (mucho) calor
   be (very) warm (*weather*)
      hacer (mucho) calor
wash lavar, (*oneself*) lavarse
watch el reloj; mirar
   gold watch reloj de oro
   watch television mirar
      la televisión
water el agua (*f.*)
way: by the —, a propósito
we nosotros, -as
weather el tiempo
   what kind of weather is
      it? ¿qué tiempo hace?
wedding la boda
   wedding anniversary
      aniversario de bodas
week la semana
   last week la semana pasada
   next week la semana que
      viene, la semana próxima
weekend el fin de semana
welcome: you're —, no hay de
   qué, de nada
   welcome! ¡bienvenido, -a!
well *adv.* bien; pues, bueno
   very well muy bien, está
      bien
what? ¿qué? ¿cuál? ¿cómo?
   what color is (it)? ¿de qué
      color es?
   what's (his) name? ¿cómo
      se llama (él)?
   what's new? ¿qué hay de
      nuevo?
what a . . . ! ¡qué . . . !
when cuando

when? ¿cuándo?
where donde
where? ¿dónde?, (*with verbs of*
   motion) ¿adónde?
   where is (George) from?
      ¿de dónde es (Jorge)?
whether si
which que, el (la, los, las) que,
   el (la) cual, los (las) cuales
   which (one)? ¿cuál?
   which (ones)? ¿cuáles?
while el rato; *conj.* mientras
   (que)
white blanco, -a
   the white one (*m.*) el blanco
who que, quien(es), el (la)
   cual, los (las) cuales, el (la,
   los, las) que
   he (the one) who el (la)
      que, quien
who? ¿quién(es)?
whom que, a quien(es)
whom? ¿a quién(es)?
   from whom? ¿de quién(es)?
whose? ¿de quién(es)?
   whose car is it? ¿de
      quién(es) es el coche?
why? ¿por qué?
wide ancho, -a
wife la esposa
will *sign of future tense*
   will you + *verb?* ¿quiere
      Ud. (quieres) + *inf.?*
window la ventana
windy: be (very) —, hacer
   (mucho) viento
winter el invierno
   in winter en el invierno
wish querer, desear
   I wish that . . . ! ¡ojalá
      (que) + *subj.!*
with con, de, en
   with you (*fam. sing.*)
      contigo
within *prep.* dentro de
without *prep.* sin
won't you? ¿no quiere Ud.
   (quieres)?
word la palabra

work trabajar
  work hard trabajar mucho
world el mundo
  New World Nuevo Mundo
would *sign of imp. or cond. ind.*
  tense
  would that . . . ! ¡ojalá
  (que) + *subj.!*
wrap up envolver (ue)
write escribir

Y

year el año
yellow amarillo, -a
yes sí
yesterday ayer

yesterday morning ayer por
  la mañana
yet todavía
  not yet todavía no
you (*fam. sing.*) tú, (*pl.*)
  vosotros, -as; *dir. and indir.*
  obj. te, os; *after prep.* ti,
  vosotros, -as
  with you (*fam. sing.*) contigo
you (*formal*) *subject pron. and*
  after prep. usted (Ud. *or*
  Vd.), ustedes (Uds. *or* Vds.);
  dir. obj. lo (le), la, los, las;
  indir. obj. le, les, se
young joven (*pl.* jóvenes)
  the two young men los dos
  jóvenes

young man el joven
younger más joven, menor
your (*fam.*) *adj.* tu(s),
  vuestro(s), -a(s); (*formal*)
  su(s), de Ud(s). *or* Vd(s).
yours (*fam.*) *pron.* (el) tuyo,
  (la) tuya, (los) tuyos, (las)
  tuyas, (el) vuestro, (la)
  vuestro, (los) vuestros, (las)
  vuestras; (*formal*) (el) suyo,
  (la) suya, (los) suyos, (las)
  suyas, (el, la, los, las de
  Ud(s). *or* de Vd(s).
of yours *adj.* tuyo(s), -a(s),
  vuestro(s), -a(s); suyo(s),
  -a(s), de Ud(s). *or* de Vd(s).

INDEX

(References are to page numbers)

PHOTOGRAPH CREDITS

PETER MENZEL; pp. xvi, 6 *left*, 7, 12, 13, 20, 22, 23, 30, 32, 33, 40, 42 *right*, 52, 53, 63, 64, 78 *bottom*, 80, 81, 90, 94, 105, 108, 110 *bottom*, 111, 112 *bottom*, 113 *left*, 114, 115, 124, 128, 137, 139, 140, 141, 142, 143, 144, 145, 146, 147, 150, 151, 152, 153, 173, 175, 178, 180, 181, 188, 190, 195, 196, 197, 204, 206, 207, 212, 213, 224, 225 *bottom*, 228, 229, 239, 242, 243, 244 *top—bottom right*, 245, 246, 247, 257, 266, 267, 271, 272, 273, 287 *bottom*, 289 *left*, 292, 293, 297, 310, 311, 317, 320, 326, 327, 329, 342, 343, 351, 355, 357, 358, 359, 380, 386 • G. PICKOW for THREE LIONS, INC.; p. 1 • FOTO DU MONDE; p. 6 *right* • AMERICAN AIRLINES; pp. 42, 43—PHOTO BY BOB TAKIS, 107, 109 *bottom right—top* and *bottom left* BY BOB TAKIS, 110 *right*, 113 *top right—bottom right* BY BOB TAKIS • NATIONAL NUMISMATIC COLLECTION and THE SMITHSONIAN INSTITUTION; p. 44 • CHICAGO NATURAL HISTORY MUSEUM, PHOTOGRAPHY SECTION; p. 47 • SPANISH NATIONAL TOURIST OFFICE; pp. 65, 72, 75, 78 *top*, 79 *bottom left and right*, 209, 210 *top*, 211 *left and bottom right*, 282, 287 *top*, 288, 289 *right*, 291, 321, 371 • IBERIA AIRLINES OF SPAIN; pp. 68, 79 *top*—PHOTO BY C. MARRIS, 193 *bottom* • PAN AMERICAN AIRLINES; pp. 77, 177 *bottom* • TRANS WORLD AIRLINES; pp. 79 *center*, 210 *bottom* • EDITORIAL PHOTOCOLOR ARCHIVES; pp. 91, 162 *right*, 164, 225—PHOTO BY A. KELER, 290 *bottom*, 323, 325, 340 • BRANIFF INTERNATIONAL; pp. 103, 302 • MEXICAN NATIONAL TOURIST COUNCIL; pp. 109 *center*, 112 *top*, 129, 162 *left*, 163, 170 • JOHN CARTER BROWN LIBRARY; p. 118 • P. ANDERSON for BLACK STAR; p. 155 • ALEXANDER HUMBOLDT; p. 159 • THE HISPANIC SOCIETY OF AMERICA; pp. 167, 290 *top*, 336, 337, 368, 373, 374 • SCHOENFELD COLLECTION and THREE LIONS, INC.; p. 176 *top* • STANDARD OIL COMPANY (NEW JERSEY); p. 176 *left* • UNITED FRUIT COMPANY; pp. 176 *right*, 177 *top*, 185 • TERRY MCKOY; pp. 179, 193 *top*, 232, 248 • THE EMBASSY OF SPAIN, WASHINGTON, D.C.; p. 211 *top right* • ROGER COSTER, reprinted by special permission from HOLIDAY, copyright 1952, the CURTIS PUBLISHING COMPANY; p. 221 • E. M. CRAWFORD; p. 222 • ROBERT DALEY, courtesy, THE STERLING LORD AGENCY, INC.; p. 224 *top right and left* • FOTOGRAFÍA FERROVIALES; p. 236 • V. DERNER; p. 244 *bottom left* • SIMONE OUDOT; p. 256 • D. PRESTON; p. 258 • H. W. HANNAU for RAPHO GUILLUMETTE PICTURES; p. 265 • LIBRARY OF CONGRESS; p. 270 • "LA DAMA DE ELCHE"; p. 283 • BIBLIOTHEQUE NATIONALE, PARIS; p. 286 • THE METROPOLITAN MUSEUM OF ART; pp. 319—"Don Quixote and Sancho Panza" by Honore Daumier —Rogers Fund 1927, p. 370 "Portrait of a Man" by El Greco—Joseph Pulitzer Bequest Fund 1924 • BROWN BROTHERS; p. 338 • CASA MORENO, MADRID; p. 340 • MUSEO DEL PRADO, MADRID; p. 370—"Los borrachos" by Velázquez • NATIONAL GALLERY OF ART, WASHINGTON, D.C.; p. 371—"Señora Sabasa Garcia" by Goya— Mellon Collection • MUSEUM OF FINE ARTS, BOSTON; p. 372—"My Uncle Daniel and His Family" by Zuloaga • THE ART INSTITUTE OF CHICAGO; p. 372—"The Old Guitarist" by Picasso—Helen Birch Bartlett Collection • UNITED PRESS INTERNATIONAL; p. 373 *left* • S. HUROK; p. 374 *bottom* •

4 5 6 7 8 9 0

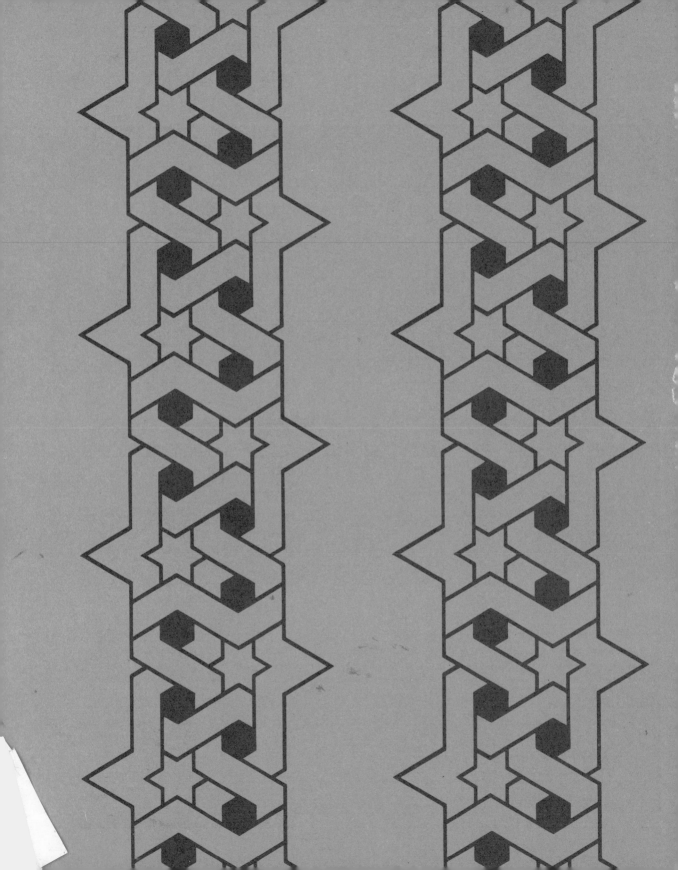